D0203213

AMERICAN FIRST LADIES

AMERICAN FIRST LADIES

★ ★ ★ ★ ★

Their Lives and Their Legacy

SECOND EDITION

Lewis L. Gould, *editor*

Routledge
NEW YORK   LONDON

Published in 2001 by

Routledge
29 West 35th Street
New York, NY 10001

Published in Great Britain by
Routledge
11 New Fetter Lane
London EC4P 4EE

Routledge is an Imprint of Taylor & Francis Books, Inc.
Copyright © 2001 by Routledge

Printed in the United States of America on acid-free paper.

All rights reserved. No part of this book may be reprinted or reproduced or utilized in any form
or by any electronic, mechanical, or other means, now known or hereafter invented, including any
photocopying and recording, or in any information storage or retrieval system, without permission
in writing from the publishers.

10 9 8 7 6 5 4 3 2 1

Library of Congress Cataloging-in-Publication Data

American first ladies : their lives and their legacy / Lewis L. Gould, editor.—2nd ed.
    p. cm.
    Includes bibliographical references and index.
    ISBN 0-415-93021-9 (acid-free paper)
    1. Presidents' spouses—United States—Biography. 2. Presidents' spouses—United States—
Pictorial works. I. Gould, Lewis L.

E176.2.A44 2001
973'.099—dc21
[B]   2001019569

Contents

★ ★ ★ ★ ★

Acknowledgments

★ ★ ★ ★ ★

Christopher Collins of Garland first asked me to embark on this project and was a source of encouragement throughout its early stages. Dr. Phyllis Korper of Garland saw the book through to completion. All of the contributors worked hard to make the book a success, but I owe special thanks to Thomas H. Appleton Jr., Stacy Cordery, Kristie Miller, and Nancy Beck Young for their individual efforts on the book's behalf. Lisa Caputo of Hillary Rodham Clinton's staff offered valuable criticisms of the essay on Mrs. Clinton. However, the responsibility for the final version of that essay is mine alone.

The staffs of the Center for American History at the University of Texas at Austin, the Jimmy Carter Library, the Dwight D. Eisenhower Library, the Gerald R. Ford Library, the Herbert Hoover Library, the Nixon Presidential Papers Project at the National Archives, the James K. Polk Birthplace, the Franklin D. Roosevelt Library, and the Harry S. Truman Library were most helpful in supplying photographs. The White House furnished the photograph of Hillary Rodham Clinton. The First Ladies Polls are included courtesy of the Siena Research Institute, Siena College, Loudonville, New York, which retains full rights to publication and reproduction of these poll results in the future.

Karen Gould was a constant source of support and care throughout the process of editing this volume.

Lewis L. Gould
Austin, Texas

THE FIRST LADY
AS SYMBOL AND INSTITUTION

★ ★ ★ ★ ★

Since the early 1980s historians, journalists, and popular writers have devoted serious attention to the role of the wife of the president of the United States in national politics and cultural life. Earlier there had been individual works that considered the place of the First Lady in American history, including Marianne Means, *The Woman in the White House* (1963), and Sol Barzman, *The First Ladies* (1970). These and other books on the First Ladies, however, drew only rarely on personal papers and original documents. For the most part they were selective and anecdotal as well.

Since the mid-1980s numerous studies of the First Lady have attempted to identify the impact of these women on American history. Authors such as Betty Boyd Caroli, *First Ladies* (1987); Myra Gutin, *The President's Partner: The First Lady in the Twentieth Century* (1989); and Carl Sferrazza Anthony, *First Ladies* (2 vols., 1990–1991) have scrutinized the institution based on extensive research into primary sources. Simultaneously, college courses on the First Lady have been offered, symposia have brought together former First Ladies to discuss their legacy, and scholarly panels have been held to measure the significance of presidential wives. By the early 1990s the outlines of a distinct research area devoted to First Ladies had emerged where history, political science, and women's studies intersected.

Despite these constructive achievements the new field lacked a reliable, up-to-date reference work that included the essential facts about each First Lady in a brief biographical essay. The purpose of *American First Lady* studies is to provide the general reading public, especially students coming initially to First Ladies, with informative entries about each of these women, entries that also indicate the location of primary sources, reliable biographies where available, and topics for further research.

Each entry on a First Lady is a self-contained unit with a chronological account of her life and an effort to assess her place in the development of the institution of the First Lady. The bibliographical essays outline where personal papers and other relevant manuscript sources can be found. They also provide a selection of the First Lady's own writings, contemporary articles or memoirs by family and friends, biographical studies of both her and her husband, and relevant newspaper stories, scholarly articles, and general surveys. In the case of deceased First Ladies, an obituary is also listed.

The editor's first task was to decide who should be included in the encyclopedia. For this volume the working definition of a First Lady is the woman or women (in the case of John Tyler and Woodrow Wilson) who were married to the president of the United States during his term of office. Previous marriages were thus ruled out, and so Alice Lee Roosevelt, Theodore Roosevelt's deceased first wife, and Jane Wyman, Ronald Reagan's divorced first wife, do not have essays devoted to them. Similarly, wives who died before their husband reached the White House have not been the subject of essays. This group includes Martha Jefferson, Rachel Jackson, Hanna Van Buren, and Ellen Herndon Arthur.

Other candidates for attention who receive coverage in books about First Ladies are the women who served as White House hostesses, what Betty Caroli has called "Young Substitutes for First Ladies" or "stand-in chatelaines." Two of his nieces served Andrew Jackson in this capacity between 1829 and 1837. Angelica Van Buren, the daughter-in-law of President Martin Van Buren, played a similar role between 1837 and 1841. Since James Buchanan was a bachelor president, his niece Harriet Lane functioned as his hostess from 1857 to 1861. Chester Alan Arthur called on his sister Mary Arthur McElroy to be his hostess between 1881 and 1885. While these women were valuable aides to the president in his social capacity, they never occupied the same status in the minds of the American people as the wife of a president. Their contributions to the institution of the First Lady were fleeting and ephemeral, and they did not merit inclusion in a volume devoted to presidential wives.

During the mid-nineteenth century a number of First Ladies relied on their daughters or daughters-in-law to aid them in the White House. These relationships, however, could be dealt with in the context of the essays about the First Ladies themselves, as the entries on Anna Harrison, Letitia Tyler, Margaret Taylor, Abigail Fillmore, and Eliza Johnson make clear.

American First Ladies seeks to provide readers with a sense of the institutional continuity and traditions of the position of the First Lady as it has evolved over more than 200 years. Accordingly, even a president's wife such as Anna Harrison, who was First Lady for only six weeks in 1841 and who never came to Washington, is still part of the continuum that runs from Martha Washington to Laura Bush in a way that Emily Donelson, hostess for Andrew Jackson, or Harriet Lane never was.

Some of the apparent gaps in the coverage of First Ladies that arise from this editorial decision are covered by the existing essays in this encyclopedia. Holly Cowan Shulman's treatment of Dolley Madison indicates how she served as a surrogate hostess for Thomas Jefferson for eight years. For the other First Lady stand-ins of the nineteenth century, researchers are referred to books by Carl Anthony and Betty Caroli, where these women are treated in detail.

Of the thirty-nine women whose lives are described in this encyclopedia, some made such a slight mark on the history of their time that only a brief essay was needed to exhaust what was known about them. Anna Harrison, Letitia Tyler, Margaret Taylor, and Jane Pierce fall into that group. With the burgeoning interest in First Lady studies, however, more information on the less renowned nineteenth-century presidential wives is likely to come to light.

For the remaining thirty-five women the editor asked the contributors to provide essays ranging between 5,000 and 10,000 words, depending on the historical importance of the First Lady herself. The length of each essay was determined by the perceived significance of the various First Ladies and their impact on the institution. Because of the greater availability of source materials and more intense coverage of their activities, the late-twentieth-century First Ladies have longer essays devoted to them.

The contributors tried to point out instances where particular First Ladies were the first members of the institution to engage in an innovative activity—to speak in public, hire a social secretary, talk on the radio, campaign for partisan candidates, testify before a congressional committee, or act as a full White House aide. They have also devoted attention to questions of education, public image, the nature of the presidential marriage, and child rearing in and out of the White House. Within the limits of the available sources and the space allotted to them, the authors have also endeavored to give a sense of the personality and individual appeal of each of these fascinating women.

Americans are ambivalent about presidential wives. The public expects the First Lady to fulfill a multitude of roles flawlessly, and there is criticism at any departure from perceived standards. At the same time the criteria for success as a First Lady constantly change as the public's view of women evolves and develops. These essays reveal the degree to which First Ladies have, from Martha Washington onward, been the subject of popular attention and controversy about their performance in the national spotlight. With the perspective that these biographical studies provide, it should now be easier to make intelligent assessments of how much future First Ladies resemble their historic predecessors.

The histories of First Ladies have common elements in the nineteenth and twentieth centuries, but there are also evident differences: The role of the president's wife has responded to changes in the nation's highest office itself and the social demands on women. During the period from 1789 to 1861 First Ladies were mostly private personages, with Dolley Madison as the notable exception and Julia Tyler a brief portent of fame to come. With the advent of Mary Todd Lincoln and her notoriety during the Civil War, the possibility of intense newspaper attention to First Ladies became a reality. None of Mary Todd Lincoln's late-nineteenth-century successors equaled her celebrity, although the coverage devoted to Lucy Webb Hayes and Frances Folsom Cleveland indicated a mounting degree of popular interest in the White House and its families.

During the early twentieth century First Ladies slowly acquired a true institutional apparatus to help with meeting the mounting demands on their time. Isabelle "Belle" Hagner represented the first social secretary to a First Lady in the modern sense when Edith Kermit Roosevelt employed her in 1902. During Mrs. Roosevelt's tenure, the role of the president's wife began to become that of social arbiter of good taste and leader of feminine fashion. Illness prevented Helen Herron Taft and Ellen Bolling Wilson from building on Edith Roosevelt's legacy before World War I.

Edith Wilson became a negative role model in her performance after President Woodrow Wilson became seriously ill in 1919. The consensus was that she had overstepped the implied limits of her position when she screened correspondence and visitors to her sick husband. Her example served as a powerful cautionary lesson against First Lady activism. Nonetheless, the impulse toward a greater visibility for presidential wives proved able to overcome the setback that Edith Wilson had dealt the institution.

As Republican First Ladies and the wives of less-than-successful presidents, Florence Kling Harding, Grace Goodhue Coolidge, and Lou Henry Hoover seem pale beside the imposing presence of Eleanor Roosevelt. Yet, as the entries on these women make clear, they each contributed to the institutional development of the role of First Lady and exploited to varying degrees their increasing status as media attractions. Florence Harding had a more feminist emphasis to her public work and paid particular attention to the media aspects of the White House. Similarly, Grace Coolidge provided a modicum of glamour and sophistication to her husband's administration and used her position to support artists and performers from all phases of the arts. Lou Henry Hoover was the first presidential wife to speak to radio audiences, and her identification with the Girl Scouts shaped her response to the economic depression that her husband faced as president. By the end of the 1920s the public had become accustomed to seeing First Ladies as more visible figures than had been the case twenty years before.

The major innovations in what a First Lady could do, of course, came with the twelve-year tenure of Eleanor Roosevelt. Her press conferences, daily newspaper column, and extensive travels made her a national personality in a way that no previous First Lady had achieved. While some of the changes she made in the institution, such as regular press conferences, did not endure, her example as an activist role model gave her successors a precedent to invoke when they wished to pursue a cause or a campaign. A full-scale examination of Eleanor Roosevelt's contributions as First Lady, based on her extensive personal papers, is one of the pressing needs of scholarship on presidential wives.

In the two decades after Mrs. Roosevelt left the White House in 1945, her successors—Bess Truman, Mamie Eisenhower, and Jacqueline Kennedy—did not embark on substantive activism or follow favorite causes. Mrs. Truman and Mrs. Eisenhower represented a return to the more traditional model of the First Lady as the helpmate, out of the public eye. Jacqueline Kennedy infused the institution with glamour and celebrity, and thus aroused popular interest in what the First Lady did, even if her own accomplishments were limited to a renovation of the interior of the White House. With the growing influence of television, the First Lady became a focus for media attention.

During the more than three decades since Jacqueline Kennedy was in the White House, a growing emphasis on activism has marked the role of the First Lady. Lady Bird Johnson identified herself with the environment and beautification. Her use of staff, her involvement with conservation legislation, and her advocacy of environmental causes laid down a style as First Lady that her Democratic successors would emulate. Following Mrs. Johnson, Patricia Nixon was less visible in her public role, but, as recent scholarship about her indicates, she was as involved in serious causes as her husband's conservative administration would allow her to be.

Betty Ford was the most feminist First Lady since Eleanor Roosevelt, in her campaigning for the Equal Rights Amendment and her general stance for a liberated and open lifestyle. The brevity of her husband's term and her own problems with chemical dependencies limited the impact of her tenure, but she pushed the boundaries of the institution in significant ways. Similarly, Rosalynn Carter was an energetic and purposeful First Lady who tried to forge a public partnership with her husband that reflected the nature of their marriage. That her strategy aroused a public backlash attested to the enduring strength of traditional ideas regarding what the wife of the president should do. Mrs. Carter's record will probably gain in historical interest as researchers investigate the materials about her activities at the Carter Library.

Nancy Reagan's controversial eight years revealed how much the popular expectation of First Lady activism had become embedded within the political culture. Faced with a public reaction against her opulent lifestyle during her first two years, she and her advisers turned to a "Just Say No" campaign against illicit drugs to validate her credentials as a First Lady with a real cause. During the second Reagan term, her influence on the presidency evoked memories of Edith Wilson and comparable criticism of her performance from male members of the press. Despite the low rankings she has received in the polls of historians, Nancy Reagan will prove to be one of the most interesting and written-about First Ladies of the modern era.

Few First Ladies can match the sustained popularity of Barbara Bush. During her four years in the position she maintained a level of public approval and applause that often saw her outpacing her husband in the polls. She benefited from following the turbulent performance of Nancy Reagan, but she also managed the media and her own image with a great deal of deftness. Her endorsement of literacy never attracted any serious criticism, and she survived the experience of being First Lady with few serious controversies. The publication of her memoirs and the opening of the Bush Library may cause some slight downward revision in her historical standing because she was more acerbic in private than her genial public posture indicated. Nonetheless, Mrs. Bush will probably be regarded as a successful First Lady because she fulfilled the several roles of the position so smoothly.

As the institution of the First Lady reaches the twenty-first century, the experience of Hillary Rodham Clinton underscored the clashing expectations that Americans still brought to the wife of the president. For independent women who had career patterns similar to that which Hillary Rodham Clinton followed, she was an inspiring model. Other women, and many men, on the right of the political spectrum regarded Hillary Clinton as a figure of such evil intentions as to render her almost devilish in character. Why she evoked such contradictory impressions will be for her future biographers to decide.

As First Lady, Hillary Clinton broadened the range of what the wife of a president can do in her role as a policy leader in the health care debate. She also encountered unprecedented legal scrutiny, including testimony before a grand jury, in the Whitewater affair. Then she made history with her successful run for the U.S. Senate in 2000. While Laura Bush may draw back from the extensive involvement in substantive issues that Mrs. Clinton practiced, there may be other presidential wives in the future who will build on the precedents she developed. In the case of First Ladies, once an innovation has occurred, it is not long before others in the White House use the example as a rationale for their course as the wife of the president. As professional women become First Ladies in the future, Hillary Clinton will probably be seen not as a dramatic departure from older norms but as the first example of how the wife of the president mirrors social trends a decade or so after they have first been noticed.

For more than two centuries the spouse of the president has been a woman. In the twenty-first century the likelihood of there being a woman chief executive will grow. How will an institution premised on the presence of a wife adapt to a "First Gentleman" or "First Mate," to mention some of the improbable titles applied to prospective presidential husbands? An encyclopedia about First Ladies cannot peer into that misty future and project how the institution will adjust to a male occupant, but there will undoubtedly have to be major changes to accommodate a male consort in the White House. Once the succession of First Ladies has been interrupted, an enduring American institution will have been changed in serious ways.

For the present, however, the historical importance of First Ladies seems ensured. These women offer a significant perspective on how their fellow citizens regard marriage, child rearing, women in society, and gender relations within the United States. The thirty-nine women included in American First Ladies have been interesting, controversial, sad, and inspiring. Americans have sensed that the wife of the president of the United States says something meaningful about the way the nation has chosen to organize its private and public affairs. The contributors to this biographical encyclopedia share this assumption, and their individual entries are designed to introduce readers to a fascinating group of women whose historical role deserves to be argued about and studied in an intelligent and thoughtful way.

BIBLIOGRAPHICAL ESSAY

There are a number of general surveys of First Ladies. Some of the older ones include Laura C. Holloway, *Ladies of the White House* (Philadelphia, 1870, 1881); Kathleen Prindiville, *First Ladies* (New York, 1942); Mary Ormsbee Whitton, *First First Ladies, 1789–1865* (New York, 1948); Marianne Means, *The Woman in the White House* (New York, 1963); and Sol Barzman, *The First Ladies* (New York, 1970). General histories of the White House in which the First Ladies are featured are Bess Furman, *White House Profile* (Indianapolis, 1951); Amy La Follette Jensen, *The White House* (New York, 1962); William Seale, *The President's House* (2 vols., Washington, D.C., 1986); and Elise K. Kirk, *Music at the White House: A History of the American Spirit* (Urbana, Ill., 1986). The most recent treatment is Betty Boyd Caroli, *Inside the White House* (New York, 1992).

For recent scholarship on the First Ladies, see Betty Boyd Caroli, *First Ladies* (New York, 1987); Nancy Kegan Smith and Mary C. Ryan, eds., *Modern First Ladies: Their Documentary Legacy* (Washington, D.C., 1989); Myra Gutin, *The President's Partner: The First Lady in the Twentieth Century* (Westport, Conn., 1989); and Carl Sferrazza Anthony, *First Ladies: The Saga of the Presidents' Wives and Their Power, 1789–1990* (2 vols., New York, 1990, 1991). Other popular treatments are James S. Rosebush, *First Lady, Public Wife* (Lanham, Md., 1987); Paul F. Boller Jr., *Presidential Wives* (New York, 1988); Diana Dixon Healy, *Amer-*

ica's First Ladies: Private Lives of the Presidential Wives (New York, 1988); Peter Hay, *All the President's Ladies* (New York, 1988); and Alice E. Anderson, *Behind Every Successful President* (New York, 1992). Ann Grimes, *Running Mates* (New York, 1990), examines the campaign of 1988 from the perspective of the women who might become First Lady. An unpublished doctoral dissertation about First Ladies is Barbara Oney Garvey, "A Rhetorical-Humanistic Analysis of the Relationship Between First Ladies and the Way Women Find a Place in Society" (Ohio State University, 1978). The fall 1990 issue of *Presidential Studies Quarterly* was devoted in part to a number of essays about twentieth-century First Ladies.

Additional scholarship includes Karen O'Connor, Bernadette Nye, and Laura VanAssendelft, "Wives in the White House: The Political Influence of the First Ladies," *Presidential Studies Quarterly* 26 (Summer 1996): 835–853, and Robert P. Watson, "The First Lady Reconsidered: Presidential Partner and Political Institution," *Presidential Studies Quarterly* 27 (Autumn 1997): 805–818. A lively and well-researched treatment of recent presidents and First Ladies is Gil Troy, *Mr. and Mrs. President: From the Trumans to the Clintons*, second edition (Lawrence, Kans., 2000). An excellent place for research on the First Ladies is the National First Ladies' Library, part of the First Ladies National Historic Site, in Canton, Ohio. Information can also be found at their website, www.firstladies.org.

CONTRIBUTORS

$\bigstar$ $\bigstar$ $\bigstar$ $\bigstar$ $\bigstar$

Carl Sferrazza Anthony lives in Los Angeles, California, and is the author of *First Ladies: The Saga of the Presidents' Wives and Their Power, 1789–1990* (2 vols., 1990, 1991), *As We Remember Her: Jacqueline Kennedy Onassis in the Words of Her Family and Friends* (1997), *Florence Harding: The First Lady, the Jazz Age, and the Death of America's Most Scandalous President* (1998), and *America's First Families: An Inside View of 200 Years of Private Life in the White House* (2000).

Thomas H. Appleton Jr. is professor of history at Eastern Kentucky University. He is co-editor of *A Mythic Land Apart: Reassessing Southerners and Their History* (1997).

Jean H. Baker is professor of history at Goucher College. She is the author of *Mary Todd Lincoln* (1987), *Private Life, Public Destinies: The Stevensons of Illinois* (1995), and *The Lincoln Marriage: Beyond the Battle of Quotations* (1999). She is currently researching and writing about the suffrage movement.

James G. Benze Jr. is professor of political science at Washington and Jefferson College. He is the author of *Presidential Management and Presidential Power: The Carter and Reagan Administrations in Historical Perspective* (1987) and has written about the career of Nancy Reagan.

Allida M. Black is editor and director of the Eleanor Roosevelt Papers and Research Professor of History at George Washington University. She is the author of *Casting Her Own Shadow: Eleanor Roosevelt and the Shaping of Postwar Liberalism* (1996) and the editor of *Courage in a Dangerous World: The Political Writings of Eleanor Roosevelt* (1999). Her next project, *First Women: Power, Image and Politics from Betty Ford through Hillary Rodham Clinton*, will be published in 2002.

Patricia Brady received her Ph.D from Tulane University. She is director of publications at the Historic New Orleans Collection and is the editor of *Nelly Custis Lewis's Housekeeping Book* (1982), *George Washington's Beautiful Nelly: The Letters of Eleanor Parke Custis Lewis to Elizabeth Bordley Gibson, 1794–1851* (1991), and co-editor of *Queen of the South: New Orleans, 1853–1862: The Journal of Thomas K. Wharton* (1999).

Charles W. Calhoun received his Ph.D from Columbia University and is professor of history at East Carolina University. He is the author of *Gilded Age Cato: The Life of Walter Q. Gresham* (1988) and editor of *The Gilded Age: Essays on the Origins of Modern America* (1996). He is completing a book on Republican party thought in the late nineteenth century.

Betty Boyd Caroli is the author of *First Ladies* (1987, exp. ed. 1995), *Inside the White House* (1992, updated ed. 1999), *America's First Ladies* (1996), and *The Roosevelt Women* (1998).

Stacy A. Cordery is associate professor of history at Monmouth College in Monmouth, Illinois, where she has won several teaching awards. She has written on women in the Gilded Age and on the career of Alice Roosevelt Longworth. She is writing "'Come Sit By Me:' The Life of Alice Roosevelt Longworth" and a book on Theodore Roosevelt.

Debbie Mauldin Cottrell is assistant dean of the faculty at Smith College. She received her Ph.D from the University of Texas at Austin in 1993, where she specialized in women's history. She is the author of *Pioneer Woman Educator: The Progressive Spirit of Annie Webb Blanton* (1993) and "Teaching Through Narratives of Women's Lives," in *Coming Into Her Own: Educational Success in Girls and Women* (1999).

Jayne Crumpler DeFiore, formerly an associate editor of the *Correspondence of James K. Polk*, taught Tennessee history in the Department of Independent Study at the University of Tennessee, Knoxville, for twenty years before retiring in 2000. She received her Ph.D from the University of Tennessee and has written a history of the University of Tennessee Medical Center.

Rebecca Edwards grew up in Smithfield, Virginia, and received her Ph.D in history from the University of Virginia. Since 1995 she has been assistant professor of history at Vassar College. She is the author of *Angels in the Machinery: Gender in American Party Politics from the Civil War to the Progressive Era* (1997) and is working on two books: "Soul Declared: The Life of Mary Lease," and "The Birth of Modern America, 1876-1900."

Julie K. Fix holds a Master's degree in history from the University of Virginia, where she specialized in pre–Civil War women's history. She has worked as a researcher and as the coordinator of the Monroe Papers Project at AshLawn-Highland, the museum at Elizabeth and James Monroe's home in Albemarle County, Virginia. She lives and works in Virginia.

Lewis L. Gould is Eugene C. Barker Centennial Professor Emeritus in American History at the University of Texas at Austin, and the editor of the "Modern First Ladies" series with the University Press of Kansas.

Myra Gutin is professor in the department of communication at Rider University. She received her Ph.D from the University of Michigan and has written and lectured extensively about First Ladies. She is the author of *The President's Partner: The First Lady in the Twentieth Century* (1989) and serves on the editorial board of White House Studies. She is writing a book on Barbara Bush.

Melba Porter Hay received her Ph.D from the University of Kentucky and served as an editor of The Papers of Henry Clay from 1980 to 1991. She is now division manager of research and publication at the Kentucky Historical Society. She has written numerous articles for journals and encyclopedias, including "1824," in Arthur M. Schlesinger Jr. et al., eds., *Running for President: The Candidates and Their Images* (2 vols., 1994), I, pp. 87–95

Kristin Hoganson is assistant professor of history at the University of Illinois, Urbana-Champaign. She is the author of *Fighting for American Manhood: How Gender Politics Provoked the Spanish-American and Philippine-American Wars* (1998). Her current research is on globalization and U.S. domesticity from 1865–1920, as manifested through household consumption, fashion, cooking, popular geography, and "Americanization" efforts.

Olive Hoogenboom was born in Calcutta, India, and graduate from Atlantic Union College. She has collaborated with her husband, Ari Hoogenboom, on a number of historical projects. She has served as an associate editor of *American National Biography*, and wrote *The First Unitarian Church of Brooklyn, One Hundred Years*.

John J. Leffler received his Ph.D in history from the University of Texas at Austin in 1991. An historical consultant, he has worked with many clients, such as the Texas Parks and Wildlife Department, the U.S. Fish and Wildlife Service, the *Austin American-Statesman*, and the Center for Archaeological Research at the University of Texas at San Antonio. He teaches history part-time at the University of Texas at Austin.

Kristie Miller is co-editor of *We Have Come to Stay: American Woman and Political Parties, 1880–1960* (1999) and author of *Ruth Hanna McCormick: A Life in Politics, 1880–1944* (1992), as well as numerous articles on women in politics.

Lynn Hudson Parsons is professor of history at the State University of New York at Brockport and the author of *John Quincy Adams: A Bibliography* (1993) and *John Quincy Adams* (1998).

Allan Peskin is Emeritus Professor of history at Cleveland State University. He is the author of *Garfield* (1978), has written numerous articles on politics and life in the Gilded Age, and is working on a biography of Winfield Scott.

John Pope is an award-winning medical/health reporter for the *Times-Picayune* in New Orleans. A Phi Beta Kappa graduate of the University of Texas at Austin, where he also received a Master's degree, Pope has written for such newspapers and magazines as *Variety*, *Preservation News*, and the *Washington Post*. In June 1999 he was a fellow at the Knight Center for Specialized Journalism at the University of Maryland.

Shelley Sallee graduated from Smith College and received her Ph.D from The University of Texas at Austin in 1998. She teaches at St. Stephens School in Austin, Texas, where she is conducting an oral history project about the school's history. She has written on American women's history during the nineteenth and twentieth centuries.

Holly Cowan Shulman is research associate professor in studies in women and gender at the University of Virginia, where she is a fellow at the Virginia Center for Digital History. She is coediting, with David Mattern, a book of the selected letters of Dolley Madison and has prepared a website at moderntimes.vcdh.virginia.edu/madison, where Madison letters can be viewed. She and David Mattern are also writing a biography of Dolley Madison.

John Y. Simon is professor of history at Southern Illinois University at Carbondale, Illinois, and is the editor of *The Papers of Ulysses S. Grant* (24 vols., 1967–). He has published more than fifty articles in scholarly periodicals and is the founder of the Association for Documentary Editing.

Kathy B. Smith professor of politics and chair of the department at Wake Forest University, specializes in the American presidency and political communication. She is co-author of *The White House Speaks: Presidential Leadership as Persuasion* (1994) and co-editor of *The President and the Public Rhetoric of National Leadership*. She publishes in anthologies and both political science and communication studies journals.

Mark Young teaches history at McKendree College. He received his Ph.D from the University of Texas at Austin in 1997 and is working on a book about Lyndon Johnson and the Democratic Party.

Nancy Beck Young is an assistant professor of history at McKendree College and is the author of *Wright Patman: Populism, Liberalism, and the American Dream* (2000). She is writing a book on Lou Henry Hoover in the "Modern First Ladies" series for the University Press of Kansas.

AMERICAN FIRST LADIES

★★★　　★★★

Martha Dandridge Custis Washington

(1731–1802)

First Lady: 1789–1797

Patricia Brady

Martha Washington was the "worthy partner," as her obituary phrased it, of the nation's first president. So entwined were their lives that she can hardly be thought of other than in conjunction with George Washington. As First Lady—although the term was not used in her lifetime—she devoted herself to domestic and social life, setting a pattern for many of the women who came after her.

Born Martha Dandridge on June 2, 1731, in New Kent County, Virginia, she was the first of eight children of John Dandridge, a modest planter and county clerk, and Frances Jones Dandridge. The Dandridges were members of the gentry class but by no means in the first rank of tidewater aristocrats. Being the oldest sister of a large family—her youngest sister was born when she was twenty-five—helped shape the matronly aspect of her character so marked in adulthood. For a woman of her time and place, Martha received an education that her parents and itinerant tutors considered quite adequate, but the vagaries of diction and grammar in her letters show its limits. A lady's education emphasized "accomplishments"—music, the arts, dress, fine sewing, dancing, demeanor, household management—to the detriment of reading, writing, mathematics, and certainly of any higher subjects that might make her seem undesirably bookish to suitors. Marriage was a Virginia woman's destiny, and charm, in the absence of fortune, was essential for attracting a husband.

Certainly, Martha was quietly charming. At the age of seventeen she caught the fancy of Daniel Parke Custis, a man twenty years her senior. He had been thwarted in earlier attempts at matrimony by his eccentric and domineering father, John Custis, who indignantly refused permission to this marriage as well. The Custises and the Parkes, Daniel's mother's family, were among the wealthiest and most prominent families in Virginia, and John Custis looked higher than little Miss Dandridge, barely out of the schoolroom and meagerly dowered, for his only son and presumed heir. Finally in 1749, through the intervention of a friend, the elder Custis acquiesced to the marriage, reportedly remarking that he was "as much enamored with her character" as Daniel was "with her person." He promptly made a will in favor of his son and died in a timely fashion.

The wedding took place in 1750 at the bride's home, and the two set up housekeeping at Custis's plantation, ironically called White House, on the Pamunkey River some thirty-three miles from Williamsburg, the colonial capital. Children arrived promptly: Daniel Parke (b. 1751), Frances Parke (b. 1753), John Parke (b. 1754), and Martha Parke (b. 1756). In 1754 young Daniel died, the first of a trail of deaths that marred their happy life. Two years later Martha's father died suddenly while traveling. In the spring of 1757 their daughter Frances died, followed three months later by Daniel Custis himself, who fell ill and died suddenly, intestate, leaving Martha Custis an extremely wealthy widow of twenty-six with two small children to rear, almost no experience of financial matters, and a tangled morass of plantation affairs and Custis family problems, including a generation-old lawsuit that threatened to beggar the estate.

Surviving documents from the period of her widowhood give a sense of the overwhelming situation facing her. Letters from agents, attorneys, and merchants refer to complex business matters; any decision about the estate might have long-lasting and possibly disastrous results. Lacking an understanding of basic finance, Martha needed someone trustworthy to look after her affairs.

And then came the tall, dignified, ambitious soldier, a few months her junior, from a respectably circumstanced family much like her own. They had probably met previously during Williamsburg's social season. It must have seemed providential for both of them when the colonel of the Virginia militia began courting the wealthy young widow. In March and June 1758, in the intervals allowed by his military duties, George Washington visited at White House, and they settled their future; he put in train renovations and a considerable enlargement of Mount Vernon, the simple manor house he rented from his brother's widow.

Washington had courted other women in his youth and had nursed a hopeless infatuation for an older, married neighbor, the glamorous Sally Fairfax. Marriage, however, was a serious matter, requiring, in his opinion, good sense, good dispositions, and sufficient financial means. In the long run, friendship was more important than a fleeting passion. Besides the attraction of her wealth, Martha Custis was good-natured and pretty, a tiny woman under five feet tall with brown hair and slanting hazel eyes. Most important, the engaged couple shared similarities of disposition and outlook that forged a forty-year marriage of extreme happiness. They agreed on the importance of dignity, good reputation, decency in human relations, and a settled family life. Neither was addicted to the vices endemic among wealthy planter families—high-stakes gambling, drunkenness, debt accumulation, and infidelity.

They were married at White House on January 6, 1759, a year and a half after Daniel Custis's death. After a visit to Williamsburg, Washington took his new wife and stepchildren to Mount Vernon, far from their family and friends in the south. Two years later, on the death of his sister-in-law, Washington became the owner of the plantation that is so closely associated with his memory.

There, for the next fifteen years, the Washingtons enjoyed lives of happiness and simple contentment, partners in, according to a letter quoted by James T. Flexner, all the "domestic enjoyments" so relished by Washington after the austerity of his youth and the rigors of military life. He became an experimental farmer of some renown, adding to his acreage and making the plantation profitable, and becoming a leader in the political and social life of the colony. Although he was troubled by the moral implications of slavery, the basis for the plantation economy, the Mount Vernon slaves were not freed until his death. The Washingtons accepted slavery as an economic necessity but dealt humanely with their unfree labor force, providing decent living conditions, keeping families together, and refusing to sell slaves against their will.

Martha Washington's concerns were primarily domestic: creating a harmonious and well-run household, managing large-scale spinning and sewing enterprises, and catering to her husband's comfort. The Mount Vernon family was very social, daily welcoming friends and acquaintances for dinner or extended visits. The influx of visitors to Mount Vernon prompted Washington in the 1770s to enlarge the house further, to its present size. To Mrs. Washington, the house seemed filled with "mirth and gaiety." Happy though they were in their marriage, the Washingtons were sorely disappointed by their failure to have children. George was a loving stepfather and a careful financial steward to the Custis children, but there was no doubt that they were Martha's children and that she would have the final say concerning them. Although Martha had been quick to criticize her own mother for spoiling a little sister, she could not see that she was similarly at fault.

Reluctant to let the children out of her sight, Martha Washington was a loving, neurotically overanxious, and much too doting mother. She spoiled her son John ("Jacky") shamefully, despite her new husband's attempts to impose some sort of discipline. Jacky grew up self-indulgent and indolent, careless of both education and

occupation. Her youngest child, Martha "Patsy" Custis, was a worry in a different way: from childhood the girl was delicate, subject to epileptic fits of increasing severity. One afternoon in June 1773, Patsy rose from the dinner table, suffered a seizure, and died in less than two minutes. "This Sudden, and unexpected blow," wrote Washington in his diary for June 19, 1773, "has almost reduced my poor Wife to the lowest ebb of Misery."

That fall, Jacky, for all his faults a loving son, returned home to be with his grieving mother. Washington succumbed to the combined entreaties of his wife and stepson, and allowed Jacky to abandon his studies at King's College and to marry Eleanor Calvert, a member of a prominent Maryland family. They were wed in February 1774.

The Washingtons' private affairs, of course, were rapidly eclipsed by history as the colonies moved toward an open confrontation with the mother country. When George rode off as a delegate to the First Continental Congress in 1774, Martha Washington struggled to accept the revolutionary changes overtaking the Virginia colony. Despite her lack of interest in politics she became a staunch defender of the patriots' cause and was scandalized by allegations that she was a Tory who opposed her husband's views.

As Washington rapidly emerged as the indispensable man of the American Revolution, he and his wife saw their placid, pastoral life disappear. For the first time since their marriage, they were separated for long periods. Washington felt compelled to accept command of the Continental Army. He wrote to his wife on June 18, 1775, informing her of his decision; his tone, which is almost apologetic, assures her that his true happiness lay with her and the family. Ever concerned for his wife's welfare, George made his will and bought Martha two suits of what he was told was the "prettiest Muslin." Upon leaving for Boston he wrote: "I retain an unalterable affection for you, which neither time or distance can change."

Losing hope for an early return to Mount Vernon, in the fall of 1775 Washington invited his wife to join him at the army's winter encampment outside Boston. For the first time in her life this retiring middle-aged woman traveled north of Alexandria, Virginia, jolting over dreadful roads to join her husband.

For the first time, too, she experienced her husband's growing celebrity. The Washingtons were respected in Virginia but had never been singled out. On this journey there were numerous public demonstrations along the way. In Philadelphia she was accorded extraordinary civilities and escorted on her way out of the city, as she dryly observed, "in as great pomp as if I had been a very great somebody."

Arriving at the camp in December 1775, Martha Washington found the preparations for war "very terable indeed" but promptly set about creating a homelike atmosphere, an oasis of peace where she attended to her needlework, welcomed the officers and their wives to her quarters, and provided emotional comfort for her hard-pressed husband. This first visit set the pattern for the Revolutionary War years. Each spring when the army took to the field, she returned to Mount Vernon and the family. Each fall she rejoined her husband wherever the army was encamped for the winter. The pleasant, grandmotherly figure became an icon of the American army, the general's lady who brought something of home and hearth to the beleaguered troops.

As the war drew to a close, Martha Washington suffered a crushing personal tragedy. Jacky Custis, who had not served in the revolutionary army, in 1781 joined his stepfather at Yorktown to enjoy the British defeat; there he contracted one of the endemic camp fevers and soon died. His wife, Eleanor, and mother, who rushed to his bedside, were devastated. Martha Washington had written on other occasions that parents of very large families were better able to bear the frequent deaths of children. It must have seemed especially painful to her that, with only two children surviving infancy, both should die before her.

Grief-stricken, Martha dreaded retirement at a Mount Vernon without children to care for. But Jacky's widow had four small children, and the Washingtons offered to adopt the two youngest, Eleanor Parke Custis (b. 1779) and George Washington Parke Custis (b. 1781). Although there was no formal adoption, Nelly and Wash, as they were known, lived with the Washingtons as their children for the rest of their lives. Their mother soon married a family acquaintance and had many more children. In the eighteenth and nineteenth centuries, such adoptions by family members were quite common. The relationship remained close and there was constant visiting back and forth between the families.

In 1783, with the Revolutionary War at a close, the Washingtons returned eagerly to Mount Vernon, attempting to pick up the strands of their previous life. Washington occupied himself with completing the embellishment of the house and restoring the land, which was sorely neglected during the war. Mrs. Washington tended to her small grandchildren, who were an endless source of interest to her. Because Washington believed girls should be as well educated as boys, the children shared a tutor, who doubled as secretary to the general. The most important of their tutors was Tobias Lear, who became a fixture of Washington family life, devoted to them and eventually marrying (in succession) two of Mrs. Washington's nieces.

Regarding Nelly, her grandmother was more of a disciplinarian than she had been with the previous generation. Her hours of music practice and studies were strictly observed, and any faults of demeanor were promptly corrected. Unfortunately, Mrs. Washington continued her permissive course toward boys—"my pretty little Dear Boy . . . it makes me miserable if ever he complains." Like his father, Wash was indolent, an indifferent student whose grandmother blamed his teachers for any lack of scholastic progress. Perhaps, though, the seeming impossibility of measuring up to Washington contributed to both Jacky's and Wash's dilatory ways.

The children's health was a constant preoccupation for their grandmother. They were not allowed to overeat or to indulge in heavy food, since Martha Washington held the firm opinion that "worms is the cause of all complaints in children." Her remedy for childhood worms—an elixir of wormseed, rhubarb, garlic, and "best wine or whiskey"—is preserved in Nelly's 1830s housekeeping book.

Not surprisingly, the endless minor complications of childhood, combined with the very real dangers of epidemic illness—smallpox, yellow fever, typhoid, and whooping cough—kept Martha Washington apprehensive. Besides her own four children, by this time she had lost five of her seven brothers and sisters, and numerous nieces and nephews. Death was very much a part of eighteenth-century life. A devout Episcopalian, she found solace in her religion; still, as she wrote to a bereaved friend, "nature will, notwithstanding, endulge, for a while, its sorrows."

The younger women in the family, including her daughter-in-law Eleanor and favored nieces from both the Dandridge and Washington families, along with the wives of Washington's aides, were essential to Martha Washington's happiness. She enjoyed a companionable social life, with a circle of young women friends to help her entertain the many visitors who found their way to Mount Vernon's hospitable door. Increasingly, these visitors were politicians as the Articles of Confederation were superseded by a federal constitution. Most Americans agreed that there was only one possible president for the new government—George Washington. Again, duty called, and when Washington was informed of his election in April 1789, he set off within two days for New York City, the temporary capital.

Mrs. Washington, who had dreamed of permanent retirement with her husband, hoping "to grow old in solitude and tranquility togather," was not best pleased by this honor. She wrote, "I think it was much too late for him to go in to publick life again," but acquiesced, as always, in his devotion to the nation. She remained a resolute patriot with all her prejudices in favor of America. As she wrote to a friend returning from a European sojourn, "I think our country affords every thing that can give pleasure or satisfaction to a rational mind."

In New York, Washington found that everything of the day-to-day business of the government was yet to be invented, and he felt his way slowly in setting precedents for the future. His governmental burden was complicated by a disconcerting social problem. There were many who believed that the nation's citizens had an inalienable right to meet their president at will and that he was obliged to entertain them. Always hospitable, Washington found, however, that this republican propensity for intruding on the president on the smallest excuse—or indeed none at all—made it almost impossible for him to carry out the work he had been elected to do.

After consultation with trusted friends and advisers, Washington fixed a formal schedule of public entertaining and refused to receive guests at other times. To limit intrusive visitors, he inaugurated a weekly levee on Tuesday afternoons, which any respectable-looking man was welcome to attend without appointment. He delegated domestic arrangements to the indispensable Tobias Lear and sent the family coach back to Mount Vernon. Martha Washington and her two young grandchildren, accompanied by her niece, as well as one of Washington's nephews, set off, arriving in New York on May 28, 1789.

Martha Washington's report on the journey reflects her usual mix of concerns, public and domestic: an agreeable trip despite Nelly's coach sickness, a reception by dignitaries in Philadelphia, shoes and stays ordered for her favorite niece. The little party was met at Elizabethtown by the president in a fine barge, culminating the "great parade that was made for us all the way we come."

Martha Washington's first care was to enroll the children in a good school. She very soon, however, discovered the tedium of constant public attention. Contrary to her usual habit at home, her hair had to be set and dressed every day and she attended much more to her clothes, putting on white muslin habits for the summer—"a good deal in the fashion."

The boundaries of social life to be observed by the president's lady were just being defined, and often the definition arrived at by her husband was not to her liking. Washington had decided that his wife would preside at a weekly drawing room for both men and women on Friday evenings. On the second day after her arrival in New York she was the hostess at the first of these parties, which continued throughout Washington's presidency. Seated, Martha Washington received her guests, who were greeted by the president and then were free to circulate among the other visitors. In addition, the Washingtons gave dinner parties on Thursdays evenings for government officials and their families, as well as for foreign dignitaries, invited in rotation.

Limiting their social life to official entertainments, Washington had announced that he and his wife would not accept invitations to private gatherings. Mrs. Washington was considerably disgruntled to find herself so fettered by political considerations. She repined and stayed at home—"I am more like a state prisoner than anything else, there is certain bounds set for me which I must not depart from—and as I can not doe as I like I am obstinate and stay at home a great deal." None of the guests attending the presidential entertainments, however, knew of her dissatisfaction. Although Washington was sometimes criticized for stiffness and ceremoniousness, his wife was always given high marks for her charm and graciousness. Even her husband's political enemies succumbed to the effortless kindness with which she made all her guests feel at ease.

Living arrangements for the presidential family were makeshift, inasmuch as both Washington, D.C., and the White House were years in the future. The Washingtons rented a three-story house on Cherry Street, large but still cramped with the many staff and servants to be housed; it also served as the working office of the president and his staff. Mrs. Washington mothered not only her grandchildren but also the several young gentlemen who were the president's secretaries and aides. In addition to their official duties, these amiable bachelors escorted her and the children on their excursions and acted as deputy hosts on all social occasions.

Besides the family and staff, Martha Washington enjoyed friendships with the wives of other government officials. Fortunately, Lucy Knox, the wife of the secretary of war, was an old friend from Revolutionary War days. An unexpected new friend, given the differences in their personal styles, was the outspoken New Englander Abigail Adams. Mrs. Adams, generally more inclined to critical observation, wrote soon after meeting her, in a letter to Mary Cranch of July 12, 1789, that "Mrs. Washington is one of those unassuming characters which create Love & Esteem. A most becoming pleasentness sits upon her countenance & an unaffected deportment which renders her the object of veneration and Respect."

There were grave doubts at home and abroad about the long-term success of what many considered to be nothing more than an experimental American government. Only Washington, it was believed, enjoyed the solid popular respect needed to lead the new nation through these years. But Washington, as his worried wife pointed out, was an elderly, if vigorous, man. During the first two years of his presidency illness threatened both his life and the shaky government. Washington was so gravely ill in 1789 and again in 1790 that he nearly died. The nation trembled, and all the more Martha Washington. Although he recovered completely both times, she was convinced that long hours, worry, and lack of regular exercise were undermining her husband's health.

At the end of 1790, after a holiday at Mount Vernon, the family moved to the interim capital, Philadelphia, the nation's leading city. They rented the large Morris mansion on High Street, and the president busied himself with household alterations and improvements, one of his abiding interests. The Custis children were settled in school, and the Washingtons again took up their schedule of official entertainments. But in Philadelphia there were many old friends and some engaging new ones. Gradually, under his wife's influence, the president's strictures against accepting private invitations were informally relaxed, and the seven years they spent in Philadelphia were filled with activity as they attended parties, the theater, church, concerts, and everything else of interest from balloon ascensions to a circular panorama of Westminster and London.

Some of the family's Philadelphia friends were extremely wealthy, well-educated, and sophisticated, to the distaste of voluble republican critics. Martha Washington, however, with her simple dignity, self-confidence, and graceful manners never found herself at a loss socially. Only about her writing ability did she suffer from any sense of diffidence. When she wanted to shine, certain letters—to the wives of foreign officials or the formidably accomplished Elizabeth Powel or her official responses to tendered gifts—were drafted for her by Washington or by Tobias Lear. She then copied these drafts and signed them as her own. But the formal correspondence with its attention to grammar and consciously literary turns of phrase lacks the charm of her own letters to her intimates—sensible, homely, and frequently lightened with self-deprecating humor.

As far as Martha Washington was concerned, her sixty-year-old husband had done all that could be expected for his country by 1792, toward the end of his first term as president. Their neglected acres at Mount Vernon needed attention, and the rising tide of partisan political attacks distressed both Washingtons. It was time for him to retire and let a younger generation of political leaders take command. Unfortunately, they were not yet prepared to do so, and both factions begged Washington to accept a second term for the good of the country. It was almost unbearably disap-

pointing to Martha Washington when her aging husband again bowed to duty. After the simple inauguration, which she and the children attended, the problems of the second term rapidly multiplied, becoming far worse than she could ever have anticipated.

The deadly yellow fever epidemic that struck Philadelphia in 1793, forcing the Washington family to take refuge in Germantown, was an ominous beginning to a troubled time. These years saw the Whiskey Rebellion, a major international crisis with Great Britain, Indian attacks on the frontier, and the tumultuous intrusion of French Revolutionary influence into American politics. Most discouraging of all to Washington was the ferocity of partisan infighting as Alexander Hamilton and Thomas Jefferson emerged as leaders of contending political factions. Republican newspaper attacks on the president grew more virulent, wounding him terribly. The family formed a lasting dislike of Jefferson for his deliberate orchestration of Washington's mortification.

Martha Washington feared that her husband would not survive the many strains of a second term. When he wrenched his back while riding during a 1794 trip to Mount Vernon, she was beside herself with anxiety. Only his return to Philadelphia prevented her from posting down on the stagecoach.

The disappointments of these years caused the president and his wife to long for their well-earned retirement at Mount Vernon. Washington had spent eight weary years building a government that could survive a change of executive, avoiding the cycles of revolution and dictatorship that would plague future republics. Remaining only to attend the inauguration of John Adams, they bade farewell to their friends in Philadelphia and loaded the family, staff, servants, Nelly's dog and parrot, as well as mountains of baggage, into two groaning coaches. The overflow—furniture and yet more baggage—was sent by ship. Despite a very heavy cold and cough, Martha Washington would hear of no delay in setting off for Virginia.

They arrived back home in March 1797 to find Mount Vernon in considerable disarray, with many of the buildings decaying. Mrs. Washington wrote to an old friend that "we once more (and I am very sure never to quit it again) got seated under our own Roof, more like new beginners than old established residenters."

Their retirement followed the pattern of previous returns to Mount Vernon. "Farmer Washington" began to bring his land back into shape after years of neglect and to oversee long-overdue building repairs. His wife devoted herself to the young people. Even though Washington Custis had remained behind for the time being at Princeton College, another young man needed her maternal attentions— George Washington Lafayette, adolescent son of the Marquis de Lafayette, sent in 1795 with his tutor to live with the Washingtons while his father languished as a political prisoner; young Lafayette remained part of the household until that fall.

Eighteen-year-old Nelly, however, claimed her grandmother's special care. By Virginia reckoning it was time to find a husband for the sprightly young brunette. She was frequently sent for extended visits with friends in Alexandria or with her older sisters, married with babies, both of whom lived in the fashionable Washington suburb of Georgetown. For a year and a half after returning to Virginia she regularly attended tea parties, the theater, horse races, and balls on these visits. Although her grandmother warned her that "one always expects more pleasure than they realize after the matter is over," balls remained her favorite amusement. When she was at home young friends from the neighborhood and acquaintances from the city were frequent callers. She attracted numerous admirers but did not immediately receive a formal offer of marriage.

The Washingtons had always entertained generously and had a large acquaintance, but now the former president's celebrity was a magnet, drawing an endless string of visitors to their door—relatives, friends, acquaintances, those who could

scrape up an introduction, and some for whom sheer gall was excuse enough. Eating dinner alone together was such a rarity that Washington mentioned the occasion in a note to Lear that summer; George and Martha Washington had last dined alone in 1785.

Ultimately the press of visitors became too great for the Washingtons' settled habits. They liked to retire early to bed, and he often wished to spend the evening in his study, arranging his papers or answering his large correspondence. He invited one of his many nephews, Lawrence Lewis, to join the family as an unpaid secretary and deputy host. Lewis was a childless widower of thirty, the son of Washington's sister Betty. He moved to Mount Vernon in 1797, relieving the Washingtons of many cares and becoming engaged to Nelly at Christmas the following year. The couple were married on February 22, 1799 (Washington's birthday), and, to everyone's satisfaction, they continued to make their home at Mount Vernon. Nelly felt too lonely away from her beloved Grandmama, and Martha Washington, as always, depended on the companionship of the young women of the family.

Washington Custis continued to present an annoying problem for George Washington, but probably not for his loving grandmother, as he neglected to apply himself at any of the colleges where he was enrolled. At his own request he was allowed to come home for good in August 1798. Martha Washington was quite satisfied to have all her young people living at Mount Vernon.

After a week-long labor Nelly gave birth to her first child, a healthy daughter, in late November 1799. Mrs. Washington's delight in her latest great-grandchild was short-lived, however. Two weeks later, despite bitter cold and snow, George Washington rode out to supervise plantation activities and became chilled; his cold soon proved to be a severe respiratory infection, and he died on December 14 with his wife and his old friend Tobias Lear at his side.

Martha Washington was devastated. She had devoted herself to her husband and she had little interest in life after his death. She closed their bedroom and moved to a small garret room. Dressed in a black gown and frilled white cap, she continued to receive the stream of callers at Mount Vernon as graciously as ever, but she had become somewhat distant and preoccupied. For her remaining two and a half years, she lived with loving companions—her grandchildren; Lear, who had remained with the family; Nelly's Frances Parke and a new baby, Martha Betty; and the many other family members who regularly made long visits. She received numerous requests for mementos of Washington and busied herself sending remembrances, including locks of his hair, to admirers. After some months of fatigue and failing health, she died in her bed, May 22, 1802, and was buried beside her husband in the family tomb at Mount Vernon.

A letter freezes a moment in time, preserving the feelings of that moment from change. Martha Washington destroyed the hundreds of letters she wrote to her husband, which might have satisfied the curiosity of later generations. Only one letter, written in 1767, escaped her fire, but that one—loving, homely, comfortable—says all there is to say. "My Dearest . . . I am sorry you will not be at home soon. . . . Your most Affectionate, Martha Washington." Her simple words reflect forty years of mutual devotion.

A few months after their marriage in 1759, George Washington wrote to an acquaintance, in a letter published in his collected papers, that he expected to find happiness with his "agreable Consort for Life." Martha Washington was certainly an agreeable consort and his partner in all domestic enjoyments. Together, they enjoyed a lifetime of quiet happiness.

BIBLIOGRAPHICAL ESSAY

Documentary sources for the life of the very private Martha Washington are sparse. No scrap of paper written by her before her first widowhood exists, and documents from that period deal largely with business matters having to do with her first husband's estate. According to family tradition, after George Washington's death, she burned all the hundreds of letters that the couple had exchanged through the years. Certainly, very few of their letters remain—four of his letters to her and only one of hers to him, accidental survivors of her determination to preserve their privacy.

Many of her letters to relatives and friends, however, were saved. Most of her papers are held by the Virginia Historical Society and Mount Vernon. Scattered letters are also to be found in other archives or in private hands. Joseph E. Fields has compiled all known papers of Martha Washington, incoming and outgoing, and published them as *"Worthy Partner": The Papers of Martha Washington* (Westport, Conn., 1994). All quotations are from this source, unless otherwise indicated. This essential resource includes an excellent short biography by Ellen McCallister Clark, formerly librarian of Mount Vernon. Fields reproduces certain well-known letters published in nineteenth-century sources while indicating that they were probably pious fakes.

The Diaries of George Washington, ed. Donald Jackson and Dorothy Twohig (Charlottesville, Va., 1976–1979), and the comprehensive collections of Washington's papers, ed. John Fitzpatrick (Washington, D.C., 1931–1944) and William W. Abbott et al. (Charlottesville, 1983–), are primary sources that contain valuable information about the daily life of the Washingtons, as do the exhaustive multivolume biographies of Washington by Douglas Southall Freeman, *George Washington* (New York, 1948–1957) and James Thomas Flexner, *George Washington* (Boston, 1965–1972). Other important sources for the private and social life of the Washington family are *Recollections and Private Memoirs of Washington* by Mrs. Washington's grandson George W. P. Custis (Washington, D.C., 1859); *The Family Life of George Washington* by Charles Moore (Boston, 1926); *The Republican Court* by Rufus W. Griswold (New York, 1855); and the annual reports of the Mount Vernon Ladies Association of the Union. Abigail Adams's comment about Martha

Washington is from a letter to Mary Smith Cranch, July 12, 1789, in Stewart Mitchell, ed., *New Letters of Abigail Adams* (Boston, 1947).

Martha Washington—often in combination with her formidable mother-in-law, Mary Ball Washington—was the subject of worshipful nineteenth-century biographies, frequently embellished with doubtful anecdotes. These include Margaret Conkling's *Memoirs of the Mother and Wife*

of Washington (Auburn, N.Y., 1850); Benson J. Lossing's *Mary and Martha* (New York, 1886); and Anne Hollingsworth Wharton's *Martha Washington* (New York, 1897). In the twentieth century *Washington's Lady* by Elswyth Thane (Mattituck, N. Y., 1977) is a fictionalized but carefully researched work. There is no scholarly biography of Martha Washington. Her obituary can be found in the *Alexandria Advertiser and Commercial Intelligencer*, May 25, 1802.

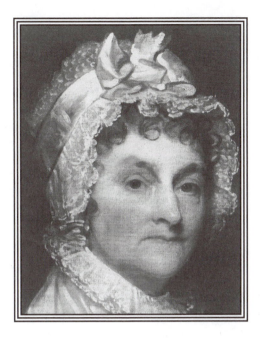

★★★　　★★★

Abigail Smith Adams

(1744–1818)

First Lady: 1797–1801

Lynn Hudson Parsons

Abigail Smith was born on November 11, 1744, in Weymouth, Massachusetts, and died a little less than seventy-four years later in nearby Quincy, on October 28, 1818. She was the daughter of a Congregational minister, William Smith, and of Elizabeth Quincy Smith, and the granddaughter of John Quincy, a prominent citizen of colonial Massachusetts, for whom she named her eldest son. In 1764 she married John Adams, then a virtually unknown attorney from Braintree, who became the second president of the United States in 1797. They had four surviving children, one of whom, John Quincy Adams, became the sixth president of the United States in 1825. She thus became the first woman to be both the wife and the mother of a president.

Abigail Smith, like all American women of her time, did not enjoy the benefits of formal education. She did, however, have access to her father's extensive library of classical literature, of which she took full advantage with the help of Richard Cranch, a suitor, and eventual husband, of Abigail's older sister Mary. It was through Cranch that Abigail first met John Adams. Although her orthography and spelling were unique, those who have read her letters to her husband, her children, and her network of friends and relatives inevitably appreciate the breadth of her intellect, the variety of her interests, and the strength of her character. One can only speculate as to what degree her horizons could have been expanded had she been given the educational opportunities provided to her father, brother, husband, and sons.

Abigail Adams was the first First Lady to take an active interest in politics before, during, and after her husband's term of office. And she was nothing if not opinionated. In later years she recalled that her father regarded her as a "sausy" child. Today she is perhaps best remembered for her famous letter to her husband, written in 1776, on the eve of the Declaration of Independence, in which she admonished John Adams to "remember the ladies" in setting up the new republic. Yet both the context of the letter and the course of her life indicate that she accepted the domestic role women of her time were expected to play, and she played it exceedingly well. Within that role, however, she chafed at the denial of opportunity for women to grow intellectually, to travel independently, and to share in the exciting public events of the time. She managed to overcome many of these restrictions herself, and thus played a significant role in the history of American feminism as well as in that of America's First Ladies.

As her husband emerged as a leader in the protest against Britain's new imperialism in the 1760s, Abigail Adams provided encouragement. Since John Adams's legal practice often required him to be on the road, riding the judicial circuit, she kept him informed, beginning a rich correspondence that would continue for the next thirty-five years. The separations engendered by his circuit-riding proved to be insignificant compared with what was to come. John Adams was selected to represent Massachusetts in the First and Second Continental Congresses, which met in Philadelphia and elsewhere from 1774 through 1777. His wife regularly reported the progress of the war for independence in Massachusetts, observed with seven-year-old John Quincy Adams the Battle of Bunker Hill from atop one of the hills on their farm, and several months later relayed the triumphant news of the British withdrawal from Boston.

Shortly thereafter Abigail Adams penned her "remember the ladies" letter to her husband:

I long to hear that you have declared an independency—and by the way in the new Code of Laws which I suppose it will be necessary for you to make I desire you would Remember the Ladies, and be more generous and favourable to them than your ancestors. Do not put such unlimited power in the hands of the Husbands. Remember all Men would be tyrants if they could. If perticular care and attention is not paid to the Ladies we are determined to foment a Rebelion, and will not hold ourselves bound by any Laws in which we have no voice, or Representation. (A. A. to J. A., March 31, 1776)

The accusation "All men would be tyrants if they could" is borrowed from Daniel Defoe. It is not clear how seriously Abigail Adams was pushing this agenda, turning as she did orthodox republican and Lockean rhetoric against the all-male Continental Congress. Certainly, she had no intention of organizing a "Rebelion." Years later she read Mary Wollstonecraft's *Vindication of the Rights of Women* and found in it much that she agreed with, and much that she did not. She never wavered in her insistence on greater parity between men and women within marriage, and saw to it that her daughter—also named Abigail—received much the same education at home as did her three sons. Yet she never advocated the vote for women nor challenged what later would be called the "cult of domesticity." "However brilliant a woman's tallents may be, she ought never to shine at the expence of her husband," she later told her son.

Abigail and John Adams were brought up in the culture of "civic virtue" typical of Americans in the late eighteenth century, which emphasized one's duty to the public first and to oneself second. Her husband was passing up a lucrative legal career. As for herself, she explained to a friend, she had been taught by her husband's "precept and example to sacrifice every private view to the publick good" (A. A. to Daniel Roberdeau, December 15, 1777). But,

I have often experienced the want of his aid and assistance in the last 3 years of his absence and the Demand increases as our Little ones grow up 3 of whom are sons and at this time of life stand most in need of the joint force of his example and precepts.

And can I sir consent to be separated from him whom my Heart esteems among all earthly things, and for an unlimited time? My life will be one continued scene of anxiety and apprehension, and must I cheerfully comply with the Demand of my Country? (A. A. to James Lovell, December 15, 1777)

From 1777 through 1785, John Adams went from representing Massachusetts to representing the United States in a variety of diplomatic posts in Europe, ending with his appointment as the first American minister to Great Britain. In his absence from Braintree, his wife assumed most of the responsibilities that normally fell to men, including the managing of their farm; hiring, supervising, and occasionally firing servants and hired hands; deciding which crops to grow where; and investing whatever profits there were at the end of the year. Her husband heartily approved of her decisions.

Their longest separation lasted six and a half years, from December 1777 to July 1784. It was broken by a few months in 1779 when John Adams returned from his first mission to France, only to leave again before the end of the year. In these years Abigail Adams not only dealt with approaching middle age (she was thirty-three when her husband left for France; she would be nearly forty when she rejoined him), but also defended him against critics both at home and abroad. Her husband had managed to run afoul of French diplomats who preferred to take the lead in negotiating any peace with Great Britain, and who vastly preferred the more amiable and cooperative Benjamin Franklin. John Adams had grown increasingly critical of Franklin's allegedly sybaritic lifestyle and lack of attention to detail, and Franklin's defenders were quick to respond. Abigail Adams promptly sent forth a stream of letters critical of Franklin and defending her

husband to friends and political contacts in Massachusetts and Philadelphia. "When he is wounded I bleed," she said (A. A. to James Lovell, June 30, 1781).

By late 1782, hearing from her husband only by infrequent and infuriatingly short letters, Abigail Adams was as close to complete depression as she ever would be. The news of Cornwallis's surrender at Yorktown and its promise of a successful end to the War for Independence did little to cheer her. She wrote despondently to her husband of their now-distant youth:

I recollect the untitled Man to whom I gave my Heart, and in the agony of recollection when time and distance present themselves altogether—wish he had never been any other. Who shall give me back Time? who shall compensate to me those *years* I cannot recall? How dearly have I paid for a titled Husband; should I wish you less wise that I might enjoy more happiness? (A. A. to J. A., October 25, 1782)

By 1783 neither spouse could stand it any longer. Leaving their two youngest sons in the care of relatives, Abigail Adams and her daughter embarked on the vessel *Active* for London in June 1784. There they were met first by seventeen-year-old John Quincy Adams and then by John Adams himself. They then went to Paris, where they lived for a year while Adams, along with Thomas Jefferson, negotiated commercial treaties with Britain and France, and then moved to London after Adams received his appointment as minister to Great Britain.

Not only had the Adamses been brought up in the culture of "civic virtue," they were also products of New England puritanism, albeit somewhat diminished in the more secular eighteenth century. As such, their reactions to both French and British society were mixed at best. In contrast to their genial colleague Jefferson, Abigail Adams disliked France generally and Paris in particular. Like many Americans before and since, she thought the French were hedonistic, frivolous, and lazy. Formerly the mistress of a seven-room cottage, she now found herself in charge of a thirty-room mansion outside of Paris with an entourage of servants, no one of whom, she thought, worked as much as their American counterparts. The French seemed not to take marriage seriously, and prostitution was an accepted fact of Parisian life, as the hundreds of abandoned children in the foundling hospitals she visited readily attested. Upon attending a ballet, she wrote: "I felt my delicacy wounded, and I was ashamed to bee seen to look at . . . girls cloathed in the thinnest silk and gauze . . . perfectly shewing their Garters & draws, as tho no peticoat had been worn" (A. A. to Mary Cranch, February 20, 1785; quoted in Withey, 169).

London was a little better, the English appearing to be more serious and businesslike. The city was cleaner and more prosperous than Paris, but this was offset by the thinly veiled hostility much of London society felt toward Americans. Whatever their faults, the French never hesitated to profess the respect and admiration for all things American, even in the waning days of Bourbon absolutism. Added to this was the expense of court appearances before King George III and his family, whom Abigail Adams found "in general very plain ill-shaped and ugly" (A. A. to Mary Cranch, June 24, 1785; quoted in Withey, 178). She was both pained and amused by the way in which London society revolved around the royal family. "I never expect to be a Court favourite," she told her sister (to Mary Cranch, September 30, 1785; quoted in Withey, 183).

The Adamses made contact with the small colony of Americans then living in London and with the minority of British "republicans" who were not attracted to monarchical ways. Abigail Adams also carried on a lively correspondence with her husband's counterpart in Paris, Thomas Jefferson, who had become a family favorite while they had been in Paris. "He is one of the choice ones of the earth," she once remarked. When Jefferson's nine-year-old daughter Polly was sent from Virginia to

join him, she was committed to Abigail Adams's care in London before traveling on to Paris. But in spite of her circle of friends in London and elsewhere, Mrs. Adams was happy when her husband determined that he could be of no further use in the hostile climate of the English court and determined to return home in 1788.

The return coincided with preparations for the adoption of the new Constitution of the United States, hammered out the year before at Philadelphia. It was assumed that George Washington, a Southerner, would be the unanimous choice for president of the new nation, so most agreed that the vice presidency should go to a Northerner. John Adams's name quickly rose to the top of the list. By now Abigail Adams had accepted the fact that her husband could never function well outside of public affairs, and with her children grown and no longer needing her, she became his most enthusiastic advocate. Custom forbade any hint of public or private "campaigning" for the office, but both Abigail and John Adams would have been bitterly disappointed if the nation's second highest office had gone to anyone else.

With the national capital located temporarily in New York, the Adamses made plans to move there in 1789. They settled in a sumptuous home, Richmond Hill, located in what is now the heart of Greenwich Village. Since neither Martha Washington, the nation's first First Lady, nor Abigail Adams, the nation's first "Second Lady" had much guidance in the way of precedent to govern matters of protocol, their pattern followed closely that of British royalty, with formal receptions, visiting cards, and dinners at which members of Congress and other government officials were entertained. Both Adamses believed that the new government needed to be supported with as much formality and deference as was possible in a republic, and for this they were criticized. John Adams in particular found himself in trouble for publicly expressing his belief that the presidency needed a grandiloquent title similar to European royalty in order to instill respect, and his wife agreed. Neither was a monarchist in any meaningful sense of the word, but from this point forward they never were able to escape the charge that their residence abroad had somehow corrupted them into "monarchical" thinking.

The following year found the Adamses in Philadelphia, the new temporary capital that was to be their home during the remainder of John Adams's vice presidency and most of his presidency. They lived for one season outside the city and then moved to Philadelphia proper, in order to more conveniently entertain guests and, for the vice president, to preside over the Senate. Abigail Adams found the routines of entertainment and formal receptions to be both boring and arduous, and it was with great eagerness that she looked forward to spring and the move northward to Quincy—as the north parish of Braintree was now called—and the company of relatives and friends. She valued these contacts so much that she chose not to return to Philadelphia during her husband's second term as vice president. As for John Adams, his summation of the vice presidency remained a classic for many years: it was the most "insignificant office . . . ever . . . contrived."

Their discontent was aggravated by the growing cleavage in American political culture that would eventually result in partisan warfare between the Washington administration and its critics. Those who supported Washington's policies called themselves "Federalists," appropriating the name once applied to all supporters of the Constitution. Not to be outdone, the critics began calling themselves "Republicans," implying that Federalists had abandoned their Revolutionary heritage. John and Abigail Adams soon found themselves on the Federalist side of many disputes with former friends like Mercy Otis Warren, John's cousin Samuel Adams, and finally even Thomas Jefferson. The last was most painful for Mrs. Adams, for whom the Virginian was no longer "one of the choice ones of the earth." Many of their former friendships were affected as Federalists and Republicans quarreled over the interpretation of their new Constitution, the definition of true

"republicanism," and their proper role in the growing war between Great Britain and Revolutionary France. Frightened, as were many of her fellow citizens, by the alleged excesses of the French Revolution, Abigail Adams turned increasingly partisan and conservative, denouncing critics of the Washington administration as being little more than foreign agents. Gone was her earlier Anglophobia, as Great Britain appeared to more and more Americans to be the only bulwark against a Reign of Terror in America.

In the midst of the rising political tumult, Abigail Adams again ran the family farm in Quincy, much as she had in the days when her husband was in Europe. Again, John Adams was willing to offer advice if asked, but was even more willing to let his wife handle their financial affairs, including the investment of the farm's profits in government bonds and real estate. She also supervised the remodeling and expansion of the house in Quincy that they had purchased upon their return from Europe, and where they would spend the remainder of their lives.

George Washington's decision to retire from the presidency in 1796 resulted in the first contested presidential election in American history, with John Adams facing his former friend Jefferson for the succession. The Virginian had come to lead the opposition to the Washington administration, especially its financial policies as put forth by Alexander Hamilton and its accommodationist approach to Great Britain as typified by Jay's Treaty. Though John Adams was not entirely comfortable with either one, he represented those in America who favored a continuation of both. Adams won the election by a narrow margin, with Jefferson, under the rules at that time, becoming vice president.

Abigail Adams now began to doubt her abilities as a First Lady. She knew she had a reputation for frankness, both in public and in private. "I have been so used to a freedom of sentiment," she explained to her husband, "that I know not how to place so many gaurds about me . . . to look at every word before I utter it, and to impose a silence upon my self, when I long to talk." She would not be able to retreat this time to the Quincy farm, as she had for the previous four years. Although not present at the inauguration in March 1797, Abigail Adams joined her husband later that spring, occupying the house in Philadelphia used by the Washingtons before them. There she resumed her role as hostess, at one time entertaining the entire United States Senate and the president's cabinet simultaneously. She was anxious to return home that summer.

In the meantime, events were unfolding abroad that would define the Adams administration's successes and failures. The president had appointed a three-man delegation to smooth over relations with the French, which had deteriorated following Jay's Treaty in 1795. This resulted in the infamous XYZ Affair, in which the three Americans were confronted in Paris with hostility, mixed with demands for bribes. When the news of the affair arrived back home, the president denounced the French and angrily withdrew his representatives. A wave of Francophobia swept the nation, followed by demands for war. For perhaps the only time in his life John Adams was a national hero, as the Republican opposition wisely retreated into silence.

For Abigail Adams, the XYZ Affair and its aftermath provided justification for the Federalist cause and that of her husband. "The people are daily becomeing more firmly decided and united," she proudly told her diplomat son, "more disposed to repel insult with due energy, and having failed in our attempts to negotiate, I think will unite to defend our Country and protect our Commerce." Congress approved funds for a revitalized army, with George Washington agreeing to command it should war be declared, but turning its command over to Alexander Hamilton in the meantime. For good measure, in 1798 Congress passed the Alien and Sedition Acts to deal with what most Federalists, including Abigail Adams, believed to be an internal threat of subversion by French agents and their Republican allies.

Mrs. Adams's role as a partisan defender and advocate of her husband was recognized by both friend and foe. Office seekers deluged her with letters seeking her influence on their behalf. Not surprisingly, a Republican critic maintained that "the President would not dare to make a nomination without her approbation." She regularly supplied newspapers with pro-Federalist material, often taken from the letters of John Quincy Adams, then minister to Prussia. She was critical of Congress for stopping short of war with France in 1798. She was a firm supporter of the Alien and Sedition Acts, believing the threat from "Jacobins" to be real enough to justify the jailing of many critics of her husband's administration. She became fearful of French influence, especially some of the trends in women's fashion. The "Empire style" featured low necklines and short sleeves, so that, as she told her sister Mary, when in her drawing room a woman curtsied as custom required, "every Eye in the Room had been fixed upon her, and you might litterally see through her." Too many of them "look like Nursing Mothers."

Those who had hoped for war with France and had assumed John Adams's loyalties lay with Great Britain were doomed to disappointment. "We will have neither John Bull nor Louis Baboon," he told his wife shortly before becoming president. In a move that alienated significant portions of his own Federalist Party, Adams, after receiving indirect assurances from the French, renewed diplomatic contacts with Paris. Upon learning that his Secretary of State Timothy Pickering was undermining his policies, he fired him. Thus Adams was faced with hostility from two sides: Republicans who were attacking the Alien and Sedition Acts as unconstitutional breaches of the rights of free speech and free press, and "High Federalists," led by Hamilton and Pickering, who fought his attempts to restore relations with the French. In the end, his diplomacy was successful but his bid for reelection was not. The better-organized Republicans, again with Jefferson as their candidate, prevailed over the divided Federalists, although Adams proved to be far more popular than his party.

As for Abigail Adams, the year 1800 turned out to be tragic personally as well as politically. The marriage of her only daughter was less than successful; her husband, William Stephens Smith, was constantly in pursuit of the quick killing in real estate that would forever elude him and would eventually land him in debtors' prison. Worse still, Charles, the middle son in the family, fell victim to alcoholism and depression, and died in New York City shortly after his father's defeat. Mrs. Adams almost welcomed her husband's loss as she looked forward to a peaceful retirement.

Abigail Adams was the first presidential wife to live in what would later be called the White House, when the seat of national government moved to the new "city" of Washington in the summer of 1800. She did not look forward to the experience. Built on a swamp, the new capital seemed more a forlorn village than the seat of a future world power. Few public buildings had been completed when the Adamses arrived. Traveling separately from her husband that fall, Abigail Adams and her party managed to get lost in the woods between Baltimore and Washington, and were obliged to put up for the night at the home of a stranger.

She found the White House, like everything else in Washington, incomplete. The rooms were drafty, requiring thirteen fires to maintain warmth in the approaching winter. The East Room was little more than a cavern suitable for drying laundry, the use to which Abigail Adams proceeded to put it. But if one looked past the stumps on the lawn, one had a magnificent view of the Potomac River and Virginia beyond it. The house was, she conceded, built "for ages to come," not for her own nor that of her husband.

Although John Adams and the Federalists had been defeated in the presidential election of 1800, it was not yet clear that Jefferson had won. Under the rules of that day, each presidential elector cast two votes, so every Republican elector dutifully voted for Jefferson and his running mate, Aaron Burr. The result was that the two men tied for the office. Not caring to wait for the result, Abigail Adams left Washington a month before her husband. It was only as she was passing through Philadelphia that she learned the House of Representatives had chosen Jefferson over Burr as the third president of the United States. A week later she returned to Massachusetts for the last time.

In the years of "retirement" that lay ahead of her, Abigail Adams never lost her interest in politics and public affairs. At first she continued in her resentment against Jefferson, the Republicans, and a good portion of the American people for their opposition and eventual ouster of her husband. She pitied, she wrote to her sister Elizabeth, the "infatuated deluded multitude who are hastning upon themselves more missery than they have enjoyed of tranquility & happiness for twelve years past" (Levin, 392). She worried, too, whether her husband could adjust to his retirement, and whether the family could make ends meet on the income from their farms and limited investments. The latter problem turned acute in 1803 when the London firm in which they had placed a considerable portion of their assets went bankrupt. Eventually they recovered their funds, but in an age in which former presidents did not receive pensions, finances were always of concern.

In 1804 Abigail Adams read in the newspapers that President Jefferson's younger daughter, Polly, had died at the age of twenty-five. This was the daughter who, as a young girl, had been entrusted to her care in London before she went to Paris. Affection for her old friend triumphed over partisan resentment, and (without telling her husband) she wrote a note of condolence to the grieving president. Jefferson responded graciously enough, but unwisely concluded his letter with a reference to John Adams's "midnight appointments," the only act, he said, of his former friend that he had felt to be personally unkind. This provoked a response from Mrs. Adams, and there ensued a polite but spirited exchange of opinions in letters that threatened to reopen the old wounds. At that point she chose to end the correspondence; only then did she show the letters to her husband.

In these years Abigail Adams turned increasingly toward her role as mother and grandmother to a sometimes troubled family. Her son Charles was survived by two daughters who needed to be provided for, and Abigail and John Adams took both them and their widowed daughter-in-law under their wing. Likewise, their daughter's fortunes continued to decline, along with those of her ne'er-do-well husband. They had four children. Thomas Boylston Adams, the youngest Adams son, and his wife had seven. John Quincy Adams returned from Europe in 1801 with his wife, Louisa Catherine, and a new son, George Washington Adams, the first of three. As her grandchildren matured, Abigail Adams engaged most of them in lively correspondence, firing off advice on matters including dress, deportment, penmanship, and, to her teenage granddaughters, the choice of a husband.

Following his return, John Quincy Adams entered politics as a Federalist senator from Massachusetts. In time, however, he came to disapprove of what he believed to be the overly pro-British tendencies of that party, and eventually broke with them, supporting instead the foreign policy of President Jefferson. Abigail and John Adams heartily approved, supporting Jefferson's policies and those of his successor, James Madison. Following his break with the Federalists, John Quincy Adams was named minister to Russia by Madison. This was a mixed blessing for the senior Adamses, for it meant another prolonged absence from his parents, with every expectation on their part—John Adams was seventy-four and Abigail was sixty-five—that they would not see him again. When he, his wife, and an infant son left Boston for St. Petersburg in 1809, Abigail was too overcome by emotion to see them off.

Almost as soon as her son had arrived in Russia Abigail Adams determined that he could not afford the high cost of living there and began an unsuccessful campaign to bring him back. She even wrote to President Madison, asking that her son be recalled. As it was, John Quincy Adams would progress from his post in Russia to head the American delegation that negotiated an end to the War of 1812. From there he went on to become American minister to Great Britain, the post his father had held thirty years before. He returned to America in 1817 as President Monroe's new secretary of state. Contrary to her fears, his mother was there to meet him.

Part of her concern was generated by her correspondence with her daughter-in-law, Louisa Catherine Adams, who kept her informed of their situation in the Russian capital. At first Abigail Adams had been dubious about the English-born Louisa's ability to measure up to Adams family standards, at one point predicting that Louisa's frail health would not permit her to survive the Massachusetts climate. Louisa was extremely intimidated by her mother-in-law, particularly on the frequent occasions when she saw fit to offer advice on what to feed and how to clothe her grandson. In time, however, the tensions between the two eased, and transformed into mutual respect and affection. When in the winter of 1815 Louisa and her eight-year-old son Charles Francis Adams dashed from St. Petersburg to Paris in a single carriage to meet her husband, Abigail Adams was full of admiration, as was the rest of the family.

At Quincy, Abigail Adams continued writing letters to the rest of her extended family and the dwindling number of surviving friends from the days of the Revolution. When her husband at last began his famous correspondence with Thomas Jefferson in 1812, she occasionally scribbled a note at the end of the letters. The death of her daughter in 1814 provoked a sympathetic response from Jefferson, who recalled the similar circumstance of 1804. Although often complaining of headaches, rheumatism, and chronic bronchial congestion, Abigail Adams did not permit her health to keep her from her daily routines for very long. She often rose at 6 A.M., made her own fire, and awakened the servants. "Life stagnates without action," she told her sister.

Two years after they celebrated their fiftieth wedding anniversary, John Adams could write to his son that his mother still "must take upon herself the Duties of her Grandaughter, Neice, Maids, Husband and all. She must allways be writing to You and all her Grandchildren" (Levin, 479). "Your Father, and I have Lived to an Age, to be sought for as Curiositys," Abigail Adams told her son John Quincy a few weeks later (Withey, 309). Yet she lived in constant awareness of her advancing years, by 1818 having outlived all of her siblings and two of her grown children. That summer, Secretary of State John Quincy Adams and his wife arrived for a brief visit before returning to Washington. It would be the last time he saw his mother. Abigail Adams died on October 28, after a brief battle with typhoid fever. She was buried in the Quincy churchyard, eventually to be joined by her husband, her son, John Quincy, and her daughter-in-law.

Nearly two centuries have elapsed since her death, yet Abigail Adams has remained fixed in the public's imagination as the best-known female symbol of the early republic, the prototype of the "Republican Mother." She invariably ranks among the top three First Ladies. Her sharp wit, her inquisitive intellect, her patriotism, and her loyalty to her family, her son later wrote, "gave the lie to every libel on her sex that was ever written."

BIBLIOGRAPHICAL ESSAY

Of the many biographies of Abigail Adams, the three best—in order of length—are Charles W. Akers, *Abigail Adams: An American Woman* (Boston, 1980); Lynne Withey, *Dearest Friend: A Life of Abigail Adams* (New York, 1981); and Phyllis Lee Levin, *Abigail Adams: A Biography* (New York, 1987). See also Lyman H. Butterfield's essay on Adams in *Notable American Women 1607–1950: A Biographical Directory* (Cambridge, Mass., 1971); the essays by Edith Gelles collected in her *Portia* (Bloomington, Ind., 1992); and Gelles's *First Thoughts: The Life and Letters*

of Abigail Adams (New York, 1999). A good, albeit somewhat romanticized, picture of Abigail and John Adams is in Irving Stone's double biography *Those Who Love* (New York, 1965). Paul Nagel's *Descent from Glory: Four Generations of the John Adams Family* (New York, 1983) and *The Adams Women: Abigail and Louisa Adams, Their Sisters and Daughters* (New York, 1987) offer what one scholar has described as the "Abigail-as-shrew" perspective.

Scholarly essays that deal with Abigail Adams include Joan Hoff Wilson, "The Illusion of Change: Women and the American Revolution," in Alfred E. Young, ed., *The American Revolution: Explorations in the History of American Radicalism* (DeKalb, Ill., 1976); Linda Grant DePauw, "The American Revolution and the Rights of Women: The Feminist Theory of Abigail Adams," in Larry R. Gerlach et al., eds., *The Legacy of the American Revolution* (Logan, Utah, 1978); and Joseph E. Illick, "John Quincy Adams: The Maternal Influence," *Journal of Psychohistory*, 4 (Fall 1976): 185–195.

The complete collection of Abigail Adams's letters to her many correspondents will eventually be published in Richard Ryerson et al., eds., *Adams Family Correspondence*, 6 vols. (Cambridge, Mass., 1963–, of which only letters through 1784 have appeared. These may be supplemented by Stewart Mitchell, ed., *New Letters of Abigail Adams*, (Boston, 1947); and Lester J. Cappon, ed., *The Adams-Jefferson Letters*, 2 vols. (Chapel Hill, N.C., 1959).

Most of the Abigail Adams manuscripts are available in research libraries in the form of the Adams Papers Microfilm Project, issued in 1954 under the auspices of the Massachusetts Historical Society and the Adams Family Manuscript Trust. Additional collections of her letters are at the American Antiquarian Society in Worcester, Mass., and the Houghton Library at Harvard University.

The extant portraits of Abigail Adams are in Andrew Oliver's *Portraits of John and Abigail Adams* (Boston, 1967).

★★★ ★★★

Dolley Payne Todd Madison

(1768–1849)

First Lady: 1809–1817

Holly Cowan Shulman

Dolley Payne was born on May 20, 1768. Her mother, Mary Coles, was descended from Isaac Winston, an early Quaker settler in Virginia who was the grandfather of the American patriot Patrick Henry, and from William Coles, an immigrant from Wexford County, Ireland. Her father, John Payne, came from an Anglican family of middling success. Dolley's parents were married outside the Quaker faith in 1761, but three years later her father applied and was admitted to the Quaker Monthly Meeting in Hanover County, Virginia.

In 1765 the Paynes moved to Rowan County, North Carolina. Dolley Payne was thus born in North Carolina, near where Guilford College stands today. Dolley was one of eight children, four boys (Walter, William Temple, Isaac, and John), and four girls (Dolley, Lucy, Anna, and Mary). The family, however, did not thrive, and, a year after Dolley's birth, they returned to Virginia. Three years later they settled into a house on the estate of her mother's family, the Coles Hill plantation. As a young girl Dolley grew up in comfort in rural eastern Virginia, deeply attached to her mother's family.

With the Revolution over in 1783, John Payne emancipated his slaves. Soon afterward he took his family to Philadelphia, where he attempted to establish himself as a merchant in the laundry starch business. The move, however, would soon bring tragedy. In 1785 the Paynes' eldest son, Walter, perished. Philadelphia was a city in transition, where spiraling costs and contracting trade imposed crushing expenses on small businessmen. In 1789 John Payne's venture failed and he retreated into his home. He died a broken man on October 24, 1792.

Dolley's mother survived initially by opening a boardinghouse for the leaders of the new nation. In 1793, however, Mrs. Payne retired. She moved with her two youngest children, Mary and John Coles, to western Virginia to live with her daughter Lucy, who in 1792 had married George Steptoe Washington, a nephew of George Washington.

In January 1790 Dolley Payne married her first husband, a young Quaker lawyer named John Todd. Todd provided her with much-needed financial security. The couple prospered and produced two boys in rapid succession, John Payne Todd (b. 1790) and William Temple Todd (b.1792).

In the fall of 1793 yellow fever struck Philadelphia. It was a devastating epidemic. Five thousand people died within a few weeks. Dolley Todd took her two children to a resort on the outskirts of the city. Her husband remained in the city, at first attending to his business and then helping his ailing parents, who soon perished. Then he fell ill and, on October 24, 1793—the very day of the first anniversary of her father's death—John passed away in Philadelphia. Their infant son William Temple also succumbed to the plague. She lost her husband, her in-laws, and her infant son all within the space of one week.

After she had recovered from the initial shock, Dolley Todd returned to Philadelphia and settled into a new life. She was a widow at the age of twenty-five, concerned with the future of her surviving son and surrounded by friends anxious to help her. Young and attractive, she soon became popular.

In May 1794 James Madison asked his friend Aaron Burr to introduce him to Dolley Todd. Anticipating their meeting, Dolley wrote to her friend Eliza Collins Lee that "Aaron Burr says that the great little Madison has asked to be brought to see me this evening." Madison was seventeen years

her senior and, at the age of forty-three, a long-standing bachelor. A member of a Virginia planter family, he had played a large role in the framing of the Constitution and the Bill of Rights, and then was elected to the House of Representatives from central Virginia. From there he became a leader of the emerging Republican Party. He "was a little man with small features rather wizened when I saw him, but occasionally lit up with a good-natured smile," wrote British diplomat Augustus John Foster, who first knew James Madison as secretary of state, in his "Notes," later published as *Jeffersonian America*.

During the summer of 1794 Madison courted Dolley Todd. It was a good match: he was charming and witty among his friends (if often shy and remote in public); brilliant and successful; a man without his own children who was anxious to care for hers. And he had fallen passionately in love with her. As her cousin Catherine Coles wrote to her on June 1, Mr. Madison "thinks so much of you in the day that he has Lost his Tongue, at Night he Dreams of you & Starts in his Sleep a Calling on you to relieve his Flame for he Burns to such an excess that he will be shortly consumed. . . ."

Four months after their first meeting, Dolley Todd and James Madison were married. The wedding took place on September 15, 1794, at her sister Lucy's estate, Harewood, in Virginia. "In the course of this day," Dolley wrote to her friend Eliza Collins, "I give my Hand to the Man who of all other's I most admire." The Quakers disowned her on December 12, 1794. She was now the wife of a prosperous, slave-owning, Virginia planter who was definitely not a Quaker. And she moved onto the national stage as the wife of a leader of the emerging Republican Party.

The Madisons lived in Philadelphia for the next three years. Their home was a large, fashionable, red-brick house in the middle of the city. Dolley Madison brought with her not only her four-year-old son, John Payne Todd, but also her younger sister, Anna, who had lived with her from the time that she married John Todd and had become like a daughter. Philadelphia was a lively city, full of balls and parties. The Madisons' house was filled with a whirling social life, gossip, and the latest in French fashion. Mrs. Madison loved the new European styles, with short sleeves and revealing necklines, the sort of dress an older, primmer, Abigail Adams thought outrageous and indecent.

Amidst the excitement of her new social life, Mrs. Madison lost two of her remaining brothers. In 1795 William and Isaac died. Only one brother, John, remained. She left behind no letter recording her emotions.

Nor did she or James Madison ever write down what it meant to them to remain childless. There is no hint of disappointment or sadness. This circumstance, however, did leave her in the unusual position of having only one child to raise.

When John Adams became president in 1797, the Madisons retired to Montpelier, the family estate of 5,000 acres in Orange County, Virginia. There they expected to remain as planters, living quietly in the country. In 1800 Dolley's youngest sister, Mary, wed a member of the Virginia House of Delegates, John G. Jackson, who would in 1803 be elected to Congress from what is now West Virginia.

In May 1801, at the request of the newly elected president, Thomas Jefferson, the Madisons once again shifted—this time to the new capital of Washington, D.C. The day after his presidential inauguration, Jefferson nominated James Madison as secretary of state. Madison accepted immediately, but the family delayed moving for several months, as James Madison was ill and his father died.

Upon their arrival in the federal city in May, the Madisons stayed first with Jefferson in the White House, later moving to a row house between the White House and Georgetown, and finally settling in at 1333 F Street, Northwest, two blocks east of the president's house. It was a comfortable brick home with plenty of bedrooms, entertaining space, living quarters for servants and slaves, storage space for wine and fuel, and a carriage house in the rear.

During the eight years that he served as secretary of state, Madison engaged in a series of complex negotiations with France, Britain, and Spain. The country's major foreign-relations issues—the revolution in St. Domingue (now Haiti), the depredations of the Barbary pirates, the dangers of a possible French empire west of the Mississippi River, the American claims to Spanish Florida, and, after 1805, the intensifying conflict between France and Britain as the world's two superpowers—were discussed at home and are occasionally referred to in Mrs. Madison's letters, but they did not form the cornerstones of her life. The important events lay in her private sphere and with her public obligations.

The circumstances of her family were often emotionally difficult, although for the first years in Washington life proceeded without any major problems or shifts in her daily routine. Then, on March 30, 1804, her sister Anna married Richard Cutts, a congressman from Maine who had first been elected in 1801. Anna's marriage was a seismic event for Dolley Madison, as intense as any grief she had yet experienced—and she was quite clear about the pain in her letters.

Soon thereafter Mrs. Madison began a long bout with an ulcerated knee, which by 1805 needed serious medical attention. That summer she went to Philadelphia to be treated by the eminent Dr. Philip Syng Physick. For much of the time her husband remained by her side—writing, but also relaxing and visiting—until September, when business called him back to Washington.

It was the only time in their marriage that the Madisons spent more than a day or two apart, and their often-quoted letters from these weeks have a tenderness that speaks of a mutual affection. Dolley Madison began the correspondence on October 23, 1805, writing, "A few hours only have passed since you left me my beloved, and I find nothing can releave the oppression of my mind but speaking to you in this *only* way." Mr. Madison responded five days later by asking his wife to "let me know that I shall soon have you with me, which is most anxiously desired by your ever affectionate James Madison."

It was her first visit to Philadelphia since she had left the city in 1797. She spent a great deal of time renewing old friendships. Returning to Philadelphia as a leading woman of Washington, however, also clarified how much her life had changed, and the importance of her public role.

The Madisons traveled very little. Jefferson, the Monroes, and the Adamses, for example, had spent years in Europe, as had a score of the leading figures of the early Republic and their wives. James Madison loathed traveling. The Madisons shuttled between their plantation in Orange County and their home in Washington, with an occasional visit to a friend or relative in Virginia. This insularity intensified Mrs. Madison's concentration on her immediate roles: doyenne of Washington and mistress of Montpelier. It also helped her create a special blend of high fashion and popular American culture. She interpreted European dress, manners, and food through a purely American filter.

By 1805 her only surviving brother, John C. Payne, had become an alcoholic and a reckless gambler. In 1806 the Madisons sent him to Tripoli as secretary to the American consul there. For Dolley Madison, who always wanted as much of her family as close as possible—while they increasingly moved to more and more remote regions—this was another loss. Later that year, two of her nieces died. In 1807 her mother passed away and, a year later, her sister Mary succumbed to tuberculosis, after years of illness. Her immediate family was thus reduced to her two surviving sisters, Anna and Lucy, her wastrel brother John, her son, and her husband.

She remained very close to her sisters, Anna Cutts and Lucy Washington, and Mary's widower, John G. Jackson. The entire Cutts family often spent the months Congress was in session in Washington, and, after 1809, the year Madison was elected president, they actually lived in the White House. The two women were thus often together. When Anna Cutts was back

in Maine, Dolley Madison missed her. While apart they wrote each other often, filling their correspondence with news about children, family, and their various illnesses.

Nevertheless, the situation had its strains. As the spring of 1812 drew to a close, President Madison began to count votes in Congress for a declaration of war. Richard Cutts wrote that he could not attend the congressional session; he had been thrown from a carriage in the Boston Wharf in the fall of 1811, and he was in too much pain to make the long trip. Whether this was the truth is uncertain; however, Cutts had other problems. A New Englander, Cutts was faced with the fact that his constituency opposed open conflict with England. In addition, he had speculated quite heavily in a shaky shipbuilding deal, and he feared that war would ruin him. He showed up shortly after the vote for war had been taken. Despite the strains, however, when Richard Cutts was defeated that fall, President Madison appointed him superintendent of military supplies. Cutts and his family, now part of the civil service, moved into their own home, a large and comfortable house on Lafayette Square, across from the White House.

Richard Cutts, however, suffered severe financial losses from his speculations over the course of the War of 1812. In an attempt to pay his debts he borrowed heavily from both Madison and John G. Jackson. Cutts finally went bankrupt and was sent to debtors' prison. His assets were sold to pay his debts, although Madison bought the Cutts house and furnishings so that the family could remain there. After the Madisons retired to Montpelier in 1817, the Cutts house was the family residence in Washington.

Although Mary had died in 1808, her husband, John G. Jackson, remained in Congress and proved an extraordinarily strong supporter of the president, as well as a close friend of both Madisons. While Mary was alive, the couple rented rooms in a boardinghouse close to the Madisons, at the corner of Fifteenth and F streets. Like the Cuttses, the Jacksons were active in Washington social life, and the three sisters were often together, although Mary and Dolley were never as close as was Dolley to her sister Anna.

The bond between them was, nevertheless, tight enough so that Jackson wrote to his new fiancée in 1810 that he considered Dolley Madison his confidante "in all things." He named a daughter by his second marriage Madisonia, and a son James Madison. In July 1809 Jackson rose to Federalist bait and accepted a challenge to a duel to defend the honor of Madison's administration. Jackson was wounded in the hip and temporarily retired from Congress in 1810. By 1813 he was back and, unlike brother-in-law Cutts, very much a War Hawk. Though Mrs. Madison herself was closer to the Cutts family, the president felt a warmer tie with Jackson.

The fourth sister, Lucy Washington, was widowed in 1809. She spent much of the next three years living in the White House. Prominent in the city's social scene, in 1812 she married Supreme Court Justice Thomas Todd, a forty-seven-year-old widower from Kentucky. Their wedding, held March 29, 1812, was the first ever to take place in the White House. The Madisons approved of the match, but Mrs. Madison was, again, saddened to see a sister move so far away.

Her brother's problems seemed without end. He was a failure as secretary to the American consul in Tripoli, and continued to drink and gamble. In 1811 John C. Payne returned home, sick with malaria. Mrs. Madison tried to find him a job in the army, but the military would not have him. The Madisons finally sent Payne to Kentucky to live with the Todds. Jackson found him a job as assistant to the quartermaster in Clarksburg, Virginia. By May 1816 Payne was married, sober, but poor.

During this time, however, problems also began to emerge with her only surviving son, (John) Payne Todd. He had proven an indifferent student, unready to go to college, despite the Madisons' wish that he follow in his stepfather's footsteps and attend Princeton. Instead, he returned from boarding school to Washington, where he idled around the White House, playing cards and the horses, drinking, and leading an increasingly dissolute life.

In an effort to curb this debauchery, in May 1813 the Madisons shipped Payne Todd off to Russia on a diplomatic mission, under the guidance of their friend Albert Gallatin. However, in Europe he was treated as American royalty, rarely doing a day's work. Initially reluctant to leave home, a few years later he had enjoyed himself so greatly he was loath to return, both times worrying his mother enormously. While abroad he ran up expenses and gambling debts of $6,500, which he sent home to the Madisons to pay. When he finally reached the United States, his mother assumed he would go back to Montpelier with them in 1817 and take up his obligations as a planter. He did move back to Orange County, but by that time he had resumed his reckless lifestyle—a disaster in the making.

On June 13, 1813—a little more than a month after Payne Todd departed for Europe—James Madison fell very ill, with what was then called a bilious fever. The doctors said he was near death. Mrs. Madison stayed by his bedside night and day for nearly five weeks, and even after that she kept watch over him—as she told Hannah Gallatin on July 29—"as I would an infant." For Dolley Madison it must have been a very difficult time indeed: her son gone; her husband hovering on the brink of death.

If her private life was complex, her public life consumed her. Dolley Madison was the most famous and the most beloved of all the First Ladies of the nineteenth century. It is, then, important to examine the basis upon which that reputation lies. To begin with, generously defined, her term as First Lady extended over a sixteen-year period, 1801 to 1817. She was unquestionably the most important woman in Washington throughout the years of Jefferson's administrations (1801–1809) as well as Madison's (1809–1817). Her reputation, moreover, rested squarely on two major areas of accomplishment: decorating the White

House and her role as a hostess. She played a critical role in defining the public social space for the executive branch of the federal government, and she helped formulate a style of etiquette appropriate to a new republic.

The lives of women in the new republic were familial and private. In public they were adjuncts to their husbands. Dolley Madison, however, was not merely an appendage to her powerful husband. She created, instead, a kind of third world between public and private. In society—on those occasions when government is run through the social forms of dinners, parties, and other ceremonial forms of entertainment—she was more important than her husband. The drawing rooms of the White House were *her* rooms and not his. She presided over that world as no First Lady had done before, and created a precedent that her successors could follow.

Dolley Madison's public image was created in part through the public space of the White House. With her husband's approval, and in partnership with architect Benjamin Henry Latrobe, she decorated the presidential mansion during the first two years of her husband's first administration.

Presidents John Adams and Thomas Jefferson had already put money into the White House. Congress allocated $14,000 during Adams's four months in Washington, and gave $29,000 to Jefferson during his eight years. But much of that had gone into painting and plastering and finishing off staircases.

Jefferson had solved the problem of how to furnish the White House by bringing his own things from Monticello. In part, this was an easy solution to the problem of creating his living and working spaces. But it also enabled Jefferson to create his own public image, and to do so with great speed and no controversy. His strategy was to appear a man of simple republican virtues. Toward this end he did not want a large and formal state dining room. Instead he used a small room for dining, decorated with small round tables. He hired a French chef, served European haute cuisine, and stocked

his wine cellar with the best imports he could find. It was not, in other words, a matter of depriving himself of the finer things in life, but of devising an image to impress upon both supporters and opponents how greatly he adhered—even in his daily ceremonial routines—to his political ideology.

When Jefferson retired, he shipped his furniture back to Monticello. The Madisons thus moved into a cavernous and largely unfurnished mansion. They needed to act.

Madison entrusted the job to his wife. This was an unusual decision. Since great homes were public arenas for important men, their decoration was predominantly a man's job. It was George Washington, and not Martha Washington, for example, who personally chose the wallpaper, carpets, tables, and sofas for Mount Vernon. However, since Madison was swamped with work, he gave over supervision of redecorating to his wife.

Her taste had slowly changed over the years. When she married James Madison, she shed the simple furniture with which she had lived as the wife of a young Quaker lawyer. During their years in Philadelphia the Madisons began a pattern of collecting French furniture through American diplomats stationed in Europe, especially James Monroe, who was in Paris and who took the time to buy up as much of the worldly goods as he could from the auctioned-off estates of the nobles of the ancien régime. Mrs. Madison grew to love French taste, in furniture as in clothes. French styles were beautiful. French goods were a symbol of status and taste. French objects befitted good Republicans, who approved of all things French and disdained all things British.

The Madisons redecorated Montpelier with French fashions. And once in Washington they outfitted their house on F Street with care, as a center for Washington society. Mrs. Madison, moreover, became friends with the wives of the French ministers, who furthered her education in French high style.

The White House, however, required decorating in earnest. Benjamin Latrobe was an architect who was already surveyor of public buildings, and therefore on the public payroll. He knew Mr. Madison well, and his wife was well acquainted with Mrs. Madison. The two set to work even before the president-elect had been inaugurated.

They needed to furnish a dining room for large state dinners. That meant buying not only furniture, but also china, glassware, and serving pieces. They created a parlor, where Mrs. Madison could receive her callers. They decorated the Oval Room for large official functions. And they did this all both quickly and relatively inexpensively. Congress gave the Madisons very little money to work with. In their five years in the White House—before the British burned them out—Congress budgeted only $20,000 for renewal and upkeep of the executive mansion.

Extravagance was out of the question. So was French furniture. Like Jefferson, the Madisons had to construct a public image. Theirs had to be woven out of conflicting strands. They had, first, to appease a populist Republican constituency. For these people the Madisons needed homespun American goods. They had, second, to counter Federalist opponents. For these men the Madisons required formality and elegance suitable to older traditions of the symbols of power. They had, finally, both to accommodate and counter the European powers with missions in Washington. For these diplomats the Madisons required a blend of European-style conventions and down-home American comfort.

Dolley Madison and Benjamin Latrobe worked rapidly. They bought high-quality American-made goods, largely manufactured by Philadelphia craftsmen who were the most sophisticated in the nation. They made the presidential palace both beautiful and comfortable. But Dolley Madison's genius lay not with the speed at which she worked. Nor was it with the way she handled Latrobe, albeit she did so with great grace and with an ability to soothe his feathers when they became ruffled. Nor was it with her "taste"—as an abstract expression of beauty and elegance. It lay in her ability to construct a middle ground between Republican simplicity and Federalist high fashion—through her choices of chairs and tables, wallpapers and water goblets. She molded a presidential palace just fine enough for Federalist ideas, just sophisticated enough for the new nation's international image, and yet simple enough to soothe Republican fears. It was a great accomplishment.

The Madisons did not live out their full two terms at 1600 Pennsylvania Avenue, however. On August 24, 1814, the British invaded Washington and burned the White House to a shell. The story of the British assault on Washington and how Dolley Madison saved Gilbert Stuart's portrait of George Washington has been told many times. It is probably the single "action" for which she is most famous—along with serving ice cream in the White House, a delicacy Jefferson had brought to America from France.

The war had been going on for two years. The city had long been full of rumors about a coming invasion. More than a year before, in a letter dated May 13, 1813, Mrs. Madison had written to her cousin Edward Coles that "the City & G.[eorge] Town (except the cabinet) have expected a visit from the enemy, & were not lacking in their expressions of terror and reproach." By July 23, 1814, Mrs. Madison complained to her close friend Hannah Gallatin that "we have been in a state of perturbation here, for a long time." The city was in chaos. "Such a place as this has become I cannot describe it." She was indignant at the criticisms hurled against her husband for not protecting the capital, and, she angrily explained to Mrs. Gallatin, a good deal more disgusted at her fellow Washingtonians than afraid of the British. "I am," she avowed, "determined to stay with him."

Then, on August 17, a British fleet landed thirty-five miles from the capital. Slowly British troops began to walk toward Washington, but at first they moved so slowly it was hard to believe they were ever going to reach the city—or even meant to do so. As late as August 21, President Madison thought the British would not attack.

By August 22 he had changed his mind. He left the city to review the troops. Mrs. Madison stayed on at the White House, ready to pack up the government papers and secure them from harm. Madison wrote to his wife that she "should be ready at a moment's warning" to get into her carriage and flee. The enemy was coming in full strength. "It might happen," he warned her, "that they would reach the city with intention to destroy it."

The day of August 23, Madison was still out of town. Mrs. Madison was in the White House. As she prepared to evacuate the building, she wrote a letter to her sister Lucy. "I have pressed as many Cabinet Papers into trunks as will fill one carriage," she scribbled. "Our private property must be sacrificed, as it is impossible to procure wagons for its transportation. I am determined not to go myself until I see Mr. Madison safe, and he can accompany me, as I hear of much hostility towards him . . . disaffection stalks around us."

The next day the president was still absent, and she was still guarding the gates of the executive mansion. "Since sunrise," she wrote to her sister, "I have been turning my spy-glass in every direction and watching with unwearied anxiety, hoping to discern the approach of my dear husband and his friends, but, alas, I can descry only groups of military wandering in all directions. . . ." She waited anxiously for hours but, by that afternoon, British troops were approaching too fast to be ignored. She filled a wagon with silver and other valuables that she could stuff in and sent it off to the Bank of Maryland for safekeeping— "or fall into the hands of British soldiery, events must determine." And then she decided that she had one more task to accomplish. "I insist on waiting until the large picture of Gen. Washington is secured," she penned, as the events were taking place, "and it requires to be unscrewed from the wall. This process was found too tedious for these perilous moments; I have ordered the frame to be broken, and the canvass taken out it is done, and the precious portrait placed in the hands of two gentlemen of New York, for safe keeping. And now, dear sister I must leave this house, or t[he] retreating army will make me a prisoner in it. . . ."

Mrs. Madison fled to Virginia. A day later she finally met up with her husband and, on August 27, they returned to the city. The British had torched the White House and the Madisons had not a roof to put over their heads.

Initially they moved into the Octagon House, the second-largest residence in the city. It belonged to John Tayloe III, the richest man in the capital. They remained there for less than a year. In August 1815 they moved again, this time to the corner of 19th Street and Pennsylvania Avenue, a corner house in a group of buildings known as the "Seven Buildings." Perhaps they decided it was wiser not to stay too long in the home of one of the city's staunchest Federalists.

Mrs. Madison continued to entertain with great energy and style. But a new note of worry crept into her correspondence. The new house on 19th and Pennsylvania was empty. Mrs. Madison had therefore to furnish it from scratch, and do so on almost no budget. Their own funds were simultaneously being stretched to support the Cutts family and to pay off Payne Todd's debts. Mrs. Madison once again returned to her practice of buying whatever secondhand furniture she could acquire through members of the American legation in France, and turned to her old friends the Gallatins to purchase what she could from the home they were closing up in Washington. She accomplished her goals and entertained successfully until Madison left office and the couple returned to Montpelier in March 1817.

Dolley Madison's other great achievement lay in her role as a hostess. She created public ceremonies appropriate for the new republic—which took place in *her* public spaces. In her role as official hostess, however, her job began in 1801 as the woman the widower Jefferson most often called upon to assume that task.

Her setting was a newly created capital, ugly and barren. A few brick houses erected with little plan and less design sat cheek by jowl with wooden hovels, while town lots filled more by mud than trees awaited developers. Only those blessed with a splendid imagination could picture a grand city; for most there were half-finished buildings set amid ungainly trees on swampy grounds.

By 1800 there were 14,093 people living in the District of Columbia, about half of whom lived in pre-Revolutionary George-town. The population of the central city had reached only between 3,000 to 4,000, and of these only 233 men had personal or real property with a value of more than one hundred dollars. When the Madisons moved to 1333 F Street, there were only 109 brick houses in the whole of the city.

Washington's permanent elite was composed of town-dwelling Southern planters, congressmen—many of whom lived in boardinghouses without their families—cabinet officers and a few other high civil servants, and the few foreign diplomats who were paid high salaries and cost of living allowances that enabled them to live on a grander scale than almost any American could do. In a city that was largely either poor, or—among the members of Congress—almost exclusively male, mixed company with enough wealth to entertain and to create "society" was confined to a very small number.

Washington presented a blank slate upon which to write new republican social messages. The newly installed President Jefferson expressed his republican virtue by flouting contemporary rules of attire, dressing for visiting dignitaries, for example, in rumpled old clothing and dirty woolen socks. His garb, a senator complained, made the president look more like a servant than a president. To do so was Jefferson's intention. He stripped away formal rules of protocol. He thus eliminated drawing room evenings, for example, and invited guests for small, informal dinners.

There is one particularly famous social incident that describes Jefferson's goals and methods. It also articulates something about the role Dolley Madison played during the Jefferson years, her character, and her education as the nation's most important hostess.

In 1803 the British sent their first minister, Anthony Merry, to Washington. Dressed in formal diplomatic attire, Merry called upon President Jefferson, who received him wearing slippers. Merry was offended. A few days later, Jefferson asked Merry and his wife to dine at the White House. Mrs. Merry cared a great deal for both fashion and her own status. When it was time to go in for dinner, Jefferson—who should have escorted Mrs. Merry—turned to Dolley Madison and offered her his arm. Merry was again upset. Shortly thereafter the president issued a statement, the "Cannons of Etiquette," in which he declared the "rule of pele-mele." It befitted America, Jefferson wrote to James Monroe on January 8, 1804, "that no man here would come to dinner where he was to be marked with inferiority to any other. . . ."

A few days later the Madisons had the Merrys to dinner. This time, James Madison extended his arm to the wife of the secretary of the treasury. Again the Merrys were offended. Merry and the minister from Spain decided to boycott the White House. The French head of legation refused to go along with the plot. The incident developed into a matter of international consequence. Perhaps Jefferson intended it to do so. Certainly Henry Adams argued that "the seriousness of Jefferson's experiments in etiquette consisted in the belief that they were part of a political system which involved a sudden change of policy toward two great Powers."

Federalist newspapers had a field day with the conflict. Mrs. Merry vented her wrath on Dolley Madison when she described dinner at the Madisons' as a harvest home supper. Mrs. Madison coolly responded that "the profusion of my table so repugnant to foreign customs arises from the happy circumstances of abundance and prosperity in our country."

During the years her husband was secretary of state (1801–1809), Dolley Madison developed a reputation as the most important hostess in the city. In part she excelled because Washington was a small Southern city and she was a Virginian. Her mother's experience running a boardinghouse provided a model of tact and public demeanor. Philadelphia in the 1790s was the best training ground in the American social graces. And she was a woman who was anxious to please, with a talent for reaching out to people in an open-hearted and unpretentious way. According to one of her biographers, Mrs. Madison once wrote that "I confess I do not admire contention in any form, either political or civil. I would rather fight with my hands than my tongue."

On March 4, 1809, James Madison became the fourth president of the United States. On March 29, the Madisons gave their first evening party at the White House, a practice they continued on a semiweekly basis. They returned—in a new sort of way—to the older forms of entertaining practiced by Washington and Adams, and dropped Jefferson's studied informality, which admitted no room for a woman of Dolley Madison's talents and personality— or for James Madison's shyness.

In a republic, the reasoning went, the president should be available to any person who wanted to see him. But if there were no schedule, he would receive constant interruptions, leaving no time for work. The Madisons scheduled large events. They changed the name from "levee" to "drawing room," reducing the formality of the event but retaining the general structure.

They placed announcements in the newspaper, as had the Washingtons and Adamses. Mrs. Madison rearranged the use of the rooms in the White House to accommodate large numbers of guests. At dinners she took the head of the table and placed her cousin and husband's secretary, Edward Coles, at the foot, leaving the president to sit in the middle. They carefully invited as many and as broad a range of people as possible. It was a tradition of entertainment that lasted until the 1930s.

Alexander Dick, a member of the British legation in Washington, described his first "drawing room" in his journal in June 1809. "We went this Evening & found a Crowd of Ladies and Gentlemen Walking thro the Apartments which were all thrown open & a band of Military Music playing." The food was rather simple, he complained, and there was neither dancing nor cards, "but in a place like Washington where there are Scarcely any public places at all, Such a Meeting seems to be much relished, & there is the honor of Seeing the President & his Lady." The wife of a later British minister, Charles Bagot, wrote:

> The women usually sit stuck around the room close to the wall. The men— many of whom come in boots & perfectly undone & with dirty hands & dirty linen— stand mostly talking with each other in the middle of the rooms. Tea and coffee & afterwards cold punch with glasses of Madeira & cakes are handed around & by ten o'clock everyone is dispersed.

The British held the provincial Americans in disdain. This contempt, however, partly explains the level at which the Madisons pitched their dinners and drawing room evenings.

The other side of the Madisons' equation emerges from the comments of a Pennsylvania congressman, Jonathan Roberts, who was living in a boardinghouse on Capitol Hill. On December 2, 1811, Roberts wrote a letter to his brother. He was having difficulty making up his mind whether or not to attend a presidential dinner. He wavered, feeling that "it is not pleasant to encounter new scenes where it is not easy to be prepar'd for all that passes & where embarrassments may arise that may subject one to the sneers of the narrow minded." He worried that his manners were not up to the occasion and feared that he would embarrass himself.

Roberts went, however, and told his brother about it. He was met at the door by a French servant. After dropping off his hat and coat he proceeded in to the room where the company was assembled. There "we found Mrs. Madison & her widowed sister [Lucy] Washington & perhaps [eight] or ten gentlemen." Mr. Madison had a bad toothache and was not there. "At about ten feet distance," Roberts went on, "rows of chairs with stuffed purple silk velvet cushions were extended in parallel lines from the two ladies seats." He approached Dolley Madison and her sister, bowed, and retreated to the seats, where he awkwardly plunked himself down on an empty chair. After about thirty minutes, dinner was served. Escorted by the two men nearest them, the two women were seated for dinner.

> Thro the whole entertainment the good Lady preservd her character as the efficient head of table. There was no want of variety or plenty but the soup Meats pastry and dessert were plain and economical. There was Porter [beer] for drink & five kinds of wine none of which I believe could be called good wines.

Roberts's attendance had been a compromise between conflicting feelings. He was not sure how closely associated with the White House he should be. But he wrote with general approval of the proceedings.

Roberts also commented on White House drawing room parties. On those occasions some men put on their best suits. John G. Jackson, for example, wore a "superfine-blue-cloth" coat with trimmings of silver vellum lace, pleated buttons, and white pantaloons in the summer, and a black coat, silk waistcoat, cravat, and black velvet pantaloons in the winter. The Baltimore *Whig* used the canons of dress as political ammunition, and accused Mrs. Madison of barring men with boots from her drawing room—an allegation that she was not living up to her republican ideology. Roberts described the required dress simply by writing that "those who aspire to distinguished gallantry do not appear in boots. . . ." He did not approve of such airs—after all, boots were good republican footwear. But he did admit (contrary to the Baltimore *Whig's* libel) that one *could* attend shod in one's boots. "Mrs. Madison," he concluded, "I understand has unequivocally declar'd she is a democrat tho the world have strong doubts about it."

A wide gulf of experience and culture lay between the reactions of Dick and the Bagots on the one hand and Roberts on the other. The Madisons were required to entertain foreign ministers and their wives, who expected the formal standards of Europe. Yet they also needed to meet the expectations of their domestic political constituency. They carefully invited each member of Congress to a least one dinner every legislative session. They appeared as heads of state—but as leaders who were not too elegant or too refined in their manners and dress. It was a difficult line to walk.

It is precisely here that Dolley Madison proved brilliant. This is the reason her reputation was so great. She was elegant and stunning in a simple and unaffected way. It is notable that her supporters called her "queenly." Her Federalist detractors accused her of being an innkeeper's daughter. She created a social mecca in Washington for diplomats, congressmen, and Washington society. She had a knack for reaching out to people, finely honed skills of conversation, and warmth that made people feel good. Her actions as First Lady made the White House a social center.

There were times when Dolley Madison found company exhausting. Keeping up with the daily demands of housework required an endless routine. In the mornings she wore a plain, Quaker-style gray dress, white apron, and white kerchief. She supervised food preparation, cleaning, laundry, and whatever else needed attending that day. She did her own shopping, sometimes accompanied by her sister. And when all of this had been completed, she dressed up in her fine clothes and went into the sitting rooms, where she attended the ceaseless rounds of company. At times she did all these tasks while she felt anxious about her brother or distressed over her son. She hated entertaining when Anna and Lucy were not with her. She suffered terrible headaches and was afflicted with bouts of rheumatism.

William C. Preston—who would later become a congressman, but was then only eighteen years old—lived for a few weeks in the White House in 1813. He kept a journal, recording his impressions of Washington life. It was the first winter of war, and the Madisons had a full house. Living with them at that time was one of the president's nephews, Edward Coles's sister Betsy, another young woman from Richmond, and the Cutts family. White House social obligations had meanwhile increased to accommodate men in newly minted uniforms.

Preston's arrival at the executive mansion came about through a visit with an army general. According to custom he was presented to the First Lady, whereupon she stretched out her hand and asked him if he was not the son of an old friend and a not-too-distant relative. She took him under her wing, introduced him around, and told him that while in the city he should stay on in the White House as their guest.

Preston did stay on at the White House. In his journal he describes the president's labors as "incessant." Of Mrs. Madison he wrote that she admitted not only to worrying about her husband's health, but that she herself "was wearied of it [entertaining] to exhaustion." It was unusual for Mrs. Madison to be so open with anyone except her sisters or close family, but Preston's single sentence opens up a window onto her personality. Her demeanor was consistently calm, warm, and accepting. She understood politics and the importance of tact and discretion. She carefully confined her public role to forms and ceremonies, and with equal care, she left no written record of her personal philosophy.

In March 1817, James Madison retired from office. The Madisons remained in Washington for another month, going to parties, saving good-bye to friends, and packing up their belongings. The Monroes had moved straight into the White House, left vacant since the British burned it. On April 6 the Madisons left Washington and returned to their estate in Orange County, Virginia.

Montpelier was a beautiful and gracious home, which the Madisons had steadily improved over the past sixteen years. They had added one-story wings on each side, a four-columned portico, and limestone plaster over the whole of the original brick. Inside it was light and airy. Friend Margaret Bayard Smith wrote in 1828 of "airy apartments—windows opening to the ground, hung with light silk drapery, French furniture, light fancy chairs, gay carpets. . . ." There were paintings by Gilbert Stuart and busts of Washington, Franklin, Jefferson, and Adams. And Mr. Madison's study held the core of a library of over 4,000 volumes. The grounds were equally splendid. Planted with silver poplar, weeping willows, boxwood, and walnut trees, rimmed with roses and white jasmine, the grounds extended beyond farm buildings and slave quarters, past pear orchards and grape arbors, to fields of grain and tobacco.

For James Madison it was permanent retirement. He lived nearly twenty years more, but he never again visited Washington. Only once did he make any sort of extended trip, and that was to Richmond in 1829.

Dolley Madison stayed by her husband's side, and so for her, too, the next twenty years were spent exclusively at Montpelier. As she wrote to her cousin, Sarah Coles Stevenson, in 1826, "A spell rests upon me, and withholds me from those I love most in this world; not a mile can I go from home; and in no way can I account for it, but that my husband is fixed here, and hates to have me leave him." Whether or not she cast her fixed station in such strong terms to appease a cousin she dearly loved and so hated to disappoint—the Madisons would stay with cousin Sarah during their single visit to Richmond—or she found her years in Montpelier confining, is difficult to know.

The Madisons stayed in place, but the world came to them. There was, of course, family. James Madison's nieces and nephews flocked to the family estate. Dolley Madison's relations were even more welcomed. Her brother John C. Payne moved, with his wife and eight children, to a small farm nearby, a family appendage and permanent dependent. Lucy Todd visited regularly. Anna Cutts and her children clustered there. When not in attendance, Anna wrote her sister on a weekly basis.

There were streams of other visitors. Ninety guests came to a Fourth of July picnic. Younger political leaders, such as Daniel Webster, rode to Montpelier to discuss politics. European writers, such as Harriet Martineau, traveled to see the former president and his wife. "At this moment we have only three and twenty [guests]," Mrs. Madison wrote to Margaret Bayard Smith in 1828, indicating twenty-three as a small number. They were never short of people with whom to spend their time, or out of touch with national politics and Washington gossip.

Entertaining, however, cost money. And money became increasingly short of supply. The Madisons had retired to Montpelier with sizable assets and substantial savings. But the 1820s and 1830s proved hard times for them—as they did for most Virginia planters, who suffered from a serious, and ultimately disastrous, agricultural depression. Many planters sold all or some of their land. They trafficked in slaves, shipping them to the more prosperous regions of Georgia, Alabama, Mississippi, and Louisiana. They moved out West themselves. Or they slid slowly into poverty. A few members of the Madison family moved to Alabama, Louisiana, and Illinois. Their neighbors Thomas Jefferson and James Monroe went broke.

James and Dolley Madison were financially stable until the 1830s. But by then the toll of their gracious life, combined with their refusal to sell off their slaves, began to erode their resources. The ultimate source of financial ruin, however, was the combination of these general problems—mixed with the profligacy of Payne Todd.

Todd never settled into a planter's life, or made Montpelier his home. He drifted. He was restless. He traveled to New York, Philadelphia, and Washington, and then back again. He drank and gambled. He piled up debt after debt after debt.

The Madisons sent him money. But it proved impossible for them either to stop him or to keep up with his mounting obligations. In the winter of 1824–1825, he accumulated a debt of $700—in 1824 dollars. Over the course of the years between 1813 and 1836, when he died, James Madison quietly shipped his step-son $20,000, never telling his wife so as to spare her the mortification and pain. Together they gave him an additional $20,000. Todd cost them a total of $40,000 in those years.

Despite their efforts, Todd went to debtors' prison in Philadelphia in 1830. The escalating costs of sustaining Payne Todd forced James Madison to sell off his land in Kentucky and mortgage half his Montpelier estate—all of which, when he retired from politics in 1817, he had owned free and clear. And still, Madison wrote to Edward Coles in February 1827, "with all the concealments and alleviations I have been able to effect, his mother has known enough to make her wretched." Twenty-five years later, during an interview with William Cabell Rives, who in the mid-1850s was writing a biography of James Madison, Edward Coles would describe Payne Todd as the "serpent in the garden of Eden."

Despite Payne Todd's many faults, Dolley Madison loved her son and missed him. But not only was she hurt, she was also embarrassed by his behavior and his long absences from Montpelier—without a job, wife, family, or any other visible proof of a productive life. As early as December 1824 she wrote to him that "I am ashamed to tell, when asked, how long my only child has been absent from the home of his mother. Your father and I entreat you to come to us. . . ." And a year later, in November 1825, James Madison told his stepson that "it is painful to utter reproaches; yet how can they be avoided."

Partly to create an inheritance fund for his wife, and partly to preserve the historical record, James Madison began arranging his papers. He saved the correspondence he received and began retrieving letters which he himself had written to others. He then added the various notes he had made for speeches and state papers.

It was time-consuming work, and Madison needed secretarial help. He enlisted his brother-in-law and his wife. Mrs. Madison spent hours every day working on his project, adding to her busy schedule as housewife and hostess. As she wrote to her cousin Sarah in 1826, "The business seems to accumulate as he proceeds." Before he died, James Madison had arranged and edited his papers through 1787. These became the three-volume Madison Papers published in 1840 under congressional supervision. Beyond that, Dolley Madison organized his papers into folios, with the intention that these, too, she would sell.

By the mid-1830s, James Madison was increasingly ill. Mrs. Madison committed her time to his health. "My days are devoted to nursing," she wrote to her niece Dolly Cutts on May 11, "and comforting my sick patient." Her husband died on June 28, 1836.

Dolley Madison remained at Montpelier for the whole of the following year. Her niece Anna Payne—one of John C. Payne's children—came to live with her, and remained Mrs. Madison's companion until her death thirteen years later. Payne Todd came home for a stay, and Mrs. Madison mobilized her household to finish copying her husband's papers.

She moved forward with the sale of the *Madison Papers*. President Andrew Jackson recommended that the government acquire the manuscript, and Congress authorized $30,000 in payment.

In the fall of 1837 Dolley Madison departed from Orange County, leaving her son in charge of the plantation, and moved into the Cutts house on Lafayette Square in Washington. Anna had died in 1832, a loss that brought Mrs. Madison great anguish, especially as it followed on the heels of her son's imprisonment. With only her niece as company, Dolley Madison, now approaching seventy, took up her old life as doyenne of Washington as best she could. She soon began entertaining, holding dinner parties and evening parties, and going out with great regularity, sustaining her old friendships and forging many new ones.

Moving to Washington helped alleviate her loneliness; it eased such burdens of widowhood as a life without a husband of forty-odd years. But it did nothing to solve the impending crisis of economic insolvency.

Payne Todd, instead of managing the family estate, was rapidly deteriorating from alcoholism. He suffered from pains in his legs, pains in his teeth, pains in his back, heartburn, nausea, and innumerable mysterious inflammations. He slept at all hours, rose at all hours, and ate at all hours. He took to slumbering rolled up in a blanket in front of the fireplace and to not moving for days. Under his guidance Montpelier steadily declined, leaving both mother and son with debts rather than income from the farm.

By 1842 Mrs. Madison had decided that she needed to mortgage her house in Washington. She took a trip to New York City—for the first and only time of her life—and while there negotiated a loan from John Jacob Astor, an old friend who was one of the wealthiest men in America. She signed the note that August.

She continued to peddle the remaining Madison papers. At first she hoped to sell them to a publishing house. But she left the negotiations to her son, and he botched the job. By the winter of 1843–1844 she decided that she would never find any other buyer than the federal government, and wrote to Congress, offering to sell her late husband's papers.

Although Congress had bought the first batch, this time it refused her offer. The reason, at least in part, was that her son had persuaded her to try to get him an appointment as American consul to Liverpool. President Tyler had turned her down. "Mr. Todd," Tyler explained, "is not fitted for the office." Soon the sale of James Madison's correspondence became enmeshed with the seamy life of his ne'er-do-well stepson.

Over the summer of 1843, in ever greater need of financial relief, Dolley Madison sold off part of Montpelier and rented out the house. But then in July 1844 she learned that Mr. Madison's younger brother William was suing the estate for $2,000. She received a letter from one of her slaves informing her that the county sheriff was trying to sell the slaves to "negro buyers" to raise money to pay off William Madison. Dolley Madison quickly sold the whole of the estate to pay off the debt and prevent the dismemberment of her slaves' families. But it was not without pain. "No one," she wrote to Henry Moncure on August 12, 1844, "I think can appreciate my feeling of grief and dismay at the necessity of transferring to another a beloved home." Thereafter, she lived only in Washington.

She remained an active hostess to the end. She was, William Preston noted of these later years, even in her poverty and without her husband, "the same good-natured, kind-hearted, considerate, stately person, that she had been in the hey-day of her fortunes." And, he added, "[her] manner was urbane, gracious, with an almost imperceptible touch of Quakerism." She became good friends with Secretary of State Daniel Webster, who began to look after her. He bought—and then emancipated—Paul Jennings, Madison's valet and now one of her slaves in Washington. As Dolley Madison's poverty increased, Webster, worried that she had not even enough to eat, would send Jennings to her house laden with a basket of food.

Finally, in 1848, Congress agreed to purchase the rest of James Madison's papers, for a total sum of $25,000. But they would do so only by putting the money into a trust, so that her son could not spend it. Regardless of these provisions, immediately upon sale of the papers, Todd showed up on her doorstep, desperate. He went around the city, vaguely threatening vengeance against the trustees. She was miserable at his conduct. "At this moment," she wrote him on June 29, 1848:

> I am much distressed at the conversations you held, and the determinations you expressed, on the subject of bringing suit against my Trustees. . . . Your mother would have no wish to live after her son issued such threats which would deprive her of her friends, who had no other view in taking charge than pure friendship.

Yet still she sank deeper into poverty.

Dolley Madison fell fatally ill in July 1849, lingered for five days in bed, and died on Thursday evening, July 12. The most beloved First Lady of the new nation, she had known every president from George Washington to Zachary Taylor. In her declining years she had become friends with the youthful Julia Tyler and the serious and politically capable Sarah Polk. She was the last living icon of the Founding Fathers.

Dolley Madison had transformed the role of First Lady. She was determined not to emulate Martha Washington and Abigail Adams and their Federalist, "monarchical" formality. She could not imitate the widower Thomas Jefferson. She needed to create new ceremonial forms and an appropriate ceremonial setting for the new republic. She did so with flair, charm, and tact. She was a great First Lady.

Her funeral took place on July 17. It was a state occasion, attended by the president, the cabinet officers, the diplomatic corps, members of the House and Senate, justices of the Supreme Court, officers of the army and navy, the mayor and city leaders, and "citizens and strangers." At half-past five that afternoon a large and imposing funeral procession wound its way to the Congressional Cemetery, where, the city's *Daily National Intelligencer* announced, "[Dolley Madison's body] will remain until it is removed to its final resting place at Montpelier."

BIBLIOGRAPHICAL ESSAY

The largest collection of Dolley Madison papers—and the one from which the quotes used in this essay were drawn—is in the Papers of James Madison, Alderman Library, University of Virginia, Charlottesville. There are also Dolley Madison papers in the Library of Congress and at the Greensboro Historical Museum in North Carolina. Although a sizable amount of her correspondence exists, many of her personal letters and those of her husband have not survived. Moreover, Mrs. Madison often did not date her letters beyond a mere "Sunday" or "March 10." Dating her correspondence, therefore, requires careful analysis and often must be done according to internal evidence.

While there are only scattered letters of Richard Cutts, the papers of John G. Jackson are at Indiana University. The diary of Mrs. Madison's neighbor and friend, Anna Marie Thornton, is at the Library of Congress, and the letters of Margaret Bayard Smith are contained in the J. Henley Smith Papers at the Library of Congress. Copies of the correspondence of foreign diplomats present in Washington during the years 1801–1817 can also be found at the Library of Congress.

Students who wish to study the importance of Dolley Madison's influence on material culture of that time period should examine her lists of household furnishings and her work on decorating the White House. The papers of Benjamin Latrobe are located at the Maryland Historical Society in Baltimore. There is a published three-volume edition of these papers, edited by John C. Van Horne (1986). Jumping ahead to secondary sources, the student should begin with Conover Hunt-Jones, *Dolley and the "Great Little Madison"* (Washington, D.C., 1977).

There are a number of biographies of Dolley Madison, as well as children's books, novels, and all sorts of articles. Caroline Holmes Bivins authored a bibliographical study, printed by the Blue Ride Quick Print Company (Brevard, N.C., 1982). There is a copy in the Library of Congress and another with the Papers of James Madison.

The first two biographies were written in the style of "life and letters" and reprint selections from Dolley Madison's personal correspondence. These two books are Lucia B. Cutts, *Memoirs and Letters of Dolly Madison* (Boston, 1886); and Allen C. Clark, *Life and Letters of Dolly Madison* (Washington, D.C., 1914). In both volumes the letters have been heavily edited. Other biographies include Maud W. Goodwin,

Dolly Madison (New York, 1896); and Ethel Stephens Arnett, *Mrs. James Madison: The Incomparable Dolley* (Greenville, N.C., 1972).

The most useful biographies of James Madison are Irving Brant, *James Madison* (6 vols., Indianapolis, 1944–1961); and Ralph Ketcham, *James Madison* (New York, 1971). See also Henry Adams, *A History of the United States During the Administrations of Thomas Jefferson and James Madison* (9 vols., New York, 1889–1891). For the War of 1812, consult Reginald Horsman, *The War of 1812* (New York, 1969). On Washington, D.C., see the early volumes of the Columbia Historical Society Records. Useful books include Margaret Bayard Smith, *The First Forty Years of Washington*, ed. Gaillard Hunt (New York, 1906); W. B. Bryan, *A History of the National Capital* (Washington, D.C., 1914); Constance McLaughlin Green, *Washington* (Princeton, N.J., 1962); Barbara G. Carson, *Ambitious Appetites: Dining, Behavior, and Patterns of Consumption in Federal Washington* (Washington, D.C., 1990); and James Sterling Young, *The Washington Community* (New York, 1966). On material culture and fashion, see Richard Bushman, *The Refinement of America* (New York, 1962). For women during the early republic, see Linda Kerber, *Women of the Republic* (Chapel Hill, N.C., 1980); Linda Grant DePauw and Conover Hunt, *Remember the Ladies* (New York, 1976); Jan Lewis, *The Pursuit of Happiness* (Cambridge, Mass., 1983); and Catherine Allgor, *Parlor Politics: In Which the Ladies of Washington Help Build a City and a Government* (Charlottesville, Va., 2000).

A useful Ph.D. dissertation on the Washington scene during the era of Dolley Madison is Catherine Allgor, "Political Parties: Society and Politics in Washington City, 1800–1832," (Yale University, 1998). A fuller bibliography of writings about Dolley Madison is available at the National First Ladies Library at *www.firstladies.org*.

★★★　　★★★

Elizabeth Kortright Monroe

(1768–1830)

First Lady: 1817–1825

Julie K. Fix

Elizabeth Kortright was born on June 30, 1768, the second of five children of Captain Lawrence Kortright, a merchant and former captain in the British colonial army, and his wife, Hannah Aspinwall Kortright. Elizabeth, along with her brother, John, and sisters Hester, Maria, and Sarah, grew up in New York City. Hannah Kortright died the year Elizabeth turned nine years old. Hester Kortright, Elizabeth's paternal grandmother, played a significant role in forming the young girl's character after the death of her mother. A strong and independent woman, Hester Kortright started and maintained her own business after her husband's death, refusing all offers of matrimony.

As a daughter of the well-established, wealthy, and socially prominent Kortright family, Elizabeth grew to be a cultured and attractive young woman. Dark haired and only five feet tall, throughout her life she was known for her youthful beauty. In 1785, at the age of sixteen, Elizabeth Kortright met James Monroe, a young representative from Virginia who had come to New York, then the capital city of the new American nation, to attend his first session of Congress. They were married the following year on February 16, 1786, at Trinity Episcopal Church in New York and honeymooned on Long Island. On the surface, the marriage seemed to be a mismatch. Elizabeth was the seventeen-year-old daughter of a wealthy

Tory sympathizer, while James Monroe was a twenty-seven-year-old lawyer from backcountry Virginia who had earned a commendation from General George Washington during the Revolutionary War. Indeed, the bride's friends confided that they had expected her to do better. Of the four Kortright daughters' marriages, Elizabeth's seemed the least successful at first. In contrast, James Monroe's friends saw Elizabeth Kortright as an appropriate match, but some disliked her New York air, which, they felt, made her seem aloof.

For the first three years of their marriage the Monroes lived in Fredericksburg, Virginia, where James Monroe practiced law. In order to earn his living as a lawyer, Monroe spent much of his time traveling the lengthy circuit from court to court. Elizabeth Monroe, after the birth of her first daughter, Eliza, in December 1786, frequently made the journeys with her husband. It was the beginning of a long life of traveling together; James Monroe's later public service would require that they reside in many different cities and countries over the years. The small family moved to Charlottesville in Albemarle County, Virginia, in 1789.

In 1790, the death of William Grayson left a vacant seat in the first United States Senate. Monroe replaced Grayson as a senator from Virginia. His concern for his wife's happiness influenced his decision, at least in part. Since Philadelphia served as the capital city of America in 1790, Monroe's presence at sessions there would allow Elizabeth Monroe the opportunity to visit her family in New York for the first time since her marriage four years earlier. Monroe served four terms as a senator, with his wife and daughter accompanying him on most of his trips to Philadelphia.

In 1793 Monroe purchased a plantation in Albemarle, Virginia, near Thomas Jefferson's Monticello home, but the Monroes would not take up residence at their new home, which they called Highland, until several years later. In 1794, Monroe, known as a Francophile, was named U.S. minister plenipotentiary to France by President Washington. He and his family moved to the diplomatic residence on the Folie de la Bouexiere in Paris.

Elizabeth Monroe's experiences in France deeply influenced her later years as the president's wife. In the decades following the Revolutionary War, the government of the new United States was desperate for recognition from foreign states. American leaders felt it was important that America be seen as a sophisticated and powerful country rather than a bumbling political version of the nouveau riche. The precedents set during the years of the early republic would form the basis of American relationships with other countries for decades to come. As the American representatives in France, James and Elizabeth Monroe were determined to uphold the dignity of their country as well as its republican virtues. Aware that aristocratic foreign powers put great stock in social sophistication as a measure by which to judge political maturity, the Monroes combined casual American manners and social customs with the more formal and stylized protocols of Europe.

Although the Monroes did not entertain frequently, because of financial constraints and the turbulent political situation in France during the years immediately following the 1789 French Revolution, Elizabeth Monroe became known as a highly successful hostess in Paris. The French called her *la belle américaine* for her manners as well as her physical beauty. It may have eased the Monroes' entrée into French society that they enrolled their daughter Eliza in Madame Jeanne de Campan's school in St. Germain-en-Laye, near Paris. Mme. de Campan had been Marie Antoinette's chief lady-in-waiting, and Eliza's classmates included such members of the French elite as her lifelong friend Hortense de Beauharnais, the daughter of Josephine de Beauharnais. (Josephine de Beauharnais later married Napoleon Bonaparte, and Hortense de Beauharnais eventually became queen of Holland through her marriage to Louis Bonaparte.)

Other Americans were not so conversant with French social mores and not as willing to adapt to them. As a harbinger of difficulties to come, Monroe was called upon to smooth over a prickly social situation that developed when an American tourist complained because Elizabeth Monroe, as the American minister's wife, had not greeted the newcomer upon her arrival in Paris. Monroe explained that, according to French custom, it was incumbent on the new arrival to make the first visit. In the world of the late eighteenth century, social niceties played a significant role in establishing an individual's status. Whereas Elizabeth Monroe's failure to call on someone was seen as a grievous insult, because of her position as wife of the American minister, individuals she did call upon gained status and power through her visit.

Elizabeth Monroe and her husband learned the true power of social niceties during the course of their attempts to save Adrienne de Lafayette. French politics in the 1790s were highly volatile. The executions by guillotine of French aristocrats that followed the 1789 revolution continued during the Monroes' sojourn in France. One of the aristocrats slated to be executed was Adrienne Noailles de Lafayette, the wife of the Marquis de Lafayette, who had been a hero in the American Revolutionary War. James Monroe felt that it would be poor gratitude to the marquis for Americans to let his wife be executed if there were any way to save her. However, in order to keep relations between the U.S. and French governments peaceful, it was necessary to approach the problem delicately. Gouverneur Morris, the former minister to France, had already tried to secure Adrienne de Lafayette's release and failed.

It is unknown to what extent Elizabeth Monroe contributed to the formation of the plan to free Adrienne de Lafayette, but she was integral in carrying it out. In 1794 the French Committee of Public Safety was holding Adrienne de Lafayette in Le Plessis prison. The Monroes acquired a sumptuous carriage, refurbished it, and equipped it with liveried servants. Elizabeth Monroe, elegantly dressed and appearing the epitome of a powerful minister's wife, rode in this carriage through the streets of Paris to Le Plessis in a very public visit to the prisoner. The vehicle attracted an audience, as the trappings of the aristocracy had all but disappeared from the city in the wake of the bloody revolution. Adrienne de Lafayette's mother, sister, and grandmother had already been taken to the guillotine, and when she was called to emerge from her cell, she feared that she was also about to be executed. When she discovered that a visitor rather than the headsman awaited her, Adrienne de Lafayette burst into tears. The dramatic and very public scene swayed opinion in Paris enough that James Monroe succeeded where Gouverneur Morris and his purely political arguments had not. Mme. de Lafayette was released from prison on January 22, 1795.

The Monroes returned to the United States in 1797, and James Monroe resumed his political career when he was elected governor of Virginia by the General Assembly. He served three one-year terms between 1799 and 1803. For Elizabeth Monroe that meant traveling with her daughter Eliza to Richmond, where she found the governor's palace so decrepit as to be uninhabitable. Poorly compensated public service mired James Monroe deeper and deeper in debt. He was too busy and too distant from Highland to ensure a good yield from his plantation, and his salaries for his various offices, when paid, rarely covered the debts he incurred while serving his country. Although Elizabeth Monroe's father had died in 1794, any hopes the Monroes might have had of a sizable inheritance were frustrated. Captain Kortright's financial affairs were in hopeless disarray, and Elizabeth's sisters, in an attempt to organize their father's financial assets, had to appeal to James Monroe for assistance.

In May 1799 Elizabeth Monroe gave birth to a son whom she and her husband named James Spence Monroe. The child died from whooping cough only sixteen months later. Elizabeth Monroe's health had never been very good, and, exhausted from tending to her son during his final illness, she was sick for several months after his death. She recovered eventually, and in early 1803 she gave birth to her third and last child, a daughter named Maria Hester.

In 1803 Monroe was sent back to France to conduct negotiations for the Louisiana Purchase with Napoleon Bonaparte. To finance the voyage, Monroe sold much of his silver and furniture to his friends and neighbors James and Dolley Madison. He needed to furnish their new residence in France, and his financial situation would not allow him to keep two complete households.

The Monroes spent the next four years living abroad in Paris and London. Elizabeth Monroe far preferred Paris. In London, for the first time, she and her husband were socially snubbed. As a penurious minister of a neutral country not involved in Europe's power plays, Monroe's political and social status made him and his wife nonentities in Britain. Monroe had even been insulted as minister to England from the United States when he had been seated at a diplomatic dinner between representatives of two very minor German principalities. His placement at the table reflected his lack of political importance in the eyes of his host. In France, Elizabeth Monroe had learned about the vital link between protocol and politics; in London, she learned that she could survive social ostracism.

After their return to the United States the Monroes enjoyed a respite of several years at Highland, their plantation in Albemarle. Eliza Monroe married a prominent Virginia lawyer named George Hay in 1808, but the occasion was marred by the absence of James and Dolley Madison. A serious two-year rift had developed in the friendship between James Monroe and James Madison when Monroe allowed himself to be nominated as the 1808 Republican presidential candidate running against Madison. Madison won the election, to become the fourth president of the United States. Eventually, Monroe and Madison resolved their differences, and the two were publicly reconciled in 1810.

Also in 1810 James Monroe was elected to the Virginia General Assembly and, the following year, to his fourth term as governor of Virginia. He would leave Virginia before completing his term, however, when President Madison named him secretary of state in 1811. A year passed before Elizabeth Monroe could join her husband in Washington, D.C. Even after her arrival the Monroes rarely entertained, though they both attended official and public functions. Not only were they still deeply in debt from James Monroe's public service, but, sensitive to social undercurrents, they were not eager to strain Madison's newly regained friendship by upstaging the president or his wife in any way. Elizabeth Monroe retained the reserved manners that had served her well in France. Whereas Dolley Madison followed the American custom of calling on the wives of the senators and congressmen, Elizabeth Monroe made the first visit only to friends or acquaintances, though she would return calls. Dolley, as the president's wife, was outgoing, open, and casual; Elizabeth, as the wife of the secretary of state, remained retiring, reserved, and very formal. Although they lived in the capital city for several years before James Monroe was elected president, the Monroes still seemed like strangers to Washington society. On December 4, 1816, after serving a brief stint as both secretary of state and secretary of war simultaneously, Monroe was elected the fifth president of the United States; he took office on March 4, 1817.

Because of the exigencies of her new role, almost as soon as her husband was elected president Elizabeth Monroe began to rely on her daughter Eliza to help with her social commitments. However, her reliance on Eliza soon led to conflict. Quiet Maria Hester Monroe would have been a better choice than Eliza Monroe Hay to act as her mother's stand-in, but Maria Hester was away at school in Philadelphia. Despite her excellent French education, or perhaps, in light of the accusations of aristocratic tendencies because of it, Eliza Hay managed to alienate virtually all members of Washington society. Neither Eliza nor anyone else in Washington was certain of her exact status. Although she frequently acted in her mother's capacity, she was clearly not the president's wife. In her impatience with social niceties and her rather fumbling efforts to define her role, she often appeared high-handed and dictatorial.

On December 29, 1817, President James Monroe held a cabinet meeting to discuss the protocol of receiving diplomats in Washington. Elizabeth Monroe and Louisa Adams, the wife of the new secretary of state, John Quincy Adams, also met to consider their social strategy.

Elizabeth Monroe decided to integrate the formal social customs that had marked her as the wife of the American minister to France and later as the wife of the secretary of state into her new role as the president's wife; she realized, after her experiences abroad, the importance Europeans placed on protocol. Despite the insult much of Washington society would inevitably feel as a result of the Monroes' use of some European conventions, it was necessary that visiting dignitaries and the diplomatic corps resident in Washington respect both the country and its president.

Elizabeth Monroe understood that her social status was nearly as great as her husband's and that she as well as the president must weigh the political implications of attending social events. In addition, she subscribed to the traditional belief of the nineteenth century that a woman, particularly the president's wife, should remain in the shadow of her husband. In one instance, when James Monroe refused an invitation tendered to him by the French minister, Elizabeth Monroe was invited to take his place. She declined because she felt that if the president's presence at the affair would create a politically sensitive situation, then the same would be true for her.

In addition to her concern over the political impressions that America's social customs conveyed to visitors, the wife of the new president chose to institute a distant and reserved etiquette for a more prosaic reason. Elizabeth Monroe had never enjoyed a sound constitution, and she was plagued continually with health problems, including rheumatism and headaches. She may have had several miscarriages, and she

apparently suffered occasionally from fits that recent scholars speculate may have been epileptic seizures. On one such occasion she fell into a fireplace and was badly burned. Elizabeth Monroe also contracted several serious fevers during her residence in the marshy and unhealthy capital city of Washington.

Paying calls was exhausting even for someone in perfect health, and still more so in a city that lacked paved roads. In the early years, before many congressmen's wives traveled with their husbands to the capital, the number of calls a president's wife was expected to make may have been manageable. As the city developed, however, more and more of the distaff branch of Congress took up residence in Washington. Indeed, John Quincy Adams wrote in his diary that Dolley Madison's experiences in attempting to fulfill her social obligations had been torturous. Dolley Madison was known for her energy and her vivacity; Elizabeth Monroe, for her passive elegance. In part the knowledge that she could not be another Dolley Madison may have influenced Elizabeth Monroe's decision to rewrite the social rules.

While foreign visitors approved of and appreciated Elizabeth Monroe's formality, the same was not true of Americans. A storm began to brew in Washington society as the congressmen's wives and daughters felt themselves snubbed by the First Lady. Rumors circulated that Elizabeth Monroe fancied herself a queen. The fine French pieces with which the Monroes furnished the White House indicated to critics that the First Family had aspirations to aristocracy. (Initially, many of these pieces were furnishings purchased in Paris when James Monroe was French minister, after the Monroes had been forced to sell their own furniture to make the price of the ocean voyage.) Americans in the early republic were sensitive to charges of harboring monarchical aspirations, having spent much of the Revolutionary War asserting their independence from the British Crown.

In 1819 the women of Washington socially boycotted Elizabeth Monroe, and also Eliza Hay and Louisa Adams, who had followed Elizabeth Monroe's example: they refused to pay calls on or accept invitations from the White House. Maria Hester Monroe's wedding to Samuel Lawrence Gouverneur at the White House in 1820 was a further cause of contention. The wedding, which most residents of the capital felt should be the social event of the year, was held in "New York style," with only family and close friends attending. Eliza Hay, infuriated over the boycott, made it clear that she felt the new couple should refuse calls from the women who had snubbed her and the First Lady. It became necessary for Secretary of State John Quincy Adams to step in and inform members of the diplomatic corps on behalf of President Monroe that their wives would be welcomed by the Gouverneurs. The Monroes and the Gouverneurs planned a series of balls to celebrate the wedding and assuage the hurt feelings of their neighbors. The first, very successful, revel was held at the home of Commodore Stephen Decatur. Unfortunately, the popular Decatur was mortally wounded in a duel the following morning and died the next day; the remaining balls were canceled out of respect.

The quiet battles fought over etiquette became so fierce that they began to affect the domestic political atmosphere in Washington. John Quincy Adams noticed that the issues raised by the women were used by the men for political purposes and that they caused dissension between himself and the senators. The president had somewhat sidestepped the issue by adhering strictly to George Washington's policy of not accepting invitations to events at the homes of cabinet officials or to other affairs with political overtones, leaving it to his wife to accept or refuse other social advances. Whereas Monroe had Washington's precedent to follow, his wife was creating a precedent for subsequent First Ladies. In 1819, however, the president held a cabinet meeting to discuss common rules of etiquette.

Elizabeth Monroe persevered in the face of harsh criticism, attempting to reach an acceptable compromise. Dinners at the White House were formal and served in the European style, with one waiter per guest. At the same time, the Monroes retained the American custom that had been known as the "presidential levee" under George Washington. Thomas Jefferson had abandoned the custom, but the Madisons revived it and it came to be called simply the "drawing room." "Drawing rooms" occurred about every two weeks while Congress was in session. The White House was opened to anyone suitably dressed for an evening party who cared to meet the First Family. Contemporary accounts of these events show that they were often rowdy gatherings characterized by guests who were unfamiliar with the fine points of manners and courtesy.

Having established the rules for social etiquette, Elizabeth Monroe maintained them rigidly to avoid charges of favoritism. On one occasion, she turned a close relative away from the White House for violating the "drawing room" dress code. Possibly in anticipation of further criticism, whereas Martha Washington had gone by the title of "Lady" and Dolley Madison that of "Presidentress," Elizabeth Monroe preferred to be addressed simply as "Mrs. Monroe" (the term "First Lady" was not used at the time). Eventually her patience and perseverance succeeded, and Washington society abandoned its boycott against the president's wife and her circle. By James Monroe's second term in office, Washingtonians had begun to accept his wife's policy of restricting the First Family's social obligations to receiving guests. The social customs Elizabeth Kortright Monroe developed became the core of White House protocol today.

Elizabeth Monroe's health grew worse throughout her husband's second term as president, and her public appearances became increasingly rare. In 1824, after one of many prolonged illnesses, she presided over a state dinner honoring the Marquis de Lafayette, whose wife she had been instrumental in saving. A few months later Elizabeth Monroe attended her last official public function, the New Year's Day reception at the White House. On both occasions, visitors commented on her gracious manners and her youthful beauty, despite her weakness. When John Quincy Adams became president in March 1825, the Monroes were unable to vacate the White House for several weeks until Elizabeth Monroe felt well enough to travel. By June 1825 the couple had retired to Oak Hill, in Loudoun County, Virginia. James Monroe had refurbished the farm and built a new home there between 1820 and 1823. Oak Hill was closer to Washington than Highland, the Albemarle plantation, and it was an easier journey for Mrs. Monroe.

On September 23, 1830, Elizabeth Kortright Monroe succumbed at Oak Hill. Eliza Hay, who had been attending her husband on his deathbed only two days earlier, arrived at Oak Hill after her husband's demise, just in time to witness her mother's death. James Monroe was devastated by his wife's passing. He confided to Egbert Watson, a visitor at Oak Hill at the time, that he did not think he would live long without her. Monroe ordered a double vault at Oak Hill, one that was to contain his remains as well as those of his wife, and he delayed her funeral until it was completed. Despite his years in the public eye, James Monroe was a very private man. He almost never expressed his personal feelings in writing. In an unusual letter to James Brown dated December 9, 1830, Monroe referred to the death of his wife:

> We have both suffered the most afflicting calamity that can befall us in this life, and which, if time may alleviate it, it cannot efface. After having lived, with the partner of your life, in so many vicissitudes of life, so long together and afforded to each other the comforts which no other person on earth could do, as both of us have done, to have her snatched from us, is an affliction which none but those who feel it can justly estimate.

James Monroe lived with his daughter Maria Hester Gouverneur in New York until his death only a few months later, on July 4, 1831. He was buried in New York, but his remains were reinterred in the Hollywood Cemetery in Richmond, Virginia, in 1858. In 1903, Elizabeth Monroe's remains were finally reinterred. She lies beside her husband in Richmond.

Unfortunately, James Monroe's desire for privacy left his wife with no voice in history. According to family tradition, James Monroe burned all of the letters he and his wife had written to one another. To date, only one letter is documented as having come from the pen of Elizabeth Monroe, and it is neither lengthy nor revealing. Despite the paucity of sources, Elizabeth Monroe still emerges as a sympathetic figure. A brave and tenacious woman, she hid beneath her quiet, retiring surface a backbone of iron that allowed her to face grief, penury, social ostracism, and chronic illness with grace and composure. Despite her poor health and her belief that a woman should not make her presence strongly felt in public, except in support of her husband, Elizabeth Monroe had a decided and lasting impact on Washington society and on the role of First Lady. She shaped the core of the First Lady's social obligations in the face of furious opposition. Though faded with time, the mark she made on protocol and diplomacy in Washington is still visible.

BIBLIOGRAPHICAL ESSAY

Only one letter remains that is known to have been written by Elizabeth Monroe. Family tradition holds that James Monroe burned his wife's correspondence after her death, including his own letters to her. Elizabeth Monroe's name appears in James Monroe's papers primarily in postscripts concerning her health. Some of his papers are available on microfilm at the Library of Congress, while others are scattered throughout repositories across the country. Monroe's papers are not indexed, but the Monroe Consortium is in the process of compiling a calendar to improve access to them. Even James Monroe's autobiography had little to say about their private life. Mentions of Elizabeth Monroe in John Quincy Adams's diary provide probably the single most reliable and comprehensive contemporary source of information about her. Adams's diary was edited by Allan Nevins: *The Diary of John Quincy Adams 1794–1845: American Political, Social, and Intellectual Life from Washington to Polk* (New York, 1928). Though few, Adams's references to her are more extensive than those in James Monroe's papers.

Most general histories of First Ladies confine their accounts of Elizabeth Monroe's life to a few pages, primarily listing basic information such as her date of birth and the year Monroe was elected president. The only biography of any length pertaining to her is the slim volume *Elizabeth Kortright Monroe*, written by James E. Wootton, the curator of Ash Lawn-Highland, and published by Ash Lawn-Highland, College of William and Mary, in 1987 (Ash Lawn-Highland, James Monroe Parkway, Charlottesville, Virginia 22901). Harry Ammon's *James Monroe: The Quest for National Identity* (New York, 1971) is currently the definitive work on James Monroe; it contains some material concerning Elizabeth Monroe.

★★★　　★★★

Louisa Catherine Johnson Adams
(1775–1852)

First Lady: 1825–1829

Lynn Hudson Parsons

Louisa Catherine Johnson was born in London on February 12, 1775. Her father was Joshua Johnson, an American merchant, and her mother was an Englishwoman whose maiden name was either Catherine Nuth or Catherine Young. Despite assiduous research by Henry Adams and others, the origins of Louisa's mother remain clouded. There is evidence that the Johnsons were not married until 1785, when Louisa was ten years old. She thus is the only First Lady to have been born abroad, and may also be the only First Lady to have been born out of wedlock.

Louisa's father was born in 1742, one of eleven children in an up-and-coming Maryland family. His brother Thomas later became governor of Maryland and an associate justice of the United States Supreme Court. A partner in the mercantile firm of Wallace, Davidson, and Johnson, Joshua arrived in England in 1771 and stayed there until 1778. At that point he deemed it prudent to move to France along with his family, settling in the commercial port of Nantes. There the young Louisa received her first formal education in a Roman Catholic boarding school, where she became as fluent in French as she was in English. Her family spent five years in Nantes, where they received prominent visitors such as the American diplomat John Adams, who was in 1779 accompanied by his solemn twelve-year-old son, John Quincy. Louisa was then four years old.

Following the end of the War for Independence, Joshua Johnson returned to London. His financial situation apparently had not suffered in the interval, for he moved into a large house in Cooper's Row, near Tower Hill. By this time he had sired six children, with three more yet to come. With one exception, all were girls. Louisa, the second eldest, was placed in a boarding school near London, along with two of her sisters, Nancy and Caroline.

In 1788 Joshua Johnson's fortune took a turn for the worse, resulting in an end to his daughters' stay at school. Their education was continued by a governess who instructed them in the expected upper-class female skills of the day: music, singing, and embroidery. Despite precarious finances, the Johnsons continued their outwardly affluent style of living. When President George Washington appointed Johnson the U.S. consul in 1790, the house in Cooper's Row became a gathering place for visiting Americans. Often in the evenings Louisa would join her older sister Nancy at the piano or the harp to entertain her father's guests after dinner. It was on such an evening in mid-November 1795 that those guests included the young American minister to the Netherlands, John Quincy Adams, now a twenty-eight-year-old bachelor.

Adams had been sent to England from The Hague to arrange for the ratification of the controversial Jay Treaty with Great Britain, something he found had already been accomplished by the time of his arrival. While awaiting further instructions, Adams had little to do other than visit the London theaters and socialize with other Americans of his age. The Johnson family found Adams good company once he overcame his initial reserve, and they viewed him as a prospective husband for one of their marriageable daughters, although the Southern-born consul believed that Yankees made bad matches. By the time of John Quincy's return to the Netherlands in the spring of 1796, Louisa Johnson and John Quincy Adams were engaged to be married.

They would not, however, be married for more than a year—an unusually long engagement by eighteenth-century standards. John Quincy's formidable mother, the future First Lady Abigail Adams (who had already broken up an earlier romance between her son and a young Massachusetts girl), soon learned of the engagement and questioned whether his fiancée's "foreign" background would stand up to the harsh demands of American republicanism. As the anxious Johnson family watched, Adams seemed to retreat from his commitment. He sent forth to London a remarkable series of letters bluntly critical of Louisa's temperament, lifestyle, reading habits, and vocabulary. Even when he learned that President Washington had promoted him to the post of minister to Portugal—thus doubling his salary—Adams still pleaded lack of financial security for an immediate marriage, suggesting at one point that Louisa join her family in its planned move to the United States. There she could wait for him until he had completed his three-year tour of duty. He did not seem particularly disappointed at the prospect. "Let us consider it as one of those counterchecks in the affairs of life which happen to all," he breezily wrote (December 5, 1796), "which all must endure whether they will or not." When Louisa not unreasonably suggested that he might think about placing their future happiness ahead of his career, she was rebuked. "To serve my country at her call, is not merely an ambition, but a duty," he told her on February 7, 1797. "My duty to my country is in my mind the first and most imperious of all obligations; before which every interest and every feeling inconsistent with it must forever disappear." No one could say that Louisa had not been warned.

But Joshua Johnson forced the issue with Adams by making him an offer he could not refuse: if he would come to London for the wedding, Johnson would provide the newlyweds with a private vessel to take them on to Lisbon. Adams had run out of excuses. He left the Netherlands in early July 1797, and on the twenty-sixth day of that month the couple were married at a church, as his grandson later said, "in the shadow of the Tower of London." Upon learning of the marriage, and with the unpopular Jay Treaty in mind, an irreverent opposition newspaper, the *Boston Independent Chronicle*, reported on September 14, 1797, that "Young John Adams' Negotiations, have terminated in a Marriage Treaty with an English lady. . . . It is a happy circumstance that he made no other Treaty."

Just before leaving the Netherlands for London, Adams had learned that the new president of the United States—his father, John Adams—had changed his appointment from minister to Portugal to minister to Prussia. Berlin, not Lisbon, would be their first home. Matters were further complicated by the news that Joshua Johnson's business affairs had deteriorated to an extent that necessitated a hasty departure from London—and from his creditors. This left the impression, at least in Louisa Adams's mind, that her new husband might think he had been tricked into marrying a woman whose financial position was nowhere near what he had anticipated. Although John Quincy Adams never mentioned it, his wife brooded over the matter for years.

The young Adamses left England in October 1797. The new bride was in great discomfort, suffering from what would turn out to be one of several miscarriages she would experience in Berlin before giving birth to her first son, George Washington Adams, in 1801. Her frequent indisposition, combined with her husband's minuscule salary, prevented the couple from living up to the scale of most of the rest of the diplomatic corps and from participating in the glittering social life of the Prussian court. But when she did appear, Louisa Adams's youth, beauty, and fluency in French made her an asset to her husband. She was fond of dancing and often was the first to begin and the last to conclude the evening's festivities. She became a favorite of the Prussian royal family, and when she was entering the confinement that would lead to the birth of her son, the king of Prussia closed off traffic outside the Adamses' home so that she would not be disturbed.

Privately, the tensions that had surfaced before their marriage remained, compli- cated now by Louisa Adams's ill health. The degree to which her illnesses and miscarriages were psychosomatic is not clear. In the view of one twentieth-century authority, many of her symptoms were consistent with the nineteenth-century definition of "hysteria." Those included persistent fatigue, lethargy, and frequent illness after receiving bad news. In any event, her husband was emotionally ill-equipped to deal with them.

While in most ways a faithful and devoted husband, John Quincy Adams was too wrapped up in his work to create an atmosphere in which his wife's emotional needs could be satisfied and in which she could develop self-confidence. Despite the example set by his own mother, Adams did not take women seriously until very late in his life. Moreover, adversity in whatever form was invariably seen as a test of inner strength. Adams thus welcomed their spartan existence in Berlin as evidence of proper republican simplicity in the face of Old World decadence. He even refused to let Louisa wear rouge to public events.

When President John Adams was defeated by Thomas Jefferson in the election of 1800, he recalled John Quincy from Berlin to spare his son the indignity of being dismissed by his successor. In the summer of 1801 Louisa Adams, now a proud mother, eagerly looked forward to the transatlantic voyage and a reunion with the Johnson family in America. She probably looked forward less eagerly to her first meeting with her Adams in-laws. Years later, when she wrote her autobiographical fragments, the impressions of the initial encounter with her husband's family and friends were still fresh in her mind: "Had I stepped into Noah's Ark I do not think I could have been so utterly astonished." While having long since accepted and indeed embraced her son's marriage, Abigail Adams was still dubious, and tensions were never far from the surface. Whereas Abigail was a no-nonsense "republican mother" who had spent years alone, managing her household in the absence of her itinerant diplomat-husband, Louisa Adams, by her own admission, was ill prepared for the domestic responsibilities of private life. "The qualifications necessary to form an accomplished Quincy Lady," she wrote in 1840, "were in direct opposition to the mode of life which I had led. . . . I hourly betrayed my incapacity and to a woman like Mrs. Adams, equal to every occasion in life, I appeared like a maudlin hysterical fine Lady. . . ." Her health was a source of concern for Abigail, who at one point declared to a friend that Louisa's "frame is so slender and her constitution so delicate that I have many fears that she will be of short duration." Mitigating the tension between mother-in-law and daughter-in-law was the instant affection established between Louisa and the elder John Adams, which endured until the former president's death a quarter of a century later. John Adams later remarked that the wisest decision his son ever made was to marry Louisa.

In Boston, John Quincy Adams reluctantly resumed the practice of law that he had eagerly abandoned eight years before. It did not take long for him to plunge into politics, running successfully as a Federalist for the Massachusetts State Senate in the spring of 1802, then unsuccessfully for Congress the following fall. A few months later he was elected by the Massachusetts legislature to the United States Senate. In the meantime Louisa Adams had again become pregnant, with all of the ominous implications that went with another pregnancy. This time, however, the pregnancy ended happily with the birth of a second son, John Adams II, born on July 4, 1803.

Joshua Johnson died nearly penniless in 1802, unable to provide for any of his family in his will, and the senior Adamses received a severe financial setback the following year with the failure of a London bank. Louisa Adams thus found herself settling in to the routine of an American wife under economic circumstances drastically reduced from those of her childhood. Accordingly, when her husband's election required a move to Washington, the junior Adamses lodged at the home of Louisa's sister Nancy and her family. Catherine John-son, the women's widowed mother, was residing there as well. Summers were sometimes spent in Washington with Louisa's sister, other times in Massachusetts with her in-laws. It would be many years before she had a home of her own.

John Quincy Adams's single term as a U.S. senator was marked by increased estrangement from the Federalist Party, largely over foreign policy. Perhaps sensing that his senatorial career would not be long, he accepted appointment to Harvard College in 1805 as Boylston professor of rhetoric. When Congress adjourned for the summer, Adams immediately left for Massachusetts, taking the family with him but immersing himself in preparations for his academic responsibilities the following year. When Congress adjourned the following spring, Adams again rushed north, leaving his wife behind although she was seven months pregnant. Letters between Louisa Adams and her husband indicate that she was not happy with what she called "this separation life" (August 12, 1804). In 1806, with her husband hundreds of miles away, Louisa Adams suffered another miscarriage. "Mon Amie," she wrote plaintively a few weeks later, "I grant as you have undertaken the business that it is necessary to attend to it but your family have some call on you as well" (July 20, 1806).

At no time, however, did Louisa Adams question her husband's ambition for public service. Indeed, acccording to a letter written from Berlin to her brother-in-law on October 6, 1798, when Adams attempted to write out his resignation owing to the financial strains of his position, Louisa burned the document. When he contemplated quitting the Senate in 1806 for the more lucrative practice of law, she reminded him that his destiny lay in public life, not the law. In fact, her husband needed little persuading, but the tension continued. "I can neither live with or without you," she wrote on November 25, 1806, after yet another separation. The following year she gave birth to a third son, Charles Francis Adams, this time with her husband present.

The summer of 1807, John Quincy Adams was later to write, marked the turning point in his career, for it was then that his break with the Federalist Party became irreparable. His support of Thomas Jefferson's foreign policy and his participation in the Republican caucus of 1808 led to his resignation from the Senate and a return to private life. But not for long. In early 1809, while Adams was in Washington to argue a case before the Supreme Court, James Madison, the new Republican president, offered him the post of minister to Russia. Without consulting his wife, or anyone else, Adams accepted on the spot. The following August, Louisa Adams found herself on a vessel bound for St. Petersburg. It would be eight years before she returned.

When she came to write her memoirs in 1840, Louisa Adams would maintain that the Russian mission had been against her will and that she had been virtually hustled away from her two eldest sons, George and John, who remained behind in the care of relatives. She also claimed that she had been prevented from seeing her father-in-law at the last minute, for fear that the two might combine to somehow prevent the voyage from taking place. While there can be no doubt that she had misgivings about the matter, there is no record of disagreement over the decision to leave the two older boys behind and to take the two-year-old Charles Francis with them.

The Adamses arrived at St. Petersburg in October 1809 after an adventurous voyage across the Atlantic during the height of the Napoleonic Wars. By January 1810 Louisa Adams was writing to her mother-in-law that she was ready to return home. "I do not like the place or the people," she said. Abigail must have agreed that the mission was a mistake, for that summer she wrote to President Madison on her own, asking that he recall her son. Madison complied, but left the decision up to Adams, sending him a letter of recall to be used at his discretion. He later followed it up with an appointment to the Supreme Court in 1811 that Adams declined, much to the regret of his wife and parents. The official reason given was his

wife's pregnancy. In August of that year Louisa Catherine Adams II was born, the first American citizen born in Russia.

In spite of her later recollections of St. Petersburg, which were mostly unpleasant, Louisa Adams was again a social success and an asset to her husband's standing in what was the most elegant court in Europe. Her fluency in French allowed her to converse with most diplomats and their wives, something not true of all diplomats' spouses. Tsar Alexander I took particular notice of Louisa, and singled her out as a dancing partner on more than one occasion. Yet, as in Berlin, their financial situation often prevented them from appearing in court. Louisa's health was affected by the brutal winters. Notwithstanding her successful pregnancy she suffered two further miscarriages, and she developed erysipelas—a painful skin condition—every winter.

In September 1812 the infant Louisa died, a victim of dysentery. More than anything else this colored Louisa Adams's memories of Russia in later years. She began a diary full of self-recrimination, resentment of her husband, and distaste for Russia. Shaken by his daughter's death, John Quincy Adams resolved to have the family united once again, and he sent for his two older sons. It would be another three years before he and his wife would see them, owing to the outbreak of the War of 1812.

In 1814, President Madison appointed Adams to lead the delegation that would try to negotiate an end to the war. From April of that year through the following March, Louisa Adams again found herself alone, this time in a foreign country. During that period she demonstrated inner strength that she had not shown before. She continued to entertain guests at their home. She took charge of the family's finances. Her letters to her husband showed a new self-confidence as she teased him about his celibate condition during her absence from him. Although, as she wrote in one letter, "there are some wounds which are not easy to heal," she declared later, "it seems to me now that I want you more than ever." After Adams and his colleagues negotiated the

"Peace of Christmas Eve" on December 24, 1814, she got her wish; Adams directed her to join him in Paris as soon as possible. She sold most of their personal possessions and made all the necessary social and financial arrangements for departure.

On her fortieth birthday, February 12, 1815, Louisa Adams began the most exciting six weeks of her life. Traveling by carriage with seven-year-old Charles Francis Adams and two servants, she raced from St. Petersburg to Paris. Despite the risks of travel in the dead of winter, she urged her frightened servants on, often by night as well as by day, until she reached Berlin. There she was briefly reunited with old friends from the days in Prussia, fifteen years before. Then, as she moved toward the French border, she learned of Napoleon's escape from Elba and his rumored return to Paris. In a carriage with Russian markings, she was in danger of being mistaken for either a Russian or an Englishwoman—in either event an enemy of France. Once again her French saved her as she addressed suspicious soldiers in their own language and shouted "Vive Napoleon" from her carriage. From then on there were no problems. She rolled into Paris on March 23, 1815. When she arrived at their hotel, her husband was at the theater.

Although John Quincy Adams was deeply impressed, Louisa seemed not to think much at the time of what she had done. "My journey from St. Petersburg was performed with as little uneasiness and as few misfortunes as could possibly be anticipated and I have really acquired the reputation of a heroine at a very cheap rate," she reassured her increasingly respectful mother-in-law on June 12, 1815. But in 1836, twenty-one years later, feeling the need to justify herself to her family and others, Louisa wrote her "Narrative of a Journey from Russia to France, 1815," which was published long after her death by her grandson Brooks Adams in *Harper's Magazine*.

John Quincy Adams had asked her to meet him in Paris because he was expecting a new appointment from President Madison as minister to Great Britain. With the

cessation of hostilities, the Adamses were also looking forward to a reunion with their two older sons. Both of these events came to pass, and Louisa was to spend the next two years in the city of her birth, courtship, and marriage. They may well have been the two happiest years of her life. Her health improved and her self-confidence grew as she assumed more and more responsibilities for running the household. The Adamses grew closer to one another as they mixed in London society and took over supervising the education of their three boys. Her husband was following in the footsteps of his father, who had served in the same diplomatic capacity thirty years before—which, of course, had led to the presidency of the United States.

While in London, both Louisa Adams and her husband had their portraits painted by the young American artist Charles Robert Leslie. Louisa's portrait shows the contentment and relaxation she enjoyed during this period of her life. Although her husband disagreed, she wrote on November 11, 1816, that she thought both portraits "most striking likenesses."

The following year, John Quincy Adams was appointed secretary of state by the new president, James Monroe, and Louisa Adams returned to the United States with greater self-confidence than she had displayed in 1801. She prevailed upon her husband not to repeat the nomadic existence they had followed during his tenure in the Senate, and, accordingly, he purchased a house on F Street in Washington in which they lived, off and on, for the next thirty years. With the death of Abigail Adams in 1818 Louisa became the matriarch of the family, maintaining close ties with her aging father-in-law and anxiously watching the careers of her sons, all of whom entered Harvard College.

In Washington, where First Lady Elizabeth Monroe received only limited numbers of visitors due, in part, to her own fragile constitution, the Adamses' house soon became the social center. Well aware that her husband could, like many previous secretaries of state, succeed to the presidency, Louisa Adams was a willing, even enthusiastic, participant in what became a seven-year effort to line up support for John Quincy. Every Tuesday evening while Congress was in session, the house on F Street was thrown open to visitors. Charles J. Ingersoll, a Pennsylvania congressman, described the Adamses' house in 1823 as "a great watering place, where amusement is a business, a need, to which almost every body is given up from 5 o'clock till bed time." Another was less enthusiastic: "Mrs. Adams is, on the whole, a very pleasant and agreeable woman," wrote a Massachusetts senator, Elijah Mills, to his wife on December 24, 1820, "but the Secretary has no talent to entertain a mixed company, either by conversation or manners."

In 1819 Louisa Adams, along with First Lady Elizabeth Monroe and the other cabinet wives, engaged in an "etiquette war," in which they squared off against the wives of congressmen and senators over who was to pay the first visit at the outset of each social season. Although the senators passed a resolution supporting their wives and the matter became the subject of at least one cabinet meeting, Mrs. John Quincy Adams and the others successfully stood their ground.

As a hostess, Mrs. Adams thus played a significant role in her husband's quest for the presidency in 1824. While deeming it unseemly to engage in outright intrigue for the office, John Quincy Adams hungered for it as much as or more than any of his rivals: Henry Clay, William Crawford, John C. Calhoun, and Andrew Jackson. He paid close attention to the invitation lists drawn up by his wife. In 1824 the Adamses' social schedule predictably accelerated. In January they threw a mammoth ball at their home in honor of General Jackson on the anniversary of his victory over the British at New Orleans nine years earlier. It was the talk of Washington society for weeks before and for years after.

In fact, the ball was an ill-concealed attempt on the part of the secretary of state and his wife to court Jackson, seeking either his outright support for the presidency or to convince him to run for vice president

with Adams (suggested slogan: "Adams, who can write, and Jackson, who can fight"). In that sense it was a failure, and later in the year John Quincy Adams found himself second in both popular and electoral votes to the general. Nevertheless, with the help of another rival, Henry Clay, Adams was chosen president by the House of Representatives in March 1825.

Historians and biographers agree that the presidency of John Quincy Adams was the least successful of his three "careers." The circumstances under which he obtained the office, his own ineptitude in communicating with the public, and the rise of the second two-party system combined to doom it from the start. Louisa Adams, no less than anyone, sensed this from the moment she entered the White House. The successful organizer of balls and soirees quickly and unaccountably turned into a recluse, like her husband shunning the public, and complaining that the presidential mansion was a "dull and stately prison." To her son George she wrote: "There is something in this great unsocial house which depresses my spirits beyond expression and makes it impossible for me to feel at home. . . ." Relations between the First Lady and her husband, after several years of relative harmony, steadily deteriorated during his unhappy presidency. In the summer of 1826 they took separate vacations. By the following year they were barely communicating at all.

Louisa Adams's change may have been because of her sensing the political rocks upon which her husband's presidency was foundering, but many of her biographers, both male and female, have attributed it to what one of them called "a long menopause." This is what the president was told when he sought medical advice concerning his wife's condition in 1828. Her youngest son, Charles Francis Adams—who, like all good Adamses, was keeping a diary—remarked that his mother had lost her "elasticity of character." It was at this time that she began the first of her two melancholy autobiographical fragments, "The Record of a Life, or My Story."

While in the White House, Louisa Adams also wrote plays, evidently intended to be read and acted out by members of the family on the few occasions when they were together. Significantly, one of them—entitled "The Metropolitan Kaleidescope"—concerned the life of a fictional English family named Sharpely. Lord Sharpely was a highly talented statesman, "a fond father, a negligent but half indulgent husband," who had good qualities; "but ambition," she wrote pointedly, "had been the first object of his soul." On the other hand, Lady Sharpely "had been a spoilt child" who "was the oddest compound of strong affections and cold dislikes; of discretion and caprice; of pride and gentleness, of playfulness and hauteur . . . irritable one moment, laughing the next. . . ." There can be little doubt that Louisa Adams had both her husband and herself as models for the Sharpelys.

Louisa Adams did not limit herself to the writing of plays. Her papers from this period include reflections on the relationship between the sexes in America and her growing dissatisfaction with it. A wife, Louisa wrote, was "made to cook [her husband's] dinner, wash his clothes, gratify his sensual appetites" in exchange for which she was expected to "thank him and love him for permission to drudge through life, at the mercy of his caprices." The Adamses in particular, she told her niece (and future daughter-in-law) Mary Hellen, were particularly hard on their women and ignored their particular wants and frailties (August 19, 1827). Her respect for her late mother-in-law, Abigail, grew, especially after reading the letters she had written years before to her husband, John, and her son John Quincy. Louisa Adams hoped someday to see the letters published. Reading them, she said, would "gladden the hearts of many a timid female whose rays too feebly shine, not for want of merit but for want of confidence. . . ." The world might realize that the mind of a woman "is as capable of solid attainment as that of man." Yet Louisa Adams was no early nineteenth-century feminist. She accepted conventional nineteenth-century notions of women's "frail-

ties" and was not above taking advantage of them when it suited her purpose.

Louisa Adams had little impact on the "office" of First Lady. The Adamses rarely entertained and, when they did, the guests were not particularly grateful. Senator Mills related to his wife how he had been invited to stay for dinner one evening with the president. "I went with him to the supper-room, where we found Mrs. A. and her two nieces, and had a supper of roast oysters in the shell, opening them ourselves, which of course was not a very pleasant or *cleanly* process. . . ." The toll taken on Louisa Adams during her husband's presidential years is exemplified by a portrait of the First Lady painted in 1826 by the venerable Gilbert Stuart. Compared with the middle-aged serenity so evident in her earlier portrait in London, Stuart's rendering shows a prematurely aging woman in ill health. Members of the family were horrified, but Louisa wrote after seeing it that it "looks very much as I looked, like a woman who was just attacked by the first chill of death and the features stiffening into torpor." (July 13, 1827). "It speaks too much of inward suffering and a half broken heart."

But her unhappiness as First Lady never turned to disloyalty. At no time was Louisa Adams uninterested in her husband's political fortunes or opposed to his reelection as president. Indeed, the year before the nasty election of 1828, she herself became involved when a Jackson paper alluded to her English birth and presumably unrepublican ways. Never before, with the possible exception of her mother-in-law, Abigail, had a First Lady been seen as an appropriate political target. She defended herself in an unsigned article giving the true circumstances of her background, describing herself in the third person as "a woman of unassuming manners, fond of reading, writing and knitting, and detesting politics, and in such general bad health that she seldom leaves her chamber." Yet she wanted it to be known that "Mrs. Adams is the daughter of an American Republican Merchant." And she was well-enough informed to question her husband's refusal to promote himself as a candidate for reelection. On more than one occasion she urged him to show himself more among the people, but he almost always refused. The result was a humiliating defeat in 1828.

Yet, in all probability, Louisa Adams did not regret her husband's defeat, even though it came at the hands of their former friend Andrew Jackson. Now she could look forward to a long and dignified retirement, similar to that of Abigail and John Adams after a similar defeat at the hands of Thomas Jefferson in 1800. Like her in-laws, she hoped to be able to sit back and enjoy her children and grandchildren. This proved to be a miscalculation. Within five years two of her three sons died, and her husband, far from being content with a dignified retirement, reentered the political world as a congressman.

George Washington Adams died in 1829, a probable suicide. Although possessing a good intellect (he had won the coveted Boylston Prize at Harvard in 1820, beating out the young Ralph Waldo Emerson), his life went downhill after his graduation. He became an attorney after studying in the law offices of Daniel Webster, briefly entered politics with little success, and dabbled in poetry. By 1828 he had lapsed into a life of dissipation and drink, and had fathered an illegitimate child by a servant girl. When his parents summoned him to Washington to help them move back to Massachusetts, he apparently was unable to face them. He either jumped or fell off a steamboat on the journey south in April 1829. His body was found several weeks later.

John Adams II died in 1834 under mysterious circumstances. He, too, had attended Harvard, but he did not graduate, having been expelled in 1823 for his role in leading a student riot. He became his father's secretary and, in early 1828, married his cousin Mary Hellen, daughter of Louisa's older sister, Nancy. When his father invested in a Washington flour mill, John took over its operation, but a combination of bad luck and poor management resulted in continual losses. By 1834 it was clear the investment was a disaster, and the strain brought about by the failure contributed to his death later that year.

The loss of her two eldest sons rekindled Louisa Adams's spark of resentment against her husband and against their decision years earlier to leave George and John behind while the rest of the family went to Russia. "In no way as you know have I ever been consulted or have I even participated in the settlement of my children," she reproached her husband in a letter written July 16, 1834, shortly before John's death. A few years later she began writing "The Adventures of a Nobody," which spelled out in more detail her accumulated resentments. She convinced herself that, beginning with the trip to Russia in 1809, she had been afflicted with a "succession of miseries only to cease with existence." She had by then concluded of her early courtship that "[h]appy it would have been for Mr. Adams if he had broken his engagement, and had not harnessed himself with a wife altogether so unsuited to his peculiar character."

At first Louisa Adams resisted her husband's reentry into public life, refusing, as she said, to return to the "Bull Bait" of politics. To return to Washington merely to gratify what she called her husband's "insatiable passion" for public life was more than he had a right to ask. She even threatened to stay behind in Massachusetts, but upon further reflection, and giving in to the urgings of her sons, she agreed to go. "I was born for a controversial world and cannot escape my destiny," John Quincy Adams once explained. He found his destiny in the next sixteen years as "Old Man Eloquent," enlisting in the ranks of the antislavery movement, defending the right of petition against the pro-slavery "Gag Rule," opposing the Jacksonian Indian removal policy, resisting the annexation of Texas, and opposing the war with Mexico with almost literally his last breath. In time, Louisa Adams grudgingly accepted, and even supported, John Quincy Adams's new career. She came to realize what the rest of the American political world of that day already knew: that political affairs were to her husband what oxygen was to normal human beings, and that to deprive him of that atmosphere would be equivalent to a death sentence.

She maintained a close communication with her son Charles—then starting his own political career in Massachusetts—informing him of his father's activities. In the midst of the great struggle for the right of petition, she and her widowed daughter-in-law, Mary, assisted John Quincy Adams in filing and cataloging the antislavery petitions (many of which came from women). When the congressional pro-slavery forces threatened to censure her husband for introducing a disunionist petition in 1842, Louisa rallied to his defense. "To be *his* Wife, and *your* Mother, is all the Dignity I can crave," she wrote to her son on February 5, 1842.

During these years Louisa Adams began a careful study of the Bible and came to challenge the prevailing Scripture-based justification for the subordination of women. This led to a correspondence with Sarah Grimké, whose *Letters on the Equality of the Sexes and on the Condition of Women* she had read and admired. "Man may subvert woman for his own purposes," she told Grimké, in a letter dated January 11, 1838, but he "cannot *degrade* her in the sight of God, so long as she acts up to those great *duties*, which her Nature and Constitution enforce. . . ." But in spite of her resentments Louisa Adams was still no feminist. She continued to frown upon women who traveled alone, showed their ankles in public, or asked men to dance with them. Along with her husband, she was a product of the conventions of her day. Unlike her husband, she was not always comfortable with them.

That there were disagreements within the Adams family apparently was no secret. The abolitionist Theodore Dwight Weld, who married Sarah Grimké's sister Angelina, reported to his wife in 1842 that he had visited the Adamses at their F Street home, where the former president had introduced him to Louisa. "In doing so I was glad to hear him call her 'my dear,' as I think you told me they lived unhappily together." That was not quite the case. Louisa and

John Quincy Adams loved each other, but in their own fashion, and rarely gave ground. As late as May 14, 1845, the seventy-year-old Louisa could tell her seventy-eight-year-old husband:

I like very well to adopt my husband's thoughts and words when I approve them, but I do not like to repeat them like a parrot, and prove myself a nonentity. . . . When my husband married me he made a great mistake if he thought I only intended to play echo.

For many Americans, the best-known description of Louisa Adams is found in her historian grandson's famous *Education of Henry Adams*. To the young Henry

she seemed singularly peaceful, a vision of silver gray, presiding over her old President and her Queen Anne mahogany; an exotic, like her Sèvres china; an object of deference to every one, and of great affection for her son Charles; but hardly more Bostonian than she had been fifty years before, on her wedding-day, in the shadow of the Tower of London.

"Singularly peaceful" she may well have appeared to her grandson and others, but behind the exterior there was a troubled soul, buffeted about by regrets and tragedies that at times threatened to overwhelm her both physically and mentally. Indeed, a more accurate description of her situation was penned by her son Charles, when he declared, "The history of my family is not a pleasant one to remember. It is one of great triumphs in the world but of deep groans within, one of extraordinary brilliancy and deep corroding mortification." In the words of Lyman Butterfield, for many years editor in chief of the Adams Papers, Louisa Adams "lived an extraordinarily varied and arduous life and survived a marriage of more than five decades to one of the most trying of men."

Until the twentieth century, no other First Lady traveled as far as she, nor met so many kings, queens, tsars, and ambassadors.

She seemed ideally suited for the role of First Lady in the still-young republic. But, as with her husband, the years she spent in the White House proved to be disappointing both personally and politically. Louisa Adams lived in two worlds: a public one of glitter and grace, and a private one of self-doubt and frustration. Possessing an intellect more than competitive with those of most men of her day, it was her fate to be bound to a family whose understanding and appreciation of female achievement was limited by both their times and their temperament. Her term as First Lady, like her husband's as president, was marked by political wrangling and personal unhappiness.

Most of what is known about the early life of Louisa Catherine Adams is found in two memoirs she composed in her mature years. The first, which she entitled "Record of a Life, or My Story," was written in 1825 while her husband was president. The second, "The Adventures of a Nobody," was written around 1840. By the latter date her marriage had experienced a mixture of triumph and tragedy, both personal and political, and much of what she had to say about her past was colored by events that had taken place in the intervening years. She made no effort to conceal resentments that had accumulated against her husband and his family. Yet at the same time she was quick to defend him against others and to acknowledge those qualities of personal integrity and patriotism that in time became John Quincy Adams's major claim to fame. For his part, her husband wrote a summation of their marriage after fourteen years that could have applied at virtually any time. "Our union has not been without its trials," he told his famous diary in 1811, "nor invariably without dissensions between us." But, he added, "[s]he has always been a faithful and affectionate wife." He never wavered in his fidelity, and gave his affection as best he knew how.

By the mid-1840s time was running out on Louisa and John Quincy Adams. In 1846 he suffered a debilitating stroke. He recovered enough to celebrate their fiftieth wedding anniversary in the summer of 1847, and took his seat in the House of Representatives the following January. He suffered a second and fatal stroke while on the House floor and died on February 23, 1848. "The Madame," as Louisa Adams had come to be called, continued on, living in the F Street house. She, too, was stricken and left partially paralyzed in 1849, but she continued to receive visitors, especially every New Year's Day. Presidents, senators, diplomats, and ordinary well-wishers would stop by to pay their respects to what must have appeared to them to be a relic of another age. She died on May 15, 1852, aged seventy-seven.

Congress adjourned on the day of her funeral, the first time that had ever been done in behalf of a former First Lady, or indeed any woman. Her son Charles took her body back to Quincy, Massachusetts, where it was interred next to her husband's and those of John and Abigail Adams in the First Congregational Church. He wrote the following inscription, which may be read by visitors today:

LOUISA CATHERINE
Daughter of
Joshua and Catherine (Nuth) Johnson
Born, 12 February, 1775,
Married, 26 July, 1797,
Deceased, 15 May, 1852,
Aged 77.
Living through many vicissitudes, and
Under high responsibilities,
As a Daughter, Wife, and Mother,
She proved equal to all;
Dying, she left to her family and her sex
The blessed remembrance
Of a "Woman that feareth the Lord."

BIBLIOGRAPHICAL ESSAY
Louisa Adams's papers can be found in the Adams Papers Microfilms (Massachusetts Historical Society, 1954), which are available at major research libraries throughout the United States. All of the quoted letters and diary entries from Adams family members found in the above essay may be located there, or in the two works by Paul C. Nagel: *Descent from Glory* (New York, 1983) and *The Adams Women* (New York, 1987). Letters written to her husband and

other members of the family can be found among the "Letters Received and Other Loose Papers." Her account of her trip from St. Petersburg to Paris in 1815 was published by her grandson Brooks Adams as "Mrs. John Quincy Adams's Narrative of a Journey from St. Petersburg to Paris" in *Scribner's Magazine* 34 (October 1903): 449–464. Her grandson Henry's recollections are in his *Education of Henry Adams* (Boston, 1918), chapter 1.

There is no published scholarly biography of Mrs. Adams, but Jack Shepherd's *Cannibals of the Heart* (New York, 1980) is an attempt—not always successful—to describe the relationship between Mrs. Adams and her husband. Most other biographical studies, including Dorothie Bobbé's *Mr. and Mrs. John Quincy Adams* (New York, 1930) and Meade Minnigerode's *Some American Ladies* (New York, 1929), were written without benefit of the Adams Papers, and are not authoritative.

The only doctoral dissertation that deals with Louisa Adams is Joan Challinor's "Louisa Catherine Johnson Adams: The Price of Ambition" (American University, 1982), which unfortunately ends with her return from Europe in 1817, thus excluding her term as First Lady. See also Challinor's "The Mis-Education of Catherine Johnson," Massachusetts Historical Society *Proceedings* 98 (1986): 21–48; "'A Quarter-taint of Maryland Blood:' An Inquiry into the Anglo/Maryland Background of Mrs. John Quincy Adams," *Maryland Historical Magazine* 80 (Winter 1985): 409–419 (which discusses the confusing marital status of Mrs.

Adams's parents); and Katherine Corbett's "Louisa Catherine Adams: The Anguished 'Adventures of a Nobody,'" in *Women's Being, Women's Place: Female Identity and Vocation in American History*, ed. Mary Kelley (Boston, 1979), 67–84.

Also recommended are Lyman Butterfield's article on Mrs. Adams in *Notable American Women 1607–1950*, Vol. 1, 12–15; Butterfield's delightful analysis "Tending a Dragon Killer: Notes for the Biographer of Louisa Catherine Adams," *Proceedings of the American Philosophical Society* 118 (April 1974): 165–178; and Betty Caroli's brief account of Louisa Adams as First Lady in *First Ladies* (New York, 1987). All the existing portraits of Louisa Adams are discussed in Andrew Oliver's *Portraits of John Quincy Adams and His Wife* (Cambridge, Mass., 1970).

Samuel Flagg Bemis's two volumes, *John Quincy Adams and the Foundations of American Foreign Policy* (New York, 1949) and *John Quincy Adams and the Union* (New York, 1956), are still the basic sources for his life, but they have little to say about his wife. Mrs. Adams plays a much larger role in Marie Hecht's *John Quincy Adams: A Personal History of an Independent Man* (New York, 1972). There are a number of letters to Louisa Adams from her husband in W. C. Ford's *Writings of John Quincy Adams* (7 vols., New York, 1913–1917) but not many from her to him. In any event, this edition does not include correspondence later than 1823, having discontinued publication during World War I.

★★★ ★★★

Anna Tuthill Symmes Harrison

(1775–1864)

First Lady: March 4–April 4, 1841

Nancy Beck Young

Anna Tuthill Symmes was born on a farm bordering the Flatbrook River in Sussex County near Morristown, New Jersey, on July 25, 1775, to John Cleves Symmes and Anna Tuthill Symmes. Her sister, Maria, had been born thirteen years earlier. Anna's father, an associate justice on the New Jersey Supreme Court (1778–1785), had married her mother on October 30, 1760, at Southhold, Long Island, New York.

Born and raised on the East Coast, Anna led a life representative of that of many other American women of her era. During her life she experienced four wars: the American Revolution, the War of 1812, the Mexican War, and the Civil War. She staked her fortunes on the opportunities in the West as opposed to the security of the more settled East. Yet she retained ties with friends and family on the East Coast throughout her life. Later in life she chose to remain in Ohio rather than travel to the nation's capital when her husband was elected president. Her choice to remain behind groups her among the wives of six presidents between 1829 and 1869 who chose not to assume the duties of the First Lady. William Henry Harrison's untimely death leaves the question open as to whether his wife would have journeyed to Washington and taken over as First Lady. Had her husband lived, she most likely would have joined him at the White House but probably would have delegated the formal entertaining duties to her daughter-in-law, who had already assumed the role of "hostess" for her father-in-law. The concerns Mrs. Harrison harbored about her training as a hostess were common among presidents' wives in the mid-1800s.

Despite her short tenure and the fact that she never actually lived in Washington, D.C., Anna Harrison achieved many "firsts" for American First Ladies. She was the first president's wife to have received a formal education as a child. At age sixty-five she was the oldest woman to become First Lady. She never assumed any of her duties as First Lady and was the first woman to become widowed while her husband was in office. After President Harrison's death, Mrs. Harrison received the first pension given to a former First Lady. She was also the first First Lady to be the grandmother of a president, Benjamin Harrison (1889–1893).

Anna's mother passed away at the family homestead, "Solitude," on July 25, 1776, exactly one year after Anna was born. From 1776 to 1779 her father commanded the garrisons along the New Jersey frontier. He looked after his daughter for three years before entrusting her care to her maternal grandparents, Mr. and Mrs. Henry (sometimes Daniel) Tuthill, who lived in Southhold. Concern for young Anna's well-being during the Revolutionary War prompted this move. While holding the rank of colonel in the army, John Symmes disguised himself as a British officer and carried his young daughter on horseback through British lines east to Southhold. Anna lived with the Tuthills for the duration of her childhood. Her father returned to his troops to fight the remainder of the war, and Anna did not see him again until 1783, when he made a brief visit. Her grandmother provided Anna with the best education available. Anna studied at the Clinton Academy, located in East Hampton, where she received both classical and English training. She probably attended classes in the latter division, as very few young women of that period were trained in Latin and Greek.

Anna's grandmother also introduced her to religious affairs and stressed the importance of a serious outlook on life. The Tuthills followed the religious convictions of the Great Awakening and raised Anna as a devout Presbyterian. She never developed a taste for high society. Mrs. Tuthill taught her young charge to engage both her hands and her mind actively with the world around her. The lessons did not go unheeded, and Anna developed a lifelong passion for knowledge. Nor did her formal education cease at the Clinton Academy. Her father and her grandparents arranged for her to matriculate at a New York City boarding school. The proprietor of the school, Isabella Graham, had been trained at Edinburgh, Scotland, and was an early New York educator and social worker.

Following the end of the Revolutionary War in 1783, Anna's father, not content to return to New Jersey and live out his life, instead saw the opportunity available in Western land speculation and farming. Judge Symmes developed an interest in the Northwest Territory while serving in the Continental Congress from 1785 to 1787 under the Articles of Confederation. He bought the one-million-acre Miami Purchase, located between the Great and the Little Miami rivers near present-day Cincinnati, and organized a land company of former military officers to settle the area. On February 19, 1788, Congress appointed Symmes judge for the Northwest Territory. Also in 1788, Anna's sister, Maria, married Peyton Short, and the couple established housekeeping in Lexington, Kentucky. Symmes's record as a colonizer was mixed. Careless record-keeping resulted in the sale of duplicate titles and land outside the boundaries of his Miami Purchase. Furthermore, on September 30, 1794, Symmes received a patent for only 311,682 acres after he could not raise the funds for the entire acreage. After spending seven years in Ohio, Judge Symmes returned to New York to reclaim his younger daughter and take her west with him.

Some time after his first wife's death, Symmes had married Mary Henry Halsey of New Jersey; little is known about that union. He later married Susanna Livingston, daughter of New Jersey Governor

William Livingston. Anna developed a close relationship with her new stepmother. Arriving in the region called North Bend, sixteen miles west of Cincinnati, on January 1, 1795, Symmes, his new wife, and daughter began a new life together. Anna was not yet twenty. Petite in build, she had dark hair and eyes, a full mouth, and a cleft chin.

Anna and her stepmother spent part of their first winter in Kentucky with the Short family. There Anna met Lieutenant William Henry Harrison, who was on leave between military campaigns in Ohio. He had entered the military in 1791 after abandoning plans for a medical career. The couple found they had romantic feelings for each other and their closeness grew.

Judge Symmes distrusted the ability and the character of the military in the Northwest Territory, comparing them with criminals. In June 1795 Symmes wrote, stating his hesitations about Harrison's courtship of his daughter:

> I know not well how to state objections, save that as yet we are all too much strangers to each other, the young man has understanding, prudence, education, and resource in conversation, about £3,000 property, but what is to be lamented is, that he has no profession but that of arms.

According to contemporary correspondence, Anna Symmes and William Henry Harrison exchanged vows in the Symmeses' home on November 25, 1795. Judge Symmes was away on business. In his correspondence Symmes appeared resigned to the union by December 1795, and he looked for reasons to approve the match. Four months after the marriage Symmes wrote to his friend Robert Morris:

> [I]f I knew what to make of Captain Harrison, I could easily take proper arrangements for his family, but he can neither bleed, plead, nor preach, and if he could plow I should be satisfied. His best prospect is in the army, he has talents, and if he can dodge well a few years, it is probable he may become conspicuous.

Over time Symmes gained respect and admiration for William Henry Harrison, referring to his son-in-law affectionately in correspondence and naming him one of the executors of his estate in 1813.

Anna's marriage to William Harrison reflected the more relaxed social mores of the frontier. Theirs was a relationship built on love and respect. Throughout their years together she called him "Pah" and he addressed her as "Nancy." She was the more religious of the two, but he respected her spiritual teachings as they affected secular affairs. She was not particularly interested in social contacts but, instead, was willing to live out her years as a gentleman farmer's wife. Yet the couple associated with many of the wealthy and powerful figures in Ohio and Indiana.

In 1796 Harrison gained command of the garrison in Fort Washington, to the south of the Symmeses' North Bend Home. On September 29, 1796, Anna Harrison gave birth to Elizabeth Bassett, the first of ten children. Two years later she delivered a second child at Fort Washington, John Cleves Symmes, named for his maternal grandfather. After earning a promotion to captain in 1797, Harrison resigned from the army in 1798 and, with the proceeds from his inheritance, purchased 169 acres of land in North Bend, where they constructed a log cabin. On July 6, 1798, he was appointed secretary of the Northwest Territory, a job with an annual salary of $1,200 that he held for approximately one year.

In 1799 Harrison was elected territorial delegate to the U.S. House of Representatives in Philadelphia. Judge Symmes campaigned actively for his son-in-law. In Congress, Harrison chaired the Committee on Public Lands and stalled action on a proposal that would have brought legal proceedings against Symmes. Mrs. Harrison and their two children went to Philadelphia and, from there, traveled to Richmond, Virginia, to visit the Harrison family. A third child, Lucy Singleton, was born in Richmond in 1800.

Although she enjoyed her stay in the nation's capital, Anna Harrison was happy to learn, on May 13, 1800, that President John Adams had appointed her husband territorial governor of Indiana and ex officio superintendent of Indian affairs. He held that post until the outbreak of war with Great Britain in 1812, when he reentered the military. Harrison had hoped for appointment as governor of the Ohio territory but instead was given the Indiana territory, a region farther west and less civilized.

In January 1801 the Harrisons arrived in Vincennes, Indiana, originally a French fur-trading post on the Wabash River. Despite a salary of only $2,000 a year, Harrison engaged in land speculation and other investments in the region. He purchased land nearby and, in 1804, he built a brick home for his wife. Grouseland, as their residence was named, served as the social and cultural gathering place for settlers in the territory. Grouseland's architectural style was reminiscent of Berkeley, the Harrison family estate in Richmond, Virginia, with the appropriate additions to permit its use as a fortress. Thirteen rooms on two and a half floors made for a large mansion.

Susanna Symmes made the trip to Vincennes with the Harrison clan so Anna Harrison would have female companionship. After a series of disputes with her husband —Judge Symmes—Mrs. Symmes returned to New York in 1808. Despite these marital disagreements, Susanna Symmes remained close to her step-daughter. The Harrison family expanded in Indiana with the birth of five more children—William Henry (b. 1802), John Scott (b. 1804), Benjamin (b. 1806), Mary Symmes (b. 1809), and Carter Bassett (b. 1811). John Scott, a Lexington physician who had served in the army with Harrison, attended Mrs. Harrison for each of the births.

Anna Harrison took primary responsibility for the children as well as management of the land holdings of her husband, whose finances often ran a negative balance. With occasional help from her husband, she directed her children's formal education, while the spiritual needs of the family were

tended by a Methodist circuit rider. She kept the family afloat but never turned a large profit because, like her father, she was a careless financial manager. Nevertheless, she fulfilled the official responsibilities of a politician's wife on a shoestring budget. While she would later have doubts about the duties required of the wife of a president, Mrs. Harrison functioned as hostess of the Indiana Territory without complaints. As the wife of the territorial governor, she entertained their guests with great skill. The only request she made of her husband was that he forgo official business meetings on Sunday. She witnessed her husband's often difficult negotiations with Native American leaders, including Tecumseh and his brother, Tenskwatawa, the Shawnee Prophet.

As governor of Indiana, Harrison followed Thomas Jefferson's policy of opening Western territory to white settlers. He preferred making individual treaties with the Native Americans, but these policies increased tensions between himself and Tecumseh. In 1811 Harrison defeated Tenskwatawa at the Battle of Tippecanoe. He believed an increased American military presence in Indiana was required to safeguard the western movement of white settlers. War with Great Britain provided the perfect opportunity. Passed over for appointment as brigadier general in the regular army, Harrison was eventually appointed major general in the Kentucky militia. By August 1812, he had been promoted to brigadier general in the regular army and assigned to defend Indiana and Illinois.

During the War of 1812, Anna Harrison took her children to Cincinnati, where their safety could be assured. Since Judge Symmes's North Bend home had been burned, leaving him without any financial resources, father, daughter, and children rented a house and remained in Cincinnati for the duration of the war. A ninth child, Anna Tuthill, was born in 1813. In Cincinnati, Mrs. Harrison joined the First Presbyterian Church, where she enjoyed the benefits of regular worship services. Religion provided her with refuge from her worries over her father's failing health and finances and over her husband's safety.

Harrison's campaign ended in October 1813 after he defeated the British and gained control of the Northwest in the Battle of the Thames. The general spent most of 1814 in Cincinnati. That year Harrison resigned from the military after disagreements with War Department officials. He and his wife assumed operations of her father's farm in North Bend after Judge Symmes's death on February 26, 1814. His estate was in disarray and many of his holdings had been depleted. With no home on the land, the couple moved their log cabin, named "the Bend," to the new site and began an extensive process of remodeling and expansion that eventually included twenty-two rooms. Harrison also turned his attention to financial investments. In 1814 the oldest Harrison child was married and their last child, James Findlay, was born.

The Harrison home became a stopping point for visitors curious to meet the military hero. Mrs. Harrison welcomed traveling preachers and opened the grounds for their worship services. She often invited the entire congregation of her church home for the noon meal after Sunday worship services. At Grouseland, potential conflicts with Native Americans had been the greatest threat to the Harrisons' existence. At the Bend a new challenge arose: the cost of maintaining a public presence. Mrs. Harrison's responsibilities increased with her husband's departure for Washington after his election to Congress in 1816. He remained there until his election in 1819, to the Ohio State Senate, where he served until 1821, at which time he returned to his wife in North Bend. Three years later, in 1824, he returned to Washington as a United States senator from Ohio. Despite fragile health and her husband's frequent absences, Mrs. Harrison ran her household, oversaw her children's education, and, with the help of a tutor, established a school for area children in her North Bend log cabin.

The death of her infant son, James Findlay, in 1817 caused Anna Harrison much grief. Her loss was tempered by her religious convictions, which would be tested over the years as other loved ones died. Anna Harrison's thoughts are expressed in a letter to her son William, who was attending Transylvania College:

I hope my dear, you will always bear upon your mind that you are born to die and we know not how soon death may overtake us, it will be of little consequence if we are rightly prepared for the event. . . . While you remember us, I hope you will not suffer yourself to forget your dear little brother who has left us for the world of spirits. . . . May the God of all mercies bless, protect you, and keep you in the paths of virtue.

As the Harrison children grew, so did their household expenses. Between weddings, dowries, college tuition, and extravagant lifestyles, General Harrison was forced to mortgage much of his property to keep his businesses afloat and to provide for his children. He sought and received an appointment as minister to Colombia from President John Quincy Adams on May 29, 1828, but he did not depart until November. Anna Harrison did not join her husband for the mission. The added income from the new post did not last. Soon after his election, Andrew Jackson recalled Harrison from diplomatic service and replaced him in September 1829.

In the 1820s and 1830s the Harrisons suffered a series of tragedies. Their daughter Lucy Singleton died in 1826. The general's finances were in disarray, but matters worsened when their son William Henry, Jr., an alcoholic, was forced by mounting debts to abandon the legal profession for farming. He later died in 1838. The death of their son John Cleves in October 1830 left William and Anna Harrison responsible for a $12,000 debt to the government and care for his wife and six children. Two more sons died in 1839 and 1840.

When Harrison entered the race for the presidency in 1836, his wife realized his chances for victory were slim. She knew the two Whig candidates—Daniel Webster and Hugh L. White—and her husband, running on the Anti-Masonic ticket, stood little chance against Martin Van Buren, the Democrat. Van Buren's election caused Anna Harrison little regret; she enjoyed her life in Ohio and worried about her ability to meet the demands of life in Washington.

Four years later Harrison was the sole standard-bearer for the Whig Party on a ticket balanced with a Southern Democrat for vice president—John Tyler. The two men handily defeated Van Buren in a campaign that featured debate over economic policy and glorification of Harrison's log cabin roots and military victories. In the previous contest, the newly formed Whig Party had failed to grasp the importance of grassroots political organization. The 1840 contest was a different story. Harrison became the sole Whig candidate in a contest with the unpopular Democratic incumbent, Van Buren. Harrison had no clearly stated political views but instead was a popular military hero capable of stirring the masses.

Despite claims such as those found in *Presidential Wives* (1988) that Anna Harrison "rules the General, apparently," her voice over his decisions was fairly limited. Had she had a choice in the matter, he would not ever have been a candidate for the presidency. Yet she did carry some weight in deciding how her husband would campaign. Harrison refrained from any electioneering on Sunday in deference to his wife. The candidate reportedly told a group of partisans that "I should be most happy to welcome you on any other day, but if I have no regard for religion myself, I have too much respect for the religion of my wife to encourage the violation of the Christian Sabbath.

The spate of deaths in the family left Anna Harrison in a weakened emotional state. She did not relish the thought of moving to Washington. Of her husband's new position, she wrote: "I wish that my husband's friends had left him where he is,

happy and contented in retirement. At age sixty-five and in poor health, she postponed her departure. Worried about her abilities to manage the duties of First Lady, she arranged for her daughter-in-law, Jane Irwin Harrison, the recent widow of William Henry Harrison, Jr., to function as hostess until weather permitted her departure for Washington. Several other female relatives lived in Washington and helped Jane Harrison perform her duties, including Mrs. Jane Findlay, the adopted mother of Jane Harrison, and a friend of the Harrison family. President Harrison received many petitioners for office during the first month of his administration, and the extensive schedule he kept, combined with the pneumonia he caught during the inauguration, hastened his death on April 4, 1841. These circumstances kept Anna Harrison out of the nation's spotlight for good.

Interest in the deceased president did not wane. In fact, Anna Harrison received numerous requests over the years for her husband's autograph, which she obliged as long as she had a supply of his letters and personal documents. Settling her husband's estate proved to be a lengthy and difficult task, which she postponed for some time. Her surviving son, John Scott Harrison, shared the duties with her son-in-law John Cleves Short, a nephew who had married Elizabeth Bassett, the Harrisons' oldest daughter, in 1814. The two men lived some distance apart and had trouble deciding how to handle certain bills. Short recommended that his mother-in-law use part of the proceeds from her pension to settle some of the outstanding accounts. Throughout the remainder of her years, Anna Harrison went to her son-in-law when she was short of funds.

As a widow, Anna Harrison's devotion to Christianity increased. She worked hard to bring her remaining loved ones "into the Fold of Christ," as she wrote to a niece in 1846. She lived in North Bend until around 1855, when her log cabin home, the Bend, burned to the ground. As a result she moved in with her only living offspring, John Scott Harrison, the father of the future president

Benjamin Harrison. Her three remaining daughters—Elizabeth, Mary Symmes, and Anna Tuthill—had died within six years of their father's death. She relied on her religious faith to sustain her in her losses. She told her pastor, "And now what shall I say to these things; only, 'Be still and know that I am God.' You will not fail to pray for me. . . . For I have no wish for my children and grandchildren than to see them the humble followers of the Lord Jesus."

Despite continued medical problems, Anna Harrison closely followed political and military developments after her husband's death and throughout the Civil War era. As a former First Lady she received free franking privileges—a service she used for her mail the remainder of her years. She stayed informed of the policies of John Tyler's administration as well as those of his successor, James K. Polk. She questioned the direction of the Democratic Party on national policy but recognized that Tyler had been helpful to her and her family. She relied on Tyler and Polk to help her grandsons receive military commissions. She opposed slavery and encouraged her grandsons in their military careers with the Union Army during the Civil War. She told one grandson:

> [Y]our country needs your services. . . . Go and discharge your duty faithfully and fearlessly. I feel that my prayers in your behalf will be heard, and that you will be returned in safety. And yet, perhaps, I do not feel as much concerned for you as I should: I have parted so often with your grandfather under similar circumstances, and he was always returned to me in safety, that I feel it will be the same with you.

Anna Harrison died on February 25, 1864, in her son's home. The Reverend Horace Bushnell conducted the funeral services. Mrs. Harrison was interred beside her husband's grave on the bank of the Ohio River in North Bend.

Family had played an important role throughout her life. She had never hesitated to include even the most extended relations in her close-knit circle. For example, when her sister and her daughter died, she welcomed the new brides of both her brother-in-law and her son-in-law as friends. Likewise, Mrs. Harrison's concern for her fellow human beings was played out in numerous acts of anonymous kindness. As a historical figure, her life was representative of the role of elite American women on the frontier in the nineteenth century.

BIBLIOGRAPHICAL ESSAY

Anna Harrison's personal papers were destroyed in the fire that consumed her home in North Bend in the 1850s. The papers of William Henry Harrison, housed in the Library of Congress, Manuscripts Division, contain important correspondence pertaining to Mrs. Harrison. The Short Family Papers in the Library of Congress, Manuscripts Division, also contain numerous references to Anna Harrison. Two books reprinting the letters of her father, John Cleves Symmes, include significant information about Mrs. Harrison. See Beverley W. Bond, Jr., ed., *The Correspondence of John Cleves Symmes: Founder of the Miami Purchase* (New York, 1926), and *The Intimate Letters of John Cleves Symmes and His Family Including Those of His Daughter Mrs. William Henry Harrison Wife of the Ninth President of the United States* (Cincinnati, 1956). The Cincinnati Historical Society's James Albert Green/William Henry Harrison Collection provides useful background on Anna Harrison's life.

For background on William Henry Harrison, see Dorothy Burne Goebel, *William Henry Harrison: A Political Biography* (Indianapolis, 1926); Freeman Cleaves, *Old Tippecanoe: William Henry Harrison and His Time* (Port Washington, N.Y., 1969); and James A. Green, *William Henry Harrison: His Life and Times* (Richmond, Va., 1941). For information on Harrison's presidency, see Norma Lois Peterson, *The Presidencies of William Henry Harrison and John Tyler* (Lawrence, Kans., 1989). Carl Sferrazza Anthony, "Anna Symmes Harrison: Frontier First Lady," *Traces of Indiana and Midwestern History* (Fall 1990) is a recent brief study.

Mrs. Harrison appears in several collective studies of First Ladies. See Laura C. Holloway, *Ladies of the White House* (New York, 1870); Kathleen Prindiville, *First Ladies* (New York, 1942); Mary Ormsbee Whitton, *First First Ladies, 1789–1865: A Study of the Wives of the Early Presidents* (New York, 1948); Sol Barzman, *The First Ladies* (New York, 1970); Paul F. Boller Jr., *Presidential Wives* (New York and Oxford, 1988); and Diana Dixon Healy, *America's First Ladies: Private Lives of the Presidential Wives* (New York, 1988). Most of these sketches follow similar lines of argument, with some more detailed than others. The more useful accounts are found in Holloway and Whitton. Information concerning the dates of birth for the Harrison children is sometimes elusive and difficult to reconstruct. Several previous accounts repeat the errors.

★★★ · ★★★

Letitia Christian Tyler

(1790–1842)

First Lady: 1841–1842

Melba Porter Hay

Letitia Christian was born on November 12, 1790, at Cedar Grove plantation, twenty miles east of Richmond, Virginia, and about fourteen miles from Greenway, the plantation of John Tyler's family. Her father, Robert Christian, was a well-to-do planter who was prominent in Federalist politics, and her mother was Mary Browne Christian. Letitia was the third of eight daughters and the seventh of twelve children. Little is known of her life before she met and married John Tyler. She apparently had the minimal education afforded most women of her day. By all accounts, she was a very beautiful and gracious, but introverted, woman who preferred the company of her family and close friends, and enjoyed such simple pursuits as knitting and garden-

ing. She was completely devoted to her children and they to her. Religion also played an important role in her life.

Perhaps because none of her letters survived, Letitia "never really emerges from the mists of history," in the words of Robert Seager II, one of her husband's biographers. Most of what is known about her stems from Tyler's references to her in his own letters and comments about her in her children's letters.

John Tyler met Letitia about 1808, after he graduated from the College of William and Mary in Williamsburg, Virginia, and while he was studying law. The Christians' Cedar Grove plantation was near the road leading from Greenway to Richmond, and Tyler undoubtedly availed himself of the opportunity to visit there whenever he traveled to the capital after his father became governor in 1809, and when he himself was elected to serve in the Virginia House of Delegates in 1811. The courtship lasted for nearly five years and was apparently an undemonstrative relationship during that time. Tyler repeatedly made the statement that he had not dared to kiss Letitia's hand until three weeks before the wedding. The one surviving love letter he to wrote her before their marriage is dignified and philosophical:

> You express some degree of astonishment, my L., at an observation I once made to you, "that I would not have been willingly wealthy at the time I addressed you." Suffer me to repeat it. If I had been wealthy, the idea of your being actuated by prudential considerations in accepting my suit, would have eternally tortured me. But I exposed to you frankly and unblushingly my situation in life—my hopes and fears, my prospects and my dependencies—and you nobly responded. To ensure to you happiness is now my only object, and whether I float or sink in the stream of fortune, you may be assured of this, that I shall never cease to love you. (Seager)

Although Tyler wrote his fiancée a few sonnets, he apparently approached the marriage without either fear or excitement. He wrote to his friend Henry Curtis on the eve of the wedding that "I had really calculated on experiencing a tremor on the near approach of the day; but I believe that I am so much of the old man already as to feel less dismay at a change of situation than the greater part of those of my age." The ceremony took place at Cedar Grove on Tyler's twenty-third birthday, March 29, 1813.

Both of Letitia Tyler's parents died soon after her marriage, and her inheritance was valuable in helping the young couple establish themselves at Mons-Sacer, a 500-acre section of Greenway that Tyler inherited from his father. The alliance also strengthened Tyler's ties to the influential families of the peninsula. After living at Mons-Sacer

for two years, they sold it and moved to a neighboring tract, where they built a residence called Woodburn. Six years later, in 1821, they bought Greenway, the estate where Tyler had grown up, and moved there.

Scarcely four months after their marriage, Tyler left his bride to serve in the War of 1812. He was appointed captain of the militia group known as the Charles City Rifles, which had been raised to defend Richmond and its river approaches from a British raiding party. The Charles City Rifles were attached to the Fifty-second Regiment of the Virginia Militia and were sent to Williamsburg. They soon found themselves transferred to a new unit, the Second Elite Corps of Virginia, an assignment that lasted until the British raiding party withdrew from the Hampton area a month later. The little militia unit then disbanded and the men returned home without ever having encountered the enemy.

The Tylers were able to resume their normal pattern of life. An ever-increasing number of children soon followed: Mary (b. 1815), followed by Robert (b. 1816), John, Jr. (b. 1819), Letitia (b. 1821), Elizabeth "Lizzie" (b. 1823), Anne Contesse (b. 1825), Alice (b. 1827), and Tazewell (b. 1830). All survived their mother except Anne Contesse, who lived only three months, and a ninth child who either was born dead or died in early infancy.

When Tyler was elected to the U.S. House of Representatives in 1816 and to the U.S. Senate in 1827, his wife chose to remain at home with the children, except for the winter social season of 1828–1829. She apparently had no interest in politics and no desire to live in the nation's capital. At home, by all accounts, she excelled in the role of plantation mistress, supervising the housekeeping and cooking, sewing clothes for the slaves, and nursing the sick. She made only one trip to the watering places of the North but occasionally enjoyed trips to some of Virginia's springs. Even if she had been inclined to travel or take part in her husband's political life, Mrs. Tyler probably believed her place was at home with the children. Burdened as she was by a large family and an economic situation that was frequently precarious, she likely felt she had to take whatever measures possible to economize. The family was land-rich and cash-poor, as were many in the planter class, and this situation was worsened by Tyler's propensity for lending money to friends and relatives, many of whom often failed to repay him, forcing him in times of dire need to resort to the embarrassing task of pressuring people for repayment.

Mrs. Tyler's main foray into public life occurred during the years 1825–1827, when her husband served as governor of Virginia. During that time, she presided over the governor's mansion with charm and set a high standard for social life in the state capital. The one drawback was lack of money. During the years in Richmond, she found that entertaining at the governor's mansion, despite her attempts to keep social functions as simple as possible, proved very expensive. On one occasion, in an attempt to persuade the legislature to increase his salary, the governor invited members of the legislature to a banquet where only Virginia ham, corn bread, and cheap Monongahela whiskey were served. The ploy failed, however, and by the time he was elected to the U.S. Senate, the family was in serious financial difficulty. Even when Tyler resigned from the Senate in 1836 over the principle of legislative instruction, it was a sacrifice of his family's well-being, because they still needed his salary.

Among the most revealing evidence of Letitia Tyler's character are letters written by her husband to their daughter Mary and subsequently published by Lyon G. Tyler in *Letters and Times of the Tylers*. In one such letter, dated March 4, 1830, Tyler wrote that he could not give her a better pattern to imitate than her mother. He added that Mrs. Tyler's actions were never precipitate, but rather considered judiciously and prudently. In a letter of March 11, 1832, he advised Mary to make her mother her only confidante and to have confidence that she would never be betrayed into error. To his son Robert he wrote on March 15, 1832, that he was mortified by Mrs. Tyler's com-

plaint that Robert and John, Jr., were not treating their mother with proper respect. He reminded them that she had cared for them, nursed them, and would give her life for them. He concluded by ordering Robert to obey his mother's every wish.

In 1837, after resigning from the Senate, Tyler moved his family to Williamsburg. By this time Mary had married Henry Lightfoot Jones, a young tidewater planter, in an elaborate ceremony that further diminished the Tyler coffers. John, Jr., became the second child to marry when he wed Mattie Rochelle in October 1838. This union eventually proved to be an unhappy alliance, due in part to John's drinking habits and lack of reliable employment. Daughter Letitia married James A. Semple, a James River neighbor, in October 1838. That marriage, too, ended unhappily, with Tyler appointing Semple a purser in the navy in 1844, an arrangement that kept his son-in-law at sea much of the time. After the Civil War, a formal separation took place. A more successful union was the marriage, in September 1839, of Robert to the beautiful actress Priscilla Cooper. Priscilla's father was the famous tragedian actor Thomas A. Cooper, and she had followed in his footsteps. She won Robert Tyler's attention in Richmond when she played Desdemona while her father played Othello. The panic of 1837 and the depression that followed wrecked the American theater, so Priscilla had experienced real hardship by the time of her entry into the family. Despite the Tylers' straitened circumstances, such an alliance must have come as a relief to her. The Tylers seem not to have minded Robert's bringing an actress into the family, as Robert informed Priscilla that there was no one else in the world his mother would rather have him marry. Yet the happy occasion was marred by the absence of Mrs. Tyler, who shortly before the wedding had suffered a stroke that left her partially paralyzed.

Priscilla Tyler developed a deep love for her mother-in-law. She wrote a thorough description of Letitia Tyler, who then was aged forty-seven:

[She] must have been very beautiful in her youth, for she is still beautiful now in her declining years and wretched health. Her skin is as smooth and soft as a baby's; she has sweet, loving black eyes, and her features are delicately moulded; besides this, her feet and hands are perfect; and she is gentle and graceful in her movements, with a most peculiar air of native refinement about everything she says and does.

Even though Mrs. Tyler remained in her bedchamber after her illness, Priscilla noted that she somehow still managed to run the household and supervise the staff while sitting in a large armchair. A small stand beside her chair held her Bible and prayer book—the only things she read after her illness. Always a devout Episcopalian, she became even more religious after the stroke.

When Tyler was elected vice president of the United States on the Whig ticket in 1840, he planned to continue living in Williamsburg, where his wife would be more comfortable. This quiet life came to an abrupt halt, however, when William Henry Harrison's death a month after taking office propelled him into the presidency. During Harrison's weeklong illness, the vice president had not been informed about the seriousness of the president's condition. After Harrison died, Fletcher Webster, son of Secretary of State Daniel Webster, was sent to Williamsburg to inform Tyler that he had become the nation's tenth president (the first vice president to succeed to that office). Young Webster aroused the household at sunrise on the morning of April 5, 1841, to give them the news. Within two hours, Tyler, who would be christened by his detractors "His Accidency," was on the road to Washington.

The family decided that Robert and Priscilla would follow within the week, but no immediate decision was made about the removal of Mrs. Tyler to Washington. Soon it was agreed that she would move into the White House, but it was obvious she was unequal to the task of serving as White House hostess. Almost by default, Priscilla assumed that role. As an experienced actress, she directed White House entertaining with dignity and verve, ably advised by Dolley Madison, who was then in her seventies and living in a state of poverty in Washington. While Congress was in session, two formal dinner parties were held each week: the first usually had twenty guests made up generally of persons visiting Washington; the second had forty guests, composed of the highest-ranking members of the government, military, and diplomatic corps. Each evening during the session the reception rooms were thrown open to informal visitors until 10 p.m. This became so burdensome that, in early 1842, the evening receptions were held only twice a week. Sometimes there were small private balls, and each month a great public levee was held with up to 1,000 guests in attendance. Special receptions occurred on New Year's Day and the Fourth of July. On warm summer evenings, concerts by the Marine Band were held once a month on the south lawn. Much of this entertaining was done at the president's personal expense.

Very early in his administration, John Tyler, in sentiment really a states' rights Democrat, came into conflict with nationalist-oriented leaders of the Whig Party in Congress. During much of his term he was locked in bitter combat with the party that had elected him, over such issues as a national bank and a protective tariff. His veto of the first Whig bank bill resulted in an outburst by partisan demonstrators at the White House on the evening of August 16, 1841, in which guns were fired, bugles blown, and the president burned in effigy. After he vetoed the second Whig bank bill in September 1841, the entire cabinet, which the president had retained from the Harrison administration, resigned, except for Secretary of State Webster. Tyler was formally read out of the Whig Party two days later.

Such events must surely have had an adverse effect on Letitia Tyler's already poor health. Moreover, her husband's fight with Congress prevented his acquiring any funds for redecorating and cleaning the White House or its furnishings, which had become dirty and dilapidated to such an extent that a New York *Herald* correspondent proclaimed them a disgrace. Indeed, the usual sums appropriated for the upkeep of the mansion were not provided. The president was forced to pay much of the lighting, heating, and maintenance of the establishment out of his own pocket.

One of the happier moments of the Tyler presidency was the marriage of Elizabeth Tyler to William N. Waller of Williamsburg on January 31, 1842. It was a small affair, attended by Dolley Madison, members of the cabinet, and a few friends and family members. It was the only occasion that Letitia Tyler appeared downstairs during her life in the White House.

As 1842 progressed, Mrs. Tyler's health continued to decline, and she suffered a second stroke. In early July, Tyler wrote to one of his daughters that his wife's health was bad and "her mind is greatly prostrated by her disease." By September she apparently sensed her coming death and sent Robert to New York to get Priscilla, who was there visiting her sister. They were too late, reaching Washington after Mrs. Tyler's death on September 10, 1842. Priscilla wrote that Robert suffered great anguish when told that his mother's eyes had constantly turned to the door, watching for him. Mrs. Tyler's last act was to pluck a damask rose from a vase beside her bed. She died holding the rose in her hand. Her funeral was conducted in the East Room of the White House on September 12 by the rector of St. John's Episcopal Church, and she was interred at Cedar Grove two days later. The Washington *Intelligencer*, a bitter critic of her husband and his administration, wrote of her that she was "loving and confiding to her husband, gentle and affectionate to her children, kind and charitable to the needy and afflicted." It was a fitting epitaph for a woman whose health and disposition prevented her from making a contribution to the institution of First Lady.

BIBLIOGRAPHICAL ESSAY

No letters or personal papers written by Letitia Tyler have ever been uncovered. The paucity of sources and her physical incapacity while in the White House have resulted in relatively little being written about her. References to her may be found in the John Tyler Papers located at the Library of Congress and at the Duke University Library, as well as in the Tyler Collections at the Alderman Library, University of Virginia, and the College of William and Mary.

Many of the most important family letters were published by Lyon Gardiner Tyler, one of John Tyler's sons by his second wife, in the three-volume *Letters and Times of the Tylers* (Richmond, Va., 1884–1896), in which he sought to defend his father's reputation as president and secessionist. One of the earliest assessments of Letitia Tyler is found in Laura C. Holloway, *Ladies of the White House* (Philadelphia, 1881), but much of her account of life in the White House is based on letters in which chronology and facts are questionable. Margaret Brown Klapthor's *First Ladies* (Washington, 1981), published by the White House Historical Association, also contains the major points of Letitia Tyler's White House tenure.

The most thorough consideration of Letitia Tyler can be found in Oliver Perry Chitwood, *John Tyler: Champion of the Old South* (New York, 1939); and Robert Seager II, *And Tyler Too: A Biography of John and Julia Gardiner Tyler* (New York, 1963). Most quotations, except where noted, are from the Seager work. The next-to-last quotation is from Norma Lois Peterson, *The Presidencies of William Henry Harrison and John Tyler* (Lawrence, Kans., 1989).

★★★　　★★★

Julia Gardiner Tyler

(1820–1889)

First Lady: 1844–1845

Melba Porter Hay

Julia Gardiner was born May 4, 1820, on Gardiners Island, New York, and grew up in East Hampton, Long Island. Her father, David Gardiner, was a direct descendant of Lion Gardiner, who emigrated from England to Connecticut in 1635 and subsequently purchased from the Indians the 3,300-acre island off the eastern tip of Long Island. Julia's mother, Juliana McLachlan Gardiner, was the daughter of a wealthy Scottish brewer from New York City. David Gardiner, a Yale graduate, practiced law in New York City from 1807 to 1815 and then leased and managed Gardiners Island from 1816 to 1822, while the heir apparent to the family estate was a minor. In 1822 he moved his family to East Hampton and thereafter spent his time managing his wife's extensive property holdings in New York City and giving legal advice to family members. A supporter of John Quincy Adams, Gardiner was elected in 1824 to the New York State Senate, where he served until 1828.

In 1835 Julia entered Madame N. D. Chagaray's Institute on Houston Street in New York City, where she followed a curriculum of music, French literature, ancient history, arithmetic, and composition. She remained there as a boarding student until 1837 or 1838. Considered beautiful by the day's standards, she was short and plump with black hair and large, dark eyes. The high point of her teenage years was her first formal dance when she was fifteen. She became practiced in the art of flirtation and soon acquired a string of suitors. Virtually all the doors of society were opened to her because of her family's prominence.

The third of four children and the Gardiners' first daughter, Julia acquired from her father a deep fear of economic insolvency, which she retained throughout her life. She was even more strongly influenced by her mother, a highly opinionated woman who dominated her husband and attempted to control the lives of her four children. Although she and Julia were close, Juliana Gardiner had less success in controlling her elder daughter than she did her other children—David Lyon Gardiner (b. 1816), Alexander (b. 1818), and Margaret (b. 1822). All the children were brought up to believe in their own social superiority, in the importance of maintaining propriety at all times, and in the value of marrying someone with money.

Always high-spirited and adventurous, Julia, on at least one occasion, exceeded the bounds of propriety. Having finished her formal education by 1839, she grew bored and restless in East Hampton. Possibly as a strategy for escaping the confines of Long Island, she appeared in a cheap advertising lithograph by Bogert and Mecamly, a dry goods and clothing business in New York City. The advertisement depicted her standing in front of the store with a sign in the shape of a lady's handbag that read: "I'll purchase at Bogert and Mecamly's, No. 86 Ninth Avenue. Their Goods are Beautiful and Astonishingly Cheap." Pictured with her was an older man, and the ad was captioned "Rose of Long Island." It was the first occasion in which a lady of the upper class had personally endorsed a business enterprise. The incident was humiliating to the staid and proper Gardiners. They were further embarrassed by publication in the May 11, 1840, Brooklyn *Daily News* of a poem titled "Julia—The Rose of Long Island," written by someone using the pseudonym "Romeo Ringdove."

The episode was perhaps the catalyst for removing Julia from the New York City area for a while. The family traveled to White Sulphur Springs, Virginia, in August 1840, while a trip to Europe was being planned. Mr. and Mrs. Gardiner, Julia, and Margaret then sailed for Europe on September 27. They went first to England, then to France. They traveled extensively for a year and Julia engaged in a series of romances before they returned home in September 1841.

In January 1842 David Gardiner took both his daughters to Washington, D.C., for the winter social season. Their wealth and position assured that they were invited into the top circles of Washington society. Julia met President John Tyler's son Robert. Then, on January 20, the Gardiners were invited to the White House, where they were greeted by Robert's wife, Priscilla Cooper Tyler, and they met the president.

After returning to East Hampton, Julia again became very bored. She was able to persuade her father to take them back to Washington in December 1842. They boarded at Mrs. Peyton's, where Julia found herself so besieged by beaux that they soon had to rent an extra room to use as a parlor for entertaining visitors. Congressman Francis W. Pickens of South Carolina, Supreme Court Justice John McLean of Ohio, and Congressman Richard D. Davis of Saratoga County, New York, were all believed to be in love with Julia. Her most constant escort was Richard Waldron, a young naval officer whom she had met during her previous visit. Although the White House was still mourning the death of the president's wife, Letitia, Priscilla Tyler invited Julia and Margaret there for some quiet activities. The recently widowed president apparently became interested in Julia very quickly. He invited the Gardiners to dine at the White House on Christmas and, by late January 1843, the Tylers and Gardiners were very close. By February he was courting Julia in earnest.

A coquette accustomed to leaving men with broken hearts, Julia skillfully played off her other suitors against the president. At a ball celebrating Washington's Birthday on February 22, Tyler proposed. Julia refused, later professing to have been very surprised. Three days later the Gardiners had tea at the White House, and the president escorted Julia to a concert later in the evening. Since it was the first time he had been out all winter, it fueled much gossip. In March, Tyler again proposed, this time in the presence of Margaret. When her parents heard about the proposal, they decided to linger in Washington. Before they left the capital on March 27, another proposal was forthcoming, and Julia accepted. Tyler wanted to set a date for the fall of 1843, but Mrs. Gardiner insisted that Julia have more time to make certain she knew her own mind. Both the Gardiners were concerned about the thirty-year age difference between the two; the president was nine years older than Juliana Gardiner and had three children older than Julia, but that seems not to have worried Julia. There was a definite understanding before the Gardiners left Washington, but no date was set for the wedding.

The Gardiners returned to Washington for the next winter's social whirl. On February 28, 1844, Julia, Margaret, and their father accompanied President Tyler on an excursion aboard the USS *Princeton* to Mount Vernon. On the third firing of the huge gun on the *Princeton*, the breech of the gun exploded, killing David Gardiner, along with the secretary of state, the secretary of the navy, and several others. Within seven weeks of the disaster, Julia informed Tyler that she was ready to marry him. She later remarked that after her father's death her feelings for the president changed, and no younger man seemed as agreeable as he. She came to adore Tyler, adopting his causes as her own, praising his writing, speeches, and oratory, and defending him against all criticism. On April 20, Tyler wrote to Mrs. Gardiner, formally asking for Julia's hand.

Julia's brother Alexander began to make arrangements for the secret wedding. With only a few family and friends present, the couple exchanged vows on June 26 at the Church of the Ascension on Fifth Avenue in New York City. After a wedding breakfast at the Gardiner home they took a tour around the harbor in the ferryboat *Essex*, then disembarked at Jersey City and caught

a train to Philadelphia. They traveled to Washington, then to Old Point Comfort, Virginia, and ended their honeymoon trip at Sherwood Forest, an estate Tyler had purchased in Charles City County, Virginia, in 1842. The president had whimsically named the plantation Sherwood Forest in reference to his outlaw status with the Whig Party. Located only two miles from Greenway, his old home, it was to be the final Tyler family home.

All four of Tyler's daughters were completely stunned by the wedding. Mary Tyler Jones, the eldest, soon adjusted to the marriage. Twenty-one-year-old Elizabeth and seventeen-year-old Alice had more difficulty, but eventually they came to love and admire their young stepmother. All the boys, from fourteen-year-old Tazewell to John, Jr., and Robert, liked her from the start; however, Letitia Tyler Semple, who had been serving as White House hostess since Priscilla and Robert moved to Philadelphia in March 1844, never lost her hostility toward her stepmother.

The second Mrs. Tyler made no secret of her pleasure in her new role. Though her husband had only eight months remaining in his term when they married, she made the most of that short time. The White House was suddenly filled with fun and gaiety, and the entertainments were lavish and formal. The president, who had been subdued by the illness and death of his first wife and his violent political fights, regained his natural sense of humor and seemed much younger.

Little could be done to redecorate the White House, which was in deplorable condition because of Congress's refusal to appropriate funds for upkeep, but the new bride made her best efforts to get the place cleaned up. She ordered expensive French wine and furniture at their personal expense, often using Gardiner money. She introduced the polka and the waltz to the White House, though Tyler had previously thought the waltz immoral. Newspapers called her the "Lady Presidentess," and a New York musician composed "The Julia Waltzes." Perceiving the importance of a favorable press, the new First Lady cultivated F. W. Thomas, a New York *Herald* reporter, so successfully that he virtually became her personal press agent.

Julia Tyler attempted to imitate European court manners in her formal entertainments, causing some to say critically that she was putting on airs and attempting to behave like a queen. Her "court" consisted of Margaret, her cousins Mary and Phoebe Gardiner, and Alice Tyler. She outfitted the White House coachmen and footmen in expensive new livery. She directed her sister to send her diamonds and pearls from New York, and she got her husband to buy her an Italian greyhound. She initiated the custom of having musicians greet the president with "Hail to the Chief." Some thought her extravagant when she traveled in a carriage drawn by four horses and self-centered when she entertained seated on a raised platform with feathers in her hair and a long-trained dress. Most seemed to enjoy the display, however, and her husband obviously doted on her. Her first large public reception, held on New Year's Day 1845, was attended by more than 2,000 guests. The president reportedly became jealous upon observing former suitor Justice McLean looking at Mrs. Tyler in her regal attire, even though McLean was now married.

Most, but not all, of the White House entertainments were a success. A dinner on January 10 to honor the Supreme Court justices and their wives proved disappointing because the attorney general had already invited many of the same people for the same evening, and Mrs. Tyler had to fill her guest list with others less notable. But nothing could rival the great final ball she gave before Tyler left office. She selected February 18 for the event, and because her own handwriting was so poor it was often illegible, she pressed her sister Margaret into the role of social secretary for compiling the guest list and writing invitations. Two thousand guests were invited, but 3,000 came. Margaret had arranged for eight dozen bottles of champagne and for wine by the barrel. When congratulated on the success of the event, the president,

referring to his exclusion from the Whig Party, exclaimed: "Yes, they cannot say now that I am a *President without a party!*"

Unlike Tyler's first wife, Julia Tyler took an active interest in political affairs. Her family had once owned slaves, so she had no problem supporting the peculiar institution, and she adopted her husband's states' rights beliefs. She was especially ardent in her support of Texas annexation and did much lobbying for it at the White House social events. When annexation was accomplished in the last days of the Tyler administration, she gave a lavish dinner party to celebrate the victory.

The Tylers left the White House on March 3, 1845, to stay in a hotel until after the inauguration of the new president, James K. Polk. Once back at Sherwood Forest, Mrs. Tyler set about making their home one of the showplaces among the James River estates. Because Charles City County was a Whig area, many of their neighbors were initially cold, but Mrs. Tyler soon won them over with her gracious entertaining.

Despite the Gardiner money, Mrs. Tyler's spending caused her husband to fall into even greater financial difficulty. In 1845 she bought an expensive new carriage and outfitted the coachman and footman in new livery. She also had a small boat, *Pocahontas*, given Tyler by Commodore Beverly Kennon, and she outfitted her oarsmen in elegant attire. She frequently made trips to spas such as Old Point Comfort and White Sulphur Springs, and regularly visited her family in New York. On the corn and wheat plantation she often nursed sick slaves and always made a point of seeing that they were clothed and fed. Still very much influenced by the advice of her strong-minded mother, she always kept a white housekeeper.

Mrs. Tyler's role as a stepmother to her husband's first set of children frequently caused her dismay. Elizabeth Tyler Waller and especially Letitia Tyler Semple insulted her at every turn, while the former president supported his wife and tried to smooth the situation. Alice Tyler, too, failed to show proper deference to her young stepmother. The drinking and brawling of John, Jr., was yet another problem and a continual embarrassment to the family. Not until the mid-1850s did he finally settle down and practice law with his brother Robert in Philadelphia.

In 1846 gossip circulated for months that John and Julia Tyler had separated. In fact, the rumors actually originated with John, Jr.'s, marital problems and were exacerbated because Julia had gone to East Hampton to give birth to the first of her seven children. The baby, David Gardiner Tyler, was born on July 12, 1846. His mother doted on him and constantly bragged about him. "Gardie" eventually became a lawyer, judge, and congressman. A second son, John Alexander Tyler (Alex), was born April 7, 1848. The first daughter, Julia Gardiner, (Julie) Tyler, was born on December 25, 1849, followed by Lachlan on December 9, 1851, Lyon Gardiner on August 24, 1853, Robert Fitzwalter (Fitz) on March 12, 1856, and another daughter, Pearl, on June 13, 1860. Lyon Gardiner became a historian and served for many years as president of the College of William and Mary. Like his mother, he devoted much of his life to defending his father's administration and reputation.

The family had become too large by 1853 to make the usual trips to East Hampton, Saratoga, or even White Sulphur Springs. In 1858 Julia Tyler used her own money to purchase property in Hampton, Virginia, near Old Point Comfort, where they could escape the unhealthful summers on the James River. She named the house Villa Margaret after her sister, who had died the previous year at the age of thirty-five.

Much of Mrs. Tyler's time after leaving the White House was devoted to defending Southern rights and her husband's administration. In February 1853 the *Southern Literary Messenger* published a letter she had written to the Duchess of Sutherland, the Countess of Derby, Viscountess Palmerston, the Countess of Carlisle, and Lady John Russell in reply to an open letter the British women had written urging Southern women of quality to take the lead in demanding an end to slavery. Mrs. Tyler denounced the image of slavery recently

depicted in *Uncle Tom's Cabin* and denied the right of British critics to intervene in an American institution. She noted that slavery had been established in America by the English colonial system and urged the British to concentrate on the problems of the poor in their own realm, especially the merchant and naval seamen and the starving Irish.

By 1858 the former president was feeling his years. He frequently complained of aches and pains and did not like to leave Sherwood Forest for fear that he might die in unfamiliar surroundings. He drew up a will in 1859 leaving everything to his wife and her children. The family finances were still swimming in a sea of debt, and Gardiner resources often saved them from embarrassment. Despite his wife's extravagance, however, Tyler continued to dote on her, once proclaiming that the honeymoon had never ended.

By 1860, the impending sectional crisis was affecting the Tyler family. Both husband and wife were ardent supporters of the Southern position, but the former president attempted to follow a moderate course in an attempt to preserve the Union. When a Peace Convention was called to meet in the nation's capital in 1861, Tyler was named one of Virginia's commissioners. As Julia Tyler planned their return to Washington for the first time in sixteen years, she hoped to reconquer the city where she had known her greatest social triumphs. On February 5, Tyler was elected president of the Peace Convention. While he attempted to find some form of compromise, his wife kept an exhausting social schedule. The proceedings and ultimate failure of the Peace Convention convinced Tyler there could be no compromise. Thereafter, the former president and his wife both became ardent secessionists.

Mrs. Tyler welcomed her husband's election to the Confederate Congress in November 1861. When he left home for Richmond in early January 1862 to take his seat, she planned to follow the next week after brief visits at the Brandon and Shirley plantations. However, on January 9, she had a dream that caused her to change her plans and go straight to Richmond. In her dream, Tyler lay dangerously ill in the Exchange Hotel in Richmond. She believed dreams served as avenues for thought transference, and so she hastened to her husband's side. On her arrival she found him well. On January 12, however, she awakened to find him ill. He said he had a slight chill and was going to the dining room for a cup of hot tea. Rising to leave the dining room, Tyler lost consciousness. After he was revived, he stumbled back to their room, and Dr. William Peachy was summoned. The doctor diagnosed what was undoubtedly a stroke as a bilious attack of bronchitis. The patient seemed fairly well for a few days except for a cough and headaches, but, when his strength did not completely return, Dr. Peachy advised him to return home. Before they could leave for Sherwood Forest, Tyler grew worse. He woke gasping for breath and died at 12:15 A.M. on January 18, 1862, at the age of seventy-two.

Her husband's death was a great blow, and it left Mrs. Tyler alone at an extremely critical time. She had seven children to rear, a 1,600-acre plantation, seventy slaves, and a mountain of debt. In April, both she and her son Fitz fell seriously ill from influenza; the boy almost died. The Civil War was already pressing close to Sherwood Forest, and by May the plantation lay well within Union territory. Through the intercession of Mrs. James I. Roosevelt, a prewar friend in New York, General George McClellan placed a guard at the plantation. Field hands began to leave the estate, and in July, Mrs. Tyler became ill with malaria. By October she had concluded it would be best to take the children to safety in New York. Working through friends, she was able to obtain a federal pass, so she and all the children except Gardie went to Staten Island.

Shortly after New Year's Day 1863, Mrs. Tyler, Fitz, and Pearl returned to Virginia. She planned to sell Sherwood Forest, place Gardie in school, and return with the two youngest children to Staten Island for the duration of the war. Gardie enrolled at Washington College in Lexington, Virginia, but his mother was unsuccessful in selling the plantation. She did manage to sell the wine cellar for $4,000 and two horses for $800 in Confederate money. She hired John C. Tyler, her husband's nephew, as plantation manager and by mid-May was ready to return to Staten Island. Unable to get a pass to the North without taking an oath of allegiance to the Union, she began to plan how to leave illegally. Finally, on October 28, she sailed from Wilmington, North Carolina, for Bermuda by blockade runner.

Mrs. Tyler reached New York on November 24 and joined the crowded Gardiner household, which then consisted of her, her mother, her brother David Lyon Gardiner, his wife, and nine children, one nurse, one live-in servant, and four servants who lived out. Tensions soon flared to the point of violence between Julia Tyler, who had strong Confederate sympathies, and her brother, who was a Unionist. In an attempt to protect her daughter, Juliana Gardiner removed all her business affairs from her son's hands and ordered him and his family from the house. He never saw his mother alive again.

From the time Mrs. Tyler arrived on Staten Island, she became active in a Copperhead group, which distributed peace pamphlets, conducted relief activities in Southern towns occupied by the Union army, and sent money and clothes to needy Confederates. Her main project was to try to obtain the release of Captain R. H. Gayle, whose ship had taken her to Bermuda and who had been captured on his return voyage to North Carolina and sent to Fort Warren Prison. She worked through General John A. Dix to secure Gayle's exchange, all the while sending him letters, food, wine, and other amenities. His letters to her grew increasingly personal, and he asked for and received her picture. In October 1864 he was exchanged for a Union naval officer and was soon on the Wilmington-Bermuda run. In January 1865 his ship, the *Stag*, became the last ship captured attempting to run the Union blockade. Gayle was returned to Fort Warren, and Mrs. Tyler began a new crusade in his behalf. She also worked for the election of General McClellan, the Democratic nominee, to the presidency in 1864. Despite the way the war was going, she continued to believe in the ultimate defeat of the Union.

The Tylers were among the first Southerners to lose property during the Civil War, when Villa Margaret was seized by Union troops early in the war and used as barracks. In May 1864 Sherwood Forest, too, was occupied by Union forces. Some outbuildings were burned and farm buildings were raided. Tyler's son-in-law James A. Semple and nephew John C. Tyler managed to get the former president's papers, the silverware, and family portraits to a warehouse and a bank vault in Richmond before the house was sacked. That effort proved futile, however, because, before the war ended, the warehouse and bank where the valuables were stored went up in flames. Fortunately, the house at Sherwood Forest was not harmed except for some broken windows and doors.

Mrs. Tyler was undoubtedly concerned for the welfare of her two sons who participated in the war. Gardie and his fellow cadets at Washington College became involved in the war effort in 1864. Alex, at age sixteen, wanted to join his brother but did not succeed in doing so until the war was nearly over. In April 1865, when General Robert E. Lee evacuated Richmond, both Gardie and Alex marched west with him. On Alex's seventeenth birthday, the Army of Northern Virginia was surrounded at Appomattox Court House, Virginia, where, two days later, April 9, 1865, Lee surrendered to Grant. The Southern troops were paroled, including the two Tyler boys.

The previous fall, Mrs. Tyler had suffered a major loss with the death of her mother in October. Mrs. Gardiner had made a new will on her deathbed, leaving substantially more of her estate to her daughter than she had in her previous will. David Lyon Gardiner promptly challenged the new will, charging that his sister had brought "undue influence" on their mother. The case was in court for years. In 1867 the New York Court of Appeals declared the will void, and the following year the New York Supreme Court made the final division of the estate. Mrs. Tyler received the Castleton Hill house on Staten Island and three-eighths of the real estate in downtown New York City; David Lyon Gardiner received three-eighths of the same, and Harry Beeckman, Margaret Gardiner Beeckman's son, received one-fourth.

Mrs. Tyler experienced financial difficulties and was very poor—at least by Gardiner standards—until the settlement of her mother's will was reached. She financed her children's education and the family's living expenses by borrowing. Moreover, Union victory in the Civil War brought threats to the family's safety because of their known Confederate sympathies. A group of local thugs broke into Mrs. Tyler's home on Staten Island on April 15, 1865, in search of a rebel flag. Not finding the nonexistent flag, they tore down a piece of cloth hanging over a portrait. After President Lincoln's assassination, there were further threats to burn the house. Because of these events, Mrs. Tyler considered moving to Europe, but she ultimately decided to stay and fight for Sherwood Forest, Castleton Hill, and the Gardiner estate. She did, however, send her sons Alex and Gardie and her nephew Harry Beeckman to school in Germany.

Mrs. Tyler developed an innovative plan of creating a medieval manorial system to revive Sherwood Forest. She hired a Swede in New York to manage the plantation, using immigrant farmers. When this effort failed, she turned to the sharecrop system using former slaves, as did most Southerners. From 1865 to 1874 she was involved in many lawsuits, such as claims against John Tyler's estate and her attempts to get Villa Margaret back. For a time Villa Margaret was controlled by the American Missionary Society and used for housing teachers of the Freedmen's Bureau. In October 1868 the War Department authorized a rent of four dollars per month. When Mrs. Tyler regained control of the property in 1869, it was in terrible shape. She sold it in 1874 for $3,500, less than one-third of its 1860 value.

In 1866 Mrs. Tyler sent her older daughter, Julie, to the Convent of the Sacred Heart in Canada. An incorrigible flirt like her mother before her, Julie in 1869 married William H. Spencer. When she died in childbirth in 1871, at the age of twenty-one, her death was a devastating blow to her mother, whose only consolation was in taking the child, Julia Tyler Spencer, called "Baby," and rearing her as her own. They moved to Georgetown, D.C., where Fitz and Pearl enrolled in Catholic schools.

During these years Mrs. Tyler began studying religion as she searched for something to give her life meaning and security. Reared a Presbyterian, she had since joined John Tyler's Episcopal Church. After much searching, in 1872 she converted to the Roman Catholic Church along with her daughter Pearl.

The panic of 1873 compounded Mrs. Tyler's financial woes, as income from her Manhattan properties dropped from an average of $750 per month to virtually nothing by 1878. Sale of Villa Margaret enabled her to save Sherwood Forest from being sold to pay the Bank of Virginia's note against the Tyler estate. In 1874 Mrs. Tyler and Baby moved back to Sherwood Forest in order to save money. Gradually the family fortunes improved, and by the end of the 1870s the children had all finished school and Sherwood Forest was again productive. In 1879 "Mrs. Ex-President Tyler," as she styled herself, launched a campaign to get Congress to appropriate a pension for presidential widows. She asked for the same $3,000 per year Mary Todd Lincoln received and was, instead, given a pension of $1,200 a year. In 1882, following President Garfield's assassination, all presidential widows were awarded $5,000 a year. She also received a pension of eight dollars per month for widows of veterans of the War of 1812. The money enabled her to move to Richmond, where she lived for the last years of her life.

Mrs. Tyler had always been uncommonly healthy and active; however, as the 1880s progressed, her health declined. In 1883 she fractured an arm that bothered her the rest of her life. In 1885 she suffered an illness that rendered her unconscious and near death for five days, and in 1887 she experienced another such attack. Yet, in 1889 she was able to attend the ball and first commencement exercise over which her son Lyon Gardiner Tyler presided as president of the College of William and Mary. Returning to Richmond on July 7, Julia Tyler and Baby decided to stay at the Exchange Hotel because her house had been closed during their trip to Williamsburg. On July 8 she fell ill, and two days later suffered a stroke and died at age sixty-nine. She was only a few doors from the room where John Tyler had died in the same hotel in 1862. On July 12 she was buried at Hollywood Cemetery in Richmond beside her husband and her daughter Julie.

BIBLIOGRAPHICAL ESSAY

Important primary sources concerning the life of Julia Tyler include the Gardiner Family Papers at Yale University Library, New Haven, Connecticut; the Gardiner Papers, Long Island Collection, at the East Hampton Free Library, East Hampton, New York; the John Tyler Papers at Duke University Library, Durham, North Carolina, and at the Library of Congress; and the Tyler Collections at the University of Virginia, Charlottesville, and at the College of William and Mary, Williamsburg, Virginia. Many of the important family letters were published in Lyon Gardiner Tyler's *Letters and Times of the Tylers*, 3 vols. (Richmond, Va., 1884–1896).

For Julia Tyler's letter to the British ladies who were criticizing slavery, see "To the Duchess of Sutherland and the Ladies of England," *Southern Literary Messenger* 19 (February 1853). Also of significance is her "Reminiscences," published in the Cincinnati *Graphic News* (June 25, 1887), and later reprinted in the Richmond *Dispatch* (July 21, 1889).

Much has been written by or about the Gardiner family. Some of the more significant works are Curtiss C. Gardiner, *Lion Gardiner and His Descendants* (St. Louis,

1890); John Lion Gardiner, *The Gardiners of Gardiners Island* (East Hampton, N.Y., 1927); Sarah D. Gardiner, *Early Memories of Gardiners Island* (East Hampton, N.Y., 1947); and Margaret Gardiner, *Leaves from a Young Girl's Diary* (privately published, 1925).

There are numerous secondary works dealing with First Ladies or with John Tyler and his administration that include information about Julia Gardiner Tyler. A few of the more important are: Oliver Perry Chitwood, *John Tyler: Champion of the Old South* (New York, 1939); Paul F. Boller, *Presidential Wives* (New York, 1988); Margaret Brown Klapthor, *First Ladies* (Washington, D.C., 1981); Betty Boyd Caroli, *First Ladies* (New York, 1987); Norma Lois Peterson, *The Presidencies of William Henry Harrison and John Tyler* (Lawrence, Kans., 1989). By far the most detailed biography of Mrs. Tyler and one that is based on all known primary sources is Robert Seager II, *And Tyler Too: A Biography of John and Julia Gardiner Tyler* (New York, 1963). All direct quotes come from the Seager work. There is an obituary in the *New York Times*, July 11, 1889.

★★★   ★★★

Sarah Childress Polk

(1803–1891)

First Lady: 1845–1849

Jayne Crumpler DeFiore

Sarah Childress was born near Murfreesboro, in Rutherford County, Tennessee, on September 4, 1803. Her father, Joel Childress, was a prominent merchant, planter, tavern keeper, and land speculator. Born in Campbell County, Virginia, Childress moved in the 1790s, to Sumner County, Tennessee, where he met Elizabeth Whitsitt. The two were married on January 17, 1799, and settled in Rutherford County in 1803. The third of their four surviving children, Sarah had an older brother, Anderson, an older sister, Susan, and a younger brother, John Whitsitt Childress. Two other children born to the Childresses, Benjamin and Elizabeth, died in infancy.

Sarah strongly resembled her mother in appearance and, no doubt, in manner.

Throughout her life, Elizabeth Childress occupied a prominent position in the lives of her children and grandchildren. Her husband died at the age of forty-two and she survived him by forty-six years—a fate she would share with her daughter Sarah, who outlived her husband by forty-three years. Death came early to Elizabeth's eldest son, Anderson, and his wife, Mary Sansom Childress, leaving the responsibility of rearing their only child to Elizabeth Childress.

The family occupied a frame house about two miles from the center of Murfreesboro, which was designated Tennessee's capital from September 26, 1819, to October 15, 1825. On friendly terms with the state's leading politicians, the Childresses often opened their home to visiting dignitaries, among whom were Andrew Jackson and

Felix Grundy, one of the state's premier attorneys and politicians. As a result, Sarah was exposed at an early age to politics and political discussions, as well as to the proper techniques for entertaining political worthies.

Three essential elements composed the child-rearing ethos of Joel and Elizabeth Childress: education, a good name, and a high moral character. While some of their contemporaries might have believed that education beyond the essentials of successfully supervising a home was wasted on the female children of the family, the Childresses did not discriminate with regard to their children's education. Both Sarah and her older sister Susan initially attended the Daniel Elam School in Murfreesboro. Beyond that, Sarah's parents engaged Samuel P. Black, the principal of Bradley Academy, to tutor the young girls privately at the school after the boys had finished their lessons and departed for the day. Both girls, then, received a primary education that was separate but nearly equal to that of the young boys in the community.

James Knox Polk, Sarah's future husband, spent a year at the Zion Presbyterian Church Academy in Columbia before continuing his education at the Bradley Academy in Murfreesboro, during which time he boarded with a local family. Small for his eighteen years, James was behind the other students in his studies because of illness, a painful case of urinary bladder stones. His father, Samuel Polk, took young James to Danville, Kentucky, in 1812 to seek relief. Ephraim McDowell, the West's foremost surgeon, removed Polk's bladder stones, but probably left him sterile. Despite his educational shortcomings, when Polk enrolled as a pupil at Bradley Academy, he applied himself to his lessons and in two years was ready to enter college. It is hard to imagine that the studious eighteen-year-old James K. Polk, though probably acquainted with the Childresses, had any romantic interest at that time in eleven-year-old Sarah.

At the age of twelve or thirteen, Sarah and her sister were sent to the Abercrombie School in Nashville to acquire the accoutrements deemed necessary for the young daughters of a prominent Middle Tennessee family. For entertainment, the sisters dressed in stylish silk gowns to attend balls, one of which was held in the home of Andrew Jackson.

Concluding two years of study at the Abercrombie School, the Childress sisters returned to Murfreesboro for a brief stay. By the time Sarah returned from Nashville, James Polk had already completed his studies at the Bradley Academy and had entered the University of North Carolina at Chapel Hill. A short time later, Sarah and Susan began an arduous journey to Salem (now Winston-Salem) North Carolina, to attend the Moravian Female Academy, known for its high standards of piety and morality. Escorted by their older brother, Anderson, the two young women rode horseback for the 500 miles between Murfreesboro and Salem, a journey that lasted about a month.

The curriculum at the Moravian Female Academy was a blend of courses in grammar, syntax, history, geography, English, and Bible instruction, with painting and music also offered. At a cost of $200 per year per student, the Moravian Female Academy would have been economically out of reach of all but the wealthiest frontier families. The Childress sisters matriculated at the academy from June 1, 1817, through May 27, 1819, when they were called home to be with their father, who was very ill. Upon his death, Joel Childress left his family a substantial estate.

When Sarah and Susan returned home, Murfreesboro was teeming with activity, as Tennessee's legislators thronged the newly designated capital. Enjoying a construction boom, the town now boasted of fourteen saloons and four hotels that marked off the boundaries of the public square. Legislative sessions attracted such well-known Tennessee politicians as Samuel Houston and David Crockett.

Polk, having graduated with honors from the University of North Carolina in 1818, returned home to Columbia, Tennessee. His father's business acumen had resulted in prosperity, and the family moved to an elegant two-story home near the center of town. Polk's reunion with his family lasted for only a brief interval before he left for Nashville to study law with Felix Grundy. Polk's political opportunity came in 1819, when Grundy urged another young attorney in his office to seek the state senate clerkship at the next legislative session in Murfreesboro. The young man refused the offer, and Polk asked to go in his place. Polk was elected clerk of the state senate in 1819. He was reelected in subsequent legislative sessions until 1822. Between the 1819 and 1820 legislative sessions, Polk was admitted to the Tennessee bar.

Annual General Assembly meetings usually lasted about a month and provided the occasion for Polk to renew his acquaintance with Sarah Childress. The diligent young man was no doubt attracted to Sarah's dignity and reserve, coupled with an untempered wit and charm. Additionally, she exhibited the most valued qualities of her sex and station that a young man of the early nineteenth century could hope for in a wife. Above all, a wife was to be pure, pious, submissive, and domestic. Their courtship ripened into betrothal, and Sarah began preparations for her bridal trousseau in 1823. Probably with their future in mind, at the end of a special session of the General Assembly convened in 1822, James announced his candidacy for the state legislature.

Conducted between legislative sessions, Polk's budding law practice in Maury County, Tennessee, involved covering the superior court circuit in the nearby counties. Valuable for its voter contacts, his law practice opened the way for his political career. His clerkship enhanced his political astuteness by enabling him to observe firsthand the maneuverings of the two political factions in the one-party (Republican) state of Tennessee. Indefatigably, he rode through the district gathering support from the locals for his election. Following his election as representative from Maury County, Polk charted a middle course between the two factions. He cast his lot with the harbinger of Jacksonian democracy in Tennessee, Governor William Carroll, in all instances except on the question of presidential succession. In that matter he unequivocally supported Andrew Jackson. If he asked Sarah for her opinion, she too would have supported Jackson—a man she had known since childhood.

At the conclusion of the 1823 legislative session, James Polk and Sarah Childress finalized plans for their wedding. The couple exchanged vows on January 1, 1824, in the bride's home. After the ceremony and a series of dinners, the newlyweds left Murfreesboro bound for Columbia to begin another round of festive gatherings in their honor. The first of these was held at the home of Sarah's in-laws, Samuel and Jane Knox Polk. Sarah's mother-in-law dutifully introduced the new bride to the Polk relations. Not considered a beauty according to the judgment of the times, Sarah nevertheless made a positive impression on the townfolks and, according to Mrs. A. O. P. (Caroline) Nicholson, even evoked a comment from one gentleman regarding the "spicy appearance" of her eyes.

Sarah Polk's new hometown, Columbia, was half the size of Murfreesboro and probably a great deal less exciting than the capital had been. Still, her husband's family was among its earliest settlers and had rapidly risen to prominence. Polk's parents had joined the westward migration from Mecklenburg County, North Carolina, in the early 1800s. Sam Polk had been instrumental in the creation of Maury County in December 1807.

The couple soon settled into a routine. Their first home was a rented cottage, in which they remained for one year before moving across the street from Polk's parents. Sarah Polk supervised their household while James tended to his law practice and legislative duties. If Sarah Polk missed the company of her sister, she was certainly not lacking in female companionship. Her husband was the eldest of ten children, with four sisters varying in age from twelve to twenty-six, three of whom lived in Columbia. At the outset of their marriage, Sarah Polk established the couple's Sunday routine of attending the Presbyterian church, often accompanied by James's mother, Jane. The couple also tried to keep in close touch with Sarah Polk's relatives in Murfreesboro, traveling there periodically to visit.

James Polk's legislative career attracted interest from the state's leading politicans; with their support and a diligent canvassing effort in the district, he was elected to the House of Representatives in 1825. Polk made his congressional debut in Washington without his wife. Upon his return home in the spring of 1826, he sought to solidify his political position by attending militia celebrations in his district. For the entire fourteen years he spent in Congress, Polk followed this routine whether or not opposed for reelection. Sarah Polk, therefore, became accustomed to her husband's being away from home for extended periods early in their marriage.

Sarah Polk accompanied her husband on his second journey to Congress. It was customary in Washington for the legislators to gather in what they referred to as a "mess" at a local boardinghouse. The Polks joined a mess in a house on Pennsylvania Avenue. Immediately, Sarah Polk was drawn into the political and social life of Washington. She was a keen observer and gradually evolved to become the eyes and ears of her husband. Again, she insisted upon regular Sunday attendance at the First Presbyterian Church. Although Polk attended the Presbyterian church with his wife, he was captivated by the sermons of a Methodist evangelist, John B. McFerrin, whom he heard at a camp meeting in the summer of 1833. There was no such response in his wife. Indeed, it is doubtful that she ever attended a Methodist camp meeting. She formally declared her affiliation with the Presbyterian church in Columbia.

At the close of the congressional session in 1827, Polk divided his time between campaigning in his district and tending to his father, whose health was rapidly deteriorating. Upon his father's death in November 1827, Polk became the head of two families, because his mother and his younger siblings looked to him to guard their welfare. Unfortunately, Sarah Polk's older brother had mishandled her father's estate and, before the problems could be ironed out, Anderson Childress died. James Polk, therefore, assumed responsibilty for the Childress estate as well. Failure to have children of their own resulted in the Polks' increasing role as surrogate parents in behalf of their nephews, nieces, and Polk's younger brothers. Financially, Polk eventually accumulated enough wealth to acquire land, first in West Tennessee and later a plantation in Mississippi.

Near the end of 1827, the Polks returned to Washington accompanied by two newly elected congressmen from Tennessee, John Bell and Robert Desha. Over the years, Polk's friendship with Andrew Jackson deepened. When Sam Houston left Washington to seek Tennessee's gubernatorial chair in 1827, Polk moved up in Jackson's esteem, becoming a close adviser in Jackson's 1828 presidential election bid. Their growing friendship encourged Jackson to place Polk in charge of his route to Washington for the inauguration. It must have been an exciting journey, but Sarah Polk was too tired to enjoy it fully. She had contracted a severe case of the measles and was still recuperating when they left Columbia for Washington. Once she reached Washington she recovered rapidly and, with her sister-in-law, Ophelia Polk, she attended a reception at the White House given by the outgoing president, John Quincy Adams. Andrew Jackson's inauguration on March 4, 1829, ushered in a new era in American politics and eventually a second two-party system.

Although Sarah Polk adhered to her husband's guidance in Washington in the early years of their marriage, she soon asserted herself in the matter of Peggy Eaton. A suspected liaison between Senator John Eaton and Peggy O'Neale Timberlake precipitated a social uproar in Washington when President Jackson appointed Eaton to his cabinet. Although Eaton, under President Jackson's directive, married Peggy after the death of her husband, rumors of a romantic tryst before their marriage continued to make the rounds in Washington. The wife of Vice President John C. Calhoun led the cabinet ladies in refusing to mingle socially with Peggy. Even Mrs. Andrew Jackson Donelson, the official White House hostess, refused to have anything to do with the wayward Peggy Eaton. Sarah Polk, understandably, sided with the cabinet wives to defend the tenets of established morality. This created a dilemma for her husband, since Andrew Jackson expected unfettered loyalty from his partisans in all cases. Polk refrained from joining a delegation of Democrats that tried to dissuade Jackson from keeping Eaton in his cabinet. Saved by congressional adjournment, the Polks left Washington for Tennessee, temporarily sidestepping the dilemma.

No doubt James and Sarah Polk discussed the situation, especially with regard to Jackson's expectations. Nevertheless, when the couple returned to Washington in November 1829, Mrs. Polk persisted in her course of ostracizing Mrs. Eaton. Observers concluded that, because of Sarah Polk's behavior, her husband must be henpecked. If Polk was concerned for his political future, so was his wife, who readily understood how important questions of propriety were in Washington's social circles. Under increasing strain, Polk managed deftly to maneuver among the members of Jackson's administration.

Once more, congressional adjournment in May 1830 allowed the Polks to extricate themselves from further political entanglement. Even though Polk still had Jackson's confidence, he must have decided that another session in Washington, with his wife supporting the cabinet members' wives, was too risky. For the second and last time during their marriage, Sarah Polk did not accompany her husband to Washington. Polk inferred accurately that the social situation among Jackson's cabinet members had become untenable, resulting in a irreparable rift between Jackson and Calhoun and Eaton's resignation from the cabinet. Polk wrote to his wife at the end of the congressional session that he missed her counsel and companionship—indeed, he

expected to arrive home before the letter. There was never any doubt after the spring of 1831 that Sarah Polk would be by her husband's side in Washington.

In Washington in 1834, Polk made an election bid for speaker of the House of Representatives. Although Polk had Jackson's support, John Bell defeated him. By this time Sarah Polk had carved out her own niche in the Washington social scene. Her interest in politics was well known among Polk's closest political associates. Samuel H. Laughlin, editor of the Democratic newspaper in Nashville, referred to her in a letter as "membress of Congress-elect."

In the fall of 1835, Washington politics became more animated than usual as a growing schism developed between the members of Congress who supported John Bell and Hugh Lawson White of Tennessee and those who supported President Jackson and Martin Van Buren. Bell had made an irretrievable break with Andrew Jackson in June and, in Tennessee, Bell's followers determined to defeat Congressman Polk before the session convened. Polk feverishly covered his district during the summer. His election victory encouraged him to challenge Bell for the House of Representatives speaker's chair again. He won the coveted position on December 7, 1835.

Polk's elevation to the speakership also meant a shift to greater responsibility for his wife. Required by the new position to entertain larger groups of people, the Polks moved to larger quarters. Another visible sign of their prominence was a new and luxurious coach, fitted with the latest fashions and lined inside with red satin. Increasingly a political asset to her husband, Sarah Polk was included in invitations issued by wives of men who held views opposite to those of the speaker. In March 1838, the Polks gave their own party, issuing hundreds of invitations. It was a smashing success, and Sarah Polk was singled out as having given the preeminent party of Washington's winter season. Sarah Polk's strict adherence to her Presbyterian principles kept her from two places in Washington. One was the horse races and the other was the theater. But her being absent from those places only enhanced appreciation for her piety.

All was not parties and finery during Polk's speakership. The Bell group attempted to discredit Polk at every turn. Partisan newspapers gave notice in advance of their merciless verbal attacks on the speaker, resulting in a packed visitors' gallery. Publicly, Polk bore up well under the vicious attacks, and Sarah Polk conducted herself in her usual exemplary manner, even though she must have suffered for her husband. Despite the discomfort of the situation, Polk maintained the president's confidence. At the end of Jackson's second term, the Polks escorted the former president to Tennessee.

In the 1837 state elections, the Whigs in Tennessee handed the Democrats a political drubbing, requiring Polk to make a critical political decision. His choices were either to stay in his safe congressional seat or run for governor of Tennessee in an effort to redeem the Democrats. He chose the latter. The Whigs in Congress tried once more to embarrass the speaker by denying him the usual vote of appreciation at the end of his term. Not only did they fail, but Supreme Court Justice Joseph Story, in a poem he composed for her, honored Sarah Polk with a special tribute.

In March 1838, Polk launched a two-month-long campaign tour. Sarah Polk was used to her husband's extensive travels in his congressional district, but he had never before been away from home for such an extended period. Polk instructed his wife to send documents pertinent to his congressional record. Sarah Polk unofficially orchestrated her husband's campaign in concert with his political associates. She also fretted about his health, knowing how taxed he was by his strenuous schedule. It was during this time that Polk's affection for his wife deepened into respect.

The enthusiasm generated in the political campaigns between 1839 and 1844 made possible an increased role for women throughout the state, but carried out within the strict limits of proper womanhood. Sarah Polk's involvement in her husband's campaign was never brought to the public's attention, because she would have been subjected to ridicule. Victorious, the Polks spent the next two years in Nashville, while Polk guided Tennessee's government.

The Tennessee Democratic Party's plan to include Polk as the vice presidential candidate on the 1840 presidential ticket with Martin Van Buren failed to materialize and presaged two more political setbacks in Polk's career. William Henry Harrison's smashing presidential victory in 1840 stunned the Democrats and left Polk with no other choice than to run for reelection as governor.

The 1841 gubernatorial race opened with Polk's announcing the most elaborate speaking schedule any candidate had ever undertaken in Tennessee. The Whig opponent, James C. Jones, matched Polk's schedule at every turn. During the backbreaking campaign, Polk twice became ill, a source of great concern for his wife. Still, she kept him apprised of anything that needed his attention as governor, and, upon his request, forwarded newspapers and documents. For the first time, she openly expressed uncertainty about her husband's quest for the governorship. She was troubled that obtaining the office might cost him his health. During the entire campaign he was home only four days, and she visited the Democratic leaders in Nashville to make sure they were carrying out her husband's instructions. She also oversaw his business as governor, sorting out matters requiring his immediate attention upon his return. Polk lost the election by a narrow margin. Samuel Laughlin later wrote to Sarah Polk, counseling that, where her husband or his friends are concerned, "a wife never gives up the ship."

The loss was the first in Polk's long political career. In October 1841, the Polks left Nashville to return to Columbia. Polk renewed his law practice while keeping up a lively correspondence with party leaders. Throughout this interregnum, Sarah Polk closely guarded her husband's health, and tried to persuade him to strike a balance between work and leisure. The campaign of 1841 had brought them even closer as a couple, and she had proved her worth again as a companion and political confidante.

This pleasant interlude ended when Polk opened his third gubernatorial campaign in April 1843. A few days after he declared his candidacy, he published a list of seventy-five speaking engagements, exceeding even his own record set in 1841. His four-month absence from home weighed heavily upon his wife. She had enjoyed having him at home and was saddened by his departure. She did not bother to hide her feeings of dread. In a letter to his wife, Polk urged her to become more cheerful. Following a five-day break in the campaign, she noted that he was too absorbed to pay her much attention. The voters reelected the incumbent, Jones.

If Sarah Polk was despondent during the campaign, her husband was after it. The results of the election put Polk's position as head of the Tennessee democracy in doubt. If Sarah Polk harbored any relief that her husband's political career might be over, she would have kept it to herself.

Although his prospects for the vice presidential nomination appeared dimmer than ever, Polk was determined to make the effort. At the very least, he would have to build solid support behind Martin Van Buren in Tennessee to be considered for the presidential ticket of 1844. One of Polk's strengths was that he could count Andrew Jackson among his ardent supporters. When Polk's name arose for consideration as a presidential candidate at the Democratic nominating convention in May 1844, delegates questioned Tennessee's representatives concerning the suitability of Sarah Polk as First Lady. On that score, she won the endorsement of all who were her acquaintances, as well as those who knew her only by reputation. The convention was a triumph for Polk's partisans, and he emerged as the party's first "dark horse" nominee.

Once the Democratic nominee was known, Polk's longtime friend Supreme Court Justice John Catron urged the Polks to journey to Nashville for a Democratic rally. Catron believed that both should be seen, but not heard, because presidential candidates did not actively campaign. He believed Sarah Polk's presence would be an asset to her husband and would put to rest any ugliness concerning the president's wife stemming from Andrew Jackson's campaign. Sarah Polk, he wrote, was needed to win "the women, the young men," and "the vain old ones." Despite Catron's appeals, Polk declined the invitation, preferring to adhere to the traditional presidential campaign in which the candidate did not appear in public. In Polk's behalf, Andrew Jackson put a shaky pen to paper, claiming that he would sacrifice his life if necessary to see Sarah Polk beside her husband at the head of government. Toward the end of the campaign, Sarah Polk's despondency returned as doubts clouded the outcome of the election in Tennessee. Polk lost his home state, but managed to stem the Whig tide in New York State, which swung his presidential victory.

On the first leg of their travels to Washington for the inauguration, the Polks took a steamboat to Louisville, Kentucky. Sarah Polk's reputation as a proper lady was enhanced when she requested that visitors be denied access to her husband on the Sabbath. She also requested that a band greeting the presidential party on Sunday cease playing. From Wheeling, West Virginia, the presidential party boarded carriages and in a winding procession journeyed to Cumberland, Maryland, where the Polks entrained for Washington. Torchlight parades, banner-bearing crowds, cannon salutes, and fireworks greeted them everywhere.

One of Sarah Polk's early obligatory functions as First Lady was to call on former First Lady Dolley Madison. Sarah Polk was the subject of intense scrutiny on each of these social occasions, and won the admiration of all who came in contact with her because of her dignified comportment. She emitted an air of command not only of herself but, as one observer not acquainted with their political partnership charged, of her husband. Sarah Polk presented a stark contrast to the youthful former First Lady, Julia Tyler, whom many had criticized for being too involved in worldly amusements.

Immediately following the inauguration on March 4, 1845, the Polks opened the White House to visitors. Newspaper reporters unreservedly praised Sarah Polk. She seemed to personify the elegance, charm, and dignity that marked the pinnacle of true womanhood, in the opinion of many the greatest attainment for an upper-class woman in the mid-1840s. She was gracious to all who entered the White House and did not distinguish between Democrats and Whigs. It was predicted in the *Nashville Union* of March 16, 1845, that she would have a "successful, popular and happy career in the sphere of domestic and social relations of life," and Sarah Polk never disappointed the public's expectations of her.

Routinely, the Polks held two evening receptions each week. The White House welcomed visitors, who were able to shake hands with the president and his wife. Because no formal invitations were issued for these functions, the rooms set aside for guests frequently overflowed, and the Polks often stood in a line for hours greeting swarms of visitors. During the spring and summer, Wednesday evenings were set aside for concerts by the Marine Band on the White House lawn. Special receptions were held on New Year's Day and the Fourth of July. Sometimes work constraints kept the president in his office, whereupon his wife took charge and informed him afterward of the guests who had attended the receptions. She was particularly adept at scrutinizing the behavior of cabinet members who sometimes reflected their displeasure with her husband's decisions.

The Polks made it their policy not to speak ill publicly of even the bitterest of their political enemies. Their popularity could not be ignored, even by Polk's rancorous political enemy John Bell. Bell called on the president in January 1848 to make amends. The two men had not spoken since their races for speaker of the House of Representatives in 1834 and 1835. While President Polk and John Bell easily healed their wounds, Bell predicted that Mrs. Bell's reconciliation with Mrs. Polk would probably not go so smoothly. He implied that the problem would be on the side of his own wife rather than the president's. Etiquette required Mrs. Bell to make the first call upon the president's wife.

Polk's work schedule kept him from reading the newspapers faithfully, so he charged his wife with keeping him informed of public opinion—a duty she had performed in the past. She read and marked items of interest for her husband in the newspapers in a manner calculated to save him energy. Close friends understood that Polk worked relentlessly, and they urged Sarah Polk to maintain vigilance in that regard. Periodically, she would send someone to fetch him from his office to witness an entertainment held at the White House in order to extricate him from his duties.

The president seldom left Washington during his term. The exceptions were visits to Mt. Vernon, Fort Monroe, New England, and his alma mater, the University of North Carolina at Chapel Hill. At the many intermediate stops en route to North Carolina, local citizens greeted the president and First Lady enthusiastically with bands and parades, then ushered them to separate quarters to receive visitors. While on tour of the university, Polk showed his wife his former room and the Dialectic Hall.

Both Polks experienced a number of illnesses during their four years in Washington. In 1846, Sarah Polk became gravely ill for several days and, after much prodding from her husband, agreed to allow a physician to attend her. In May 1847 she again developed chills and fever—a common but often serious malady. The president became very ill in September 1847, to the extent that he conducted presidential business from his bedchamber instead of his office. Sarah Polk again fell victim to chills and fever after her husband's illness. Repeatedly, the president sustained attacks of illness. Over time, the Polks became unwilling to risk their health. If the weather was inclement or if either felt in the least indisposed, they refrained from leaving the White House.

The president ended his term in triumph. For most of Polk's presidency the Mexican War had occupied his attention, and he rejoiced when a peace treaty was signed in February 1848. No sooner had peace been restored than Democratic delegations called on Polk to reconsider his decision to be a one-term president. He unequivocally refused. An unusually large crowd attended the New Year's Day reception in 1849 and the Polks' final reception in February. Several thousand people arrived at the White House to bid them farewell.

Sarah Polk's keen understanding of propriety was rewarded. A Nashville newspaper singled her out as a model of propriety, who properly eschewed the follies and amusements of the world and thereby conferred dignity upon the position of First Lady. She was praised especially for abolishing dancing at the White House, in accordance with the tenets of her religion. A Washington newspaper printed a special farewell tribute to Sarah Polk. All assessments of her accomplishments as First Lady spoke with a single voice of commendation.

The Polks were unprepared for the outpouring of enthusiasm that greeted them on their return journey to Tennessee. At each stop huge crowds met the presidential party and conveyed them to the heart of the city. They were deluged with visitors. While cannons boomed in the distance, receptions, parades, balls, bands, brilliantly illuminated houses, and dinners met them everywhere they went, each event finer than the one before. The pair and their entourage shook the hands of literally thousands of people. Between the constant deluge of visitors and the difficulties associated with travel, the Polks barely got any rest. Reports of cholera in New Orleans added to the strain of the journey. Sarah Polk's health held up, but her husband's did not. Fatigue took its toll on him, and he became ill. On March 18, the Polks learned that a passenger on their steamboat had died of cholera. At Smithland, Kentucky, the presidential party disembarked, unable to go any farther because of the state of the former president's health. When the Polks finally arrived in Nashville on April 1, it was obvious that Polk was seriously debilitated.

His flowing gray locks made him appear much older than his fifty-three years.

Polk's health improved gradually until early June, when he again became ill. He died at 4:40 in the afternoon on June 15, 1849. Funeral services were held on June 16. Polk's body, followed by a procession of carriages filled with the city's leading politicians and citizens, was conveyed to a temporary grave.

In May 1850, the former president's remains were moved to the grounds of his home at Polk Place, to a tomb erected for that purpose. Polk's will reflected once more his full confidence in his wife. In his final tribute to her, he summarized their relationship, saying that she "constantly identified with me in all her sympathies and affections, through all the vicissitudes of both my private and public life."

After her husband's death, Sarah Polk became a recluse. Except to attend church, she rarely left her home. Mrs. Polk's mother, sensing the depth of her daughter's sorrow, brought Sarah's grandniece, Sarah Polk Jetton ("Sallie"), to live at Polk Place. Sallie grew up in her aunt's home and later married George William Fall. The couple and their daughter, Saidee Polk, resided with the former First Lady.

On August 12, 1891, Sarah Polk became gravely ill. She died two days later at 7:30 A.M., at the age of eighty-eight. Nashville's most revered citizen had passed away. Her funeral was held on Sunday, August 16, and her remains were entombed beside those of her husband. Two years later, in a solemn, dignified procession, the remains of the former president and his wife were removed from the tomb and reinterred on the grounds of the capitol in Nashville.

Within the confines of proper womanhood, Sarah Polk strengthened the role of First Lady. Publicly she dignified the office in a manner her contemporaries held in highest esteem. Privately, she was her husband's most valuable political ally. Not since Abigail Adams had a wife shared so intimately in the details of her husband's political career. Though silently, she operated as a political equal to her husband, who awarded her his full measure of confidence. Sarah Polk was so universally admired that it is extremely unlikely anyone would have questioned her reputation as an outstanding First Lady.

BIBLIOGRAPHICAL ESSAY

There are several published primary sources that provide information on Sarah Polk's life. Her own words are found in the letters she wrote to her husband during his political campaigns in Tennessee. These are housed in the James K. Polk Papers at the Library of Congress. Additionally, the letters are published in the series of volumes that compose the *Correspondence of James K. Polk*, currently being edited at the University of Tennessee, Knoxville. Quotations, unless otherwise noted, are contained in the published correspondence. Anson and Fanny Nelson recorded Sarah Polk's recollections of her life shortly before her death and published *Memorials of Sarah Childress Polk* (rpt., Spartanburg, S.C., 1980). Then there is the diary of James K. Polk. It begins in August 1845 and concludes the day before Polk was struck with a fatal illness. See Milo Milton Quaife, ed., *The Diary of James K. Polk During His Presidency*, 1845 to 1849 (4 vols., Chicago, 1910).

The Tennessee State Library and Archives also contains primary material in its Polk Family Papers, including letters from Sarah Polk's nieces while they were at the White House during James K. Polk's term as president. The collection also includes President Polk's will, newspaper clippings bearing on the disposition of Polk Place after Mrs. Polk's death, her obituary, genealogical information, family correspondence, photographs, and a number of other items of interest. Not specifically touching on the Polks but valuable nonetheless is the firsthand account of Tennessee politics and frontier living found in the "Reminiscences of an Octogenarian (Mrs. A. O. P. Nicholson) Published in Maury Democrat 1894," also at the Tennessee Archives. John R. Bumgarner, *Sarah Childress Polk: A Biography of the Remarkable First Lady* (Jefferson, N.C., 1997) is the only modern biography.

By far the most outstanding secondary sources of information on Sarah Polk are Charles Sellers's works, *James K. Polk: Jacksonian 1795–1843* (New Jersey, 1957) and *James K. Polk: Continentalist 1843–1846* (New Jersey, 1966). The *Tennessee Historical Quarterly* has two indexes that assist in finding articles containing information about Sarah Polk. Robert W. Ikard's article on Polk's surgery is in that journal. One source for nineteenth-century attitudes regarding proper womanhood is Barbara J. Harris, *Beyond Her Sphere: Women and the Professions in American History* (Westport, Conn., 1978).

A visit to Samuel Polk's home in Columbia proves rewarding, since many of the items used by the Polks in the White House and afterward at Polk Place are there, including furniture, the family Bible, and portraits. This site is available on the Internet at www.jamespolk.com. Sarah Polk's genealogy is under intense investigation even now by her descendants.

There are a few histories of Columbia in Maury County, and Murfreesboro in Rutherford County, Tennessee, that portray the mid-nineteenth-century frontier towns. Among those are Jill Knight Garrett, *Maury County, Tennessee: Historical Sketches* (Columbia, 1967); Carlton C. Sims, ed., *A History of Rutherford County* (Murfreesboro, 1947); and Mabel Pittard, *Rutherford County* (Memphis, 1984).

Margaret Mackall Smith Taylor

(1788–1852)

First Lady: 1849–1850

Thomas H. Appleton Jr.

Margaret Mackall Smith was born on September 21, 1788, at St. Leonard's in Calvert County, Maryland. She was the daughter of Ann Mackall (pronounced Maykle) Smith and Walter Smith, a prosperous planter and Revolutionary War officer whose great-grandfather, Richard Smith, was named attorney general of Maryland during the reign of Oliver Cromwell. Although little is known of Margaret's earliest years, she evidently received more than the rudimentary education typical of a plantation daughter of that time.

In autumn 1809, while visiting her older sister and brother-in-law, Mary and Samuel Chew, in Kentucky, Margaret met twenty-five-year-old Zachary Taylor. An army lieutenant four years her senior, Taylor was then on leave at Springfield, his parents' home outside Louisville. After a courtship of some seven months, the young officer persuaded "Peggy" (as he called her) to marry him. They were wed on June 21, 1810, in a double log house close to the Taylor family estate.

For most of the next forty years, Margaret Taylor lived in a succession of frontier outposts. Without the benefit of West Point training and connections, her husband was perennially assigned to remote forts ill-suited for wives or children. Yet she

Note: No authenticated photo or portrait of Margaret Taylor is known to exist. Photo of White House in the late 1840s courtesy Library of Congress.

insisted on accompanying him whenever possible—from Fort Crawford in the North to the Everglades in the South and Fort Smith in the West. Documentary evidence offers occasional hints of the monotonous life Mrs. Taylor endured as an army wife. Writing to his brother Hancock from Fort Knox at Vincennes in December 1813, Taylor, then a brevet major, remarked, "Peggy . . . says she is very lonesome, and is in hopes that you will be as good as your word in paying us the visit you promised. . . . If you come over[,] Peggy says you must bring her some cotton for [k]nitting which [she] wants mother to have spun for her. . . ." At that moment the Indiana fort boasted a garrison of forty-six officers and men.

The Taylors had six children, including five daughters: Ann Mackall (b. April 1811), Sarah Knox (b. March 1814), Octavia Pannill (b. August 1816), Margaret Smith (b. July 1819), and Mary Elizabeth "Betty" (b. April 1824). Their sixth child and only son, Richard, arrived in January 1826. "Dick" would later serve as a lieutenant general in the Confederate Army.

Tragedy struck the family in July 1820, when daughter Octavia, at age three, succumbed at Bayou Sara, Louisiana, to what her absent father termed "a violent bilious fever." Two months later Mrs. Taylor fell gravely ill, and her husband did not expect her to survive. As he rushed to be with her, Taylor wrote a superior: "At best her constitution is remarkable [sic] delicate. . . ." Gradually Mrs. Taylor regained her strength and in time was able to nurse two other daughters back to health. Fifteen-month-old Margaret, however, died in October. The death of two children within four months was devastating to both parents.

From 1832 to 1836, Margaret Taylor and her youngest children, Betty and Dick, lived at Fort Crawford, Michigan Territory, at what today is Prairie du Chien, Wisconsin. As wife of the fort commandant, Margaret Taylor partook of amenities that had been absent at more spartan outposts. The family lived in a two-story frame house, complete with a kitchen and a pantry in the basement. Mrs. Taylor ran the household with the help of two slaves, Will and Sally, whom she brought from Louisville. Although Taylor himself seldom drank anything more potent than iced milk, he maintained for the convenience of their guests what New York author Charles Fenno Hoffman pronounced a "hospitable" wine cellar. In 1832, another visitor to the Taylor home described Mrs. Taylor as "a most kind and thorough-bred Southern lady. . . . She and her children," he added, "were communicants of the Episcopal church."

Margaret Taylor often lived apart from her children. Determined that her daughters and son receive the best education possible, she sent the four East to be schooled. The eldest, Ann, attended a female academy at Lexington, Kentucky; Sarah Knox studied in Louisville and Cincinnati; Betty enrolled at a boarding school in Philadelphia; and Dick graduated from Yale at the age of nineteen.

Having witnessed firsthand the hardships that befell an army wife, Margaret and Zachary Taylor attempted without success to dissuade Ann from marrying Robert Crooke Wood, the assistant surgeon at Fort Crawford. When the two were wed in September 1829, the bride was barely eighteen. The couple soon departed to take up an assignment at Fort Snelling in what is today Minnesota.

Much to her parents' dismay, Sarah Knox also found romance in the chilly clime of Fort Crawford. Sometime in 1832, eighteen-year-old Knox (as her relatives and friends called her) fell in love with Lieutenant Jefferson Davis, a West Point graduate five years her senior. The Taylors steadfastly objected to their daughter's marrying into the military. "I will be damned if another daughter of mine shall marry into the Army," Colonel Taylor reportedly told Major Stephen Kearny. "I know enough of the family life of officers. I scarcely know my own children or they me." Furthermore, Taylor considered Davis, in particular, to be unsuitable; for whatever reason, he bore an intense dislike for the junior officer.

Despite her parents' disapproval, Knox became engaged to Davis, whom she continued to see in the homes of friends. The couple's romance survived a two-year separation while Davis served in what is now Oklahoma. Then, in 1835, in part to counter her parents' objections, the Mississippian resigned from the army. Yet the Taylors remained opposed to the marriage. Knox had reached twenty-one, however, and she no longer required parental consent. She and Davis were married on June 17, 1835.

Given the prominence that Margaret and Zachary Taylor and Jefferson Davis would later achieve, historians and tale-spinners alike have distorted the circumstances of Knox's wedding for their own purposes. Some writers persist in perpetuating the traditional lore that Knox and her fiancé eloped—it's frequently said through a window—an action that particularly grieved an often "delicate" Margaret Taylor. In truth, the couple married with the full knowledge if not the blessing of the Taylor parents. The nuptials took place in the home of the bride's paternal aunt near Louisville, in a ceremony attended by Knox's older sister Ann and numerous cousins. Her father's elder brother gave the bride in marriage.

That mother and daughter were not estranged, and communicated at the time of the marriage and thereafter, is certain. Two letters written by Knox to her mother have survived. In the first, penned on her wedding day, the bride informed her mother that she would be married "as you advised" in a bonnet and traveling dress. With sister Ann beside her, Knox continued, "I shall not feel so entirely destitute of friends." She expressed gratitude for her father's "kind and affectionate letter," accompanied by a "liberal supply of money." The young bride encouraged her "dearest Mother" to write to her in Mississippi. "I shall feel so much disappointed and mortified if you do not."

Later, on August 11, a pleased Knox wrote to her mother from the Davis plantation below Vicksburg: "I have just received your affectionate letter forwarded to me from Louisville; you may readily imagine the pleasure it afforded me to hear

from you. . . . How often, my dear Mother, I wish I could look in upon you [at Fort Crawford]. I imagine so often I can see you about attending to your domestic concerns—down in the cellar skimming milk or going to feed the chickens. . . ." The newlywed closed with a reassurance to her mother: "Do not make yourself uneasy about me; the country is quite healthy."

Margaret Taylor was soon plunged into grief, however, when word arrived that both Davises had contracted malarial fever. Though Jefferson Davis recovered, his wife did not; Knox died in her husband's arms on September 15, 1835. The couple had been married just shy of three months.

The Taylors struggled with their grief and coped with the isolation of Fort Crawford, and then Jefferson Barracks, Missouri, as best they could. Finally, in March 1837, Colonel Taylor requested a six-month leave of absence to attend to "private affairs," including "visiting my Children who are at school in Philadelphia and Kentucky, and who have been absent from us for . . . several years." Although granted leave, Taylor was unable to accept it. Recurring Indian hostilities in Florida, known collectively as the Second Seminole War, led to Taylor's being ordered to Fort Brooke at Tampa Bay. For his defeat of the Seminole and Mikasuki Indians in the Battle of Okeechobee on Christmas Day 1837, Taylor was promoted to brevet brigadier general. Some months later Margaret Taylor sailed from New Orleans to join her husband at Tampa, where she is said to have tended the sick and wounded. By January 1840 the Indian hostilities had largely subsided, as the general, out on maneuvers, remarked in a note to his brother: "I recd. a letter from Peggy the 25th ulto, all well at Tampa, but very dull there. . . ."

As a result of the Florida campaign, Zachary Taylor earned a well-deserved nickname—Old Rough and Ready—and the furlough for which both he and his wife had been longing. In May 1840, the Taylors sailed to Pensacola and on to New Orleans. They proceeded leisurely to Baton Rouge, then to Louisville and Washington, before being reunited with their daughter Betty in Philadelphia, where she was attending a private boarding school. Betty and her parents toured through upstate New York as far as Niagara Falls before heading to Kentucky for a six-week stay with relatives.

In November 1840 Margaret Taylor accompanied her husband to the post of Baton Rouge, just north of the town of that name. Except for occasional forays to such frontier outposts as Fort Gibson and Fort Smith, Arkansas, Mrs. Taylor would remain in Louisiana for the next seven years. At Baton Rouge she declined the more fashionable quarters to which she, as the wife of the post commander, was entitled. Instead, she delighted in restoring a small, neglected cottage, located directly on the banks of the Mississippi, that had originally been built for the Spanish commandant. Aided by her two slaves and various off-duty soldiers, Mrs. Taylor transformed the dilapidated wooden building into a comfortable residence. By all accounts, the Taylors and their daughter Betty relished living in the four-room shaded cottage surrounded on all sides by a cozy veranda.

Devoutly religious, Mrs. Taylor felt keenly the absence of an Episcopal church at Baton Rouge. She located a room inside the garrison that could be used as a chapel and persuaded a rector to offer occasional services. She later participated actively in the establishment of the parish and church of St. James.

The outbreak of hostilities with Mexico shattered the Taylors' domestic bliss and forever changed Margaret Taylor's world. As tensions between the United States and its southern neighbor heightened, Taylor, a general in 1845, was ordered to secure a position "on or near the Rio Grande." For seven months he commanded an army of occupation at Corpus Christi. After war was declared in April 1846, he led American forces to victory at Palo Alto, Resaca de la Palma, and, above all, Buena Vista. Old Rough and Ready emerged from the war as the undisputed hero of the day.

Throughout the war, Margaret Taylor busied herself in her beloved "Spanish cot-tage" at Baton Rouge. She tended her garden, prayed in the chapel, and doted on her four grandchildren when daughter Ann Taylor Wood came to visit. She worried incessantly that Taylor would be killed in battle. Legend has it that she made a vow to forsake society and fashion if her husband were returned safely to her.

Margaret Taylor and her daughters boarded the *Mary Kingsland* on December 2, 1847, as the steamer bearing General Taylor made its way toward New Orleans. The next day, the Crescent City lavished on Zachary Taylor the most elaborate tribute in its history since Andrew Jackson's defeat of the British a third of a century earlier. Several days later the Taylors reached the "Spanish cottage." There the family would spend most of the following thirteen months.

Content in her surroundings—which often included her three children, four grandchildren, and numerous kinspeople—Margaret Taylor, age fifty-nine and in "feeble health," hoped to live in retirement with her husband. That was not to be, however. His battlefield victories propelled Old Rough and Ready to national prominence, and a movement was already under way to draft him for the presidency. For Margaret Taylor, the prospect of life in the White House had no appeal; she would far prefer to have remained in her Louisiana cottage, caring for her roses. Although she made no public expression of her feelings, Mrs. Taylor remarked to friends that she prayed each night that the presidency would fall to someone other than her husband. In November 1848, to her sorrow, Zachary Taylor was elected the twelfth president of the United States.

As she had done throughout their thirty-eight-year marriage, Margaret Taylor followed her husband as he assumed yet another assignment for his country. A portent of the role she would play as wife of the president may be seen in her first days in the capital. The family made the Willard Hotel its headquarters during the week that preceded the inauguration. On March 1, 1849, when the outgoing president, James K. Polk, entertained some forty persons at dinner, Mrs. Taylor declined the invitation, remaining at the Willard while the president-elect attended with their daughter Betty. Nor did the new First Lady appear at any of the three inaugural balls. Again the vivacious Betty, twenty-four years of age and striking in a simple white gown, elicited rave reviews from diarists.

Yet it would be a mistake to conclude that Margaret Taylor became a recluse during her time in the White House. She was hardly the "phantom" some writers have described. Although frail, she attended Episcopal services almost daily at St. John's Church on Lafayette Square. As her husband's biographer Holman Hamilton observed, "Exceedingly devout, and at least as concerned with the hereafter as with life on earth, Mrs. Taylor was little interested in White House pomp and ceremony." She was content, therefore, to turn over the duties of hostess to her daughter Betty, who sat beside her father at official functions throughout his administration. (Betty, ironically, became the Taylors' third daughter to marry an army officer. Shortly after the election, in December 1848, she wed her father's longtime aide, Colonel William W. S. Bliss.)

Though she seldom appeared at official functions, Margaret Taylor enjoyed entertaining an intimate circle of relatives and friends upstairs in the private quarters of the White House. Members of the president's family from Kentucky paid extended visits. One Taylor niece, Becky, a teenager, even lived at the mansion when not at boarding school. The Taylors' eldest child, Ann Wood, frequently came over from Baltimore with her two daughters. One of Mrs. Taylor's favorite visitors was Varina Howell Davis, the second wife of her son-in-law Jefferson Davis, with whom the family had become reconciled during the Mexican War. Mrs. Davis recalled in her 1890 memoir that she had especially enjoyed "Mrs. Taylor's bright and pretty room where the invalid, full of interest in the passing show in which she had not the strength to take part, talked most agreeably and kindly to the many friends who were admitted to her presence." Biographer Holman Hamilton

concluded, "Far from forbidding in Taylor's regime, White House corridors rang with laughter and echoed the patter of little feet."

Many observers of the Washington scene who were accustomed to seeing the wife of the president in a more social role wondered why Margaret Taylor remained largely out of view. Rumors circulated that she was a coarse, common woman whose years on the frontier made her unfit to preside over polite society. Like Rachel Jackson, another wife of a military hero who became president, Margaret Taylor was depicted as smoking a corncob pipe. In truth, the slender woman of medium height and graying hair was "gentle" and "refined," according to Varina Davis. What is more, neither she nor her husband smoked, a grandson later recalled, because tobacco smoke made her "actively ill." Yet familiar images die hard; as recently as 1937 a story in the *New York Times* portrayed Mrs. Taylor leisurely puffing away at her pipe.

In a June 1850 letter to his son, President Taylor reported that Margaret Taylor's health was "about as usual." Ever solicitous of his wife's welfare, the president encouraged her to make an excursion from Washington. Along with her daughter Betty, Margaret Taylor began planning a July trip to Old Point Comfort on Chesapeake Bay. Perhaps there the Taylor ladies could escape the suffocating heat and Asiatic cholera that had sickened so many in the capital.

Ironically, it was not the fragile Margaret Taylor but her husband whose health took a sudden turn for the worse. On July 4, the president participated in the laying of the cornerstone of the Washington Monument. After sitting hatless for two hours under the broiling sun, he returned, famished, to the White House. He consumed large quantities of raw fruits and vegetables, accompanied by frigid liquids. Some hours later Taylor complained of nausea and cramps. Although attending physicians assumed that the president, too, was suffering from "cholera morbus," the ailment was actually acute gastroenteritis. By July 9, death appeared imminent.

The Taylors' two daughters and sons-in-law (three in number, counting Jefferson Davis) maintained vigil upstairs. Around 10 P.M. the president asked to see his wife, urged her not to grieve, and lapsed into unconsciousness. Within a half hour he was dead.

Margaret Taylor collapsed under the burden of grief; she could not stand or walk without support. A distraught Betty Bliss reportedly said, "We had thought of our mother's dying, for she is . . . seldom well; but our father . . . we never expected him to die!" Neither mother nor daughters were able to attend the funeral service conducted in the East Room. The widow remained upstairs in her sitting room with Varina Davis.

The new president, Millard Fillmore, invited Mrs. Taylor to remain for a time at the White House. She declined, moving out on the evening of her husband's funeral. She had resided at the executive mansion for one year and 131 days. Yet she never mentioned the White House again for the remainder of her life.

On July 18, 1850, Mrs. Taylor left the capital, never to return. She traveled first to Baltimore for a lengthy visit with her eldest daughter, Ann Wood, and Ann's husband, Robert. "Mrs. Taylor and all the family are well," Dr. Wood wrote two weeks after the president's death, "and as composed as could be expected." After a three-month stay in Baltimore, Mrs. Taylor departed with Ann Wood and Betty Bliss to meet their brother Dick in New Orleans. There the Taylor estate—worth an estimated four million dollars in 1995 currency—was divided among the president's heirs, with the bulk of the assets apportioned to the children. Mrs. Taylor received several income-producing warehouses and property in Louisville, bank stock, proceeds from the sale of household furniture used in Washington, and five slaves.

The president's widow lived with the Bliss family in obscurity in East Pascagoula, Mississippi, until her death on August 14, 1852, at the age of sixty-three. She had survived the president by two years and thirty-six days. Eventually, she was buried beside her husband on the Taylor family property in Louisville in what is today the Zachary Taylor National Cemetery. For Margaret Taylor there could be no more fitting epitaph than the words penned by a devoted husband while in the remote outpost they shared: "I am confident the feminine virtues never did concentrate in a higher degree in the bosom of any woman than in hers."

BIBLIOGRAPHICAL ESSAY

"What's in a signature?" one collector recently asked. "If it's First Lady Margaret Taylor's, plenty! One can name any price and probably get it." The only "catch," he continued, was finding one, "because hers is one of the rarest of all presidential wives." In "From Margaret Taylor's Pen," published in the summer 1993 issue of *Manuscripts*, pp. 193–98, Walter A. Ostromecki, Jr., declared that "not a single letter" from Mrs. Taylor apparently has survived, though she is known to have been "a typical letter writer" of her day. What happened to her correspondence is not known. It is conceivable that the intensely private Margaret Taylor destroyed such materials following her husband's death. There is also the possibility that her papers may have been lost during the Civil War. In a November 1890 letter recently offered at auction, her daughter Betty Taylor Bliss Dandridge remarked that "all" her father's papers "were destroyed when my mother's house was burned by Federal troops during the war where they had been placed for safe keeping." A copy of the letter is in the Margaret Mackall Smith Taylor Biographical File, Kentucky Historical Society. Regrettably, the visual record is equally sparse. There is no authenticated portrait, sketch, or daguerreotype of Margaret Taylor.

Information must therefore be gleaned from others. During the 1930s and 1940s, her husband's foremost biographer, Holman Hamilton, gathered and published much of Taylor's correspondence in *Zachary Taylor: Soldier of the Republic* (Indianapolis, 1941) and *Zachary Taylor: Soldier in the White House* (Indianapolis, 1951). All quoted material appears in those volumes.

Supplementing Hamilton's work are Brainerd Dyer, *Zachary Taylor* (Baton Rouge, La., 1946); Silas Bent McKinley and Silas Bent, *Old Rough and Ready: The Life and Times of Zachary Taylor* (New York, 1946); and K. Jack Bauer, *Zachary Taylor: Soldier, Planter, Statesman of the Old Southwest* (Baton Rouge, La., and London, 1985). Particularly helpful on the relationship of Jefferson Davis and the Taylors is Holman Hamilton, *The Three Kentucky Presidents: Lincoln, Taylor, Davis* (Lexington, Ky., 1978).

The August 17, 1852, issue of the New York Times contained a one-line obituary: "Mrs. General Taylor, relict of the late President, died at East Pascagoula, on Saturday night."

★★★　　★★★

Abigail Powers Fillmore

(1798–1853)

First Lady: 1850–1853

Kristin Hoganson

Abigail Powers was born in the town of Stillwater, in Saratoga County, New York, in March 1798. She was the daughter of Abigail Newland Powers and Lemuel Powers, a Baptist minister. Two years after her birth, her father's death left the family in financial straits. Abigail's mother decided to move westward with a group of relatives and friends, in an effort to stretch her meager resources. The widow resettled her family in the frontier town of Sempronius, in Cayuga County, New York.

Little is known of Abigail's childhood in Sempronius, except that she was educated by her mother. She developed a passion for reading and worked her way through the extensive library left by her father. When she was sixteen, she began to support herself as a teacher, even as she continued her own studies. Reportedly, she helped establish a circulating library in Sempronius. Abigail grew to be a tall, thin young woman with a fair complexion, light auburn hair, and a love of books that lasted throughout her life.

When Abigail was nineteen, she met Millard Fillmore, who was briefly a student of hers at the New Hope Academy in Sempronius. Fillmore was the son of a poor New York farm couple and was two years younger than Abigail. He had been apprenticed as a clothmaker but decided that he wanted to become a lawyer instead. Like Abigail, he taught school to support himself while he continued his own studies. The two young scholars shared an eagerness to learn and often studied together. In a later autobiographical essay, published by the Buffalo Historical Society, Fillmore remembered that at New Hope he was "stimulated by the companionship of a young lady whom I afterward married." Throughout their life together, Abigail and Millard were intellectual partners who sparked each other's desire to learn.

The couple became engaged in 1819 but did not marry until 1826 because Fillmore was studying law and was unable to support a family. For three years of their courtship they lived about 150 miles apart and did not see each other once. Their relationship was kept alive through letters, now lost. Besides the obstacles of poverty and distance, the couple had to overcome the objections of Abigail's mother and older brother—a judge—who considered Fillmore socially inferior. The Powerses may have been poor, but they were proud of their genteel New England ancestry.

After winning familial approval, Abigail Powers married Millard Fillmore on February 5, 1826, in her brother's house in Moravia, New York. Fillmore was Episcopalian at the time, and an Episcopalian minister officiated. Following their marriage, the couple lived in Aurora, in Erie County, New York, close to Fillmore's family. Abigail Fillmore continued to teach for two years after her marriage while her husband established himself professionally. Her labors helped make ends meet. Years later she would be remembered as the first First Lady to hold a paying job after marriage. Abigail Fillmore stopped teaching in 1828, when her husband was elected to the state legislature and she gave birth to their first child, Millard Powers Fillmore, whom they called Powers. From that time on, she applied her talents to educating her children and advancing her husband's career.

In 1829, when Fillmore went to Albany as a legislator, his wife stayed in Aurora. Although the Fillmores had spent much time apart while engaged, this first separation of their married life was difficult, as a letter written by Abigail Fillmore to her husband on January 17, 1829, indicates. In the letter, located in the Fillmore Papers in Oswego, New York, Mrs. Fillmore told her husband: "You have scarcely been out of my mind during the day." She expressed a desire to have him there to read to her and study with her. She thanked Providence for "so tender a friend," but also expressed concern that his affections might change in her absence, especially if he beheld "fairer and more accomplished females." She concluded her January 17, 1829, letter on a more confident note, saying she was certain that his heart was firm "and that no fascinating female can induce you to forget her whose whole heart is devoted." Despite their frequent separation, the Fillmores remained close. To help cope with their separation, Abigail Fillmore located her husband's boardinghouse on an Albany map so that she could imagine where he was.

After serving two years in the state legislature, Fillmore decided to open a law practice in Buffalo with his friend Nathan K. Hall. Abigail Fillmore moved with her husband to Buffalo in 1830. The law firm prospered, and the Fillmores purchased a house in the city. For the first time in their lives, Abigail and Millard Fillmore were financially comfortable. They joined the Unitarian Church, helped establish a lending library, and worked to improve public education. Abigail Fillmore studied French, practiced the piano, and cultivated flowers in the conservatory the couple had added to their house. She also continued to read voraciously. When her husband returned from business trips, he always brought home more books, thus establishing the core of a family library that eventually contained over 4,000 volumes. In 1832, Abigail Fillmore gave birth to her second and last child, Mary Abigail, nicknamed Abby.

Also in 1832, Fillmore was elected to the House of Representatives as an Anti-Masonic candidate. He served for two years in Washington while Mrs. Fillmore remained in New York. In 1835, he returned to Buffalo and resumed his law practice. In 1836 he was reelected to his old seat in Congress, this time as a Whig; for the first time, Abigail Fillmore accompanied her husband to Washington. Their children—Millard, age eight, and Mary Abigail, age four—remained in New York with relatives. Their decision to leave the children behind was based on several factors: their boardinghouse had no yard in which to play, the Washington heat could be oppressive, and they considered the schools inferior.

From 1836 to 1842, while Congress was in session, the Fillmores lived apart from their children, with the partial exception of 1840–1841, when their daughter Abby accompanied them to Washington. Abigail Fillmore's letters to her children reveal her commitment to the ethic of self-improvement. In letter after letter, she admonished them to study diligently and to work hard to improve themselves. Above all, she warned them not to spend their time "foolishly and idly." Mrs. Fillmore often positioned herself as a teacher in these letters: she chided her children for their carelessness in penmanship and their lack of attention to punctuation and grammar. To help improve their spelling, she listed the words they spelled incorrectly in their previous letters, along with the correct spellings. She repeatedly advised her son to use his dictionary when he did not know how to spell a word. "Take pains my dear little boy," she wrote on January 19, 1838, "that every letter we receive from you is written better than the last one." She encouraged her children to compete against one another by telling them that she was going to keep track of who improved more in their writing during the course of the year. Her critiques were balanced by praise for well-written letters and with requests that her children report on what they had learned in their lessons.

In 1838, when her son asked if she was homesick, Mrs. Fillmore replied that, although she wanted to see her children and New York friends, she was not. "I am as contented as I expected to be," she wrote on January 26, 1838. Nonetheless, the separation often was difficult for her. "I want to see you very much more than I can tell you," she wrote to her son on June 24, 1841. "I am so anxious to see you I scarcely know how to wait," she wrote to him three months later. In a July 1841 letter she wrote that she wished to be with her children, but that their father was "anxious to have me remain with him." Torn between her husband and children, Abigail Fillmore stayed with her husband.

Perhaps the most painful aspect of her separation from her family was the death of her mother in February 1838. After hearing the sad news, Mrs. Fillmore was distraught that she had been too far away to see her mother one last time. "O that I could have been there and seen her once more!" she wrote to her son in early March. She wanted to go home immediately, but could not do so because the Hudson River was still frozen and she was unable to find a traveling companion.

Abigail Fillmore took an active interest in her husband's political career and served as an adviser to him. As the wife of a congressman, she kept herself well informed on political issues. She listened to Senate and House debates in the Capitol, read newspapers, and participated in political discussions in their Washington boardinghouse. Her interest in politics was reflected in her letters to New York, which often included comments on various bills and debates. (Mrs. Fillmore followed congressional affairs especially attentively toward the end of each session, because, always eager to return to Buffalo, she wanted to know when Congress would adjourn.) Her husband appreciated her political acumen and acknowledged that he consulted her on important matters.

In addition to serving as her husband's confidante, Mrs. Fillmore played the social role of a congressional wife conscientiously. She attended parties and funerals and left her calling card at the households of government officials and foreign ministers. Once she accompanied her husband on a ceremonial visit to a navy gun ship in Annapolis. Although she avidly followed politics, Abigail Fillmore avoided placing herself in the public eye. She reportedly refused an invitation to speak at the dedication of a building, and she was not a luminary on the Washington social scene.

Mrs. Fillmore accepted the responsibilities that would further her husband's political career, but she preferred small tea parties to large social events. She was particularly interested in intellectual and musical pursuits. She enjoyed visiting galleries, listening to concerts, and viewing the curiosities on display in the Department of State. On Sundays she attended church services, weather permitting. And, as she did throughout her life, Abigail Fillmore continued her quest for self-improvement by reading and attending lectures. Despite her studious nature, Mrs. Fillmore had a lighter side. In 1841, for example, she went to the races with her daughter, bet a pair of gloves, and lost. During the Fillmores' stay in the boardinghouse, Mrs. Fillmore was relieved of some housekeeping responsibilities. Nonetheless, she spent much of her time on domestic tasks such as sewing, embroidering, and shopping. "I have been very busy," she wrote to her sister on June 19, 1837. "I scarcely find time to mend my stockings and gloves, and keep my caps etc. in order."

In 1842 Millard Fillmore declined renomination to Congress, and the Fillmores returned to New York. That summer Abigail Fillmore injured her foot when she slipped on an uneven sidewalk and it turned inward. After two weeks she began to walk, but that caused her injured foot to become more inflamed. She was confined to her bed the entire autumn, and to her room for many months after. For two years, she relied on crutches to move about. One of her greatest concerns was that her confinement would injure her health further, because it prevented her from exercising as much as she was accustomed to. In hopes of healing her foot, she consulted a doctor in New York City and traveled to Saratoga Springs. The treatments reduced the swelling, but for the rest of her life, she found it painful to walk or to stand for long periods of time.

In 1844, after failing to secure the Whig vice presidential nomination, Millard Fill-

more ran for governor of New York and narrowly lost. He continued to practice law until 1847, when he was elected state comptroller. Mrs. Fillmore accompanied him to Albany, where they again stayed in a boardinghouse. When he wrote to arrange for their lodgings in late November 1847, Fillmore explained that "my wife's health is too poor to think of troubling her with the cares of housekeeping for the present." He requested a quiet place, so that the rush and bustle would not disturb her.

While the Fillmores lived in Albany, their son, Millard, studied in Cambridge, Massachusetts, and their daughter, Abby, attended boarding school in Lenox, Massachusetts. Abigail Fillmore missed her children's company but she wanted them to secure the best education possible. In a January 11, 1848, letter she expressed concern that if her daughter stayed in Albany, her time would be "frittered away and I know not what kind of acquaintances [she] might make by seeing so much company in the parlor." Mrs. Fillmore continued to write frequently to her children. "I fear you have too much care about your dress," she wrote to her daughter on July 7, 1848. "You seem to be wanting something new all the while." She reminded her daughter to continue to keep her studies uppermost in her mind. Abigail Fillmore believed that women, like men, should work hard to cultivate their minds.

In Albany, Abigail Fillmore maintained her passion for intellectual pursuits. After speaking with a visiting theology professor, she commented in a July 25, 1848, letter: "I do not recollect when I have had such a mental treat." Besides continuing her studies through reading and attending lectures, Abigail Fillmore was drawn into the Albany social whirl. She found constant company in the boardinghouse and frequently attended parties. Her letter of January 30, 1848, stated that she was "almost worn out with dissipation." Although she socialized extensively with the Albany elite, her letters reveal her dissatisfaction with fashionable society. When she vacationed in Newport, Rhode Island, with her son in the summer of 1848, she noted that the "very gay fashionable society" there was fun to observe, but she considered it frivolous. "It is amusing to look on and see the great variety of costume, and the great effort made to rival each other at display in dress. But it does not interest me," she wrote on August 20, 1848. At Newport, she spent only a little time each day in the parlor of the boardinghouse and always returned to her room at an early hour.

In 1848, Millard Fillmore was nominated for vice president on the Whig ticket with Zachary Taylor. About that same time, Abigail Fillmore's health deteriorated even further. She developed headaches and a cough as well as back and hip problems, which her family attributed to a spinal disorder or rheumatism. She sometimes stayed in her room for days. "I almost despair of her ever enjoying health again," wrote her husband on January 4, 1849. When Fillmore moved to Washington to assume the vice presidency, his wife stayed in Buffalo for health reasons. "It seems a great task to me to pack up and move from here. I could not do it now, but I hope to be better," she wrote to her husband on March 11, 1849. After Fillmore moved to Washington, Mrs. Fillmore noted that she missed her husband "more than I ever did before in my life." Despondent at being separated from her family, Abigail Fillmore felt alone. Even when Abby was home visiting, the teenager spent little time with her mother and instead studied or socialized in the parlor. After spending a lonely birthday, Abigail Fillmore reflected in a March 14, 1849, letter to her husband that "perhaps ere another anniversary I shall be numbered with the dead. I feel a presentiment that I shall not see many more." She attributed this presentiment to her "low spirits." During this time Mrs. Fillmore received a number of visitors, however, and she made calls. She also continued to read books and kept careful track of proceedings in Washington by reading the newspapers. On March 7, 1849, she complained to her husband that she was being "beset by office seekers," but she did intercede with him in several patronage cases. Despite the distance between them, she continued to support

her husband, counseling him on March 15, 1849, to "take courage" as he faced the trials and vexations of Washington.

After a brief visit to Washington, Abigail Fillmore returned to Buffalo in April 1850. Her husband wrote to her regularly to comment on political developments and his loneliness. "You have scarcely been out of my mind," he wrote in an April 1, 1850, missive. "How I wish I could be with you!" he exclaimed. That wish was granted unexpectedly. On July 9, 1850, President Zachary Taylor died suddenly. Millard Fillmore was inaugurated president the next day. At the time, Abigail Fillmore and their two children were vacationing at a seaside resort in New Jersey. Millard Fillmore, now president, joined them in September, and the family traveled to Washington together. By October 1850, Abigail Fillmore was in Washington, ready to assume the responsibilities of the president's wife.

When she moved into the White House, Abigail Fillmore was not enthusiastic about Washington's social life and was afraid that Washington socialites would find her dull. A few years later her obituary in the *New York Daily Tribune* characterized her as such: "Mrs. Fillmore was not fitted by nature to dazzle in a ball room nor to win admiration from casual observers; nor did she find delight in crowds or ostentatious display." In a January 5, 1851, letter her friend Kate Williams worried that Abigail was "so domestic" and so fond of "a quiet home" that she would be unhappy in the White House.

Mrs. Fillmore was able to escape some of the social obligations of her position by pleading poor health. She let her more vivacious daughter serve as hostess at a number of White House events. Nevertheless, Mrs. Fillmore generally attended several weekly functions: Tuesday morning receptions, Friday evening levees, large dinners on Thursday evenings, and smaller dinners of about twenty people on Saturdays. Because of her injured ankle, standing at official functions was a particularly burdensome ordeal. Sometimes she would spend the day before a levee in bed in order to be able to stand the next day. Although Abigail

Fillmore worried that she would be considered dull, she was a lively conversationalist in smaller gatherings. Furthermore, despite her retiring character and desire to avoid the spotlight, she was regarded favorably by the public. Copies of her daguerreotype sold well, especially to women.

Perhaps Abigail Fillmore's greatest contribution during her time in the White House was establishing a library there. After moving in, she was disappointed at the lack of books in the White House. Previous occupants had brought their own and had packed them up again upon departure. Shocked at this state of affairs, Mrs. Fillmore had her husband ask Congress to fund a White House library. He did so, and Congress appropriated $2,000. With the money, Abigail Fillmore purchased several hundred volumes—sets of Shakespeare and Burns, travel narratives, biographies, histories, law treatises, religious works, and novels, including some by her favorite authors, Thackeray and Dickens. The Fillmores designated a second floor oval parlor as the library and had the room completely redecorated. Mrs. Fillmore placed her piano and her daughter's harp in the library and enjoyed having her friends over for evenings of music. One such visitor wrote to Mrs. Fillmore in February 1852, thanking her for the "many pleasant hours in social chit-chat by your cheerful fire side, sometimes over our cup of tea and the music of the evening contributing not a little to our enjoyments." Besides entertaining small groups in the library, Mrs. Fillmore also relished spending hours alone there, reading. Despite her relinquishment of some official duties, she found that she was still left with little time to read. Once, after receiving a volume titled *Female Poets of America*, Abigail sorrowfully noted that she had not had time to read it because of "the multiplicity of engagements which surround me."

Although Mrs. Fillmore regretted some of her obligations, she relished the opportunities to meet cultural leaders that her position afforded her. After hearing the famous "Swedish Nightingale," Jenny Lind, sing in Washington in 1850, Abigail Fillmore invited the singer to visit. She also entertained some of her cherished authors—William Thackery, Charles Dickens, and Washington Irving. Mrs. Fillmore worked to make the White House a center of culture during her husband's presidency.

Other aspects of being the president's wife also appealed to Mrs. Fillmore. As First Lady, she was not obliged to return visits or attend parties outside the White House. She was happy to be reunited with her husband and her children, both of whom stayed in the White House during their father's term. She and her husband often drove around Washington and the surrounding countryside in a coach and team given to the Fillmores by some of their New York supporters.

Mrs. Fillmore's domestic responsibilites were lightened by the White House staff, which took care of most of the housework. A friend in New York helped her find a seamstress and a maid who had studied hairdressing at a fashionable New York establishment. To make the White House more comfortable, the Fillmores enlarged the heating system and rewallpapered some of the rooms. They also had the first iron range installed in the kitchen, where all the cooking previously had been done in an open fireplace.

The Fillmores had only a few visitors stay with them in the White House, one of whom was Millard Fillmore's elderly father. The death of her sister in February 1851 was a heavy blow to Abigail Fillmore. After her sister's death, Mrs. Fillmore corresponded mainly with her brother, a niece, and some New York friends. Both of the summers during her husband's presidency were spent traveling back to New York to visit friends and relatives.

As First Lady, Abigail Fillmore received a number of letters from acquaintances and strangers, who asked her to intercede with the president in their behalf on issues ranging from admission to West Point to pensions and patronage jobs. Several of these supplicants later wrote effusive thank-you letters, thus suggesting that she did indeed speak for them. That her brother, David Powers, won a patronage job despite the president's opposition to nepotism suggests a powerful influence over her husband. Mrs. Fillmore also received a number of letters from church groups, benevolent associations, and individuals asking for money and other favors. One young dressmaker in New York City beseeched her to place an order to help her win a following among fashionable women, and Abigail Fillmore did so. The nature of Mrs. Fillmore's correspondence during this time suggests that the public viewed her as an accessible and sympathetic woman and social leader.

As president, Millard Fillmore worked long hours. The support he received from his wife and children made his job easier. He also benefited from his wife's continued counsel. The single most important issue of President Fillmore's term was the Compromise of 1850. A major component of the compromise was the admission of California as a free state. To pacify the South in a time of great sectional tensions, the compromise charged federal officials with capturing and returning runaway slaves in the North. Abigail Fillmore reportedly counseled her husband not to sign the Fugitive Slave Act. She was morally opposed to it and believed it would end his political career. Although the story cannot be verified, Fillmore would have been wise to follow such counsel. After the president signed the law, Northern abolitionists protested passionately, and the Whigs did not nominate him for reelection in 1852.

During her final months in the White House, Abigail Fillmore looked forward to returning to New York and spending more time with her family. She and her husband planned improvements to their house and arranged to tour the South while their possessions were moved back to Buffalo. Those plans collapsed after she caught cold during the outdoor inaugural ceremonies for Franklin Pierce in March 1853. Mrs. Fillmore had been ill during the winter, and her slight cold turned into pneumonia. Her husband summoned the best physician in the city. The doctor cupped and blistered

her several times, surely adding to her problems. Abigail Fillmore stayed in the Willard Hotel for three weeks as her condition continued to worsen. She found it hard to breathe or talk. In her final days, her family remained by her side. They talked and read to her until she passed into unconsciousness. Abigail Fillmore died of bronchial pneumonia on March 30, 1853, at the age of fifty-five.

As a sign of respect, Congress adjourned, public offices closed, and President Franklin Pierce suspended his cabinet meeting for the day. Mrs. Fillmore lay in state at the Willard Hotel, and Washington leaders came to pay their respects. Newspapers ran laudatory obituaries. The *Boston Journal* characterized her as "a lady of great strength of mind, dignified manners, genteel deportment, and much energy of character." The *New York Daily Tribune* praised her for blending "good sense with high principle." It commented on her "earnest piety" and "unaffected humility." The *Daily National Intelligencer* of Washington, D.C., described Mrs. Fillmore as "meek, unostentatious, gentle, and dignified," as an "affectionate wife, a tender and dutiful mother, and a most amiable and beloved friend." The Washington, D.C., *Union* commented on her "benevolence of character" and "unassuming" manner. An admirer from North Carolina wrote to Millard Fillmore to say that Mrs. Fillmore had served as First Lady "in a manner acceptable and admired throughout the country."

Abigail Fillmore lived in the White House at a time when women were expected to avoid activist public roles and instead devote their energies to domestic matters. Although she was well educated and politically informed, she did not challenge that expectation. Rather, she worked so that her political counsel was always behind the scenes and her image approximated that of the mid-nineteenth-century ideal of an apolitical woman devoted to home and family. Her obituaries were uniformly positive because Abigail Fillmore adhered to prevailing ideas about women's sphere. Her conventionality made her a great asset to her husband's political career. It also meant that she did not significantly reshape the position of presidential wife or refocus ideas about women's roles.

Following Abigail Fillmore's death, the Fillmore family chartered a train to take her remains back to Buffalo for burial. Her despondent husband wrote on April 12, 1853: "I feel that I have no strength, no resolution, no energy. The prospect is gloomy. My home is deserted." The family suffered yet another blow in July 1854, when the Fillmores' daughter died suddenly of cholera. Their son never married, but in February 1858, former president Millard Fillmore married once more. His second wife was Caroline McIntosh, an Albany widow.

BIBLIOGRAPHICAL ESSAY

Many of Abigail Fillmore's papers have been lost or destroyed, although a number of letters to and from her can be found among the Millard Fillmore papers, available on microfilm. Much of this essay is based on those papers. The Fillmore papers are described in the *Guide to the Microfilm Edition of the Millard Fillmore Papers*, edited by Lester W. Smith (Buffalo, N.Y., 1975). Most of the originals pertaining to Abigail Fillmore are located in the Library of the State University College, Oswego, New York. The Fillmore family letters cited in this essay come from that collection. The Buffalo and Erie County Historical Society owns the letterbooks pertaining to Millard Fillmore's presidency, but they do not contain many references to Abigail Fillmore. Some of Millard Fillmore's papers, including his reminiscences on meeting his wife, have been published in a two-volume set by the Buffalo Historical Society titled *Millard Fillmore Papers*, edited by Frank H. Severance (Buffalo, N.Y., 1970).

There are no comprehensive biographies of Abigail Fillmore. She is mentioned briefly in books about her husband, including Benson Lee Grayson's *The Unknown President: The Administration of President Millard Fillmore* (Washington, D.C., 1981) and Elbert B. Smith's *The Presidencies of Zachary Taylor and Millard Fillmore* (Lawrence, Kans., 1988). General treatments of the First Ladies also include information on Abigail Fillmore, much of it undocumented. *The Ladies of the White House*, by Laura C. Holloway (New York, 1870), contains comments on Abigail Fillmore written by one of her friends. Mary Ormsbee Whitton's *First First Ladies, 1789–1865* (New York, 1948; rpt. 1969) contains information often cited in later histories of the First Ladies. More recently, Betty Boyd Caroli, in *First Ladies* (New York, 1987), interprets Abigail Fillmore's invalidism as an excuse for avoiding a public role. Carl Sferrazza Anthony, in *First Ladies: The Saga of the Presidents' Wives and Their Power, 1789–1961* (New York, 1990), disagrees, arguing that her genuinely poor health did not prevent her from assuming a public role. Another source of information on Abigail Fillmore, particularly on her establishment of the White House library, is William Seale's history of the White House, *The President's House*, vol. 1 (Washington, D.C., 1986).

The obituaries of Abigail Fillmore were generally formulaic and contained little information on her life. Two of the better ones are found in the *New York Daily Tribune*, March 31, 1853, and the Washington, D.C., *Daily National Intelligencer*, March 31, 1853.

★★★   ★★★

Jane Means Appleton Pierce

(1806–1863)

First Lady: 1853–1857

Debbie Mauldin Cottrell

Jane Means Appleton was born in Hampton, New Hampshire, on March 12, 1806, the third of six children of Elizabeth Means Appleton and Jesse Appleton. The Appleton family enjoyed their status as prestigious New Englanders with connections to business, religion, law, and academics. Jane's father, a Congregational minister, served as president of Bowdoin College in Brunswick, Maine. After the death of her father in 1819, Jane's mother moved her family to the Means Mansion in Amherst, New Hampshire. During her teenage years, Jane enjoyed close relationships with her sister Mary, who married and moved to nearby Lowell, Massachusetts, and her sister Elizabeth, who married a Bowdoin professor, Alpheus S. Packard.

Little is known of Jane's educational background, but she apparently received some general training and was particularly fond of literature. As a young girl, her mental capacities were much stronger than her physical ones, which marked her as frail, nervous, and sensitive.

Jane met Franklin Pierce through Packard, who had taught Pierce at Bowdoin. At the time the two met in 1826, the twenty-two-year-old Pierce was about to begin his legal career. During the courtship, Pierce, a Jacksonian Democrat, was elected to the New Hampshire House of Representatives and to the United States Congress. He found Jane charming and delicate, and she returned his affection despite the obvious superior social standing of her family. While she was never comfortable with his profession, Jane accepted Franklin's marriage proposal and seemed determined to stand up to her mother's disapproval of her choice for a spouse. The couple married on November 19, 1834, in Amherst.

In late 1834, the newlyweds moved to Washington, D.C., where Pierce continued to serve in Congress. From her earliest days as a politician's wife, Mrs. Pierce exhibited a combination of characteristics that would affect her future role in the White House. Shy and retiring, she also projected the image of a well-bred New England woman with a strict sense of propriety. Plagued by ill health, she often was unable to participate in the social life expected of her. Regardless of her health, she had little interest in the world of politics, finding it a sordid and demeaning career that bore an ill influence on her husband. The tendency of her husband to join other politicians in heavy drinking particularly concerned her.

In the first few months of her marriage, Mrs. Pierce showed a cautious approach to embracing her new life and role. She wrote to her father-in-law soon after arriving in the nation's capital in 1834 that she and her husband "have both generally been very well and not very unhappy." Yet she also made clear that she was not overly fond of Washington and preferred quiet dinners at home to the various social invitations they received from well-known politicians. She visited the White House for a New Year's Day reception in 1835 and was impressed both with its furnishings and its occupant, Andrew Jackson, whom she described to a relative as "mild and chastened . . . a venerable and fine-looking old man." Davy Crockett, on the other hand, offended her New England aristocratic sensibilities, and she described him as "conceited, stupid, silly."

Before the end of 1835, Mrs. Pierce's frail nature caused her to leave Washington to stay with her mother in Amherst. The Pierces had acquired a home in Hillsborough, New Hampshire, but she spent little time there and left the running of the household to others. Thus, less than one year into their marriage, the Pierces began to spend a good deal of time apart. He wrote her daily from Washington and expressed sincere concern over her health. She appeared to miss him deeply, but not the city where his work required that he be. While visiting family at Lowell in February 1836, she gave birth to their first child, Franklin, Jr. The child died three days later, beginning a series of personal tragedies for the Pierces and their offspring.

After the loss of their son, the Pierces relocated their New Hampshire home from Hillsborough to Concord, largely to accommodate Mrs. Pierce's desire for a different locale. She continued to experience health problems, even returning to Lowell to undergo treatment with leeches to improve her constitution. By 1837, Mrs. Pierce found her health little improved, and her outlook darkened when the state legislature of New Hampshire elected her husband to the U.S. Senate. She grudgingly returned with him to Washington, but made it clear that she was eager for him to find another career that would allow them more income in a more desirable city. During her husband's years as a senator, Mrs. Pierce gave birth to Frank Robert (b. September 1839) and to Benjamin "Bennie" (b. April 1841). With the arrival of her sons, Jane Pierce argued strongly for their need to find a more wholesome environment in which to raise a family.

Franklin Pierce completed his Senate term in 1842 and left public office, briefly providing his wife with some of her happiest married days. The Pierces returned to Concord, where he practiced law. The family worshiped regularly at South Congregational Church, and Jane Pierce's disposition brightened away from the world of politics and Washington. Pierce stayed active in New Hampshire politics, chairing the state Democratic Party and serving as a federal district attorney in the state. But, out of deference to his wife, he declined other political appointments, including offers to return to the U.S. Senate, run for governor of New Hampshire, and become President James K. Polk's attorney general. Although Mrs. Pierce's health initially improved upon their return to New Hampshire, she remained frail and, by 1845, was weaker than she had been in 1842. The death of their older son from typhus fever in 1843 worsened Mrs. Pierce's condition and distanced her from her husband.

It was with some difficulty, then, that Pierce determined in 1846 that, despite his wife's health and her lack of support, he would enlist to fight in the war with Mexico. He did so with great concern for her health, even arranging for live-in assistance while he was away. At the same time, he believed that issues of patriotism and conscience required him to leave her. Mrs. Pierce never supported his decision with any enthusiasm, but she did come to accept it and looked forward to the regular letters he sent her, which usually began with the endearment "Dearest Jeanie." When he returned after the war a local hero, the Pierces enjoyed several years of serenity in Concord. Her health improved and she devoted herself to raising Bennie and enjoying his youthful spirit. Their only surviving child was close to both parents, but he shared many of his mother's personality traits and developed a particularly close bond with her.

Their time of relative happiness was shattered in 1852, when Pierce received the Democratic Party's nomination for president. Word of the nomination came to the Pierces while they were taking a ride outside of Boston, where they were visiting. Although this development was not a complete surprise, Pierce had downplayed its likelihood to his wife and had in fact received the nomination only on the party's forty-ninth ballot as a compromise candidate. Her shock and displeasure were evident in her immediate response: she fainted. Later, Bennie indicated that he, too, was unhappy with the news because he knew his mother did not like it.

Throughout the campaign of 1852, Jane Pierce stayed out of the public's eye and prayed that her husband would be defeated. She had no interest in returning to Washington and believed that life as the president's wife would only be worse than her previous unhappy stints as a politician's spouse. Although she was relatively healthy during this time, she remained susceptible to frailty and ill health, and the prospect of fulfilling the responsibilities of the president's wife was certainly a daunting one to her. Pierce's victory over Whig candidate Winfield Scott in November 1852, then, depressed her, and it was with great reservations that she began to make plans to occupy the White House.

In her already downtrodden frame of mind, Mrs. Pierce next suffered the one thing she was least capable of sustaining— the loss of her only remaining child. On January 6, 1853, the Pierces, along with their eleven-year-old son, boarded a train in Massachusetts, where they had been visiting relatives, to return to New Hampshire and make final preparations for the move to Washington. The train traveled a short distance before derailing. Although his parents were uninjured, Bennie was crushed in the wreckage and died before their eyes.

Whatever limitations and hesitations Mrs. Pierce exhibited about being a public figure before Bennie's death now only deepened and worsened as she fell into great despair and depression just as she was elevated to the White House. The loss was great for both parents, and it had a traumatic impact on their marriage. While her husband blamed himself for Bennie's death and saw it as a form of punishment for his own weaknesses, Mrs. Pierce interpreted the loss as God's way of removing a distraction to his presidency. She did not see any positive will of God in this matter, but rather a necessary act from above to allow her husband to pursue the career on which he insisted. In her eyes, her husband's political career continued to disrupt their lives and inflict tragedy upon them. She found some solace in religion and worship, but she remained steadfast in her grief and saw no need to overcome it or find healing through her new position.

Jane Pierce did not attend her husband's inauguration on March 4, 1853. She stayed in Baltimore during the festivities, with the assistance of her late uncle's second wife and a close friend, Abby Kent Means. Her relationship with her husband suffered further during this time when she learned from a cousin that although Pierce had told her he did not want or seek the presidential nomination, he had actually worked very hard to be selected as a candidate. She resented his misrepresentation and his covert effort to take their family back into politics. Coupled with her grief, this anger at her husband took her into the White House a few weeks later a most unhappy woman.

As the president's wife, Jane Pierce found little to occupy her time. A New Hampshire hotel proprietor and his wife oversaw the day-to-day operations of the White House. Other workers tended the gardens and stable, and Abby Means, who moved into the White House with the Pierces, served as a hostess when social duties were required. Mrs. Pierce held no evening receptions, rarely dined with guests, and entertained only a few close family members and friends from New Hampshire.

Taking refuge in her grief, she secluded herself—often writing letters to her dead son—and insisted on one of the most limited social calendars the White House had ever known. Family members worried about her depression and ill health. They also worried about her inability to give her husband the strength and support he needed as president. As Roy Franklin Nichols, a later biographer of her husband, noted a little more than a century later, First Lady Jane Pierce surrendered herself "to an all-enveloping melancholy."

There was little change in her approach and style during her years in the White House, although she gradually became more active. She continued to find some comfort in religion, worshiping regularly with her husband at Washington churches. She also encouraged workers in the White House to do the same. She would not attend concerts or other cultural events in Washington with the president, but she did occasionally sail with him on the Potomac and vacation with him and a few close friends in Virginia. Mrs. Pierce developed a friendship with Varina Howell Davis, wife of Secretary of War Jefferson Davis. Varina Davis became an active hostess during the Pierce administration, which, further subduing social life at the White House, included among its cabinet members three widowers. Mrs. Pierce appreciated Mrs. Davis's willingness to take a lead in Washington's social life, and she enjoyed the Davises' young son.

Toward the end of her husband's administration, Mrs. Pierce dined with a few diplomats and even received guests in the White House to inaugurate Washington's social season. Those who met her found her gracious and warm. Still, this small stirring of activity did not offset her overall reluctance or inability to assume any full-time role as the president's wife. Her health did not improve while she lived in the White House, and, as her husband's political fortunes fell over slavery politics, the Pierces quietly completed their years in Washington in early 1857.

Mrs. Pierce remained in ill health after resuming private life. She and her husband made an extended trip to Europe late in 1857, but her continued grief over Bennie, as well as the recent death of Abby Means, offset any sense of rejuvenation that might have afforded. By 1860, the Pierces had reestablished residence in Concord, although Jane Pierce also spent much time with relatives in Massachusetts. Mrs. Pierce's health continued to decline, although letters written between the Pierces during this time indicate that she had some interest in the politics of the unfolding Civil War. These and other letters also reflect ongoing concern for her health. As she wrote to her niece in an unpublished letter on August 15, 1862: "[M]y health at its best is uncertain."

Jane Pierce died at age fifty-seven on December 2, 1863, in Andover, Massachusetts. The official cause of death was consumption. Upon her death, Nathaniel Hawthorne, her husband's college classmate and her New England friend, attended the former president and joined him in mourning. Jane Pierce was buried beside her children in the Concord, New Hampshire, cemetery.

Known to Americans as a sad, grieving, invalid First Lady, she did little to overcome or change her image or to enhance the role of the president's wife. Much of her disdain for the tasks she faced in this role were well established before the death of her third son, but that tragedy allowed her to minimize the expectations and activities of the First Lady. For a shy, frail, aristocratic New Englander, marriage to the politically aspiring Democrat Franklin Pierce presented challenges that complicated the lives of both husband and wife. Jane Pierce never enjoyed sustained happiness or health, but she remained steadfastly religious and committed, in her own way, to her marriage. Her husband's tenderness and affection did not overcome the differences and tragedies in their lives, but Mrs. Pierce accepted them and seemed to understand that her husband truly loved her. For a biographical entry of Mrs. Pierce compiled by Laura Holloway, the former president wrote of his wife shortly before his own death in 1869 that "her natural endowments were of a high order. . . . She inherited a judgment singularly clear and correct, and a taste almost unerring."

Many Americans sympathized with Jane Pierce during her lifetime. She was not subject to excessive public scrutiny or criticism for her approach, and contemporary observers noted a sense of heroism and strength to her character as she dealt with the tragic loss of her third child while living in the White House. Even after the turn of the century, Alexander K. McClure wrote very kindly of her in his *Recollections of Half a Century* as a "highly cultivated and accomplished woman" who was "always most happy in the circle of her own home." Surveys conducted in the 1980s and 1990s indicate, however, a less benevolent view of her. Whether being judged for her overall effectiveness, background, value to the United States and her husband, integrity, intelligence, independence, or courage, Jane Pierce is consistently ranked in the bottom quarter of First Ladies.

BIBLIOGRAPHICAL ESSAY

The largest collection of Jane Pierce's letters resides in the Amos Lawrence and Amos A. Lawrence Papers at the Massachusetts Historical Society. Several family letters concerning Mrs. Pierce are reprinted in Annie M. Means, *Amherst and Our Family Tree* (Boston, 1921). The disappearance of much of the correspondence between Franklin and Jane Pierce has led to speculation that the former president destroyed the letters before his death.

No full-length biography exists of Jane Pierce. Roy Franklin Nichols, in *Franklin Pierce: Young Hickory of the Granite Hills* (2nd ed., Philadelphia, 1958), considers her throughout his work. The quotation from Jane Pierce's 1834 letter to her father-in-law is on page 77 of Nichols's book. Larry Gara, *The Presidency of Franklin Pierce* (Lawrence, Kans., 1991), is a more recent study of the president, although its treatment of Mrs. Pierce is much more brief than Nichols's. The entry on Mrs. Pierce in Laura C. Holloway, *The Ladies of the White House* (Philadelphia, 1881), is based on contemporary letters and memories.

Helpful material is also found in Lloyd C. Taylor, Jr., "A Wife for Mr. Pierce," *New England Quarterly* 28 (September 1955): 339–348, from which the quotations about Mrs. Pierce's 1835 White House visit are taken. Taylor also wrote the entry for Jane Pierce in *Notable American Women*, vol. 3 (Cambridge, Mass., 1971). Alexander K. McClure, *Recollections of Half a Century* (Salem, Mass., 1902), contains his assessment of Jane Pierce as First Lady. Jane Pierce's letter to her niece of August 15, 1862, appeared in a Vintage Cover Story autograph catalog, a copy of which is now in the Center for American History, University of Texas. An obituary for Jane Pierce appeared in the *Boston Recorder* on January 8, 1864.

★★★   ★★★

Mary Ann Todd Lincoln

(1818–1882)

First Lady: 1861–1865

Jean H. Baker

Mary Ann Todd was born in Lexington, Kentucky, on December 12, 1818. Her parents, Robert Smith Todd and Eliza Parker Todd, already had two daughters when Mary became the unspecial third daughter in a growing family. Soon after Mary was weaned, her mother became pregnant with a first son, and there followed in eighteen- and twenty-two-month intervals another daughter, Ann, and a son, George Rodgers Clark Todd, who was born in 1825. After her younger sister's birth, the middle name Ann was dropped from Mary's name. Immediately after George's birth, Eliza Parker Todd fell ill of puerperal sepsis—the bacterial fever that nineteenth-century women called "the childbed fevers." Mary was an impressionable six when her mother died.

Both of Mary's parents were members of the wealthy gentry of Lexington, a city that aspired to be "the Athens of the West." Her father was the son and nephew of Lexington's founding triumvirate of Todd brothers who, in 1775, named the new community after a distant revolutionary battle fought in Massachusetts. During his life, Mary's father was a well-known Whig politician. He was also, at various times, a partner in a dry-goods firm, a banker, and the owner of a factory near the Ohio River that produced cotton yarn and coarse fabrics. Along with his wife and aided by the ten slaves who lived with the family, he was known for the hospitality extended in the parlors of his substantial three-story brick home near the center of Lexington.

The Parkers, from whom Mary's mother was descended, also held a respected place in Lexington. Through intermarriage, the Todds and Parkers created a circle of close kin. Mary's maternal grandmother lived next door throughout her childhood.

Two years after his wife's death, Mary's father married Elizabeth Humphreys—a woman whom Mary and her older sisters Elizabeth and Frances despised. Promptly another set of infant Todds arrived in a family that eventually numbered fifteen. Often at odds with her stepmother, Mary spent a good deal of time with her grandmother Parker. At school she stood out among her siblings, cousins, and friends for her lively intelligence and her interest in the academic studies considered irrelevant to the lives of the sociable ladies of antebellum Lexington.

Mary attended the Shelby Female Academy, later known as Ward's. In 1832 she began to board—in a most unusual arrangement that suggested friction at home—at Madame Charlotte Mentelle's select family boarding school in Lexington. There she became fluent in French and learned decorative needlework, along with the traditional subjects of reading, writing, arithmetic, and history.

Mary's twelve years of schooling place her among a handful of early American women in terms of education. Throughout her life she continued to display an interest in intellectual matters. An avid reader, Mary was a lively conversationalist whose schooling was displayed in the carefully crafted letters that she wrote to friends and family.

Another of Mary's youthful interests revolved around the unladylike concerns of politics. One story has Mary riding her pony to Senator Henry Clay's nearby Ashland estate, where she told the recently defeated presidential candidate that someday she, too, expected to live in the White House. Another reports her arguing with a boyfriend over her conviction that the Whigs were a better political party than the Democrats. In the meantime her father had begun his political career as a Whig legislator. Robert Todd was campaigning for the Kentucky State Senate when he died of cholera in 1849.

In 1832 Mary's older sister Elizabeth married a lawyer and aspiring politician, Ninian Edwards, and moved to Springfield, the new capital of Illinois. Soon her sister Frances followed, marrying William Wallace, a physician. Briefly in 1837, and then permanently in 1839, twenty-one-year-old Mary Todd left the crowded, unfriendly household established by her stepmother. Her plans for this time are unclear, although she may have intended to become a schoolteacher. Moving to Springfield, she lived with her sister Elizabeth and led a lively social life. Her brother-in-law Ninian Edwards, then an Illinois attorney general, once described Mary as so attractive as to make a bishop forget his prayers.

In the Edwards household, most of the men Mary Todd met were interested in public affairs. They included several local politicians as well as Stephen Douglas, later an Illinois senator and Democratic presidential aspirant in 1860. She was most attracted to Abraham Lincoln. Lincoln won a seat in the Illinois legislature and moved to Springfield from New Salem in 1837. Mary's sisters opposed their courtship, finding them an oddly matched couple. She was short, ruddy, plump, tempestuous, and aristocratic—a self-described "ruddy pine knot with periodic exuberances of flesh"; he was tall, gaunt, often depressed, and plebeian. Mary's sister Frances called him the ugliest man in Springfield.

Like many couples, Mary Todd and Abraham Lincoln had a sometimes stormy courtship. This was a time in American history when romantic passion, common interests, and congeniality, rather than considerations of land and cows and family determined the choice of a spouse. Lincoln hesitated to marry because he was uncertain that he could afford to support a wife. His earnings from his law practice fluctuated around $1,500 a year. Lincoln felt he must be the breadwinner for his family, and, even at thirty-one years of age in 1841, he was uncertain of his prospects.

On the other hand, Mary Todd, like many other young women, hesitated to make a commitment because courting was a rare time of power for her. Once married she would lose her independence and her legal and economic rights under the doctrine of coverture. She must also be certain about her husband's habits and commitment. Marriage at a time in which divorce was not an established legal procedure was forever. Only twenty-three years old in 1841, Mary was also having a good time as one of the most popular single women in Springfield.

By 1842, what Mary Todd called "lover's eyes" had prevailed. On a rainy night in November, she married Abraham Lincoln in the home of her sister Elizabeth.

Next followed nearly two decades of invisible domesticity, as Mary Todd Lincoln lived a traditional middle-class female life in Springfield, a thriving community of 5,300. The Lincolns began their married life, as did many American couples of the era, in a boardinghouse. Soon Mrs. Lincoln was pregnant, and their first son, Robert Smith Todd, was born on August 1, 1843. Edward Dickinson Lincoln followed in March 1846. Young Eddie was sick most of his short life. In the second of a series of devastating losses, Eddie died in 1850 of tuberculosis. Almost immediately Mary Lincoln was pregnant with her third son, William Wallace Lincoln, who was born in December 1850. Because Willie must have a playmate, according to his mother, she was soon pregnant again. In April 1853 the last Lincoln son, Thomas ("Tad"), was born.

By this time Mary and Abraham Lincoln had moved into a one-story, five-room cottage with a loft on an eighth of an acre at the corner of Eighth and Jackson streets in Springfield. Her father had helped with the purchase of this house. Later, again with financial help from her father, the Lincolns finished off the upstairs. Under her tasteful direction, an artisan's cottage became a proper middle-class home with two parlors, a dining room, and four new second-story bedrooms.

Like most women of her status, Mary Lincoln had intermittent domestic help, usually from the daughters of farmers who came to town to earn some money. At one point an Irish woman lived with the family. But, for the most part, Mary Lincoln was responsible for the female chores of cooking, cleaning, sewing, doing the wash (which took most of Monday and Tuesday), entertaining at her famous "strawberry parties," nursing sick members of her family, and raising her sons. In Springfield she was remembered as an engaged mother who played games with her sons and organized birthday parties for large numbers of their friends.

Besides running the household, Mary Lincoln also contributed to her husband's career by teaching him the etiquette and good manners expected of middle-class Americans. Having grown up among Lexington's gentry, she was well equipped to instruct the head of the household in how he should look and act. She was quick to correct him whenever he answered the door in shirtsleeves, rubbed his hands along his trousers after eating, or used the wrong knife; in this regard Mary Lincoln sought to gentrify a man who had grown up in the country. She also supervised the clothes of a man who, before his marriage, wore denims eighteen inches above his shoes and sometimes unmatched socks.

During these years Lincoln was often away, following the court sessions to the tiny courthouses in the Seventh Judicial Circuit, which stretched through central Illinois. In 1850, for example, he was away from home over half the year, and, during these absences, Mary Lincoln was in charge of the household. Abraham Lincoln also remained active in time-consuming Whig politics and was elected to four terms in the Illinois legislature. In 1846 he won a seat in the 30th United States Congress as one of seven representatives from Illinois. His wife and children accompanied the new congressman to Washington and lived across from the United States Capitol in a boardinghouse.

In later years such a move would not be considered unusual, but, even after the Civil War, most wives, especially those with young children, remained at home. In Washington, Mary Lincoln several times watched the sessions of Congress from the galleries. During a spring 1848 visit to her family in Lexington, Mrs. Lincoln wrote and received letters reflecting a mutual affection: "I shall be impatient till I see you," the thirty-nine-year-old congressman wrote, to which his wife replied: "How much I wish we were together this evening."

Upon returning to Springfield, Mary Lincoln continued to encourage her husband's political career. In 1850, when Abraham Lincoln sought a patronage job, in her careful handwriting she wrote his letters of solicitation to well-placed Whigs. When Lincoln was offered the governorship of faraway Oregon, Mary Lincoln successfully opposed a move to the frontier—which would have reduced his opportunities to become a national leader of the new Republican Party. She actively campaigned in 1854 and 1858 when her husband ran for a seat in the U.S. Senate—a position that, at the time, was determined by the vote of state legislators.

At the time, the two-party system in the United States was undergoing a realignment. Issues relating to the expansion of slavery in the territories caused a shift in traditional allegiances. The Illinois Senate seat was contested by Whigs, Free-Soilers, Democrats, and the new party that Lincoln joined—the Republicans. Not only did Mary Lincoln discuss politics with her husband, but she also joined with him in filling several tiny notebooks with the name and partisan allegiance of each legislator. When the legislature voted in January 1855, Mary Lincoln and her sister Elizabeth were in the gallery of the state capitol. They looked on as Lincoln released his delegates to Lyman Trumbull in order to break a deadlock and prevent the election of a Democrat.

Mary Lincoln's greatest contributions came in the years after her husband's first defeat for the U.S. Senate. In this period she encouraged his public career. A newspaper reporter who shared a ride with Lincoln during the 1850s quoted him as saying that his wife insisted that he would be senator and even president of the United States, at which Lincoln shook with laughter.

In 1858 Mary Lincoln's predictions became more realistic when Lincoln again ran for the U.S. Senate. This was the occasion of the Lincoln-Douglas debates, and she traveled to Alton to hear the last debate, in which her husband took the ethical high ground, arguing that his opponent, Stephen Douglas, did not care about the immoral institution of slavery. Douglas, a former suitor of Mrs. Lincoln's, won the vote from the legislature.

Throughout the 1850s, there is other evidence of Mary Lincoln's unusual interest in and support of her husband's political career. She wrote to friends in Kentucky to clarify his position on slavery. She explained his ideas about the Know-Nothing party, which opposed the immigration of Irish and Catholics. More likely to have opinions on specific issues rather than a formal belief system, Mary Lincoln was nonetheless ahead of her time in her interest in the Republican Party platform. She took an active role in discussing with her husband the political prospects of his competitors, perceptively noting in the mid-1850s that the Democrats were losing ground in the state of Illinois.

By 1856, Abraham Lincoln had a national reputation. That year he received 110 votes for vice president at the Republican convention. In 1860 Mary Lincoln's efforts were rewarded when, though a dark horse among better-known candidates such as New York's William Seward, Lincoln was nominated for president at the party's national convention in Chicago. During the long, hot summer before the election, she became—as she would remain for the rest of her life—public property. When reporters and national figures came to Springfield to survey the candidate, she was available for comment and sometimes a tour of the Lincoln house. Having no reservations about her new status, Mary Lincoln welcomed her husband's victory. In Springfield, Lincoln's friends remembered that after he heard the Republican electors had won in Pennsylvania, he hurried home, calling out: "Mary, Mary, we are elected."

Even before the Lincolns—eighteen-year-old Robert, eleven-year-old Willie, eight-year-old Tad, and forty-three-year-old Mary—accompanied the new president to Washington, Mary Lincoln signaled what she intended to be her future role as her husband's adviser. She wrote one of her husband's campaign managers about an aspirant for a cabinet position, condemning Norman Judd, who had been one of Lincoln's earlier competitors in Illinois. As the disruption of the Union approached, she began to receive threatening letters from the South with skulls and crossbones. Even as she exulted about the realization of her ambitions, Mary Lincoln experienced anxiety about what lay ahead for the family that was the center of her life.

Before her husband's inauguration in March 1861, Mary Lincoln began preparations for her role as the mistress of the White House. Sensitive to patronizing, uninformed newspaper accounts of her husband's plainness and her own vulgarity, she traveled to New York to buy new clothes. At a time when most wives of public officials were invisible, Mary Lincoln was determined to make her mark as a hostess and as a symbol of good taste.

Mary Todd Lincoln's tenure in the White House coincided with the most brutal war in American history. Her four years in Washington began with the newly formed Confederacy's firing on Fort Sumter in April, just weeks after her husband's inauguration in March. They ended with her husband's assassination in Ford's Theatre, just four days after the Southern commander Robert E. Lee surrendered the Army of Northern Virginia. At a critical moment in the nation's history, Mary Todd Lincoln inhabited not only the male sphere of public affairs in her efforts to influence patronage and to improve the White House. She also lived in the more traditional private female domain of domesticity—raising her children, managing a home (which happened as well to be a public place), and supporting her husband in the upstairs rooms that were the customary domain of the presidents' wives.

Immediately after her husband's inauguration, Mary Lincoln planned the interior improvements to the White House that

would stand as one of her important, if untimely, accomplishments. Many citizens were repelled that she would attempt such a transformation during wartime. But, like many Americans, she was shocked at the condition of the thirty-one-room mansion, including broken furniture, peeling wallpaper, fifty-year-old soiled rugs, and tawdry decorations. In the state dining room there was matched china service for only ten. This First Lady (and Mary Lincoln was the first president's wife to be called by that title) began immediately to plan for the mansion's refurbishing.

By this time the Union was at war, and rumors persisted that the president's family would be kidnapped by Confederate forces stationed across the Potomac in nearby Alexandria, Virginia. Mary Lincoln stood her ground and refused to leave her husband. Instead, as the Union Army was recruited and then trained in Washington, she grew accustomed to living with troops camped in the East Room. In late April, when Northern regiments finally reached Washington and paraded past the White House, she waved her relief from a second-floor window.

By the middle of May, despite continued warnings that journeys through Maryland were not safe, the First Lady left for Philadelphia and New York to buy wallpaper and furnishings. Her ambitious intentions were both private and public. The latter was especially crucial during a time in which she believed the home of the president must stand as a symbol to foreign ambassadors of the continuing power of the American republic. A correspondent for the *London Times* began the practice of referring to Mrs. Lincoln as "First Lady," while some American papers called her "the American Queen." With the French and British uncertain of their neutrality, she believed that her job was to make the White House express the authority of a legitimate, if imperiled, government.

In doing so, Mary Lincoln reversed the customary arrangement between the commissioner of public buildings, who usually did the buying for the White House, and previous presidents' wives, who had played little role in the process of decorating the White House. In the spring and summer of 1861, she led the way into the stores and made her selections. A merchant was dispatched to Paris to buy elegant French wallpaper. From Alexander Stewart's department store in New York she chose rugs and curtains. The existing White House china had been purchased ten years before, during President Franklin Pierce's administration. Mary Lincoln picked a 190-piece French Limoges service decorated with royal purple and double gilt with the arms of the United States on each piece. Testifying to her own politics, the gold border with its two entwined lines signified the North and South. Unable to resist a bargain, she ordered a duplicate set of the porcelain for the Lincoln family, replacing the seal of the United States with her own initials.

Soon visitors marveled at the improvements in the White House, which included heavy, gold-fringed draperies in the Green Room, French wallpaper costing over $3,220 in the Gold Room, and new damask curtains and an expensive carpet in the East Room. The exact cost of this refurbishing is unclear, though Mary eventually made eleven trips to New York to buy furnishings for the White House. What was soon obvious, however, was that Mary Lincoln had overspent an allowance expected to last four years. In actuality the commissioner of public buildings signed the vouchers; yet the very visible and unconventional Mrs. Lincoln was held responsible. Her arrival in Washington came at a time when Americans demanded strict economy. Public money must go to the war effort, not what her husband called "flub-a-dubs."

Mary Lincoln's spending complicated her relationship with her husband. Lincoln was furious about the bills. In Springfield his wife had run her home without much interference from him, in an example of the domestic feminism that led many American women to control aspects of household management by the mid-nineteenth century. In Washington the president confronted her with expenditures that he announced would "stink" in

the land. Other officials argued on the floor of Congress that the government must "place every last dollar in the war chest." As it would in other instances, the ambivalent, public-private status of the First Lady led to confusion and conflict.

Eventually, money from other public projects was redirected to pay White House bills. A new commissioner of public buildings was appointed. In previous administrations deficiency allowances were buried in civic appropriation bills and no one held the president's wife responsible, as Mary Lincoln would be. Meanwhile the First Lady found her own ways of trying to pay off the overexpenditure by holding a sale of secondhand White House furniture and even by trying to sell the manure from the stables where her sons kept their ponies. She also pared the staff of the White House in order to achieve some savings. There is some evidence that the White House gardener padded his expense accounts for the grounds and returned money to the First Lady to pay off the overexpenditures generated by refurbishing the interior.

Unlike some nineteenth-century presidents, Lincoln had nothing to do with the White House, as his wife organized and ran the mansion. Several times before his wife left town, the president asked her advice about the administration of the household. Longtime White House employees were astonished, as one later explained, that Mary Lincoln was "the absolute mistress of all that part of the White House inside the vestibule and of all the upper floor east of the folder doors."

Throughout her four years in Washington, Mary Lincoln refused to spend her husband's $25,000 salary on household expenses. In the past, most presidents had retired poorer than when they arrived. Under Mary Lincoln's direction, however, her family saved money, which became the bulk of Lincoln's estate—and her $38,000 inheritance after his assassination.

Mary Lincoln also intended to make the White House a center of social importance. At first, with Washington full of Southern sympathizers, this ambition was difficult to achieve. In time, however, Mrs. Lincoln's parties became elegant affairs. According to the influential *New York Herald*, "[Mary] is more self-possessed than Lincoln and has accommodated more readily than her taller half to the exalted station to which she has been so strangely advanced from the simple social life of the little inland capital of Illinois."

State dinners, usually arranged by public officials, had long been a staple of the Washington season. Customarily the secretary of state hosted the first dinner of a new administration in honor of the diplomatic corps. Instead, Mary Lincoln organized the dinner, much to the irritation of Secretary of State William Seward.

Mary Lincoln further changed White House entertainment by organizing evening parties intended to raise the spirits of both her husband and the members of the government during a grim war. As many as 4,000 guests attended her receptions on what she referred to as her "handshake days." It was generally recognized that during her tenure the White House was, in the words of one of the mansion's longtime employees, "more given over to the public than in any other [administration]." This aspect of domesticity—serving as hostess—became part of her role as a public figure.

Elegantly dressed in the New York clothes for which she sought donors, Mary Lincoln circulated among the guests in her lavish, but tasteful, gowns. Like many leaders of fashion, she was criticized for her high taste and, sometimes, her low necklines. In 1861, soon after her arrival in Washington, she posed for Matthew Brady, the popular photographer, in an expensive off-the-shoulder, heavy silk gown, onto which her seamstress, Elizabeth Keckley, had sewed hundreds of velvet bows and dots. With her attention to style, the First Lady became a celebrity closely watched by the corps of journalists. The latter, now including a few women, were stationed in Washington awaiting news from the battlefield. Mary Lincoln made good copy for them.

Most of Mary Lincoln's public appearances took place during the traditional twice-a-week winter and spring receptions, when visitors crowded into the East Room, sometimes snipping material from the damask curtains. There were also the exhausting levees on New Year's Day and holidays, with special entertainments for the diplomatic corps, judiciary, and Congress. In August 1861 she entertained a member of Europe's royalty when France's Prince Napoleon, the nephew of Napoleon Bonaparte, arrived at the White House for dinner and was admitted, to his surprise, by young Willie Lincoln. That evening Mary Lincoln spoke the French that she had learned many years before at Madame Mentelle's boarding school.

In time she placed her stamp on the White House entertainments, with her evening soirees of elegant buffet dinners and fancy ices from caterers. Irritating the Washington caterers and merchants, she gave her functions a cosmopolitan flair by extending the White House trade to Philadelphians and New Yorkers. At one party in 1861 the caterer was from New York, and in another innovation the Marine Band played its new polka, "The Mary Lincoln Polka." Certainly, the First Lady was unique in the creation of an American salon where intellectuals, including Massachusetts Senator Charles Sumner, and literary figures, such as Nathaniel Willis, gathered after dinner for conversation in the Blue Room.

During one of her parties, Willie Lincoln lay ill upstairs and both parents spent most of the evening by his bedside. Ten days later, in February 1862, the third and most accomplished of the Lincoln sons died, probably of typhoid fever. Again Mary Lincoln faced a tragedy. Suffering from what her seamstress and friend, the African-American former slave Elizabeth Keckley, called "paroxysms of grief," marked by weeping, shaking, and weakness, she stayed in her bed. Unable to attend Willie's funeral in the East Room, Mary Lincoln never recovered from her favorite son's death.

Wearing the mourning clothes of the bereaved, months later she had sufficiently recovered to move to the family's summer quarters—the Soldiers' Home—three miles from the White House in the northern part of the city. The family moved there every summer to avoid the stifling heat and dangerous vapors of Washington. At the Soldiers' Home, the Lincolns' life was less formal and more private.

Most summers the First Lady also traveled north with her youngest son. Determined to protect Tad, she sought out resorts in New Hampshire and New Jersey and waited for word that the capital's diseases had disappeared with the cooler weather. After Willie's death, she became interested in spiritualism and met with its practitioners in Boston and New York.

The possibility of raising the dead became a popular consolation for many parents whose sons died in the war. Convinced that, with the help of seancers, Willie Lincoln returned to the White House and spoke to her of his happy life across the river, she invited spiritualists to the White House. A curious president watched one seance. She also made frequent visits to the home of a spiritualist in nearby Georgetown. Like so many of her activities, the First Lady's dalliance with spiritualism brought ridicule, especially from members of established religions.

The war brought other losses to Mary Lincoln. Two months after Willie's death her half brother, Sam Todd, a soldier in the Confederate Army, was killed leading a charge at the Battle of Shiloh in Tennessee. Later, her half sister Emilie's husband, General Benjamin Hardin Helm, died during the Battle of Chattanooga. Like many other American families during the Civil War, especially those in border states such as Kentucky and Maryland, the Todds were divided in their allegiance. Some members of the family, including Mary and her sisters Elizabeth Edwards and Frances Wallace, supported the Union, while others, like her younger half brothers, joined the Confederate Army.

Mary Lincoln suffered for her family's Confederate ties. In Washington scurrilous gossip circulated that the First Lady was a traitor, intent on influencing her husband toward defeatist, proslavery policies. The charges were untrue and unfair. But, when her favorite half sister, Emilie Todd Helm—having become a destitute widow—came to live temporarily in the White House in December 1863, the newspapers renewed their charges of Mary Lincoln's supposedly secessionist principles. When Emilie Helm demanded a license to sell cotton, while refusing to take an oath of allegiance to the Union, Lincoln refused. The sisters' close relationship was severed after Emilie wrote an angry letter to both Lincolns blaming them for her husband's and brother's deaths.

While her brothers were dying on the battlefield and her sisters were exiling themselves through their intractable commitment to the Confederacy, Mary Lincoln was also losing the attention of her husband. In many ways his years in the White House kept Lincoln home more than he had ever been before. But the exhausting circumstances of leading the country through myriad military, political, and economic problems turned an always absent-minded man into a distracted, weary one. The president—the man whom Mary Lincoln once described in one of her letters as "truly my all-Always lover-husband-father and all, all to me"—was surrounded during the day by his secretaries, advisers, and generals. In the evenings he worked in his second-floor office. It was not unusual for him to hold midnight meetings with cabinet officers and congressmen.

As the war continued, the First Lady acknowledged that she considered herself fortunate if she and her husband could meet to discuss the day's events at eleven o'clock at night. Yet deep bonds of affection, despite the couple's differences and the strain of living in the White House, kept the Lincolns close throughout their marriage.

In the traditional role of female comforter, Mary Lincoln encouraged afternoon carriage rides as a source of relaxation for the president. Both Lincolns enjoyed the theater and often attended plays with their son Tad in Washington. Their other remaining son, Robert, was at this time a student at Harvard. Mrs. Lincoln also enjoyed the opera and, ever an engaged mother concerned with her children's education and entertainment, she once brought Tom Thumb to the White House to entertain Tad and his friends.

Especially after General Ulysses Grant's forces moved into northern Virginia in 1864, the First Lady enjoyed reviewing the troops. Once she arrived on the battlefield to see her husband on horseback, accompanied by the wife of one of the commanding generals. Unable to deal with the constant spotlight of public attention and, ever imagining herself Lincoln's political partner, Mary Lincoln lost her temper and verbally attacked her husband in front of the entire Union Army command for not waiting for her.

Among Mary Lincoln's other intrusions into areas previously reserved for men were her persistent efforts to influence patronage matters—an area that had interested her since her courtship with Lincoln in Springfield. Sometimes she intervened in behalf of a friend or acquaintance from Springfield or even Kentucky. Certainly she encouraged her husband to appoint her two Democratic brothers-in-law, Ninian Edwards and William Wallace, to official posts, actions that led to complaints that the president placed his whole family in government jobs.

Believing that woman's intuition afforded her sex a better understanding of human character, she continued to try to influence her husband's appointments until the public men of Washington acknowledged a role that kept her at her desk writing as many as three letters a day. "Mrs. Lincoln," wrote a reporter for the *New York Times*, "is making and unmaking the political fortunes of men and is similar to Queen Elizabeth in her statesmanlike tastes."

The patronage seekers who clustered in the upstairs hall of the White House recognized that this First Lady had influence. Some pressed their claims with her for positions in the army as well for the civilian jobs that multiplied during the Civil War. But hers was not a popular role, and the First Lady was humiliated by the press reports about her boldness in these matters.

Mary Lincoln may even have initiated an exchange of her influence with Lincoln for

bills from rich merchants who were pleased to have her wearing their dresses. After 1861 she owed money for her handsome gowns and shawls—items that she considered an important adjunct to her role as First Lady. By 1864, Abram Wakeman, an ambitious New York lawyer, was renegotiating her bills with the merchants of New York.

Many of her interventions in patronage matters were not self-serving, but, rather, were dedicated to the correct proposition that some of the men around Lincoln connived against him. Once she recommended to Secretary of State Seward that he buy Kentucky horses. In 1863, when conservative Republicans pressed for General Nathaniel Banks's appointment to the cabinet, Mary Lincoln encouraged several friends, including Senator Charles Sumner, to write to her husband of their opposition. Such attention to the public matters considered beyond the private sphere irritated Lincoln's advisers, especially Secretary of War Edwin M. Stanton, who once came to the White House to lecture the First Lady on her "proper" duties.

The First Lady was more traditional in other activities that took her beyond the confines of the White House. During the Civil War, she joined thousands of other American women in visiting hospitals crowded with wounded Union soldiers. "Among the many ladies who visit hospitals none is more indefatigable than Mrs. Lincoln," praised the *Washington Star*. To the wounded and dying she delivered flowers, special food, and sympathy. She also wrote letters to their relatives. An active participant in the Sanitary Commission fairs, which raised money for soldiers, Mary Lincoln made generous donations to the cause.

In an unusual gesture for a white woman, the First Lady extended these activities to the most needy of all—the former slaves who flooded into Washington during the war. Called contrabands of war before they became known as freedmen, these refugees lived in appalling conditions in unsanitary camps. Mary Lincoln raised money for the Contraband Relief Association on her trips to New York and Boston. With her friend Elizabeth Keckley, she purchased bedding and clothing for freed African Americans. Such generous behavior suggests the degree to which she shared her husband's commitment to both emancipation and the improvement of living conditions for what she called "the oppressed race."

In the summer of 1864, the First Lady was in Washington when Confederate troops again threatened her safety. During that summer General Jubal Early's troops drove Union forces from Lynchburg, Virginia. Then, in early July, Early undertook a bold raid on Washington after defeating the Union Army in western Maryland. For the Confederacy, it was a last offensive. From the Soldiers' Home both Lincolns watched civilian refugees taking flight down 7th Avenue. Mary Lincoln was asked to leave the city and again refused to do so. Instead she rode with her husband to Fort Stevens, one of the earth fortifications ringing Washington. Afterward she informed Secretary of War Stanton that the forts were inadequate.

That fall Lincoln ran for a second term as president—this time against the Democratic Union general George Brinton McClellan. As usual, the First Lady involved herself in politics, even encouraging state leaders to mobilize Republican voters. To some Americans, Mary Lincoln herself became an election issue because of her bills and spending on the White House. Despite fears that he would lose the election, Lincoln won reelection with 55 percent of the vote. Now a proud Mary Lincoln could look forward to another four years in the White House.

During the next few months in the White House, the president and Mary Lincoln traveled several times to Virginia, where the defeat of the Confederate Army seemed imminent. A couple who had seen so much tragedy talked of their future. As the Confederate Army retreated and, in April 1865, evacuated Richmond, Mary Lincoln toured the Confederate capital. Upon their return to Washington they enjoyed the city's celebration, which included a huge gaslight transparency that sparkled from the Capitol with the legend of victory: "This is the Lord's doing."

Five days later, on April 14, the Lincolns took a carriage ride together and, that night, attended the Ford's Theatre production of *Our American Cousin*. An hour and a half after their arrival and the show-stopping applause that greeted them, John Wilkes Booth shot Abraham Lincoln in the back of the head. Everyone in the theater remembered Mary Lincoln's anguished cries of "Oh, my God, and have I given my husband to die!"

The remaining years of Mary Lincoln's life were lonely and unhappy. Absorbed in grief over her husband's death, she stayed in the White House for over a month before moving to Chicago with Tad. Uncertain about her inheritance, she lived in hotels. In 1866 she bought a home, which she soon found she could not afford. She was also humiliated by the rumors surrounding Anne Rutledge, a young acquaintance of the Lincolns. Early Lincoln biographers, who disliked Mary Lincoln, told the public that young Rutledge had been the president's only love.

Mrs. Lincoln's financial situation worsened. At one point she hired a lobbyist to make her case to Congress for a pension on the grounds that, without one, she would have to live forever in a boardinghouse. Eventually Congress passed a law giving Mary Lincoln an annual pension of $3,000.

Throughout the remainder of her life, Mary Lincoln fought for an increase in her pension to $10,000. As the president's widow, Mrs. Lincoln served as a symbol of a government debate over the issue of welfare extended to the widows of war veterans. Some congressmen argued that giving Mary Lincoln a stipend honored the dead president, while others, agreeing with some support for women who had lost their breadwinners in battle, bridled at her campaign to increase her annual pension to $5,000. She had earlier received the unpaid balance from Lincoln's salary in 1864 and her portion of Lincoln's estate of $38,000, which was divided with her two surviving sons.

Twice she traveled to Europe, spending two years in Germany with Tad and visiting spas in England and in France before the

Franco-Prussian War, her money worries, and her homesickness led her to return to the United States. When Mary Lincoln returned to Chicago, Tad was ill with pleurisy. Her youngest son died in 1871 of what the papers called compression of the heart. Once again struck by grief, she lived for a time with her son Robert and his wife. Mostly she traveled—to visit friends and to see the spiritualists who continued to console her.

In 1875, at the urging of her son Robert, who was by that time a prosperous lawyer in Chicago, Mary Lincoln was brought to public trial, as required by Illinois law, on the grounds that she was incompetent. A conservator was appointed to run her estate, and after testimony from her son of her supposed insanity, she was sent to a private mental institution outside of Chicago. She remained at the institution for less than four months, when, through the intervention of Myra Bradwell—one of the nation's first female lawyers, who was convinced she was not insane—she was able to regain her freedom.

Convinced that her son would try to send her back to an insane asylum, Mary Lincoln fled to Pau, a French resort city near the Pyrenees, where she lived alone for four years. Eventually her declining health forced her to return to the United States. She lived quietly with her sister Elizabeth in Springfield until her death on July 16, 1882, from a stroke at sixty-three years of age.

Mary Todd Lincoln was an important and controversial First Lady who summarized some of the themes of domestic women caught in public roles during the Civil War. Her interpretation of her status as First Lady involved an expansion of that role's authority as she straddled the male sphere of public affairs and the female's secluded habitat of homemaker. Her husband's prominence made her public property at an especially trying time in American history. While she insisted that she was a domestic woman, as First Lady she also had ambitions for the White House, which she greatly improved, and for herself. Ahead of her time, she saw herself as a vanguard of American fashion and

intellectuality. She was often criticized for her trespass onto male territory, obscuring her contributions.

Today, Mary Todd Lincoln still ranks at the bottom of historians' rankings of First Ladies, while her husband remains near the top. Such a status reflects the inaccurate stereotype created by early students of her husband's career, who asserted that the Abraham Lincoln who dealt so generously with the afflicted during a devastating war learned his moderation and patience through his private life with a shrew. Such a malign, unbalanced view overlooks Mary Lincoln's contributions and her modern view of her role as First Lady.

BIBLIOGRAPHICAL ESSAY
Mary Todd Lincoln's letters are scattered, and every year at least one new letter is discovered. The bulk of her correspondence has been published in Justin and Linda Levitt Turner's *Mary Lincoln—Her Life and Letters* (New York, 1972). There are few letters surviving from the years before 1861. Some are found in the Robert Todd Lincoln Collection of Lincoln Papers, now on microfilm.

Earlier biographies focused on the First Lady's life as Lincoln's wife, and because she was so modern in her approach to the White House, the views of Lincoln's biographers are often harsh. Family remembrances are contained in Katherine Helms's *Mary, Wife of Lincoln* (New York, 1928), and there is an important collection of materials relating to Mary Todd Lincoln in the Helm Papers in the Kentucky Archives. A firsthand account appears in Elizabeth Keckley, *Behind the Scenes* (New York, 1868).

The best of the earlier biographies is Ruth Painter Randall, *Mary Lincoln: Biography of a Marriage* (Boston, 1953). Mark Neely and Gerald McMurtry have provided an analysis of the trial and imprisonment in *The Insanity File: The Case of Mary Lincoln* (Carbondale, Ill., 1986). The most recent biography, Jean H. Baker, *Mary Lincoln: A Biography* (New York, 1987), considers Mary Lincoln's life from her perspective, rather than that of male stereotypes. Quotations in the text are taken from that volume. There are also a number of fictional accounts of some of the dramatic episodes in Mary Lincoln's life, including her trial. An editorial obituary appeared in the *New York Times*, July 18, 1882.

★★★   ★★★

(1810–1876)

First Lady: 1865–1869

Nancy Beck Young

Eliza McCardle was born on October 4, 1810, to John McCardle, a shoemaker of Scotch-Irish descent, and Sarah Phillips McCardle in Greeneville, Tennessee. She was an only child. Her parents were married on April 23, 1809 and, typical of the settlers in the eastern Tennessee mountains, never knew economic fortune or success. In 1824 Eliza's father was an innkeeper in Warrensburg, Tennessee. Two years later he died, leaving his wife, Sarah, with the responsibility of rearing their daughter. Sarah McCardle remarried in 1833, to Moses L. Whitesides.

Immediately after McCardle's death in 1826, mother and daughter returned to Greeneville. Without financial resources, Sarah McCardle worked as a weaver. Eliza made crazy quilts and hand-woven sandals. Her formal education was limited to efforts by her mother with the assistance of neighbors with private libraries and study at the Rhea Academy in town. As a young lady of fifteen, Eliza had brown hair with soft curls, blue eyes, and delicate features.

In September 1826, Eliza met Andrew Johnson. Johnson, along with his mother, Mary McDonough Johnson Doughtry, and stepfather, Turner Doughtry, had arrived in Greeneville in search of work and shelter. Johnson worked for a period of time in George Boyle's tailor shop, and he and his family rented rooms. According to some reports, Johnson met Eliza and several other girls when he first came to town. This incident prompted other girls to tease Eliza, who then said of Johnson: "He's all right, I might marry him someday" (Barzman, *The First Ladies*). Although this and other similar anecdotes are probably apocryphal, Eliza and Andrew quickly developed feelings for one another. Johnson and his parents moved on to Rutledge, where they remained for six months. Andrew and Eliza corresponded frequently, and in the spring of 1827, he returned to Greeneville to establish his own business and plan his future with Eliza. The couple exchanged vows on May 17, 1827, in Warrensburg. Mordecai Lincoln, a local justice of the peace and cousin of Abraham Lincoln's father, performed the ceremony for the two teenagers. Andrew Johnson was eighteen and Eliza Johnson was sixteen. The newlyweds moved into a two-room frame structure in the middle of town. Johnson used the front room as a shop for his tailoring business. The other room served as private quarters.

Eliza saw great potential in her husband. The myth persists that she taught Andrew to read and write. That was not the case. Andrew Johnson learned the alphabet and the basics of reading and writing while still a tailor's apprentice in Raleigh, North Carolina. According to a letter recently offered at auction, the Johnsons' older daughter, in September 1881, recalled that "it is a mistake she [Mrs. Johnson] taught my father [President Johnson] the alphabet as this he had acquired before leaving Raleigh. . . . But little has been written about my mother as she always opposed any publicity concerning her private life.—She was the stepping stone to all the honor and fame my father attained." Eliza Johnson's own words corroborate this version. Her only biographer quoted the former First Lady in an unpublished manuscript, "Tennessee Johnson's Eliza," as saying, "I taught him to form the letters, but he was an apt scholar and acquired all the rest of it for himself." Often, in public appearances, he credited his wife with advancing his education. The couple stayed up late into the night honing his oratorical skills. At her suggestion, he joined the Greeneville College debating society. One year after their marriage, Johnson cam-

paigned for, and was elected to, the office of town alderman. He later became mayor.

Eliza Johnson gave birth to four of her five children within the first seven years of her marriage: Martha (b. October 25, 1828), Charles (b. February 19, 1830), Mary (b. May 8, 1832), Robert (b. February 22, 1834). The Johnsons purchased a brick home in 1831 and a separate structure for Johnson's business, which had grown quite lucrative. Mrs. Johnson took charge of the household duties and proved skillful in managing the accounts.

When Johnson was elected to the state legislature in 1835, Eliza Johnson remained at home and managed the family's financial affairs, which expanded with the addition of a farm and a few slaves. She also attended to her children's education in the basic subjects. In 1842 Johnson was elected to the House of Representatives. His wife did not join him in Washington. In 1851 they purchased a large home on Main Street in Greeneville. The added space proved useful. When Johnson's stepfather died, his mother moved in with the family. She remained with the Johnsons until her death in 1856. Furthermore, Eliza Johnson gave birth to her last child, Andrew, Jr. (nicknamed Frank), there on August 5, 1852.

Mrs. Johnson's responsibilities as a parent increased as her two older sons—Charles and Robert—grew to maturity. Both suffered from alcoholism. By 1853, when her husband was elected governor of Tennessee, Eliza Johnson's health had deteriorated to the point that she could not travel to Nashville. She never fully regained her health. Correspondence between family members and friends alternately indicates improvement and weakening of her condition; however, consumption limited her activities for the remainder of her life. Adding to Mrs. Johnson's emotional and physical burdens, her mother passed away in April 1854. That same year, the Johnsons' younger daughter, Mary, married Daniel Stover. Their older daughter, Martha, wed David T. Patterson in 1855.

In 1857, Andrew Johnson was elected to the U.S. Senate. Eliza Johnson again remained in Tennessee, where she continued to manage the family's financial affairs, including the activities of their slaves. The slaves—never numbering more than eight or nine—served as a status symbol for Johnson. Finally, in 1860—sixteen years after Johnson was first elected to the House of Representatives—Eliza Johnson traveled to Washington. She was accompanied by her sons Robert and Frank. They remained in Washington until spring 1861, when the Civil War broke out and Johnson returned with the family to Tennessee. Johnson's passionate speeches against secession in his native state produced several threats on his life from Confederates in the South. In 1862 the senator returned to Washington, hoping that he could persuade Union forces to defend and assist the people of East Tennessee who lived under Confederate control but remained loyal to the North. Confederates confiscated the Johnson home in Greeneville and used it as a barracks and hospital. The Confederacy filed a writ of attachment against the Johnsons' holdings and enjoined Eliza Johnson from disposing of any of their possessions. During this time Mrs. Johnson lived with her daughter Mary Stover in Carter County, Tennessee, except for a month that she spent in Nashville with the governor. Though she was never in as much danger as her husband implied in his public addresses, Eliza Johnson, as the wife of the only Southern senator loyal to the Union, did have reason to worry about her safety. President Lincoln heard Senator Johnson's pleas for the well-being of his family, and appointed him military governor of Tennessee.

Confederate general E. Kirby Smith, who commanded the region of Eastern Tennessee, on April 24, 1862, gave Eliza Johnson thirty-six hours to depart from his jurisdiction. According to Andrew Johnson's published papers, his wife replied to Smith, on April 28, that "in my present state of health, I know I can not undergo the fatigues of such a journey; my health is quite feeble, a greater portion of the time being unable to leave my bed." On September 19, she told authorities that her health would permit her to travel. At that time she asked for the necessary passports. Eliza Johnson, along with her sons Frank and Charles and the Stover family, made the difficult journey through Confederate territory. Confederate general Nathan Bedford Forrest forced the party to remain in Murfreesboro until further permission came from Richmond for them to continue to Nashville. Finally, they arrived in Nashville on October 13, 1862.

Eliza Johnson traveled on to Cincinnati that November. There she visited her son Robert, whom she had not seen for about a year. His alcoholism had gotten him into trouble with his military unit, and she hoped to rectify the situation. The next stop for Mrs. Johnson and her daughter Mary was Vevay, Indiana, where they enjoyed the local springs. Eliza Johnson hoped this treatment would improve her health. Upon arriving in Louisville with the Stovers, she decided against travel to Washington because of concern over the impact of that climate on her health. As recorded in his published papers, Johnson wrote to his wife in Louisville from Washington on March 27, 1863:

> I feel sometimes like giv[in]g all up in dispare! but this will not do[.] we must hold out to the end, this rebelion is wrong and must be put down let cost what it may in the life and treasure[.] I intend to appropriate the remainder of my life to the redemption of my a[do]pted home East Tennessee and you and Mary must not be weary, it is our fate and we Should be willing to bear it cheerfully. . . . Give my love to all and accept for yourself the best wishes of a devoted husband's heart[.]

Eliza Johnson did not return to Nashville until May 1863. While in Nashville she occupied the home of Lizinka C. Ewell. A further tragedy came in 1863, when her son Charles died after being thrown from a horse. Then, in 1864, her son-in-law, Daniel Stover, died from consumption. In August 1864 Eliza Johnson and her remaining sons, Robert and Frank, journeyed to New England. The exact purpose of the journey is unclear. Records indicate they vacationed at the Pigeon Cove resort northeast of Boston, but it is also probable that they sought treatment for Robert's drinking problem at Dr. Dio Lewis's sanitarium in Lexington, Massachusetts.

By March 1865, Eliza Johnson was back in Nashville when her husband was sworn in as vice president. News of President Lincoln's assassination a month later on April 14, 1865, traumatized Mrs. Johnson. According to Johnson's published papers, Martha Patterson wrote to her father on April 15, inquiring, "Are you safe, and do you feel *secure?* . . . Poor mother she is almost deranged fearing that you will be assassinated." The new president realized, for both reasons of public scrutiny and personal support, that his family should join him in Washington as soon as possible. Previously in her husband's career Eliza Johnson had followed the pattern of the majority of congressional wives by not moving to Washington. But expectations for the new First Family were heightened. Eliza Johnson did not relish the thought of becoming First Lady. Following Mary Todd Lincoln only increased her apprehensions. Mrs. Lincoln had been severely criticized for her role in affairs of the state. Though they put off the journey until late summer, Mrs. Johnson and her surviving children prepared for life in Washington. Arriving in Washington on August 6, 1865, the group included Eliza Johnson, her sons Frank and Robert, her daughter and son-in-law Martha and David Patterson and their two children, and her daughter Mary Stover and her three children.

Mrs. Johnson sequestered herself in a small corner room upstairs in the White House and spent her time reading, doing needlework, and visiting with family and close friends. The president worked in a room across the hall from his wife. Mrs. Johnson kept a close watch on her husband's temper, never failing to admonish him for excessive displays of anger. The First Lady urged her husband to act with greater tolerance and gentleness. She made sure he dressed appropriately and ate properly. William H. Crook, a former White House bodyguard, recalled in his memoirs that when Mrs. Johnson wanted to influence her husband she would touch his arm and say, "now, Andrew."

Ill health limited Eliza Johnson's ability to function as hostess and First Lady. Martha Patterson, her older daughter and the wife of Tennessee Senator David T. Patterson, shouldered those responsibilities. As a girl, Martha had spent several holidays in the White House during the James K. Polk administration. During Johnson's years in Congress, she had been enrolled in the Georgetown Visitation Convent.

When the Johnson family moved into the White House, they found the executive mansion in a dilapidated condition. Four years of war, combined with the onslaught of sightseers following Lincoln's death, had left the White House in bad shape. Bugs and insects had damaged much of the furniture and could be found throughout the mansion. Furthermore, stains from tobacco juice soiled the walls and floors, leaving the drapes and rugs in need of replacement. Martha Patterson oversaw the restoration of the White House. Congress had appropriated $30,000 for repairs—much less than required for the project. Martha Patterson stretched the money as far as possible. With new wallpaper and linen slipcovers for the furniture, the public areas of the executive mansion were again pleasing to the eye. As an added touch, Martha Patterson regularly distributed freshly cut flowers throughout the White House. She even covered the carpets with muslin cloth for each of the receptions her family hosted. The president's elder daughter herself joined in the cleaning process. Each morning she donned a calico work dress and helped the staff with the restoration. Martha Patterson procured two Jersey cows and milked them daily so that the White House would have fresh dairy products. On January 1, 1867, the Johnsons hosted the first of many receptions and levees. Martha Patterson did not indulge elaborate tastes; instead, these affairs were noted for their simple charms. According to Mary Clemmer Ames's *Ten Years in Washington*, the president's daughter stated, "We are plain people from the mountains of Tennessee, brought here through a national calamity. We trust too much will not be expected of us."

During her husband's administration, Eliza Johnson attended only two White House affairs—a reception for Queen Emma of the Sandwich Isles in August 1866 and the president's sixtieth birthday party in December 1868. For her father's birthday, Martha Patterson planned a juvenile soiree—the first children's ball ever held in the White House. Julia Dent Grant, the wife of Ulysses S. Grant and a frequent guest at Washington social affairs, described Eliza Johnson in her memoirs as

> a retiring, kind, gentle, old lady, too much of an invalid to do the honors of the house, which care and pleasure she gladly transferred to her two daughters, Mrs. Patterson and Mrs. Stover, but she always came into the drawing room after the long state dinners to take coffee and receive the greetings of her husband's guests. She was always dressed elegantly and appropriately.

The Johnson family's hospitality, dispensed evenly throughout the president's difficulties with Congress, generated favorable reviews.

With the assistance of her daughter and the White House staff, Eliza Johnson maintained a regular schedule of activities with her family. Martha Patterson and the small staff of the executive office handled her correspondence. Eliza Johnson received numerous letters and petitions for employment from people hoping for an audience with the president. For example, in a letter among Andrew Johnson's personal papers dated August 28, 1867, C. F. Sussdorff implores Mrs. Johnson to give his best wishes to the president:

> I take the liberty once more to inclose to your address a few lines to your much beloved husband, with the respectful request that if it please you and after perusing it you think it worthwhile to hand it to the President to do so, otherwise to destroy it as wastepaper. I would not deprive him one moment from his recreations or add a

feathers weight to his duties by this communication but my wish and intent is to cheer him in my humble capacity.

Other letters routed through Mrs. Johnson to the president adopted a similar tone of deference.

The First Lady's routine included breakfast alone in her quarters, after which she toured the family's living quarters of the White House, occasionally stopping to visit her husband in his office. She spent a good deal of time with her grandchildren after they completed their lessons. Eliza Johnson was careful about her appearance, dressing simply but in expensive costumes created by the finest Washington dressmakers. She kept a close eye on the well-being of White House employees. She kept busy in other ways. In 1867 she made a donation to an orphans' home in Baltimore. That same year she traveled to Boston, New York, Philadelphia, Pittsburgh, and Louisville.

Andrew Johnson's relations with Congress deteriorated as the executive and legislative branches of government quarreled over the development of a policy for reconstruction of the former Confederate states. Moderate and radical Republicans lost patience with the chief executive when he vetoed two bills—one extending the life of the Freedman's Bureau and the other a civil rights bill that did away with the black codes. As a result, Congress took responsibility for the reconstruction and placed the Southern states under the jurisdiction of five military districts. Johnson, on the other hand, dismissed government officials favorable to the newly enacted congressional policies. His actions ultimately convinced Republicans in Congress to push for his impeachment and removal from office in 1868.

Eliza Johnson worried profusely about the efforts to remove her husband from office. She followed the congressional proceedings closely. The president sought moral support from his wife each morning during this period. She read many newspapers and clipped material for the president's perusal, giving him favorable articles at each day's end and critical accounts the following morning. Martha Patterson made herself available to the president throughout the day. One historian has argued that the president sought advice from his wife and daughters instead of political figures in Washington. William Henry Crook notes that Mrs. Johnson once remarked that she preferred memories of her early married life with the president in Tennessee to her days in the White House: "It's all very well for those who like it—but I do not like this public life at all. I often wish the time would come when we could return to where I feel we best belong" (*Memories of the White House*).

Crook described the First Lady's reaction to her husband's acquittal at the impeachment proceedings:

> The frail little lady . . . rose from her chair and in both her emaciated hands took my right hand. Tears were in her eyes, but her voice was firm and she did not tremble once as she said: "Crook, I knew he'd be acquitted; I knew it. Thank you for coming to tell me." That was all she said, and I left a moment later; but I shall never forget the picture of that feeble, wasted little woman standing so proudly and assuring me so positively that she had never doubted for one instant that her beloved husband would be proved innocent. (*Memories of the White House*)

The family returned to Greeneville in March 1869, at the end of Johnson's term. Adoring crowds greeted the president and his family along the way. The former president, though, languished in the slow-paced life of Greeneville. Worries about his wife's health punctuated his correspondence with their children. Tragedy struck soon after their return to Tennessee, when their son Robert, who never overcame his drinking problem, committed suicide in April 1869. Yet, the family had reason to celebrate. Afterward, their only remaining son, Frank, then a student at Georgetown College, promised his mother he would never take alcohol. That same month, Mary Johnson Stover married William R. Brown.

In January 1875, Johnson was elected to the U.S. Senate from Tennessee. Eliza Johnson was glad for the vindication of her husband's public record, but the excitement associated with the contest placed a great strain on her health. The former First Lady went to visit her daughter Mary Stover Brown on a nearby farm, where she hoped to recuperate. Johnson stopped to visit her on his way to Washington, D.C. While there he suffered a stroke and died on July 31, 1875. Eliza Johnson's weakened condition prohibited her from attending his funeral. Many mourners extended their condolences to the former First Lady. Despite her health she was named executor of her husband's estate, which was valued at over $100,000. In the discharge of those duties she was bonded for $200,000. Eliza Johnson died six months later, on January 15, 1876. Both the Johnsons were interred at the Andrew Johnson National Cemetery in Greeneville.

Eliza Johnson's tenure in the White House revealed very little about her life. Already ill for many years by the time of Abraham Lincoln's assassination, Mrs. Johnson saw no reason to assume the duties of First Lady, especially when her daughter, Martha Johnson Patterson, was there to perform as White House hostess. Eliza Johnson, therefore, had little contact with the general public or government officials during her husband's administration. Her daughter Martha Johnson Patterson established a quaint and friendly tone for White House affairs that drew rave reviews from social critics. More important, the Johnsons' elder daughter saw the executive mansion through a period of needed restoration following the Civil War. Ultimately, Eliza Johnson had little impact on the development of the institution of the First Lady. Some historians have argued that several First Ladies in the nineteenth century consciously used their physical condition to avoid their official responsibilities. In the case of Mrs. Johnson, however, she had never taken an active role in her husband's public life. Instead, throughout Andrew Johnson's long career in politics, Eliza

Johnson remained at home, where she looked after their children and their financial accounts. Others have suggested that Andrew Johnson quickly eclipsed his wife, who benefited from a superior education. But this assertion is not borne out by the evidence. Often hidden from view, Eliza Johnson played an important role in managing the day-to-day tasks of their life. In the White House she maintained a calming influence over the president and remained his most trusted adviser. Other historians have speculated about the quality of their marriage. Early writers describe the couple as a perfect match. But the years of separation, as noted by more recent scholars, must have been difficult to bear. Yet those few letters between the two that survive are laced with affection and respect. Thus, Eliza McCardle Johnson's greatest importance rests with the gentle nurturing she provided for her husband, children, and grandchildren over the years.

BIBLIOGRAPHICAL ESSAY

Eliza Johnson's personal papers have not survived. The papers of Andrew Johnson, housed in the Library of Congress, Manuscripts Division, contain important correspondence pertaining to his wife. Researchers should also consult the published papers of Andrew Johnson. This edition includes a thorough index that references documents that mention Eliza Johnson but were not to or from the former first lady. See LeRoy P. Graf and Ralph W. Haskins, eds., *The Papers of Andrew Johnson* (Knoxville, Tenn., 1967–1986). Fay Brabson prepared a biography of the former president. The Brabson Papers, located in Special Collections, University of Tennessee Library, Knoxville, Tennessee, contain useful documents about Eliza's life. Margaret Gray Blanton worked for some time on a biography of Mrs. Johnson. Her manuscript, "Tennessee Johnson's Eliza," was never published but can be found in Special Collections, University of Tennessee Library. The University of Tennessee Library also has the Blanton Papers, which contain the author's research notes, a

Johnson family genealogy, and photographs of interest to scholars. The letter cited from Martha Johnson Patterson is reprinted in part in the catalog for *Walter Burk's Autographs and Coins*. A copy of this catalog can be found in the Eliza Johnson file at the Center for American History, University of Texas at Austin.

Several memoirs provide insight into Eliza Johnson's years in Washington. See, for example, William Henry Crook, *Through Five Administrations: Reminiscences of Colonel William H. Crook, Body-Guard to President Lincoln*, compiled and edited by Margarita Spalding Gerry (New York and London, 1910); and *Memories of the White House: The Home Life of Our Presidents from Lincoln to Roosevelt, Being Personal Recollections of Colonel W. H. Crook, Sometime Bodyguard to Lincoln, Since Then Disbursing Officer of the Executives*, compiled and edited by Henry Rood (Boston, 1911); and Mary Clemmer Ames, *Ten Years in Washington: Life and Scenes in the National Capital, as a Woman Sees Them* (Hartford, Conn., 1875).

For background on Andrew Johnson see Fay Warrington Brabson, *Andrew Johnson: A Life in Pursuit of the Right Course, 1808–1875, the Seventeenth President of the United States* (Durham, N.C., 1972); and Hans L. Trefousse, *Andrew Johnson: A Biography* (New York, 1989). For information on Johnson's presidency see Albert Castel, *The Presidency of Andrew Johnson* (Lawrence, Kans., 1979). For two accounts of Johnson's impeachment see Eric L. McKitrick, *Andrew Johnson and Reconstruction* (Chicago, 1964);and Michael Les Benedict, *The Impeachment and Trial of Andrew Johnson* (New York, 1973).

Eliza Johnson appears in several collective studies of First Ladies. See Laura Carter Holloway, *The Ladies of the White House* (New York, 1870); Kathleen Prindiville, *First Ladies* (New York, 1942); Sol Barzman, *The First Ladies* (New York, 1970); Betty Boyd Caroli, *First Ladies* (New York, 1987); Paul F. Boller, Jr., *Presidential Wives* (New York and Oxford, 1988); Diana Dixon Healy, *America's First Ladies: Private Lives of the Presidential Wives* (New York, 1988); and Carl Sferrazza Anthony, *First*

Ladies: The Saga of the Presidents' Wives and Their Power, 1789–1961 (New York, 1990). The more useful accounts are found in Caroli, Boller, and Anthony.

Further information about Eliza Johnson can be found in Lately Thomas, *The First President Johnson: The Three Lives of the Seventeenth President of the United States* (New York, 1968); and Ronald Vern Jackson, *Andrew Johnson and Eliza McCardle Ancestry* (Utah, 1980).

★★★   ★★★

Julia Dent Grant

(1826–1902)

First Lady: 1869–1877

John Y. Simon

Born in St. Louis on January 26, 1826, Julia Dent was raised on the family estate of White Haven in south St. Louis County. Her father, Frederick Dent, called "colonel" by courtesy, was born in Maryland in 1786; her mother, Ellen Bray Wrenshall Dent, was born in England and brought to Pittsburgh by her parents. Julia's grandfather John Wrenshall was both a Methodist preacher and an importer. Julia's mother came from a cultured and pious home. Her parents sent her to Philadelphia to school; from there, her husband carried her to frontier Missouri. She gave birth to four sons, then to four daughters. Except for one daughter, all survived infancy.

Frederick Dent prospered as a St. Louis merchant and was able to buy the thou-sand-acre White Haven estate while maintaining a downtown residence. Gradually he withdrew from business, enjoyed rural life, and his rather considerable wealth began to erode. Nonetheless he maintained the attitudes of a Southern gentleman, used slaves for farm labor, and never doubted his own opinions. Julia, the eldest daughter, grew up amid the comfort and security of a family with high social standing. She attended a local school kept by John F. Long, where, she later recalled, she never did master those "dreadful roman numerals." She then spent seven years at the Mauro boarding school in St. Louis, where she remained indifferent to mathematics and delighted in reading novels. Among her favorites was *The Dashing Lieu-*

tenant; she told friends that she hoped someday to marry a soldier.

In the spring of 1844, eighteen-year-old Julia returned from school in St. Louis to the Dent family estate. There she met twenty-two-year-old Brevet Second Lieutenant Ulysses S. Grant, stationed at nearby Jefferson Barracks and a frequent visitor to the parents of his West Point roommate, Julia's brother Frederick T. Dent. If the initial meeting of Ulysses and Julia did not spark love at first sight, it came close enough to qualify as the first chapter in a great American love story. The "dashing lieutenant" who entered her life shared her love of novels. Both Ulysses and Julia had mothers who were strict and fervent Methodists.

Ulysses Grant captivated Julia but alarmed her father, who expected his daughter to marry someone better able to support her in comfort. When Grant was ordered away to Louisiana, where his regiment assembled to prepare for anticipated hostilities with Mexico, the young couple became informally engaged, but they lacked courage to confront Colonel Dent. One year later, Grant obtained leave and won reluctant consent.

During the Mexican War, Grant wrote frequently to Julia, and she less often to him, but they maintained their attachment and intention to marry. After three years of separation, Grant returned to St. Louis for a wedding in the Dent townhouse in St. Louis on August 22, 1848. All three of Grant's groomsmen later fought for the Confederacy. The most prominent of them was James Longstreet, Grant's close friend and a cousin of the Dents.

Grant had arrived at Jefferson Barracks three years earlier hoping to return to West Point as an instructor of mathematics—a subject at which he excelled—and he had even pursued a course of study to bolster his qualifications. During the prolonged buildup of hostilities with Mexico, and an equally lengthy period between the end of the fighting and the negotiation of a peace treaty, Grant lost his opportunity to return to the academy but not his wish to leave the army.

During their first four years of marriage the Grants lived at Detroit and Sackets Harbor, New York. Julia Grant learned to cook and keep house—skills that had been unnecessary amid the slaves of White Haven—and flourished in the social circles of the junior officers. On May 30, 1850, her first child, Frederick Dent Grant, was born in St. Louis. She had gone home for the birth on the advice of the army surgeon at Detroit.

Julia Grant was pregnant again in the summer of 1852 when Grant's Fourth Infantry was ordered to the Pacific Coast. She remained behind with Grant's family in Ohio, where Ulysses S. Grant, Jr., was born on July 22, 1852. Family slaves later nicknamed the boy "Buckeye" or "Buck" for his Ohio birth, and the second version remained his lifelong nickname. Grant had no reason to question his decision to leave his wife and child behind. Many of the women and children who accompanied the regiment died in the steamy jungles of Panama, along with many of the officers and men. Once on the Pacific Coast, Grant found his army pay inadequate to reunite his family; every enterprise he tried to earn extra money collapsed. After two years of separation, Grant was stationed at isolated Fort Humboldt, California, as part of a small garrison commanded by Colonel Buchanan, a martinet who disliked him. Plagued by malaria and bad teeth, unlikely to gain promotion for many years, and painfully lonely, Grant received his commission as captain and resigned the same day. Army gossip held that Grant's drinking led to his resignation, but he had plenty of other reasons to return to his family.

Grant found his wife and the children at White Haven, where Colonel Dent, generous even when impecunious, gave the Grants enough acreage for a farm. There Grant built the rough log house he named Hardscrabble, and Julia Grant coped with the life of a farmer's wife with the aid of four slaves her father provided. Grant's farm enterprise foundered in the depression of 1857, and the Grants moved to White Haven to help Colonel Dent after the death of his wife left him devastated. Colonel

Dent's shaky finances collapsed as well, and Captain Grant sought employment in St. Louis, once again leaving his wife and children behind. Now there were four: Ellen (Nellie) Grant was born on July 4, 1855, and Jesse Root Grant on February 6, 1858. Everything Grant tried to do to earn money turned out badly. In desperation he turned to his father and accepted employment at the family leather goods store in Galena, Illinois, managed by his two younger brothers, Simpson and Orvil. For Ulysses and Julia, Galena represented an unattractive prospect, redeemed only by the assurance of keeping the family together.

The Grants had lived in Galena less than a year when the Civil War began. Educated as a soldier, with fifteen years of army experience, and outraged by the Confederate assault on the flag, Grant barely hesitated before volunteering his services. "I know it is hard for men to apparently work with the Republican party," Grant wrote to Colonel Dent on April 19, 1861, "but now all party distinctions should be lost sight of and evry true patriot be for maintaining the integrity of the glorious old *Stars & Stripes*, the Constitution and the Union." Colonel Dent, however, supported the Confederacy, despite the fact that his son Fred fought for the Union. As for his "Federal son-in-law," said Dent, "There shall always be a plate on my table for Julia, but none for him." Julia loved her father but never wavered in supporting her husband.

During the Civil War, Julia Grant accompanied her husband whenever possible. She joined him at Cairo, Illinois, after the Battle of Belmont (November 7, 1861) and later in 1862 at Memphis and Holly Springs, Mississippi, where he had established headquarters with some degree of permanence. From Holly Springs, Mrs. Grant, her son Jesse, and one of her female slaves moved to Oxford, where they were at headquarters when Confederate general Earl Van Dorn raided Holly Springs. A party stopped at the house recently occupied by the Grants, hoping to capture the general's wife. She came no closer to danger during her wartime visits, which were numerous and of obvious importance to both her and her husband. "Do stop digging at this old canal," she told him when she reached Vicksburg. "You know you will never use it." Grant was delighted to receive such amusing advice from so unlikely a source. His wife's visit relieved his spirits after months of frustrating efforts to reach the enemy on dry ground.

Julia Grant left Galena in 1861 and did not return until her husband's triumphant welcome home in 1865. When not with her husband she remained nearby with her father in St. Louis, a relative in Louisville, or the Grants in Covington, Kentucky. The Confederate sympathies of her family and their neighbors near St. Louis troubled her visits there, and old antipathies in the Grant family clouded visits to Covington. In fact, Julia Grant missed being with her husband as much as he missed her. She sent the three older children to stay temporarily with a relative in St. Louis. Fred, now a teenager, accompanied his father through the last stages of the Vicksburg campaign. Fred was only eleven when he joined his father on the general's first march across Illinois, then had been sent home before the regiment crossed into hostile Missouri. Julia Grant disapproved, arguing that the future Alexander the Great had been no older when he accompanied Philip of Macedon during the fourth century B.C. When Vicksburg surrendered, Mrs. Grant was so proud of her husband that she told an army officer that "she would rather be Mrs. Grant than the wife of the President."

In March 1864, when Grant was promoted to lieutenant general and given command of all Union armies, Julia Grant followed him to Washington, where she met the Lincolns. She was becoming something of a celebrity herself and seemed to enjoy attention more than did her husband. At a New York charity fair, where those who donated money were entitled to vote on whether an ornate ceremonial sword should be presented to Grant or to General George B. McClellan, the former general-in-chief and impending Democratic candidate for president, Julia Grant gallantly cast her votes for McClellan, an act that drew favorable newspaper coverage. Her husband approved the act but deplored the publicity.

By the fall of 1864, Grant's campaign against Robert E. Lee had settled into a long siege at Petersburg, Virginia. Grant occupied a simple cabin at City Point, a few yards from a large and commodious mansion that he declined to occupy. The Grants lived simply in the cabin, pleased to be together. Sometimes officers who brought messages during the evening found them holding hands.

In late January, three Confederate peace emissaries arrived at City Point, prepared to negotiate an end to the conflict. Both Grants received them cordially, and the general encouraged President Lincoln to meet them informally. Lincoln offered liberal treatment once the rebels abandoned fighting and recognized the death of slavery. Confederates declared that tantamount to unconditional surrender and responded with nothing save an ill-conceived scheme to unite the two armies to drive the French from Mexico. Although the conference ended in failure, Confederates noted Julia Grant's cordiality, mistaking it for sympathy with the Southern cause rather than an attempt to wheedle the release of her brother John Dent, a Confederate sympathizer who had rashly visited the South and had been taken prisoner. Grant refused to sanction an exchange of one rebel for another, and Dent languished in captivity.

Building on Julia Grant's cordiality, a conference between Union general Edward O. C. Ord and Confederate general Longstreet, held to discuss the exchange of civilian captives, concluded with a scheme for Mrs. Grant and Mrs. Longstreet to exchange visits. Both Ord and Longstreet believed that this simple initiative would broaden into discussions between leaders of both armies and culminate in a negotiated settlement of the war. Grant called the proposal "simply absurd. The men have fought this war and the men will finish it." His words left Julia "silent, indignant, and disappointed." His judgment concluded the issue without changing her views.

Julia Grant's cordiality received a severe test late in March, when the Lincolns arrived at City Point. Grant had appointed the Lincoln's son Robert to his staff late in the war and thought that his parents would want to visit him. Mary Lincoln, already exhibiting the bizarre behavior that clouded her last years, insulted and snubbed Julia Grant and put on a disgraceful scene during a review of the troops. Mrs. Lincoln made another unpleasant scene on April 13, when she and Grant rode through Washington to see the illuminations celebrating Lee's surrender. Cheers for Grant provoked Mary Lincoln's jealous wrath. Both Grants welcomed an opportunity to beg to be excused from accompanying the Lincolns to the theater the next evening so that they could visit their children, then in school at Burlington, New Jersey. The news of Lincoln's assassination reached them en route. Julia Grant later believed that a mysterious stranger had stalked her during the day, and her husband received an anonymous letter from someone claiming to have followed them on the train as part of the assassination plot, only to be foiled by a locked door. Whether the Grants were pursued on April 14 remains unknown. John Wilkes Booth originally expected to find them at Ford's Theatre.

Lincoln's death left Grant the greatest living hero of the war and the nation's foremost celebrity. Admirers had presented the Grants with a comfortable home in Galena, where they had rented a cottage before the war, and another in Philadelphia, where they planned to live after the war. Grant detested the political climate of Washington and found the refinement of Philadelphia more to his taste, but duties as general-in-chief demanded his presence in Washington so frequently that commuting proved onerous and Julia disliked being separated from her husband. Reluctantly they moved to Washington, first into a rented house in Georgetown, then into a substantial mansion presented to them by wealthy New Yorkers. At last, thought Julia, she could enjoy domestic pleasures with her husband by her side. All four children were at home and attended nearby schools until Fred left for West Point in the summer of 1866.

The political turmoil that Grant feared soon engulfed him. Lincoln's successor, Andrew Johnson—who was once expected to punish treason harshly—now pushed for rapid restoration of the Southern states without fundamental changes that recognized the emancipation of former slaves. Reconstruction under such conditions offended Grant as commander of the army that tried to enforce congressional mandates despite presidential efforts at circumvention. As commander of an army that had won the war with black troops as well as white, Grant objected to trampling the civil rights of the freedmen. Above all, Grant resented Johnson's attempt to harness the enormous popularity of the victorious commander to otherwise unpopular administration policy. Johnson tried to entangle Grant in efforts to oust Secretary of War Edwin M. Stanton, a radical favorite, by defying Congress and replacing Stanton with Grant as secretary of war during a congressional recess. When Congress reassembled and insisted on Stanton's reinstatement, Grant immediately acquiesced. In doing so he quarreled irreparably with Johnson and became the inevitable Republican nominee as his successor.

Grant maintained a circumspect silence during Johnson's impeachment trial, and soon after it ended, accepted the Republican nomination. Privately, he wrote that he had been "forced into" nomination "in spite of myself." Accepting the presidency meant abandoning the lifetime tenure of military command and the privacy he cherished. Julia Grant may have shared some of his reservations, but the enormous pride she took in her husband's abilities and accomplishments influenced her attitude. During the presidential campaign, Grant avoided politicians and reporters by living in out-of-the-way Galena, his first and last extended use of the house presented by civic boosters to secure his residence.

When Grant took office on March 4, 1869, Julia Grant "listened with pride and emotion to the first inaugural address of my husband, the President." She had badgered him repeatedly but unsuccessfully for the names of his cabinet appointments, and their announcement came as a surprise to her, the rest of the nation, and most of the nominees. Elihu B. Washburne of Galena, the local congressman who had furthered Grant's career early in the Civil War, was appointed secretary of state but served only a few days before resigning for health reasons and embarking for Paris as minister. His successor, Hamilton Fish, an aristocratic New Yorker, served throughout the remainder of the two terms of the Grant administration, and Mrs. Grant found Mrs. Fish, also named Julia, an invaluable guide to the social duties of the First Lady. Although Julia Grant had lived in Washington for more than three years before entering the White House, neither Mary Lincoln nor Eliza Johnson had provided a role model. Mrs. Johnson, reclusive and something of an invalid, had abandoned social responsibilities to her two daughters. Furthermore, the estrangement of Grant and Johnson limited Mrs. Grant's visits to the White House. Johnson did not even attend the inauguration of his successor.

Like her husband, Julia Grant viewed life in the White House as temporary. When her husband arranged sale of their Washington house to Washington's mayor, Mrs. Grant refused to sign the deed. Only when wealthy New Yorkers—essentially the same crowd that had bought the house for the Grants—offered a higher price for the house, intending to present it to General William T. Sherman, did Julia Grant acquiesce. She found the White House "in utter confusion." The public rooms were shabby and abused. The furniture needed reupholstering and the carpets had to be replaced. Mrs. Grant ordered male servants to wear dress suits and white gloves and not to smoke on duty. As a Missouri farm wife, Julia Grant had forced her husband to leave the house to smoke his pipe; now she imposed the same rule on White House servants even though she could do nothing about her husband's cigars.

Mrs. Grant hired an excellent chef and brought in caterers for state dinners, served elegantly on fine new china. Expensive wines and liquors accompanied these feasts in a profusion that would have shocked her Methodist forebears. She tried consciously to restore elegance to the White House and succeeded to the extent that some condemned the Grant years as ostentatious and garish. Guided by Julia Fish, the First Lady received guests on Tuesday afternoons. All comers were admitted, including government clerks who arrived by streetcar. Asked by an usher about what to do "if any colored people call," she answered: "Admit all who call." Apparently, however, some callers were discouraged by ushers behind Julia Grant's back, including those "colored people." None ever appeared, "thus showing themselves modest and not aggressive," she reported. Despite a policy of open receptions, the drawing rooms contained few beyond the elegantly dressed and bejeweled. Mrs. Grant, stout and cross-eyed, unpretentious and genuinely friendly, put visitors at ease.

Julia Grant's chief goal in the White House was to create a comfortable home for her family. Colonel Dent moved in, and the crusty old Democrat enjoyed sitting in the waiting room, sharing outrageous political opinions with Republican visitors. Here, as at the family dinner table, the Grants regarded Dent as a delightful relic of an older day. Grant's mother, Hannah, on the other hand, never visited Washington, and Jesse Grant stayed in hotels. During the harsh years of the late 1850s, both Grants had come to view the Dents as their true family and mourned Colonel Dent's death in 1873. Of Julia Grant's four brothers, Fred stayed in the army, officially assigned to the staff of General Sherman but unofficially reassigned to Grant's staff, on which he had served since 1864. John Dent, onetime Confederate sympathizer, received a lucrative Western post tradership. George Wrenshall Dent became appraiser of merchandise at the customhouse in San Francisco. Lewis Dent ran for governor of Mississippi with the support of the Democ-

rats. Once Grant declared opposition, however, Dent lost but moved to Washington to practice law, trading heavily on executive connections—real or imagined. Julia Grant's younger sister Ellen (Nellie) had married Dr. Alexander Sharp, appointed marshal of the District of Columbia, and the youngest sister, Emily (Emma), had married James F. Casey, appointed collector of customs at New Orleans. A few years earlier, President Johnson, in a heavy-handed effort to gain Grant's goodwill, appointed his father, Jesse, as postmaster at Covington. The old man was something of an embarrassment to his son; Johnson might have done better by appointing a Dent to office.

Julia Grant brought her two youngest children to live in the White House. She closed off the back lawn to visitors to provide eleven-year-old Jesse room to ride his velocipede. In addition, Jesse had a playhouse on the grounds, where he and his friends formed a club that published its own newspaper. Jesse ran through the corridors of the White House as unchecked as Tad Lincoln years earlier. When sent to school in Pennsylvania, Jesse begged, successfully, to return home. Even so, he stayed away longer than his sister, Nellie, who had been sent to Miss Porter's School in Farmington, Connecticut, in 1870. Fifteen-year-old Nellie left school immediately. She clearly enjoyed the social whirl of Washington, which she had entered prematurely, far more than any educational environment. On a European tour she fell in love with an Englishman, Algernon Sartoris. Their White House wedding became a public event that inspired poetry from Walt Whitman and a lavish shower of wedding gifts from across the country.

The Grants' oldest child, Fred, also married during his father's presidency, and his first child, named Julia, was born at the White House. The Grants' second son, Buck, entered Harvard in 1870, scraped through to graduation, and returned to the White House to serve as his father's secretary. The Grants formed a close knit and affectionate family. Critics complained that Julia Grant indulged and spoiled the two younger children; Mrs. Grant believed that she was far stricter a disciplinarian than was her husband. At family dinners, Grant rolled bread into small balls with which he pelted his children. He enjoyed teasing his wife, who, in turn, enjoyed the attention. By 1877 the Grants had come to think of the White House as a comfortable home that they hated to leave.

Comfortable, that is, for three seasons of the year. During the oppressive summer heat, the Grants went to Long Branch, New Jersey, a seaside resort where they acquired a large house labeled a cottage, as were seaside mansions at Newport, Rhode Island. Surrounded by her family, Julia Grant sat on a large porch overlooking a private beach. In response to her husband's teasing, Mrs. Grant once emulated Buck by vaulting over the porch railing to the ground below, an amazing feat for one of her age and size. The quiet and leisure of Long Branch refreshed both the president and his wife. Few visited at Long Branch except invited guests, and those were almost always old personal friends.

So far as the Grants were concerned, Julia Grant's role was that of wife and mother rather than First Lady. Despite their wishes and intentions, she was inevitably drawn into the controversies of the period. In 1869, Grant's brother-in-law Abel Rathbone Corbin, the elderly husband of Grant's sister Jennie, joined the unsavory team of Jay Gould and Jim Fisk in a scheme to corner the gold market, push prices sky-high, and profit handsomely from persons contractually obligated to pay debts in gold. The scheme depended upon persuading government officials to cooperate by not selling gold to lower the price. Corbin's role was to secure Grant's cooperation. Learning of the scheme, Grant asked his wife to write a letter to Jennie urging her to persuade her husband to abandon the enterprise. Grant then arranged the sale of government gold that ended the panic, which became known as Black Friday. Because Julia Grant had penned the letter to Jennie, rumors persisted that she had been involved in the conspiracy and stood to profit.

In general, Mrs. Grant played a far smaller role in the events of the period than rumor reported. Because Grant kept his own counsel, as he had with his cabinet selections, people wondered where he got his ideas. After a desperate effort to discover how Grant thought, Henry Adams began to question that he thought at all. Believing that his ideas came from outside, some attributed Grant's policy to his wife. In reality, policy interested her very little; people, however, interested her very much. At the funeral of Chief Justice Salmon P. Chase, Julia Grant spotted the blond curls of New York Senator Roscoe Conkling, notorious Republican spoilsman, and mused how well they would look against the black robe of the chief justice. She shared her thoughts with her husband, who was already prepared to offer the post to Conkling for barely more sensible reasons. Fortunately, Conkling rejected the offer.

Mrs. Grant tended to personal views of those people close to the president, expecting their complete loyalty and resenting any deviation. Postmaster General Marshall Jewell, formerly a Connecticut governor favored for rescuing Nellie Grant from Miss Porter, attributed Republican setbacks in the 1874 election to administration policy and supported the efforts of Secretary of the Treasury Benjamin H. Bristow to investigate Whiskey Ring scandals. Bristow followed a trail that led to White House private secretary Orville E. Babcock. Afterward, Jewell could not leave the cabinet quickly enough to suit Mrs. Grant.

In 1876, Secretary of War William W. Belknap barely escaped impeachment for selling post traderships. Evidence pointed to the involvement of Belknap's former wife, who had died while he was in office, and to his second wife, a sister of the first. Julia Grant thought of Belknap as a gallant gentleman who had sacrificed himself to protect a woman's honor—a belief rarely shared at the time and even more rarely by posterity. Belknap evaded impeachment chiefly because the president had accepted his resignation before he was charged. Perhaps Grant acted rashly, but certainly without his wife's advice. Mrs. Grant took a passionate interest in the fortunes of the Grant administration, yet it is difficult to discern how she influenced them.

By 1874 many Republicans believed that Grant should receive yet another nomination, despite traditional sentiment against a third term. In congressional elections of that year, Democrats campaigned against a third term for Grant, something few Republicans dared mention. In May 1875 Grant wrote to delegates to a Pennsylvania Republican convention, disavowing all interest in a third term. "I did not want the first," he remarked. Before mailing the letter, Grant had called a rare Sunday afternoon cabinet meeting, at which he read the letter without asking for comment. As soon as the meeting ended, Julia Grant called her husband upstairs, but he stalled until a messenger had deposited the letter in a mailbox. She upbraided him in vain. To allow her to read the letter before it reached the sanctuary of a mailbox would have invited her disapproval. As it was, he had to face only her sulky disappointment.

Following the presidential election of 1876, supporters of both Republican Rutherford B. Hayes and Democrat Samuel J. Tilden claimed victory, throwing the country into turmoil. Mrs. Grant recalled that her "policy would have been to hold the fort until another election could be held." Her husband retorted that it was lucky for the country that she was not president. On Inauguration Day, Mrs. Grant served luncheon to incoming President and Mrs. Hayes, a gracious gesture mixed with a wish to remain in her beloved White House as long as possible. Neither Mary Lincoln, with her queenly airs and irrational behavior, nor Eliza Johnson, reclusive and ill, had succeeded in making the White House into either a comfortable family home or a republican mansion. Julia Grant had succeeded in both. She received praise for restoring "elegance and dignity" to the White House.

Julia Grant wept as she left Washington. After residing in the White House for eight happy years as First Lady, the longest she had lived anywhere with her husband, she now departed for a trip around the world but without a home in the United States. She felt, as her *Memoirs* record, like a "waif." She longed for the comfort of a settled life, but she would go anywhere with her beloved husband, Ulysses.

Because Grant was the youngest man elected president in the nineteenth century and had not yet reached the age of fifty-five when he left office, he faced the problem of what to do next. First, however, came a trip around the world. Neither Grant nor his wife had ever traveled beyond North America, and both looked forward to it. For two and a half years the Grants circled the globe, welcomed everywhere by heads of state in honor both of Grant's accomplishments and as a tribute to the people he represented. Amid strange people with unfamiliar customs, Julia Grant passed some of the happiest days of her life. Near the end of 1879, the Grants docked at San Francisco. Ironically, they returned too soon. The triumphant welcome they received across the country on their way back to Philadelphia, where the trip had begun, faded before Republicans met in June to nominate their presidential candidate. More than 300 Republican stalwarts voted for Grant ballot after ballot before James A. Garfield won the nomination. The problem of what to do remained.

The Grants moved to New York City, to a town house off Fifth Avenue. Their son Buck had entered the world of Wall Street as a partner of Ferdinand Ward—considered a genius of finance—and his father joined the firm as a silent partner. Many potential investors believed that the name of the firm came from the general himself and that its operations reflected Grant's own upright integrity. Unfortunately, they reflected instead the swindles of Ward, who attracted ever increasing funds by proclaiming fabulous returns on earlier investments. Eventually the entire scheme collapsed, burying Grant under a mountain of debt and severely damaging his reputation. Grant owed $150,000 to William H. Vanderbilt, to whom he turned over all his real estate and the souvenirs of his career. When Vanderbilt tried to return the property, putting it in Mrs. Grant's name to save it from other creditors, Mrs. Grant joined her husband in declining the offer. Bankrupt and desperate, Grant soon felt the pain in his throat that was eventually diagnosed as an inoperable cancer. Finding no way to support his family except to write for money, Grant grimly tackled the writing of his memoirs.

During the final year of Grant's life, he exhibited the courage and determination that had made him an American hero. His children joined their mother in caring for him. When Grant realized that he had completed the memoirs, he finally relinquished his struggle on July 23, 1885, at the summer cottage at Mount McGregor, New York, where he had gone to escape the heat of New York City. Her husband's death devastated Julia Grant. Overcome by grief, she could not attend the massive public funeral in New York. Her life had been so thoroughly entwined with that of her husband that she seemed to be paralyzed.

A few years later, however, she recovered sufficiently to begin to dictate her memoirs. Afflicted with strabismus, Julia Grant always avoided both reading and writing. Before the Civil War it had been Grant who read aloud to the family in the evenings. Influenced by the enormous financial and critical success of the *Personal Memoirs of U.S. Grant*, Julia Grant hoped to recount what her husband had omitted and to complete the story of their life together. Grant's account did not go beyond the Civil War, and his wife began her dictation with memories of the trip around the world. Mrs. Grant's memoirs were not published in her lifetime because of her ambivalence about their frankness. No other president's wife had written such a book.

In her final years, Julia Grant lived qui-etly in Washington with her daughter Nellie, whose marriage had long since failed, and she traveled frequently to visit family. Public appearances usually involved the dedication of statues of her husband or reunions of his former troops. To the end, which came on December 14, 1902, she thought of herself as Mrs. Ulysses S. Grant, and she was buried, as both had wished, by his side.

BIBLIOGRAPHICAL ESSAY

Julia Dent Grant preserved and cherished the letters she received from her "dashing lieutenant" and continued to save those of her husband. These letters have been printed in *The Papers of Ulysses S. Grant* (20 vols., Carbondale and Edwardsville, Ill., 1967–). Letters from Julia Grant to her husband, less often found, appear in the same volumes along with other letters written by or addressed to her. Other letters written by Mrs. Grant sometimes appear in manuscript collections but remain scarce because she avoided writing.

The Personal Memoirs of Julia Dent Grant (New York, 1975) supply a charming introduction to a fascinating person. The preceding sketch frequently draws upon her interesting comments. The only biography is Ishbel Ross, *The General's Wife: The Life of Mrs. Ulysses S. Grant* (New York, 1959). Ross wrote without access to important sources yet researched diligently and unearthed considerable obscure material. The bibliography is especially useful. Ross also wrote the sketch of Mrs. Grant in *Notable American Women* (Cambridge, Mass., 1971). For an obituary, see the *New York Times*, December 15, 1902, followed by accounts of her funeral and burial on December 19 and 21–22.

★★★   ★★★

Lucy Ware Webb Hayes

(1831–1889)

First Lady: 1877–1881

Olive Hoogenboom

Lucy Ware Webb was born in Chillicothe, Ohio, on August 28, 1831, to James Webb and Maria Cook Webb, who had been married five years and already had two sons. Lucy's father, a medical doctor, was antislavery, even though he was from the South. In 1833 he returned to his family's home in Lexington, Kentucky, to free fifteen to twenty slaves he had inherited from his aunt. When he arrived there, he worked day and night caring for the sick in a cholera epidemic, in which his parents and brother died. Dr. Webb, too, became a victim of the epidemic, dying before his wife reached his bedside. Lucy proudly recalled her mother's response to friends' advice that she sell the slaves her husband had come to free: Before she would sell a slave, her mother said, she would take in washing to support her family.

At first Maria Webb and her children continued to live near her family in Chillicothe. Her father, Isaac Cook, a state legislator, promoted state-supported schools and was a temperance advocate. He successfully urged Lucy and his other grandchildren to sign a pledge to abstain from using alcohol. Among Lucy's early teachers was a Miss Baskerville, who refused her students recess, keeping them at their desks all day with only a short break for lunch. When Lucy invited her little cousin Joe to school one day, he misbehaved and Miss Baskerville started to hit him. "How dare you whip Joe," Lucy fearlessly cried out, "I brought him to school to visit, and you shan't touch him."

When Lucy was thirteen, her mother moved the family to Delaware, Ohio, where Lucy entered the preparatory department of what is now Ohio Wesleyan University. Later, even though young women were not usually allowed to study there, she took courses in the college department, where her brothers were enrolled. (Like her father, Lucy's brothers both became medical doctors.) It was near the popular sulfur spring on the school's campus that Rutherford B. Hayes, a young lawyer visiting his hometown, first saw "bright-eyed," "clever," and "sunny hearted" Lucy, whom his mother especially wanted him to meet. But Hayes found fifteen-year-old Lucy "not quite old enough to fall in love with." A few months later, fearful that her daughter would be "carried off" into marriage by some graduating Methodist minister, Maria Webb transferred her to Cincinnati Wesleyan Female College—one of the first colleges in the United States to give degrees to women. There Lucy excelled, and in 1850, during her last year, she was elected a member of the exclusive Young Ladies Lyceum.

That same year Hayes, who had moved to Cincinnati, stopped by Lucy's college to visit her. His older sister, Fanny Platt, had described her to him as "so frank, so joyous," and "remarkably intelligent," and reported that she "would be handsome only that she freckles." Late that summer Lucy and Rutherford were members of a wedding party, and seeing her "bright eyes and merry smile" again gave him such a "peculiar" feeling that he gave her the prize—a gold ring—that he found in his piece of wedding cake. When they were secretly engaged the next summer, Lucy put the wedding-cake ring on his finger, and Hayes wore it the rest of his life. With about thirty relatives and friends present, Lucy and Rutherford were married at her home in Cincinnati on December 30, 1852. Following the wedding, they spent a month-long honeymoon at his sister's home in Columbus, where, during the first week, Hayes argued a case before the Ohio Supreme Court.

When the Hayeses returned to Cincinnati, they shared her mother's home, where, within a year of her marriage, Lucy Hayes gave birth to a son, Birchard "Birch" Austin. In all, she would have eight children, five of whom would survive infancy. Influenced by his wife's antislavery sentiments, Hayes, who had thought abolitionists too radical, began defending runaway slaves who had crossed the Ohio River from Kentucky. The Hayeses were so identified with the cause of black freedom that, a month after they settled in their own home near downtown Cincinnati, an abandoned black baby in a bandbox was placed at their door. Lucy Hayes remained in contact with the former slaves of her father's family and often employed them or their descendants in her home. With her in Cincinnati was a former slave, Eliza Jane Burrell, whom she taught to read. The most enduring relationship Lucy Hayes had with any of these workers was with Winnie Monroe—an excellent cook and nurse—who would accompany the Hayeses to the White House. She was the daughter of "Aunt Clara," one of the Kentucky slaves whom Maria Webb had freed, and the mother of Mary Monroe, who, encouraged by Lucy Hayes, attended Oberlin College.

Just after the frigid winter of 1856— when Hayes's work for runaway slaves had increased because more of them could escape across the frozen Ohio River to Cincinnati— Lucy Hayes's second boy, Webb Cook, was born. A few months later Hayes's sister Fanny Platt—who had sparked his political ambition and interested Mrs. Hayes in woman's suffrage—died following childbirth. Earlier Lucy Hayes and Fanny had heard Lucy Stone speak on women's rights. The logic of Lucy Stone's arguments surprised Lucy Hayes, who left the lecture agreeing that reform was needed. If Fanny had lived, she might have influenced Lucy Hayes to work for women's rights, but, despite the efforts of two of Lucy Hayes's aunts, who were active in the women's movement, neither she nor her husband became advocates of women's suffrage.

In 1858, after the birth of her third son, Rutherford "Rud" Platt, Lucy Hayes developed a severe case of rheumatism. During the remainder of her life she was occasionally troubled by it and periodically suffered from migraine headaches. Thanks to her mother and brother Joe, who were append-ages to her home, she was freed from the constant care of her children, who always had an adult lap to climb onto and a live-in physician to see them through childhood diseases. Young Birch felt sorry for his Aunt Fanny's children, who lacked an Uncle Joe.

In 1860, leaving her little boys with her mother and brother Joe Webb, Lucy and Rutherford Hayes took a month-long trip to Canada and the eastern states. Before returning to Cincinnati they stopped in Fremont, where Hayes's uncle, Sardis Bir-chard, was building a fine brick house on a twenty-five-acre wooded triangle he called Spiegel Grove. While he proudly showed them his new house, Birchard told them it would belong to them someday. It became their treasured home and, later, the site of the first presidential library.

During every stage of his political career, Hayes was helped by his wife, who was inter-ested in politics and had an agreeable way with people. Her mother-in-law praised her treatment of "old people," calling it "a rare and excellent trait of character," and a niece never forgot her introduction to "Aunt Lu," who conversed intimately with her during a large party and later brought laughter to her motherless home. After Abraham Lincoln won the 1860 election, Lucy Hayes went with her husband to Indianapolis to accom-pany Lincoln to Cincinnati on the presiden-tial train.

When Southerners attacked Fort Sumter on April 12, 1861, Lucy Hayes patriotically insisted that if she had been there with a detachment of women, it would not have surrendered. She enthusiastically sup-ported her husband's decision to volunteer for the Union Army, in which her brothers became surgeons. Just before Hayes and the Twenty-third Ohio Regiment left for what would become West Virginia, Lucy Hayes spent the night with him in camp. Together they walked from campfire to campfire and talked with the soldiers who were cooking rations for three days. On this night—as throughout the war—Mrs. Hayes especially sympathized with common soldiers. She also sympathized with the brave people who

were striving to win their own freedom. "Above all things Ruddy," she wrote her husband in an unpublished letter of Octo-ber 1861, "if a contraband [runaway slave] is in Camp—dont let the 23rd Regiment be disgraced by returning [him or her] or any thing of the kind."

In late December 1861, eight months after the war's beginning, Lucy Hayes gave birth to her fourth boy, Joseph, who was a very colicky baby. With three little boys to take care of as well as the new baby, Lucy Hayes told her husband on March 13, 1862, in a letter preserved in her papers, that she sometimes thought that "drilling a regi-ment would be play." Despite being busy with the children, she laid aside a lifetime distaste for writing letters and in sprightly snatches of sentences kept Hayes informed about her feelings and those of their boys. She yearned to do something personally to help the North win the war and to stop slav-ery. "It is a hard thing to be a woman—and witness so much and yet not do any thing," she wrote to her brother Joe in an unpub-lished letter of April 23, 1862, while admonishing him to be kind to the sick and wounded. Continuing to search for ways to help, Lucy Hayes began visiting the soldiers who were filling the hospitals in Ohio. Meeting men from the Twenty-third Ohio who had not received their pay while recov-ering from battle wounds, she urged that a system be worked out to get them their back pay promptly. After setting up beds in her "back parlor" for two wounded and two sick soldiers who had missed their train to Chicago, Lucy Hayes imagined in a letter to her husband how he would feel "in a strange country—wounded and trying to get home." In a few months he would indeed be in that situation.

In September 1862—during the Anti-etam campaign—a musket ball hit Hayes's left arm while he and the Twenty-third led the assault that opened the Battle of South Mountain. Severely wounded, he was taken to the home of strangers in Middletown, Maryland. Unknown to him, his first tele-gram was not sent to his wife, and his sec-ond one—"I am here, come to me. I shall not lose my arm"—mistakenly gave Washington as its place of origin. After searching frantically for her husband in the numerous makeshift hospitals in Washington, Lucy Hayes discovered he was in Middletown. She caught the first train to the area of the recent battle, and, after standing most of the way, shared a seat with a woman who despaired of finding her husband alive, because he had lost both legs. "Lucy is here," a pleased Hayes wrote to his Uncle Sardis on September 26, 1862, in a letter printed in his *Diary and Letters*. "She visits the wounded and comes back in tears." In two weeks' time Colonel and Mrs. Hayes and a few other wounded soldiers were able to travel back to Ohio.

After Hayes recovered sufficiently to return to his regiment, his wife—sometimes accompanied by her mother and children and always participating fully in camp life—repeatedly joined him. Adored by young officers and common soldiers, she often helped her brother Joe, the surgeon of Hayes's regiment, to care for the sick. Twenty-year-old William McKinley, then a lieutenant in the regiment, spent hours tending the evening campfire because Lucy Hayes was seated near it. But not all her days in camp were idyllic; there she also spent the "bitterest hour" of her life—when her infant son Joe sickened and died.

Even though Mrs. Hayes was back in Ohio when her fifth boy was born, in September 1864, she felt so much a part of the war that she named him for Hayes's commander, General George Crook. Shortly after that baby's birth, the newspapers reported that Hayes had been killed in the Battle of Cedar Creek. Fortunately, Lucy Hayes did not see the papers until after a telegram arrived saying: "The report that your husband was killed this morning is untrue. He was wounded, not dangerously, and is safe."

Like everyone else in the North, Lucy Hayes's "great joy" at the Confederate surrender at Appomattox turned to "sorrow and grief" when Lincoln was assassinated five days later. "I am sick of the endless talk of Forgiveness," she wrote to Hayes, "tak-ing them back like brothers. . . . Justice and Mercy should go together." In mid-May 1865, Hayes, who had been elected a congressman even though he had refused to leave his troops to campaign, wanted to share the closing scenes of the war with his wife, who had recently recovered from a severe bout of rheumatism. Together they stopped at New Creek, his last army post, where he filled out his resignation papers. Next they went to Washington for the Grand Review of the Union Army. Sitting with her husband in the congressional stand, Lucy Hayes borrowed his field glasses to get a better look at President Andrew Johnson and General Grant. She especially liked the way Grant's boys leaned on him. While her heart filled with joy at the thought of the destruction of slavery, she could not forget the thousands of soldiers who would never come home, especially those who had died in the Twenty-third Ohio.

While Hayes was in Congress, Mrs. Hayes divided her time between Washington and Cincinnati. On their second night out, during her first stay in Washington, the Hayeses went from General Ulysses and Julia Grant's first reception to one given by Senator John and Margaret Sherman. As Hayes told his mother in a letter of February 4, 1866:

> I have always wanted to be the first, the very first at a big party. I never heard of anybody who was first. We did it at Grant's. There were a goodly number of ladies and gentlemen in the clothing-rooms all waiting for somebody to break the ice. Lucy and I hurried off our things and got down first. It was right jolly. General and Mrs. Grant, a sister, and a staff officer's wife waiting anxiously for an attack. We charged and had a good merry time of it all to ourselves.

While in Washington, Mrs. Hayes regularly attended the House of Representatives, wearing a checkered shawl Hayes could easily spot in the chamber's diplomatic gallery.

Lucy Hayes was back in Cincinnati with her boys in mid-April 1866 when Birch came home from school with scarlet fever. The disease quickly moved through the family, and twenty-month-old George, after nearly getting well several times, died from its effects in late May 1866. When Hayes won a second term in Congress, Mrs. Hayes traveled with him and other congressmen (most of whom were, like Hayes, radical Republicans) and their wives to to the scene of recent race riots in Memphis and New Orleans. Despite the Civil War and because of the riots, white Southern women tried to make as favorable an impression as possible and talked cordially and freely with Lucy Hayes at social gatherings.

In 1867, while Hayes campaigned to become governor of Ohio, his wife awaited the birth of her sixth child. To everyone's joy the baby was a girl, named Fanny for her father's sister. When Hayes was elected governor, the family rented a home in Columbus so near to the State House that when Fanny learned to talk, Hayes could hear her call "bye-bye" as he mounted the steps to the governor's office. Lucy Hayes had a difficult time regaining her strength in early 1871 after the birth of her seventh child, an eleven-pound boy whom they named Scott Russell.

During Hayes's two terms as Ohio governor, Lucy Hayes regularly visited hospitals for the mentally ill, reform schools for boys, and other state institutions. Remembering the soldiers she had befriended during the Civil War, Mrs. Hayes secured state funding for an orphanage she had started for veterans' children. Hayes acknowledged her help. "My life with you has been so happy—so successful—so beyond reasonable anticipations," he told her, "that I think of you with a loving gratitude that I do not know how to express." Deciding against a third term as governor, Hayes and his family left Columbus after a farewell reception in January 1872.

The birth of Lucy Hayes's eighth child, at Spiegel Grove on August 1, 1873, left her weak and surprised her older sons, who had no idea that she was pregnant. Named for General Manning F. Force, the new baby was only thirteen months old when he died, probably of dysentery, on Lucy Hayes's forty-third birthday. "With all our changes and sorrows," she managed to write to Webb, who was away at college, "a happy and blessed family we have been and are." After Hayes, following a brief retirement, was pressed by his party to run for governor a third time and was victorious, the *Ohio State Journal* wrote: "Mrs. Hayes is a perfect queen of a woman, and demonstrated as of old that she is equal to any emergency."

When the 1876 Republican National Convention met in Cincinnati, Hayes was Ohio's favorite son and the second choice of many delegates. After the front-runners fell short, he received a majority of the votes on the seventh ballot. Following her husband's nomination for the presidency, Lucy Hayes became the subject of many newspaper articles. "Mrs. Hayes is a most attractive and lovable woman," the *New York Herald* announced. "She is the life and soul of every party. . . . For the mother of so many children she looks . . . youthful." Mrs. Hayes and four of her children fondly remembered the Ohio Day observance at the Centennial Exposition in Philadelphia as the high point of the campaign. "It was one of the happiest days in your mother's life," she wrote her son Rud, who had missed the event. "The expressions of pleasure and joy at your father's appearance touched the old wife who has known his *merits* for many years."

When Hayes and his wife retired on election night, November 7, 1876, they thought that he had lost the race. Apart from their personal disappointment, they felt intense anxiety about black Americans in the South and feared that the Fourteenth and Fifteenth Amendments, which guaranteed civil and voting rights to former slaves, might be nullified. The Hayeses soon learned, however, that nothing had been decided. Both parties claimed to have carried South Carolina, Florida, and Louisiana, and to deserve their electoral votes; and one electoral vote in Oregon, which Hayes clearly carried, was contested on a technicality. To win, Hayes needed all these states' electoral votes, while his opponent, Samuel

J. Tilden, needed only one additional vote. To determine the winner in the states where the returns were disputed, Congress established an Electoral Commission, but, because it awarded disputed state after disputed state to Hayes, the Democrats in Congress delayed the counting of the electoral votes while they pressed for concessions. They delayed the count so long that Hayes, his wife, and their family had to start for Washington by train before they were certain that he had been elected.

On March 2, 1877, a few hours after the disputed election had been decided in Hayes's favor, he and his family were cheered as they arrived in Washington. Newspaper correspondents noted that Lucy—the first president's wife to have graduated from college—was striking and self-confident, and, for the first time, they used the term First Lady regularly in their reporting. A few days later, when Mrs. Hayes was seated at the inauguration with her younger children, Fanny and Scott, on either side, her "gentle and winning face" and the "tender light" in her dark eyes provoked comparisons with the Madonna. But if Lucy Hayes were indeed a Madonna figure, she was an unusually vivacious one, whose happiness was readily reflected in those around her. *The Cleveland Plain Dealer* reported that White House servants were "now all smiles and politeness."

Always fond of people and entertaining, Mrs. Hayes invited young relatives and friends from Ohio to help make large White House events more friendly and less formal. Although her state dinners were described as brilliant, she found them intimidating. Hayes observed in his diary on December 15, 1880, that Mrs. Hayes "*hates* state dinners." At her first one—given for Russian Grand Dukes Alexis and Constantine—she surprised Washington society with her stunning cream-and-gold dress, fringed with pearl embroidery and ribbon rosettes. There were fifteen different dishes on the menu, and at each place setting, besides a water glass and a small bouquet, were six wine glasses, which angered temperance organizations. Realizing the importance of

the temperance vote to the Republican Party and abhoring drunkenness, Hayes decided not to serve alcoholic drinks at the White House again. Because Lucy Hayes was a Methodist teetotaler, she was blamed for her husband's decision. Although no one called her "Lemonade Lucy" at the time, the alliteration—made evident in a contemporary newspaper poem entitled "Lemonade"—is probably responsible for the later widespread use of the nickname.

Mrs. Hayes was best at informal gatherings. "She has the reputation of fascinating her visitors," the *New York Graphic*'s correspondent observed on March 18, 1878, "because . . . she is so vivacious and so responsive that everybody leaves her presence with a vague idea that he is the one person whom she was longing to see." On Sunday evenings, Lucy Hayes, an unusually strong contralto who sometimes accompanied herself on the guitar, gathered friends and family to sing with her around a piano, often played by Secretary of the Interior Carl Schurz. Vice President William A. Wheeler—with whom Mrs. Hayes sometimes went fishing—was almost always a member of this group, and General William T. Sherman and his brother John, the secretary of the treasury, also attended.

In keeping with her egalitarian ideas, Lucy Hayes invited the telegraph operator and all the White House secretaries and their families to her first Thanksgiving dinner in the White House. It took three turkeys and a roast pig to feed them all. After dinner, the children joined Fanny and Scott in a game of blind man's buff, while the adults kept them from bumping into the large bouquets of flowers that decorated the parlors. When Christmas came, Fanny received an enormous, three-story, six-room doll house, built by the White House carpenter. At the sounding of a bell, she and Scott raced to bring presents from the Red Room to the library, where not only their family but all those who worked in the White House waited for their gifts.

On December 30, 1877, came the Hayeses' twenty-fifth wedding anniversary—their grandest celebration—when

Ohio relatives and friends filled the White House and nearby hotels. With Lucy wearing her wedding dress (let out a bit at the seams), the Hayeses repeated their marriage vows to the minister who had married them. The festivities continued on New Year's Eve, when the Marine Band played Mendelssohn's "Wedding March" as Mr. and Mrs. Hayes and their Ohio guests came down the stairs. Next came the traditional New Year's Day reception, which "Miss Grundy," in the *Washington Post* of January 5, 1878, called "the most brilliant ever known to Washington." On New Year's Eve, Mrs. Hayes's flower conservatories were ablaze with gas jets for the first time. These deluxe greenhouses grew to twelve in number during the Hayes years, and one dollar out of every four dollars appropriated for White House upkeep was expended on them. Caring for the flowers in the conservatories occupied ten people, including a woman with a horse and cart to deliver bouquets to hospitals and friends.

From New Year's to Lent, the official Washington social season was in full swing. During that time Mrs. Hayes held receptions every Saturday from three to five. She organized the wives of cabinet members to assist her at each season's first and last reception. At those in between, she asked the wife of one cabinet member to greet the guests with her. She urged everyone to wear street clothes and encouraged lively conversation by stationing her young Ohio house guests in the various parlors.

Lucy Hayes—who characteristically exhibited childlike joy, even jumping up and down when something especially pleased her—was the happiest when she was surrounded by young people and animals. Of her older boys, only Webb, who served as an unofficial secretary to Hayes, lived in the White House. Birch and Rud, away at school, seldom had a bedroom to themselves when they came home. With the White House usually crowded, the Hayes children and their visiting friends often had to sleep on cots in hallways, couches in reception rooms, or even in large bathtubs. Pets included the country's first Siamese cat, a loud-singing

mocking bird, two dogs, and a goat who hauled Scott around the White House grounds in a cart. Because Congress no longer permitted area children to roll eggs on the Capitol grounds, Mrs. Hayes invited them to use the White House lawn on Easter Monday, and that activity, which started in 1878, has become a First Lady tradition.

In Washington, Lucy Hayes continued her work for veterans and young people. She often visited Gallaudet College for the deaf and Hampton Institute near Norfolk, Virginia, where she furnished a scholarship for an Indian girl. When she heard that Major Bailey, an old soldier, was sick and without funds, she persuaded cabinet members to contribute $125 for him, and, in the month of January 1880 alone, she and Hayes gave $990 to help the poor in Washington.

It bothered Lucy Hayes to see from the south windows of the White House the abandoned, one-quarter-finished monument to George Washington, begun forty years earlier. Congress had recently appropriated money to complete it but had insisted that the foundation be strengthened before construction was resumed. With his wife's concern added to his own interest, Hayes consulted experts—who advised that a hoop skirt be added to the foundation to support the enormous weight of the planned obelisk. Hayes then began work on the project, and made its completion his hobby.

Deciding to celebrate American flora and fauna in a new set of White House dishes, Lucy Hayes asked Theodore R. Davis, an artist noted for his knowledge of American plants and animals, to design them. The realistic results, he admitted, were "curiosities of ceramics." After dining on them, Clover Adams, a celebrated Washington hostess and letter writer, complained that she had difficulty eating her soup calmly with a coyote springing at her from a pine tree. Lucy Hayes partly agreed with those who thought that the new dishes belonged more in a museum than on a dinner table. "One almost feels as if such Ceramic Art should be used for no other purpose except to gratify the eye," she wrote the artist. But her young guests loved eating from the new dishes—one of them, writing to her family back in Ohio, called them "superb."

The Hayeses traveled so much that the *Chicago Times* of September 6, 1878, called the president "Rutherford the Rover." During an 1877 trip to New England, they met the historian John W. Burgess, who insisted that they made such a perfect couple that anyone "who ever saw them together could never think of speaking of them apart." The success of that trip convinced them to travel south in an effort to help unify the country. Southerners received them enthusiastically. "Mrs. Hayes," the *Richmond Dispatch* reported, "has won the admiration of people wherever she has been in the recent tours of the President."

The Hayeses' California trip kept them away from Washington for seventy-two days near the end of their White House years. It was the first time that a president and First Lady had ever visited the West Coast while in office, and their presence caused excitement. When they reached Utah, they rode in the engineer's cab to better see Echo Canyon, rising high above the train tracks. Later, on a stagecoach to Roseburg, Oregon, General William T. Sherman, who accompanied them, rode shotgun on the box beside the driver. They made a side trip to visit Sarah Winnemucca, a young teacher who was a Piute chief's daughter. (Sarah had been vaccinated for smallpox, along with Lucy Hayes and White House guests, when she was part of an Indian delegation to Washington.) While the presidential party was at Winnemucca's school, the *Daily Oregonian* of October 7, 1880, observed that she petitioned Hayes so eloquently to gather her people at "one place where they could live permanently and be cared for and instructed" that Lucy Hayes was moved to tears. The next day's *Oregonian* noted that at Walla Walla in the Washington Territory, dancers from the Umatilla Nation performed an hour-long war dance, "wild and fantastic beyond comprehension," which proved "the

most novel and interesting scene of the entire trip."

After stops in Seattle, San Francisco, Yosemite, and Los Angeles, the president, his wife, and their party headed back east by train until the tracks ended in New Mexico. Getting into horse-drawn wagons and army ambulances, they covered 172 miles in three arduous days before reaching another railhead. During the first sixty-four miles of this journey, they were accompanied by a heavy military guard, as they were traveling through dangerous country dominated by Apache war parties and bands of outlaw cowboys. In Santa Fe they attended a colorful fiesta before boarding a train for St. Louis. Early on the morning of November 1, 1880, they were back at Spiegel Grove.

During Mrs. Hayes's last months in the White House, the whole country poured out its love and affection for her. She was described as the most widely known and popular president's wife the country had known. Always great entertainers, the Hayeses had so many visitors during their last three months in Washington that their steward, William T. Crump, claimed that they averaged thirty-seven guests for each dinner during this period. On February 24, 1881, all the rooms of the White House, including the flower conservatories, were opened to provide room for over 2,000 guests who attended the reception for the Diplomatic Corps.

When Lucy Hayes's last week in Washington arrived, everyone was sad. According to Hayes's diary of September 1, 1885, Elizabeth Bancroft, the wife of the historian George Bancroft, claimed that there had never been a White House mistress "so well fitted for her place," and Chief Doorkeeper Thomas Pendel encountered more weeping people than he had seen during his thirty-six years at the White House. On her last day there, Lucy Hayes served lunch to the Garfield family, just as Julia Grant had served lunch to the Hayes family four years earlier. As soon as she could get away, Mrs. Hayes left the table for a hurried inspection of the White House. "All was lovely and serene," she later commented. "It was well I was so hurried for the goodbyes would have overcome me, for I grew to love the house."

Back in Spiegel Grove, Lucy Hayes continued her duties as national president of her church's Woman's Home Missionary Society—a position she had held since 1880. The society's goal was to improve the home life and condition of women in the United States, and Mrs. Hayes regularly addressed its annual meeting in cities such as Philadelphia and Detroit. In her retirement, young people and animals continued to crowd around her. She told her husband's cousin that her beloved greyhound with "his dignified trot" was always beside her carriage, causing children to shout: "Oh there is Mrs. Hayes and Gryme." While seated at a bay window sewing and watching Fanny and her friends play tennis, Lucy Hayes suffered a stroke. She died at home a few days later on June 25, 1889, and was buried at Oakwood Cemetery. Hayes died three and a half years later and was buried beside his wife. In 1915 their remains were moved to Spiegel Grove. Below them are the graves of Gryme and two favorite horses, Old Whitey and Old Ned.

For Lucy Webb Hayes, the hardest part of being First Lady was reading unfair comments about her husband. "I keep myself outwardly very quiet and calm," she told him, "but inwardly (some times) there is a burning venom and wrath." But she forced herself to hide her occasional anger "under a smiling and pleasant exterior." Possessing an acute sense of history, she felt connected with the First Ladies she followed and influenced those who followed her. She visited Sarah Polk at her home near Nashville, Tennessee; took pleasure in sleeping at Martha Washington's Mount Vernon home; admired the immense trees at Montpelier, the home of Dolley Madison; had Julia Tyler officiate with her at a February 1878 White House reception; was on friendly terms with Julia Dent Grant, Lucretia Garfield, and Ida Saxton McKinley; and in 1877 introduced to White House living seventeen-year-old Helen "Nellie" Herron, who would marry William Howard Taft in 1886 and become First Lady in 1909.

BIBLIOGRAPHICAL ESSAY

The Lucy Webb Hayes Papers, 1841–1890, are at the Hayes Presidential Center, Spiegel Grove, Fremont, Ohio. Also located there are the papers of her husband, children, and other members of her family. The center's material on Lucy Hayes's forebears can be augmented by items in the Cook Collection, Western Reserve Historical Society, Cleveland. The papers of some of Rutherford B. Hayes's cabinet members and other associates are at the Hayes Presidential Center, as are copies of letters in other depositories concerning the Hayes administration and members of the Hayes family. Located at the center is the original typescript of "Lucy's Search for Her Husband," the account of her difficulty in finding Hayes after he was severely wounded during the Civil War, which she dictated to a typist during her White House years. Also housed at the center are remembrances of her by her contemporaries. Among these are Mrs. John (Eliza Given) Davis, *Lucy Webb Hayes: A Memorial Sketch* (1890); Laura Platt Mitchell, "Lucy Webb Hayes: Reminiscences for Her Grandson by One of Her Nieces" (1890); and Lucy E. Keeler, "Lucy Webb Hayes: Her Family, Life, and Letters" (1904).

The most complete biography of Lucy Hayes is Emily Apt Geer, *First Lady: The Life of Lucy Webb Hayes* (Kent and Fremont, Ohio, 1984). All quotations in this entry, unless otherwise indicated, are found in her book. Also of interest is Watt P. Marchman, "Lucy Webb Hayes in Cincinnati: The First Five Years 1848–1852," *Bulletin of the Historical and Philosophical Society of Ohio* (January 1955). Much can be learned about Lucy Hayes in T. Harry Williams, ed., Hayes: *The Diary of a President, 1876–1881* (New York, 1964); and Charles Richard Williams, ed., *Diary and Letters of Rutherford Birchard Hayes: Nineteenth President of the United States* (5 vols., Columbus, Ohio, 1922–1926). She is also frequently mentioned in books covering aspects of her husband's career, including T. Harry Williams, *Hayes of the Twenty-third* (New York, 1965); and works published by Kenneth E. Davison (Westport, Conn., 1972) and Ari Hoogenboom (Lawrence, Kans., 1988) that share the title *The Presidency of Rutherford B. Hayes*. Lucy Hayes's life can also be traced in the following biographies of her husband: Charles Richard Williams, *The Life of Rutherford Birchard Hayes: Nineteenth President of the United States* (2 vols., Columbus, Ohio, 1914); H. J. Eckenrode, *Rutherford B. Hayes* (New York, 1930); Harry Barnard, *Rutherford B. Hayes and His America* (Indianapolis, 1954); and Ari Hoogenboom, *Rutherford B. Hayes: Warrior and President* (Lawrence, Kans., 1995). An obituary is in the *New York Times*, June 26, 1889.

★★★ ★★★

Lucretia Rudolph Garfield

(1832–1918)

First Lady: March 4, 1881–September 19, 1881

Allan Peskin

Lucretia Rudolph was born on April 19, 1832, in Garrettsville, a village near Hiram, in Portage County, Ohio, a rural corner of the New England–influenced Western Reserve district. Her mother, Arabella Mason Rudolph, was from Vermont and her father, Zebulon Rudolph, a well-to-do farmer and carpenter, was born in Virginia of German descent. They were pious, kindly, but undemonstrative parents, not given to outward displays of affection.

Lucretia (inevitably nicknamed "Crete"), the eldest of four children, passed a sickly childhood, suffering from some sort of respiratory ailment that often left her bedridden. These periods of enforced isolation intensified her bookish tendencies, and she grew into a serious, dutiful but emotionally repressed adolescent.

The Western Reserve's New England tradition encouraged the education of women, and the region's struggling schools could ill afford to turn away prospective students. Lucretia was sent to the Geauga Seminary, a Baptist-affiliated academy at nearby Chester. There she met James Abram Garfield, who was also enrolled as a student. Once she exhausted the academy's offerings, she enrolled at the newly opened Western Reserve Eclectic Institute. Located at Hiram, this semicollegiate institution was run by her own denomination, the Disciples of Christ. In fact, her father helped establish it and was a member of the board of trustees.

At the Eclectic Institute, Lucretia's path again crossed that of James Garfield. Her senior by only half a year, Garfield was a social step beneath her. Born in a log cabin, reared by a widowed mother, he led an aim-less youth, culminating in a short stint on the rowdy Ohio Canal, where, he later real-ized, he was "ripe for ruin . . . ready to drink in with every species of vice." He was spared by his religious conversion—to the Disciples of Christ—and by his immense capacity for learning, a capacity that pro-pelled him, whatever his social drawbacks may have been, to the position of acknowl-edged intellectual leader of the Eclectic's student body.

Lucretia remembered James from their time together at Geauga Seminary, but their acquaintance remained casual while each pursued other adolescent romantic interests. He became attracted to a pretty but insipid schoolgirl, and she became pre-occupied with an infatuation for a hand-some but dissolute young man who scarcely noticed her. When those relationships soured, Lucretia and James began to pay closer attention to one another. She was already his prize Greek student, and he could hardly fail to have noticed her liquid black eyes, her high, chiseled cheekbones, and her jet-black hair, drawn tightly back in the severe fashion of the day.

The courtship began in a stiffly formal manner in November 1853 with the inau-guration of a correspondence, initially on the subject "The Study of Dead Lan-guages." Gradually the letters became more personal, and by springtime it seemed set-tled. "We love each other, and have declared it," Garfield told his diary. Yet, at the same time, he was also expressing reser-vations: "There is no delirium of passion nor overwhelming power of feeling that draws me to her irresistibly," he noted.

Part of his misgivings may have been prompted by the essay "Women's Status," which Lucretia wrote for the school literary magazine. The essay displayed a disturbing degree of independence. "Is it equitable," she asked, "that the woman who teaches school equally well should receive a smaller compensation than man, who is so much more able to support himself in other ways?" By 1854, however, this brief rebel-lious mood had been quashed and a subdued

Lucretia docilely agreed that "Woman's province is her home."

A more serious impediment was Lucre-tia's reserved demeanor, molded by her stiffly formal upbringing. Garfield was impetuous and passionate, given to soulful introspection, moody effusions, and extrav-agant flights of rhetorical fancy. His emo-tions ran deep, and he enjoyed baring them for others to share. "I am so constituted," he confessed in his diary, "that I cannot enjoy a cool formal friend (a misnomer) but must be as a brother or sister to enjoy them." Did Lucretia, he wondered, possess "that warmth of feeling that loving nature which I need to make me happy"? Actually, she did, but her tightly controlled emotions were revealed only to the pages of the private diary, in which her passion for her "noble James" was expressed with a rapture she would not allow herself to reveal in person.

After commencement their paths diverged: his took him to Williams College in Massachusetts, to continue his education in a more prestigious setting; hers took her in a direction not customary for her time and station, to various northern Ohio commu-nities where she taught school. This demon-stration of independence was satisfying but temporary, as it was generally assumed that she and James would eventually marry.

That prospect seemed clouded when James's first visit home produced a strained and chilly reunion. In desperation, Lucre-tia drew her diary out of its hiding place and allowed him to read her secret thoughts. Overwhelmed by this revelation of hitherto concealed emotional depths, Garfield returned to Williams in an exultant mood. "My every thought goes winging westward," he dramatically proclaimed, "singing like a golden seraph, its song of rejoicing and love."

In Massachusetts, away from Lucretia's presence, James's affections strayed for a time to another. But after graduation, when he returned to Hiram, first as professor of ancient languages and then as college pres-ident (at the age of twenty-five), his com-mitment to marry Lucretia could not be evaded. He left all the arrangements to his betrothed, saying curtly, "I don't want much parade about our marriage. Arrange that as you think best."

Lucretia and James were married on November 11, 1858, in a simple ceremony at the Rudolph home, then located in Hiram. There was no honeymoon. The bridal couple took rooms at a local boardinghouse, which Lucretia Garfield tried to make into a home for her reluctant spouse.

It was not the most auspicious beginning for "life in union." The bride continually fought back tears as her husband bluntly told her that their marriage was probably "a great mistake." He found ways to busy himself elsewhere, first in college duties and then in a new career as state senator. That required even more frequent absences while he boarded in Columbus during legislative sessions.

In 1860, the birth of a daughter, Eliza (named after James's mother, who lived with them), brought the Garfields closer together. Little Eliza's father doted upon "Trot," as the baby was nicknamed, but the coming of the Civil War broke up the family circle. James went off to war, first as colonel of the Forty-second Ohio Volunteer Infantry and soon as brigadier general of volunteers.

The next summer he returned home, not in triumph, but near death from jaundice and dysentery. His wife lovingly nursed him back to health in an isolated farmhouse they had secured at nearby Howland Springs. In that secluded setting they enjoyed the first extended privacy they had ever known. During this long-deferred honeymoon, Lucretia Garfield's coldness finally melted, and her husband rejoiced in the change. "It is indeed," he told her, "a baptism into a new life which our souls have received and which, after so many years of hoping and despairing has at last appeared in the fulness of its glory."

It was a false dawn. With his health now restored, Garfield was ordered east to await a new assignment. It was probably at this time, lonely and bored while he was waiting for a decision from the War Department, that he made the acquaintance of Lucia Calhoun, a previously married New Yorker with literary aspirations. Apparently "the fire of . . . lawless passion" (as Lucretia Garfield called it) was briefly kindled between them. Little is known of the episode because Garfield was able to retrieve and destroy the incriminating papers, but he did later admit that this was the occasion on which he had "come closest" to betraying his marriage vows.

When Lucretia Garfield learned of her husband's lapse, she bitterly reproached him: "James, I should not blame my own heart if it lost all faith in you. I hope it may not . . . but I shall not be forever telling you I love you when there is evidently no more desire for it on your part than present manifestations indicate." Her errant husband at first attempted to bluster his way through the crisis, but memories of their recent Howland Springs idyll melted his pose of cold formality, and he pleaded for "a truce to sadness" and a fresh start.

Their reconciliation had to be conducted mainly by correspondence, as Garfield had finally received his long-awaited assignment to the front. While he was serving as chief of staff of the Army of the Cumberland and winning glory (and a major general's star) at the Battle of Chickamauga, his wife held down the home front, giving birth to a second child, Harry Augustus (b. 1863). Garfield made his son's brief acquaintance in the fall of 1863, during a hurried family reunion squeezed in between his resignation from the army and the assumption of the seat in the U.S. House of Representatives that he had won the previous fall.

Then tragedy struck. On December 1, 1863, three-and-a-half-year-old Eliza suddenly died. Her father was so distraught that he considered returning to the army to escape his sorrow, but Lucretia Garfield, displaying the emotional strength expected of nineteenth-century women, reconciled him to life without "our blessed little Trot." It was a hard lesson. "He was never quite the same after the death of Trot," she later said.

In at least one respect, he was better. Garfield's affections never again strayed from home and family. The redemptive power of a child's untimely death was one of the standard themes of the era's literature. The Garfields often shed sentimental tears over fictional tragedies. Now a real-life loss linked them together with bonds of shared suffering.

Not even the glamour of Congress could shake Garfield from his depression. When he returned to rented rooms in Washington, "more alone than ever before in my life," his thoughts dwelled obsessively upon his lost daughter. His wife, who was no stranger to loneliness, had a remedy. One evening, when he was visiting home, she silently handed her husband a slip of paper on which she had jotted a set of figures. They documented that in their nearly five years of married life they had spent only twenty weeks together. No more needed to be said. When Garfield returned to Washington, his wife accompanied him. Never again would they live apart.

At first the Garfields rented rooms but, after a few elections, it became clear that Garfield's hold on his constituents was so strong that he could consider Washington a permanent home. In 1869 they built a house on the corner of 13th and I streets and settled down—for the first time—in their very own home.

They were not alone, of course. Lucretia Garfield's mother-in-law, a frail but tough-minded old lady, always lived with them, as did the occasional servants and governesses needed to help with the ever-growing Garfield brood. Harry was followed by James Rudolph (b. 1865), Mary, called "Mollie" (b. 1867), Irvin (b. 1870), Abram (b. 1872), and Edward, called "Neddy" (b. 1874). Neddy's death in 1876 ended the cycle.

Lucretia Garfield presided over what her husband called "this sweet circle" with dignity and efficiency, transforming her home into a model of Victorian-era middle-class domesticity. She had become, her now-contented husband belatedly acknowledged, "the solid land on which I build all my happiness and hope." Their adolescent yearnings for a "delirium of passion" had given way to mature serenity. "The tyranny of our love is sweet. We waited long for his coming, but he has come to stay."

To a twentieth-century observer, Mrs. Garfield's surrender to domesticity represented the tragedy of "an intellectually alert, capable, feminist-inclined young woman who was nearly erased into nothingness." Lucretia Garfield would have found this harsh judgment simply incomprehensible. Her hard-won family bliss was so precious to her that she had no patience with feminist demands for the right to vote or even for dress reform if they would threaten, even slightly, the sanctity of home and marriage. Far from feeling "crushed into nothingness," she felt as important as those Roman matrons she had studied in Latin class who instilled virtue in their children and courage in their husbands.

Nor was her intellectual development stifled by the demands of family life. She remained an avid reader of poetry, especially Burns and Tennyson, and of novels, eagerly following the serialization of Henry James's *Portrait of a Lady* as it appeared chapter by chapter in the *Atlantic Monthly*. Throughout her life her correspondence and diary would be peppered with well-chosen literary allusions, attesting to her continued involvement with the life of the mind.

By her own choice, Lucretia Garfield did not share in her husband's Washington swirl of banquets and dinner parties; however, she was not simply a passive homebody. "The General"—as she usually called her husband—regularly turned to the woman he called "the best woman I have ever known" for encouragement and advice on the course of his career. In the summer of 1880, that career took a sudden and unexpected turn.

The Republican Party was at a crossroads. Although it had controlled the presidency ever since the Civil War, the party's support had recently eroded, as attested by the narrow victory (if, indeed, it could be called a victory) of Rutherford B. Hayes four years earlier under disputed circumstances. Hayes's refusal to seek a second term threw the nomination wide open. The leading candidate was former president Ulysses S. Grant, who was supported by a group of prominent "Stalwart" senators, most notably New York's imperious Roscoe Conkling. Grant's nomination was opposed by a number of Republicans, particularly Maine's James G. Blaine and Ohio's John Sherman, who feared that a return to Grantism would sink the party.

As a congressman, Garfield was on friendly terms with Blaine and, as an Ohio delegate to the Republican convention, he was committed to Sherman, but he was also on cordial enough terms with leading stalwarts that he might prove an acceptable compromise choice, should the convention deadlock. Garfield himself disclaimed any such ambition. His wife agreed. "I don't want you to have the nomination merely because no one else can get it," she told him. "I want you to have it when the whole country calls for you. . . ." But with the deeply divided Republican Party unable to agree on a nominee, some sort of compromise was inevitable. On the thirty-sixth ballot the delegates impulsively turned to Garfield, overriding his protests that he was not a candidate.

Lucretia Garfield did not know "whether to be sad or rejoice" over her husband's nomination, but she dutifully settled into the role expected of her. Nineteenth-century Americans did not believe that would-be presidents should actively campaign. The fiction was still maintained that this office should seek the man. Except for a few fence-mending forays into the East, the candidate remained at his Mentor, Ohio, home, pretending to lead a normal life.

That home in Mentor had been acquired in 1876 as a permanent Ohio residence to replace the summer homes the Garfields had rented ever since they had left Hiram. Previously a run-down farmhouse on 160 acres of land east of Cleveland, their new home was finally expanded and made presentable by mid-1880, just in time for the presidential campaign. Because convention prevented Garfield from sallying forth to meet the voters, the voters were expected to come to him, in what was called a "front-porch campaign." Daily delegations arrived at "Lawnfield" (as the newspapers grandly dubbed the farmhouse) to pay their respects. While there they trampled the grounds and gawked at the house and its inhabitants. The Garfield family served as a background

prop, a sort of tableau of rural family life, designed to assure the public that the candidate shared its values and lifestyle.

Lucretia Garfield and her family endured this ordeal with good grace and even found themselves enjoying it at times. Republican victory in November 1880, however, brought fresh problems. It was not merely the flurry of shopping trips and dressmakers' fittings required for the family's new position in the social limelight, but also the hard decisions required in shaping the new government. The president-elect solicited suggestions from all quarters of his party, but he paid particular attention to the advice of his wife.

That advice was moral as well as political. Exercising woman's traditional prerogative as custodian of home and family, Mrs. Garfield scrutinized potential cabinet appointees for their domestic and social fitness. Thaddeus Pound of Wisconsin flunked this test because of a youthful scandal that had once touched his wife. Lucretia Garfield was more forgiving toward James G. Blaine, whose first child had appeared awkwardly close to his wedding date. Satisfied that Blaine had been man enough to make an honest woman of his wife, Mrs. Garfield raised no further objections to his appointment as secretary of state.

With that impediment removed, Lucretia Garfield became Blaine's champion, serving as a conduit through which Blaine's views were transmitted to her husband. While on a preinaugural shopping trip to New York City (using the pseudonym "Mrs. Greenfield" to avoid publicity), Lucretia Garfield stayed at the home of Whitelaw Reid, Blaine's chief New York crony. Both men were anxious to put an end to the control of the state party organization exercised by their hated rival, Conkling. They took this opportunity to fill their houseguest's ear with lurid tales of Conkling's duplicity and ingratitude. Lucretia Garfield did not need to be persuaded. She already distrusted Conkling because of his well-publicized extramarital affair with Washington beauty Kate Chase Sprague (whom she had long resented because of a suspected wartime flirtation with her own husband).

Garfield was hoping to harmonize all factions of his party, but his wife, at Reid's prodding, urged that he side with Blaine to crush the Stalwarts. The only way to deal with Conkling's friends, she insisted, was to "fight them *dead*. You can put every one of them in his political grave if you are a mind to. . . ." Garfield's subsequent break with Conkling, which nearly paralyzed his administration, was due more to the New York senator's arrogance and intransigence than to the First Lady's prompting, but her encouragement certainly helped to stiffen the president's resolve.

The president-elect and his family arrived in Washington on March 1, 1881. The preinaugural days were crowded with such intense emotions that, as Lucretia Garfield told the diary she had started up again after a lapse of twenty-five years, only "the tears would tell of the strange excitement that had touched my heart." This emotional high would peak on March 4, during the ceremony at which her husband was sworn in as chief executive. All eyes were on the Garfield family, especially his aged mother, but Lucretia saw and heard nothing but her husband, who "became in the magnificence with which he pronounced his Inaugural almost superhuman."

The ceremony was followed by an exhausting round of parades, balls (though the First Couple begged off from dancing), and receptions. At one reception Lucretia Garfield stood at the head of a seemingly endless line of well wishers, shaking hands and mumbling greetings. She later complained in her diary:

> Before the first hour was over, I was aching in every joint, and thought how can I ever last through the next long sixty minutes. But the crowd soon made me forget myself, and though nearly paralyzed the last hour passed more quickly than the first.

For such a private person, all this public exposure was a new and somewhat intimidating experience. Unlike many previous First Ladies, who had been the wives of governors or cabinet ministers, Lucretia Garfield had been sheltered from the great world behind her self-erected walls of domesticity. She turned for advice to Mrs. Blaine, in much the same way her husband leaned on Secretary Blaine. Mrs. Blaine, like her husband, never suffered from a lack of confidence and briskly set the First Lady straight on matters of political and social protocol.

The most troubling of these matters was a legacy from the Hayes administration. President Hayes had initiated a controversial practice of banning all alcoholic refreshments, including wine, from the White House table. Old Washington hands, reputedly a hard-drinking lot, ridiculed this policy and derisively dubbed his wife (its perceived promulgator) "Lemonade Lucy." Temperance advocates, a significant element of Republican support, revered Mrs. Hayes as a moral exemplar and urged her successor to follow the path she had blazed.

Lucretia Garfield was torn. Though she sympathized with the reformers' goals, she was put off by their fanaticism. There was also the dignity of the White House to be considered, especially in the eyes of foreign diplomats. The Blaines advised the president and his wife not to let "the usages of village society" interfere with the administration's social success. Their advice was decisive and, though some face-saving compromise was possible, alcohol was once more available to brighten White House evenings.

With this crisis surmounted, the First Lady was free to turn to the project closest to her heart—making the White House a home for her family. Despite its outward magnificence, the old mansion was in a shabby state, with tattered drapes, worn carpets, and even structural flaws. To repair these defects she enlisted expert help "to support me or rather the President" (a revealing turn of phrase illustrative of how she perceived her subordinate status) in lobbying Congress for funds.

While planning for the mansion's future, Lucretia Garfield also immersed herself in its past, learning all she could about the lives of its previous occupants.

These little scraps of reminiscences that I gather up now and then lend to this old place a weird charm that I fancy might grow into a solemn silence with me, did not my live boys go tumbling through it with their hand-springs and somersaults.

Little Abe and Irvin delighted in riding their high-wheeled bicycles through the White House hallways, scattering the lines of office seekers and callers. James Rudolph was usually closeted with tutors, preparing for college in the fall. Harry, who was also supposed to be studying, was too smitten with an adolescent romance to pay much attention to his studies or to anything else. This was the sort of intense passion for which his father had once yearned, but neither the president nor Harry's mother, who took him aside for long talks, was able to understand or control it. Mollie seemed more tractable. Her mother beamed with pride as she watched her daughter organize luncheon parties for her little friends, but no one noticed the soulful glances she directed at Joseph Stanley-Brown, the president's private secretary, whom she would one day marry.

Care for her husband's health and well-being remained, as always, Lucretia Garfield's prime concern. Then, suddenly, their roles were reversed. On May 4, 1881, the president's wife was stricken with a serious illness. The doctors called it malaria, but exhaustion undoubtedly played a part. Chills were followed by racing pulse and a dangerously high fever, soaring at times to over 104 degrees. For a time the doctors despaired of her life and the distraught president sank to his knees on the Red Room floor, alternately sobbing and praying. During an earlier illness he had told his wife: "When you are sick, I am like the inhabitants of countries visited by earthquakes. They lose all faith in the eternal order of things." Now he personally took charge of her care, canceling his appointments and nursing her through bouts of fever and carrying "the dear one," when she was able to sit up, from room to room. He was made "tearfully proud" when she told

the doctors that he was "much the best nurse" she had.

Although Lucretia Garfield passed the crisis, she remained bedridden in a state of "nervous prostration" for over a month. By June 18, 1881, she was strong enough to travel. Her husband sent her to Long Branch, New Jersey, in the hope that rest and the refreshing sea breeze would restore her to full health.

Mrs. Garfield was recuperating at the Jersey shore on July 2 when word was flashed across the nation that her husband had been shot by a demented assassin. She immediately returned to Washington on a special train that was placed at her disposal. There she found the wounded president in his White House bedroom, surrounded by physicians who convinced him that he could not live out the day. Tearfully, he prayed that he might be spared long enough to see his wife once more. When she arrived that evening, he drew her close and tried to whisper his final instructions for rearing the children after his death. She cut him short. "Well, my dear," she said with an assumed air of brisk confidence, "you are not going to die as I am here to nurse you back to life; so please do not speak again of death."

And nurse him she did, throughout the hot Washington summer. Her own illness was put aside as she tended her stricken husband with the help of a battery of overworked doctors and attendants. For months the most powerful man in America lay helpless as a baby. He had to be lifted, turned, dressed, fed, and even changed. The First Lady took charge of his care and, under her supervision, the patient rallied and seemed to regain some of his strength.

The entire nation avidly followed the daily bulletins issued from the White House sickroom. The ordeal of the fallen leader and his wife, "the bravest woman in the universe," captured the public imagination as had no event since wartime.

All this effort was unavailing. After each deceptive rally the president sank ever closer to death. By September a change of scene was decided upon. It was hoped that the sea breeze would work upon him the same magic it had for his wife. On September 6 he was transferred in a specially fitted train to Elberon, New Jersey. It was too late for fresh air or anything else. At 10:35 P.M. on September 15, 1881, the president died. His wife was at his side.

Displaying the same strength she had demonstrated during his illness, the president's widow took charge of the funeral arrangements, a massive display of public mourning. When that was over, she supervised the planning of the monumental tomb in Cleveland's Lake View Cemetery that would house his remains.

As she had spent the past quarter-century as James A. Garfield's wife, so she lived out the rest of her days as the president's widow, arranging his papers for posterity, writing letters on black-bordered stationery, and indignantly denying all rumors that she might remarry. Supported by the income from a nearly $360,000 trust fund raised by popular subscription, she lived at Mentor surrounded by children, grandchildren, and memories. Family remained the focus of her life, and she basked in the reflected glow of her children's successes. Harry became president of his father's alma mater, Williams College, in Massachusetts. James would be secretary of the interior during the Theodore Roosevelt administration.

As Lucretia Garfield grew older, the Ohio winters proved too taxing, and she established a second home in Pasadena, California. Active and alert, she attended the first Rose Bowl Parade, rolled bandages for the Red Cross during World War I, and—at last showing her independent streak—supported a Democrat, Woodrow Wilson, in 1916. Two years later, on March 13, 1918, Mrs. Garfield died in Pasadena at the age of eighty-five. She was laid to rest beside her husband in the basement crypt of the Garfield Monument.

As the wife of the president with the second shortest term of office (next to that of William Henry Harrison), Lucretia Garfield scarcely had a chance to make her mark on the White House. Her career, like that of her husband, was richer with possibilities than with accomplishments—a dramatic and tragic interlude in the story of First Ladies.

BIBLIOGRAPHICAL ESSAY

The indispensable sources for the life of Lucretia Garfield are in the Library of Congress, Manuscript Division. Her own papers are especially valuable for the periods of her youth and widowhood. The collections of her sons, Harry and James R. Garfield, are useful for family matters. The massive collection of her husband's papers (also available on 177 reels of microfilm) chronicles their life together, though specific correspondence between them is sparse except during their rare periods of separation. A charming and revealing selection from that correspondence can be found in John Shaw, ed., *Crete and James: Personal Letters of Lucretia and James Garfield* (East Lansing, Mich., 1994). The most comprehensive printed source consists of the four volumes of Harry J. Brown and Frederick D. Williams, eds., *The Diary of James A. Garfield* (East Lansing, Mich., 1967–1981). Lucretia Garfield's White House diary is included as an appendix to the final volume of this remarkably well edited set.

The standard biographies of President Garfield are Margaret Leech and Harry J. Brown, *The Garfield Orbit* (New York, 1978); and Allan Peskin, *Garfield* (Kent, Ohio, 1978). The former is especially strong on personal relationships; the latter stresses public affairs. It is also the source of all the quotations in the preceding essay, unless otherwise noted. For an illuminating discussion of the Western Reserve environment of Lucretia Garfield's early years, see Hendrik Booraem, *The Road to Respectability* (Lewisburg, Pa., and London, 1988). See also the comprehensive bibliographic survey compiled by Robert O. Rupp, *James A. Garfield: A Bibliography* (Westport, Conn., 1997), esp. 139–140.

General studies of First Ladies include an anecdotal collection, Paul Boller, *Presidential Wives* (New York, 1988), which is the source for Lucretia Garfield's schoolgirl essays, and Betty Boyd Caroli, *First Ladies* (New York, 1987), whose modern-day feminist evaluation is cited in the preceding essay. An extensive obituary was published in the Cleveland *Plain Dealer*, March 14, 1918.

★★★　　★★★

Frances Clara Folsom Cleveland

(1864–1947)

First Lady: 1886–1889, 1893–1897

Rebecca Edwards

Born on July 21, 1864, Frances Clara Folsom became the nation's youngest First Lady at the age of twenty-one, when she married President Grover Cleveland. Celebrated for her beauty, thoughtfulness, and social grace, she focused most of her energy on her private roles as wife and mother. This reflected her own preference as well as the political views of her husband, who argued that the president's wife had no public position. Ironically, however, Frances Cleveland's years in the White House marked a turning point in the First Lady's role. Frances Cleveland became a national celebrity and symbol of her generation, modernizing the public image of the Democratic Party and serving as a popular trademark in the world of commercial advertising.

Frances Folsom was born into a well-to-do family in upstate New York, the daughter of Emma Harmon Folsom of Medina and Oscar Folsom of Folsomdale. Her father and Grover Cleveland had established a law partnernership in Buffalo, where they were known as an excellent team with contrasting backgrounds and personalities. Cleveland, the fifth child of a poor Presbyterian minister, had been unable to pursue a college education because of his father's early death. He had moved to Buffalo in 1855 to live with an uncle, and eventually read law and passed the bar. He was serious, shy, a dogged worker, and a meticulous researcher. Folsom was merry and popular, fond of sports and fast horses, and he maintained a cavalier attitude toward the more esoteric points of law. Cleveland called him "irrepressible," and he seems to have enjoyed drinks and social gatherings in the shadow of his convivial friend.

During Frances's childhood, Cleveland became her family's benefactor in two important ways. The first was, at the time, kept as quiet as possible. In 1873 a widow named Maria Halpin bore a son whom she named Oscar Folsom Cleveland. She sought child support from both law partners. Cleveland stepped forward and assumed responsibility, paying the mother for some time and arranging for the child's adoption. When the affair later came to light, during Cleveland's first presidential campaign, he reported that other men could also have been the child's father— among them, undoubtedly, Oscar Folsom. Friends explained that Cleveland had accepted sole responsibility because he was a bachelor. He thus shielded from blame his married partner, whom Buffalo society would have considered more culpable.

A year later, in July 1874, Oscar Folsom died suddenly in a carriage crash, while driving recklessly. He was only thirty-seven years old; his daughter Frances had just celebrated her tenth birthday. She and her mother were at the Harmon family estate in Medina when the news arrived. With the proceeds of a generous insurance policy, and with wealth in both her own and her husband's families, Emma Folsom did not face the financial difficulties that beset many a husbandless woman. Nonetheless, the lives of widow and daughter were thrown into turmoil. Grover Cleveland, whom Oscar's will named as executor, handled Emma and Frances's financial affairs and took a continuing interest in their welfare.

The Folsoms had been looking for a house in Buffalo when Oscar died. Emma and Frances first went to live with relatives in St. Paul, Minnesota, but after six months they moved back to Medina, New York, and returned to Buffalo four years later. For the rest of her teenage years, Frances spent summers with her paternal grandparents in Folsomdale, school years in Buffalo, and winter holidays in Michigan, where her maternal grandparents had moved after selling their New York estate.

Frank, as the family called her, in honor of an aunt and an uncle with that nickname, received an excellent education by the standards of her day, starting at Madame Brecker's French Kindergarten and Miss Bissell's School for Young Ladies. After her father's death she attended various private schools as she and her mother moved from place to place, and she ended up at the Central School in Buffalo. Unenthusiastic about high school, Frank dropped out during her senior year, in October 1881, possibly because she was depressed over a broken engagement. Worried, her mother and Grover Cleveland arranged for her to transfer to Wells College in Aurora, New York, certifying that she was ready for the college's course of study. She arrived there in February of her class's freshman year.

Frank flourished at Wells, enjoying both her studies and a lively social life. During her sophomore year she turned down one marriage proposal and broke an engagement. Grover Cleveland wrote to her regularly at college, with the formal permission of Emma Folsom and of Wells's "lady principal," who supervised the students' social lives. While Frank progressed at college, Cleveland rose from the post of Buffalo mayor to become governor of New York in 1882. Frank received letters, clippings, and weekly bouquets from the governor's mansion—sent, all assumed, in Cleveland's capacity as a family friend. Frank and her mother visited the governor's mansion on several occasions. They were present when Cleveland formally accepted the Democratic presidential nomination in the summer of 1884.

Grover Cleveland later expressed regret that his wife, "poor girl, never had any courting like other girls." But he added that "he did say some things to her one night" when she and her mother visited the White House in March 1885. During this stay, the couple took evening walks in the East Room and Cleveland expressed his desire for marriage. At the time, rumors abounded of possible partners for the "bachelor president," but attention was deflected from

Frank by her youth. Instead, several Washington sources identified Oscar's widow—Frank's mother—as a potential bride for the forty-seven-year-old president. Only close relatives knew the truth. A few months after the Folsoms' White House visit, when Frank had graduated from Wells, Cleveland wrote to her with a formal marriage proposal. Frank promptly accepted.

The engagement remained secret for over a year, and even Frank's close friends knew nothing of it. Though Frank wanted to marry immediately, Cleveland insisted that his fiancée continue with her plans to tour Europe with her mother, which she did after a second White House visit in September. Traveling through seven countries, Frank ended the trip in Paris to assemble her trousseau. In the United States, sensational speculation had by this point arisen over the rumored engagement. Cleveland's adviser Daniel Lamont dispatched the U.S. consul and his wife from Antwerp to shield the Folsoms from the press. Though the consul and Frances's cousin, Ben Folsom, managed to decoy journalists from the U.S.-bound steamer, the Folsoms were greeted in New York by reporters in boats, and led them on a chase through the harbor. At a Decoration Day parade in New York City, Cleveland made a brief appearance and then welcomed home his bride-to-be. Bands in the parade played the current hit from Gilbert and Sullivan's *Mikado*: "He's Going to Marry Yum-Yum."

In the meantime, Cleveland had sought advice from female relatives on how to proceed. He insisted that the wedding was a matter "purely personal to me" and worried about subjecting Frank to an "ordeal," reflecting his own anxieties more than hers. He wrote to one of his sisters, "I have my heart set on making Frank a sensible, domestic American wife. I should be pleased not to hear her spoken of as 'the First Lady of the Land' or 'mistress of the White House.' I want her to be happy . . . but I should feel very much affected if she lets many notions in her head." After discussing New York City and Folsomdale as possible wedding sites, the couple agreed

on the White House. Rose Cleveland, the president's unmarried sister and White House hostess, arranged for the service to be simple and small.

The circumstances of the wedding must have been stressful for Frances (the name she used after her marriage). Only a few days after returning to the United States, she and her mother were spirited to Washington by the late train on the night of June 1, 1886, arriving at 5:30 A.M. on the wedding day. The president worked his usual schedule on June 2, joining the Folsoms only for breakfast and lunch. In the midst of other duties he sent last-minute wedding invitations to his cabinet members and their wives. At 7 P.M., with fewer than two dozen guests present, a Presbyterian minister read the ten-minute service. Following a brief reception, the couple slipped out the back door of the White House to be whisked away in a carriage.

Frances Cleveland thus began life with a husband who had known her since her birth, but with whom she had spent only a few weeks of her adult life. The couple took a short wedding trip to Deer Park, Maryland, where they were besieged by reporters seeking to fulfill insatiable public demand for news of the wedding. Though virtually barricaded in their rustic cottage, the couple nevertheless managed to arrange walks and afternoon carriage rides. Cleveland's friend Daniel Lamont and his wife, Julie, both of whom had helped with wedding preparations, visited during the honeymoon. After five days the president, who was famous for his devotion to work, felt that duty required him to return to the capital.

Arriving with him, the new First Lady faced a difficult situation. Her shy husband was bewildered and indignant at the enormous fuss made over his wife. Frances Cleveland, who had a wide circle of friends and was thoroughly schooled in social graces, nonetheless faced the daunting task of overseeing White House affairs as an outsider who had only twice set foot in Washington. At age twenty-one she was far younger than any of the cabinet wives or other women who wielded social influence. In fact, she was close in age to many of their daughters, and younger than the six First Ladies who succeeded her. (Grace Coolidge, who was born in 1879 and whose husband became president in 1923, was the next First Lady born after Frances Cleveland.)

Mrs. Cleveland handled this awkward situation with grace and fortitude, negotiating between her husband's intense desire for privacy and the demand of citizens to see and meet her. She declined an invitation to present flags to the New York fire department, explaining that the president's wife could not act in an official capacity separate from her husband's. Yet she attended charity balls in Washington and Baltimore when her husband chose to stay at home, and her fame contributed to the success of these public occasions. She kept close ties with classmates from Wells College, maintaining a circle of young women who shared her interests. On some occasions she left Washington for two-week visits with friends. At the same time she sought the advice of Washington social arbiters such as Harriet Lane, who had served as White House hostess for her brother James Buchanan in the late 1850s.

The results probably far surpassed what the president had imagined. After greeting ten thousand people at her official presentations to the diplomatic corps and to the public, the new First Lady organized an ongoing series of noon receptions, assuaging the desire of multitudes to meet her. She redecorated the White House in a style widely praised for economy and taste; she initiated a lively social calendar, charming visitors with her up-to-date menus and gowns, and impressing diplomats with her fluent French. With the departure of Grover Cleveland's sister Rose, a temperance advocate, wine and liquor reappeared at White House functions—undoubtedly a factor in Frances Cleveland's social success. In late 1887 she joined her husband on an extended tour of the South and West, waving to thousands who thronged the streets of many cities, and shaking so many hands that her arm was perpetually swollen.

Under Frances Cleveland's guidance the Clevelands lent their name to the arts, becoming honorary members of the Washington Choral Society and patrons of music at the White House. The First Lady, whose tastes ranged from piano sonatas to Wagner's operas, won praise for elevating Washington culture. She sponsored the young violinist Leonora Jackson to study in Berlin—a city where Frances Cleveland had stopped during her European tour. In an era when women struggled to claim a place as professional musicians, Jackson became the first American to win the Mendelssohn Stipendium, a prestigious scholarship named in honor of the great composer.

Observers noted a marked transformation in Grover Cleveland. "What a change has come over the President since he was married!" wrote Frank Carpenter, Washington correspondent for the *Cleveland Leader*, in early 1887. "From being almost a recluse where the fair sex was concerned, he has become almost gallant. . . . Mrs. Cleveland has accomplished much in little time. Her husband now dresses faultlessly under her watchful eye. He has become gentler and more polite and even seems to enjoy the pleasantries of social intercourse. Instead of appearing to be bored with his state dinners, he apparently finds them agreeable. At the last big evening reception, he did not look straight ahead and plunge unseeing through the crowd as before, but stopped now and again to say a gracious word to one or another of his guests." At the same time, the press hailed Mrs. Cleveland as "a lovely and perfect type of the flower of womankind—an American girl," who was "sensible, affectionate, talented, and refined."

Frances Cleveland's glowing reviews were partly a result of circumstance. There had been no First Lady since Lucretia Garfield, who was widely admired for her devoted care of her husband and her courage upon his death, but who remained a symbol of tragedy. Chester Arthur had been a widower. Rutherford and Lucy Hayes, who had left the White House in 1881, were thus the last happy couple associated with the mansion. Frances Cleveland was the first bride of an incumbent president. She was also among the first women of the post—Civil War generation to achieve national celebrity. Born too late to remember the war, she represented the nation's fresh start after it. The theme of reunion was reinforced by the Clevelands' tour through the South, the first undertaken by a presidential couple since the Confederacy's defeat. Not surprisingly, Frances Cleveland was wildly popular among white Southerners, for whom she symbolized sectional harmony under Democratic rule.

In a decade when American women were making new advances in education, employment, and public affairs, the young First Lady offered something for both traditionalists and progressives. She was a polished, well-traveled college graduate who demonstrated the benefits of women's education and, in a vaguer way, young women's progress in cultural and public affairs. On the other hand, she reassured those who were anxious about "the woman question" by devoting her energies to marriage, motherhood, and the duties of a social hostess. She enabled young Americans to feel that their generation had arrived while she charmed their elders by choosing a portly, forty-nine-year-old groom. At receptions, more than one aging hero of the Union cause was known to linger over the First Lady's proffered hand.

Frances Cleveland, though, deserves personal credit for her popularity. By all accounts she had a gracious disposition and a talent for thoughtful gestures, as well as a "wonderful memory for faces" and a firm belief that the least visitor to the White House should be treated as respectfully as the greatest. By the time she left Washington, dozens of stories about her circulated: at a White House reception, she had pressed her fresh handkerchief upon an elderly lady who had dropped her own and found it trampled; she had stopped in a ballroom, mid-waltz, to pin the gown of a distressed young dancer; on a bitter winter day she had offered strangers a hot drink in the family's private rooms. Returning visitors to the executive mansion were astonished when the First Lady greeted them by name, and delighted to hear her

gently chide guests who tried to make third or fourth turns through the reception line. Frances Cleveland made frequent use of White House greenhouses to send flowers to invalids, and sick children who came to her attention often received toys or delicacies.

Such stories held special poignancy in Grover Cleveland's second term, when his policies were widely blamed for the devastating depression of 1893. In the sunny first years of her marriage, however, Frances Cleveland's public image served other purposes. Allegations about Grover Cleveland's illegitimate child had surfaced in the 1884 campaign, and though the charges did not prevent his election, anxieties remained about a man whom prominent newspapers had labeled "a moral leper," "an enemy of the family," and "a coarse debauchee who would bring his harlots with him to Washington." The president's marriage helped dissolve these clouds of social opprobrium. Respectable Americans could breathe a sigh of relief: their president was now a good family man.

Intentionally or not, the marriage also served partisan ends. As leader of the first Democratic administration since the Civil War, Grover Cleveland encountered an array of Republican practices and values that had become entrenched during the party's quarter-century of dominance. One aspect of Republican Party culture was a commitment to female-centered domesticity and women's moral influence. Republicans had, from the emergence of their party onward, portrayed Southern Democrats as violent, lascivious tyrants, abusive both at home and in public affairs. Less bitterly, perhaps, but no less often, Republicans deployed the same stereotype against Democratic men in the North, especially Irish immigrants. By contrast, Republican men presented themselves as self-controlled Christians who heeded the moral guidance of mothers, sisters, and wives. The Democrats' most frequent defense was telling: they ridiculed their opponents as weak, effeminate men and attacked Republican women for meddling where they should not.

This battle raged at the highest level in presidential elections, starting in 1856, when Jessie Frémont became a prominent symbol in her husband's campaign against bachelor James Buchanan. Republicans celebrated First Ladies Lucy Webb Hayes (mother of eight children) and Lucretia Garfield (mother of seven) for their elevating influence on the nation's "home life." A remarkable number of Democratic presidential hopefuls were bachelors. The wives and children of those who were not, found little place in the party's campaign literature or rhetoric. Between 1861 and 1884, Democrats attacked every succeeding First Lady—each a Republican—for alleged shrewishness, tyranny over her husband, and interference in party affairs.

Partisan concerns thus profoundly shaped the public debate over Grover Cleveland's alleged illegitimate child, in addition to influencing his own attitude toward the proper role of the First Lady (a term first used by Republicans, in the Lincoln years). The marriage of this "bachelor president" to a young and beautiful woman propelled his party, grudgingly at first, into a shift on matters domestic. Frances Cleveland was the first president's wife to be celebrated widely in Democratic Party literature. A popular wedding account, Francis Williams's *Bride of the White House*, was inserted in its entirety into Democratic campaign handbooks in 1888. The same year saw publication of Lydia L. Gordon's *From Lady Washington to Mrs. Cleveland*, the first history of White House women from a Democratic perspective. In it, Republican First Ladies were still criticized for overbearing behavior, but Democratic First Ladies were rescued from long neglect.

Frances Cleveland's popularity also grew from the ground up. In 1888, many a Democratic home displayed her portrait in the window. Buttons, banners, quilts, and milk pitchers featured her image. Campaign posters often included her—in one instance front and center, with the presidential and vice presidential nominees behind her, on the sides. In dozens of cities and towns, especially in the Midwest, young Democratic women organized Frankie Cleveland clubs and demanded a role in presidential campaign rallies. Though the First Lady now used the name Frances, campaign clubs emphasized her youth by resurrecting her boyish nickname. Frankie Cleveland clubs joined dozens of campaign parades, their members riding on horseback or marching with men. In response, Republican women began to organize Carrie Harrison clubs. The result was a rapid expansion of women's roles in Midwestern campaigns.

Far from endorsing the use of his wife's name and image, Grover Cleveland was annoyed by it and sought to set limits. In 1892, when a New York woman asked permission to create a national association of Frances Cleveland Clubs, the president flatly refused. Like other Democratic leaders, he deplored women's activity in partisan campaigns—discouragement that, in the long run, gave Republicans an edge in using female volunteers for local organizing. Throughout his presidency, Grover Cleveland maintained a hostile attitude toward any use of his wife's likeness. After the birth of the couple's first daughter, he forbade anyone other than close family friends from sketching the baby or taking her photograph. Those few who did so had to swear never to release the resulting images to the public.

Frances Cleveland's impact on electoral politics, as a symbol of Democratic domesticity, is hard to measure. As the Maria Halpin scandal did not prevent Cleveland's election in 1884, so his wedding did not prevent his subsequent defeat. Yet widespread admiration for Frances Cleveland and public celebration over the birth of the couple's first child, Ruth, in October 1891 sustained Grover Cleveland's popularity. Historian Allan Nevins has ranked the wedding as the most popular act of the president's first administration. In intangible ways, Grover Cleveland's softer public image as a father and family man may have contributed to his second election in 1892.

The impact of electoral politics on Frances Cleveland, on the other hand, must have been painful. Republican attacks on Cleveland as a sexual monster, so prevalent in 1884, did not entirely cease after his marriage. In 1888, rumors that he beat his wife circulated so widely that Frances Cleveland took the unusual step—no doubt highly distasteful to her husband—of issuing a public statement denouncing these "wicked and heartless lies." "I can wish the women of our country no greater blessing," she wrote, "than that their homes and lives may be as happy, and their husbands may be as kind, attentive and considerate, and affectionate as mine." Despite her popularity, more subtle rumors also circulated. Republican journalist Nellie Bly claimed that Frances Cleveland was "cut off" by leaders of Washington society—a clear attack on the president's reputation by way of his wife.

In addition to enduring partisan insults, the First Lady found her personage appropriated in the burgeoning world of Gilded Age commerce. Advertisements featuring her face, and often her alleged endorsement, abounded in the late 1880s, when news of her was most in demand. Salesmen used her image to sell needles and thread, headache remedies, digestive aids, soap, beauty products, and even arsenic pills ("the secret of her beautiful complexion"). One indignant columnist denounced "the persecution of Mrs. Cleveland by the patent-medicine men, pill-peddlers, soap-makers, and other unscrupulous advertisers. . . . But what can Mrs. Cleveland do?" he added. "She cannot enter suit and put herself on the witness stand. She evidently feels that noticing such slander would be beneath her. She has no other course than to suffer this outrage in silence." The marketing frenzy extended in 1891 to "Baby Ruth" Cleveland, whose name graced a new candy bar.

Of the Clevelands' second term in the White House, a senator's wife later observed that "there was much less disposition to entertain during President Cleveland's second term. . . . Mrs. Cleveland had become so much engrossed in her domestic cares and motherly duties that she manifested less interest in social functions." In September 1893 and July 1895 the Cleve-

lands' second and third daughters, Esther and Marion, became the first children born to an incumbent president. Motherhood offered solace to Frances during a decade fraught with private and public agonies. The terrible depression of 1893, beginning soon after Cleveland resumed office, made him bitterly unpopular. In June 1893, with the crisis worsening, the president was found to have cancer of the mouth. Fearful of further unsettling unstable financial markets, he underwent a secret operation on a yacht belonging to a wealthy New York friend. Frances, seven months pregnant with Esther, took Ruth to Gray Gables, the family's summer home on Buzzard's Bay, Massachusetts. She bravely parried reporters' questions while waiting to hear whether her husband had survived. He returned five days later, weak but with the cancer removed.

In July 1894, Frances Cleveland wrote privately that "the poor President is under a fearful strain and responsibility," and described him as "worried and anxious." She was frightened when household staff discovered mysterious men lurking around Gray Gables. With public anger at the president mounting, she feared that her children might be the target of an attack or a kidnapping plot. "I don't want to be silly," she wrote to a White House official, going behind her husband's back to request extra security without adding to the president's burdens. "But the times are so queer and everything seems so uncertain."

As the 1896 presidential campaign approached, the president seemed increasingly distant from the majority of his party. Decisively rejecting Cleveland's policies, the Democratic National Convention chose for its candidate William Jennings Bryan, a young Westerner whose financial proposals the president loathed. In a major intraparty split, Cleveland played little role in the ensuing campaign except as a target of abuse from all quarters. Understandably, Frances Cleveland was overjoyed to leave the White House and settle into private life. After her husband's 1888 defeat, the couple had moved to New York City. This time they located a suitable house in Princeton, New Jersey, where they had friends and where Frances Cleveland, according to an acquaintance, felt marriage prospects would be excellent for her daughters. In Princeton she gave birth to two sons: Richard Folsom Cleveland in October 1897 and Francis Grover, in July 1903.

The tragedies of Frances Cleveland's life were not yet over. In January 1904 their oldest daughter, Ruth, died suddenly during a bout of diphtheria that was not thought to be life-threatening. Mrs. Cleveland's health was poor at the time, including problems with her eyes that later left her almost blind. She was so devastated by the loss of her daughter that friends feared for her life. For years she grieved deeply for Ruth, refusing to go to Gray Gables, which the Clevelands had bought just before Ruth's birth and which held many memories of her eldest child. Though Grover Cleveland was saddened by the abandonment of the summer home, he continued to go there for his beloved summer fishing trips. His wife never returned.

Grover Cleveland died in June 1908, at the age of seventy-one. His death was not unexpected; he had long been in ill health, and he apparently had believed he was dying for several months beforehand. In the last days, Frances Cleveland left their four surviving children with her mother, who was staying at the Clevelands' new summer home in the mountains of New Hampshire, and returned with her husband to Princeton. She stayed by his bedside through the long night of June 23 until his death the following morning. He was buried in Princeton, beside Ruth's grave, in a modest family plot. Frances Cleveland insisted that the funeral include nothing of a "military character," even asking that state militiamen, who guarded the grave for several days, not appear in uniform. Her mother, now twice widowed, lived with the family in Princeton for several years afterward, except for a few months when the rest of the family went to Europe. Frances Cleveland wore mourning for more than four years, finally appearing

"in colors" in November 1912, at her daughter Esther's debut.

Recovering from the deaths of her daughter and husband, and later undergoing a successful cataract operation that restored her sight, Frances Cleveland remained active in civic and social affairs. Her most important public position, which she held for over fifty years, was as a trustee of Wells College. In this capacity she served her alma mater faithfully, taking a term as chair of the Wells College Endowment Fund in 1922. She helped persuade Wells to hire a good friend of the Clevelands, Thomas Jex Preston, Jr., as professor of art and archaeology. Preston had received his bachelor's, master's, and doctoral degrees from Princeton after leaving a business career to return to college. On February 10, 1913, Frances Cleveland and Thomas Preston were wed in a private ceremony—her second marriage and his first.

One of Grover Cleveland's controversial acts in his retirement had been to publish, in *Ladies Home Journal*, articles in which he criticized women's clubs for taking women too far outside the domestic sphere, and denounced the movement for woman suffrage. Both, he asserted, were "harmful in a way that directly menaces the integrity of our homes." Despite her first husband's views, Frances Cleveland carved out a modest place for herself in public work. She joined the Needlework Guild of America, which during the depression of the 1890s organized sewing drives for coats, mittens, and other warm clothes. She continued her involvement for many years, serving a term as national president. She was a member of the Colony Club of New York City and the Present Day Club of Princeton, both of which took an interest in current affairs. During World War I Mrs. Cleveland took charge of the speakers' bureau of the National Security League, organizing public addresses and rallies in support of the war effort. Yet she took no political stances, other than maintaining, well after her first husband's death, that she was "against suffrage for women."

Frances Folsom Cleveland Preston lived to see her daughters marry and her son Richard follow in his father's footsteps by becoming a lawyer. While visiting Baltimore for Richard's fiftieth birthday, she died in her sleep on October 29, 1947. She was buried in the Princeton cemetery beside her first husband and her daughter Ruth. She was remembered as a First Lady who demonstrated the traditional womanly attributes of beauty, social grace, and devotion to home and family. She was most significant, perhaps, as a child of the post—Civil War era who established a place among an elder generation, whom she long outlived, and at the same time became a heroine for Democratic women closer to her own age. Thus, Frances Cleveland helped carry forward the values of domesticity into a new era of economic turmoil and social change.

BIBLIOGRAPHICAL ESSAY

The Grover Cleveland Papers, held by the Library of Congress and available on microfilm with an index, include letters by Frances Cleveland to friends and admirers. Scattered letters from Frances Cleveland also exist in other collections at the Library of Congress and the New York State Library. Wells College Library, in Aurora, New York, holds information on Frances Cleveland's role as trustee.

Newspaper accounts give extensive coverage to the Clevelands' wedding, honeymoon, and inauguration balls, and to the births of Ruth, Esther, and Marion. Francis Howard Williams published his account of the wedding as *Bride of the White House* (Philadelphia, 1886); several Democratic campaign biographies of Grover Cleveland, published in 1888 and 1892, reprinted this. See also Lydia L. Gordon, *From Lady Washington to Mrs. Cleveland* (Boston, 1888), which clearly was written with the presidential campaign in mind.

Frances Cleveland's denial of rumors that her husband abused her appeared widely on June 6, 1888; see, for example, the *New York Evening Post* of that date. Nellie Bly's interview was printed in numerous Republican papers, such as the *San Francisco Chronicle* (September 9, 1888). Among accounts by contemporaries, two are especially helpful: Frank G. Carpenter's columns, collected in *Carp's Washington* (New York, 1960); and "The Anecdotal Side of Mrs. Cleveland," *Ladies' Home Journal* (June 1898). Grover Cleveland's articles "Woman's Mission and Woman's Clubs" and "Would Woman Suffrage Be Unwise?" appeared in *Ladies Home Journal* (May and October, 1905, respectively). Frances Folsom Cleveland Preston's obituary appeared in the *New York Times* (October 30, 1947).

Allan Nevins's multivolume *Grover Cleveland: A Study in Courage* (New York, 1932) is the most thorough biography of the president and acknowledges Frances as a factor in her husband's popularity. Also helpful is Nevins's edited collection, *Letters of Grover Cleveland* (New York, 1934). Sue Severn's biographical article, in the first edition of *American First Ladies*, draws on interviews with Cleveland friends and family members that were conducted by the late William I. Severn.

Elise Kirk, *Music in the White House* (Urbana, Ill., 1986), documents Frances Cleveland's interest in music. On "Frankie's" uses as a symbol of Democratic domesticity, see Rebecca Edwards, *Angels in the Machinery: Gender in American Party Politics from the Civil War to the Progressive Era* (New York, 1997), chapter 3. On her popularity in campaigns and advertising, see Edith P. Mayo, "Campaign Appeals to Women," in *American Material Culture: The Shape of Things Around Us*, ed. Edith P. Mayo (Bowling Green, Ohio, 1984); Roger A. Fischer, *Tippecanoe and Trinkets Too: The Material Culture of American Presidential Campaigns* (Urbana, Ill., 1988); and H. Wayne Morgan, *From Hayes to McKinley: National Party Politics, 1877-1896* (Syracuse, N.Y., 1969). The First Ladies exhibit at the National Museum of American History, Smithsonian Institution, Washington, D.C., includes a wonderful collection of advertisements and commercial products bearing Frances Cleveland's image and name.

★★★   ★★★

Caroline Lavinia Scott Harrison

(1832–1892)

First Lady: 1889–1892

Charles W. Calhoun

Caroline Lavinia Scott was born in Oxford, Ohio, on October 1, 1832, to John Witherspoon Scott and Mary Potts Neal Scott. Her parents were married in 1825, and she had two sisters—Mary and Elizabeth—and two brothers—John and Henry. Her father had trained for the Presbyterian ministry. At the time of Caroline's birth, he taught mathematics and natural science at Miami University. Her mother was the daughter of a Philadelphia banker and businessman.

Although as a teacher and preacher John Scott remained a man of modest means, he and his wife sought to rear their children in an atmosphere of culture and refinement, emphasizing not only religious training but nurture of the intellect as well. Caroline was

a happy child who enjoyed having fun but also had a strong sense of sympathy for others. At an early age she developed a fondness for English and American literature, which she maintained as an adult. She showed exceptional skill at music and was teaching piano before she was twenty years old. Her greatest artistic interest, however, lay in painting. Her talent, especially for china painting, matured through the years, and she remained passionately committed to the craft to the end of her life.

Caroline's formal education proceeded under her father's watchful eye at a school for females that he established in Cincinnati while he was teaching chemistry and physics at Farmers' College in that city. It was there that she first met Benjamin Harrison, a student at Farmers' who paid frequent calls at the Scott home. The diminutive Harrison immediately took notice of the petite, slightly plump Caroline with her kindly eyes and profusion of exquisite brown hair. True to the adage that opposites attract, the serious-minded, ambitious young man enjoyed the company of the warmhearted and sympathetic young woman whose vivacity and playful sense of humor drew him out of his solemn introspection. Their friendship quickly ripened into romance. Within a year, however, her father moved his school to Oxford, where he established the larger Oxford Female Institute. By then Benjamin had become so enamored of Caroline, ten months his senior, that he decided to complete his college work at Miami University at Oxford. During his senior year the couple were engaged to be married.

Caroline witnessed Harrison's graduation in June 1852. A few months later he left for Cincinnati to begin reading law. Remaining at Oxford to finish her studies, Caroline also began to teach piano at the Institute. The regular piano teacher, a relative and close friend, had fallen ill, and Caroline not only took over her teaching duties but devoted much time to nursing her as well. The strain of overwork eventually began to take its toll on Caroline's own health, moving Harrison to push for an early marriage date. With a typically nineteenth-century mixture of romance and morbidity, Harrison convinced himself that if they were not soon married, she would die of overwork and anxiety. Caroline was also eager, and the two were married by her father on October 20, 1853.

The young couple began married life at North Bend, Ohio, at the Harrison family homestead, where Benjamin's grandfather, former president William Henry Harrison, lay buried. His father, John Scott Harrison, had recently been elected to Congress and was absent during much of their stay. In early 1854 Benjamin won admission to the bar, and by spring he and his wife decided to settle in Indianapolis. In April they set off for the city they would call home for the rest of their lives. Able to ship all their worldly goods in one large box for ninety-one cents in freight charges, the couple endured their first two years of marriage in severely straitened circumstances.

When the Harrisons arrived in Indianapolis, Mrs. Harrison was in the fifth month of her first pregnancy. After a fire drove them from the house where they were lodging, they decided that Mrs. Harrison, who needed rest and medical attention, should return to her parents' home at Oxford until the baby was born. Harrison stayed on in Indianapolis to pursue clients for his fledgling legal practice. On August 12, 1854, Mrs. Harrison gave birth to a boy, Russell. Mother and son joined Harrison in Indianapolis in October. But because Mrs. Harrison was ill much of the time and Harrison was unable to hire regular help, she and Russell returned for an extended stay with Ohio relatives in early 1855.

Harrison's practice still attracted few clients or fees, and so the family rented a modest house on Vermont Street consisting of only three rooms: kitchen, dining room, and bedroom. Mrs. Harrison did all her own housekeeping. There was little time or money for diversions.

The family's big break came in the spring of 1855 when William Wallace, a successful local attorney and son of a former governor, invited Harrison into partnership. Campaigning for the Marion County clerkship, Wallace needed someone to look after his firm's business: the twenty-one-year-old lawyer jumped at the chance. Wallace lost the election but kept Harrison on. Thanks to the senior partner's connections and the junior's high intelligence and willingness to work hard, the firm of Wallace and Harrison prospered.

In light of Harrison's eagerness to marry Caroline to relieve her of the necessity to teach, it was clear that she would not work outside the home. Nor would the social station to which they aspired permit remunerative labor for Mrs. Harrison. Instead, she focused much of her energy on domestic concerns. By all accounts she became a model housekeeper, displaying talents and proclivities that later influenced her performance as First Lady.

In college Harrison had considered entering the ministry before opting for the law, and afterward religion continued to be a dominant force in both Harrisons' lives. Friends noted, however, that Benjamin's somber Calvinism was softened somewhat by his wife's gaiety and fun-loving spirit. Prayers and Bible reading formed an important part of the daily routine of their household. One of the first things they did when they arrived in Indianapolis was to join the First Presbyterian Church. There Mrs. Harrison applied her musical talent in working with the choir. She also became the teacher of the Sunday school's infant class, whose grown-up graduates decades later still remembered her gentle but stimulating instruction in simple Bible lessons. In these years the Harrisons' social life revolved around the church, with its cycle of socials, donation parties, oyster suppers, and festivals.

Their improved financial circumstances allowed the Harrisons to move into a larger house on New Jersey Street, and while they lived there, Mrs. Harrison gave birth to their second child, Mary, on April 3, 1858. Even with this added responsibility, hired help permitted Mrs. Harrison to give increasing attention to social and charitable activities. She was particularly interested in the Indianapolis Orphans' Asylum. In 1860 she took a seat on its board of managers—a position she retained until her death.

While Harrison's legal practice flourished, he began to take part in politics. Elected city attorney in 1857, he became secretary of the Republican State Central Committee the following year. With a fast-growing reputation as an able stump speaker, he received the Republican nomination in 1860 for reporter of the state supreme court and won by a comfortable majority. The position entailed considerable labor piled on top of an already demanding load from his private practice, and he found less and less time for home and family. Still, his new prominence rendered Harrison's professional standing and the family's financial position all the more secure, and Mrs. Harrison became pregnant for the third time. This time, however, their eager anticipation ended in their first great sorrow as a married couple, when, in early June 1861, their baby girl died at birth.

The Harrisons soon experienced another great pain—that of separation. The Civil War had already begun, and although Harrison's commitment to his court reporter's job delayed his enlistment for over a year, in the summer of 1862 he became colonel of an Indiana regiment in the Union Army. The couple had recently purchased a large two-story residence on North Alabama Street. With her husband gone to the field, Mrs. Harrison shouldered the burden of managing this new household, as well as caring for their two small children. Like countless women throughout the country, she followed war news with nervous anxiety and eagerly welcomed each letter from Benjamin as confirmation of his safety. She was a faithful correspondent in return, reporting how she and the children were getting along without him.

On the home front, Mrs. Harrison did her part for the war effort through such organizations as the Ladies Patriotic Association and the Ladies Sanitary Committee. She showed particular solicitude for wounded soldiers at hospitals in Indianapolis, where she helped with the nursing and did her best to cheer the men up. She also participated in drives to gather food, clothing, and medicines, and personally distributed them to the soldiers.

When circumstances permitted, Mrs. Harrison visited her husband in camp. In 1862 and 1863 she journeyed to his headquarters in Kentucky and Tennessee, where she and other officers' wives mended their husbands' uniforms and did other chores about camp. In September 1864, she welcomed Benjamin home for his first extended leave, but she and the children were forced to share his time. Renominated for supreme court reporter, Harrison set off on a statewide speaking tour culminating in his reelection in October. The following January, Harrison was again home on furlough, and he and Mrs. Harrison decided to use his return trip eastward as a second honeymoon with the children. Unfortunately, while they were staying with relatives at Honesdale, Pennsylvania, all four Harrisons came down with scarlet fever and were placed under quarantine. They recovered in due time, but Caroline Harrison and the children returned to Indianapolis while Harrison went on to rejoin his troops.

The family was reunited for good when Harrison returned home in mid-June 1865. Mrs. Harrison was justly proud when Harrison's military exploits earned him a hero's salute from the city. But she also worried that his popular acclaim would soon be translated into a political office that would again take him from her. Like many soldiers' wives, Mrs. Harrison had borne the separation of the war years with difficulty, fearful that his prolonged absence betrayed a decline in his affection for her. Now talk of his election to Congress, with the prospect of prolonged absences in Washington, filled her with dread. But even before returning home, Benjamin had assured her that he intended to forgo such honors and that he would devote much more time to the family circle than he had before.

In the years after the Civil War, the Harrisons enjoyed an ever-advancing prosperity—financially, socially, and politically. Harrison finished his term as supreme court reporter and then bent his labors full time to his practice, soon becoming one of the most sought-after lawyers in the state. Five years after the war, the Harrisons were listed among the top 10 percent of Indianapolis's taxpayers. In 1874–1875 they superintended the construction of a new house on fashionable North Delaware Street. The massive brick home had sixteen rooms and cost over $21,000 to build. The planning, fitting, and decorating of this imposing residence provided Mrs. Harrison with experience she later applied in the White House.

In these years, Mrs. Harrison continued to take considerable pleasure in domestic concerns and accepted full responsibility for managing the household. Although the family enjoyed the help of servants, she did her own marketing and much of the housework and gardening as well. A talented seamstress, she made clothing for her children and rarely showed up at a club meeting without some bit of needlework to occupy her hands.

Caroline Harrison also performed the duties and enjoyed the pleasures of a society matron. On January 1 each year she held the customary New Year's Day open house. Church functions continued to dominate her social calendar, and she played a leading role in the First Presbyterian Church's missionary society. She took a literature class once a week and, perhaps feeling a measure of intellectual frustration, she was the founding spirit of the Impromptu Club—a group of men and women who gathered regularly for readings, discussions, and dramatizations of English and American literature.

Amid Mrs. Harrison's varied activities, painting continued to be her consuming pursuit. Despite considerable talent, she still thought of herself as a student and took art lessons twice a week. Every chance she got, she turned to her well-lit studio on the north side of the Delaware Street house, where she executed watercolors or, more often, painted flowers on china. Using models from her own garden, she spent long hours perfecting her technique and often invited other artists to join her. She regularly exhibited her works at Indianapolis art shows and frequently donated them to institutions around the city or gave them as presents to relatives and friends.

The two decades in Indianapolis after the Civil War formed the happiest period in Caroline Harrison's life. She lived comfortably, had lots of friends, and watched Russell and Mary grow to maturity. She also became reconciled to her husband's blossoming political career and lent him all the support she could from the sidelines. When he contemplated running for governor in 1872, she encouraged him to seek the Republican nomination. He came in a respectable second in the state convention balloting. Four years later, when ethics charges forced the gubernatorial nominee from the ticket, the Republican State Committee tapped Harrison to complete the race. For Mrs. Harrison, this meant losing her husband to yet another extended speaking tour and also playing political hostess at the Delaware Street house. Despite their combined efforts, however, Harrison lost a close race.

The Harrisons had clearly emerged as one of the first families of the state, and Caroline Harrison was growing increasingly accustomed to her role as a politician's wife. An eastern vacation trip in June 1877 included a call upon the newly elected President and Mrs. Rutherford B. Hayes at the White House. Two years later, Mrs. Harrison was able to return the hospitality when the Hayeses paid a visit to Indianapolis. Hayes spent an evening at the Harrison home, and Mrs. Harrison entertained the president and his wife at a lawn party that scored a social and political triumph.

By 1880, Harrison had set his sights on the U.S. Senate. Once more, Caroline Harrison sent him off on a stump speaking tour of Indiana, the Midwest, and the East. In one particularly telling speech, he defended presidential nominee James A. Garfield against Democratic attacks. Mrs. Harrison sent a copy of the speech to Garfield, who sent a warm thank-you note to Harrison. Garfield won Indiana and the election, and when he invited Harrison to his Ohio farm to discuss cabinet possibilities, he urged him to bring his wife along. A few days before they were to go, however, a fall on the ice gave Mrs. Harrison two black eyes and prevented her from helping out on this important political mission.

Garfield would have liked to have Harrison in his cabinet, but the Hoosier preferred the Senate seat to which the legislature had just elected him. In early March 1881, Mrs. Harrison, along with twenty-six-year-old Russell and twenty-two-year-old Mary, joined Harrison in Washington for his swearing-in. Later that year, Mrs. Harrison and Mary found a suitable lodging of four rooms and a bath at a boardinghouse on Vermont Avenue. Despite the relative modesty of this residence, her position as a senator's wife gave her an easy entry into Washington society. Even so, she had neither the inclination nor the means for sumptuous entertaining, and bouts of ill health prevented her from doing much more than giving simple receptions and dinners. This low-keyed approach to entertaining persisted even after the couple moved into a roomier apartment in the Woodmont on Iowa Avenue. Continuing her interest in charitable work, Caroline Harrison played an active role as a member of the board of lady managers of Washington's Garfield Hospital.

In these years Congress remained in session only about half the year, and Mrs. Harrison was perfectly content to leave Washington for her own home in Indianapolis or various vacation spots during the summer. When Harrison lost his bid for reelection to the Senate in 1886, Mrs. Harrison decided to remain at home for his last session in the winter of 1886–1887. The election loss resulted from a Democratic gerrymander of the Indiana legislative districts, and in no sense signaled an end to Harrison's career. Indeed, two years later he emerged as a strong contender for the Republican presidential nomination.

Although Mrs. Harrison never assumed as influential a role as political adviser to her husband as have some other politicians' wives, she was keenly aware of Harrison's prospects as she anxiously watched the nomination race in the spring of 1888. Privately, she was critical of newspapers, particularly in Chicago, that she believed misrepresented Harrison's record and views. She recognized that his hopes rested largely on his securing endorsement from the supporters of 1884 nominee James G. Blaine. She believed that a rumored attempt to bring Blaine forward again would spur deep resentment among the announced candidates and wreck the Republicans' chances of taking the presidency back from Democrat Grover Cleveland.

The proprieties of the era kept both Harrisons in Indianapolis while the Republicans met in convention at Chicago. On the gathering's decisive day, Harrison huddled with advisers around the telegraph in his law office while Caroline Harrison stayed at home with her daughter. Looking out the window, she saw the crowds massing on her front lawn and knew the result. Her life would never be the same again.

For once in his political life, Benjamin Harrison stayed home during a campaign. Day in and day out, he and his wife greeted delegations of well-wishers whose carefully orchestrated visits occasioned brief speeches by Harrison that were reported around the country. This "front-porch" strategy taxed Mrs. Harrison's political skills to the limit. She stalwartly stood by her husband, reviewing endless campaign parades with marchers sometimes numbering 75,000. Countless nights she turned down the beds for visiting dignitaries at the Delaware Street house. Throughout the summer and fall she watched a steady stream of Republicans pass by the punch bowl on her dining room table. The picket fence disappeared, carpets wore thin, furniture broke, and through it all she kept her equanimity. With characteristic good humor, toward the end of the campaign she remarked (according to a newspaper account in the Harrison Papers at the Library of Congress), "Well, it's the White House or the poorhouse with us now."

During the campaign, Mrs. Harrison became a focus of public interest second only to her husband. With his victory, the scrutiny grew exponentially. Her last New Year's Day reception in Indianapolis drew a thousand callers. When she and her daughter traveled to New York to shop, reporters dogged their every step. Through them she assured the nation that her inaugural gown and other dresses would be American made.

In some ways, Mrs. Harrison was astounded at the celebrity she experienced as First Lady. Soon after the election she joked that the newspapers revealed more about the Harrisons than they knew about themselves, but at least she would not have to write many letters to friends. Reporters wanted her opinion on whether the bustle should go, what blossom should become the national flower, whether women should propose marriage, and on and on. Letter

writers asked her intercession for appointments, veterans' pensions, and other presidential favors. After it was known that wine would grace the White House table, temperance advocates showered her with advice reminding her of the good example set by her predecessor Lucy Webb Hayes. Church groups and others solicited recipes for their fund-raising cookbooks, while others begged for scraps from her dresses to sew into crazy quilts. "You might as well shake a red rag at a bull as say crazy quilt to me," she said in one newspaper clipping preserved in the Harrison Papers.

Although Mrs. Harrison was an experienced political hostess, nothing had quite prepared her for the magnitude of the social responsibilities she encountered in the White House. The crush of receptions in the first three weeks sent her to bed fatigued and ill. Early in the administration she eliminated the customary handshaking in her receiving lines, a decision that met with general approval in the press. In addition, she soon decided to divide her hostess responsibilities with her daughter and daughter-in-law, both named Mary, and nieces living in the household. This latter course offended both the wife of the vice president, Mrs. Levi P. Morton, and the wife of the secretary of state, Mrs. James G. Blaine, who believed that protocol accorded them access to the First Lady. Harriet Blaine, sharing her husband's disappointment that they never occupied the White House, considered the "Hoosiers" living there her social inferiors. She privately mocked Mrs. Harrison as "her American majesty" (a remark recorded in a letter published by her daughter), but she was nonetheless pleased when the First Lady sent her flowers. Being a smashing social success had never been Caroline Harrison's chief goal in life, and her premier position and self-possession freed her from being much disturbed by the cattiness of others in Washington society.

To the degree the demands of her situation permitted, Caroline Harrison sought to re-create the kind of life she had led in Indianapolis. Determined to continue her painting, especially of china, she transported her kiln and other art equipment to the White House, where the botanical conservatories established by former First Lady Lucy Webb Hayes provided abundant subjects for her work. She even persuaded the German-born artist Paul Putzki, with whom she had studied painting in Indiana, to move to Washington. She took three lessons a week and also organized a painting class for cabinet wives and other Washington women.

With Putzki's help, Caroline Harrison designed new formal china for the White House. The new service bore a patriotically sentimental depiction of the arms of the United States in the center, bordered by corn and goldenrod to symbolize the nation's abundance and natural beauty. In assembling china for use by the White House, Mrs. Harrison searched through the closets and attics for remnants of previous sets and discovered a remarkable array of items from past administrations. She had the pieces cleaned and repaired, and they formed the nucleus of the White House China Collection—which, to this day, remains one of the chief public attractions of the Executive Mansion.

Mrs. Harrison's focus on domestic concerns generally won her a favorable treatment in the press, and she continued to be a political asset to her husband. She usually accompanied him on political trips, including the April 1889 celebration of the centennial of George Washington's inauguration in New York. On the Harrisons' cross-country tour to California in the spring of 1891, the First Lady was warmly greeted at stops along the way.

Not all of her press coverage was complimentary or pleasing, however, and one incident in particular evoked a storm of criticism. In the summer of 1889 she and the president spent a weekend with Postmaster General John Wanamaker at Cape May Point, New Jersey. The First Lady was so taken by the seaside resort that, the following spring, Wanamaker put together a group of subscribers who commissioned the construction of a twenty-room cottage,

which they presented to the First Lady in June 1890. Thrilled at the prospect of spending summers at the pleasant spot, under her own roof, Mrs. Harrison accepted the gift, with little apparent notion of the political difficulties it might raise for her husband.

When news of the cottage became public, editorial writers said that the transaction opened the president to accusations of being a bribe-taker, and reporters and others demanded to know who the subscribers were. Most were wealthy business friends of Wanamaker from Philadelphia, and none expected an appointment or other official favor from Harrison. To defuse criticism, Cape May officials offered some 300 reporters a free excursion to the resort. During their visit Mrs. Harrison held a levee at her cottage for the excursionists. Several returned to their home papers and prepared favorable portraits of the resort with straightforward descriptions of the Harrison cottage.

Even so, press opponents charged that the Harrisons had played into the hands of Cape May developers who, in fact, did begin to tout the village as the summer home of the president. Attempting to redeem the situation in a press interview, Mrs. Harrison probably made matters worse. Without mentioning Grover Cleveland by name, she noted that, early in his term, the former president had bought a summer house in the Washington suburbs, which he had sold for a substantial profit upon leaving office. Her husband, she said in the interview, preserved in the Harrison papers, had "decided scruples" against following a similar course. Accepting the cottage, she said, "does not involve the President in any money-making for his personal benefit. How others may be benefited does not concern us. If our presence at Cape May Point may be a benefit to any persons they are welcome to it." In the end, Harrison gave Wanamaker a check for $10,000 for the cottage, but the public relations damage was already done.

Journalistic attention to First Family doings often offended Caroline Harrison, who resented what she considered an invasion of their privacy. Reporters had a field day with Benjamin Harrison McKee, "Baby McKee," the president's favorite grandchild, who enjoyed frolicking on the White House grounds. Most distressing to Mrs. Harrison, however, was the imputation that the family welcomed such attention as a way of winning public favor. After nearly three years as First Lady, she wrote to Mrs. James S. Clarkson (a copy of the letter is at the University of Texas at Austin), "I have about come to the conclusion that political life is not the happiest—you are [so] *battered* around in it that life seems hardly worth living."

But being among family made life worth living for Caroline Harrison, and she took to the White House as many members of her family as she could. Resident in the private quarters were her daughter and son-in-law, Mary and J. Robert McKee, and their two children, Baby McKee and his sister, Mary. Daughter-in-law Mary Harrison and granddaughter Marthena also lived in, joined by son Russell Harrison whenever he could escape his business obligations in Montana. Caroline Harrison also offered a home to John Scott, her ninety-year-old father, who was scrimping along on a Pension Office clerkship when the Harrisons arrived in Washington. Rounding out the household was Mrs. Harrison's thirty-one-year-old widowed niece, Mary Lord Dimmick. The Harrisons' Indianapolis house had nine bedrooms, but, for these eleven family members, the White House offered only five bedrooms and two bathrooms. By contrast, the attraction of the cottage at Cape May was obvious.

For years, the private second floor of the executive mansion had witnessed the encroachment of official functions. Now fully two-thirds of the rooms had been converted to offices, and the only space available for an upstairs sitting room was a section of a hallway. Previous First Families, most of them smaller than the Harrisons', had unsuccessfully requested expansions of the mansion, but Caroline Harrison was determined to get something done. She invited congressional committees on Buildings and Grounds to the White House to view firsthand the mansion's inadequacy as well as its dire need for repair. She argued that Congress could afford to be liberal, especially in light of the addition of the magnificent Senate and House wings to the previously inadequate Capitol Building. She courted public support through interviews and tours of the house with reporters, observing that she sought the enlargement not merely for the comfort of the Harrisons, who would soon be gone, but to create a residence worthy of all presidential families to come. Drawing on the patriotic feeling surrounding the Washington centennial, she argued (as recorded in a clipping in the Harrison Papers) that the expansion "would be a fitting memorial to the growth of the republic during the first hundred years."

To give substance to her suggestions, Mrs. Harrison enlisted the aid of Washington engineer and architect Fred D. Owen, who prepared three alternative plans. The first called for the construction of an entirely new house on 16th Street, and the second for modest additions to the current structure. Owen's third proposal, embodying Mrs. Harrison's views, called for the preservation of the existing mansion and the addition of two complementary wings perpendicular to it. The west wing would be devoted to offices, thereby freeing the original White House for private use and public entertaining. The east wing would house an art gallery, which Mrs. Harrison defended on the grounds that the national government had reached the point where it ought to do more to support the arts. Connecting the two new wings at the opposite end and at a lower grade would be an enlarged botanical conservatory. The resulting quadrangle would enclose a large garden with an allegorical fountain commemorating Christopher Columbus's discovery of America.

Later historians of the White House and of architecture have considered the scheme a monstrous violation of the integrity of the original building, but at the time, Mrs. Harrison won the support of the Buildings and Grounds Committee chairs in both the House and the Senate. In January 1891,

Senator Leland Stanford of California sponsored a bill appropriating $950,000 to carry the plan into effect. In the rush of legislation in the waning days of the 51st Congress, however, the bill failed to win consideration. The Republicans lost the congressional elections, and little hope for passage remained for the rest of Harrison's term. Major expansion did not come until after the turn of the century.

Although her expansion project had failed, Mrs. Harrison continued to direct the major overhaul and refurbishing of the mansion that she pushed throughout her term. Known as a careful, even fastidious, household manager in Indianapolis, she was horrified at the dilapidated conditions she found at the White House. Curtains were discolored and tattered, upholstery threadbare and soiled, and carpets worn thin. Discarded books and papers as well as rubbish cluttered the attic and other storage areas. The White House harbored one of Washington's largest rat colonies and other vermin.

Mrs. Harrison's first step was to order a thorough cleaning, top to bottom, with the enlistment of a team of ferrets to go after the rats. She had the contents of every room including storage areas inventoried. Often personally inspecting furniture and other items in the dusty attic or grimy basement, she carefully earmarked those worthy of preservation. Old floors, some five layers deep of rotting materials, were torn up and replaced with cement, bricks, and wood. Workmen gutted the kitchen and rebuilt it with modern equipment. Bathrooms were installed and rooms reconfigured on the second floor. Public rooms on the first floor received fresh coats of paint, new curtains, carpets, and upholstery. Mrs. Harrison secured four special appropriations which, minus ordinary operating expenses, gave her $52,000 for restoration and refurbishing. Of that sum, $13,450 paid for the installation of electric lighting.

The First Lady's focus on family and domestic functions identified her as a traditionalist, described by White House Chief Usher Irwin Hoover in his memoirs as "a nice 'homey' person, kind and motherly."

Even so, she took some interest in matters of concern to women. As the head of a Washington-based committee, she helped lead a national effort to raise funds for a medical school at the Johns Hopkins Hospital in Baltimore. Composed largely of professional and society women, the group stipulated that its fund-raising would go forward only on the condition that the school would admit women on an equal footing with men—a condition the hospital accepted. Besides lending the prestige of her name to the effort, Mrs. Harrison played an active role, including hosting fund-raising receptions at the White House.

Mrs. Harrison also agreed to head the newly formed Daughters of the American Revolution (DAR) as its first president-general. Celebrating its centennial under the Constitution, the nation witnessed an upsurge of patriotic sentiment in this era. At the Washington centennial in New York, President Harrison made his famous suggestion that every schoolhouse in the land fly the American flag. Many educated and socially prominent women, unwilling to see patriotism become the exclusive province of men, founded the DAR in 1890, with the avowed purposes of perpetuating the memory of the Revolution, supporting historical preservation, and promoting citizenship education. Sympathizing with these goals, and also frankly recognizing the political returns, Mrs. Harrison accepted the position of president-general. Although she insisted on appointing an assistant who would handle most affairs of her office, she was no mere figurehead. She gave close attention to the selection of the society's other officers, opened the White House to its functions, and presided or spoke at many of its meetings. She told the group's First Continental Congress (as reported in the first issue of its *American Monthly Magazine*) that study of "the early struggle of this country" showed "that much of its success was due to the character of the women of that era. The unselfish part they acted constantly commends itself to our admiration and example."

Personal rivalries plagued the society's early organizing group, and Mrs. Harrison's willingness to become its head did much to neutralize those controversies and help launch what grew into a powerful lobbying organization and conservative women's voice. For decades after her death, DAR members continued to revere her as their founding patron, adopting her favorite flower—the orchid—as their special symbol.

During her stay in the White House, Caroline Harrison was frequently ill with colds or other respiratory ailments that some outsiders variously attributed to her spending too much time rummaging through the clammy mansion basement or being exposed to the noxious effects of her painting pigments. In the spring of 1892 she suffered an attack of influenza that was soon diagnosed as tuberculosis. At the suggestion of doctors, the president took her to a retreat in the Adirondack Mountains. There she rallied in the early summer, but then her condition worsened. In September she asked to be taken back to the White House, where she died on October 25, 1892. After funeral ceremonies in Washington, her body was buried in Crown Hill Cemetery in Indianapolis. Two weeks after her death, Benjamin Harrison lost his bid for reelection.

Four years later, Harrison married Mary Lord Dimmick, Mrs. Harrison's niece, who had lived with the family during virtually all their time in the White House. Russell Harrison and Mary McKee adamantly opposed the union, refused to attend the private wedding service in New York, and saw little of their father afterward. Some observers at the time and in later years speculated that Harrison's love for Mrs. Dimmick originated during the White House years. Contemporary news accounts noted that although the niece had moved into the White House to assist the First Lady with social responsibilities, Mrs. Dimmick became something of an informal adviser to the president, helping with correspondence and appointments and even conferring on some matters of state. At the time of the wedding, several newspapers quoted Harrison to the effect that while he was president, he enjoyed having Mrs. Dimmick around because she was quiet and was the only woman who would

not talk when he was trying to think. Reporters further noted that Harrison, who took long walks for exercise, frequently invited Mrs. Dimmick to join him, and that the two occasionally took afternoon carriage rides together. But contemporary accounts also attest to a continuing love between the Harrisons in the White House, as illustrated by the president's gifts for his wife, his openly affectionate greetings when she returned from trips, and the devastating loss he felt at her death.

When the second marriage was announced in early 1896, Harrison's former secretary of war, Stephen B. Elkins, writing in a letter preserved in the Whitelaw Reid Papers, Library of Congress, discounted the whispered rumor that "Mrs. Harrison in her life [had been] disturbed at the fondness of the President for Mrs. D—." But five years later, Republican official Perry Heath told George B. Cortelyou, private secretary to President William McKinley, that Harrison's son-in-law, J. R. McKee, had said that Caroline Harrison was so distraught that she threatened to move out of the White House. According to a memorandum of Heath's conversation in Cortelyou's papers (Library of Congress), McKee dissuaded her from leaving the president only after convincing her of the great damage such a move would unleash. For her part, the second Mrs. Harrison kept a carefully annotated scrapbook of news clippings regarding her marriage to the former president, a scrapbook now in the Harrison Papers. In one clipping a reporter speculated that the elderly Harrison was marrying again mostly for companionship rather than romance; next to this story the second wife wrote: "How little this reporter knew how great a love match this was! It was a romance!" She left unstated, however, when the romance began. Ten months after the marriage, she gave birth to Harrison's third child, Elizabeth.

No evidence suggests that Mrs. Harrison ever asked her niece to leave the White House. Indeed, Mrs. Dimmick traveled with the First Lady, accompanied her on shopping trips, and served as a constant nurse during her last illness. While the true nature of the relationship remains obscure, the innocent explanation may well be that the hardworking president found in the young and energetic Mrs. Dimmick a likable helper and companion, and that the lonely, widowed, politically rejected former president found in her a woman he knew well and one he could easily love.

If, on the other hand, the stories of domestic turmoil in the Harrison White House are true, they bespeak a deep suffering on Caroline Harrison's part that simply throws into higher relief her achievements as First Lady. Without setting out to transform the institution, she was, nonetheless, an activist in her own way and accomplished a good deal. She found the White House rat-infested, shabby, and filthy, and left it a modern and attractive residence worthy of the nation's chief executive. She effectively highlighted the need for an expanded mansion, not only for the comfort of the First Family but also to provide enough room for the more efficient operation of the increasingly complex office of the president. She launched the program to preserve china, furniture, and other artifacts from the mansion—a program that in the twentieth century made the White House a leading force for historical preservation in the United States. Although she relished her domestic role and never occupied a place in the vanguard of feminism, Caroline Scott Harrison nonetheless lent her name and her labor to an assortment of women's organizations and causes that clearly suggested that women of the future should play a variety of roles beyond the purely domestic.

BIBLIOGRAPHICAL ESSAY

The papers of Benjamin Harrison, in the Manuscript Division of the Library of Congress, contain a good bit of material on Mrs. Harrison. Her correspondence in the collection consists primarily of letters she received from her husband during the Civil War and routine letters she received at the White House. More useful are the collection's clipping scrapbooks that contain numerous newspaper stories about specific events during the period Mrs. Harrison was

First Lady, as well as several sketches of her life and obituaries. The Office of the Curator of the White House holds documents dealing with her efforts to improve the Executive Mansion. The Benjamin Harrison Home in Indianapolis, Indiana, has a small collection of family papers, including Caroline Harrison's diary of her first year in the White House as well as family letters that touch on Caroline's children's dismay at the ex-president's second marriage. The Whitelaw Reid papers and the George B. Cortelyou Papers, both at the Library of Congress, also have information about tensions in the Harrison marriage.

No full-length scholarly biography of Caroline Harrison exists. She received sympathetic treatment in Harry J. Sievers's *Benjamin Harrison* (3 vols., Indianapolis and New York, 1952, 1959, 1968), which is the major biography of her husband. Short, nonscholarly biographies include Harriet McIntire Foster, *Mrs. Benjamin Harrison: The First President-General of the National Society of the Daughters of the American Revolution* (n.p., 1908), and Ophia D. Smith, "Caroline Scott Harrison: A Daughter of Old Oxford," National Historical Magazine 75 (April 1941): 4–8, 65. Caroline Harrison's obituary appeared in the *New York Times*, October 26, 1892.

Caroline Harrison's refurbishing and preservation efforts figure in general studies of the evolution of the White House. Of considerable value for her expansion and improvement efforts are William Seale, *The President's House: A History* (2 vols., Washington, D.C., 1986); and William Ryan and Desmond Guinness, *The White House: An Architectural History* (New York, 1980). See also *Extension of the Executive Mansion*, House Report 4042, 51st Cong., 2nd sess. The Smithsonian publication *Official White House China, 1789 to the Present* (1975), by Margaret Brown Klapthor, chronicles Mrs. Harrison's china painting and collecting and her preservation work. Irwin H. (Ike) Hoover, *Forty-two Years in the White House* (Boston, 1934), includes an assessment of Mrs. Harrison.

★★★   ★★★

Ida Saxton McKinley

(1847–1907)

First Lady: 1897–1901

John J. Leffler

Born in Canton, Ohio, on June 8, 1847, Ida Saxton was the daughter of James A. Saxton and Katherine "Kate" Dewalt Saxton. Her family was prominent in the life of her native town. Ida's paternal grandfather, John Saxton, began publishing his Canton newspaper, the *Ohio Repository*, in 1815, and continued to serve as its head until his death in 1871; her father was a wealthy banker and businessman. Through wealth and inclination, the Saxtons were also active in the development and governance of the local Presbyterian church.

The second of three children in her family, Ida had an older brother, George, and a younger sister, Mary. What little is known about Ida's childhood suggests that she was indulged by her parents, particularly by her father, a man who "lived in a large and easy way," as biographer Josiah Hartzell put it. She was an intelligent child whose views were shaped by her parents' Presbyterian faith. Ida attended the Canton public schools and private schools in Delhi, New York, and Cleveland, Ohio. When she was nineteen, her parents, determined to provide her with a fashionable education, sent both of their daughters to board at Brooke Hall Seminary in Media, Pennsylvania. Brooke Hall was a "finishing school" rather than a center of serious education, but Ida later had fond remembrances of the time she spent there; while First Lady she invited Brooke Hall alumnae to a White House reception, and offered to help one of her old teachers obtain a position with the post office.

By all accounts, Ida was an attractive, witty, and energetic young woman when she returned from Brooke Hall and reentered Canton society. In March 1868 she won the popularity prize for a part she played in an entertainment held at Schaefer's Opera House to raise funds for the Presbyterian church. In October she dressed as the Queen of Hearts for a masquerade attended by fifty members of Canton's social elite. She was also teaching Sunday school for her church at about that time. At a picnic she met Major William McKinley, a handsome and ambitious young man who was beginning to make a mark for himself in the area. There is no evidence that any sparks flew between the two at the time.

In the summer and fall of 1869, Ida and her sister joined a small group chaperoned by Jeanette Alexander, a Canton schoolteacher, for a "Grand Tour" of Europe. Landing in Ireland in June, Ida and her companions traveled for about six months through Scotland, England, Holland, Belgium, France, Germany, Austria, Switzerland, and Italy at a sometimes exhausting pace. The trip was designed to be an educational experience for the young women (Miss Alexander's expenses were paid by Ida's father), and virtually every day was filled with trips to museums, art galleries, castles, and other points of interest. The extended letters Ida and Mary wrote to their parents during the course of the trip offer interesting insights into Ida's character and capabilities at this stage in her life; they are particularly significant because no comparable evidence exists by which to understand Ida in later years, after she became an invalid.

From her letters, Ida emerges as practical, competent, and independent. While her younger sister often waxed romantic in her descriptions of scenery and mentioned various books she was reading, Ida's letters were usually shorter and more matter-of-fact in tone. Though Ida mentioned music, art, and scenery in her letters, many of her discussions focused on matters relating to money. She was comfortable with handling large sums of cash, and accounted her expenses meticulously; she was constantly

searching for bargains and learned quickly to negotiate with shopkeepers for the best possible prices. She clashed with Jeanette Alexander, the chaperone, over money and activities. While the beleaguered chaperone saw Ida as a headstrong, "spoiled" young woman, Ida, twenty-two years old at the time, thought the teacher was too restrictive and unreasonable. As she wrote to her parents on October 10, 1869, "Miss A. does not like to have us suggest anything that would be an improvement on her plans. . . . She is very self-willed."

Considering the symptoms of the affliction that would plague her later life, it may be significant that, beginning in August, Ida began to suffer from chronic headaches, and she intimated that she had been troubled with them in the past. On August 21, 1869, for example, she told her parents that she was not feeling well: "[H]eadache is all the trouble," she wrote. "I have been having so little headache, that now I cannot stand much." The headaches seem to have continued, at least intermittently, for much of the rest of the trip. On August 29 she reported feeling "sick last evening with a hard headache so could not write." Again on October 27 she told her parents: "I am sure to have the headache if I do not take tea for breakfast."

The letters also contain evidence that Ida formed a romantic attachment to a young man before leaving for her tour of Europe. On several occasions she noted that she received letters from a Mr. Wright (the man has since been identified as John W. Wright of Canton). Ida wrote to him regularly, and purchased a card case for him inscribed with the letter *W*. He had planned to travel to New York to greet her when the trip was over. On September 26, however, Ida received an emotional shock when she learned that Wright had died about three weeks earlier. Her sister told their parents that she found Ida standing on the veranda "feeling very badly. . . . I am so sorry for her because she thought considerable of him. . . . [S]he feels very badly and looks quite pale, but I think traveling and seeing so much will take her mind from it and make her feel better." After Wright's tragic death, a more thoughtful side of Ida began to surface in her letters. Her descriptions of natural beauty became more detailed and appreciative, her observations of local customs more acute and empathetic. Traveling through Switzerland in early October, for example, she marveled at the scenery but also noted that "The women are made slaves of in this country, it is terrible to see how hard they work in the field and the loads they carry on their poor backs."

Ida and her sister returned home to Canton in early 1870, carrying with them various treasures they had picked up during their travels, including furs, false hair pieces, and music boxes. Many of their purchases were made for friends and members of the family; Ida also remembered to buy a small gift for every student in her Sunday school class. Later that year she began to work in the Stark County Bank, owned by her father. It was an unusual move for a woman at the time, but Ida displayed an aptitude with figures, and James Saxton apparently encouraged his daughter to develop her independence. She began as a clerk, then was promoted to cashier; according to some sources, she was occasionally entrusted with managing the bank in her father's absence. After her return, Ida also reestablished her position in Canton society, and the Saxton house was a center of social activity. Though pursued by several suitors (some of whom, according to legend, carried flowers to her cashier's window), Ida at first resisted them all; quite likely, she was still recovering from the death of Mr. Wright. At the bank, at her house, or during a public lecture (the stories conflict), she met William McKinley again, however. She soon fell in love with him, and he with her.

McKinley (also known as "the Major"), then twenty-seven years old, was a Civil War hero who had established an excellent moral reputation in Canton after building a law practice in the city. Though the Major had little money, he had recently been elected Stark County's prosecutor, and was clearly a man with a future. Their courtship was brief but intense. According to biographer Margaret Leech, McKinley was "madly, devotedly in love, with all the repressed passion of his deeply emotional nature." Ida was equally taken. Once, when she had arrived at a social event before McKinley, she could not conceal her anxiety, and questioned every guest on his whereabouts: "Have you seen the Major? Do you imagine the Major is sick? Has the Major been called [away] from the city?" To some she seemed overly possessive, and seemed jealous of another woman whom McKinley had previously attended. On a moonlit night the couple took a buggy to the top of a hill near the city, and McKinley proposed marriage. Ida accepted, and her father, who had known McKinley for some time, gave his consent. McKinley wrote to Rutherford B. Hayes, his friend and mentor, that Ida was everything he could hope for.

The bride wore a white satin gown edged with lace when the two were married on January 25, 1871, in the city's Presbyterian church. Over a thousand people attended, packing the church so full that many of the well-wishers had to stand through the wedding. Though Ida McKinley would later switch to her husband's Methodist congregation, the ceremony was conducted by ministers of both faiths. The newlyweds traveled to New York for their honeymoon, then returned to Canton. After living for a short time in the St. Cloud Hotel, they settled into a rather small house on North Market Street that had been given to them by the bride's father.

William and Ida McKinley worked together to establish their household, and, by all accounts both seemed happy during the first two years of their marriage. Ida McKinley called her husband "Major" in public, but in private it was "dearest." On Christmas Day 1871, Ida McKinley gave birth to their first child, Katherine, named after Ida McKinley's mother. About six months later, she became pregnant again. Katie, as the first baby was called, became the center of the household. William was delighted with his little blonde daughter, while Ida McKinley seemed to shift some of her possessiveness concerning her husband into attentiveness for her child. She posed Katie for a photographer and then paid to have one of the pictures duplicated in an oil painting. She watched over every aspect of the child's life with a devotion that sometimes verged on overprotection.

In early 1873, just after little Katie's first birthday, Ida McKinley's mother died. Less than a month later, before she had recovered from the profound shock of her mother's death, Ida McKinley underwent a hard labor during the birth of her second child. The baby, named Ida, was sickly and died in less than five months, on August 22, 1873. Still depressed and very ill from the delivery, Mrs. McKinley was not prepared for the blow; her health and her psyche were seriously damaged. She suffered from severe headaches, convulsions, and seizures accompanied by blackouts; though nerve specialists and other physicians were consulted, they could effect no change in her condition. It was whispered that she had epilepsy, though the disease was poorly understood at the time. She spent many days in her bed, physically limited by other symptoms that her doctors explained with a diagnosis of phlebitis. Irritable and anxious, Ida McKinley grew increasingly morose, and her protectiveness toward young Katie became more intense, even obsessive. She wondered out loud whether this cherished part of her life would be taken from her, too. Had she offended God somehow? According to author Thomas Beer, Katie's uncle Abner once saw his little niece playing outside and invited her on a walk. "No, I mustn't go out of the yard," she replied, "or God'll punish Mama some more."

Once a vivacious, energetic woman, Ida McKinley quickly became an invalid. William McKinley's hope that his wife would eventually recover was almost destroyed on June 25, 1875, when three-year-old Katie died of typhoid fever. Mrs. McKinley's nerves were shattered, and she never completely recovered. Even twenty-five years later, during her years in the White House, she remained periodically subject to unpredictable seizures and intense headaches,

and the crippling phlebitis continued to limit her movements severely. She was also prone to a number of other ailments, including an irregular menstrual cycle, digestive problems, and stubborn colds. Her illnesses took their toll in other ways, too. Ida McKinley seemed to age prematurely. Her face often seemed strained, and she had her hair cut short to eliminate the weight of braids and pins pulling on her head. The bromides prescribed by her doctors sometimes left her dull and listless.

The traumatic events surrounding the birth and death of little Ida, and the subsequent death of Katie, fundamentally altered the character of Ida McKinley's marriage. Afraid that she would somehow lose the husband she truly loved, Ida McKinley demanded a great deal of his time and attention, and became extremely jealous of other women. She commissioned a portrait of him and had it hung on the wall opposite her bed. William McKinley responded to the new circumstances with a dutiful selflessness that led others to admire the depth of his character. He cut back his business obligations as much as possible, and no longer exercised with his usual long walks and horseback rides; he tried his best to accommodate his wife's demands and to allay her anxieties. McKinley was never known to criticize his wife or to complain about his lot in life. He became accustomed to the seizures, and learned to adopt the nonchalance of a medical professional when they occurred. At the onset of an attack, he would simply place a handkerchief or napkin over her face and proceed as if nothing important had occurred. Friends and visitors came to understand that they were expected to react in a similar fashion. The McKinleys never had another child, but they both came to be confident in their love for each other.

Ida McKinley was aware of at least some of the burdens she placed on her husband, and tried hard to mitigate them as best she could. Despite her deep-seated fears and anxieties, an element of her old independence remained. Not wanting to be labeled an invalid, she attempted to keep her spirits up and attended to household duties as far as her health allowed. She struggled to maintain her health by taking various medicines to sustain her strength and by traveling to consult with various doctors in Ohio and on the East Coast. Ida McKinley fought against the temptation to seal herself off from the world, and despite the constant risk of personal embarrassment, she continued to keep their house open to the social functions necessary to her husband's career. She ignored (if she heard them) the whispers about her "fits." James Saxton helped to shore up the family finances. In May 1873, not long after the troubled birth of the McKinley's second child, Saxton placed his legal affairs in McKinley's hands, and, in December of that year, the *Repository* carried a notice announcing that Major McKinley had been chosen to be the manager of his father-in-law's bank.

Ida McKinley must have known that her life as a politican's wife would be particularly difficult, considering her illnesses and anxieties, yet she took an active interest in her husband's budding political career and insisted that William continue to pursue his political ambitions. During the early years of McKinley's career, his wife often remained at home battling with her illness, while speaking engagements and other commitments took her beloved husband away from her. She endured it, and encouraged him to continue. As William McKinley pushed to expand his political horizons, Ida McKinley also helped to shape his views. She kept herself well-informed on the issues of the day, and was perfectly capable of presenting her ideas in a convincing manner. According to McKinley biographer Charles Olcott, Mrs. McKinley's opinions were often so "sound and sensible" that her husband could only respond, "Ida, I think you are right." It was partly because of her interest in the temperance issue that McKinley became actively involved in Canton's temperance movement in 1874.

In 1877, after William was elected to Congress, the McKinleys sold their home on North Market Street and moved into a modest suite at the Ebbitt House in Washington, D.C.; they remained at the Ebbitt until 1891, after McKinley's failure to win reelection. Because Ida could not stand fresh air, they rode in closed carriages and their suite was stuffy. McKinley conducted much of his congressional business in a room he rented across the hall, and hired a nurse to watch over his wife while he was working there or at the Capitol. If he had to work late in the House, he was always careful to send Mrs. McKinley a note so that she would know when he would be home. He spent virtually all of his free time with his wife and woke up early each morning so that he could get in a couple hours of work before having breakfast with her. McKinley was addicted to cigars but did all of his smoking outside their rooms, or contented himself indoors by chewing the end of a Garcia.

Ida McKinley spent much of her time during these years alone with her nurse, sitting in a rocking chair while embroidering patterns or crocheting, surrounded by pictures of her husband that she had mounted on the walls. In some ways, she seemed, by then, to have resigned herself to the status of an invalid. Despite the number of different medicines and treatments prescribed for Mrs. McKinley during McKinley's years in Congress, her condition showed no signs of general improvement. On one occasion in 1888, while visiting in Canton with her sister, she had an attack so severe and so protracted that her doctors feared for her life, and her husband was called from Washington to see her. The timing of some of the attacks seemed almost too convenient. In 1881, Ida McKinley experienced a seizure just after her husband mentioned seeing a particularly attractive woman at President Garfield's funeral. According to Thomas Beer, Ida McKinley felt she was being neglected by her husband at that particular time. In contrast, she seems to have handled the death of her father in 1887 fairly well. There is no evidence to suggest that she suffered inordinately, although she was in Canton without her husband when the death occurred.

Though Ida McKinley's capacity for socializing was limited by her condition, she did attend a number of social functions during this part of her husband's career. She

particularly enjoyed several visits to the
White House while Rutherford Hayes, the
Major's longtime mentor, was president.
Lucy Webb Hayes, the president's wife,
developed an affection for both McKinleys;
once, they stayed at the White House for
two weeks to look after the Hayeses' children while the president and his wife were
traveling. After Hayes left office in 1881, Ida
McKinley lost an important social outlet,
but she and the Major occasionally entertained visitors in their rooms. Constituents
from Ohio dropped by, as did various congressmen, who sometimes brought their
families. Like her husband, Mrs. McKinley
was extremely fond of children, and she
doted on them when they came with their
parents to see her. She also enjoyed traveling. She took two trips to California with
her husband while he was in Congress, and
went to Canton without him at least twice
in the late 1880s. In 1890, she and the Major
took some time off to go to Chicago for what
they called their second honeymoon.

Though Congressman McKinley was
defeated in his 1890 bid for reelection, in
November 1891 he was elected governor of
Ohio. He and his wife moved into the Chit-
tenden House, an old hotel near the capitol
building in Columbus. Later, after the Chit-
tenden burned down, they lived in a larger
set of rooms in the Neil House. By all
accounts Ida McKinley's health noticeably
improved during her four years in Columbus. She seemed more calm and relaxed,
and though she continued to have seizures,
the attacks were much less violent. At least
part of the reason for her apparently increasing good health and placid demeanor,
however, may have been the drug treatments—the sedatives—prescribed by Dr. J.
N. Bishop of New York, whom she probably met in 1893 during yet another eastern
search for help with her problem. Ida
McKinley continued to spend a great deal
of her time with her crochet needles.

While it was understood in Columbus
that Mrs. McKinley was an invalid, the
McKinleys nevertheless began to enjoy
something like a normal social life. Ida

McKinley developed a small set of friends,
and encouraged William to invite people
home to their apartment. The Major took
up horseback riding again, and he and Mrs.
McKinley spent weekends in the mansions
of friends in Cincinnati and Cleveland.
Though Ida McKinley usually appeared
only briefly at official receptions while her
husband was governor, near the end of his
term she successfully hosted a large formal
affair that included dancing.

By this time, Mrs. McKinley's social
refinements helped to alter the rather austere approach to life that William brought
to their marriage. From Mrs. McKinley the
Major learned to appreciate fine lace, flowers, and jewelry, and through her he also
came to enjoy music and stage dramas; he
liked Shakespeare and sometimes read the
plays before watching them performed.
The couple frequently attended operas in
Cleveland while McKinley was governor,
taking advantage of a box reserved for them
by political friend and sponsor Mark
Hanna, and they became acquainted with a
number of the stars of the stage.

Ever the devoted husband, McKinley
continued to guard against his wife's anxieties, and he devised a system of signals to
let her know he was thinking about her as
he went about his duties as governor. Each
morning, after he left the house, he would
wave his handkerchief to his wife from a
particular spot across the street from their
apartment; every afternoon, at exactly three
o'clock, he would open his office window,
clearly visible from the Neil House, and
wave again. When sitting with her, McKinley was always alert for the slightest sign of
discomfort from his wife, and some observers were astonished by the speed of his
responses to her needs. In the evenings,
when he and his wife often played cribbage,
he contrived ways to make sure she won.

In 1893 the McKinleys unexpectedly
found themselves in serious financial trouble. Some time earlier, the Major had
cosigned some promissory notes to help
Robert Walker, one of his boyhood friends,
start a business. McKinley had thought that

the notes obligated him for only a few thousand dollars, at most, if Walker's enterprise ever failed; instead, when he was informed in February 1893 that Walker's business had gone down, he also learned that he had been misled. After the final accounting was done, McKinley learned that his share of Walker's debts amounted to more than $100,000: he was on the brink of financial and political ruin. Mrs. McKinley, visiting in Boston when she heard the news, immediately left for Ohio to support her husband. Against the advice of many of her friends, she selflessly offered her own money (including her inheritance, she could raise about $92,000) to help her husband. Ultimately, the money was paid by a pool of friends organized by Mark Hanna, but Ida McKinley's gesture, thought foolish by some, was widely admired, and it demonstrated the depth of her commitment and love for her husband.

In 1896, at the end of McKinley's second term as governor, the McKinleys returned to Canton and rented their former home on North Market Street, where many years before they had experienced both happiness and tragedy. By this time McKinley was a strong contender for the Republican nomination for the presidential race that year, and more than ever, he and his wife were in the public eye. On January 17, 1896, a crowd of about a thousand people were waiting for them when they arrived at the train station in Canton; the next day, the McKinleys were escorted by a parade of citizens to the center of town, where a huge crowd gave them a noisy welcome. In the beginning of February, the couple held a lavish party to celebrate their silver wedding anniversary. Over 500 people attended, and Ida McKinley performed flawlessly as the smiling hostess. If the party had been intended partly to demonstrate that Mrs. McKinley was not a hopeless invalid, it did not completely succeed.

The election of 1896, which pitted McKinley against William Jennings Bryan, was one of the most virulent and intense political contests in American political history. As presidential politics heated up that

year, Ida McKinley became the target of a vicious whispering campaign intended to undermine her husband's candidacy. Various rumors intimated that she was actually an English spy, a mulatto, a Catholic, a battered wife, or a lunatic. Others claimed that her husband was a common drunkard, an agent of the pope, a swindler. Though some strategists in the Republican camp believed that publicly responding to the rumors about the candidate's wife would do more harm than good, ultimately the Republican Party funded a campaign biography of Ida McKinley in an attempt to offset some of the damage done by the rumors.

The sixty-one-page pamphlet, *Sketch of the Life of Mrs.William McKinley* by Josiah Hartzell, was only one part of a massive mailing campaign conducted by the Republicans that year. It was the first campaign biography of an American presidential candidate's wife ever published. Through a preliminary discussion of her grandfather's accomplishments, the pamphlet linked Mrs. McKinley with America's hardy pioneer past and established the respectability of her roots. The rest of the book portrayed her life as a sentimental tragedy, though the author was careful to emphasize that the candidate's wife had emerged from her trials as a purer, more wholesome spirit. The pamphlet ended with a paragraph describing the nation's mood when William McKinley won the Republican nomination and "the telegraph poured forth its torrent of yellow slips, harbingers of the joy of the people, until late in the night." The messages of congratulation came, Hartzell wrote:

> Not from men alone, to the Governor, but from men and women to Mrs. McKinley; from friends she had known, and from another multitude of those whose hearts had been melted by the pathos in her story, and in whose aspirations her husband's name stood transfigured as the symbol of deliverance and hope.

While William Jennings Bryan stormed around the country preaching the gospel of free silver, McKinley conducted his campaign from the front porch of the house on North Market Street. Hundreds of thousands of visitors traveled to Canton to see the candidate and shake his hand. Mrs. McKinley, although she usually remained out of sight, sometimes emerged from the house to pose for photographs with various delegations who came to pay their respects to her husband. The Major occasionally left the premises when tactless questions about his wife were posed by visitors.

In early March 1897, after McKinley's decisive victory, the McKinleys traveled to Washington with about fifty friends and relatives. The couple stayed at the Ebbitt while preparing for the inauguration. Ida McKinley was reportedly in very poor health at this time. She remained in her room, resting in bed, while her sister Mary dealt with reporters and other visitors who called at their rooms. When she and her husband were invited by the outgoing president, Grover Cleveland, and his wife, Frances, to an informal White House dinner on the evening before the inauguration, McKinley went alone. The new First Lady looked sickly and pale during McKinley's inaugural address on March 4, 1897, and her appearance at a ball that night was cut short halfway through the reception line. The new president and his wife spent the rest of the evening in the White House.

Mrs. McKinley's health made it impossible for her to meet the full social responsibilities of her position as First Lady. The sometimes grueling routine of duty in reception lines and state dinners taxed her strength and her nerves. Her continuing susceptibility to unpredictable seizures also limited her role. While protocol demanded that she sit opposite her husband at state dinners, for example, the president decided early in his administration to sit next to his wife so that he could attend to her if necessary. He was encouraged to do so by Jennie Hobart, the vice president's wife, who often tactfully helped Mrs. McKinley carry out the duties of her position. The Hobarts lived in the "Cream White House" across from the Executive

Mansion, and virtually every day Mrs. Hobart visited the White House, lending her unassuming support, which earned the respect and gratitude of the president and his wife. Because phlebitis and general weakness prevented Ida McKinley from standing for long periods of time in reception lines, she sat in a chair positioned next to the president. Mrs. Hobart stood nearby to gently guide people past her and send them down the line. Occasionally Jennie was also hurriedly called by the president to help him with White House functions when his wife was too ill to appear, or when she needed the company of a woman she could trust.

The First Lady's moods fluctuated with her health and the medications she took. She could be charming, witty, and entertaining on some days; more often, she seemed irritable and testy. In her book, *I Would Live It Again*, acquaintance Julia Foraker related a number of the uncomfortable moments she had spent in the White House. Once, when Mrs. Foraker introduced a group of women to the First Lady and commented on the beautiful fall weather, Mrs. McKinley snapped at her: "Beautiful? I don't see anything beautiful about it. We've had nothing but rain, rain, rain." On another occasion, at a White House dinner party, Mrs. McKinley turned to the ladies surrounding her and abruptly insisted that Mrs. Alger (the wife of the secretary of war) wanted her position. Henry Adams, who witnessed the scene, thought her comment was perceptive; but the moment was, nevertheless, disagreeable. Though most people in the country knew Mrs. McKinley's health was delicate, the general public was unaware of her actual condition; and when heavily sedated, as she often was, the First Lady could leave a disturbing impression. In her diary, later published under the title *Washington Wife*, Ellen Maury Slayden described her visit to the White House in 1897:

The first glimpse of Mrs. McKinley made me feel ashamed of coming. She sat propped with pillows in a high armchair with her back to the light. Her color was ghastly, and it was wicked to have dressed her in bright blue velvet with a front of hard white satin spangled with gold. Her poor relaxed hands, holding some pitiful knitting, rested on her lap as if too weak to lift their weight of diamond rings, and her pretty gray hair is cut short as if she had had typhoid fever. . . . We all shrank from being there with a poor, suffering woman who ought to have been hidden from the gaze of the curious. Her voice was gentle and refined, and her face almost childishly sweet.

Mrs. McKinley's love for children was well publicized, and she encouraged her friends and acquaintances to bring their children to the White House. Many mothers, encouraged by the publicity, took their young ones to see the First Lady, hoping to give them a memorable experience. She continued to spend a good deal of her time crocheting, and gave more than 3,500 bedroom slippers she had made to charities (slippers personally knitted by the First Lady brought good prices at charity auctions). Ida McKinley also knitted slippers for people she liked, carefully choosing the colors for each pair to fit her idea of the recipient's personality.

When she was feeling well, the First Lady enjoyed entertaining at the White House. In early 1898, for example, she held a number of receptions in the Executive Mansion, inviting people from Canton and other cities. During the same period she brought visitors into the White House to enjoy a series of musicals that she had arranged. She also made short trips alone to New York and Baltimore. Receptions and entertainments held at the White House during the McKinley administration reflected Mrs. McKinley's taste for luxury and refinement. She traveled extensively during these years for diversion, for shopping, for health reasons, and to accompany her husband on political trips. Boston, Chicago, Canton, Atlanta, Virginia Hot Springs, New Orleans, San Antonio, and Los Angeles were just a few of the places she visited.

Though the First Lady did not direct the refurbishment of the White House that took place during the McKinley administration, she did help to choose the colors of the paint and silks that were applied to the walls of the old mansion during the renovation. The McKinleys enjoyed being surrounded by flowers, and during their stay in the White House, the rose beds in the conservatory adjoining the west wing of the mansion were expanded. The First Lady liked to place flowers in every room when possible, and some areas of the White House were adorned with several arrangements. At dinner parties the tables were always decorated with blossoms.

Everyone who knew the president and his wife was impressed by the depth of their mutual affection. Even during the Spanish-American War, while pressed into an extremely demanding schedule of work, the president continued to devote himself to his wife's comfort and well-being. Retiring for the evening, exhausted at two o'clock in the morning, he often found his wife wide awake and nervous; setting aside his own fatigue, he would sit on the bed beside his wife and hold her until she slept. In her book, titled *Memories*, Jennie Hobart described the McKinleys' relationship as "one of those rare and beautiful things that live only in tradition." In 1899, the McKinleys repurchased the old house on North Market Street in Canton. Together they spent three days planning to remodel it for their life together after the presidency. McKinley later told one of his aides that those three days were some of the happiest of their lives, that it was like having another honeymoon. After so many years of living in hotels, even life in the White House did not stop the two from looking forward to the day they would have a home of their own.

Mrs. McKinley idolized her husband and was always quick to defend him. She could also be intensely partisan in her outlook. On one occasion she discovered that two of her guests were Democrats, and subjected them to a long and bitter discourse to explain why Grover Cleveland had been a poor president. She felt that he had degraded the presidency when he sold his Washington house for a profit. On the other hand, as Henry Adams observed, she could be quite perceptive in her evaluations of character. Opha Moore, McKinley's stenographer when he was governor of Ohio, believed that Mrs. McKinley was a better judge of men than her husband was.

The First Lady's influence with the president sometimes shaped his decisions concerning appointments and policies. Early in the McKinley presidency, for example, newspapers announced that Captain H. O. S. Heistand, a U.S. Army officer who had become a close friend of McKinley's in Ohio, would be appointed as a military aide to the president. The appointment never happened, however, because Ida McKinley had developed a dislike for Heistand's wife. On the other hand, General Leonard Wood received his appointment to command American forces in Cuba in 1899 partly because of his friendship with Ida McKinley, which had developed during his assignment as White House physician. The First Lady also helped arrange the appointment of a member of the Daughters of the American Revolution to a government commission concerned with the Philippines. Mrs. McKinley's interest in sending missionaries to the Philippines to "civilize" a tribe in northern Luzon has led some to speculate that she helped influence McKinley's decision to annex the islands after the Spanish-American War. Colonel Benjamin Montgomery, a military aide to the president, was one who believed that she played a part in the decision. Though the available evidence is inconclusive, Ida McKinley's views almost certainly encouraged her husband's ultimate inclination toward annexation and expansion.

In the spring of 1901, at the beginning of McKinley's second term of office, Ida McKinley set out with her husband on an extensive tour of the nation. One of her fingers became infected early in the trip, and the problem worsened after her doctor attempted to lance it. Though she stoically withstood the pain during their reception in Los Angeles in early May, the infection led to an inflammation of her heart. For several days in San Francisco she remained so dangerously ill that her life seemed in danger; her husband remained close by, standing by her bed until the worst was over. Although she recovered rather quickly, the trip was cut short, and by July the McKinleys were in Canton for an extended rest.

Four months after Mrs. McKinley's brush with death in California, she stood over her husband as he lay on his own deathbed, mortally wounded by an anarchist assassin. According to biographer H. Wayne Morgan, the president's first thoughts after being shot were for her: "My wife, be careful how you tell her—oh be careful!" he said. McKinley lingered for eight days after being shot. Like the president, many people close to Ida McKinley feared her response to the awful news. To virtually everyone's surprise, she bore up rather well, although her diary entry for September 13, the day before he died, indicated her despair: "I hope the Lord will take me with my Precious, I do not want to live with out him." As Ida McKinley was led to her husband's bed to say good-bye for the last time, her face was etched with pain but no sobs emerged. His last words to her were whispered in tones too low for others in the room to hear.

Mrs. McKinley maintained her dignified composure during the following difficult days while her husband's body lay in state. She attended the funeral without the aid of sedatives, then returned to Canton and the house on Market Street. A week after McKinley's death, Ida McKinley's doctor told a reporter for the *New York Times* that she was "bearing up bravely" but was crushed by grief, and that he did not feel confident about her condition. Ida McKinley lived almost six years longer, however, and her health steadily improved; according to some sources, she never had another seizure after her husband's death. She spent these last years of her life in the Market Street house, often traveling out by carriage to visit her husband's grave. Her last illness began in early 1907. According to her obituary in the *New York Times*, she was heard to say "He is gone, and life is dark to me now," as her health rapidly deteriorated. She died May 26, 1907, and was buried next to her husband. Later that year their bodies were moved to the McKinley Mausoleum on Canton's Monument Hill.

Poor health prevented Ida Saxton McKinley from fully carrying out her social responsibilities as First Lady and restricted her opportunities to encounter the public. In any case, despite her independent outlook as a young woman, her concept of the role itself seems to have been limited to the pattern she inherited from her nineteenth-century predecessors. She did not publicly promote any particular cause, and she remained comfortably in the shadow of her husband. Although she possibly influenced her husband on the question of American involvement in the Philippines, her influence on his ultimate decision is difficult to gauge. Her primary contribution lay in the ways her social refinements, her support, and even her infirmities helped over the years to shape the sensibility and outlook of her husband. Although her illness limited her husband's activities, in an odd way the burden may actually have helped his political career. McKinley's unselfish devotion to his wife was often cited as the best evidence of his integrity—perhaps his most valuable political asset. Historians polled by the Sienna Research Institute in 1993 ranked Ida McKinley thirty-second of thirty-seven presidential wives, a better overall score than either Nancy Reagan or Mary Lincoln received.

BIBLIOGRAPHICAL ESSAY

No full-length study of Ida Saxton McKinley has yet been written, but much of her life is discussed extensively, though not always sympathetically, in Margaret Leech, *In the Days of McKinley* (New York, 1959), and in H. Wayne Morgan, *William McKinley and His America* (Syracuse, N.Y., 1963). The Leech book contains photostats of some of the diary entries Mrs. McKinley wrote just after her husband's assassination. Charles Olcott, *The Life of William McKin-*

ley (2 vols., Boston and New York, 1916), contains a somewhat more sympathetic portrait of the early Ida, as well as additional material, and should also be consulted. Her letters to her parents from Europe were compiled by Henry S. Belden in *The Grand Tour: Ida Saxton McKinley and Sister Mary Saxton Barber, 1869* (Canton, Ohio, 1985). Josiah Hartzell's *Sketch of the Life of Mrs. William McKinley* (Washington, D.C., 1896, 1897) is a brief and romantic biography written during the presidential campaign of 1896.

"Usurping Cuckoo," the chapter on Ida McKinley in Carl Sferrazza Anthony, *First Ladies: The Saga of the President's Wives and Their Power, 1789–1961* (New York, 1990), is a short and generally hostile, but nonetheless interesting, overview of her life. Betty Boyd Caroli discusses Mrs. McKinley in a cultural context in her book *First Ladies* (New York, 1987); part of her discussion centers around a contemporary article, "Comparison of Mrs. McKinley and Mrs. Bryan," *Harper's Bazaar* 33 (August 11, 1900): 954–956. Edward Thorton Heald, *The William McKinley Story* (Canton, Ohio, 1964), contains useful material about the McKinleys gathered from sources in Canton. Murat Halstead's article "Mrs. McKinley," *Saturday Evening Post* 175 (September 6, 1902): 6–7, and his book *The Illustrious Life of William McKinley, Our Martyred President* (n.p., 1901) provide additional information about McKinley's deathbed scene and Mrs. McKinley's later life. Ida McKinley's obituary in the *New York Times* (May 27, 1907) is also useful. Other sources include Thomas Beer, *Hanna* (New York, 1929); Mrs. Garrett [Jennie] Hobart, *Memories* (Mount Vernon, 1930); Julia Foraker, *I Would Live It Again* (New York and London, 1932); Walter P. Webb and Terrell Webb, eds., *Washington Wife: Journal of Ellen Maury Slayden from 1897–1919* (New York and Evanston, Ill., 1962); William Seale, *The President's House: A History* (2 vols., Washington, D.C., 1986); and Col. W. H. Crook, *Memories of the White House: The Home Life of Our Presidents from Lincoln to Roosevelt* (Boston, 1911).

Ida McKinley's childhood home in Canton, Ohio, is now a part of the First Ladies National Historic Site (established by an act of Congress in 2000), which includes the National First Ladies' Library. Ida lived there from 1850 until 1871 and then, after her marriage to William McKinley, from 1878 to 1891.

★★★ ★★★

Edith Kermit Carow Roosevelt

(1861–1948)

First Lady: 1901–1909

Stacy A. Cordery

On August 6, 1861, Edith Kermit Carow was born to Gertrude Tyler Carow and Charles Carow. Edith was the first daughter and the first living child of the wealthy Carow family. Edith and her younger sister, Emily, should have had an idyllic childhood, and in some respects they did—their pedigree and their money insulated them from most trials. Several misfortunes, nevertheless, marred their young lives. Charles Carow, Knickerbocker scion of the New York City–based international shipping family, was a gambler and an alcoholic whose failed business precipitated a family life that Edith would later seek to forget. Gertrude Tyler Carow, in the face of the strain, retreated to hypochrondia and became a distant and selfish mother, preoccupied with her husband and their mounting troubles. Edith seldom spoke of her parents in later years, and she did not regale her children with stories of their grandparents. By nature, Edith was a loner who often preferred books to people. Her acquaintances labeled her haughty and imperious. She guarded her privacy—so much so that in later life she burned many of her letters and left few traces of the pain of her early life. Thus her youth is difficult to reconstruct—except in reference to her childhood companion and future husband, Theodore Roosevelt.

As a little girl, Edith grew up within the the large and playful circle of her family's neighbors—the Roosevelts. Charles Carow had been a longtime friend of Theodore

Roosevelt, Sr., and Edith attended school in the Roosevelts' mansion in New York City. There a Roosevelt relative taught reading, writing, and needlework. With the Roosevelt children, Edith learned etiquette and dancing at the Dodsworth School. In 1871, the Carows moved, from their home near the Roosevelts on East Fourteenth Street, uptown to West Forty-fourth Street. That year, Edith enrolled in Miss Comstock's school for girls. Her circle of friends expanded, as did her understanding of the world. Louise Comstock instilled in Edith a devotion to religion and ethical behavior that increased her gravity and aloofness. At Miss Comstock's school she studied English, history, Latin, French, music, and a smattering of the sciences. Her favorite subject was English literature, particularly Shakespeare and poetry—enthusiasms she would retain throughout her life.

In 1873, the Roosevelt family joined the Carows and other New Yorkers in their flight uptown. This enabled Edith to see more of Corinne and Theodore Roosevelt—her two closest friends. The Roosevelts had spent the previous year traveling around the world, and had returned with a new seriousness. Theodore, then fifteen, echoed Edith's high moral code. He was preparing to enter Harvard. Corinne, age twelve, re-created a literary club similar to one she belonged to in Dresden. She invited her friends—Edith among them—to be the charter members of P.O.R.E., or Party of Renowned Eligibles. This literary society pursued wisdom by writing and then reading aloud their own works of prose and poetry.

Edith spent her summer vacations with her Tyler relatives in Monmouth, New Jersey, and with the Roosevelt family at Oyster Bay, Long Island. She enjoyed the solitude of the beaches, took long walks, and learned to identify wildflowers. While visiting Oyster Bay, Edith entered fully into the rambunctious yet intellectual life of the iconoclastic Roosevelt family. They rode across the island, rowed across the bay, staged theatricals, and discussed literature around the campfire. Young Theodore

christened his rowboat *Edith*, and asked its namesake to create a nautical flag for him to fly.

As teenagers, Theodore and Edith were drawn together. They saw their idealism and intellectualism reflected in one another and they enjoyed the absence of tension that came from growing up together. For Theodore, this attraction had some ambivalence. He nicknamed Edith "her Ladyship" and was wary of her moodiness. She unabashedly admired the charming scholar, even though, in proper nineteenth-century fashion, she did not disclose this to him.

Theodore's father died in February 1878. In the wake of this blow, Theodore sought Edith's company during their summer holiday at Oyster Bay. They spent some part of every day together for four days. Then they quarreled. The reasons for the spat are unclear. One theory is that Theodore proposed and Edith rejected him because she was too young (she was seventeen in 1878). Edith maintained, however, that Theodore had asked her to marry him several times in 1877 and 1878. Corinne, in later life, refuted this by stating that her father had warned Theodore not to marry Edith because of Charles Carow's alcoholism. Perhaps they fought because both Theodore and Edith had fiery tempers. Edith never satisfactorily explained the incident. For his part, Theodore returned to Harvard for his junior year and fell in love with a beautiful, athletic Bostonian, Alice Hathaway Lee. Drawn to her vigor and ebullience, he secretly proposed to her in 1879, but she hesitated.

In July 1879 the Carows moved once more, to East Thirty-sixth Street. Edith missed the Roosevelt family's near-constant company. She graduated from Miss Comstock's school and, customarily, consoled herself with Victorian novels. Edith received a book as a birthday present from Theodore, and the two lunched together on December 26. Not long after, Alice Lee accepted Roosevelt's proposal. Theodore Roosevelt told his family and notified Edith before the formal announcement was issued. Edith was devastated, shocked, and hurt. She confessed none of her pain to Theodore and none of it to her diary.

By October 13, 1880, Edith had recovered sufficiently to host a dinner party for Theodore and his bride-to-be, and two weeks later, she attended the exclusive Brookline wedding. It would not be the last she would see of the new Mrs. Roosevelt. Their social circle was identical, and they attended the same parties and balls. Edith's strain in this situation was eased slightly when Theodore won election to the New York State Assembly in 1881. The Roosevelts moved to Albany, and, although Edith longed for Theodore's intellectual company, it is unlikely she missed Alice.

The New York social season regulated Edith's life. She danced at balls, enjoyed the opera and the theater, frequented museums, and made social calls. Except to see her relatives, and unlike many of her friends, Edith did not travel. Instead, she cared for her ailing father and her increasingly invalid mother. On March 17, 1883, Charles Carow died of illnesses brought on by excessive drinking. The family's financial future was uncertain, as Carow's gambling and lavish spending had depleted his savings. While not bankrupt, the family found itself impoverished by New York standards.

Meanwhile, Edith could not help but be affected by the Roosevelt family's fortunes. Theodore Roosevelt excelled as an assemblyman—a job he relished. Corinne married in 1882, and Alice became pregnant in 1883. She gave birth to a healthy daughter on February 12, 1884, but was gravely ill with Bright's disease, diagnosed too late. On February 14, Alice Lee Roosevelt died. The morning of the day of her death, Theodore Roosevelt's mother also died, of typhoid. Roosevelt wrote in his *Memorial* that the light had gone from his life forever. Barely cognizant of his infant daughter, Alice, Theodore turned her care over to his eldest sister, Anna Roosevelt (called Bamie or Bye), and buried himself in his work. Edith's feelings can only be conjectured. She attended the double funeral, but Theodore was inconsolable. In fact, as if to put as much space as possible between his sorrow and himself, Roosevelt went west, to his ranch in the Dakota territory.

In September 1885, politics brought Theodore back to New York. It had been a year and a half since Edith and Theodore had seen one another, having studiously avoided one another on his few trips home. In an era when the upper classes married only once, he placed a premium on constancy. She, presumably, did not want to distress him by her physical reminder of their youthful romance. Sometime after his arrival he visited his daughter at Bye's house and bumped—unexpectedly—into Edith. They met regularly in private, and then ultimately to attend New York social events together. On November 17, 1885, Theodore asked Edith to marry him. She immediately said yes. They kept their engagement a secret even from their families because it had been less than twenty-four months since Alice's death.

While Edith and Theodore discussed their future plans, Gertrude and Emily Carow had decided to move to Europe. They reasoned that they could live there in a more genteel manner, despite their poverty. Edith was expected to accompany her mother and her sister. As their engagement remained a secret, Theodore and Edith agreed that she should go abroad to help Gertrude and Emily establish their residence. When that chore was accomplished, more time would have passed, and Roosevelt would have completed his book on Thomas Hart Benton and put his business affairs in the West in order.

During the difficult eight-month separation, Edith wrote to her fiancé regularly, telling him of her reading, sharing her introspections, and alerting him to the preparations she was making for their wedding. She learned from his letters that he had accepted the long-shot Republican nomination for mayor of New York City. During the autumn, Roosevelt clumsily informed his sisters of his engagement. In the face of their surprise, he wrote to his sister Bye on September 20, 1886. He told her that she could keep the twenty-month-old Alice and that he would pay for her expenses.

Just after his anticipated electoral loss, Theodore and Bye sailed for England and the wedding.

Edith Kermit Carow and Theodore Roosevelt were married at a private ceremony in St. George's Church in London on December 2, 1886. A shipboard friend, Cecil Spring-Rice, was best man. They traveled through Europe for their honeymoon, exploring England, France, and Italy. The newlyweds visited Gertrude and Emily Carow, who had settled in Florence. When they meandered back to London in the early spring, they happily entered into the city's social scene.

On March 27, 1887, Mrs. and Mr. Roosevelt arrived back in New York. Their first order of duty was to see Theodore's daughter, Alice, at Bye's home. At the same time, they reacquainted themselves with their friends in New York, especially Roosevelt's Republican associates, including Henry Cabot Lodge. Two weeks later the Roosevelts went to visit the Tyler relatives in Philadelphia, and then Roosevelt went out West to ascertain the damage done by the terrible blizzard of 1886–1887 to his livestock holdings in the Dakotas. The monetary losses were extremely high, and the couple began their married life with approximately $20,000 less than they had anticipated.

Yet another challenge confronted the newlyweds. Alice, then two years old, was devoted to her Auntie Bye, whom she later called "the single most important influence on my childhood." Edith Roosevelt made the decision to rear Alice as her own child and to remove her from her secure and lively home with Bye. She also insisted that Alice call her "mother." Mrs. Roosevelt's Victorian sensibilities placed the family at the center of her world, and she considered it her Christian duty to raise her husband's child. This decision provoked some unease between Edith and Bye. It would also prove to be a difficult choice for Alice, who maintained in later life that she always felt an outsider in the Roosevelt family.

Alice was referred to as "Sister" because she soon had company in the nursery. On September 13, 1887, Mrs. Roosevelt gave birth to a son, Theodore, Jr., known as Ted. Edith Roosevelt suffered from postpartum depression. She did not send for Bye until October. Instead, to help manage the children, she summoned the woman who had been her own nursemaid, Mary (Mame) Ledworth. Mame became a fixture, nursing all of the younger children until Roosevelt assumed the presidency in 1901.

The family moved into a large, rambling house at Oyster Bay, Long Island, originally built, and called Leesholm, for Alice Lee. Roosevelt renamed it Sagamore Hill. It became the site of an annual summer retreat from the glare of public life—a sustaining oasis amid the increasingly hectic existence of the Roosevelt family. Edith Roosevelt loved Sagamore Hill, and all of the children had fond memories of the family homestead. There were Roosevelt cousins in the vicinity, and a village not far away with a church and a school that the boys attended. The summers were filled with swimming, picnicking, horseback riding, yacht races, hikes, tennis tournaments, parties, and polo matches. The Roosevelts also kept a home in New York City, where they lived during the winter, maintaining their social and political contacts.

In August 1888, Mrs. Roosevelt suffered a miscarriage and was bedridden for almost two weeks. When she arose, Theodore left for a monthlong Western hunting trip. He checked in on his wife but then left immediately on a campaign trip to gather votes for presidential candidate Benjamin Harrison. Edith Roosevelt by then felt well enough to accompany him, and she learned a great deal about the public side of politicking. Roosevelt liked writing—his naval history of the War of 1812 was famous, and he had recently completed a biography of Gouverneur Morris and the first volume of *The Winning of the West*—but he loved politics. While Mrs. Roosevelt avoided the public eye, Mr. Roosevelt sought it. After Harrison won the presidency, he rewarded the jubilant Roosevelt with the post of civil service commissioner. This job entailed the family's living in Washington in the winter, rather than New York. While Edith Roosevelt supported her husband's decision to accept the position, she lamented that her third pregnancy would detain her at Sagamore Hill.

Roosevelt plunged with customary zest into his new job, returning to Sagamore Hill infrequently. He left for the Dakotas again in August. Edith Roosevelt's letters of the time demonstrate her devotion to her husband and her fears about motherhood. She delivered a son prematurely. This time, Bye was at her side, but Theodore had returned to Washington, D.C. Kermit Roosevelt was born on October 10, 1889. Nearly three months later, Edith felt strong enough to venture to Washington to establish their household there. On New Year's Day, 1890, the commissioner and his wife attended the Harrisons' White House reception. It was the first of many official and semiofficial gatherings the two would experience in their lives together. Mrs. Roosevelt enjoyed herself most when the guest list included an author or some other intellectual luminary like Henry Adams. Edith Roosevelt quickly became a favorite of the acerbic Adams, and she spent many happy hours at his house in the company of others who shared her passion for literature and art. As the wife of a midlevel government appointee, Mrs. Roosevelt hosted suppers and tea parties. No matter who the guests were, Theodore Roosevelt always occupied center stage.

When summer came, Edith Roosevelt, as usual, gathered the children and released them to the joys of Sagamore Hill. Roosevelt joined the family in August, just before his western trip. That year he took his wife, his sisters Corinne and Bye, plus Corinne's husband, Douglas Robinson, and Bye's friend Bob Ferguson, as well as a sixteen-year-old friend of the family. Edith Roosevelt fell in love with the rough, wild scenery of the Badlands and Yellowstone. Her health, always precarious, improved with the trek across country. That winter she became pregnant again, and, on August 13, 1891, after a difficult labor, her first daughter, Ethel Roosevelt, was born. On April 9, 1894, Edith gave birth to Archibald Bulloch Roosevelt, her third son.

In late summer 1894, Republican reformers in New York City asked Roosevelt to run for mayor. He solicited his wife's opinion. Edith Roosevelt much preferred Washington and their relatively stable life there to New York and a job at the whim of the voters. Even though Roosevelt wanted to accept the nomination, he bowed to his wife's wishes and declined. It was only later that Mrs. Roosevelt understood the true extent of Theodore's wish for the mayoralty. He confided his full desire to his sister Bye. A remorseful Edith Roosevelt wrote to her on September 28, "[I]f I knew what I do now I should have thrown all my influence . . . and helped instead of hindering him. You say that I dislike to give my opinion. This is a lesson that will last my life, never to give it for it is utterly worthless when given."

Perhaps Mrs. Roosevelt's stand against the mayoralty was strongly influenced by her domestic situation. The strenuous biannual work of moving the large family back and forth to Sagamore Hill was accomplished by Edith Roosevelt alone. Her husband was rarely by her side to help with the day-to-day care of the five children. Although the nurse, Mame, offered some assistance, the burden of tending to the usual round of childhood illnesses, excesses, and enthusiasms fell to Mrs. Roosevelt. She complained of migraine headaches and eventually had to take a break from the family after Christmas 1894. She spent two weeks at the estate of her sister-in-law, Corinne Roosevelt Robinson, in New Jersey. That spring, the Roosevelts' circumstances changed dramatically. Roosevelt became New York City police commissioner. The salary was nearly double the starting salary of the civil service commissioner, but it meant that Edith Roosevelt would have to leave the secure and absorbing circle of friends in the nation's capital that she had painstakingly constructed during their six-year residence.

In April 1895, as the Roosevelts moved to their new home at 689 Madison Avenue, Gertrude Carow died. Edith Roosevelt was saddened, but not surprised, as her mother had complained for years of various ailments. Emily came to stay with the family for six months beginning in June. The sisters mourned their mother together, and Emily temporarily provided another pair of hands to help with the move and the children.

Edith Roosevelt reentered New York's familiar social world, attending the opera, the theater, and art museums. She enrolled both Alice and Ted in Mr. Dodsworth's dancing school and chaperoned them herself. Roosevelt was a very successful police commissioner, but in the process, he made a number of enemies because of his decision to enforce the hated law that forbade alcohol sales on Sunday. Roosevelt became a popular speaker on behalf of the Republican Party and shortly set his sights on another governmental post under the new president, William McKinley.

Roosevelt was rewarded for his work in behalf of the party in April 1897, when President McKinley nominated him as assistant secretary of the navy. Although she was glad to be returning to Washington, Edith Roosevelt had to make the trek while pregnant. In August, she chose a house on N Street to rent before relaxing at Sagamore Hill for the rest of the summer. Roosevelt remained in the capital, and the family rejoined him in October. On November 9, 1897, Edith gave birth to Quentin Roosevelt. Her recovery was slower after this pregnancy, and during the Christmas holidays, she fell ill with what was eventually diagnosed as an internal abscess. Not until early spring did she undergo the operation that initiated her recuperation, and, between January and May, her life was punctuated by a series of domestic and national crises.

Edith Roosevelt's sickness was so severe that the younger children were sent to stay with friends while Alice and Ted sojourned with their Auntie Bye in New York. Alice, just turned fourteen, was enrolled for the first time in school, but that did not stop her from "running the streets uncontrolled with every boy in town," as Edith Roosevelt put it in a letter to her sister on February

15, 1898. Alice had grown to be a stubborn and lively young woman who regularly challenged her parents' authority. In New York, Alice blossomed under Bye's care. Ted, who suffered from nervous headaches, also benefited from the change in scenery. Away from home and under the ministrations of a New York City physician, he began to mend. The doctor's diagnosis was that Roosevelt had exerted too much physical and mental pressure on Ted, expecting from his eldest son the sort of perfection that he wanted from himself.

The day after Alice was sent to Bye's, the U.S.S. Maine exploded in Cuba's Havana harbor. The cry for war against Spain rose from every quarter of the nation, but nowhere was it louder than in the Roosevelt household. Theodore Roosevelt blamed the explosion and consequent loss of American lives on the Spanish; he tried to think of a way he could join the fighting that seemed sure to erupt. Congress declared war against Spain on April 25. Despite his wife's condition, Roosevelt offered his complete support. He later recalled to his military aide, Archibald Butt, that he "would have turned from [his] wife's deathbed to have answered that call." On May 6, 1898, Roosevelt resigned his position as assistant secretary of the navy and organized the First Volunteer Cavalry Regiment—later known as the Rough Riders. By that time, Mrs. Roosevelt was well enough to see him off. The younger children returned home to rally around their soldier-father and wave him good-bye. He stopped by his sister's home in New York to bid Alice and Ted farewell.

When their training in Texas was complete, the Rough Riders shipped off to Florida in preparation for Cuba. Lieutenant Colonel and Mrs. Roosevelt made arrangements to meet one last time before he went to war. On June 1, 1898, Edith Roosevelt left for Tampa. She rendezvoused with her husband and they spent almost a week together. During her stay, Mrs. Roosevelt met the unusual men who made up the Rough Riders—cowboys and Native Americans from Roosevelt's days in Dakota, old schoolmates from Harvard, New York City policemen—and toured the campsites. Putting aside her worries, she stoically said good-bye to her husband again and returned home to the children.

She spent the next month in uncertain health, fearful of her husband's destiny. Colonel Roosevelt was a favorite of the press, and she could at least follow his exploits through the newspapers. The letters that she did receive from him were not always reassuring. He wrote of battles, terrible living conditions, vultures wheeling over the dead, and the valor of his Rough Riders. At home, though, his heroism was paving the way for greater political success. When she came across a letter to the editor of the *New York Sun* advocating Roosevelt as governor, Edith sent it to him in Cuba.

The couple were reunited secretly in mid-August when the Rough Riders were shipped home to Montauk, Long Island. Edith defied a quarantine to meet Theodore. She volunteered as a hospital assistant and worked for four long, hard days treating the men who had been wounded in battle or stricken with yellow fever. Finally, Roosevelt was given permission to leave the camp, and he escorted his wife back to Oyster Bay, where crowds of people met them. Roosevelt's popularity soared as word of his leadership in the Battle of Kettle Hill and of his solicitous treatment of his men circulated. More and more reporters asked about his political plans. Mrs. Roosevelt was surprised one day to return from a swim to find photographers lying in wait. It foreshadowed the battle she would fight with newsmen in the White House. An intensely private woman, she loathed the incandescent gaze of the press.

True to the intimations of prominent Republican Party leaders, Theodore Roosevelt was nominated for governor of New York in early October 1898. This marked the beginning of Mrs. Roosevelt's own public life and the eventual end of her valued privacy. She attended the political meeting in Carnegie Hall at which Roosevelt commenced his gubernatorial campaign. She did not accompany him on the campaign trail, though—partly out of her desire to avoid publicity, and partly because she had the children to nurture. Instead, she and Alice assisted Roosevelt's secretary with his mail. Mrs. Roosevelt soon assumed the lion's share of the duties, sorting and answering the vast quantities of fan mail for the colonel. On November 8, 1898, the family's work paid off: Theodore Roosevelt won the governorship of New York.

Inauguration Day was January 2, 1899. It was a cold but exciting morning. People came from all over to watch the inaugural parade, to see the governor sworn in, and to shake his hand at the governor's mansion. Edith Roosevelt and Alice sat together to watch Theodore Roosevelt take the public oath of office and to hear his inaugural speech. That afternoon, Edith Roosevelt stood next to the governor in the receiving line. Six thousand people paid their respects. While Governor Roosevelt shook hands, his wife began a tradition she would maintain throughout her years in the public eye: she held a bunch of flowers with both hands and smiled warmly as the citizens filed by.

The Roosevelt family settled happily into the enormous governor's mansion. Mrs. Roosevelt hired a governess to oversee Alice and Ethel, sent Ted and Kermit to the Albany Military Academy, and retained Mame for the younger boys. Her first task was to modernize and make comfortable the rambling old Victorian house. She created a bedroom out of a cloakroom, turned the billiard room into a gymnasium for Theodore and the children, rearranged the furniture and the paintings, and began to entertain the denizens of Albany. In this last endeavor, she had the assistance of the governor's aide, Colonel Treadwell. He attended to the food, music, and seating protocol, perhaps setting the precedent for Mrs. Roosevelt's delegating those same responsibilities when she became mistress of the White House. As the governor's wife, she traveled around the state with her husband, and they enjoyed more time together than at previous junctures in his career. In her spare time she joined a local women's club, the Friday Morning Club, whose members read and discussed papers on topics of interest. She spent time with an old childhood friend, Fanny Smith Parsons, a noted botanist and author who shared Mrs. Roosevelt's enthusiasm for wildflowers. In March 1900, Edith Roosevelt went with her sister Emily on a tour of Cuba, where they were official guests of Governor General Leonard Wood. In response to the query by their old friend, diplomat Sir Cecil Spring-Rice, Edith Roosevelt responded later that month: "We like being Governor very much, thank you."

When Roosevelt's name began to appear in connection with the vice presidency early in 1900, Mrs. Roosevelt hoped that he would not be nominated. She enjoyed life in Albany. When she longed for intellectual company, she invited old friends to Sagamore Hill, where they still spent their summers, or she took the train to New York City. Always uppermost in her mind was the state of the family's finances. Edith Roosevelt had been the family accountant for years. Not until the Spanish-American War concluded did she cease worrying about how to make ends meet with her large brood. After the war, Roosevelt commanded high fees for his articles and speeches on that subject, and because the governor's mansion was provided to them, they did not have to pay rent on a house. The position of the vice president would entail decreasing his salary by $2,000 (the governor's salary was $10,000) and the expense of renting a house. And because public figures paid for most entertaining out of their own pockets, costs would be higher in Washington than they were in Albany.

Republican leaders who disliked the governor's reform legislation wanted Roosevelt in the relatively powerless position of vice president. Roosevelt himself was reluctant to be relegated to the vice presidency. In June, the Roosevelts attended the Republican Convention so that Roosevelt, a delegate, could place President McKinley's name in nomination. Mrs. Roosevelt sat attentively throughout. She watched with mixed emotions as the delegates overwhelmingly selected her husband as the vice presidential choice the following day. She

confided to her stepdaughter that month that she was "feeling very uneasy about the Vice Presidency but trust it may all come right in the end."

Their last days in Albany were hectic. Roosevelt spent much of his time on the campaign trail. As usual, the household and child-rearing duties fell to his wife. She also continued the secretarial chores for his campaign, sorting through and helping to answer his mail. In November 1900, William McKinley was elected for a second term, with Theodore Roosevelt as his vice president. Mrs. Roosevelt began to keep a diary as she entered this most public phase of her life. She loosened her ties to New York with the New Year's Day reception at the governor's mansion. To unwind after the strain of the campaign, Roosevelt went on a hunting trip, leaving his wife to prepare for the family's move to Washington and their two-day visit for the inauguration.

The Roosevelt family, with the exception of Quentin, saw Roosevelt take the oath of office in the Senate chamber. The three-year-old joined them for lunch at the White House with the McKinleys and other dignitaries. Mrs. Roosevelt rented a room above a manicure shop on Pennsylvania Avenue so that she and the children could watch the inaugural parade. The inaugural ball capped off the whirlwind trip, and Edith Roosevelt and the children departed the next morning for New York. Roosevelt later joined his family at Sagamore Hill for an eventful summer. In late August, Edith Roosevelt took her children on a vacation in the Adirondack Mountains. Roosevelt was on a speaking tour, and Alice soon separated from the family to join friends of her own also on holiday at a nearby resort. Roosevelt was expected to meet up with the family when his tour ended, but instead he telephoned his wife to inform her that President McKinley had been shot and was teetering on the brink of death. Roosevelt was standing by the president's sickbed. Three days later McKinley's condition improved, and Roosevelt left to join his family—only to be interrupted by an urgent message that the president had relapsed. Roosevelt rushed to Buffalo, New York, on September 13, 1901. The next morning he sent his wife a telegram: "President McKinley died at 2:15 this morning." Suddenly Edith Roosevelt was the First Lady and her husband was the youngest man ever to become president.

The circumstances of Roosevelt's coming to office were sad. As the country mourned the loss of the popular William McKinley, Edith Roosevelt boarded a train unaccompanied to attend the state funeral. Her husband joined her after escorting the body of the slain president to the White House. Roosevelt stayed for the next week and a half at his sister's house, giving Mrs. McKinley time to pack her belongings. Edith Roosevelt returned to Sagamore Hill to gather the children. On September 23, 1901, Theodore Roosevelt moved into the White House. Mrs. Roosevelt arrived with Ethel, Quentin, and Archibald on September 25. Alice lingered with Auntie Bye, and the older boys were still in school.

With the country in mourning, the new First Lady could do no official entertaining. She turned her attention, instead, to the pressing problem of where to put her family of eight in the too-small White House. Ted, age fourteen, was usually away at Groton School, but everyone else needed a room. The Executive Mansion's living quarters were then on the second floor with the offices. Edith Roosevelt loathed this configuration, and as Roosevelt wrote in a letter to a friend, "Edie says it's like living over the store." She gave herself a "library"— really an office—next to the president's private office. It had an adjoining door so that they could talk throughout the workday. From this vantage point the First Lady read through magazines and newspapers, clipped out articles that she thought would interest her husband, and deposited them on his desk. Next to her library was a room shared by Quentin and Archie, and theirs was adjacent to the Roosevelts' bedroom. Alice's large room was across the hallway; Ethel's, next to hers in a small corner room. Kermit's room, the guest room, and a tiny room for the two maids completed the living

quarter assignments. As soon as she had opened the windows, rearranged the furniture, and placed flowers throughout the house, the First Lady fell into an exhausted, two-day sleep.

The children explored their new domain. Alice eventually rejoined the family at the end of the month and, even though she was nearly eighteen years old, took part in discovering the delights of the Executive Mansion. Chief among their pleasures was an exhilarating slide down the stairs on large tin trays borrowed from the pantry. They rode bicycles and tottered on thin stilts in the upstairs hallway. The basement made a perfect roller skating rink. Even Theodore joined in the ongoing games of hide-and-seek. The children liked to secret themselves in the center of the upholstered circular seats in the East Room and pop out to scare unsuspecting visitors. Alice's blue macaw lived in the conservatory, and the other pets that composed the Roosevelt menagerie also found their way to Washington. Aside from their leisure activity, Kermit and Archie were enrolled in Washington public schools, while Ethel attended the local Cathedral School. Alice was too old for school, and Quentin too young.

Mrs. Roosevelt may have been thrust into the role of First Lady unexpectedly, but that did not stop her from effecting immediate and long-lasting changes in the position. Early on she wrote to Alice that the McKinley "household was disorganized to the last degree." She eliminated the office of housekeeper, performing that supervisory function herself. She counted upon the chief usher to monitor the staff, and he reported directly to her. In another break with the previous administration, Edith Roosevelt hired caterers to fix and serve the meals. Even though the expense was high and paid for out of the president's salary, the First Lady determined quickly that she did not want to be bothered endlessly with details. She had counted upon Colonel Treadwell for similar service in Albany, and here the house was smaller and her public position more time-consuming. Mrs. Roosevelt also initiated weekly musicales, preceded by dinner for twenty, with both famous and unknown performers serenading the hundreds whom the First Lady favored with invitations.

Every Tuesday, Mrs. Roosevelt hosted the wives of the cabinet officers in her upstairs library. Gathering these influential women together, she maintained a grasp of Washington social life and laid down certain rules. According to future White House military aide Archibald Butt, the First Lady let it be known that she would not invite men or women who were involved in adulterous relationships or whose morals were lax in other ways, no matter what their political or social prominence. Mrs. Roosevelt also used the meetings of the cabinet wives to release decorating and culinary information about upcoming White House events, to set a standard for other enterprising hostesses. That sort of news leak would help her to guarantee that White House functions were not eclipsed.

Edith Roosevelt made a major institutional change when she hired a social secretary. Isabelle Hagner was the first social secretary to serve a First Lady, but only one of several unmarried women of good background who worked in that demanding position for leading Washington families. Isabelle had worked previously for the family of McKinley's first secretary of war, Russell A. Alger, and had been a part-time secretary to Bye. Initially, Isabelle's job was to help organize Alice Roosevelt's January 1902 White House debut. It was the social event of the season, and the debutante herself could not be counted on to assist with the details. Soon, though, Mrs. Roosevelt came to depend upon the charming and sympathetic Miss Hagner to help her screen out morally suspect visitors and protect the family's privacy by speaking to the female society-page reporters. Isabelle released photographs of the Roosevelts at the First Lady's request—Edith Roosevelt's plan to thwart what she called the "camera fiends." Isabelle also served as a sounding board when Mrs. Roosevelt debated which worthy charities might best use her quiet patronage. She often sat as an "extra woman"

at dinner parties, where her warmth and impeccable manners were appreciated. According to a letter Archibald Butt sent to his mother on June 30, 1908, he believed that "the fact that everything has gone as smoothly as it has is due more to her than every one else put together about the Executive Mansion." Butt characterized Isabelle's job as "head aide, general manager, and superintendent."

It was even more than that, however. Isabelle Hagner kept up with the wayward jewels, pets, friends, shoes, and even gentlemen callers of the Roosevelt family. Hagner's private papers document her closeness to all the Roosevelts. In 1902, Ethel wrote, "Dear Miss Hagner—will you please send me out ten cents as soon as you can with the scrap basket and a large piece of chocolate with it." Upon the arrival of the Archbishop of Canterbury in September 1904, Edith Roosevelt implored her secretary: "We are short two women on the dinner of the 24th so please look about and see if any, good church women preferred, are in town and telegraph me." Alice wrote to Isabelle in 1905 in a characteristic fluster because she had lost some charms that did not belong to her: "Could you ask some of the men about the house to look for them or ask if they have seen them. Oh but please don't tell a word of this to another soul." On March 19, 1909, Edith Roosevelt wrote to Isabelle's father of "all that Belle has been to me these past eight winters in the White House. In joy and in sorrow she has stood beside me with the love and loyalty of a very dear daughter." Isabelle Hagner remained a lifelong friend to all the members of the family. She continued to assist the Roosevelts even while she officially served the family of President Woodrow Wilson. Her myriad and evolving duties set a precedent for all other First Ladies' social secretaries.

Isabelle Hagner did not become a permanent member of the White House staff until after the First Lady's renovation of the executive mansion in 1902. This much-needed improvement was one of Edith Roosevelt's most important legacies. The Roosevelts' plan was to expand and modernize the White House, separate the living quarters from the offices, and restore the entire building to its original eighteenth-century look—both inside and out. Edith Roosevelt engaged the architectural firm of McKim, Mead and White to draw up blueprints. Their design so impressed Congress that it appropriated the necessary funds, over half a million dollars. While the first family moved out of the mansion in June 1902, the architects began work. The First Lady, understanding that she oversaw a national treasure, involved herself intimately in every decision. The job was not without its frustrations. "Mr. McKim is coming here on Monday," Mrs. Roosevelt wrote to Isabelle Hagner in July, "and we shall have a heart-to-heart talk. I do get very angry with him." She found it particularly difficult to convince him of the historicity of the mansion. She saw the White House as a national treasure sheltering irreplaceable reminders of American history. Edith Roosevelt wanted the mansion to be a patriotic showcase as well as a comfortable and modern home and work space for the president and his family.

Her adamant stance paid off. The new West Wing housed offices exclusively. The East Wing provided guest rooms and the family's living space. The plumbing, lighting, and heating systems were upgraded. The landscaping was redone, the greenhouse torn down, and a tennis court built. The State Dining Room was enlarged and the Cabinet Room was suitably dignified. The Green Room, the Blue Room, and the East Room were all stripped of the ornamentation that Alice Roosevelt in her autobiography characterized as "late General Grant and early Pullman." The furniture was mostly antique, much of it with symbolic value. Edith Roosevelt, in consultation with the architects and her family, chose the wall coverings, the carpet colors, the paintings. The public response to her changes was overwhelmingly positive.

The renovation gave birth to two more of Edith Roosevelt's legacies: the White House China Collection and the First Ladies' Portrait Gallery. In order to serve everyone who could now fit into the remodeled State Dining Room, Mrs. Roosevelt needed to order a new set of china. Her set, consisting of 120 place settings, was traditional, elegant Wedgwood featuring the Great Seal of the United States. It produced many compliments, even from such stern judges as Helen Herron Taft, wife of William Howard Taft, then secretary of war. Reserving the Wedgwood for formal use, Mrs. Roosevelt began searching for other sets of presidential china. A Washington journalist, Abby Gunn Baker, assisted the First Lady as she displayed the collection from twenty-five administrations in cabinets along the ground floor hallway. The White House China Collection is still on display and still being augmented.

Another lasting gift to the nation from Edith Roosevelt began as the redecorating commenced in the renovated White House. In August, she asked McKim to gather together all of the portraits of former First Ladies and hang them as a group along the ground floor corridor where the china was displayed. Her act of resurrecting the scattered portraits from the ignominy of storage was widely praised. The hallway served as a channel for guests as they queued to be received by the president and the First Lady. The interesting china and the fascinating portraits eased the wait.

While receiving universal praise for her conduct as First Lady, Edith Roosevelt found some of the concomitant duties of the role irksome. She wrote to Alice of the annual White House Easter egg rolling festival: "There is a howling rabble rolling eggs or rather romping outside in our garden. I suppose it will look like a pigpen tomorrow." She occasionally asked her more famous, celebrity stepdaughter to stand in the receiving line with her, or in her stead. It was always the press that caused the most annoyance. She did not see why newspapers needed news or photographs of the First Family and wearied of the game they all had to play to elude the cameras. Mrs. Roosevelt tired of journalists' incessant requests for descriptions of her gowns, and she and Alice rapidly grew expert in confusing reporters by describing the same dress in many different ways.

What was important to Edith Roosevelt was her family and her privacy. She continued to read to the children, as she had done all their lives. She provided Sunday school instruction for the younger children and a moral rudder for all. Edith Roosevelt embraced motherhood with a zeal born of her Victorian-era upbringing. Even after Archie's birth, she longed for more children. While First Lady, she suffered two miscarriages before deciding that her childbearing years were over. She was a loving, if firm, mother. She had to be the disciplinarian because her husband was, in her words, "her fifth boy." She enjoyed the respect and love of all of her children and took enormous pride in their accomplishments. While her relationship with her stepdaughter was complex, it was not without a great deal of affection on both sides.

Edith Roosevelt's relationship with her husband also matured. Contemporary commentators believed that Mrs. Roosevelt exerted a real but subtle influence over the president. In the White House, Mrs. Roosevelt spent the hour from 8 to 9 A.M. alone with the president, and she took frequent horseback rides with him around the countryside. They walked daily in the White House gardens. She spoke her mind freely with him and he admitted that, whenever he failed to follow his wife's advice, he paid for it. Her judgment of men was often better than his, and she closely watched the issues that interested her. The 1902 congressional off-year elections worried the First Lady. In a letter preserved in the Churchill College Archives, she wrote to Spring-Rice on October 12: "Everyone foresees a great Republican defeat next month, but the thing one can't bear to think of is the suffering which this means for the poor in the great cities." Edith Roosevelt maintained an excellent association with the president's assistant, William Loeb and, with his help, could often sway Roosevelt to her viewpoint. According to biographer Sylvia Jukes Morris, Isabelle Hagner asserted in a May 24, 1933, *Boston Transcript* article that the

legislation creating the National Gallery was passed because of the First Lady's influence. One of the most enduring roles Mrs. Roosevelt played as First Lady was that of diplomat. When the Russo-Japanese War began in 1905, President Roosevelt thought it imprudent to write directly to his most trusted source on Russia's activities, because that source—his former best man, Sir Cecil Spring-Rice—was not the official British ambassador. Roosevelt supported a year-long correspondence in which the Englishman wrote detailed reports to the First Lady, who forwarded them to him. Mrs. Roosevelt also communicated with Whitelaw Reid, the U.S. ambassador to England. His epistles were filled with intelligence from Europe meant for the president. Morris's biography quotes novelist Owen Wister's summation of Edith Roosevelt: "She was the perfection of 'invisible government.'"

Life in the White House was punctuated by splendid dances, receptions for visiting royalty, and glorious musicales, but by and large the social seasons were regulated by official functions. The annual New Year's reception of 1903 introduced the curious public to the renovated White House. Cabinet dinners followed in regimental fashion. The First Lady thrived in her roles as hostess and mother. The president successfully encouraged Congress to pass most of his reform legislation. The Roosevelts were flourishing. By 1903 they all looked confidently to the upcoming election, eager for four years more as America's official family. The Republican Party nominated Roosevelt without controversy.

Edith Roosevelt and the children summered at Sagamore Hill while the president remained in Washington. On election night, Edith and Theodore Roosevelt hosted a gathering of friends and family who celebrated with them as the returns proved the president's landslide victory. The only sour note was the statement Roosevelt made that night to the press. In the course of his remarks, Roosevelt maintained that he would not be a candidate for president in the future, since he had served three and a half years of McKinley's term. Roosevelt wanted to honor the tradition established by George Washington to serve only two terms. Mrs. Roosevelt suspected that this would turn her husband into a lame duck with Congress.

The inauguration in March 1905 proceeded smoothly, and the First Lady's spirits were high. Soon she would assume the diplomat's role as war erupted between Russia and Japan. Her other preoccupations included a rough vacation cabin she bought in the middle of Albemarle County, Virginia, and the burgeoning relationship between Alice and her eventual husband, Nicholas Longworth. Edith Roosevelt purchased the cabin, "Pine Knot," from a Carow relative for $195, which included five acres of surrounding land. She thought the rustic cabin essential for her husband's mental and physical health. Pine Knot superseded Sagamore Hill as the couple's idyllic haven away from the throng of the press. To reach it, they had to ford a stream and walk through woods and meadows. There was no road to the front door. The First Lady, ever mindful of her husband's welfare, arranged for two Secret Service men to watch over their slumber at night—unbeknownst to the president.

In July 1905, the president assigned his friend, Secretary of War William Howard Taft, to lead a congressional junket to the Philippines and the Far East. Alice Roosevelt accompanied the congressmen and their wives as a goodwill ambassador to the recently demilitarized Philippine Islands and, particularly, to Japan. Japan and Russia had agreed in late June that they would allow President Roosevelt to mediate peace talks. Also along on the junket was Ohio Representative Nicholas Longworth. A shipboard romance ensued between the twenty-one-year-old Alice and her thirty-six-year-old suitor. A full month after Alice returned from her victorious mission, she informed her stepmother. Edith Roosevelt gave her blessing to the match, even though she had doubts about Longworth's suitability as a husband because of a perceived drinking problem. Stepmother and step-daughter together planned the wedding, which turned into a spectacular social event. Seven hundred invitations were issued, but many thousands more watched from outside as "Princess Alice" married Nicholas Longworth in a simple White House ceremony on February 17, 1906. Edith Roosevelt, Isabelle Hagner, Ethel Roosevelt, and several family friends were exhausted by the preparations, the wedding day, and the writing of the thank-you notes—of which the bride did very little.

Mrs. Roosevelt celebrated more good news: Theodore Roosevelt negotiated a successful end to the Russo-Japanese War. He basked in congratulations from around the world. The First Lady shared his triumph and its culmination: the awarding of the Nobel Peace Prize in December 1906. When the wedding and the war were over, the president and First Lady vowed to take a long vacation. Roosevelt was forty-eight years old, suffering from arteriosclerosis, obesity, a bad leg, and a recently blinded left eye. Ted, Jr., was the cause of further concern when he was put on scholastic probation at Harvard. Independent eight-year-old Quentin was also misbehaving at school. On November 8, 1906, the day before Quentin's ninth birthday, Theodore and Edith Roosevelt left on an extended trip, but it was not exactly a holiday. They sailed for Panama to survey the building of one of Roosevelt's greatest accomplishments, the Panama Canal. While it did not leave either of them particularly rested, Mrs. Roosevelt thoroughly enjoyed the jaunt.

President Roosevelt, as popular leader of the Republican Party, could hand-pick his own successor for the office. As much as he now regretted his Election Day statement about never running again, he had to abide by it. His choice fell eventually on William Howard Taft. Taft was a corporate lawyer and a judge currently serving as secretary of war. Edith Roosevelt felt that Taft was too weak, too much of a yes-man, and would not prove to be the standard-bearer that her husband so fondly hoped. Helen Herron Taft, the secretary's assertive wife, wanted Taft to be president, even though her husband preferred a seat on the Supreme Court. The remaining year in Roosevelt's final term would be plagued, for Edith Roosevelt, by worries over her husband's faith in Taft, and his own postpresidential plans, as well as by Quentin's difficult time as a boarder at Episcopal High School, and by Mrs. Taft's inappropriate eagerness to set her own mark on the White House. A new assistant appeared in April, White House military aide Major Archibald Butt. The tactful, loyal aristocrat soothed the trials of Edith Roosevelt's final year in the White House.

On November 3, 1908, Taft easily won election to the presidency. At first, Edith Roosevelt celebrated the Republican victory. But she soon ran into the first pangs of leave-taking when Major Butt informed her that Mrs. Taft had asked him to remain in the service of the president and First Lady but would make sweeping changes in the rest of the White House staff. Dedicated as she was to the men who had served them so well, Mrs. Roosevelt asked if Butt could reduce the number of men Mrs. Taft would dismiss. Mrs. Taft refused to speak with Edith Roosevelt about her plans. Mrs. Taft also informed Major Butt that she would no longer hire caterers, but would have every meal prepared in the Executive Mansion.

When it came time to leave the White House, Edith Roosevelt sought only two token reminders from her seven and a half years as First Lady. She had been given a pair of Sèvres glass figures by the French in 1902 and had grown very fond of them. As she had the documents to prove that they were a present to her and not to the United States, taking these evoked no outcry. The other memento, however, brought on a hailstorm of criticism, through a series of misunderstandings. In 1901, the First Lady had purchased a small antique sofa to put in the White House. It brought back memories not only of pleasant White House days, but also of long afternoons spent prowling through Washington antique shops—a particular passion of the First Lady's. Edith Roosevelt wanted to have a copy of the sofa made to leave in the Executive Mansion;

however Theodore—without his wife's knowledge—wrote to the Speaker of the House, Joseph Cannon, asking for permission to remove the sofa. Somehow the gist of the letter was leaked to the press, who wrote of it as though the First Lady were attempting to steal White House furniture. She abandoned the attempt at moving the sofa because, during the public ordeal, all of the good associations had turned to bad.

When the time approached for the final leave-taking, and the Roosevelt family had to say good-bye to the White House, Edith Roosevelt was speechless. Major Butt chronicled the scene for his sister on February 21, 1909:

> She stood among all those weeping women Friday apparently as unmoved as if she were an iceberg, and yet I knew that her heart was being torn just the same as theirs, yet she retained her dignity and composure through all and never let down once; only later Belle Hagner told me that when she went to her room she had one good wholesome weep, and when I saw her later she was smiling through her tears.

Theodore Roosevelt invited the Tafts to share their final night in the White House. It was a dismal dinner party. One month later, on March 22, Edith was still missing the White House, as she wrote to Isabelle Hagner: "It is nice having [the family] all together at home, but we are not feeling very gay."

The remaining gaiety disappeared under a facade of bravery as, early the next morning, the family gathered to send Theodore and Kermit off on a year-long safari across Africa. The plans for this expedition had been carefully organized during the previous year. A similar scheme was concocted for Edith Roosevelt's return to private life. Less than two weeks after Theodore and Kermit left, Edith Roosevelt, along with Ethel, Archie, and Quentin, embarked upon a lengthy tour of Europe. They went first to Italy and France. In September, Archie and Quentin returned to school in the United States, and Edith Roosevelt and

Ethel set out to see Switzerland before landing in Italy at the home of Mrs. Roosevelt's sister Emily. In November, the women sailed home to find great unhappiness among reform-minded Republicans with President Taft, and a good deal of public longing for Roosevelt.

In March, the Roosevelts joyfully reunited in Khartoum. The prolonged absence had been torturous for both of them. Ethel and Kermit accompanied their parents as they visited local battlefields and desert sites, sometimes riding camels. The four travelers journeyed up the Nile, pausing to contemplate the Egyptian temples, and boarded a boat for Naples at the end of the month. Wherever Roosevelt went, he was hailed as a hero. Foreign governments accorded him the honors due to a sitting president. From Washington, President Taft asked Roosevelt to be the American envoy to British King Edward VII's funeral. Alice joined the family in London for the mourning ritual but also for a holiday spent among the brightest minds of England.

The Roosevelts landed in New York on June 18, 1910. A flotilla of ships met them in the harbor. President and Mrs. Taft sent Major Butt to present the Roosevelts with their letters of welcome. Reunited with the remaining members of the family—Ted and his fiancée, Eleanor Alexander; Quentin; Archie; and Nicholas Longworth—they were the guests of honor for a ticker-tape parade on Broadway. Thousands of well-wishers screamed their delight at seeing "Teddy" again. The delirium of the crowd was spurred in part by continued unhappiness with President Taft's administration and by the beginning of a split in the Republican Party. This would be reflected by the increasingly bitter relationship between Roosevelt and Taft.

On June 20, 1910, Ted and Eleanor were married. Ted began work soon after in California at the Hartford Carpet Company. Theodore Roosevelt took the position of editor at the *Outlook*, writing one article a month. He spent the rest of his time in consultation with men of national and political prominence. Roosevelt was uncertain of his next move, but politics drew him inexorably. In August he embarked on a speaking tour to muster support for local Republican candidates. In Kansas, however, he presented what appeared to be a presidential platform—a very reformist, progressive platform. The breach between Taft and Roosevelt widened. Roosevelt's oratory established him as the leader of the anti-Taft forces in the Republican Party.

He returned to Sagamore Hill, only to leave again on other speaking tours. In 1911, he would not join an attempt of Republican Progressives to nominate Wisconsin governor Robert La Follette. Instead, he continued taking his message to the people. Edith Roosevelt, who had just spent a year away from her husband, was not happy about the numerous speaking tours because of the long and disagreeable separations. So, in March, Edith joined her husband in New Mexico. The trip gave her a clear understanding of the hold Roosevelt had on Americans. She confided to Spring-Rice on April 5, 1911: "It seems as if in proportion with the hatred of Wall Street, is the love which is lavished upon him in the West. At each tiny station crowds of people assembled holding out their children, so that he might touch them." She still had no clear idea of his future, but, as the speaking tours turned into a campaign for the Republican Party nomination, Edith Roosevelt expressed ever stronger disapproval.

On February 24, 1912, she sailed for South America with Ethel. Two days later, Theodore Roosevelt announced that he was a candidate for the presidency. By mid-March, when they returned, Roosevelt was determined. "There is such a hard drive ahead that I can scarcely keep a stiff upper lip," Edith Roosevelt wrote to Isabelle Hagner on March 10. "I wish I could see you but Washington is the forbidden city for me."

In June, the Roosevelts went together to Chicago for the Republican Party convention. She perused his "Armageddon" speech and eliminated the most caustic paragraphs, which would have wounded others and himself. The speech, while improved, was to no avail, as the Taft forces controlled the convention. They nominated their man, and Edith consoled her husband. She knew him too well to think that this setback would defeat him. In August, they went to the Progressive Party convention, also in Chicago. With one voice, the Progressives nominated Roosevelt for the presidency in 1912.

Roosevelt began a furious campaign across the nation. Crowds gathered everywhere to hear him. An assassination attempt nearly killed the former president, but the bullet struck his steel glasses case and his thick, folded speech in his breast pocket. Edith beat down her own terror and stayed by his hospital bed, nursing him back to health. She was beside him throughout the remainder of the campaign, and truly mourned with him in November when he lost. Roosevelt turned finally from politics and took up the more sedentary pursuit of writing, which gave him more time with his family.

The Roosevelt children were grown up and scattered. Alice and her husband, Nicholas, were trying to maintain their marriage following Nicholas's loss of his House seat in the 1912 debacle. Ted left the carpet company and began work for a Wall Street firm. Kermit was in Brazil on a railroading venture. Ethel married a physician, Richard Derby, in April 1913. Quentin was excelling at Groton. The unhappiest person in the family was Theodore Roosevelt. To relieve the boredom, he decided to explore uncharted areas of Brazil. Edith Roosevelt sailed with him to Rio de Janeiro and traveled across the continent through Uruguay, Argentina, and Chile. Along the way they picked up Kermit, who would accompany his father on the expedition. In November, Edith turned around and sailed for home.

Charting the River of Doubt did not come without injury. Theodore Roosevelt, then fifty-five years old, hurt his leg, which abscessed. A fever followed. Edith Roosevelt read of her husband's expedition in *Scribner's*, but only when he finally returned in May 1914, did her incessant anxiety cease. That month, Roosevelt, accompanied by his elder daughter, Alice, sailed to Europe for the wedding of Kermit and Belle Willard. Edith did not go. Menopause, cou-

pled with several recent deaths in the family and Theodore's terrifying absence, made her reluctant to leave the quiet security of Sagamore Hill.

Roosevelt chafed under such a lifestyle. In 1914, he went campaigning for Progressive candidates. That losing battle was eclipsed by Roosevelt's attempts to enter World War I. Roosevelt wanted to raise a cavalry unit, as he had done in the Spanish-American War, but President Wilson turned him down. He urged Wilson to hasten American involvement in the European conflagration. Even Edith Roosevelt joined in the fray, marching alongside her daughter-in-law Eleanor Alexander Roosevelt with the Independent Patriotic Women of America. On April 6, 1917, the United States went to war. All four of Edith's sons enlisted.

The war years were sad and impatient ones for Theodore and Edith Roosevelt. While their sons distinguished themselves in battle, Ted and Archie were both wounded. In July 1918, Edith Roosevelt's worst nightmare came true. Quentin was shot down and killed behind enemy lines. While Roosevelt still shouted anti-Wilsonian sentiments before packed houses, something in him had died with Quentin. On January 6, 1919, Theodore Roosevelt passed away at Sagamore Hill.

Edith Roosevelt needed to flee from the associations at Oyster Bay. On February 5, 1919, she left for Europe to visit Quentin's grave and to mourn with her sister Emily. She returned home, but finding her grief still too intense, left again in December. This time, she ventured with Kermit to South America. In 1920, Edith Roosevelt urged Republican women to overcome their reluctance and vote. Her last twenty-eight years were spent traveling—to Spain, France, Germany, the Philippines, South Africa, Italy, South America (twice), Central America, Greece, and a trip around the world with Kermit—following the family's growth, entertaining visitors, and writing two books. With Kermit and his wife, Belle, as well as Richard Derby, Edith Roosevelt published Cleared for Strange Ports in

1927, an aphoristic travelogue. In 1928, she and Kermit edited *American Backlogs*, a primary-source history of the Tyler and Carow families. She published schoolgirl correspondence of her mother's but destroyed much of her own, particularly love letters from her husband.

In 1927, Edith Roosevelt, at sixty years of age and in worsening health, bought a large home in Brooklyn, Connecticut, called Mortlake Manor. Mortlake was an ancestral home on the Tyler side. In Brooklyn, she kept her own pace and occupations. She walked, rested, and sewed with the Needlework Guild. It was a home free of associations with Theodore and Quentin, and free also of energetic grandchildren. From that happy site she provided critical financial gifts to aging Rough Riders and others in need. The money came from the presidential widows' pension fund established by Andrew Carnegie.

The year 1932 was a galvanizing one for Mrs. Roosevelt. When the Democratic Party nominated Franklin Delano Roosevelt for the presidency, over 300 notes of congratulations came to Sagamore Hill. Disgusted and anxious to clarify the public's mistake, she decided to speak out in favor of the Republican candidate and current president, Herbert Hoover. She invited the Edith Kermit Roosevelt Republican Club members to lunch at Oyster Bay for a celebration of Hoover's birthday. Two days later, she flew to Washington, D.C., and stood beside President and Mrs. Hoover in a receiving line. On October 31, 1932, she spoke at Madison Square Garden, reminding listeners of Republican Party principles. Despite her efforts, in November Franklin D. Roosevelt swept into office. She wrote to Isabelle Hagner in August 1933: "I suddenly thought today what Franklin D. stood for. It is not Delano but *Depression*. This has given me much satisfaction."

In her old age, Mrs. Roosevelt kept the house at Sagamore Hill open for her grandchildren, wrote letters to family members and to strangers, and continued making intermittent public appearances. On September 17, 1935, she gave a speech to the Women's National Republican Club that was broadcast on the radio. Herbert Hoover was the other keynote speaker. The next month, Edith Roosevelt fell and broke her hip; she was bedridden and hospitalized for almost half a year. Though she recovered enough to live another thirteen years, the active part of her life had ended. Her world revolved around her children—whom she did not see often enough—and her memories. She enjoyed visits from Alice, Ethel, and Archie, but Kermit, who had accompanied her on many of her international travels, had become an alcoholic and committed suicide in Alaska in 1943. She was also estranged from her son Ted, and wept through his funeral in 1944. She died on September 30, 1948.

Edith Kermit Roosevelt was perpetually overshadowed by her dynamic husband, through convention and choice. She implicitly accepted the existence of nineteenth-century gender-specific spheres, which defined appropriate roles for men and women. Culturally restricted to the domestic sphere, she resisted all attempts by journalists and others to penetrate the privacy of the hearth. Her public persona, symbolized by the floral barrier she held in receiving lines, encapsulated the polite distance she deemed proper. Roosevelt, while he traveled with her and entrusted missions of quiet diplomacy to her, respected his wife and took her advice. She set high moral standards for herself and others. Her legacy as First Lady consisted of reinforcing the privacy of the First Family in the White House renovation, which looked backward to the eighteenth century; creating a visible tribute to past First Ladies in the form of a hall of portraits; and preserving the china of her predecessors. Yet she also looked forward, by appointing a full-time social secretary, a significant innovation crucial to the creation of the modern institution of First Ladies.

BIBLIOGRAPHICAL ESSAY
The primary source material on the Roosevelt family is vast. The Library of Congress holds the Theodore Roosevelt Papers,

which contain the First Lady's correspondence. The Library of Congress is also the repository for the Alice Roosevelt Longworth Collection, the Theodore Roosevelt, Jr., Papers, and the Kermit Roosevelt Papers, all of which include letters to and from Edith Roosevelt and her children. The Theodore Roosevelt Collection at Harvard University contains the correspondence of Edith Roosevelt, Corinne Roosevelt Robinson, Anna [Bye] Roosevelt Cowles, and Theodore Roosevelt. The Peter Hagner Collection at the University of North Carolina at Chapel Hill includes a lengthy correspondence between Isabelle Hagner and members of the Roosevelt clan. The Arthur Lee Papers at the Courtauld Institute in London contain Lord and Lady Lee's letters to and from various members of the Roosevelt family, including Edith Roosevelt. The correspondence between Sir Cecil Spring-Rice and Edith Roosevelt can be found at the Churchill Archives Centre at Churchill College, Cambridge. Deposited at the National Archives in Washington, D.C., is the First Lady's *White House Record of Social Functions, 1901–1909.* I am indebted to members of the Roosevelt family for access to some unpublished letters of Edith Roosevelt to her stepdaughter. Where a repository is not identified in this essay, the letter can be found in this unpublished material.

For contemporary articles about Edith Roosevelt, see Jacob Riis, "Mrs. Roosevelt and Her Children," *Ladies' Home Journal* (August 1902): 5–6; Anne O'Hagan, "Women of the Hour," *Harper's Bazaar* (May 1905): 412–416; "The White House as Social Centre," *Harper's Bazaar* (February 1908): 158–163; M. P. Daggett, "The Woman in the Background," *The Delineator* (March 1909): 393–396; Helena McCarthy,

"Why Mrs. Roosevelt Has Not Broken Down," *Ladies' Home Journal* (October 1908): 25; Charles A. Selden, "Six White House Wives and Widows," *Ladies' Home Journal* (June 1927): 18–19, 109–110, 112–113, 115; Floelle Youngblood Bonner, "Six Widows of Presidents," *National Republic* (October 1933): 5–6, 24; "Constitutionalists on the March," *Literary Digest* (September 28, 1935): 9; and Louis J. Horowitz and Boyden Sparkes, "Reshingling a Roof," *Literary Digest* (November 13, 1937): 28. For an insider's view of the First Lady and her family, consult Archibald W. Butt, *Letters,* edited by L. F. Abbot (New York, 1924), and *Taft and Roosevelt* (New York, 1930).

The best secondary source is Sylvia Jukes Morris's fine biography, *Edith Kermit Roosevelt* (New York, 1980). See also her "Portrait of a First Lady," in Natalie A. Naylor, Douglas Brinkley, and John Allen Gable, eds., *Theodore Roosevelt: Many-Sided American* (Interlaken, N.Y., 1992). Also useful are Hermann Hagedorn, *The Roosevelt Family of Sagamore Hill* (New York, 1954); William H. Harbaugh, *The Life and Times of Theodore Roosevelt* (New York, 1975); Edmund Morris, *The Rise of Theodore Roosevelt* (New York, 1979); and David McCullough, *Mornings on Horseback* (New York, 1981). For the view from her stepdaughter's side, see Alice Roosevelt Longworth's autobiography, *Crowded Hours* (New York, 1933). Betty Boyd Caroli, *The Roosevelt Women* (New York, 1998), looks at Edith Roosevelt's relationship with the other female members of her family.

Mrs. Roosevelt's obituaries include "Mrs. T. Roosevelt Dies at Oyster Bay," *New York Times* (October 1, 1948): 25; "Teddy Roosevelt's Widow Dies at 87," *Washington Post* (October 1, 1948): B-2; and "Death of a Lady," *Time* (October 11, 1948): 28.

★★★ ★★★

Helen Herron Taft

(1861–1943)

First Lady: 1909–1913

Stacy A. Cordery

Helen Herron was born on January 2, 1861, the daughter of attorney John Williamson Herron and Harriet Collins Herron. Helen—or Nellie, as she was more often called—was one of eleven children, five boys and six girls, born to a prosperous Cincinnati family. Politics and law were familiar topics in the Herron household. Helen's mother was the daughter of New York Congressman Eli Collins. Her father served in the state senate and was appointed a U.S. attorney by his old college roommate and fellow Republican, President Benjamin Harrison. The Herrons lived on Pike Street in an affluent neighborhood not far from the home of William Howard Taft.

As a girl, Helen attended Miss Nourse's school along with her sister and Taft's only sister, Fanny. Nellie most liked playing and listening to music. In her autobiography, she claimed that "music was the absorbing interest of my life in those days, the inspiration of all my dreams and ambitions." Soon she would recognize another ambition. In 1877, accompanied by her parents, Nellie took her first trip to Washington, D.C., where she spent several pleasant weeks in the White House as the guest of Rutherford and Lucy Webb Hayes. She called it the only unusual event of her girlhood, and later reminisced that she first dreamed of becoming First Lady during that visit. She promised herself then that she would find a way to marry a man "destined to be president."

Helen grew up to be headstrong, assertive, and impatient with the strictures of nineteenth-century life. She wanted to emulate her many distinguished forebears. In an era when most professions were closed to women, Nellie hoped to attain financial independence by writing critical works on art or music. Her parents encouraged her to attend her father's alma mater, Miami University, in Oxford, Ohio. An eager and dedicated student, Helen studied German, literature, history, and the sciences. After graduation she considered becoming a lawyer. She spent long afternoons in her father's office, familiarizing herself with the law by perusing the books on his shelves and helping him with his work. She learned to formulate and defend her opinions, to appreciate politics and jurisprudence, and to relish intellectual conundrums. Nellie, however, was shy and had to work hard to surmount feelings of insecurity, especially where her appearance was concerned.

Nellie unwillingly made her debut in Cincinnati society at age nineteen. She feared that she would never find a suitable husband—her standards were high—and she worried that her career plans would be thwarted. Her first season of parties and gentlemen callers proved to be agreeable enough, but she longed to work. In 1881 her wishes were fulfilled. Over her family's objections, Nellie began to teach at two local private schools. She found teaching stimulating but difficult, and her male pupils formidable. Nellie filled her diary with frustrations about her restricted state. A life of teaching was not her ideal, yet she knew that few women married "exactly right." Nellie spent tearful nights wishing she were gifted enough for a musical career. She thought about opening a school of her own. Still searching for outlets for her prodigious energy, Helen Herron and two of her friends began a salon in which invited guests could discuss pressing intellectual, political, and economic questions. This provided Helen with welcome mental exercise, and a convenient forum in which to demonstrate her skills to a dashing Yale University graduate, fellow salon member William Howard Taft.

The Herrons and the Tafts were established families in Cincinnati. John Herron and Alphonso Taft were both practicing attorneys, and they and their wives had known each other for years. Nevertheless, Helen and William did not meet until 1880, on a sledding outing, when Helen was nineteen. At that time, Taft was employed as a law clerk while attending Cincinnati Law School. In her autobiography, Helen noted that they met frequently thereafter, usually performing in amateur theatricals together, or having fun at parties in the countryside or dances in town. It was not until Helen established her salon in 1884 that the two became serious about each other. They had a rocky courtship.

She worried that he did not take her seriously, yet his letters to her were filled with reassurances that he valued her opinion and her intellect. Taft sent presents to placate her fears—histories of the world, The *Geology of the State of New York*, the novels of George Eliot—along with flowers and chocolates to build up her low self-esteem. For his part, Taft cast Helen in his mother's roles: perpetual goad, advice giver, and staunchest supporter. Helen did in fact share several traits with Louisa Torrey Taft. Both women were more ambitious and outspoken than their husbands. Both were formally educated and enjoyed scholarly pursuits; both were musically talented; and both chafed at the societal expectation of marriage. When they found their husbands, however, both Louisa and Helen recognized in them an opportunity for simultaneously pursuing their goal of intellectual freedom and gaining public status. Louisa and Nellie participated in their husbands' political and legal careers; in fact, both women interceded with presidents on their husband's behalf. Helen thus easily reproduced Louisa's job of propping up young William Taft, who also felt unsure of himself, inadequate, and wary of disappointing those who loved him.

Helen refused Taft's initial overtures of marriage, eventually accepting his proposal in 1885. This pleased both families. While she was in Washington, D.C., having her wedding gown fitted, her fiancé sent her a letter. He wondered on paper whether they might ever live in the capital in an official capacity, as his parents did when his father served as President Ulysses S. Grant's secretary of war and attorney general. Taft answered his own query by writing that of course they would live there—when level-headed Helen became secretary of the treasury. On June 19, 1886, Helen Herron wed William H. Taft. The service was conducted by the same Episcopalian priest who had married her parents.

The newlyweds left the next day for a European honeymoon. Since she had always wanted to travel, the new Mrs. Taft spent three wonderful months touring England, with a brief detour through Holland and France. Helen Taft managed their strict budget—her lifelong role—proudly writing in her autobiography that they had honeymooned on five dollars a day. While in England, Mrs. Taft asked her husband to secure tickets to a House of Commons debate. U.S. diplomat Henry White could not procure the tickets for them, but, instead, gave them passes to the popular Royal Mews. Helen Taft was no horsewoman. In 1886 she had never even ridden a horse and did not appreciate the royal stables. She was angry at missing the chance to hear the parliamentary debate, and thus was doubly disappointed with the outcome. In 1888 the Tafts embarked upon another European tour. They visited opera houses in Germany, Rome, and Florence, until William—less entranced by music than his wife—pleaded for a change.

After the honeymoon, the Tafts returned to the home they had built in Cincinnati on a lot given to Helen Taft by her father. Taft was appointed judge of the Superior Court of Ohio in 1887. On September 8, 1889, Mrs. Taft gave birth to their first child, Robert. Although Taft was very happy as superior court judge, Helen Taft found furnishing the home and taking care of her son not particularly challenging. In 1890, she was pleased when President Harrison wanted

to appoint her husband U.S. solicitor general, partly because it indicated that Taft's efforts on the bench were being rewarded, but also because it meant that the family would relocate to Washington, D.C. While Taft loved the law and dreamed of sitting on the Supreme Court, Helen Taft dreaded being stuck in what she considered the awful, boring rut of judge's wife. Taft wanted to decline the position of solicitor general, but his wife urged him to accept. She felt glad, as she phrased it, "because it gave Mr. Taft an opportunity for exactly the kind of work I wished him to do."

Taft moved to Washington, D.C., in 1890, rented a house on DuPont Circle, and began his duties as solicitor general. Helen Taft and her six-month-old baby arrived two weeks later. While she characterized their lifestyle at the time as simple, Mrs. Taft relished living in the capital. Her social circle consisted primarily of the attorney general and his wife and the Supreme Court justices and their wives. They also met Theodore Roosevelt, who was in Washington as civil service commissioner. The Tafts attended the Harrisons' 1891 New Year's Day reception at the White House. Helen Taft went regularly to listen to the debates in the House and Senate, leaving her son in the care of two maids. On August 1, 1891, she gave birth to their second child, Helen, and the burden of tending to two small children began to circumscribe her actions. What little time was not devoted to child-care duties was spent calming her husband and training his oratorical skills. The position of solicitor general involved arguing cases before the Supreme Court. Helen Taft helped William overcome his fears of speaking before the justices by urging him not to worry about their seeming indifference, not to talk overlong, and not to marshal too many arguments at once. While Alphonso Taft admonished that dramatic speeches did not win court cases, Helen Taft wanted her husband to cultivate a captivating speaking style—perhaps because she knew that her ambitions for him included giving campaign speeches.

In March 1892, another opportunity came their way. President Harrison appointed

Taft to the Sixth Federal Circuit Court of Appeals. While Taft was pleased, his wife hesitated, as the position entailed both their moving back to Cincinnati and extensive travel away from home for Taft. Cincinnati did not promise the stimulating political or artistic conversation to which she had grown accustomed in Washington. To occupy herself, Mrs. Taft reinitiated her study of history and science, joined a women's book club, became a frequent habitué of lectures and local theaters, enrolled in an art class, and aided the establishment of a new hospital and nurses' training program. She was most proud of her principal work, "the organization and management" of the Cincinnati Orchestra Association. Her superior administrative talents were fully utilized as she served as its first president and worked tirelessly to raise money and garner publicity for the creation of the Cincinnati Symphony Orchestra. On September 20, 1897, their last child, Charles, was born. The five Tafts began to holiday at Murray Bay, in Canada, where they eventually bought a vacation house. Otherwise, Mrs. Taft opined, their lives were "tranquil; quite too settled," and she was happiest of all when she learned that Taft had been appointed governor general of the Philippines.

Taft's reputation increased during the eight years he spent on the Circuit Court of Appeals. His conservative ruling in the Pullman strike case of 1894 brought him to the attention of Republican Party leaders. Taft became a popular speaker before legal and political groups, and throughout, he continued to consult with his wife regarding the content and phrasing of his speeches. Their letters from this period (Taft wrote home almost every day they were apart) brim with politics and the law. Taft solicited his wife's advice and incorporated her suggestions. Their relationship was close and caring, and he often clearly deferred to her wishes. By 1900, Taft was being considered for the position he most desired—a seat on the Supreme Court. Helen Taft, however, thought her husband would make an excellent president and she a fine First Lady; this would be the first of

several instances in which she would be instrumental in his declining the Supreme Court. As Taft wrote to a friend, he would "leave it to her to whom I owe everything and I shall abide by her decision." In 1900, President William McKinley asked Taft to become president of a commission to establish a civil government in the Philippines (and, in 1902, governor-general of the islands), with the implicit promise of a seat on the Court when the occasion arose. With Mrs. Taft's joyful approval, Taft acceded to the president's wishes.

Helen Taft immediately began to prepare for what she considered a great new adventure by reading about the islands. In 1898, the United States had gained control of the Philippines as a result of its victory over Spain. Taft's job was to convert the American-controlled military government into a civil government—despite continuing armed resistance to the U.S. presence by some Filipinos—and eventually to make the islands self-governing. This entailed mending relationships between the land-rich Catholic Church and the landless, poor, rural Filipinos. Taft regretted the missed chance at the Supreme Court, but President McKinley assured him that another opening would materialize, and that the experience of setting up a government in the Far East would be invaluable. The Tafts moved to the Philippines in April 1900. Robert was ten years old, Helen was eight, and Charlie was two. Their mother looked with keen anticipation at introducing them to the cultural benefits of living in another country. En route, Helen Taft, her children, and her sister Maria sojourned in Japan (where she was presented to the empress), China, and Hong Kong before joining Taft in Manila. While Taft brought political consensus and he improved schools, roads, harbors, sanitation, courts, taxes, civil service, and the police force, Mrs. Taft settled happily into her four-year-long role as leading lady of the Philippines. This experience profoundly shaped her White House performance.

Helen Taft wanted to re-create the comforts of home and establish a fitting base as she and her husband stepped into their positions. To do this, she grafted local customs to her own sense of American propriety. Although she shared in the genteel racism of her day and class, as the wife of the president of the commission, she set a critical precedent by beginning to dismantle the color line that existed under the military government. Her parties included leading Filipinos as well as Europeans and Americans, and her equal treatment of upper-class Filipinos did much to ease Filipino-American tensions. She studied Spanish, thereby implicitly giving equal status to the language of the country. For her Filipino coachman she designed formal white-and-green livery, to replace the casual, light-weight island garb. She frequented the Luneta, an area in Manila set aside for band concerts and promenading, which became one of her favorite places. People of all backgrounds gathered at the Luneta to enjoy each other's company and the music. Helen Taft understood the Luneta as a kind of community center in Manila and therefore seldom missed a chance to participate visibly.

Mrs. Taft spent a large part of her time in the Far East traveling. President McKinley's reelection in 1900 guaranteed the American presence in the Philippines, so the Tafts, other members of the civil government commission, and many Filipinos embarked upon a sixty-day goodwill and information-gathering tour of the southern islands. The arduous trip involved stops at more than twenty villages, and Mrs. Taft loved it. They journeyed through areas still in rebellion, seeking to establish provincial governments in their wake. At each stop the local dignitaries held parties in their honor. The Tafts always commanded the center of attention. Helen Taft reveled in her position and, despite the accompanying danger, discomfort, and exhaustion, thoroughly enjoyed her introduction to island cultures. She also welcomed her historic involvement in what she termed a unique expedition that "ushered in a new era, not to say a new national existence," for the Filipinos.

Helen Taft later journeyed by horseback for over a fortnight through the northern islands. She went with her sister Maria and a group of resident Americans. They explored undeveloped, isolated areas on the unofficial trip. This trek prompted the intrepid Mrs. Taft to learn how to ride—a task she quickly accomplished. Even though the Tafts missed one another during the weeks that she was exploring, Helen Taft could not pass up such adventure. In many areas she was the first European woman the people had ever seen. The accommodations were primitive, but she learned firsthand about living conditions in the mountains, and she recorded many scenes of natural beauty. Just before she returned to Manila, Mrs. Taft learned that her husband was to be installed as the first American governor of the Philippines on July 4, 1902.

Following the ceremony, the new governor and his family moved into Malacañan Palace, the traditional home of the ruler of the islands. Mrs. Taft found the palace much to her liking. It came with a large number of servants, sixteen ponies, twenty acres of land, and a marvelous view of the Pasig River. Taft's salary, though increased, never stretched as far as his wife would have liked because they had to carry the financial burden of state entertaining. Nevertheless, Mrs. Taft began a tradition of elaborate weekly afternoon receptions open to all inhabitants and visitors regardless of their race and station. She also held many outdoor parties with orchestras and dancing. The most impressive of these—a Venetian Carnival ball—occurred on the eve of their leave-taking. Helen Taft outlined the Malacañan with electric lights and strung Japanese lanterns through the trees. Guests arrived by boat on the Pasig, where the Tafts, dressed as the doge and his consort, received them on a landing.

While Helen Taft enjoyed herself, life as the wife of the governor was often difficult. The strains occasioned by battling the elements, arcane Filipino social codes, the uncertainty of their position following McKinley's assassination in September 1901, and the news of her mother's eventually fatal illness weighed heavily on her.

Seeking an escape from the pressures of daily life, Helen Taft journeyed to China for a much-needed rest. Without such a break, she feared that she would succumb to a nervous breakdown. Her trip was cut short, however, when she received word that Taft had undergone two operations. Leaving Shanghai, she returned to Manila to tend to him. Taft's doctors suggested he leave the island to recuperate. Taft contacted McKinley's successor, President Theodore Roosevelt, who informed him that he was needed in Washington because Congress was about to debate the Philippines. Roosevelt granted Taft a leave of absence. Helen Taft gratefully packed up the family and left the Philippines in December 1901. It was a dismal trip. Having been unable to complete her rest cure, her fears were compounded by Taft's uncertain health and the news that her mother had suffered a stroke. Her mother died before she could reach her, and soon after, her father, too, had a stroke. Helen Taft spent that winter in Cincinnati trying to recover, while her husband testified before congressional committees in Washington. Taft underwent three surgeries within five months, but the pace of their lives did not materially slacken.

Before Taft could return to East Asia, President Roosevelt sent him on an unofficial mission to the Vatican to settle the Catholic Church's disputed landholdings in the Philippines. Mrs. Taft planned to accompany him in May, but when young Robert Taft was struck with scarlet fever, she chose to remain with him in Cincinnati. One month later, Helen Taft joined her husband in Rome for another adventure. While Taft's business with the cardinals stalled, Helen Taft and the children had an audience with the pope and visited the Catacombs, St. Peter's, St. Paul's, art museums, and historic sites. It was an exhilarating month highlighted by social engagements with local aristocracy. From Rome, she and the children left for a month-long European vacation.

In September, the family—all members back in good health—reunited in the Philippines. The Tafts escaped the terrible cholera epidemic then raging, but Filipinos died in horrifying numbers. Disease was simultaneously killing farm and work animals. Governor Taft instituted measures to ward off famine. Helen Taft began procedures at the Malacañan Palace to protect its inhabitants from cholera. She imported a cow for fresh milk for the children, eventually added chickens and turkeys for their table, and put in a vegetable garden, both to help augment the governor's paycheck and to make certain they would have enough to eat. She continued her afternoon receptions and her outdoor parties because she wanted to rally people's spirits and maintain good relations—particularly between the Filipino community and the international community—during the crisis.

In October 1902, President Roosevelt offered Taft a seat on the U.S. Supreme Court, and for the second time, Taft turned down this most coveted position. He declined the offer partly because he felt he had not completed his job in the Philippines, but, perhaps most important, because Mrs. Taft did not wish to leave her position and her palace to become the undistinguished wife of a justice. Six months later, however, Roosevelt summoned Taft home to serve as secretary of war. Mrs. Taft wrote of this new proposal in her autobiography:

> This was much more pleasing to me than the offer of the Supreme Court appointment, because it was in line with the kind of work I wanted my husband to do, the kind of career I wanted for him and expected him to have, so I was glad there were few excuses for refusing to accept it open to him.

Shortly after the Tafts returned to Washington, Helen Taft met a woman she had known in Manila. The woman asked her how life as a cabinet wife compared with being the wife of the governor of the Philippines. "Why," the woman said, "out there you were really a queen, and you come back here and are *just nobody*!" Helen Taft longed for the position of First Lady, the luxurious living and total freedom from household duties. Being a cabinet wife was stressful and monotonous. Her chief activities included calling on other cabinet wives and dining out. She missed the intellectual challenge of managing the distaff side of social problems in the war-torn Philippines. The best substitute came from Taft's position. He confided in her as secretary of war and she remained one of his chief advisers.

In November 1904, Helen Taft broke the boredom of life as a cabinet wife by accompanying her husband on a diplomatic call to Panama. She found the canal-building particularly fascinating, and the Panamanians lavished them with honors. Helen Taft decided against accompanying her husband on the 1905 congressional junket to the Far East. The president's celebrity daughter, Alice Roosevelt, was destined to be the star of that trip, and Helen Taft had never been fond of the irrepressible young Roosevelt. So, after Taft departed, she and the children spent a quiet summer in England. Taft's daily missives were chatty and full of news of Alice's extravagant receptions in Hawaii, the Philippines, and Japan. Mrs. Taft's letters betrayed her impatience with Alice's antics, which overshadowed Taft's mission, and with newspaper gossip that twenty-year-old Alice and Secretary Taft had become engaged. (The truth was that Alice did find romance, but it was with Ohio Congressman Nicholas Longworth, whom she eventually married.) When the time came to leave England, Helen Taft found that her baggage was not with her. Frantic to make the boat train, which was leaving in five minutes, she ran to the station master's office "determined to overawe him by revealing to him [her] official position." She announced that she was Mrs. William Howard Taft of Washington, and asked him to hold the train for her. The station master didn't budge. "My husband is Secretary of War of the United States" elicited no response. Mrs. Taft gave it one final attempt: "You must have heard of him. He's travelling now with Miss Alice Roosevelt." At last, the train was held, the baggage found, and the boat made. She had to bear the penance of hearing her children and friends

refer to her as "*The* Mrs. Taft whose husband was travelling with Miss Alice Roosevelt."

After winning the presidential election in 1904, Theodore Roosevelt announced that he would not run again. Not until March 1907, however, did Roosevelt support Taft—who pledged to follow Roosevelt's programs—as his choice for successor to the nation's highest office. Helen Taft felt that Roosevelt had unconscionably delayed his backing, and this caused her to mistrust the president. Yet her early dream of seeing her husband in the White House could come true only with Roosevelt's assistance. She also had recently foiled another attempt to place Taft on the Supreme Court. When Justice Henry Brown retired, Roosevelt offered Taft the position. Taft wavered. Roosevelt arranged a meeting with Helen Taft, hoping to convince her to sway Taft into acceptance. President Roosevelt afterward wrote Taft that, having spent thirty minutes with Mrs. Taft, he now understood why Taft would bide his time and hope for the presidency.

Even after Roosevelt signified his intention to back him for the presidency, Taft hesitated. He wanted Roosevelt—whom he considered a friend—to run again. Mrs. Taft, though, began a quiet but determined campaign to assist the efforts of those within the Republican Party who were advocating her husband's nomination. She met with President Roosevelt, formally and socially, to urge him to throw his support publicly behind Taft. At one point in late 1906, the president reproached her for being too ambitious in her husband's behalf. Helen Taft, already suspicious of Roosevelt's motives, could not understand why he would voluntarily surrender the presidency and worried that he was using Taft as a foil for his own ambitions. As a despondent Taft began campaigning, Mrs. Taft read and corrected his speeches, monitored his popularity in the newspapers, and watched Washington politics for signs of a Roosevelt reversal. She buttressed Taft's flagging spirits and comforted him after poorly received orations. She urged him to declare himself firmly as a candidate and allow the Republican Party machinery to support him. Her vigilance extended to minute details. Once she was frantic because they had inadvertently played bridge on a Sunday and risked a newspaper scandal.

President Roosevelt sent Secretary Taft on a diplomatic mission in September 1907 to smooth tensions with the Japanese and open the first Philippine legislature. Mrs. Taft accompanied him on the eight-country tour. When they returned to the United States in December, Helen Taft worried that Roosevelt's considerable popularity with the voters might force a renomination attempt. She labored to establish her husband's independence from the president. "I do hope myself," she wrote in February 1908, "that you are not going to make any more speeches on the 'Roosevelt policies' as I think they need to be let alone for the present." As the Republican Party nominating convention approached, President Roosevelt and Helen Taft found themselves allies in the cause. Roosevelt cautioned Taft not to give impromptu speeches or to sojourn with wealthy friends while campaigning. As Republican Party leader, Roosevelt instructed his followers to bring in the necessary votes for Taft, which they dutifully did. Helen Taft followed the proceedings nervously from her husband's office, and fretted when a spontaneous demonstration for Roosevelt ran longer than the one that came when Taft was nominated. Nevertheless, she was jubilant when he won the nomination.

A stressful presidential campaign ensued. Taft sought refuge in his golf game, but Helen Taft was resolute enough for both of them. While Taft was away campaigning, she described how impatiently she waited for the evening papers to scrutinize his performance. She continually sent him advice on political topics. His other chief adviser, President Roosevelt, began to confer more and more with Helen Taft. Journalists satirized Taft as the reluctant campaigner, and neither Helen Taft—who wanted more than anything to be First Lady—nor Roosevelt—who had handpicked Taft as his successor—could afford to let Taft be nonchalant about

the nomination. Taft hated politics, loathed giving speeches, and longed for the Supreme Court. He often doubted that the Republican ticket would win. Despite his own hesitant campaign, William Howard Taft swept into the presidency on November 3, 1908. Helen Taft confessed that she had never been so happy.

She busied herself with future plans, which contributed to tensions with the Roosevelts. She called in Major Archibald Butt to discuss the White House changes she contemplated. Butt worked for the Tafts during their years in the Philippines and currently served the Roosevelts in the White House. She informed him that she intended to keep him in service at the White House, but that she would make changes in most of the remaining positions. She also told him of her decision to alter the present system of catering and to have all meals prepared in the executive mansion. Helen Taft's eagerness to supplant Edith Roosevelt symbolized to some in the Roosevelt camp the desire of the Tafts to break away from the record of the outgoing president.

On March 3, 1909, the Tafts dined at the White House and spent that night before the inauguration as guests of the Roosevelts. The president thus shattered a precedent, Helen Taft pointed out in her autobiography, but she understood it was Roosevelt's way of welcoming them to the position. Mrs. Taft remembered the dinner as strained and Mrs. Roosevelt as depressed. She herself was awake all night, reviewing inaugural plans and fretting about the terrible ice and snowstorm that blanketed the capital. The blizzard forced the ceremony indoors to the Senate chamber. Before the newly sworn-in president completed his inaugural address, Helen Taft slipped out of the Senate chamber and hastened to the Rotunda so that she could sit beside her husband on the drive from the Capitol to the reviewing stand. She was the first First Lady to do so. She reasoned that since Roosevelt broke a tradition by not accompanying the new president along the route, she, too, would break tradition and accompany him. It was the proudest moment of the day, she recalled: "Perhaps I had a little secret elation in thinking that I was doing something which no woman had ever done before."

The new First Lady determined to set her own stamp on the White House. Major Butt, who soon became indispensable to the Tafts, remained as White House military aide. She made the position of steward redundant, and hired Elizabeth Jaffray as the new housekeeper, because she believed that a woman could better help her oversee the White House. She replaced Isabelle Hagner, Edith Roosevelt's competent social secretary, with Alice Blech. After a year, Mary D. Spiers took Blech's place, but Spiers did not remain in the position long, probably because Helen Taft was a perfectionist and difficult to work for. After that— especially after the First Lady was taken ill—the position of social secretary was filled by her daughter Helen, her friends, or herself. Helen Taft experienced a cordial relationship with the press, preferring to speak with female journalists. As First Lady, she allowed newspapers to quote her directly. She told journalists that she favored equality for women, but did not think it appropriate for women to hold elected office. She supported careers, better working conditions, and higher education for women. She approved of her husband's appointment of social activist Julia Lathrop to head the federal Children's Bureau.

Because of her extensive travels and her attendance at receptions in European and Asian capitals, the new First Lady believed that the mistress of the White House should exemplify a cosmopolitan and international image. She immediately set a formal tone. She hired six African Americans, outfitted them in blue livery, and trained them as footmen. They were stationed around the clock in pairs to receive White House visitors and assist tourists. Roosevelt loyalists, and others who thought that this change ran counter to "democratic simplicity," condemned Mrs. Taft's innovation. No such criticism had arisen when her coachmen wore livery in the Philippines. Mrs.

Taft redecorated the White House in the style of the Far East, which she had grown to love during her years in the Philippines. She was finally able to display the many treasures they had bought or received throughout her husband's career. She missed the flowers that had graced the Malacañan Palace, and so Helen Taft put the White House greenhouse to good use, filling the executive mansion with an array of plants. She organized the extensive and unprotected collection of White House silver. Mrs. Taft had a silver closet built with a locked door and velvet-lined compartments for each piece. As First Lady she was "at home" three afternoons a week, when she received callers in the Red Room. She discontinued the weekly meetings of the cabinet wives, as she had never liked attending them when she was the wife of the secretary of war.

Mrs. Taft was a lavish hostess, and while she constantly worried about money, she did not stint on entertainments. She initiated the practice of following each state dinner with a musical or theatrical performance. One perquisite of being First Lady was that she could summon musicians to play and indulge her love of music. She re-created the outdoor garden parties of Manila on the lawns of the White House. Orchestral performances accompanied each of the four parties in May. An avid supporter of the arts in Washington, Helen Taft habitually attended the theater, the symphony, and the opera, often taking the president with her.

One of her proudest and most underrated accomplishments was the establishment of a Philippine-type Luneta in Washington, D.C. With Major Butt's help, and the president's support, Helen Taft converted West Potomac Park into a meeting place for Washingtonians. She renamed the long road leading up to the park Potomac Drive. Then she had a bandstand built, where the Marine Band could play, and announced to members of the public that they were invited, every Wednesday and Saturday evening, to come hear the music and visit with their friends. On April

17, 1909, President and Mrs. Taft mingled in the opening crowd of 10,000. The First Lady was very happy with her success, and public sentiment supported her venture into civic improvement.

Mrs. Taft is best known, however, as the sponsor of the cherry blossom trees that bloom along Potomac Drive every spring. She was a longtime admirer of Japan's natural beauty and, in particular, the Cherry Blossom Festival that opened the Tokyo social season. When a friend of hers, National Geographic Society board member Eliza Scidmore, suggested landscaping Potomac Drive with ornamental cherry trees, Mrs. Taft determined to make that project her own. She first attempted to replant all the cherry blossom trees in the United States in Washington, but there were only a hundred in existence. An influential Japanese scientist heard about the First Lady's plight and donated 2,000 trees. He wanted them to serve as an overdue "thank you" to the U.S. government for President Roosevelt's assistance in the 1905 Russo-Japanese peace settlement. The trees arrived as a personal gift to the First Lady, but had to be destroyed because they were diseased. Through the intervention of Taft's secretary of state and the Japanese ambassador to the United States, another lot was sent; 3,000 successful cherry blossom trees this time. Not only have the trees contributed to the beauty of the nation's capital, but they also attract thousands of appreciative tourists every spring.

Entertaining and civic improvements were always secondary to Helen Taft's involvement in her husband's career. The First Lady often sat in on Taft's conferences with politicians and diplomats, listening and contributing to them. In his memoirs, White House usher Ike Hoover reported that Mrs. Taft attended nearly all important public—and private—White House meetings. The First Lady listened to Senate and House debates, as she had done in the past. At the swearing-in of new Supreme Court justices she requested a seat within the bar of the court, and was the first woman ever to sit there. She influenced Taft directly on

at least two appointments. Taft accepted the pro forma resignation of distinguished ambassador Henry White because Mrs. Taft had never forgotten the honeymoon slight of being consigned by Mr. White to the Royal Mews instead of the House of Commons. Taft refused his Cincinnati neighbor and Republican supporter, Representative Nicholas Longworth, the ambassadorship to China. Longworth's disqualification was that he had married Mrs. Taft's old nemesis Alice Roosevelt. Mrs. Taft's rancor toward Alice Roosevelt Longworth effectively thwarted "Princess Alice's" desire to return to Asia.

In May 1909, after a day spent nursing her son Charlie through surgery, Helen Taft joined her husband and some friends on the presidential yacht. On board, however, the First Lady suffered a stroke that paralyzed her right arm and leg, as well as her facial muscles. She lost her power of speech. For a year she could not attend to any of the duties of the First Lady. The White House attempted to hide the seriousness of her illness from the public. Her daughter and sisters represented her at essential official functions. Taft's life was altogether changed. He spent hours a day teaching his wife to speak again. For a year he operated without his closest adviser. While she struggled to regain her faculties, Republicans within Taft's administration embarked upon a civil war, and the party factionalized. Taft did not disclose the extent of the rift to his wife for fear she would relapse. As she recovered, she began slowly to reassert her authority, first over the family and then over state occasions. Desperately missing politics, Mrs. Taft ate her meals behind a screen outside the State Dining Room, listening closely to the festivities within. Her first public appearances did not involve speaking.

By the summer of 1911, Helen Taft had recovered enough to plan what became her swan song as First Lady. She issued 4,000 invitations to a formal, evening celebration of their silver wedding anniversary, held on the White House lawn. This brilliant party was her last major social event as First Lady, but it provoked perhaps the final split between the Tafts and the Roosevelts. In the months that followed, relations between Roosevelt and Taft worsened, and by early 1912, the two old friends were rivals for the Republican nomination. It was an outcome that Helen Taft had both feared and expected. Although Taft received the Republican nomination in 1912, Roosevelt was determined not to give up. Running on the Progressive Party ticket, Roosevelt split the Republican Party. The factionalized party could no longer elect either candidate, and Woodrow Wilson, the Democrat, won the presidency. Taft's 1912 reelection attempt might have been successful had Roosevelt fully supported it.

Helen Taft hated to leave the White House. It was the fulfillment of all of her ambitions for herself and for her husband. Her final legacy as First Lady was to help create the Smithsonian Institution's First Ladies' gown collection by donating her inaugural dress.

Taft considered returning to private law practice, but instead joined the law faculty at Yale University. In April 1913, the Tafts moved to New Haven, Connecticut, where their son Charlie matriculated in the fall. Taft augmented his smaller paycheck by making frequent speeches and writing magazine articles. His wife scrutinized every contract. She had saved almost $100,000 from the presidential years, and, as always, she balanced the household books. Only a slight speech impediment remained as an obvious reminder of her stroke, but her health remained uncertain. Mrs. Taft entertained unostentatiously in New Haven, played golf often, and attended the theater and the symphony. The Tafts lived in four different homes in New Haven, and Helen Taft oversaw each move. In 1914, she became the first former First Lady to publish her memoirs, *Recollections of Full Years*. She invested the profits. That summer the Tafts traveled to San Francisco. He made a series of speeches and she—always interested in adventure—went sightseeing. They returned by way of Panama. At the beginning of World War I, Taft became

joint chair of the National Labor Board. Son Robert worked in the Food Administration, and daughter Helen, dean of Bryn Mawr College, turned the students into farmers and a local farm into a victory garden. Charlie Taft enlisted. Mrs. Taft supported the Red Cross, headed by her good friend Mabel Boardman.

In 1921, the Tafts were in Bermuda when they heard the rumor that President Warren G. Harding would appoint Taft chief justice of the United States. Confirmation did not arrive for several months, but by that time Helen Taft agreed he should accept the offer. Taft's lifelong dream had finally come true. The Tafts moved to 2115 Wyoming Avenue, Washington, D.C., where Helen Taft, at age sixty, still participated actively in her husband's career. They traveled to England together, where they were presented to, and later dined with, King George V and Queen Mary. As the wife of the chief justice, Helen Taft ranked second only to Florence Kling Harding, the current First Lady. She held Monday afternoon receptions, and resumed her life of reading, theater- and concertgoing, and detailed involvement in Taft's work. In 1923, Helen Taft became a member of the Colonial Dames, and that patriotic and historical organization occupied much of her time. She served as honorary vice president from 1925 and was active in the acquisition of Dumbarton House as the Dames' headquarters in Washington, D.C. Helen Taft maintained her social contacts and often traveled without her husband. He journeyed less frequently than before, partly because of his rooted position and partly because his health was failing. Taft's obesity had been a longtime problem, and for years Mrs. Taft labored to decrease his food intake. His weight seemed to reflect his job satisfaction, and while he was president, he weighed as much as 340 pounds. He had two heart attacks in 1924. The first prevented him from attending Woodrow Wilson's funeral, so Helen Taft went in his stead. Chief Justice Taft spent long hours on the bench even into his seventies. By 1929, his heart gave out. William Howard Taft died on March 8, 1930.

Helen Taft lived to see her son Robert become a U.S. senator from Ohio, her daughter Helen earn a Ph.D. in history from Yale and a J.D. from George Washington University, and her son Charlie launch a career in reform politics. She maintained a lively interest in national affairs and allowed her name to be used by her friend First Lady Lou Henry Hoover as honorary vice president of the Girl Scouts of America. In 1941 First Lady Eleanor Roosevelt honored her at a banquet for Supreme Court wives. Her later life revolved around her social circle, particularly the Colonial Dames, her intellectual pursuits, traveling, and her family. She died on May 22, 1943, at her home in Washington, D.C. With Jacqueline Kennedy Onassis, she is one of the two First Ladies buried at Arlington National Cemetery.

From the time she was a young woman, Helen Herron Taft had dreamed of someday becoming First Lady. Having traveled around the world, been entertained in the courts of Asia and Europe, and enjoyed a triumphant tenure as the wife of the governor of the Philippines during the dangerous era of conversion from military to civilian rule, she was better prepared for the position than most women who have filled it. Yet Helen Taft celebrated only two months of unalloyed happiness as First Lady of the United States before she suffered her stroke. Although she recovered most of her health after one year, she remained uncomfortable and self-conscious speaking in front of people. She always wanted her own career—admittedly an impracticable idea for someone of her class and era—but she chose instead to sublimate her desire in her husband's profession. Her influence over William Howard Taft was immense, both in and out of the White House. If she had not urged him to pass up his early chances at a seat on the Supreme Court, Taft might never have become president. Some of his biographers further speculated that Taft's administration would not have been wrecked by intraparty conflict if Helen Taft had not been such a pronounced presence in his life. He might never even have squabbled with Theodore Roosevelt. Helen Taft

could be contentious and strong-willed. If she had not suffered the stroke, perhaps she would have exerted authority in ways that might have created political problems for the president. On the other hand, if she had been healthy enough to give advice early in his presidency, Taft might have retained control of the Republican Party and been reelected in 1912. These, of course, are only conjectures. What is certain is that Helen Herron Taft was an intelligent woman and a politically astute wife who held firm opinions, certain ambitions for her husband, and the power in their marriage to implement them. As First Lady, Helen Taft is most often remembered—with gratitude—every spring as the cherry trees blossom along the banks of the Potomac.

BIBLIOGRAPHICAL ESSAY

Helen Herron Taft's correspondence with William Howard Taft is part of the William Howard Taft Papers in the Manuscript Division of the Library of Congress in Washington, D.C. (also available on microfilm). One crucial contemporary source of information on Mrs. Taft's White House years is *Taft and Roosevelt: The Intimate Letters of Archie Butt, Military Aide* (2 vols., Garden City, N.Y., 1930). Archibald Butt served both President Roosevelt and President Taft, and his letters chronicle many of the First Lady's experiences, including her illness. For other contemporary views, see George Griswold Hill, "The Wife of the New President," *Ladies' Home Journal* (March 1909): 6; "Mrs. Taft's Plans in the White House, *Ladies' Home Journal* (March 1909): 7, 72; Katherine Graves Busbey, "Mrs. Taft's Homemaking," *Good Housekeeping* (September 1911): 290–298; "First in the President's Heart— His Home," *Home Life* (April 1912): 8, 26; Charles A. Selden, "Six White House Wives and Widows," *Ladies' Home Journal* (June 1927): 18–19, 109–110, 112–113, 115; and Floelle Youngblood Bonner, "Six Widows of Presidents," *National Republic* (October 1933): 5–6, 24.

The most important published source of information on Helen Herron Taft is her autobiography, *Recollections of Full Years* (New York, 1914). The problem with this book is, of course, that it was written seven years before Taft joined the Supreme Court and twenty-nine years before her death, and so it does not tell the complete story. There is no biography of Mrs. Taft. Ishbel Ross's *An American Family: The Tafts—1678–1964* (New York, 1964), a narrative of the Taft family, includes important information on Helen Herron Taft, but much of it is derived from *Recollections of Full Years*. Historians of William Howard Taft have contributed to an understanding of Mrs. Taft, particularly Henry F. Pringle's two-volume *The Life and Times of William Howard Taft* (New York, 1939) and Judith Icke Anderson's *William Howard Taft: An Intimate History* (New York, 1981). Anderson's book is a psychobiography and devotes considerable space to Helen Taft, including a chapter on her as First Lady. For the relationship between Helen Taft and Edith Roosevelt, see Sylvia Jukes Morris, *Edith Kermit Roosevelt: Portrait of a First Lady* (New York, 1980).

For Helen Taft's obituary, see "Mrs. W. H. Taft Dies: President's Widow," *New York Times* (May 23, 1943): 43.

★★★ ★★★

Ellen Louise Axson Wilson

(1860–1914)

First Lady: 1913–1914

Shelley Sallee

Ellen Louise Axson was born in Savannah, Georgia, on May 15, 1860, to Samuel Edward Axson and Margaret Jane Hoyt Axson. Her father, a Presbyterian minister, had been ordained the previous spring, six months after his marriage to her mother, herself the daughter of a Presbyterian minister. Ellen was the first of four children born to the Axsons.

In the year following Ellen's birth, Georgia seceded from the Union, taking her father away from home for extended intervals as chaplain of the First Regiment, Georgia Infantry. In 1866 the family reunited and moved to Rome, Georgia, where her father revived the war-weary congregation of the First Presbyterian Church. The next year Ellen's brother Isaac

Stockton Keith was born, her only sibling until the birth of Edward William (Eddie) ten years later. The birth of her sister Margaret Randolph (Madge) and the death of her mother in 1881 caused one of the most pivotal periods in Ellen's life.

Ellen was twenty-one when complicated childbirth led to her mother's death. Mrs. Axson, a well-educated woman who had attended Greensboro Female College, was particularly close to Ellen. Ellen missed the affection that her mother had shown her only daughter. She also missed her mother's advice as she became responsible for her brothers. Though her Aunt Louisa Hoyt Brown raised the baby, Ellen later shared responsibility for Madge as well. In addition, Ellen's father, devastated by his wife's death, suffered from mental illness. Ellen's family responsibilities increased as her father declined.

In April 1883, Ellen still wore the requisite black mourning dress as she listened to her father's sermon. Despite the dark attire, she caught the attention of the visiting Woodrow Wilson. A young Atlanta lawyer, he had come to Rome to visit his uncle. Using his uncle's connections as an elder in the church, Wilson arranged a visit to the Axson home. The day initiated a passionate courtship.

In September, while vacationing with his mother, Wilson arranged his trip to coincide with Ellen's holiday, landing them both in Asheville, North Carolina. After convincing her to stay in town an extra day, Wilson proposed marriage just before boarding a train that would take him to Baltimore, where he was enrolled in a graduate program in history. In the midst of the busy train station, a surprised Ellen accepted his proposal.

Less than a year later, Ellen's father died. A letter from her cousin suggested to Ellen that her father had committed suicide. Aware that many people viewed suicide as disgraceful, Ellen considered breaking off her engagement. Wilson, who had been supportive throughout her father's mental illness and death, quelled her doubts.

An inheritance from her father enabled Ellen to pursue one of her own dreams. In 1884, she enrolled in classes at the Art Students League in New York, an institution known for freedom of expression. The decision revealed her intellectual independence as well as her talent for and love of art.

Although Ellen absorbed her parents' appreciation for education, her upbringing and studies at Rome Female College had made her an independent thinker who questioned their values. As a teenager, for instance, she had written her parents sharp criticism of a clergyman her grandparents had taken her to hear. Although his response to this letter is unknown, her father disapproved of his daughter's tendency to be opinionated.

Ellen's friends at Rome Female College had helped foster her independent thought.

Rosalie Anderson, Elizabeth Leith (Beth) Adams, Anna Harris, and Agness Beville Vaughn formed a female network from which Ellen found support for her ideas. Although Ellen's letters indicate strong religious conviction, she doubted the characterization formed by her parents' generation of the role of religion. As she wrote to Wilson in February 1884, "I believe that our good Presbyterian ancestors make a mistake in insisting so strongly on the duty of self-examination." She resented her parents' view that "it is always wrong to do what one wants to do." Her belief that moral obligation did not require stern religion perhaps explains why she and Beth Adams loved reading George Eliot, an English novelist who had rejected her own parents' strict evangelical values yet focused on strong moral themes.

When she was among her friends, Ellen's desire for independence often took the form of antagonism toward men. In the 1880s, few middle-class women sought livelihoods other than marriage. Almost no one seriously considered that a woman might have both a career and marriage. The belief that a woman should devote herself to her home may explain why Ellen and her friends saw ambition and marriage as incompatible. Ellen was known as "Ellie, the Man Hater" after she had confided to a close friend that if she ever fell in love, it would be against her will. A visit to Sewanee College did not change her mind. Ellen remained unimpressed with men, writing to her mother about their lack of seriousness of purpose. She and her friend Beth pledged to one another to remain single and pursue professional and financial independence.

When Ellen did fall in love, it was with a man known for his seriousness of purpose. The certainty of her love, nevertheless, did not prevent her from being unsure of how to resolve the conflict between her ambition for a career in art and a desire to be a devoted helpmate. From New York she wrote to Wilson a rationalization of her resolution to put him first. With career and marriage seemingly irreconcilable, Ellen decided that independence might ultimately mean a lonely life. The powerful emotions of being in love, coupled with cultural pressure for women's devotion to husband and family, led Ellen to rechannel her ambition. She wrote to Wilson in April 1885, "Ah! but I *am* ambitious! And the best of it is that *mine is gratified* ambition, for I am ambitious for *you*—and for *myself*, too."

Wilson always assured Ellen that he needed her. In January 1885 he wrote, "Your companionship is more essential to my *ambitions* than the books I cannot yet own or the journeys I cannot take." Unlike Ellen's father, however, Woodrow appreciated and encouraged her opinions. In letters during their engagement, they discussed art shows and works such as John Ruskin's *Modern Painters*. In a letter to his friend Heath Dabney on February 17, 1884, Woodrow praised Ellen's efforts to make money through portrait painting and her sharp, well-read mind. Above all, however, he declared her "the most *domestic* of maidens."

Wilson's compliment stemmed from a common nineteenth-century ideal that viewed a woman as a source of inspiration, a creator of beauty, a refuge. It was an ideal that shaped his profuse expressions of love in his letters to her during their engagement and throughout their marriage. She did not describe their love in such extravagant rhetoric. They both, nevertheless, drew upon their strong feelings for one another to form a meaningful partnership.

Ellen and Woodrow were married on June 24, 1885, in Savannah, Georgia. Wilson had accepted a position as associate professor of history at Bryn Mawr College, Pennsylvania, with a salary of $1,500. For the first five years of their marriage, the Wilsons lived at Bryn Mawr, followed by a brief term at Wesleyan University in Middletown, Connecticut. During these years Mrs. Wilson's time was occupied with starting a family, helping her siblings, and assisting her husband.

In April 1886, Ellen Wilson gave birth to their first child, Margaret Woodrow Wilson. Jessie Woodrow Wilson's birth followed the next year. Their family was com-

pleted in 1889 with the birth of Eleanor Randolph Wilson.

Dr. Florence Taft attended Mrs. Wilson for the last two months of the pregnancy after problems developed. During the complications that arose, Dr. Taft discovered the existence of albumin—a clue to the kidney disease that eventually killed her—in a urine analysis.

While busy with her young daughters, Ellen Wilson also provided a home to her two brothers. Eddie lived with the Wilsons full time, while Stockton joined them for extended periods. Mrs. Wilson made sure that Eddie went to a speech therapist and tutored Stockton in the German required for his teaching career. Whatever difficulties they faced, her brothers found affection and support from their sister and her husband throughout their lives.

Ellen Wilson had initially learned German to help her husband with translations. She had also become well-read in the comparative politics that he taught. This allowed them to combine work and pleasure in their precious private time together. To supplement their income, Wilson gave guest lectures at the Johns Hopkins University in Baltimore. This meant frequent, painful separations during their early married years.

In 1890 Wilson accepted an offer to teach at Princeton University, in New Jersey, at a salary double what he had made at Bryn Mawr. Before they were settled in Princeton, however, the University of Illinois tried to entice the well-published Professor Wilson to become president of the campus in Urbana. Mrs. Wilson urged her husband to use the offer of a $6,000 salary as leverage to improve his situation at Princeton. He accepted her advice and persuaded Princeton to increase his housing allowance.

As life in Princeton became more permanent, the Wilsons purchased a lot near their rented home, 82 Liberty Place. Ellen Wilson worked with the New York architecture firm of Child and de Goll to develop plans, revising them until an affordable, two-story, half-timbered Tudor house was begun. Ellen Wilson wrote her husband of the details of the developing house. From Baltimore, he carefully responded to her suggestions and questions. By the time he returned, their new home was nearly completed.

Ellen Wilson had been wise to counsel her husband to remain at Princeton. In June 1902, the board of trustees elected him president of the university. The Wilson family moved from their special home to Prospect, the president's house, which happened to stand on land donated by her great-great-great uncle Nathaniel Fitz Randolph in 1753.

Mrs. Wilson's position as mistress of Prospect provided valuable experience for later responsibilities as First Lady. She served as the chief university hostess, and her house was the center for meetings and social events. It was during these meetings that her husband won support for changing Princeton from a gentleman's club to an institution of serious education.

In her first years at Princeton, Mrs. Wilson was reluctant about the "calling" she was expected to do. Upon her husband's urging, however, she made social rounds and became an admired member of the Princeton community. Admiration perhaps stemmed from this educated community's appreciation of her personal interests in reading and art. She always found time for education. Her reading list in 1895–1896 reflected the breadth of her interests: Plato, Homer, Herodotus, Walter Bagehot, John Richard Green, Mary Wilkins Freeman, Shakespeare, Milton, Coleridge, Keats, Browning, lesser-known English poets, and any new books on art. Her liberal education made her an impressive host for university affairs.

Ellen Wilson's refurbishing of Prospect made the president's house resemble the stately mansion of its youth. She replaced the Victorian decor with antiques. Convinced that formal entertaining needed formal colors, she introduced rose and beige as the dominant tones of the most public rooms. Outside, she redesigned the conventional French garden into one with more flowers and footpaths. Apart from the center garden she created a rose garden,

later replicated at the White House. She combed the basement for treasures, and restored marble mantels and chandeliers to their upstairs positions. Her later touches, such as the addition of a stained glass window—a gift of two trustees—made it an estate particularly reflective of the Wilsons' shared vision for Princeton. The window, which she designed, shows Aristotle holding his *Ethics*, with the inscription "The human good is the activity of the soul in accordance with virtue."

After her husband's first academic procession as president of the university, Mrs. Wilson invited the faculty as well as famous guests, including Samuel L. Clemens (Mark Twain), William Dean Howells, J. Pierpont Morgan, Henry C. Frick, and—to the shock of some of her neighbors—Booker T. Washington, to a luncheon. Although she often enjoyed interesting guests, she also grew bored with the relentless entertaining; yet she dismissed it as "all in the day's work,—no use grumbling."

Her husband recognized that his new position entailed more work for his wife. In September 1903, he called her his "sweet guardian and inspirer" whose eager support was "like wine." That year the Wilsons vacationed together in Europe. Ellen Wilson returned to Europe the next year with friends and her teenage daughter, Jessie. While his wife toured Italy and wrote detailed letters home of the art and architecture that delighted her, Wilson realized even more how his happiness depended upon her. He wrote to her in April 1904: "How deeply these days make me *know* my love for my precious little wife."

The satisfaction that Ellen Wilson drew from her marriage gave her little reason to doubt her life's path. Her marital happiness, however, was called into question in 1905 by the death of her brother Eddie and, in 1907, by her husband's interest in another woman. In the spring of 1905, Edward Axson, his wife, and small son drowned in an accident. Her brother's death depleted Mrs. Wilson's physical and spiritual resources, which were already taxed by illness in her own family that year. She turned to reading Hegel, Kant, and other philosophers in search of answers.

Wilson, who, loved Eddie like a son, shared his wife's grief and sought to restore her spirits by taking the family to Old Lyme, Connecticut, for the summer. In this art community, Ellen Wilson recovered some joy as she turned to painting landscapes in oil, a departure from her previous work in portraiture. Her spirits were somewhat improved by the time she returned to Princeton in the fall. Her melancholy, nonetheless, affected her marriage and may have contributed to her husband's flirtation with another woman.

Wilson vacationed in Bermuda in 1907. While there, he caught the attention of Mary Allen Hulbert Peck, a woman with marital problems of her own. She was fascinated with him, and he, in turn, was charmed by her. While loving letters to his wife continued, he also wrote affectionately to Mrs. Peck and arranged opportunities to spend time with her after returning to New Jersey. Although he later tried to veil the extent of his relationship with her by introducing her to his wife and family, Mrs. Wilson referred to her husband's dalliance as the most painful part of their marriage.

During this stressful episode, Ellen Wilson sought respite at the Lyme Summer School of Art. For the first time since her marriage she worked with a professional instructor, Frank DuMond, who had won a gold medal at the Paris Salon in 1890. Her husband recognized her return to serious painting as a declaration of independence. His letters during the summer of 1908 ask for reassurance of her love. Ellen Wilson's letters indicate that his professed need for her was comforting and cheering. Her spirits were further buoyed by new recognition of her talents and the lively, playful atmosphere she found living among artists—including many American impressionists—at a Griswold boardinghouse. She was one of the few summer students granted a private studio. In earlier returns to painting, Ellen Wilson had concentrated mostly on portraits, such as those of George Washington, William Gladstone, and Walter

Bagehot, which hung in her husband's study. She also experimented with landscapes in watercolor and oil, and copied an English landscape by the French artist Alfred-Louis Brunet-Debaines and a Madonna by Adolphe-Guillaume Bouguereau. Although there is no indication that Ellen Wilson exhibited her work at Old Lyme in 1908, DuMond told her that her painting was developing qualities that he thought were formerly lacking. Old Lyme became a haven to which Mrs. Wilson returned whenever possible.

Although Wilson loved sharing in the domestic details of his family, he left the daily activities of caring for them to his wife. She made all of her children's clothes, preferring her own designs over the latest fashions—an attribute favorably commented upon when, as First Lady, she rejected the idea of an expensive wardrobe. On Sundays the Wilsons observed the Sabbath, and Mrs. Wilson provided the children with religious instruction. When her children were young she followed her mother's example and tutored them at home, holding regular classes every weekday from October through June.

During their years at Prospect, the Wilson daughters matured into young women with ambitions of their own. Eleanor and Jessie attended both St. Mary's Junior College in Raleigh, North Carolina, and the Women's College of Baltimore. Jessie, a kindred spirit to her mother in looks and intellectual independence, won scholastic honors. By 1909, Jessie worked in a settlement house in Trenton, New Jersey. Eleanor enrolled in illustration classes at the Pennsylvania Academy of the Fine Arts. Margaret left the Women's College of Baltimore because of a nervous breakdown. She later moved to New York for voice lessons.

In 1910, Wilson resigned from Princeton to become New Jersey's Democratic gubernatorial candidate. His final years at Princeton had embroiled him in controversy over his plans to raise educational standards and democratize Princeton. As someone who sought a moral justification for all of his actions, the emotional strain involved with his work often led him to push himself beyond his capacities. For Mrs. Wilson, her husband's reaction to stress meant offering emotional support and dealing with his depression, headaches, and stomach illnesses.

After such disappointments, the Wilsons were delighted with the gubernatorial victory in November 1910. Two years as first family of New Jersey taught Ellen Wilson to develop a public persona. She learned that her family life was now a matter of public interest and became adept at giving interviews. Her position also allowed her to publicize projects. She became chair of the Department of Art and Music of the Princeton Present Day Club, a women's educational group that she helped start. In addition, she accepted a position as honorary director of the New Jersey State Charities Aid Society (NJSCAS). Progressives had increased the need for scientific investigation of social problems with the hope that more knowledge could provoke efficient reform. As honorary director of NJSCAS, Ellen Wilson inspected institutions such as the Soldiers' Home, a state home for juvenile delinquents, the tuberculosis sanitarium, and the state reformatory.

Whereas Ellen Wilson had grown tired of the entertaining required at the university, the political crowd now attracted to her husband renewed her interest. She recognized the integral role of social occasions to political affairs. When she learned that former Democratic presidential candidate William Jennings Bryan was visiting the state, she telegraphed her traveling husband to return home. She then invited Bryan to dinner, a meeting credited with easing tensions between her husband and Bryan.

The governor himself soon became a potential Democratic presidential nominee. Ellen Wilson, in a new step for a political spouse on the national level, joined her husband during the Democratic primary campaign. When Wilson's increased popularity provoked negative criticism from conservatives within the party who found the governor too progressive, Mrs. Wilson thwarted attempts to undermine his nomination. She played a significant part in putting to rest criticism of her husband's views circulated by Henry Watterson, editor of the Louisville *Courier-Journal*.

Ellen Wilson soon discovered that the rumors were not limited to her husband. A report claiming that she condoned women's smoking appeared, at a time when women's smoking was a hotly debated issue. Ellen Wilson took her own press release to reporters to refute the claim. She understood the relationship between her stands on moral and political issues and her husband's political image.

When Wilson won the Democratic nomination in July 1912, his wife knew that he would likely be the next president. The opposition had split when Theodore Roosevelt left the Republican Party to establish the Progressive Party. On Election Day, November 5, 1912, Ellen Wilson was the first to congratulate her husband.

Despite the new political demands, Ellen Wilson gave her interest in art a chance to come to fruition. Before moving to the White House, she held her first one-woman show. The show of fifty landscapes at the Arts and Crafts Guild in Philadelphia opened in February 1913 and sold twenty-four paintings. Over the years, Ellen Wilson slowly became more confident about her artistic talents. She joined Pen and Brush, Inc., a New York organization for professional women artists, and the Association of Women Painters and Sculptors. To test herself, in November 1911 she had entered one of her works under a pseudonym in a New York exhibition. After it placed in the competition, she revealed her identity to the owner of the gallery, who looked at some of her other works and encouraged her to enter another show. In 1912, her work *Autumn* won a place in the twenty-fifth exhibition of the Chicago Art Institute. These successes gave her the confidence she needed for the one-woman show.

Women were organizing in the Progressive Era for various reform efforts and for the vote. The Women's Democratic Club invited the Wilson women to a victory luncheon at the Waldorf-Astoria. Instead of the 500 expected guests, 1,500 people showed up. Wilson did not support women's suffrage at this time but did so after his wife's death. Ellen Wilson did not take a public stand on women's suffrage, but in this heightened climate of women's activism, organized women looked to the First Lady for leadership.

Magazines such as *Ladies' Home Journal*, *Harper's Weekly*, *Collier's*, *Current Opinion*, *Independent*, and *Good Housekeeping* featured profiles, photographs, and, on one occasion, two of her best landscape paintings: *The Lane* and *The River*. Authors noted that the Wilsons were the first Southerners since before the Civil War to occupy the White House.

On April 17, 1913, the Independent's Hester Hosford wrote:

> [T]hose who know Mrs. Wilson understand that she is a conservative Southern woman with simple tastes, desiring to set an example of unostentatious living to the women of America.... I have never known a woman who ... seems to have developed harmoniously her maternal instincts, her domestic tendencies, her social inclinations and her intellectual talents.

The author added that the First Lady supported legislative reform to improve conditions for working women and children. On the most heated women's issue, Hosford indicated Mrs. Wilson's caution: "[S]he has never taken any positive attitudes either for or against women's suffrage, but she does believe in an ultimate higher destiny for women." The article showed the competing expectations for women that colored Ellen Wilson's life. It reaffirmed her domestic talents while reporting on her reform efforts.

Ellen Wilson used her influence in an area unlikely to receive much attention without publicity from the First Lady. She joined Charlotte Everette Wise Hopkins, chair of the Women's Department of the District of Columbia's National Civic Federation, to improve the deplorable living conditions of African Americans in the city. Housing was the crucial need of African Americans crowded into dilapidated shacks

in Washington alleys. Mrs. Wilson toured many of the worst areas, speaking with residents without revealing her identity. After seeing the disgraceful living conditions and listening to residents' problems, she bought stock in a newly developed Sanitary Housing Company. She also became honorary chair of the housing committee of Mrs. Hopkins's department, offering her full support of the National Civic Federation alley bill to be introduced in Congress.

Ellen Wilson also toured the Government Printing Office and the Post Office Department. After the postmaster general failed to act on her recommendations to improve substandard working conditions, she called on her husband's chief adviser, Colonel Edward M. House, for help. Ellen Wilson's heated conversation with Colonel House caught the attention of other luncheon guests, prompting him to act upon her suggestions.

Ellen Wilson enjoyed her power to publicize issues, but she did not want her efforts to conflict with those of the president. While remembered for reforms in other areas, President Wilson did nothing to dismantle Jim Crow segregation. Activists concerned with racial justice were disappointed with the president. When one of the same black newspapers that had denounced the president later praised the First Lady's work among blacks, Ellen Wilson downplayed her work.

In 1913, Mrs. Wilson oversaw renovation of the family's living quarters. A new west-wing addition provided space needed for executive offices that could then be removed from the family quarters. The wide corridors to the family rooms were not well lit, and dark walls, in addition to maroon carpeting, made the area dreary. To remove the feeling of gloom, she replaced the carpet with a soft mahogany velvet and the green walls were re-covered in gold tones of a natural grass cloth. A number of the bedrooms were also renovated.

The refurbishing of the president's room was remembered as her most unique contribution to White House decor. The entire room was redone in blue and white, using materials handwoven by women from the mountains of Tennessee and North Carolina. The First Lady's recognition of the beauty of mountain crafts brought increased interest in the work of these women. Ellen Wilson later became honorary president of the Southern Industrial Association, which sponsored events to increase the market for mountain crafts.

During her years at Princeton, and then as the governor's wife, Ellen Wilson had learned to delegate responsibility. President Wilson's first cousin, Helen Woodrow Bones, served as Mrs. Wilson's private secretary during their Princeton years. Once in the White House, Ellen Wilson inherited a responsible White House staff and hired Isabelle Hagner as her social secretary. Hagner had previously served First Lady Edith Kermit Roosevelt but was replaced when Helen Herron Taft came to the White House. Ellen Wilson thus found time from her activities and innumerable correspondences to follow her husband's political agenda and discuss with him the issues he faced.

Mrs. Wilson threw all of her energy into her new role, but failing health limited her activities. Only four months after Ellen Wilson became First Lady, the family physician, Cary Travers Grayson, recommended that she abandon active participation in philanthropic work. Bright's disease, which debilitates the kidneys, was the problem. It is unclear when Dr. Grayson revealed the cause of her illness to Mrs. Wilson. For the rest of the summer of 1913, she and her daughters retired to Cornish, New Hampshire. She loved this beautiful summer retreat and the opportunity to participate in a Cornish artists' club.

The Wilsons announced Jessie's engagement to Francis Bowes Sayre in July 1913. From their retreat, Ellen Wilson and her daughters planned the White House wedding, which took place that November. The president joined his family briefly but, as always during separations, he wrote to his wife often. Only now, he unburdened anxiety about General Victoriano Huerta's regime in Mexico, unrest in Nicaragua, and his fight for tariff reform. Mrs. Wilson

offered her ideas, but the effect of political affairs on him was her chief concern. Her support helped sustain the president, who wrote to her, "Love alone . . . makes the world of anxious business endurable."

Jessie's wedding depleted some of Ellen Wilson's physical energy, but she returned to her full social schedule. She found time among the diplomatic receptions and other social engagements to return to Princeton with the White House's head gardener, Charles Henlock. He took some of her earlier landscaping ideas from the university back to Washington. The most lasting garden alteration she and Henlock made was the addition of the Rose Garden.

Everyone had been thrilled with Jessie's White House wedding, including the Wilsons. The president and his wife, however, were disturbed when their youngest daughter, Eleanor, decided to marry Secretary of the Treasury William G. McAdoo, a man twenty-six years her senior. Although they reconciled themselves to their daughter's decision, they nevertheless detested the gossip that appeared in newspapers about all of their daughters. Rumors that Margaret, too, was engaged pained Ellen Wilson, who worried about her oldest daughter's feelings of inadequacy.

In March 1914, Ellen Wilson slipped on the floor of her bedroom and spent the following week in bed. Doctors performed a minor surgery as a result of the fall. Unaware of her disease, her family attributed her slow recovery to overexertion and stress. By April, she was well enough to take short car trips, though she remained weak and suffered from acute indigestion, making eating almost impossible. What energy she could muster went into planning Eleanor's wedding, which took place on May 7, 1914.

After the wedding, Mrs. Wilson's health deteriorated rapidly. She found some comfort each morning in sitting in the Rose Garden, watching Henlock landscape. By this time she knew the real cause behind her decline. She and Dr. Grayson maintained a pretense that she would eventually get better.

In late July 1914, Dr. Grayson moved into the White House. The president remained unaware of his wife's condition until August 3. Wilson then summoned his family to the White House and permitted the first press release on the seriousness of his wife's illness.

On August 6, the president was told that his wife had only hours to live. In and out of consciousness, she sent warm looks to her husband and daughters. Before she died, she whispered to the doctor to take care of her husband.

The next morning the *Washington Post* announced her death. The paper commended her reform work. It reported that she had told the president that she would "go away" more cheerfully if the alley improvement bill were passed. The Senate adopted the bill in silence the day she died; the House soon followed. Describing her as a "woman of simple ways" and "a woman of the old-time conservative type," the obituary praised her as a "gentlewoman of the older generation." Such sentimentalism, however, obscured the transition in women's lives that her life represented. It also neglected the sophistication that allowed her to move from Rome, Georgia, to Princeton, to the governor's mansion, and to the White House so smoothly.

Ellen Axson Wilson brought her artistic talents and a growing commitment to social reform to her term as First Lady. Her rose garden became a lasting addition to the White House landscape and has served as the preferred setting for outdoor ceremonies. In addition, her introduction of mountain crafts to the president's room increased interest in regional art. While the political climate of the Progressive Era opened opportunities for social reform, few white reformers addressed the needs of African Americans. Ellen Wilson was the exception when she talked with black residents of Washington, D.C., neighborhoods and used the prestige of her position to publicize their concerns. Her sponsorship of legislation to improve living conditions in these alleys broadened the political potential of the institution of First Lady.

Funeral services for Ellen Wilson were held at the Presbyterian church in Rome,

Georgia, where thirty-one years earlier Wilson had met and courted her. When he returned, he faced an increasingly serious world crisis, as World War I intensified. In November he wrote to Nancy Saunders Toy, a family friend, that he just wanted to escape. He shared with her one of his reflections from this time of mourning: "The love that embraces mankind does not make us happy, but only the love that gives us the intimacy of a dear one who is in fact part of our very selves." In the spring of 1915 he wrote to his daughter Jessie: "My heart has somehow been stricken dumb. . . . She was beyond comparison the deepest, truest, noblest lover I ever knew." President Wilson had depended on his wife to nourish the private life from which he drew strength and ambition for his public activities. Without intimacy in his private life he struggled to stay focused on the serious public matters that confronted him. These feelings led to his second marriage to Edith Bolling Galt later in 1915.

Ellen Wilson was what her biographer has called a "First Lady between two worlds." In her case, the transition from the nineteenth-century ideal of true womanhood to the Progressive Era's New Woman was gradual. While Ellen Axson Wilson outgrew much of the nineteenth-century world of her parents, her life blended that century's expectations for middle-class women with those of the next.

Ellen Wilson found her husband's seriousness of purpose worthy of her love and dedication. President Wilson appreciated her, drawing inspiration from their intimacy and seeking refuge in twenty-nine years of cherished domestic tranquillity. Though Ellen Wilson valued this supportive role, she also made time for her artistic interests and incorporated independent projects into the positions that became hers as a result of her husband's career. Her illness curtailed her philanthropic work and investment in social reform legislation. She entered the White House at a time when middle-class women were turning to the state with social reform agendas. Thus, Charlotte Hopkins of the National Civic

Federation had looked to the First Lady as soon as she came to the capital. If Ellen Wilson had lived longer, the role she played with the National Civic Federation might have blossomed into leadership in other social reform initiatives.

BIBLIOGRAPHICAL ESSAY

The personal papers of Ellen Axson Wilson are located with the Woodrow Wilson Papers and the Ray Stannard Baker Papers, Manuscript Division, Library of Congress, and the Woodrow Wilson Collection, Firestone Library, Princeton University. The Carnegie Library in Rome, Georgia, contains a small collection of Ellen Wilson's papers about her life in that Georgia community. Her letters to her husband, family, and friends have been printed in Arthur S. Link et al., eds., *The Papers of Woodrow Wilson* (69 vols., Princeton, N.J., 1966–1994). Eleanor Wilson McAdoo, ed., *The Priceless Gift: The Love Letters of Woodrow Wilson and Ellen Axson Wilson* (New York, 1962), is a selection of their courtship letters.

Contemporary sources on Ellen Wilson include Hester E. Hosford, "New Ladies of the White House," *The Independent* 73 (November 21, 1912): 1159–1165; Mabel Porter Daggett, "Woodrow Wilson's Wife," *Good Housekeeping* 56 (March 1913): 316–323; "New Mistress of the White House," *Current Opinion* (March 1913): 195–196; Frances McGregor Gordon, "The Tact of Mrs. Woodrow Wilson," *Colliers* 50 (March 8, 1913): 13; and Mrs. Ernest P. Bicknell, "The Home-Maker of the White House," *Survey* 33 (October 3, 1914): 19. Ellen Maury Slayden, *Washington Wife: The Journal of Ellen Maury Slayden* (New York, 1962), has some comments about Ellen Wilson. Eleanor Wilson McAdoo, *The Woodrow Wilsons* (New York, 1937), is an account by Mrs. Wilson's daughter. Frances Wright Saunders, "Love and Guilt: Woodrow Wilson and Mary Hulbert," *American Heritage* 30 (April/May 1979): 68–77, provides an account of President Wilson's relationship with Mary Hulbert during his marriage to Ellen Wilson. Saunders, *First Lady Between Two Worlds: Ellen Axson Wilson* (Chapel Hill, N.C., 1985), is a thorough biography. All quotations, unless otherwise indicated, are from Saunders. *Ellen Axson Wilson* (Washington, D.C., 1993) is a brief catalog that accompanied an exhibition of Ellen Wilson's landscape art at the White House in 1993. *The Washington Post* (August 7, 1914) has the most complete obituary.

★★★　　★★★

Edith Bolling Galt Wilson

(1872–1961)

First Lady: 1915–1921

Lewis L. Gould

Edith Bolling was born in Wytheville, Virginia, on October 15, 1872. She was the seventh of eleven children born to William Holcombe Bolling and Sallie White Bolling. The family came from the Virginia planter class, and Edith proudly traced her ancestry back to the Native American woman Pocahontas of early Virginia. During the Civil War, however, her grandfather lost his plantation and slaves. Her father studied law at the University of Virginia, went into practice, and served as a judge when Edith was a child.

Until she was in her early teens, Edith did not attend a formal school, though her sisters went to local schools. She learned to read and write at home, but was not skilled in penmanship. She was not acquainted with much literature, though she did travel with her father on occasion.

At the age of fourteen, Edith entered Martha Washington College in Abingdon, Virginia. Despite its name, the school was a rigorous preparatory institution for girls during the 1887–1888 academic year when Edith was a student. She dropped out after a single year and spent the next twelve months at home. As she approached her sixteenth birthday, Edith's youthful beauty began to attract gentlemen admirers. In 1889–1890, she attended Powell's School in Richmond. After one year, the school abruptly closed when its headmaster became ill. Edith Bolling's formal education had ended.

In 1891, Edith went to Washington, D.C., to visit her older sister, Gertrude.

Gertrude was married to a member of the Galt family—owners of a jewelry and silver store in the nation's capital that catered to the city's white elite. While in Washington, Edith caught the eye of Norman Galt, a cousin of Gertrude's husband. A careful courtship began, which lasted for more than four years. By 1896, already in her mid-twenties, Edith decided to marry Galt. It was not a deeply romantic decision, but it served her personal needs at the time.

During the decade that followed, Norman Galt became the leading figure in the operation of the family business. Several members of Edith's family relied on the store to support them. Edith became pregnant in 1903 and gave birth to a son. The child lived only three days, and the experience left her unable to have more children. Five years later Norman Galt died, and Edith inherited the jewelry business.

Edith Galt hired a manager to run the store though she oversaw its daily operation. The business produced a steady and impressive profit. She became a well-known personality in Washington as she toured the fashionable areas of the city in her electric car—one of the first women to do so. She had enough money to live a good life, and she routinely took trips to Europe with her sister and a friend, Alice Gertrude Gordon, known as Altrude, whose suitors included Dr. Cary Grayson, the physician to President Woodrow Wilson. Through Grayson, Edith Galt thus drew closer to the White House and its occupant. Edith had already seen Wilson when he delivered his first message to Congress in April 1913.

Woodrow Wilson's first wife, Ellen Axson Wilson, had died of complications arising from Bright's disease during the summer of 1914. After her death on August 6, the president seemed to his close associates a stricken man. Wilson had been deeply in love with Ellen, and his personal loss produced a period of prolonged mourning. As the months passed into 1915, the pressures of World War I in Europe, the issues arising from it, and the demands of the presidency enabled Wilson to think of a future without his beloved Ellen. Wilson's daugh-

ters and others in his entourage, sensing that he needed feminine companionship for his future emotional stability, hoped that in time he would remarry. The president had few close male friends and had become accustomed to having deferential women in his private circle. The president was also a man who felt strong physical attractions to women.

Because Edith knew Dr. Grayson, she was introduced to Helen Woodrow Bones, one of the president's cousins, who lived in the White House. One day in March 1915, Edith was invited for tea at the White House, where, in the company of Helen and Dr. Grayson, she was introduced to President Wilson. Wilson said that she should come one evening for dinner. Edith accepted his offer, and on March 23, 1915, after the other guests had left, Wilson, Helen, and Edith talked together and the president read them some poetry. Wilson and the attractive Washington widow soon felt a mutual rapport.

In her autobiography, written some years after these events, Edith Wilson described her first meeting with Wilson as an accidental romantic encounter. As Edith later told the story, she turned a corner and met her fate. Hollywood adopted the story when a movie about Wilson was made in the 1940s, and it appears in many of the popular biographies about Edith Wilson. Most likely the meeting was carefully arranged and, like so much else in her memoirs, the anecdote is misleading.

Other dinners soon followed, and the president looked for other occasions when he might speak with Edith. They attended a baseball game, but most often rode around Washington in an open car. As the weeks passed, Edith became a more frequent visitor to the White House. They talked and read together. To the president, Edith was an alluring woman. She was tall, buxom, a little on the plump side, and she gave off an aura of genteel and discreet worldliness. Wilson was soon smitten.

By early May 1915, Wilson told Edith that he was in love with her. In a letter of May 5, 1915, he referred to his "pitiful inability to satisfy you and win you, to show you the true heart of my need, and of my nature." She declined his offer of marriage at that time, but indicated that their relationship should continue. It was still the custom for women not to accept a first proposal. Wilson was frustrated at the slowness with which their courtship was developing, and he poured his feelings into the lengthy handwritten letters that he now began to send to Edith daily. "Will you come to him some time," he wrote in the same letter, "without reserve, and make his strength complete?"

Affairs of state soon overshadowed the president's budding romance when German submarines torpedoed the Lusitania on May 7, 1915. As the nation debated whether the United States should go to war with Germany because of the 124 American lives lost when the *Lusitania* went down, Woodrow Wilson turned to Edith as one of his few confidants. They talked about what he should do to resolve this foreign policy dilemma. Their shared interest in his duties intensified their passion for one another, and they exchanged letters as prospective lovers.

Wilson used affairs of state as a seductive ally in his effort to persuade Edith to marry him. He revealed foreign policy secrets to her during the spring and summer of 1915. In a letter of June 18, for example, she told him that "I feel I am *sharing* your work and being taken into partnership as it were." She resisted the president's romantic ardor at first. Later that month, however, they became lovers, and she pledged on June 29, 1915, to "trust and accept my loved Lord, and to unite my life with his without doubts or misgivings."

Throughout the summer of 1915, Wilson and Edith operated as working partners. Edith Galt was not impressed with the men around Wilson, especially his close confidant Colonel Edward M. House of Texas. She asserted herself as his most intimate adviser. The couple now wanted to announce their engagement to the world, and set a date for their marriage.

For Wilson's friends and advisers, the prospect of a presidential marriage less than a year after the death of his first wife seemed a grave political risk. In some circles a second marriage of any kind was regarded as an affront to the spirit of the deceased husband or wife. More important to several of his colleagues, his chances in the 1916 presidential contest would suffer if his romance were seen as a betrayal of his late wife's memory. Wilson's reelection was far from certain, and the public reaction to a hasty marriage might cost him the White House. The senior members of Wilson's administration met informally in September 1915 to discuss what should be done.

Part of the problem went back to Wilson's first marriage. During the years between 1907 and 1910, Wilson had been more than friendly with a woman named Mary Allen Hulbert Peck, then a resident of Bermuda, where he had vacationed. Wilson wrote Mrs. Peck letters that expressed romantic feelings. They also discussed financial loans that Wilson made to help Mrs. Peck through some personal problems. The exact extent of Wilson's friendship with Mrs. Peck is still in dispute. He later implied that no physical relationship had existed, as did she, but the letters he sent her at least suggested a more passionate tie than a married man ought to have displayed. In the years that had followed, the loans to Mrs. Peck could be read as emotional blackmail. Whatever Wilson had meant, the letters were political dynamite. In 1912, rumors about the relationship with Mrs. Peck had been circulated among Republican circles but had not become part of the election debate.

In fact, Mrs. Peck, who thought that she would be the second Mrs. Wilson in due course, had no intention of publicizing her friendship with the president. The existence of the letters, however, gave Wilson's inner circle the leverage that they hoped would deter the president from marrying Edith. The secretary of the treasury, William G. McAdoo, who was also Wilson's son-in-law, made up a story about an anonymous letter from California. The letter supposedly said that Mrs. Peck had been circulating Wilson's private letters among friends and telling others that the president had loaned her money.

Wilson did not know that the basis of the story was false. He did know what he had done with Mrs. Peck, as well as what he had written to her, and he decided to bring Edith up to date on the situation. On September 18, 1915, in an emotional letter written in a shaky hand, Wilson asked her if he might come to her house to talk with her about what he termed an "extraordinary request."

Just what Wilson told Edith cannot be known for certain. Edith's account in her autobiography, *My Memoir*, is inaccurate in many details. It is probable that Wilson gave his fiancée an edited and innocuous version of his dealings with Mrs. Peck, playing down his romantic involvement and emphasizing his innocent motives. He stressed the partisan intentions of those who were using Mrs. Peck's letters in California, and he contended that the money he had loaned to her was on an innocent and uncompromising basis. The president offered to release Edith from her pledge to marry him and thus break their engagement. In a letter to her the next day, Wilson described his dalliance with Mrs. Peck as "a folly long ago loathed and repented of."

Edith's response was all that Wilson could have hoped for. After a night of emotional turmoil, she pledged to stand by him and not to desert him at his time of trial. As she put it in a letter to him on September 19, "I am not afraid of any gossip or threat, with your love as my shield." A few days later, Wilson consulted with his close adviser, Colonel House, about the Peck letters. House advised him to go ahead with his plans to marry Edith. On October 6, 1915, Wilson himself typed out a press release announcing his engagement to Edith Bolling Galt. The president simultaneously announced his support of women's suffrage in his home state of New Jersey—a reform he had earlier opposed. The gesture was designed to lessen political reaction to his second marriage.

The marriage took place on December 18, 1915, in the White House. The Wilsons honeymooned at Hot Springs, Virginia. No major adverse public reaction to the marriage materialized, and the episode may have humanized the austere Wilson to the public. The pressures of foreign policy crises and World War I soon brought the newlyweds back to Washington and their new life together in the White House. For Edith Wilson, her duties as confidante and personal assistant to the president were extensive. To assist her in the ceremonial side of her responsibilities, she recruited Edith Benham (later Helm) as her social secretary. Benham, who became a valuable aide to the First Lady, remained for four years before she had to resign because of an illness in 1920.

Edith Wilson did not pursue any personal causes as First Lady. Her overriding interest was her husband's health and welfare. She spent as much of each day as possible at his side. She was present when he dictated letters, and he continued to share state secrets with her. She devoted great attention to the president's diet and appearance. His taste in clothes improved, and he dressed in a more fashionable manner when they went out in the evenings to the vaudeville performances that he liked.

Individuals wrote to the First Lady as a way of gaining access to the president. She took care of routine mail that did not need his own attention, and she screened some of the correspondence herself. She gradually supplanted Colonel House as the president's closest adviser, much to the colonel's displeasure. She also disliked the president's own secretary, Joe Tumulty, and she began making plans to ease him out of his position after Wilson was reelected. Because of the war, official entertaining and other social functions were kept to a minimum in 1915–1916, and then canceled altogether once the United States became a belligerent in 1917. The Wilsons did relatively little other entertaining.

The 1916 election was close and hardfought. The Republican candidate, Charles Evans Hughes, was not a good politician, but the basic strength of his party made him a strong challenger to Wilson. Angry Republicans, who regarded Wilson as weak on foreign affairs, circulated scurrilous tales about the president and his wife. Rumor had it that Wilson and his new wife had known each other before Ellen Wilson had died. Word of these tales got back to the president and the First Lady, and they bitterly resented those who spread such venom. Wilson won a narrow victory over Hughes in November 1916.

Once the president was reelected, his wife, with the assistance of Colonel House, sought to have Joe Tumulty transferred out of the White House. They persuaded Wilson to offer his secretary a job elsewhere in the government. The loyal Tumulty refused to accept the new position, and Wilson allowed him to stay on. Edith Wilson also tried to induce House to accept the ambassadorship to Great Britain, but the clever colonel would have none of that initiative.

Five months after the election, in April 1917, the United States entered World War I against Germany and its allies. Edith Wilson endeavored to set an example of frugality and economy. She asked the other wives of cabinet members to join her in buying only plain clothes and living as simply as possible. To aid the war effort, she organized a Red Cross unit at the White House and volunteered at a canteen that the Red Cross set up at Washington's Union Station. Out of her efforts came pajamas, sheets, and other clothing and supplies for the troops in Europe. As one of her charitable acts during World War I, Mrs. Wilson allowed a flock of Virginia sheep to graze on the White House lawn. That action was designed to reduce the cost of mowing. When the sheep were ready to be sheared, she arranged for the wool to be donated to the states for charitable auctions. The resulting sales raised over $50,000.

When an armistice ended the fighting in November 1918, President Wilson decided to attend the peace conference in Paris. His wife accompanied him, becoming the first president's wife to travel to Europe while her husband was in office. The American delegation departed on December 4, 1918. Edith Wilson experienced the adulation that greeted her husband, who was seen as the savior of Western Europe. The First Lady enjoyed the attention that followed her. The European press described her social secretary, Edith Helm, as a lady-in-waiting. In her memoirs, Helm recalled how crowds on the streets of Paris would shout "Vive Madame Wilson" when the First Lady passed.

During the course of the peace conference, President Wilson and Colonel House saw their close personal relationship end because of disagreements over specific provisions of the settlement. Edith Wilson had long been suspicious of the colonel, and she encouraged her husband's sense of betrayal. When Wilson became ill in late March 1919, his wife nursed him through the crisis. The president's physical resources were running out.

The Treaty of Versailles was signed on June 28, 1919, and the Wilsons returned to Washington to seek the approval of the United States Senate for the pact that contained the League of Nations with the United States as full member. President Wilson regarded the treaty as the culmination of his efforts to achieve a lasting peace, and the First Lady fully shared his deep commitment to its ratification.

It soon became apparent, however, that the treaty faced severe problems in the Senate. Henry Cabot Lodge, a Massachusetts Republican, led the opposition to President Wilson. Other senators wanted changes—or reservations—in the pact before they agreed to it. During the summer of 1919, as the chances for approval of the treaty lessened, the president decided to take his case in person to the American people. The Wilsons left on a special presidential train on September 3, 1919, for an extended campaign swing designed to pressure the Senate through aroused public opinion.

During the three weeks that followed, the First Lady watched as her husband poured his dwindling physical energies into the fight. While they were on the West Coast, she and Wilson had a brief, impersonal meeting with Mary Hulbert Peck, who was now only a fading memory from the president's emotional past. By September 25, 1919, President Wilson's campaign seemed to be gaining momentum. He made an impassioned speech in Pueblo, Colorado, that impressed many of his listeners with its warnings about what the United States would face if the treaty failed. However, his health was breaking under the strain of his exertions. After the Pueblo speech, Wilson complained of a severe headache. He awoke the next morning with one side of his face fallen and tears in his eyes. Dr. Grayson insisted that the remaining stops on the tour be canceled and that the presidential party return at once to the White House so that Wilson could rest from his fatigue. Edith Wilson decided at this early stage of her husband's illness not to disclose either to him or to the nation the extent of his physical ailments.

Within a few days, the Wilsons were once again home and medical specialists were called in to diagnose the president's condition. Before they could examine the president, he had a major stroke on October 2, 1919. He complained of some numbness in both his left leg and left arm. As Edith Wilson helped him toward the bathroom, he collapsed. Grayson rushed a specialist to the president's side later that afternoon. The conclusion was that the president had experienced a significant stroke, but the extent of his disability as a result could not be determined for some time.

Subsequent reports claimed that Wilson retained his mental faculties but lacked the physical reserves to carry on the duties of the presidency for the period extending from the early part of October 1919 through January 1920. After that, Wilson was able to function only minimally as president. His political skills were diminished and he had lost his capacity to govern with the energy and insight that had marked his administration in the past.

The role played by Edith Wilson during these events has become a matter of great historical controversy. Some writers have alleged that she functioned as the first woman president during the period of her husband's illness. In her memoirs, Edith Wilson denied that charge: "I myself never made a single decision regarding the disposition of public affairs. . . . The only decision that was mine was what was important and what was not, and the very important decision of when to present matters to my husband." Understanding how the president's wife performed during this medical crisis is central to an analysis of her historical impact on the institution of First Lady.

The first key decision that Edith Wilson made—in consultation with Grayson and the other doctors who attended the president—was that Wilson should not resign his office. At the time, there was no provision in the Constitution about the physical disability of a president. Moreover, the vice president, Thomas Riley Marshall, was not regarded as a strong political figure.

Edith Wilson asked the doctors whether the president should step down and, according to her account, they told her that staying at his post would speed his recovery most. However, it is unlikely that she actually got that advice from Wilson's doctors, and the evidence indicates that, from the first, she was determined that her husband should not leave the presidency.

A second significant judgment on Edith Wilson's part was that the public should not learn the full extent of the president's illness. She even insisted that members of the cabinet not be briefed on what was wrong with the president. She feared the political consequences of disclosing the fact that Wilson had had a stroke. The result was that the First Lady became engaged in a campaign to mislead the nation about what had happened to the president. One historian of this episode, John M. Cooper, described Edith Wilson's actions as a "cover-up that deprived the public of vital information." Recently discovered medical reports affirm the historian's claim.

In the interests of relieving the burdens on her husband, Edith Wilson took on as much of the important procedural duties of the presidency as she could handle. Significant state documents came to her and she presented them to Wilson for his consideration when he felt strong enough to look at them. She decided, however, which materials the president saw, and she also screened the few people who were allowed to visit him. Tumulty sent all the relevant documents to her, and she proceeded on the basis of the confidence she felt after having worked closely with her husband for the preceding four years.

Despite Edith Wilson's best efforts to deal with the flow of public business that poured into the White House, the machinery of government became impaired as Wilson slowly recovered. A number of significant governmental and diplomatic appointments remained vacant, and pressing domestic and foreign policy questions had to be postponed until the president could deal with them himself. Critics of Edith Wilson have concluded that the United States did not have a functioning government for much of the remainder of Woodrow Wilson's term.

The most important policy question that the Wilsons faced during this period was the issue of Senate action on the League of Nations. Here Edith Wilson acted as a go-between for her husband with the leader of the Senate Democrats, Gilbert M. Hitchcock of Nebraska. While it is unlikely that President Wilson would have compromised with his Republican opponents in any case, his wife acted in a manner that prevented him from understanding the changing facts of the situation from the time his illness began. In her memoirs, Mrs. Wilson reported that she presented the idea of a possible compromise to him in November 1919. When he told her it was "[b]etter a thousand times to go down fighting than to dip your colours to dishonourable compromise," she resolved that, from then on, she would stand firmly against anything less than the ratification of the Treaty of Versailles that her husband wanted.

In one instance, the First Lady acted to block a foreign visitor from seeing her husband. When Edward Grey, former foreign secretary of Great Britain, came to the United States to push for ratification of the peace treaty, Mrs. Wilson refused to allow him to see her husband unless he first sent home one of his close aides. The aide had reportedly repeated some indecent stories regarding Edith Wilson and the 1916 elec-

tion. Without concrete evidence, Grey refused to dismiss his subordinate, and the First Lady, for her part, would not allow him access to the president. The incident fed the Washington gossip mills.

While making sure that Colonel House did not resume his close friendship with her ailing husband, Edith Wilson also worked to undermine Wilson's confidence in his secretary of state, Robert Lansing. She had never been impressed with Lansing's talents, and resented his influence in the government. When Lansing mentioned a subject that had already been raised with the president in January 1920, Mrs. Wilson told him: "The President does not like being told a thing twice." In February, Wilson asked for Lansing's resignation on the grounds that he had held meetings of the cabinet during the president's illness without permission. Mrs. Wilson's part in the decision is not clear, but she obviously regarded Lansing as a disloyal figure.

Despite the First Lady's attempts to prevent knowledge of her husband's condition from leaking out, word inevitably reached the public regarding the true state of his health. As a result, rumors circulated that the president was being held in captivity or that his wife was, in fact, running the nation's business. The government appeared to be paralyzed. A friend of Wilson's, the journalist Ray Stannard Baker, noted in his diary for February 15, 1920, that "[i]t seemed to me as I went around Washington the other day as though our government had gone out of business."

The political difficulties that the Wilson administration confronted during 1920 posed a dilemma for the First Lady. As a presidential aide, Edith Wilson was not very successful. Had she endeavored to persuade her husband to compromise further on the Treaty of Versailles, she might well have endangered his health to an even greater extent.

The institutional legacy that Edith Wilson left for future First Ladies was the historical conviction in unofficial Washington that she had overreached the proper limits of the role of a presidential wife. Clichés about "petticoat government" and the "first woman president" became part of the conventional wisdom about her performance. Though these were exaggerations of what she had done, they were readily invoked as criticisms of Mrs. Wilson's successors when they intruded on what was believed to be the masculine realm of national politics.

The Wilson presidency ran on through 1920. Edith advised her husband to seek a third nomination from the Democratic Party. She also opposed the presidential candidacy of McAdoo, whom she blamed for the 1915 attempt to break up her relationship with Wilson. Neither Wilson nor McAdoo received the nomination, which eventually fell to Governor James M. Cox of Ohio. Cox's vice presidential running mate was Assistant Secretary of the Navy Franklin Delano Roosevelt. The Democrats lost to Republican Warren G. Harding. On March 4, 1921, the day of Harding's inauguration, the Wilsons left the White House and took up residence on S Street in Washington. They lived there until Wilson's death in February 1924. During the course of arranging for her husband's funeral services, Edith Wilson made sure that Senator Henry Cabot Lodge did not attend.

After Wilson's death, the former First Lady took charge of his historical reputation. She controlled the literary rights to his personal papers, and insisted that only those Wilsonian associates of whom she approved were allowed to consult or quote from the president's letters. When Colonel House wrote his memoirs during the mid-1920s, for instance, he was not allowed to print any of the letters he had received from Wilson. Mrs. Wilson worked closely with Ray Stannard Baker, her husband's official biographer, when he prepared his eight-volume life of the president.

In 1939, Edith Bolling Wilson published her own account of her life with Woodrow Wilson under the title *My Memoir*. Prepared two decades after the events she recounted, the book drew heavily on her romantic vision of her years with Wilson. As a result, she produced a book that evokes the spirit of their relationship but is often

prejudiced as well as inaccurate about facts and interpretation.

Later in life, Edith Wilson donated her house on S Street in Washington to the National Trust for Historic Preservation and was active in having Wilson's birthplace in Staunton, Virginia, made a national shrine. She identified herself with the fortunes of the Democratic Party and supported the presidential candidacy of John F. Kennedy in 1960. She attended the inauguration of President Kennedy in January 1961. In November 1961, Edith Wilson suffered a respiratory infection. She died a month later, on December 28, 1961, in Washington, D.C.

Because of her crucial role during her husband's serious illness from 1919 to 1921, Edith Bolling Wilson has become one of the most controversial of all the First Ladies. The extent to which she wielded presidential authority and acted as a kind of surrogate chief executive is still very much disputed though increasingly apparent. Her performance in the White House has often been depicted as an example of the dangers that might arise whenever First Ladies seek to exercise real power. Mrs. Wilson's influence over her husband's actions and her impact on his decisions represented an important aspect of the troubled last months of his presidency.

BIBLIOGRAPHICAL ESSAY

Edith Bolling Wilson's personal papers are located in the Manuscript Division, Library of Congress, Washington, D.C. The Woodrow Wilson Papers are available on microfilm in a collection that is also housed at the Library of Congress. The most convenient way to follow Edith Wilson's marriage to Woodrow Wilson and her role in the White House is in Arthur S. Link et al., eds., *The Papers of Woodrow Wilson* (69 vols., Princeton, N.J., 1966–1994). Link reprints all of the most important letters and other documents relating to the courtship and the period when Mrs. Wilson dealt with official matters after her husband's 1919 illness. Unless otherwise indicated, all quotations come from this source.

Edith Bolling Wilson, *My Memoir* (Indianapolis, 1938), provides the First Lady's recollections of her courtship and the crisis of her husband's illness. Because of the many errors it contains, it cannot be regarded as an accurate account of what took place, but it does give a strong sense of her own views and personality. There are a number of biographies of Edith Wilson. Alden Hatch, *First Lady Extraordinary* (New York, 1961), was done with Mrs. Wilson's help. Ishbel Ross, *Power with Grace* (New York, 1975), did not have the advantage of the full documentary record. Tom Shachtman, *Edith & Woodrow: A Presidential Romance* (New York, 1981), draws on the Wilson Papers, but is rather breathless and overheated in its treatment of the relationship.

Other scholars have examined Edith Wilson's performance as First Lady. Judith L. Weaver, "Edith Bolling Wilson as First Lady: A Study in the Power of Personality, 1919–1920," *Presidential Studies Quarterly* 15 (Winter 1985): 33–50, is insightful. August Hecksher, *Woodrow Wilson* (New York, 1991), has some interesting comments on Wilson's intimate relationships with both of his wives and the other women in his life. John Milton Cooper, Jr., "Disability in the White House: The Case of Woodrow Wilson," in Frank Freidel and William Pencak, eds., *The White House: The First Two Hundred Years* (Boston, 1993), 75–99, reaches intelligent conclusions about Mrs. Wilson's role. Phyllis Lee Levin is writing a new biography of Edith Wilson. An obituary appeared in the *New York Times* (December 29, 1961).

★★★ ★★★

Florence Mabel Kling Harding

(1860–1924)

First Lady: 1921–1923

Carl Sferrazza Anthony

Florence Mabel Kling was born on August 15, 1860, to Amos Kling and Louise Bouton Kling. Much of Florence's story is shrouded in uncertainty. Whether by accident, her own hand, or that of another, many primary sources about her no longer exist. Even county records regarding her father's substantial real estate and business records are not extant. Supposition and legend, therefore, have often substituted in the absence of documentation.

Florence's father, Amos Kling, was born on June 13, 1833, in Lancaster County, Pennsylvania. He was educated in Mansfield, Ohio, and later took business courses there. The origin of the Kling family is obscure. A genealogical book on a prominent Kling family, published during the

Harding administration, points out that no definitive connection could be made between the First Lady's family and the Klings of the book. What is known is that the Klings originated in southwestern Germany and, sometime in the late eighteenth or early nineteenth century, immigrated to Pennsylvania, settling in the Lancaster area before migrating to Mansfield, Ohio.

During a family visit to a friend in New Canaan, Connecticut, Amos Kling met Louise Bouton, an only child. The Bouton family history is well documented. Originating in northern France, the Boutons were persecuted as Protestants and moved to England. From there, in the 1630s, they immigrated to Connecticut, settling in New Canaan. The family was prominent in the local Methodist church, and Louise was noted as a remarkable singer in the church choir. She was educated in the local public school. Following a period of courtship, Amos Kling and Louise Bouton were married in 1859. Kling returned to Marion, Ohio, with his new wife and in-laws.

Kling soon began amassing the fortune that would make him the wealthiest man in Marion. He opened a hardware sales business on South Main Street where, above the store, his first child, Florence Mabel, was born. Two sons, Clifford and Vetallis, followed. There is little evidence, that Florence ever formed a close relationship with her brothers, although in later years she actively played the role of eldest child, directing them by letter in business and behavior.

Florence was an active child. She was an ardent bicyclist, ice skater, bobsledder, and roller skater. She was noted as Marion's best horsewoman, and won the blue ribbon in many local equestrian competitions. One account, left by her childhood friend Margaret Younkins, told of her wildly driving friends in an open carriage. Another anecdote, chronicled by later Harding coworker Jack Warwick, recounted how she had subdued her massive horse "Billy" by jumping from him, pulling the animal down, and pinning his head to the ground with her knee, until he calmed down. Her physical strength was often viewed as an oddity; few young girls of that era were encouraged to participate in such vigorous activities. Though she was often labeled "masculine" by contemporaries, Florence's lack of social convention never seemed to bother her. This may have been because she was also trained in the traditional "feminine" arts of needlepoint, housekeeping, and language by her mother.

Louise Kling, however, was an invalid, and Florence was more greatly under the influence and control of her father. By all accounts, Amos Kling was a tyrannical parent who did not hesitate to strike his children if they disobeyed his strict rules for behavior. When, for example, the young Florence was not back in the large stone

Kling mansion by her father's imposed curfew, he simply locked the door for the night. Florence was expected to fend for herself.

Florence was educated in the local public schools, but her father believed that it was important for her also to be adroit in finance. By the time Florence was a teenager, Kling's enterprises included farm horse sales, banking and investment, vast real estate leasing, and sales of both city lots and farming tracts, as well as expansion of his hardware sales business. In most aspects of his work, Kling included his daughter. She worked with him behind the counters at the hardware store and traveled with him to the outlying farm areas as he collected rents. She learned everything from the bulk price of nails to balancing accounting books.

Kling also encouraged his daughter's musical talent. Having enjoyed piano lessons since childhood, Florence was permitted to board at school. Although no exact records remain, sometime in her late teens, Florence attended at least one semester at the newly founded Cincinnati Conservatory of Music. She later recalled fondly that, while in Cincinnati, she had frequently attended opera performances.

At the age of nineteen, Florence became pregnant. In March 1880, she eloped with her beau and neighbor, Henry Atherton DeWolfe. He was also nineteen years old, and shared her interest in roller skating. It was at the local skating rink that he and Florence had courted. Her child, Marshall, was born on September 22, 1880, in the nearby town of Prospect. The couple moved to another nearby town, Galion, where Henry managed the new roller-skating rink. The details of his estrangement from Florence remain unclear, but there was a falling out. He left Florence and the child. Florence filed for divorce on June 12, 1886, citing DeWolfe's "gross neglect of duty."

After the divorce, Florence returned to Marion with her son and resumed her maiden name. Initially shunned by her father, she took rooms with a friend and worked as a piano teacher. Money and groceries were also provided to her by Henry DeWolfe's kindly father, Simon. In time,

Kling relented and, for part of the time, permitted his grandson Marshall to live with his family.

Sometime during the late 1880s, Florence met Warren Gamaliel Harding. Harding was five years her junior and was originally from nearby Blooming Grove, Ohio, but he and his family had relocated to Marion. Harding was a part owner (later the sole owner) of a small newspaper that became the *Marion Star*. There are several versions of his meeting with Florence, and how their courtship developed. One account has it that they met by chance, on the street. Another claims that it was at a Methodist church social function that Harding, a Baptist, attended. A third version says that they met at a local skating rink.

In the vernacular of the day, Harding was an avowed "sporting lady's man." It was Florence who—at least initially—pursued him. While she may have lacked what was considered physical beauty at that time, Florence possessed many other attributes, among them a keen fiscal acumen. And it was clear that she was very deeply in love with him.

To Harding, Florence represented a certain degree of social respectability, and, some suggest, financial opportunity as the daughter of Amos Kling. Kling, however, remained adamantly opposed to the match and even threatened Harding if he were to marry Florence. On several occasions, Kling attempted, without success, to stall or damage Harding's efforts at small investments and his involvement in civic activities. Despite her father's efforts to prevent the union, and as a symbol of her own independent personality, Florence Kling married Warren Harding on July 8, 1891, in the large wood home they were building on Mount Vernon Avenue.

The Hardings never had any children of their own. The reasons are unclear, although Harding's doctor later said that Harding was infertile because of a childhood case of mumps. The marriage was unconventional. Florence Harding was a working wife, unlike most middle-class women during the 1890s. Her unsalaried,

full-time position as business and circulation manager began in late 1892, following her husband's nervous breakdown. While Harding recuperated at Battle Creek Sanitarium for several weeks, the *Star*'s circulation manager quit. The next morning, Mrs. Harding rode her bicycle down to the offices and assumed responsibility. "I went down there intending to help out for a few days, and I stayed fourteen years," she later told Norman Thomas, a former newsboy who relayed the quote to Samuel Hopkins Adams in the late 1930s.

The pages of perfect columns in the account books of the *Star*, preserved at the Harding home in Marion, are all in Florence Harding's strong hand. She not only served as comptroller of the enterprise, but also created a home delivery service, enlisting dozens of local young men to serve as paperboys. Under her control, the newspaper flourished. Although recognized as the newspaper's administrative chief, she rarely involved herself in the editorial aspects of the *Star*.

Florence Harding's home life occasionally included Marshall. Considering that she chose to put all of her energy into her work at the *Star*, her part-time role as a mother is not necessarily a reflection of indifference to him. A room was provided for him in the Harding home, but most likely he continued to live with his grandfather Kling. In his 1898 high school graduation book, he is listed in one place as Marshall DeWolfe, and in another as Marshall Kling. When he later married Esther Naomi Neely in 1906 and fathered two children—Eugenia in 1911 and George Warren in 1914—Florence Harding took more of an interest in her growing family. Personal letters written after her son's death in 1915 to her grandchildren and daughter-in-law prove that she played an active role in their well-being. In 1905, Amos Kling forgave and accepted his daughter and her husband—fifteen years after their marriage. On June 26, 1906, her father married Caroline Beatty Denman. The Klings and the Hardings made their first trip to Europe together in 1907.

In Marion, as Warren Harding's prominence rose as a leading "booster" of local industry and as the *Star* became an influential daily in Ohio, Florence Harding assumed an increasingly public role. She lived with him part-time in Columbus when he served in the state senate (1899–1903) and as lieutenant governor (1904–1905). She developed a close friendship with Republican political figure Harry Micajah Daugherty, apart from his alliance with Harding. Although Harding lost in his 1910 run for governor, he nevertheless became one of Ohio's most promising Republicans. Mrs. Harding joined her husband for a conference with President William Howard Taft in 1910, and again at the 1911 White House celebration of the Tafts' silver wedding anniversary.

As he rose in political prominence, Harding also proved unconventional, in the sense that he made frequent references to his wife and acknowledged her influence over him. In 1910, according to biographer Francis Russell, Harding concluded the last speech of his campaign for governor by remarking, "I owe allegiance to only one boss—and she sits right over there in that box. She's a mighty good one too." According to Daugherty's memoirs, Florence Harding was a driving force in persuading her husband to run for the U.S. Senate, to which he was elected in 1914.

Prior to her coming to Washington, however, Mrs. Harding suffered serious health problems—all associated with her kidney functions. Shortly after her marriage, she had befriended Charles Sawyer and his wife, Mandy. Sawyer, who became the leading homeopathic doctor in Marion, opened up a famous sanitarium for the treatment of both mental and physical ailments. He became the Hardings' closest confidant in Marion, and Florence Harding relied on him greatly. In 1905, she was put under Sawyer's care at Grant Hospital in Columbus. There is indication that a surgeon may have removed one of her dysfunctional kidneys at that time. Again in 1913, she suffered a kidney attack, provoked by her weak heart, and Dr. Sawyer did not expect her to live. Again, she rallied.

Florence Harding also experienced emotional problems, resulting largely— it now seems clear—from her husband's love relationship with Carrie Fulton Phillips, a friend of Mrs. Harding's and the wife of local dry goods salesman James Phillips. The affair did not come to full public knowledge until the 1960s, when a cache of Harding's love letters to Mrs. Phillips was discovered. The Hardings and Phillipses socialized and even traveled to Europe together. The two women became close friends through a local women's social group known as the Twigs. When or how Florence Harding discovered the love affair is not entirely clear, but the letters indicate that she did know of it. The Harding marriage survived the ordeal and the love affair eventually ceased. Not only would a divorce have threatened Harding's political future, but by this time the Hardings had become, if not romantic, at least political and business, partners.

In 1915, however, when she came to Washington as the wife of a senator, Florence Harding commenced what was to become the most fulfilling companionship of her life: her friendship with the heiress Evalyn Walsh McLean. The daughter of an Irish immigrant who literally discovered a gold mine, Evalyn Walsh was married to Edward Beale "Ned" McLean, the owner of the *Washington Post, Cincinnati Enquirer*, and a multitude of lucrative investments. The McLeans owned homes in Ohio, Virginia, Florida, Maine, and Washington, D.C.

Florence Harding met Evalyn through her friend Alice Roosevelt Longworth, the daughter of former president Theodore Roosevelt and the wife of Cincinnati congressman Nicholas Longworth. Despite their twenty-six-year age difference, the two women became fast friends. Evalyn guided Mrs. Harding on the fine points of Washington society life and helped choose her increasingly extravagant wardrobe. They took motor trips and vacations together and shared a love of animals. They also found a bond in their curiosity about the occult.

During her Washington years, Florence Harding regularly consulted an astrologer,

Marcia Champrey. As notations in her schedule book indicate, she believed in zodiac readings. Later, when her husband was seeking the presidency and while he served in that office, Mrs. Harding continued to rely on her astrologer for answers to questions about cabinet members and other men serving in the administration.

On the three greatest political issues of the day, Florence Harding claimed to be prosuffrage, anti–League of Nations, and "wet" on the issue of Prohibition. Former First Lady Helen Herron Taft had expressed her support of suffrage, but Florence Harding boldly declared: "Yes, I am a suffragist." Later, during Harding's acceptance speech, he referred to the complete involvement of women in the political process, prompting a reporter to lean toward Mrs. Harding and ask: "A mark of your influence, no doubt?" She nodded affirmatively and smiled.

Florence Harding joined forces with Alice Longworth as an "Irreconcilable" Republican who did not support Woodrow Wilson's proposal for American entry into the League of Nations in any form. During the strongly anti-German sentiments of the period, Mrs. Harding attempted to deny her own German ancestry by claiming she was "Holland Dutch." Though there is no evidence to indicate that she ever indulged frequently in alcoholic beverages, Mrs. Harding nevertheless strongly opposed the Eighteenth Amendment, which brought about Prohibition.

During the Senate years, Florence Harding personally befriended some of her husband's associates, including New Mexico Senator Albert B. Fall, Harry Daugherty's informal assistant Jess Smith, and Colonel Charles Forbes. These men hitched themselves to Harding's star, but would later be at the core of the scandals that ruined his reputation as president.

During World War I, Florence Harding joined the "Ladies of the Senate." This group of Senate wives was formed by Lois Marshall, wife of Vice President Thomas Riley Marshall, who presided over the Senate. They participated in full-time Red Cross volunteer efforts in behalf of the American soldiers, including rolling bandages and knitting skullcaps, pajamas, and wool socks. Mrs. Harding worked at Union Station, as did First Lady Edith Wilson, Eleanor Roosevelt—the wife of Assistant Secretary of the Navy Franklin D. Roosevelt—Alice Longworth, and Evalyn McLean. It was Evalyn who first brought Florence Harding to the Walter Reed Hospital in Washington, where hundreds of wounded, shellshocked, and blinded soldiers were being cared for. Along with Evalyn, she quickly adopted the wards as "my boys."

Florence Harding expressed contradicting sentiments when her husband entered the 1920 presidential race. First, she pushed her husband to remain in the primaries, despite losses. Later, when he received the presidential nomination at the Chicago convention, she told reporters "I see nothing but tragedy," and indicated regret over his candidacy. She emphasized her skill at cooking waffles and housekeeping to some reporters, while focusing on her business acumen and refusal to wear the "bond" of a wedding ring to others. She eagerly served as a source for political reporters, but refused to be quoted directly on issues herself.

Whether Florence Harding knew the extent of the relationship between her husband and Nan Britton—daughter of her friend Mary Britton—is unclear. Nan Britton claimed to have had a long-term love affair with Harding and named him as the father of her child, Elizabeth Ann, born in 1919. In one campaign speech, Harding referred to his wife as a "good scout who knows all my faults and yet has stuck with me all the way."

During the campaign, conducted largely from the front porch of the Harding home, Florence Harding was a visible presence. She attended all of her husband's speeches and made a point of greeting women's groups and the spouses of men's groups. She continually affirmed her support for suffrage, triumphantly proclaiming that American women would, at last, be able to vote for president for the first time in November. She particularly encouraged women to become involved in politics.

When a strong whispering campaign broke into print that Harding had African-American ancestors, members of the campaign staff were uncertain how to respond. Coming into a meeting, Florence boldly announced: "I'm telling all you people that Warren Harding is not going to make any statement." She herself became a minor campaign issue when questions about her grandchildren raised others about her first marriage. Without mentioning divorce, she stated that DeWolfe had died before she had married Harding. That, of course, was a fabrication. She had divorced DeWolfe in 1886, and he died in 1894. She had married Harding in 1891.

On November 2, 1920, Florence Harding became the first woman to vote for her husband for president of the United States. Following Harding's victory, his wife took a role in choosing certain members of his staff and cabinet. Her influence brought about several appointments: Charles Forbes was assigned a role that would evolve into the first director of the new Veterans Bureau; Dr. Sawyer became brigadier general of the Army Medical Corps; and Ora "Reddy" Baldiner became the president's military aide. Florence Harding cajoled Andrew Mellon into accepting the post of secretary of the treasury, and she may also have encouraged the choice of Albert B. Fall as secretary of the interior. She strongly supported the choice of her friend Harry Daugherty as attorney general when word of his nomination resulted in an intraparty protest. When Harding delivered his inaugural address on March 4, 1921, it was only after his wife had blue-penciled it.

Florence Harding continued her political advisory role, sometimes overtly, as First Lady. On one occasion, she burst into the Oval Office while the president was working on his State of the Union speech and refused to leave until he had deleted a proposal to limit the president to one six-year term. She convinced her husband to rewrite a speech that indicated his willingness to consider U.S. entry into the League of Nations. She pressed her husband to support the first all-women's federal prison, an idea begun by the federal prison director and her in-law Heber Votaw. As she told one White House staff member about her professional relationship with the president, "He does well when he listens to me and poorly when he does not." The president admitted to a friend in a letter that his wife was "too busy directing the affairs of government. . . . She is full fledged in expressing her opinion as to how the Executive should perform his duties."

The First Lady's most consistent political work was also her "project," which the press and public associated with her—the care of wounded and hospitalized veterans of World War I. The public saw her accepting crafts from blinded veterans, or hosting mammoth garden parties for those in local hospitals, or making her weekly rounds at Walter Reed Hospital, where she knew many of the patients by name. However, she also worked assiduously in their behalf behind the scenes.

Whenever she privately received a complaint from a veteran or a member of his family, whether about care or placement in a federal hospital, the First Lady had the individual situation investigated. She reviewed the operating budgets and expenditures of the Veterans Bureau, from vehicles to hospital beds. With her special interest in the bureau, she also encouraged individuals within the system to inform her privately of various machinations and apparent wrongdoings. It was with her support that Dr. Sawyer continued investigating the bureau's chief, Charles Forbes, which ultimately led to the discovery of criminal activities.

Although she did not take part in any public debate about the veterans, Florence Harding did argue such issues within the official circle of cabinet members and advisers. Because of the dearth of primary source material, the degree of her success is difficult to gauge, though her expressions of serious intent about the well-being of enlisted men are clear. One 1921 letter, from Secretary of the Navy Edwin Denby, particularly suggests this, as he wrote her that "in the case of your special interest in matters pertaining to the Navy, you will express to me what you would like to have done." There is also some suggestion that she privately opposed President Harding's veto of a bonus bill for the veterans.

Florence Harding did not deliver formal speeches to the public, but she did make short addresses and frequent impromptu remarks from the south balcony of the White House, and from the back of the train on various trips with the president. Several photographs show her speaking to the crowd or delivering short remarks.

In all respects, Florence Kling Harding—as she always signed her name and insisted on being addressed—was an avowed feminist. At the White House, the First Lady highlighted active women, hosting the first all-women's tennis tournament on the White House lawn and planning a special welcoming ceremony for French scientist Madame Marie Curie. She was a strong advocate of both the Campfire Girls and the Girl Scouts because she believed that young women should be encouraged to be as physically active and fit as young men, and that girls were just as equipped for it as boys. Although she was a particularly partisan Republican, she accepted honorary membership in the progressive National Women's Party's effort to install a permanent sculpture in the U.S. Capitol building marking the contribution of women to equal rights.

In one draft letter about married women having their own careers, she wrote, "If the career is the husband's the wife can merge her own with it. If it is to be the wife's as it undoubtedly will be in an increasing proportion of cases, then the husband may, with no sacrifice of self-respect or of recognition . . . permit himself to be the less prominent and distinguished member of the combination." Frequently when Mrs. Harding was asked to attend an event in behalf of a women's group—political or otherwise—she sent a letter to the organization with permission to publish it.

Although she did not hold press conferences, Mrs. Harding openly and regularly spoke for attribution with both women social reporters and male political reporters.

Before a White House entertainment, she personally escorted groups of women reporters through the State Dining Room and described the planned event. While accompanying her husband on his official trips, she befriended the regular male press corps that covered the president's activities to the point that she knew them all by their first names.

Mrs. Harding also stayed current with the popular culture and changing technology of America during the early 1920s. She relished day excursions on speeding "machines" with Evalyn McLean, and even in the presidential limousine. On one occasion, she had a naval band play some of the new jazz tunes and at a private party, was said to have tried one of the new dance steps. On another occasion, during the transition period before the inauguration, Florence Harding suited up in a pair of pants, a helmet, and goggles, and took a ride in a "hydro-aeroplane"—something a president's wife would not do again until Eleanor Roosevelt flew in 1933. Her clothes reflected the looser styles of the era—strapless gowns, shorter skirts, and wide picture hats. She was an avid musical-theater and "moving picture" fan, and hosted a White House film premier of *The Covered Wagon* in 1923. Eventually, she willingly posed for the moving picture cameras and appeared in newsreels of the day.

Among charities, the First Lady's avid support fell to the Animal Rescue League. She frequently posed with her dog, a large Airedale named Laddie Boy. Florence Harding never denied a request from a citizen who wished to be photographed with her. In many respects, what is today called the White House "photo opportunity" began with her. During the Wilson administration, the gates of the White House were closed because of the war, and later, during Wilson's stroke and subsequent incapacitation, White House visits were kept to a minimum. The Hardings therefore made a deliberate effort to open the mansion to as much of the public as security would permit. Large groups were usually greeted with a handshake and a pose in front of the south portico. This, combined with the sophistication of camera technology, made Florence Harding perhaps the most photographed First Lady up to that time.

Her social secretary was Laura Harlan, a member of a prominent Washington family, who at different times was assisted by West Wing women stenographers. The First Lady, however, was not averse to requesting the assistance of the president's political adviser and speechwriter, Judson Welliver, or George Christian, Harding's "secretary," who served as chief of staff and press secretary. She was the first First Lady to be guarded by a Secret Service agent, Harry Barker, by her own order. Barker served as a personal aide and driver, and became almost a son to her in many ways.

As hostess, Florence Harding revived garden parties on the south lawn in the spring and summer, as well as the full entertainments of the fall and winter social season. At public events, the First Lady followed the spirit of the law and served soft drinks. In private, at the president's poker games, she personally mixed the hard liquor. She appeared at the important ceremonies of the day, including the dedication of the Tomb of the Unknown Soldier in November 1921, when she initiated the tradition of wreath placing, and the disarmament conferences of late 1921 and early 1922. The First Lady traveled with the president and made many of her own appearances in different cities, notably Birmingham, Atlanta, and New York in July 1922. She was recognized as a celebrity in her own right when she returned to Marion with the president for that city's centennial celebration.

The summer of 1922, however, proved to be one of intense stress for Mrs. Harding. With a national coal strike in progress, the First Lady received many distressing letters from miners' wives. Parodied in one cartoon with her husband as "The Chief Executive and Mr. Harding" in 1922, she was publicly criticized for sending a donation to keep "Clover"—reputedly the oldest horse in America—alive, while ignoring a plea for a contribution to an old age home

in the same Connecticut town. If the recollections of Alice Longworth are accurate, it was also during this time that the president had an assignation with Nan Britton at the home of Evalyn McLean, who was summering in Maine.

These factors created great pressure on Mrs. Harding, and by mid-September her kidney ailment not only had recurred but soon threatened her life. Through the autumn, she struggled to remain alive. Experts from the Mayo Clinic wanted to operate on her, but Sawyer refused to permit it. Finally, the poisons began to be expelled naturally and her condition slowly improved throughout the winter.

What was unusual about Florence Harding's illness from September through December 1922 was the complete honesty of the White House press office in reporting every detail in daily bulletins to the papers. Absent was the genteel propriety that had marked the illnesses of earlier First Ladies; this was the first time that the public had been so explicitly apprised of the illness of a president's wife.

By February 1923, Florence Harding had recovered sufficiently to hold an informal press conference in the private quarters. Dressed in a pink peignoir, she greeted the women reporters and answered their questions—largely health and social in nature—but, as usual, asked not to be quoted directly. By this time, however, the first of the larger scandals had begun to break.

In January, President Harding was presented with evidence of Charles Forbes's collusion and profiteering, and finally confronted him. Forbes resigned and a Senate investigation got under way in February. Forbes was later convicted and imprisoned. In March, Albert Fall resigned his position as secretary of the interior and left for business endeavors in the Soviet Union, having already obtained his illegal profits from the secret oil leasing of Elk Hills, California, and Teapot Dome in Wyoming. In May, Jess Smith committed suicide after his role in bootlegging was revealed to the president.

Mrs. Harding remained steadfast in refusing to believe that Fall would betray her and the president, but she knew the details of Smith's activities. That she and her "boys" had been betrayed by "Charley" was crushing to the First Lady, and she later told Harding intimate E. Mont Reily that the president "never recovered from Forbes's betrayal of himself and the administration."

In June 1923, Florence Harding accompanied her husband on what was billed as "The Voyage of Understanding," a transcontinental trip aboard the train Superb. The Hardings crossed many states, making longer stops in Missouri, Kansas, Colorado, Utah, Idaho, Montana, Oregon, and Washington. As the president's health began to fail visibly, the First Lady made several appearances without her husband and gave impromptu speeches—largely patriotic in nature—to assembled women and children. From Tacoma, Washington, the presidential party boarded the naval ship *Henderson* and headed to Alaska. Mrs. Harding suffered a fainting spell, then rallied, but the president's health deteriorated. Once back in the continental United States, the Hardings boarded a train for San Francisco. During its brief stops, Florence Harding addressed the crowds, telling them that the president needed to rest.

In San Francisco, the presidential party moved to the Palace Hotel. There, on August 2, 1932, while the First Lady read to him, Warren Harding suddenly died.

The gathered physicians—Dr. Sawyer, naval physician Joel Boone, American Medical Association president Ray Lyman Wilbur, heart specialist Charles Minor Cooper, and Interior Secretary Fall—agreed to list the cause of death as cerebral hemorrhage, though modern assessments indicate that it was a heart attack.

Following her husband's death, Mrs. Harding strained her own health by constant activity. From San Francisco, the train was rushed back to Washington, where the late president lay in state at the White House. She then went to Marion for the burial services at a temporary vault. Again she returned to Washington, moving to the McLean estate for several weeks. In Sep-

tember, she returned to Marion for two months. Then, in November, she came back to Washington and settled into a suite at the Willard Hotel.

On her trips to Washington and Marion, Mrs. Harding focused her attention on the president's papers. Culling them from the files, his office desk, a private safe, and bank safes, she burned what may have been a considerable amount of correspondence. Historians dispute how much and what sorts of material she deliberately destroyed but, according to a statement in the *New York Times* on September 27, 1925, she told publisher Frank N. Doubleday, who was interested in doing a book on the late president, that she burned the great majority of it because she "feared some of it would be misconstrued and would harm his memory." Her motives were probably both political and personal. Certainly, she did not want the most private of his materials to remain. Conscious of the assorted administration scandals, she may also have hoped to obstruct even the slightest suggestion that the president had been cognizant of any of them. She told military aide Reddy Baldiner that they must be "loyal" to Harding. Judging from the dearth of her own correspondence, it is also quite likely that she destroyed many of her own papers, including material predating her White House years.

In Washington, Mrs. Harding remained cloistered in her Willard Hotel suite through the winter, spring, and early summer of 1924, except for visits to the McLean family. She followed the proceedings of the Teapot Dome trial. At one point, Mrs. Harding expressed an interest in appearing before the Senate Investigating Committee and testifying as a character witness in behalf of Albert Fall, whom she maintained was innocent of any wrongdoing. Whether she decided or was persuaded against doing so by Kathleen Lawler, who now returned as her secretary, is not clear. She also unsuccessfully lobbied President Calvin Coolidge to appoint her attorney, Hoke Donithen, to a federal judgeship in Ohio. Florence Harding made only three official appearances as a former First Lady: the January 1924 congressional tribute to her late husband, the February 1924 funeral of Woodrow Wilson, and the June 1924 dedication of Harding High School in Connecticut.

Contrary to popular belief, Florence Harding was neither depressed nor sickly. Correspondence indicates that she was even considering an extended European trip in the summer of 1924, as a guest of Ambassador Richard Child. On the urging of Dr. Sawyer, however, she returned to Marion in July 1924. Because the Harding home was still being rented out, Mrs. Harding lived in several rooms in a private home at the Sawyer Sanitarium. After Sawyer's sudden death in September 1924, Florence Harding became increasingly withdrawn and ill. During an October visit by Evalyn McLean, Mrs. Harding indicated that she did not have long to live. Daily, she made visits to her husband's temporary gravesite at the Marion cemetery. On Armistice Day, she stood in a driving rain, saluting the veterans who passed in parade. About a week later, she slipped into a coma. It was shortly before this turn of events that Florence Harding had arranged for a Thanksgiving dinner to be provided for the soldiers who stood guard at the Harding grave. She died on November 21, 1924, and was buried beside her husband in the temporary vault.

The remains of both Hardings were later removed to the neoclassical Harding Memorial, dedicated on June 16, 1931. In her will, Florence Harding left the family home and all its contents to the Harding Memorial Association, which had been formed after the president's death. In 1965, the home was transferred to the Ohio Historical Society, which now maintains it.

In many respects, Florence Kling Harding was a forerunner of her activist successors—Eleanor Roosevelt, Rosalynn Carter, and Hillary Rodham Clinton. She worked in both private business and politics as her husband's full partner, advising him on political issues and assuming her own sphere of policy interest, in this case the Veterans Bureau. Ascending to the White House during the first national election in which women voted, she proved to be a popular and admired First Lady by balancing her public image between that of a traditional housewife and a contemporary working woman with political intelligence.

BIBLIOGRAPHICAL ESSAY

The best primary source on Florence Harding is the collection of her personal papers, part of the Warren G. Harding Papers, housed at the Ohio Historical Society, Columbus, Ohio. All quotations, unless otherwise indicated, are taken from Carl Sferrazza Anthony, *First Ladies: The Saga of the Presidents' Wives and Their Power*, Volume 1, *1789–1960* (New York, 1990).

Information about Florence Harding can be found in the following biographies of Warren G. Harding: Francis Russell, *The Shadow of Blooming Grove* (New York, 1968); Robert K. Murray, *The Harding Era* (Minneapolis, 1969); Willis Fletcher Johnson, *The Life of Warren Harding* (Chicago, 1923); Andrew Sinclair, *The Available Man* (New York, 1965); Joseph Mitchell Chapple, *Life and Times of Warren G. Harding* (Boston, 1924); and Samuel Hopkins Adams, *Incredible Era* (Boston, 1939). Carl Sferrazza Anthony, *Florence Harding: The First Lady, the Jazz Age, and the Death of America's Most Scandalous President* (New York, 1998), is the first full biography of Mrs. Harding.

Also of value are the memoirs of those who knew Florence Harding, including Evalyn Walsh McLean, *Father Struck It Rich* (Boston, 1936); Harry Daugherty, *The Inside Story of the Harding Tragedy* (New York, 1932); Mark Sullivan, *Our Times*, vol. 6 (New York, 1935); Irwin H. Hoover, *Forty-two Years in the White House* (Boston, 1934); and Edmund W. Starling, *Starling of the White House* (New York, 1946).

Newspaper coverage of Florence Harding can be found in the *New York Times*, the *Washington Star*, the *Washington Post*, the *Washington Herald*, the *San Francisco Examiner*, and the *San Francisco Chronicle*. An excellent obituary is in the *New York Times* (November 23, 1924).

★★★　　★★★

Grace Anna Goodhue Coolidge

(1879–1957)

First Lady: 1923–1929

Kristie Miller

Grace Anna Goodhue was born in Burlington, Vermont, on January 3, 1879, to Lemira Barrett Goodhue and Andrew Issachar Goodhue. Her father, known locally as "Captain" Goodhue, was a mechanical engineer appointed steamboat inspector for the Champlain Transport Company by President Grover Cleveland in 1886. The Goodhues were an old New England family established eight generations earlier by William Goodhue, who had immigrated to the New World from England in 1635. One descendant was a member of the first U.S. Congress in 1797. Another sailed with Sir John Franklin in 1845 to explore the Arctic Ocean—an expedition on which all had perished. Grace wrote that when she went to live in the White House, she "found in the President's study an oak desk made from the timbers of the ship on which my kinsman had sailed and presented to the government by Queen Victoria in appreciation of the American expedition sent to rescue the Franklin party."

Grace was the Goodhues' only child—born after nine years of marriage—and she later admitted that "the sun, moon, and stars, in the opinion of my parents, revolved around my infant head." She was given early opportunities to develop her interest in music, and studied piano and singing. Her family even changed their membership from the Methodist Episcopal to the Congregational Church when Grace joined the Congregational Church at the age of sixteen. She loved to "face the music" at the back of the church in Hancock, New Hampshire, and sing enthusiastically. She also studied elocution and enjoyed performing in skits.

When Grace was only four years old, her father was injured in an accident at the mill where he worked, and she was sent to stay with the nearby family of John Lyman Yale. She became attached to the Yale's older daughter, June, who served as a model for Grace as she was growing up. June Yale studied at the University of Vermont for two years, then taught at the Clarke School for the Deaf in Northampton, Massachusetts, where her father's sister, Caroline A. Yale, was principal. During vacations, June would sometimes bring home one of her pupils. By the time Grace was in her early teens, she began to help her friend look after the deaf children. She found her work with the youngsters very gratifying.

Postponing her college entrance for one year because of eye problems, Grace enrolled in the University of Vermont at Burlington in the fall of 1898. It was a coeducational school, but, in those days, according to Grace's later account, there were relatively few women students. Her father built a new house at that time, with a bedroom and a study for Grace. She often shared her rooms with a classmate, Ivah W. Gale, from Newport, Vermont, a girl Grace befriended because she seemed lonely on the university campus. Ivah later became Grace's companion at the end of her life.

Grace became one of the founding members of the Vermont chapter of the Pi Beta Phi fraternity (the term "sororities" was not used for the first Greek letter women's societies). A large open room on the third floor of the Goodhue house provided space where the young women met. Grace continued with her interest in theater, sang contralto in the glee club, and joined groups of other students in vigorous outdoor sports. She later confessed that she was more interested in current events than in her studies. As a freshman, she submitted a theme on "Life," which was returned to her with the single comment "I suggest that you

refrain from writing upon this subject until you have had more experience." This chilling remark deterred her from further literary endeavors for the next thirty years.

Grace retained her early resolve to become a teacher of the deaf. During the spring of her senior year, she wrote to Caroline Yale at the Clarke School to inquire about entering the training class. Lemira Goodhue hoped that her daughter would become a public school teacher in their own town, but eventually accepted Grace's decision to go to Northampton. Established in 1867, the Clarke School for the Deaf emphasized lipreading, or "oralism," which allowed people with hearing impairment to be integrated into the community, as opposed to the sign-language method conveyed in other schools for the deaf. Alexander Graham Bell had taught the faculty his father's system of "Visible Speech," and later married one of the school's first students.

Grace taught originally in the primary school and then in the middle school, for a total of three years. She met Calvin Coolidge in her second year of teaching. In her good-natured way, she liked to recall the humorous occasion on which she first saw her future husband. One day, as she was watering flowers outside her Clarke School residence, she looked up into the opposite house, owned by the school steward, Robert Weir, to see a man shaving himself, dressed in his hat and his union suit. She laughed and turned away. Intrigued, Calvin Coolidge asked Weir who she was. Weir obligingly introduced them. Coolidge was then able to explain that he wore the hat to keep his unruly red hair out of his eyes while he shaved.

Weir later made the suggestion that, having taught the deaf to hear, Grace might cause the mute to speak. Her friends were astonished that the warm, outgoing young woman was attracted to the silent young Coolidge. As a Vermonter, Grace was apparently unintimidated by his laconic speech, and she seemed to have discovered and enjoyed his dry wit and love of pranks. Many people failed to appreciate Coolidge's sense of humor because he always kept a straight face.

Coolidge, who was born on July 4, 1872, in Plymouth, Vermont, was six and a half years older than Grace. His father, John Calvin Coolidge, had served three terms in the Vermont state legislature and had held a variety of local offices, including those of postmaster, deputy sheriff, and notary. His mother, Victoria Josephine Moor Coolidge, died at the age of thirty-nine, after a long illness. Calvin Coolidge was twelve when his mother died. He remained devoted to her memory, and carried her photograph with him on a trip he took just before his own death. His younger sister Abigail died six years later, another blow to the sensitive young man.

Coolidge graduated from Amherst College in Massachusetts and studied law in the Northampton firm of Hammond and Field. He was admitted to the Massachusetts bar in 1897 and, the following year, opened his own law office. By the time he met Grace , he had already served as city solicitor, clerk of the courts, and chairman of the Republican City Committee. She later recalled that his first invitation to her was to attend a Republican rally at the city hall. "I accepted," she said, "and have been accepting similar invitations from him ever since."

Coolidge courted Grace persistently, accompanying her to the picnics, skating revels, and dances that were her delight, although he was seldom moved to be an active participant. Most of her friends seemed puzzled by the couple, and one friend told Grace frankly that she would be afraid of such a stern and silent man. Grace's college classmate Ivah Gale, who was shy herself, apparently approved of her friend's choice, and encouraged the relationship. During the summer of 1905, Grace Goodhue and Calvin Coolidge visited one another's homes. Although Grace charmed the Coolidges, he made a less favorable impression on the Goodhues, abruptly announcing to Captain Goodhue that he had come to ask permission to marry Grace. Although Grace's father was surprised, her mother was frankly dubious about the match, showing, as Grace later remarked, "a neutrality toward his annexation to her

dynasty which would have thrilled even Woodrow Wilson." Just as Grace had been determined to teach at the Clarke School, so she quietly persisted in the face of her mother's doubts. Grace Goodhue married Calvin Coolidge in the Coolidge home on October 4, 1905.

Grace Coolidge was of the opinion that

Marriage is the most intricate institution set up by the human race. If it is to be a going concern it must have a head. . . . In general this is the husband. His partner should consider well the policies he advises before taking issue with them.

The union of two people with strikingly different temperaments and tastes required considerable adjustment, and Grace Coolidge believed that women were, by nature, more adaptable. She also decided that exercise of this trait would gain a woman spiritual advantage as well as the love of her family.

The Coolidges' mutual affection rested on a solid bedrock of similarities. To begin with, they were both native Vermonters with college educations. Each had an impish sense of humor, although Coolidge's was so subtle that humorist Will Rogers, who appreciated this quality in him, remarked, "I bet he wasted more humor on folks than almost anybody." Both were unpretentious and unaffected. They believed in the value of hard work and the division of labor within the household. Although Coolidge did not share his wife's love of music and the theater, they both enjoyed long walks and, with her at least, he could talk easily.

Early in their marriage they had a conversation that Grace Coolidge thought significant enough to record in a memoir of her husband. He asked her when Martin Luther was born. When she said she didn't know, he was amazed. Later she wondered if her husband would have talked with her more if she had been "more serious"; apparently they seldom discussed current events, government, politics, or religion. And yet Grace Coolidge was unusually well educated for a woman of her time, and she was the first First Lady to have had a profession.

Toward the end of her life, the First Lady was asked why she had married her husband; she answered that she had hoped she could teach him to enjoy life. She admitted "he was not very easy to instruct in that way." Still, she must often have lightened the mood of the young man who had already known a great deal of sadness.

In a life of public service, Coolidge had to struggle to overcome his intense shyness. As a child, he shrank from meeting the strangers his public-spirited father was always inviting home. His wife apparently was able to give him great reassurance and to compensate for his awkwardness by gently laughing about it. She naturally supplied the warm public image that he was incapable of providing for himself.

Coolidge curtailed their planned two-week honeymoon in Canada to return to Massachusetts for his first political campaign—for the school board—which he lost. The following year, however, he was elected to the Massachusetts General Court, which met in Boston. Grace Coolidge remained in Northampton with their infant son, John, born in September 1906. Coolidge believed, and his wife agreed, that his public duties should not interfere with her efforts to give their children a normal home life. Coolidge traveled home nearly every weekend; only occasionally did she join him in Boston, where he rented a room at the Adams House. He was reelected in 1907, and another son, Calvin, Jr., was born in 1908. Their roles remained strictly divided; her husband even discouraged Grace Coolidge from attending a speech he gave at their church.

After serving two terms as representative, Coolidge returned to Northampton, where he practiced law for a year while campaigning for mayor. He won by only 187 votes, but was elected to a second term, and from then on, rose steadily in the Republican hierarchy of Massachusetts. He returned to Boston for three terms as state senator, finishing as president of the Senate. From 1915 to 1918 he served as lieutenant governor and, at the end of 1918, was elected governor of Massachusetts.

Although the Coolidges had to live very modestly—their original household furnishings came from a hotel that had gone out of business, and when Coolidge became mayor of Northampton, they had had to borrow money from his father for state clothes—Coolidge was always extravagant where his wife's clothes were concerned. He loved to shop for her, impulsively buying expensive hats and gowns.

During the many years her husband commuted from Boston, Grace Coolidge was active in community affairs. In 1912, she made her first trip to Washington, D.C., as chaperone for the senior class of Northampton High School. She worked in the Edwards Congregational Church, and sewed for the church guild. Although she considered herself an indifferent cook, she was an accomplished needlewoman, having taken up knitting during the year she stayed out of school. She often sewed or knitted while her friends played cards. She enjoyed handiwork, not only for the satisfaction of making something but also for its tranquilizing effect on her. During the war, she worked for the Red Cross as cochair of the Women's War Committee of Northampton, providing benefits and entertainment for servicemen.

Grace Coolidge's role in caring for the children and managing the household allowed her husband to focus exclusively on his career. He was considerate, though, about staying at home with the children on weekends so that his wife could socialize. Since she often had to take the place of both parents, she became adept at baseball, model trains, and carpentry. In her husband's absence, she developed friendships with other mothers and the minister of their church.

As Calvin Coolidge rose in the Republican Party, he attracted the support of other men in politics and industry, in particular Frank Stearns, a wealthy industrialist; Winthrop Murray Crane, a former governor of Massachusetts; and Dwight W. Morrow, a financier whom Coolidge knew from Amherst. Grace Coolidge also became friends with these men and their wives, and was an especial confidante of Stearns, who, as early as 1915, envisioned Calvin Coolidge as president of the United States. The Stearnses introduced the Coolidges to wider society.

Among Mrs. Coolidge's other activities during this time was her continued interest in Pi Beta Phi, her college fraternity. In 1910 she became the first president of its Western Massachusetts Alumnae Club, and at the convention in Evanston in 1912 she was elected vice president for Alpha Province, extending from Florida to Toronto. In 1915 she traveled to Berkeley, where she was elected president. While there, Grace Coolidge agreed to begin a round-robin correspondence with members of the Massachusetts group, which would continue throughout her life. It was during this time that Coolidge decided to run for lieutenant governor, and his wife curtailed her trip in order to return home to help him campaign.

Following her husband's gubernatorial inauguration in January 1919, the men dined separately while Mrs. Coolidge entertained the wives of the state officers at the University Club. In spite of her inexperience as a social leader, she proved to be popular. Stearns wrote to Dwight Morrow a few days later, in a letter quoted by Grace's biographer, Ishbel Ross, "One of his greatest assets is Mrs. Coolidge. She will make friends wherever she goes, and she will not meddle with his conduct of the office." Grace Coolidge was advised to rent a large house and hire a governess so she could entertain her husband's constituents. She insisted, however, that she wanted to be first and foremost a mother to her two boys. The Coolidges' decision to commute surprised and alienated Boston society. Governor Coolidge's work prevented him from traveling as much as before, so his wife traveled more herself, and she, too, took a room at the Adams House. Finally she persuaded her husband to buy an automobile; he agreed, on the condition that she was not to drive it. Perhaps his experience of losing the two women closest to him in childhood made him overprotective where his wife was concerned.

Coolidge's term as governor came at a time when the country was undergoing the transition from war to peace. Strikes were commonplace in 1919 as workers resisted cutbacks in wages and the loss of positions they had enjoyed under a wartime economy. The Boston police, contrary to department regulations, organized a union, and when the commissioner dropped nineteen men from the rolls, they called a strike. It was the hottest September in nearly forty years, and the city broke out in riots. At first Coolidge did nothing. According to his wife's biography, the governor responded to Samuel Gompers's request for the reinstatement of the union policemen with the message "There is no right to strike against the public safety by anybody, any time, any where." Finally, Coolidge called out the state militia and the strike was broken.

The episode brought him national attention and, together with Frank Stearns's promotional activity in his behalf, earned him consideration as a presidential candidate at the Republican convention in June 1920. Winthrop Murray Crane was desperately ill (he would die before the year was out) and at odds with Massachusetts Senator Henry Cabot Lodge over the issue of the League of Nations. Lodge, who had been scheduled to nominate Coolidge, failed to support him. In a deadlocked convention, the nomination went to Warren G. Harding, a popular senator from Ohio. Stearns encouraged Coolidge's presidential ambitions, but Coolidge was only a marginal presidential candidate. The Coolidges were in their rooms at the Adams House in Boston on June 12, 1920, adjusting to their unaccustomed defeat, when Coolidge received a telephone call announcing that he had been nominated for vice president. Calvin Coolidge felt it was his duty to accept. Grace Coolidge put aside any misgivings she may have had about the demands the new position would place on her, and joined her husband in his limited campaigning in the months that followed.

When the Republican ticket was elected in November, Coolidge consented to his family's desire to accompany him to Washington, D.C. The boys, sharing the general family feeling of sacrifice for public service, attended boarding school at the Mercersburg Academy in nearby Pennsylvania. Their mother was pleased to think she could help her husband. She wrote Stearns, "He really seems to need me." Nevertheless, she had qualms about assuming a more prominent social role, since she was not a club woman and had done little entertaining while her husband was governor.

Grace Coolidge became president of the Senate Ladies Club—a post that was concomitant with being the wife of the vice president. The Senate Ladies Club was organized during World War I as a Red Cross unit and continued after the war as a network to promote acquaintance among the wives and hostesses of senators. Grace Coolidge's predecessor, Lois Kinsey Marshall, wife of former vice president Thomas Riley Marshall, was able to smooth the way for her. Although Washington society at first worried that the little-known Coolidges would be social misfits, Grace Coolidge was admired as a college-educated woman and soon was enjoyed for her warmth and wit. The Coolidges also inherited the Marshalls' suite of rooms at the Willard Hotel, where Grace Coolidge entertained during her "at-homes" on Wednesday afternoons. She later noted that although the rooms were small and apt to be crowded, guests were happy to come.

For the first time since their marriage, Grace Coolidge appeared with her husband regularly at ceremonial occasions as well as at dinner. Coolidge nearly always accepted invitations, deadpanning, "We have to eat somewhere." His wife had a good memory for names and faces, and Coolidge proudly wrote to his father about her popularity. According to biographer Ishbel Ross, Frances Parkinson Keyes, a well-known author who was also a senator's wife, once remarked:

I doubt that any vice-presidential hostess has ever wrung so much pleasure out of Washington and given so much in return. . . . She is the only woman in official life of whom I have never heard a single disparaging remark in the course of nearly twenty years.

Despite his wife's social success, the vice president did not enjoy his job. He was unhappy about criticism leveled at him from the Lodge faction in Massachusetts, and depressed because of the insignificance of his role. In addition, a series of events began to signal that all was not well in the Harding administration. Among members of the president's inner circle there had been resignations accompanied by criminal prosecution and, in one case, suicide. Harding left for a trip to Alaska and Coolidge, accompanied by his wife, began to travel— something that was not their custom.

While they were vacationing at the family home in Plymouth, Vermont, in July 1923, the Hardings were in San Francisco, where the president became ill. Without warning, Harding died suddenly on the night of August 2. His wife had been attending him. A messenger brought the news to the Coolidge farmhouse around midnight, and John Coolidge, a notary, administered the oath of office to his son by the light of an oil lamp in their sitting room.

Grace Coolidge reacted to her unexpected new role with the sense that it was happening to someone else: "This was I and yet not I," she later wrote. The duties of the wife of the president of the United States, she realized, took precedence over her personal likes and dislikes, and Calvin Coolidge defined those duties. A woman with her education and enthusiasm might have greatly expanded the role of the First Lady at that time, but her husband did not want her to give speeches or otherwise put herself forward.

In the 1920s, American society was undergoing many changes; one of the most dramatic was in the image of the American woman. In an age characterized by free spending and lawbreaking, Grace Coolidge provided a reassuring example of a thrifty, middle-class woman who used her educational accomplishments to rear sensible children. She was also the comfortable symbol of a conventional wife, which is just what the nation needed to quell the doubts concerning recent presidents' wives— including Helen Herron Taft, Edith Bolling Wilson, and Florence Kling Harding— whose influence over their husbands had been disturbing. The advances made by feminists in the 1910s and early 1920s slowed dramatically by the mid-1920s, along with progress in other social changes, and a conservative First Lady reflected the national mood.

Grace Coolidge was also younger and in better health than any First Lady in the past fifteen years. She dressed well, and she looked good in photographs. Her preference for red created a vogue, and her position as a fashion leader became part of the First Lady's role. However, her husband prohibited any extreme fashions, such as bobbed hair or slacks or even divided skirts for hiking, although he still took a great interest in her clothes and disliked seeing her wear the same evening gown twice.

Radio and mass-circulation magazines served a large audience interested in the lives of public figures and, although Grace Coolidge did not speak publicly or officially, her activities were widely reported, and her quick wit and sense of humor won her acclaim as the most popular First Lady since Dolley Madison. She loved to dance, and knew as much about baseball as most men. An avid fan of music and the theater, she invited many performers to the White House, including Douglas Fairbanks, John Barrymore, and Sergei Rachmaninoff. The president recognized her role in providing the sophistication and fun that added an important public-relations dimension to an administration that he ran like a business. Vera Bloom, the daughter of Congressman Sol Bloom, made the controversial observation that Mrs. Coolidge was worth one million dollars a year to the Republican Party.

There is no evidence that Grace Coolidge made any attempt to change or influence her husband's attitudes about women, but she was able to encourage women's social concerns and to recognize professional women by inviting women and women's groups to the White House. Her interest in social welfare grew directly out of her own professional training. As a supporter of women's issues, she set the stage for a more activist First Lady like Eleanor Roosevelt.

Because of her interest in health care, Grace Coolidge was an active sponsor of the Visiting Nurse Association. Not much is known about the extent to which the First Lady was involved with the Clarke School after her marriage, but what is certain is that her early interest in hearing loss and other disabilities continued. She and her husband often visited the school, and Grace Coolidge was on hand to greet former students at a reunion celebrating the school's fiftieth anniversary in 1917, during Coolidge's term as lieutenant governor. In 1919 Coolidge was elected to the Clarke School board of trustees and accepted the chairmanship of the endowment committee. In 1921 his wife was elected to the board of directors of the American Association to Promote the Teaching of Speech to the Deaf.

After becoming First Lady, Grace Coolidge often invited Clarke School students and other groups of deaf people to visit and tour the White House. According to Ishbel Ross, Helen Keller was a special guest who enlisted Grace Coolidge's aid to "help brighten the dark world of the sightless."

The Coolidges continued their work in behalf of the deaf quietly, since they believed that promoting a cause that was so important to them might appear a matter of self-interest. The president chaired the Clarke School endowment committee, but would not himself sign requests for contributions. In 1927, a special endowment plan was proposed by Clarence W. Barron, manager of Dow Jones and editor of the *Wall Street Journal*, to raise $2 million and to be called the Coolidge Fund. Philanthropists such as Andrew W. Mellon, Edward S. Harkness, Cyrus H. K. Curtis, and Jeremiah Milbank contributed. Calvin Coolidge bookplates were also sold to help raise the money. The goal was met by the time the Coolidges left Washington on March 4, 1929. One-quarter of the money went to

the Clarence W. Barron research department to study experimental phonetics, the
heredity of deafness, and the psychological
difficulties of the deaf child—all concerns
of Grace Coolidge. Her involvement with
the education of the deaf influenced her
husband to become an advocate for programs to benefit people with handicaps, and
he continued to work with Helen Keller in
behalf of the blind until his death in 1933.
According to Grace Coolidge's biographer,
Dr. George T. Pratt, the principal of Clarke
School and himself the father of a deaf
child, observed: "The fact that she was so
interested made a good many people think
our work must be worthwhile."

Grace Coolidge's background in teaching
predisposed her to take a special interest in
all children's welfare. She was the first First
Lady to open the benefit fair for the Association for the Aid to Crippled Children. She
also supported the Camp Fire Girls as well
as the Hospital for Joint Diseases, the Children's Hospital, and the annual Christmas
Seal drive, the American Legion, and the
Red Cross. Her interest in the problems of
the disabled grew out of her early professional training and was not an interest
acquired after she became First Lady.

Coolidge wished to reverse the reputation of the presidency, tarnished by the
scandals of the Harding administration.
Once in office, he called for investigations
and distanced himself from the litigations
that followed. Furthermore, he wanted, by
personal example, to restore dignity to the
office. That meant that the First Lady also
needed to be a model of decorum. When
she wanted to learn to ride, her husband
told her that it would be better if, in her
position, she did not take up anything new.
The president also insisted that they both
smoke only in private, and he forbade his
wife to give interviews or speak out in public on political issues. Whereas Florence
Kling Harding, who had worked with her
husband in the newspaper business and
knew the importance of publicity, had
linked her name with those of prominent
Washingtonians and suppressed information about the state of her husband's health,

Grace Goodhue Coolidge refused to give
interviews or to be quoted publicly on any
issue at all.

The Coolidges were successful. Alice
Roosevelt Longworth, the daughter of former president Theodore Roosevelt, pronounced the White House "atmosphere as
different as a New England front parlor is
from a back room in a speakeasy." She and
the rest of Washington society liked the way
Grace Coolidge seemed to enjoy the social
life of the capital while remaining natural
and unaffected. Although Mrs. Coolidge
deliberately chose to project an image different from that of her predecessor, she kept
in close touch with Florence Harding until
Florence's death in 1924.

This success came at some cost. Three
weeks after her husband became president,
Grace Coolidge wrote, in what later
became her autobiography, "Being wife to
a government worker is a very confining
position." She herself later told the story of
a painter who had come to the White
House to do her portrait and had painted
her in a somber mood. When her son asked
the painter why he had chosen to depict his
mother in such an uncharacteristic manner,
the painter replied, "Because I once saw on
your mother's face a look of resignation."

Coolidge restricted himself as well, writing to his father sadly, "Great power does
not mean much except great limitations. I
cannot have any freedom to go and come."
His wife realized his predicament and was
eager to do what she could to make his job
easier. Once, wishing to know in advance
when he might want her to accompany him,
she asked for a list of his engagements during the coming week. Coolidge responded:
"We don't give out that information
promiscuously." After that, Grace Coolidge
made no plans for herself until she knew
whether she would be wanted.

As usual, the First Lady helped her husband by trying to keep him cheerful.
Although the president's sense of humor
soon revealed itself to members of the Secret
Service—who learned that he had a mania
for pranks—it has been suggested that
Coolidge may have been subject to depres-

sion, often sleeping eleven hours and taking naps. She could tease him gently about his social ineptitude, as after one evening when he had not spoken to two women houseguests. The following morning, he asked his wife at breakfast, "Where are my fair ladies?" She replied, "Exhausted by your conversation of last evening."

Although Coolidge did not share the details of his business with his wife, she still contributed her part to the success of his administration. For a politician who could not express his interest in the people around him, it was a real advantage to have a wife who easily expressed her warmth.

For her part, Grace Coolidge expanded the role of the First Lady by projecting a public image. Although the president objected if social duties interfered with business, he did allow his wife to appear in photographs, now widely distributed through the new mass-circulation magazines. The First Lady was thus shown taking part in numerous public events and ceremonies, riding in parades, planting trees, and laying cornerstones, as well as officially meeting with nearly every group that requested a greeting at the White House. She doubled the number of similar appearances made by Florence Kling Harding, and made such functions a permanent part of the First Lady's obligations. Daisy Harriman, an astute observer of the Washington social and political scene for many years, remarked that because of her "vivacity and savoir-faire," Grace Coolidge was "the administration's greatest success."

More than in any previous administration, the Coolidges entertained visitors including such illustrious houseguests as the prince of Wales, the queen of Romania, Will Rogers, Charles Lindbergh, the Rockefellers, and many stars of the stage and screen. Grace Coolidge, as always, enjoyed all the performing arts; in the 1920s, theater was vigorous and the film industry was expanding enormously. She attended many matinees at the National Theater and supported classical dance and music. She invited Tom Mix, Otis Skinner, Mary Pickford, Douglas Fairbanks, as well as many dance and music performers, to dine at the White House.

The First Lady also indulged her early taste in music, often inviting guests for tea and musicales. The Baldwin Company sent her a grand piano (the first ever shipped by air), then advertised the fact that she had accepted the piano—further evidence of her celebrity status. During the first Christmas the Coolidges spent in the White House, the First Lady invited the First Congregational Church choir to sing as the Marine Band played carols on the north portico. Soon people began to gather outside the fence, and Grace Coolidge invited them onto the lawn, initiating a new White House custom.

Less than a year after Coolidge succeeded to the presidency, he and his wife suffered the desolating blow of the death of their younger son, Calvin Coolidge, Jr. The boy had looked very much like the president's mother, and there was a strong bond between father and son, fostered by their mutual love of teasing. Young Calvin also shared the family values of thrift and hard work, and at the age of twelve, started working summers in the tobacco fields. After his father became president, one of his fellow workers told him, "If my father were president of the United States, I wouldn't be working in a tobacco field," to which Calvin, succinct like his father, replied, "If my father were your father, you would."

Young Calvin had been an athletic boy. Although the elder Coolidge had not wanted his wife to take up a public sport like horseback riding, Calvin, Jr., taught his mother to swim soon after they moved into the White House. He also enjoyed tennis on the White House grounds. One summer day in 1924 he was playing tennis without socks and developed a blister. It became infected, and he tried to treat it himself with iodine, not wanting to bother his parents. As the infection worsened, he developed blood poisoning and died on July 7, at the age of sixteen.

The boy's death devastated his father. He was reminded of his sister's death at almost the same age and became tortured by the thought that if he had not been in politics, his son might not have died. "When he went, the power and the glory of the presidency went with him," Calvin Coolidge later wrote in his autobiography. Adding to the nervous strain on both parents was the fact that they had received a series of death threats against their son John, then a freshman at Amherst. Grace Coolidge persuaded John Coolidge, her father-in-law, to join them in Washington as a comfort to her husband.

To help deal with her own feelings, Grace Coolidge found an outlet in contacts with other children. Her sons had attended Mercersburg Academy in Pennsylvania, and she served on its board of trustees for twelve years. She urged Alice Roosevelt Longworth to bring her baby, Paulina, for frequent visits. She also seemed to enjoy such occasions as the traditional Easter-egg roll on the White House lawn, and the May Day processions, when she could delight scores of young children. Nevertheless, as she wrote to her round-robin friends, she wished she could sometimes escape to "have one day unaccompanied just to go about unrecognized all by myself."

The tragic loss of their son had the effect of bringing the Coolidges closer to the American people. Many wrote with stories about young Calvin, and to offer expressions of sympathy. Grace Coolidge attempted to answer as many of these letters as she could herself, but soon found the task overwhelming and had to ask her social secretary for help.

Grace Coolidge made it a point to answer all of her personal letters herself, and she wrote more than any First Lady before her. As she liked to say, "A letter in my handwriting will never have any commercial value. They are too numerous." She came to use a typewriter with great efficiency. The Hardings' social secretary, Laura Harlan, the daughter of the Supreme Court justice, stayed on until October 1925, and was succeeded by Mary Randolph, who had joined the staff in 1923 and served throughout Coolidge's term of office. Randolph was knowledgeable about Washington social customs and, every morning, would discuss with the First Lady her calendar, correspondence, money requests, the press, and dinner arrangements. The work of the social secretary became more complex with the Coolidges' increased entertaining. Part of the staff handled invitations. A correspondence secretary dealt with mail and issued form letters for requests for statements, appearances, and intercession with government agencies.

Relations with the press were an increasing part of the social secretary's job. Although the president did not permit his wife to give interviews, Grace Coolidge's lively personality, attractive clothes, and interest in numerous activities generated many stories. She was comfortable with reporters, and was the first president's wife to be honored by the newly formed Women's National Press Club. Still, she was circumspect. Her only published writing as First Lady was an article on knitting that she wrote so she could donate the $250 fee to the Home for Needy Confederate Women.

In her prominent position, Grace Coolidge was able to encourage and recognize the achievements of women. When her husband delivered his first address to Congress, Mrs. Coolidge had the cabinet wives seated together as a notable group. In the election of 1924—just four years after the women's suffrage amendment was passed—she urged women to vote, and photographs were taken showing her filling out her own absentee ballot. At the reception for governors following her husband's inauguration in 1925, she warmly received Nellie Tayloe Ross of Wyoming. On April 18, 1925, she pressed a button to send a signal by telegraph to open the doors to the Women's World Fair in Chicago, organized by Ruth Hanna McCormick, to showcase the achievements of women in such non-traditional fields as plumbing, printing, and banking.

Because Grace Goodhue Coolidge had earned a college degree, she was a model for the nation's young women. In April 1924, she invited 1,300 college women to the White House for the unveiling of her portrait, which had been commissioned by the

Pi Beta Phi fraternity. Later that year, she accepted an honorary LL.D. degree from Boston University, which had just named its first woman dean, Lucy Jenkins Franklyn.

Grace Coolidge resolutely declined to plead individual causes, referring them instead to the president. She claimed to know nothing of public affairs, except what she read in the papers. Still, Mrs. Coolidge may have been more involved in the Coolidge administration than has been suspected. She attended budget meetings with her husband, watched the Senate hearings on the Teapot Dome scandal, and met with New York governor Al Smith. When C. Bascom Slemp, her husband's secretary, retired, she was the only woman invited to his farewell dinner, at his insistence.

Nevertheless, any contributions the First Lady made were done with great delicacy and restraint. Grace Coolidge had two main outlets by which to escape the suffocating feeling of restriction. One was her needlework; she liked to say that a sewing or knitting needle was like the needle of a compass for her, keeping her on course. Even while living in the White House, she continued to make her own gingham dresses. She also took long, brisk walks, covering five or six miles a day in all kinds of weather, accompanied by her Secret Service guard, Jim Haley. She particularly liked to walk around the reflecting basin in front of the Lincoln Memorial.

In this Grace Coolidge was in step with the times. There was increased interest during the 1920s in golf, tennis, swimming, boxing, and baseball, and she was the first First Lady to share the public fascination with sports. Her son Calvin had taught her to swim shortly before his death, and when Gertrude Ederle swam the English Channel, Grace Coolidge learned to do the Australian "crawl." On vacation she would get up at 3 A.M. to go pheasant hunting. She was dubbed the "First Lady of Baseball" for her enthusiastic support of both the Washington Senators and her hometown team, the Boston Red Sox.

In spite of her fitness, Grace Coolidge found the job of White House hostess increasingly wearisome. She seldom had time to read, visit friends in a leisurely manner, or be by herself. The Washington humidity aggravated a tendency to sinus trouble. The death of her son had clouded even her sunny disposition. The publicity of her position could also be very oppressive.

In 1925 there were persistent rumors that Mrs. Coolidge, at forty-six, was expecting a baby. The Coolidges refused to dignify the story with a denial, and although their social secretary, Mary Randolph, and others circulated the truth in Washington circles, the White House was inundated with caps, blankets, pillows, socks, and afghans. Even more troubling was a later rumor that she planned to divorce the president after he left office. Despite all attempts to circulate the truth, that rumor also persisted, and the Coolidges finally began to appear together not only at church and official functions, but also casually around town. Those close to them could testify to their devotion to one another. Coolidge biographer William Allen White was one of many to observe, "She is a vital part of his success, of his life, of his happiness."

Having struggled daily to restore a sense of dignity and propriety to the office of president, the Coolidges soon set about tackling another job. Shortly after moving into the White House in 1923, the president was informed that the roof was in dangerously poor condition. The original beams, installed over a century before, had sagged and been jacked up so often that they were cracking. The entire top structure needed to be rebuilt. They postponed the work until after the election of 1924. By early spring 1927, it was clear that large-scale repairs were needed. From March until June, the Coolidges lived in the grand, four-story home of Eleanor "Cissy" Patterson at 15 Dupont Circle. While there, they entertained Charles A. Lindbergh, the young American aviator who, in his plane "The Spirit of St. Louis," had just completed the first solo transatlantic flight to Paris in thirty-three and a half hours. Lindbergh invited the First Lady to take a short flight with him. She had to decline, though, as she had promised her husband that she would not fly in a plane. Lindbergh's mother, Evangeline Lodge Lindbergh, accompanied him to Washington and made the acquaintance of the Coolidges' friend Dwight Morrow. Charles Lindbergh was later invited to Mexico, where Morrow was serving as ambassador. While there he met Anne Morrow, his future wife.

The Coolidges left the Patterson residence in June 1927 for an extended vacation in the Black Hills of South Dakota while the White House repairs were being finished. The First Lady's health was another factor in their wish to escape the oppressive Washington summer. Not long after their arrival, an incident occurred that provided fresh grist for the rumor mills. Grace Coolidge left one morning at nine o'clock for her daily walk with Jim Haley, her Secret Service guard. Although she had planned to return by lunchtime, Haley, a city man, misjudged the amount of time required to return uphill, and they arrived after 2 P.M. Coolidge, always anxious where his wife was concerned, was most displeased, and he promptly transferred Haley to another post. Newspaper headlines speculated that Coolidge was a jealous husband, although his real objection was merely that the man should have known better than to guide his wife so poorly. Grace Coolidge was embarrassed by the publicity, and inconvenienced because there were few other people who could keep up with her as she hiked her six daily miles at a rate of four miles an hour.

The surprise over the Haley incident was eclipsed on August 2, when Coolidge, at his regular press conference, announced laconically: "I do not choose to run for president in 1928." As other reporters were hastening out of the room to report their story, Charles Michelson of the New York *World* asked if the president had anything else to say. "No, that's all the news in the office this morning," Coolidge replied.

Coolidge was similarly offhand when he returned home for lunch, not telling his wife of the announcement he had made, but allowing her to learn it from casual conversation with a guest. She claimed to have had no intimation of his intention, although before he had departed for the press conference, he had remarked to her, "I have been president for four years today." Grace Coolidge later wrote in what became her autobiography:

> I am rather proud of the fact that after nearly a quarter of a century of marriage my husband feels free to make his decisions without consulting me or giving me advance information concerning them.

Because of these remarks, it has generally been assumed that his not seeking reelection was the decision she had not been informed of. Probably the timing of the announcement—and not the decision itself—was what surprised her. On March 27 she had written to a friend that the president had promised her she would soon be riding in streetcars and taxicabs.

The president's increasing concern with his wife's well-being, evidenced by his agitation over her lateness in returning with Haley, may have been an important factor in his decision not to seek reelection. Her bronchitis, the wearisome responsibility of being the White House hostess, and her sadness over the loss of their son were all taking their toll. Coolidge himself had never really recovered from the boy's death, and he may have realized that his own heart was not strong. He also suffered chronically from asthma and digestive problems. William Allen White, one of Coolidge's earliest biographers, has suggested, too, that Coolidge may have realized that the country was headed for economic hard times.

Once the repairs to the White House were completed, the Coolidges returned. Grace Coolidge attempted to furnish the mansion with original period pieces but found none in storage. She did discover some antique furniture, such as a leather chair identified as "Andrew Jackson's chair," and a mahogany table inlaid with brass to represent the thirteen original colonies. These and other items were repaired, refurbished, and installed in state rooms. She had Lincoln's bed—nine feet long with a ten-foot headboard—installed in the room designated as his bedroom, then crocheted an immense coverlet for it—a project that consumed two years. A joint resolution was passed by Congress at her request, authorizing the acceptance of donations of period furniture. There were not as many contributions as she had hoped for, but before her departure in 1929, she was able to furnish the green parlor with pieces she thought were appropriate.

During the renovations a sunroom, designed especially for Grace Coolidge, was added on to the tiled roof over the south portico. There she could work or entertain close friends. She took great pleasure in the presidential mansion, and loved sharing it with guests.

Charles Henlock, the chief horticulturist, believed that Grace Coolidge was more interested in flowers than any other First Lady he had known. During her tenure, she enhanced the White House gardens with a birch tree and a water lily pond, as well as a small spruce tree from Vermont, which she had planted by the tennis court in memory of her son Calvin. Chief Usher "Ike" Hoover in his memoirs considered her "90% of the Coolidge administration," and the entire White House staff called her "Sunshine."

Grace Coolidge was also interested in other public buildings in the capital city, and followed closely the progress of the Public Buildings Act, approved in 1926 to appropriate $165 million for construction of federal buildings. She spoke often with Charles Moore, the chairman of the National Commission on Fine Arts. On at least one occasion, she quietly interceded: General Pershing had brought plans for a war memorial for her husband to view while they were vacationing in the Black Hills of South Dakota. The First Lady suggested that they reminded her of a guillotine, and the architect was asked to present a new design.

In January 1928 the Coolidges made a state visit to Cuba. Grace Coolidge enjoyed the trip with her usual gusto, but after their return, she became so ill that her husband was afraid she might die. She recovered slowly throughout the spring, then spent the summer in Brule, Wisconsin, where she seemed to recover most of her former vigor. Returning to Washington, the president and First Lady began the social season a month earlier than usual so that they would have ample time to prepare to leave their home of nearly six years.

Coolidge did little campaigning for the Republican nominee, Secretary of Commerce Herbert Hoover, who was elected easily on November 8. The Coolidges made trips over the winter to Sapelo Island off the coast of Georgia and to Mountain Lake in Florida, and prepared to vacate the White House in March. Young John Coolidge, then in his early twenties, thought that his mother had enjoyed her years in the White House but that she did not regret leaving.

William Allen White, who had known both Coolidges well, wrote of Grace Coolidge in a passage quoted by Ishbel Ross:

> To what extent Mrs. Coolidge has influenced her husband's judgment only two persons may testify. One is too silent to say, even if he realized it; and the other too smart! But Mrs. Coolidge has accepted her husband's ideals and striven with him to realize them. . . . But for Mrs. Coolidge, her husband would not have travelled the path he has climbed.

The Coolidges went directly to Union Station, where Calvin Coolidge gave a farewell message on the radio, voicing his appreciation that the Clarke School Fund of $2 million had been fully subscribed. Grace Coolidge, who had been urged all through her years in the White House to speak on the radio, turned to the microphone and said, "Good-bye, folks." She felt as though she had reclaimed her identity. They returned to their home in Northampton, but soon found that their house on a busy street was a magnet for sightseers. The next year they bought a larger house—The Beeches—well back on a large lawn behind a screen of trees.

In June 1929, Grace Coolidge received an honorary degree from Smith College, and *Good Housekeeping* named her one of America's twelve greatest women, along with Willa Cather, Jane Addams, and Carrie Chapman Catt, for her role as a national symbol of home and family life. The following June she received an honorary degree from her alma mater, the University of Vermont. In September the Coolidges attended the wedding of their son John to Florence Trumbull, the daughter of the governor of Connecticut.

Almost as soon as she left the White House—and was free to express herself—Grace Coolidge began jotting down impressions of her years in Washington. Her husband encouraged her, and acted as her agent, submitting them as articles for publication, first in *American Magazine* and later in *Good Housekeeping*. She also wrote and published verse. In 1930, Calvin Coolidge began writing a column for the McClure syndicate, although, for the most part, he refrained from commentary on the worsening economic depression or other current political topics. The following year he embarked on his autobiography. Grace Coolidge's articles and notes were collected, edited, and published by Lawrence E. Wikander and Robert H. Ferrell in 1992. She relished her newfound leisure time and resumed reading—a habit she had sorely missed during the hectic White House days.

Coolidge's years in public life seemed to have aged him. "I am too old for my years," he told Charles A. Andres, treasurer of Amherst. "I am afraid I am all burned out." His asthma and digestive difficulties worsened, and on the morning of January 5, 1933, he died quietly at home while his wife was walking around town doing errands. He was buried in Plymouth, Vermont, near his parents, his son, and his ancestors. President Hoover, who had been defeated the preceding November by Franklin D. Roosevelt, ordered thirty days of mourning.

Although her personality and her education might have enabled her to expand the First Lady's role, Grace Goodhue Coolidge's nineteenth-century upbringing led her to subordinate her wishes to those of her husband. Her biographer, Ishbel Ross, concluded, "There is no reason to think she was not comfortable with that." When her husband died, she told a friend that she felt like a lost soul. "Nobody is going to believe how I miss being told what to do. My father always told me what to do. Then Calvin told me what to do."

Nevertheless, as she outlived her husband by nearly a quarter of a century, it was inevitable that she would develop a life and a style that were more her own. For the first four years after leaving the White House, she had been primarily occupied with the care of her husband. Even so, she continued her lifelong involvement with education for the deaf and often visited the Clarke School, where she learned about experiments with high-fidelity equipment and new, larger hearing aids. The National Institute for Social Sciences awarded her a medal in 1931 for her work with the Clarke School and in behalf of social services during her time as First Lady.

In 1933, Grace Coolidge became a member of the Clarke School board of trustees, serving until her death in 1957. From 1935 until 1952 she served as chairman. In 1933, the newly constructed arts and crafts building was named the Coolidge Building in her honor. In the 1940s, Mrs. Coolidge invited John F. Kennedy, a rising young Massachusetts politician, to become a member of the National Committee of Sponsors for the Clarke School. Her influence on the future president may have prompted him later to sign a bill providing federal aid to students interested in becoming teachers of the deaf.

Grace Coolidge continued to encourage all efforts to have deaf children included in mainstream education, supporting the oral method over sign language, which, she felt, limited them severely. She also applauded the joint degrees given to graduates of the Clarke Teaching Education Department by Smith College, the University of Massachusetts, and Syracuse University.

Altogether, Grace Coolidge spent over fifty years of her life promoting education for the hearing-impaired, and she became a significant figure in that work. When, toward the end of her life, she was too weak to visit the school, the president, Dr. Augustus Galbraith, and the principal, Dr. George T. Pratt, visited her to discuss ongoing programs. Dr. Pratt wrote to her son John that his mother's influence would be felt for years, "particularly in the general field of educating the public to the fact that deafness and its attendant difficulties are respectable."

After her husband's death, Grace Coolidge spent winter vacations with her friend Florence Adams at the latter's vacation home on White Oak Mountain near Tryon, North Carolina. There she was able to indulge her taste for hiking and reading. She continued to shun the spotlight, although she did bob her hair and learn to drive a car. In 1936, she flew with Governor John Trumbull in his plane. She and Mrs. Adams also traveled to Europe, where they drove their own car in order to be spared unwelcome publicity. After their return, Grace Coolidge sold The Beeches, which she considered too large for one person, and lived for a time with Mrs. Adams in Northampton. Some of her furniture was sold at auction, and she donated the proceeds to the Red Cross for the relief of New England flood victims. Eventually she built a small house for herself—called Road Forks—in Northampton. Congress granted her an annual pension of $5,000.

Although the former First Lady enjoyed private life, she broke her long habit of reticence to speak out in favor of early intervention in World War II. In 1939 she raised money to bring refugee children from Germany to the United States, and in 1940 she was named honorary chairman of the Northampton committee to raise money for the Queen Wilhelmina Fund for Dutch victims of the Nazi invasion. She also served as honorary chairman of the Fight for Freedom Committee of Hampshire County just before Pearl Harbor. After the United States entered the war, she turned her house over to the navy for the duration. She became a "household warden," trained in blackout and air raid procedures, and worked for war-bond sales, salvage campaigns, and, especially, the Citizens Committee to present departing draftees with

books and cigarettes. At the same time, she continued to resist any special notice and declined to serve as head of the Massachusetts Women's Defense Corps because it would have made her too conspicuous.

At the end of the war, Grace Coolidge moved back into her house and resumed a quiet life, making needlepoint chair seats for her son's family while listening to baseball games on the radio. Sports commentator Red Barber wrote to her how much her interest in the national pastime was appreciated. She read widely, and continued to correspond regularly with her son's family and her friends from the fraternity. In addition to the theater and movies, she also enjoyed watching television.

Finally, as her health declined, she stopped attending baseball games in person, out of fear that she might die in a public place and horror of the resulting publicity. Ivah Gale, the college classmate and friend who was by then quite deaf, came to live with her. On July 8, 1957, Grace Goodhue Coolidge died of heart disease.

Her will expressed the hope that the Calvin Coolidge birthplace in Plymouth, Vermont, would be turned over to the state. The legislature appropriated funds to restore it and make it a memorial center, close by the Calvin Coolidge State Park, with 5,489 acres of woods.

The Siena Research Institute Poll—conducted in 1982 and again in 1993 by history professors Thomas Kelly and Douglas Lonnstrom at Siena College in Loudenville, New York—asked history professors in 102 colleges to rate First Ladies. A 1981 poll taken to rate presidents placed Calvin Coolidge at number 30; in 1982 Grace Coolidge was ranked 17. In the 1992 poll Grace Coolidge ranked 19 overall (the addition of Hillary Rodham Clinton and Barbara Bush at numbers 2 and 8, respectively, influenced Grace Coolidge's relative standing). In other measures, her status improved: from 18 to 17 as ranked by intelligence, from 32 to 26 as ranked by leadership, and from 22 to 17 as ranked by value to country.

Grace Goodhue Coolidge's influence on her husband's administration was largely in the area of public relations. She created a warm, friendly atmosphere in the White House and cheerfully performed the public tasks by which the public gets its day-to-day impression of an administration. Her interest in people with disabilities also gave national visibility to their problems and influenced her husband to work generally for programs to help the handicapped. She considered her work primarily to support her husband, and she clearly gave vital support by her understanding of one of the most individual of American presidents.

Grace Coolidge also made her own contribution to the evolving role of First Lady. She gave the institution luster after the problems associated with Edith Bolling Wilson and Florence Kling Harding. She was the most stylish First Lady between Edith Kermit Roosevelt and Jacqueline Kennedy, although she popularized mainstream designs rather than the more extreme fashions of the 1920s. By readily acceding to increased demands for photo opportunities, she was also able to express, in an indirect way, her support for women voters, sports, immigration, and children's welfare. Like many popular First Ladies, Grace Goodhue Coolidge adopted contemporary ideas without abandoning broadly accepted middle-class values.

BIBLIOGRAPHICAL ESSAY
The Forbes Library in Northampton, Massachusetts, contains unpublished material about Grace Goodhue Coolidge, including her correspondence with Therese C. Hills, one of Grace's oldest friends, and a thirty-year exchange of letters that began in the mid-1920s with Grace Graham Medinus from Chicago. Her round-robin correspondence with members of her fraternity after she left the White House is at the Coolidge Foundation in Plymouth, Vermont. There are also a few papers at the Vermont Historical Society. The Calvin Coolidge Papers at the Library of Congress, Washington, D.C., have some items about the First Lady, and there is more in the Coolidge Papers, which have been microfilmed by the Forbes Library. The collec-

tion of Dr. Joel T. Boone in the Library of Congress provides information from the perspective of the Coolidges' physician.

Soon after leaving the White House, Grace Coolidge published articles about her experiences as First Lady. These include "When I Became First Lady," *American Magazine* 108 (September 1929): 11–13, 106, 108; "Making Ourselves at Home in the White House," *American Magazine* 108 (November 1929): 20–21, 159–160, 163–164; "The Other Presidents," *Good Housekeeping* 94 (February 1932): 19–21, 135, 138, 141, 144, 146, 148; and "The Real Calvin Coolidge," *Good Housekeeping* 100 (April 1935): 38–41. The *American Magazine* articles, together with previously unpublished writings, form the core of Lawrence E. Wikander and Robert H. Ferrell, eds., *Grace Coolidge: An Autobiography* (Worland, Wyo., 1992).

Grace Coolidge was the subject of many newspaper and magazine articles during the 1920s and 1930s. See, for example, Paul A. Burns, "Profile of the First Lady," *New Yorker* (May 15, 1926): 17–18; and Anne Hard, "First Lady of the Land," *Pictorial Review* (September 1926): 7–8. Mary Randolph, *Presidents and First Ladies* (New York, 1936), is a memoir by Mrs. Coolidge's secretary.

The most thorough biographical treatment of Grace Goodhue Coolidge is Ishbel Ross, *Grace Coolidge and Her Era: The Story of a President's Wife* (New York, 1962; repr. Plymouth, Vt., 1988). Material on her also appears in Carl Sferrazza Anthony, *First Ladies: The Saga of the Presidents' Wives and Their Power*, 2 vols. (New York, 1990), as well as in his *Florence Harding: The First Lady, the Jazz Age, and the Death of America's Most Scandalous President* (New York, 1998). Charlene M. Anderson, "Grace Coolidge and the Clarke School for the Deaf," *The Real Calvin Coolidge*, 10 (1994): 5–13, looks at Mrs. Coolidge's favorite charitable commitment. Cynthia Bittinger, "Calvin Coolidge's Courting Letters, 1904–1905," and Lydia Coolidge Sayles, "Grace Coolidge: My Grandmother," both in *New England Journal of History* 55 (Fall, 1998): 69–70,

79–82, examine Grace Coolidge's personal life. Milton J. Heller, Jr., "The Boones and the Coolidges," in *The Real Calvin Coolidge*, 14 (1999), and David Pietrusza's "Wombats and Such: The Pets of Calvin and Grace Coolidge," in the same publication look at the family life of the Coolidges.

Material on Grace Coolidge can also be found in William Allan White, *A Puritan in Babylon* (New York, 1938); and Donald R. McCoy, *Calvin Coolidge: The Quiet President* (New York, 1967). See also Irwin H. Hoover, *Forty-two Years in the White House* (Boston, 1934); and Logna Logan, *Ladies of the White House* (New York, 1962). An obituary of Grace Coolidge appeared in the *New York Times* (July 9, 1957).

★★★   ★★★

Lou Henry Hoover

(1874–1944)

First Lady: 1929–1933

Nancy Beck Young

On March 29, 1874, Lou Henry was born to Florence Weed Henry and Charles Delano Henry. The family lived in Waterloo, Iowa, where Charles Henry worked as a cashier at the First National Bank. Florence Henry had been trained as a teacher, but her husband's income was sufficient to support the family without her assistance. In addition, asthma made it difficult for her to work. Eight years after Lou was born, Florence and Charles had a second daughter, Jean. In 1884 the family moved from Iowa to California, where Lou enjoyed the active life of a tomboy. As a child, she spent much time outdoors camping and hiking with her father. The family found California ideal for Charles's career and Florence's health.

Lou Henry enjoyed the benefits of a superior education. In 1890, she graduated at the head of her class from Bailey Street School in Whittier, California. She matriculated at the Los Angeles Normal School that fall but transferred to San Jose Normal School in the fall of 1892, when her family moved to Monterey. Lou earned a teaching certificate in June 1893, but she was unsure of her career choice. Her father gave her an opportunity to work as an assistant cashier at the Monterey Bank, a position she held until the spring of 1894, when she began substitute teaching in the Monterey schools. That spring she heard a lecture by a Stanford University geology professor, John Casper Branner, an event which changed the course of her life. She decided to enter Stanford that fall and major in geology. While a student in a geology lab class she met Herbert Hoover, another geology major at Stanford. The two had much in common: both were born in Iowa, both had moved to California at a young age, and both loved geology and the outdoors. Bert, as she called him, graduated in 1895 but continued his budding relationship with Lou through letters.

Lou was a persistent and dedicated student. After proving her mettle to her male colleagues, she completed the requirements for a degree in geology in May 1898 and graduated from Stanford University. Lou was one of the first women in the United States to earn a degree in geology. After completing her education, she searched briefly and fruitlessly for a job. However, she was not idle. The Spanish-American War first induced Lou Henry to participate in charitable activities. Her mother encouraged her to join the American Red Cross. She began by rolling bandages, but soon she was elected secretary-treasurer of the local chapter, giving her an opportunity to practice her leadership skills within a voluntary association.

She was still unable to find employment, so Lou's professors encouraged her to consider taking another year of study to earn a master's degree, but her life moved in another direction. When Herbert Hoover graduated from Stanford, he took his first job working for $2 a day as a laborer for a California mining company. That dedication ultimately won him a desk job in San Francisco, and subsequently he was offered a supervisory position in Australia. His hard work "down under" led to another job offer with even greater responsibility: he was appointed to oversee all mining operations in China for Bewick, Moreing and Company. Herbert did not want to go to China alone, so he wired a proposal of marriage to Lou. Lou and Bert had to arrange a speedy wedding in order to secure timely passage to China. The February 10, 1899, civil ceremony at the Henry home, which joined a Quaker and an Episcopalian, was conducted by a Catholic priest who was a friend of Lou's family. Lou later explained that in

a time and a place where settlements were sparse, denomination was less important than accessibility. The newlyweds spent their shipboard honeymoon studying Chinese language, history, and culture so that they could easily adapt to life in Tientsin.

Their arrival in China occurred one year before a violent outburst against foreign intervention into that nation's economy. With the support and encouragement of China's dowager empress, a secret society calling itself I Ho Chuan, known as the Boxers in the West, attacked foreigners engaged in trade and religious work. The Boxers feared that Western inroads would irrevocably harm the traditional Chinese culture and economy. The Hoovers and the other Westerners constructed barricades around their settlement within Tientsin. Food and water had to be rationed. A shortage of medical personnel led Lou Hoover to assist with care of those injured during the battles. The rebellion ended in July, when foreign armies put down the Boxer troops. The Hoovers spent the rest of 1900 in London and Monterey, but went back to China the following year. Lou Hoover also spent time in Japan with her sister in 1901. The years in China had a lasting impact on her. She collected fine Chinese porcelain and mastered the difficult Mandarin dialect, using the latter for the remainder of her life whenever she wanted to communicate privately with her husband in public settings. She also demonstrated her love for the outdoors and nature by frequently accompanying him on his inspection trips to the mines he was employed to supervise.

In 1902 the Hoovers moved to London, where he was made a partner with Bewick, Moreing and Company. Lou Hoover made their London home into a social center for foreigners. She gave birth to two sons during these years: Herbert, Jr., on August 4, 1903, and Allan Henry on July 17, 1907. In typical Victorian fashion she made almost no reference to her pregnancies in letters to her family in the United States. Motherhood did not inhibit her foreign travels, which included visits to Egypt, India, Burma, Australia, China, Japan, and Russia, or her activities outside the home. Lou Hoover, along with her husband, undertook the translation of a sixteenth-century mining text by Georgius Agricola, *De Re Metallica*. For five years they worked on the project, which required both scientific and linguistic expertise. The Mining and Metallurgical Society of America bestowed a gold medal upon the Hoovers in 1914 for what it termed a major scientific accomplishment. Lou Hoover also studied Egyptian gold-mining processes and the career of an important British seismologist.

The outbreak of World War I provided further opportunities for Lou Hoover to demonstrate her leadership abilities. Because her husband accepted responsibility for oversight of relief efforts in Belgium and northern France, she decided that she should help him. Since Belgium imported over 65 percent of its foodstuffs, the war portended starvation for the people of that nation without drastic intervention. Because the nation had been sacked by the Germans and was under control of the enemy, it was also subject to the British blockade. Herbert Hoover took over as the director of the Commission for Relief in Belgium.

Lou Hoover arranged for her sons' education and care with her family on the West Coast and then prepared to return to London. She sat up almost the entire night before sailing, writing a poignant letter to her sons in case she died during the war. The letter, which is preserved in her personal papers, reveals much about her values and priorities: "I *know* that if I should die, I can pray my soul to go over to my two dear little boys and to help and comfort their souls. Of course you can't see it or hear it. But sometimes you will know I am there, because your own little soul inside you will feel nice and comfy and cozy, because my bigger, older one is cuddling it. And when you are in trouble, and call for me to come to help you, and pray God to give you more force, why I can come right to you and bring along the new force he is sending to you."

When Lou Hoover returned to Europe, she served as president of the American Women's War Relief Fund and directed a variety of projects, including relief for stranded travelers, a canteen service, a hospital, and the maintenance of Red Cross ambulances. She searched for ways to complement her husband's relief efforts. The German advance through Belgium and northern France left the people there without any visible means of support. As representatives of a neutral nation, the Hoovers were able to negotiate with the Germans to permit the operation of a lace factory in Belgium, with proceeds from sales designated for relief of that country. To ensure the success of these endeavors, Lou Hoover undertook several speaking tours in the United States. In San Francisco her efforts brought $100,000.

Lou Hoover's role in World War I shifted when the United States declared war on Germany. President Woodrow Wilson invited Herbert Hoover to serve as director of the Food Administration, so the couple returned to America and took up residence in Washington, D.C. Again Mrs. Hoover tailored her activities to support her husband's work. Since the United States did not undertake a formal system of rationing foodstuffs, Hoover used his agency as a bully pulpit to encourage Americans to do without scarce items such as sugar, fats, meat, and flour by adopting wheatless and meatless days. The program relied on a propaganda blitz of posters and slogans, and was nicknamed "Hooverizing." Because the public was skeptical about this program and the Hoovers' participation in it, Mrs. Hoover cooperated with the *Ladies Home Journal* to publish a story about the Hoover family diet during the war. Among the dishes served at the Hoover table were sausage and rice cakes, potato fish loaf, and barley sponge cake.

American participation in World War I caused the federal government to undertake new responsibilities. The expansion of the government bureaucracy drew numerous young, often single, women to Washington. These women lived in boardinghouses that were often unsuitable, and found themselves without access to good nutrition or recreation. Mrs. Hoover worried about this situation, so she helped found the Food Administration Women's Club, where female clerks could go for inexpensive meals, take a room, and gather for social purposes. She rented a large house for the club headquarters. When the war ended, Mrs. Hoover turned her attention to the problems that wounded veterans would encounter on their journey home. She assisted the American Red Cross in its development of the Canteen Escort Service, a program which helped secure safe passage between the hospital ships and the trains which would deliver the veterans to their homes.

The Hoovers stayed in Washington during the 1920s because Herbert Hoover was secretary of commerce in the Warren G. Harding and Calvin Coolidge administrations. In 1921, Lou Hoover told a reporter that her family was her focus in life, but a careful review of her activities in the 1920s reveals that she was anything but her husband's silent partner. She anticipated that her husband's new post would permit her further opportunities to advocate causes beneficial to women. One of her first acts served to lessen the unnecessary social demands on cabinet wives and to provide them time to engage in more serious work if they chose. The object of Mrs. Hoover's concern was the obligatory process of leaving calling cards and hosting teas for official Washington. She and other cabinet spouses agreed to a moratorium on the practice. However, Lou Hoover was not unwilling to entertain when it seemed to have a legitimate purpose. The Hoover home became a focal point for dinner parties. One evening Herbert Hoover had arranged for three separate sets of guests and three separate parties.

However, Lou Hoover's significance in the 1920s resulted from activities that had nothing to do with hosting dinner parties. She believed women should devote their lives to more important causes than simply housework—namely, work outside the home. She rejected the view that motherhood rendered women too busy for the additional responsibilities of a career. Her

perspective was tainted in that she had never employed fewer than six household assistants, but the technological advances of the 1920s were certainly sufficient to support growing numbers of women workers, and they rose from 23 to 29 percent of the workforce. Furthermore, Lou Hoover realized that the younger generation was most likely to accept her argument, and she told teenagers to seek ways to combine marriage with a career.

These years saw an expansion of her voluntary activities as she assumed leadership posts in the Girl Scouts and the Women's Division of the National Amateur Athletic Federation, two organizations which challenged traditional roles for women and focused on outdoor and athletic activities. Mrs. Hoover was drawn to the Girl Scouts because they stressed camping and hiking, two of her favorite activities as a youth. Her involvement began in 1917, when she was named acting commissioner of scouting in Washington, D.C. By 1922, she was a troop leader in the nation's capital, a post she held until 1932. From 1922 until 1925, Mrs. Hoover was also national president of the Girl Scouts. She believed that for the organization to prosper, it would require the enthusiastic support of adult women who were willing to model alternative possibilities for young girls. However, the Girl Scout program did not overlook training young women for homemaking and motherhood.

Major components of Lou Hoover's activities for the Girl Scouts involved fundraising and the installation of a democratic leadership philosophy. The money she raised went into expanding the camping programs, providing leadership training, and publishing a magazine for the girls. She wanted troop leaders to be available to give advice when their charges needed it, but she hoped that the direction of each troop would come from the girls' own interests. However, the legacy of her involvement with the Girl Scouts was her articulation of the idea that women could, and should, plan to have a career as well as a husband and family. In the 1920s and 1930s, views such as these clearly were feminist in orientation.

Lou Hoover's involvement in women's sports was also encouraged by her feminism. She helped to found the National Amateur Athletic Federation (NAAF) in 1922 and was selected the only female vice president of the new organization. The following year she helped to found the Women's Division of the NAAF because she did not want girls to face prejudice, because she believed in the idea of play for play's sake, and because, she told the *New York Times* on October 31, 1931, "you cannot have the best functions of a good mind without a good body." She chaired the NAAF's Women's Division from 1923 to 1928 and helped ensure that it commanded more influence than its male counterpart. Mrs. Hoover remained active with the NAAF until 1940, when it merged with another entity. Her advocacy of women's sports and the Women's Division was not without conflict and controversy. For example, the organization consistently opposed women's participation in the Olympics because the contests placed too much stress on the competition among elite athletes and not enough participation for all women, regardless of ability. Mrs. Hoover worried that sports for girls would take on the negative characteristics of boys' sports, including a lack of integrity and an overemphasis on sports at the expense of academic work.

When Herbert Hoover sought the presidency in 1928, Mrs. Hoover toured with her husband, but she avoided the spotlight. Lou Hoover's erudition and grace outdistanced that of Catherine (Katie) Smith, the wife of Al Smith and the other would-be First Lady. The numerous jokes that circulated about Mrs. Smith's unfitness for the office usually highlighted her fondness for strong drink or her Lower East Side roots in New York City. Journalists for women's magazines and for news magazines cheered the Hoover election and the chance for an intellectual, strong, and dignified First Lady instead of the provincial Florence Harding and Grace Coolidge or the weak Ellen Wilson and Florence Harding. Indeed, Mrs. Hoover brought many accomplishments to her new post: she was regarded as a scholar, she had traveled more extensively

than any First Lady since Abigail Adams, and she had the respect of the numerous voluntary organizations with which she had worked.

When Herbert Hoover was inaugurated as president in March 1929, *The World's Work* described Lou Hoover as "a strong woman" with "unusual poise and great naturalness" that made her uniquely suited for the "First Lady's 'job.'" Journalists, though, had regarded her as "Hoover's silent partner" since 1917, as exemplified by a story in the September issue of *Literary Digest*. In April 1929, *Review of Reviews* proclaimed that "judging by space in popular magazines for March, it was Mrs. Hoover who was installed in the White House last month." In November 1928, a writer for *Literary Digest* had noted her feminism, which was described as "international housekeeping" because she employed a strong-minded, take-charge approach to the crises she had faced abroad—the Boxer Rebellion and the famine and relief demands during World War I.

During the Hoover years, Washington insiders credited Lou Hoover with being the first First Lady to participate publicly in her husband's administration. She was the first First Lady to speak on the radio, to give regular interviews, to be identified with a civil rights issue, and to create a political program to fight the Great Depression. But she was not Eleanor Roosevelt. Lou Henry Hoover actually did all of these things before Mrs. Roosevelt came on the national scene, but her accomplishments have been overshadowed because of the failures of her husband's presidency and the towering presence of Eleanor Roosevelt. Unlike Mrs. Roosevelt, Lou Hoover rarely challenged her husband's ideological outlook on policy questions. Contemporary journalists described her as an example of "old-fashioned wifehood," but in reality she was atypical. On the one hand, she espoused traditional gender roles, while on the other, her career exhibited most of the traits of the "New Woman"—she received an education, she was involved in social activism, and she endorsed women's political endeavors.

Most important, Mrs. Hoover continued her interests while First Lady.

Upon entering the White House, Lou Hoover set about redecorating it and compiling a history of the Executive Mansion and its furniture. The Great Depression inhibited Americans from making donations to her campaign to refurbish the White House. When it came to her own appearance and manners, though, the new First Lady took no actions to change her image. Fluent in five languages, she had no need to attempt to learn a new language, as did many of her predecessors. Nor did she go shopping to improve her wardrobe. Instead, she took pride in her age and her status as a grandmother.

One of the most noteworthy points of controversy about Lou Henry Hoover's tenure as First Lady resulted from her management of the White House domestic staff. Rumors of disgruntled employees abounded, and one or two individuals published accounts that presented negative takes on Mrs. Hoover. However, a careful review of the extensive documentation within her personal papers suggests a different conclusion. She was a demanding but fair employer. She expected her staff to perform at the high level needed to manage numerous White House social functions. Specifically, Mrs. Hoover wanted the service of her guests to appear seamless and effortless. Thus, she requested the staff to learn a complicated series of hand signals and gestures which they believed overly confusing and cumbersome. Because of the significant and difficult problems with which President Hoover contended, Mrs. Hoover sought to provide him with peace and security from criticism within their personal quarters. Her strategy included a constant stream of dinner guests, which caused further staff discontent because of the difficulty to plan for the unknown. However, all of the White House staff could count on receiving free meals as part of their employment. The Hoovers spent about $2,000 a month of their own money to cover the costs of entertaining and feeding their guests and their staff. Within Mrs. Hoover's personal papers are numerous letters testifying to deep and lasting friendships between her and the people who worked for her.

In another, more significant way Lou Hoover's entertaining in the White House resulted in a tremendous public uproar. As part of her public role as First Lady, Mrs. Hoover was expected to host a series of teas for the wives of the members of Congress. Oscar DePriest, a congressman from Chicago, was elected to the House of Representatives in 1928, the first African American to serve in Congress since Reconstruction. No African American had been a guest at the White House since 1901 when Theodore Roosevelt entertained Booker T. Washington. Most important was the political dilemma that resulted for the Hoovers. President Hoover had won the White House with the help of five Southern states. Since he hoped to build on these inroads for his party, he did not want to offend white Southerners. However, the Hoovers also realized the potential importance of African Americans to the Republican Party.

These facts suggested the likelihood for controversy should Lou Hoover include Jessie DePriest at one of the teas, but she felt strongly that Mrs. DePriest deserved the same courtesy afforded to other congressional spouses. She decided to host four separate parties instead of one large affair. To ensure that the event remained low-key, Mrs. Hoover polled several women to ensure that they would treat Mrs. DePriest with civility and respect. Twelve women rose to Mrs. Hoover's challenge, and the tea was held on June 12, 1929. The party itself was a splendid success. Congressman DePriest reported that his wife received much courtesy and respect from the other guests. However, public reaction to the tea was another matter. The volume of mail into Mrs. Hoover's office was so intense that assistants to President Hoover had to help draft responses. Many writers praised the First Lady for her courage in breaking the color barrier, but Southerners and supporters of segregation were much less kind in their choice of words. Furthermore, comment in the media was often devastating. For example, a Texas newspaper said: "Down here in Texas, white folks are white folks, whether they be Al Smith Democrats or Hoovercrats, and—negroes are 'niggers.' Every good Texan, regardless of how he cast last November's ballot, hopes that the black population of this state will understand that their social status remains absolutely unchanged by Madame Hoover's damphool desire to guzzle English tea with a member of their race." State legislatures even got into the act. Several Southern states publicly berated Mrs. Hoover for her choice of guests. For Mrs. Hoover, the criticism was devastating. President Hoover signaled his support for his wife by entertaining the presidents of both Hampton Institute and Tuskegee Institute following the DePriest affair.

Mrs. Hoover's relationship with the media was both complex and linked to its context—the Great Depression. On the one hand she avoided public exposure. Yet as First Lady, Lou Hoover redirected her position and responsibilities. She gave formal speeches because she realized the potential for power and influence that accrued to the wife of the president. The public dais, although not new to her, was a place never before occupied by a First Lady. Not only did she give speeches, but Mrs. Hoover also employed radio as a medium to transport her message nationwide. While she made her thoughts and ideas public on social policy matters in this controlled venue, Mrs. Hoover refused to break with the precedent against First Ladies giving media interviews and to engage in the reciprocity of a formal interview with the press. She did, however, visit informally with reporters before public appearances. On these occasions, she sat in her chair with the reporters seated cross-legged on the floor around her. She was willing to talk publicly when she controlled the format and the message, but not when another individual controlled the situation. As her husband's administration progressed, Mrs. Hoover struck a delicate balance with the press in which she agreed to talk about topics pertaining to the Girl Scouts. How-

ever, because for her the Girl Scouts represented the model of how Depression relief should proceed—from a voluntary organization—the interviews necessarily had wider import than their designated topic might initially indicate.

Several factors combined to render Lou Hoover unwilling to cooperate fully with the press. Ever since the media had reported her death during the Boxer Rebellion, Mrs. Hoover had held a degree of skepticism toward reporters. When journalists skewered her husband for both causing the Great Depression and lacking sympathy for its victims, she retaliated by denying reporters access to her movements. Like her husband, she allowed photographers no opportunity to capture her humanity on film, instead releasing only formal head shots to the media. One reporter who was desperate for a human interest story about the Hoovers' White House Christmas celebration went so far as to disguise herself as a Girl Scout and sneak into the Executive Mansion's family quarters for an evening of singing Christmas carols. The reporter kept careful mental notes, and after the story appeared in print, she sent a copy to Mrs. Hoover.

Yet Lou Hoover did not shrink from the spotlight. She continued to behave in a feminist way and to advocate a feminist message. She included pregnant women in White House receiving lines for the first time. She also encouraged her husband to adopt a gender-neutral policy for civil service appointments. More important, she placed herself in the public arena as an advocate for gender equality. Her June 1929 remarks to 4-H Club members were transmitted by the National Broadcasting Company to the entire United States and reprinted in the September 1929 issue of the *Journal of Home Economics*. As was typical of the woman who preferred the outdoors, Mrs. Hoover encouraged youngsters in her audience to make time for recreation. However, in the crux of the message she asked: "Just stop a second and think what home is to you boys. Is it just a place where Mother and the girls drudge a good part of the day in order that Father and the boys may have a place to come to eat and sleep? Or can or do you do anything, in your home today or in one you think perhaps you will have in the future, to make it a home?"

Mrs. Hoover took to the radio on other occasions as well (about fifteen times total during her husband's administration). She critiqued every aspect of her performance and worked with a speech coach to improve her diction. She took that action because, after one appearance, members of the audience complained that they could not hear her remarks. When news of that activity leaked to the press, the First Lady became angry. She ceased her practice sessions and had the White House staff investigate who had provided the media with the details of her activities.

Volunteerism summed up Lou Hoover's views on how best to address the poverty associated with the Great Depression. She made numerous, ongoing charitable contributions that even her husband knew nothing about. The volume of appeals that she received was such that she had to hire an additional part-time secretary for her White House staff. When the Hoovers entered the White House, they built a retreat for themselves in the Blue Ridge Mountains of Virginia, on the Rapidan River. They realized that no public education was available for the children of local residents because the parents did not earn an income sufficient to provide a tax base that would support a school. The Hoovers paid for the construction of a school out of their own resources and hired a teacher with the background necessary for dealing with her new charges.

Lou Hoover encouraged organizations of which she was a leader to engage in poverty relief work. In the fall of 1931, she conferred with the members of the General Federation of Women's Clubs and encouraged the adoption of wartime methods for dealing with unemployment relief. Mrs. Hoover believed women should play a key role in voluntary relief, and she herself participated in the Women's National Committee of the Welfare and Relief Mobilization Committee. In a typescript preserved in the subject files of her papers, Mrs. Hoover told the group that "there are going to be some millions in want, through no fault of their own," and that pride and unfamiliarity with deprivation would render them ignorant of survival skills needed to sustain their families. She added that "food and warmth and health are not enough to satisfy the desires of life. Occupation and recreation are more vital to those harassed by trouble than to the carefree." Like her husband, she accepted traditional teachings about the workings of the economy. Thus, she believed that the government's role in relief should be minimal while the private citizen should make the necessary sacrifices to ensure the continued well-being of society. To that end, Mrs. Hoover encouraged the various organizations with which she was affiliated to engage in relief efforts.

While Mrs. Hoover argued that the Girl Scouts fulfilled a very traditional function in preparing young women to be good wives, in 1931 she and the Girl Scouts undertook radically new endeavors, including the Rapidan plan, which was formulated at the Hoovers' Blue Ridge Mountains retreat, for 250,000 Girl Scouts to undertake relief work. She hoped to match up the numerous pleas for help that she received with her many contacts within the organization in order to handle the problems on a local basis. She wanted the Girl Scouts to take the lead in tackling whatever work needed to be done in their hometowns. Even when it became apparent that voluntarism alone would not solve the nation's economic dilemma, Mrs. Hoover remained steadfast in her commitment to scouting.

By the fall of 1932, it was clear that the Hoover years were over. The American people blamed the president for their economic situation, and they overwhelmingly elected Franklin D. Roosevelt to the White House in November 1932. Mrs. Hoover's post–White House life and career followed the patterns she established and maintained throughout her adult life, with much of her focus placed on volunteer work. The Girl Scouts remained an important institution to her. She again took a place on the Girl Scouts' board of directors and served as president of that organization from 1935 until 1937. She participated in various political organizations, including the nonpartisan League of Women Voters as well as several Republican committees for women. She also continued her involvement with the Palo Alto community and Stanford University, supporting that institution with financial contributions. Instead of cutting back on her activities, she took on new commitments, among them the Friends of Music at Stanford University and the Salvation Army. She also continued to indulge her interest in the outdoors, including horseback rides at age sixty-seven in 1941. Her bitterness over the media coverage of her husband's presidency showed itself in her harsh words about Roosevelt and the New Deal. Finally, she paid careful attention to the question of how best to preserve the record of her husband's public career. She purchased her husband's West Branch, Iowa, birthplace for $4,500 in 1935 and began the process of turning the property into a park commemorating his life. After attending a concert, Lou Henry Hoover died from the effects of a heart condition on January 7, 1944, at the Waldorf Astoria apartment she shared with her husband in New York City.

BIBLIOGRAPHIC ESSAY

The most important source for understanding Lou Hoover's life is her collection of personal papers, which fill 182 linear feet and cover her entire life. The papers, housed in the Herbert Hoover Presidential Library in West Branch, Iowa, are subdivided as follows: Personal Correspondence series in four chronological parts (67 boxes); Subject File series (121 boxes); Professional and Organizational Activities series (60 boxes); White House General Files (79 boxes); and White House Social Files (38 boxes). Fifty-nine feet of the papers document day-to-day White House activities. In addition to Mrs. Hoover's own papers, those of her husband flesh out the details of her life. Other important collec-

tions at the Herbert Hoover Presidential Library include those of Gertrude L. Bowman, a friend who shared Mrs. Hoover's interests in scouting and Republican politics; Philippi Harding Butler, Mildred Hall Campbell, and Ruth Fesler Lipman, all secretaries to Mrs. Hoover; and Katherine Milbank, a friend.

Since Mrs. Hoover did not write an autobiography, scholars must rely on Herbert Hoover, *The Memoirs of Herbert Hoover*, 3 vols. (New York, 1951–1952), for details of the couple's life together. Helen B. Pryor's sympathetic biography, *Lou Henry Hoover: Gallant First Lady* (New York, 1969), however, often functions as an autobiography. Pryor followed that work with a series of articles in *Palimpsest*, the journal of the State Historical Society of Iowa, all in 52 (July 1971): "Girlhood in Waterloo," 353–363; "A New Life in California," 364–368; "Homemaker in Many Lands," 369–376; "Lou Hoover: Gallant First Lady," 377–387; and "The Years Following 1933," 388–400. Pryor's book and articles are significant not so much for their scholarly contributions as because the author was a close associate of Mrs. Hoover. Scholars will have trouble using the material because Pryor did not footnote her sources.

The opening of Lou Hoover's papers for research in 1985 created a flurry of interest in her career. Dale C. Mayer's essay, "Not One to Stay at Home: The Papers of Lou Henry Hoover," *Prologue* 19 (Summer 1987): 85–93, provides an excellent introduction to the possibilities for studying Mrs. Hoover's career in biographical form. Mayer also published "An Uncommon Woman: The Quiet Leadership Style of Lou Henry Hoover," *Presidential Studies Quarterly* 20 (Fall 1990): 685–698, and he edited *Lou Henry Hoover: Essays on a Busy Life* (Worland, Wyo., 1994). This edited collection provides an overview of the gold mine awaiting the patient and meticulous biographer of Mrs. Hoover. David S. Day followed up his 1980 article, "Herbert Hoover and Racial Politics: The DePriest Incident," *Journal of Negro History* 65 (Winter 1980): 6–17, on the DePriest tea controversy, soon after the Lou Hoover papers were opened for research, and augmented the historical record with new documentation: "A New Perspective on the 'DePriest Tea' Historiographic Controversy," *Journal of Negro History* 75 (Summer/Fall 1990): 120–124. A flavor of Mrs. Hoover's White House correspondence style can be found in J. Keith Melville, "The First Lady and the Cowgirl," *Pacific Historical Review* 57 (February 1988): 73–76.

The popular press wrote frequently about Mrs. Hoover during her adult life; thus both magazine and newspaper sources extremely helpful if used with caution. Publications like *The World's Work*, *Review of Reviews*, *Literary Digest*, *Outlook*, *Saturday Evening Post*, *Delineator*, *Good Housekeeping*, and *Ladies Home Journal*, as well as newspapers, frequently covered the First Lady, and the print devoted to Mrs. Hoover was extensive for its time. However, the veracity of the stories was sometimes problematic. Mrs. Hoover often wrote reactions to inaccurate press clippings.

Several important general accounts of First Ladies provide information on Mrs. Hoover. The most important books are Carl Sferrazza Anthony, *First Ladies: The Saga of the Presidents' Wives and Their Power, 1789–1961* (New York, 1990); Betty Boyd Caroli, *First Ladies* (New York, 1986); and Myra G. Gutin, *The President's Partner: The First Lady in the Twentieth Century* (Westport, CT, 1989). For a contemporary reaction to Mrs. Hoover, see Mary Randolph, *Presidents and First Ladies* (New York, 1936). The *New York Times* published an obituary of Mrs. Hoover on January 8, 1944.

★★★　　★★★

Anna Eleanor Roosevelt

(1884–1962)

First Lady: 1933–1945

Allida M. Black

Anna Eleanor Roosevelt was born on October 11, 1884, into a family of lineage, wealth, and uncommon sadness. The first child of Anna Hall Roosevelt and Elliott Roosevelt, young Eleanor—as she was called by her family—encountered disappointment early in life. Her father, mourning the death of his mother and fighting constant ill health, turned to alcohol for solace and was absent from home for long periods of time, engaged in either business, pleasure, or medical treatment. Anna Hall Roosevelt struggled to balance her disappointment in her husband with her responsibilities toward Eleanor and Eleanor's younger brother, Hall. As the years passed, the young mother became increasingly disconsolate.

An astute and observant child, Eleanor rarely failed to notice the tension between her parents and the strain that it placed on both of them. By the time she was six, Eleanor had assumed some responsibility for her mother's happiness, recalling later in her autobiography, *This Is My Story*, that

> my mother suffered from very bad headaches, and I know now that life must have been hard and bitter and a very great strain on her. I would often sit at the head of her bed and stroke her head . . . for hours on end.

Yet this intimacy was short-lived. Anna Hall Roosevelt, one of New York's most stunning beauties, increasingly made young

Eleanor profoundly self-conscious about her demeanor and appearance, even going so far as to nickname her "Granny" for her "very plain," "old-fashioned," and serious deportment. Remembering her childhood, Eleanor later wrote, "I was a solemn child without beauty. I seemed like a little old woman entirely lacking in the spontaneous joy and mirth of youth."

Her mother's death in 1892 made Eleanor's devotion to her father all the more intense. Images of a gregarious, larger-than-life Elliott dominated Eleanor's memories of him, and she longed for the days when he would return home. She adored his playfulness with her and the way he loved her with such uncritical abandon. Indeed, her father's passion only underscored the isolation she felt when he was absent. Never the dour child in his eyes, Eleanor was instead his "own darling little Nell." Hopes for a happier family life were dashed, however, when Elliott Roosevelt died of depression and alcoholism nineteen months later. At the age of ten, Eleanor became an orphan and her grandmother Mary Hall became her guardian.

Eleanor's life with Grandmother Hall was confining and lonesome until Mrs. Hall sent Eleanor to attend Allenswood Academy in London in 1899. There Eleanor began to study under the tutelage of Mademoiselle Marie Souvestre, a bold, articulate woman whose commitment to liberal causes and detailed study of history played a key role in shaping Eleanor's social and political development.

The three years that Eleanor spent at Allenswood were the happiest years of her adolescence. She formed close, lifelong friendships with her classmates; studied language, literature, and history; learned to state her opinions on controversial political events clearly and concisely; and spent the summers traveling through Europe with her headmistress, who insisted upon seeing both the grandeur and the squalor of the nations they visited. Gradually she gained "confidence and independence," and later marveled that she was "totally without fear in this new phase of my life," writing in her autobiography that "Mlle. Souvestre shocked one into thinking, and that on the whole was very beneficial." So strong an influence did her headmistress have on the young Eleanor that, as an adult, Eleanor later wrote that Souvestre was one of the three most important influences on her life.

When Eleanor returned to her family's New York home on West 37th Street in 1902 to make her debut, she continued to follow the principles that Souvestre instilled in her. While she dutifully obeyed her family's wishes regarding her social responsibilities, she also joined the National Consumers League and, as a member of the Junior League for the Promotion of Settlement Movements, volunteered as a teacher for the College Settlement on Rivington Street. Her commitment to these activities soon began to attract attention, and Eleanor Roosevelt, much to her family's chagrin, soon became known within New York reform circles as a staunch and dedicated worker.

That summer, as Eleanor was riding the train home to Tivoli for a visit with her grandmother, she was startled to find her cousin Franklin Delano Roosevelt, then a student at Harvard, also on the train. This encounter reintroduced the cousins and piqued their interest in one another. After a year of chance meetings, clandestine correspondence, and secret courtship, the two Roosevelts became engaged on November 22, 1903. Fearing that they were too young and not ready for marriage, and believing that her son needed a better, more prominent wife, Roosevelt's mother, Sara Delano Roosevelt, planned to separate the couple and demanded that they keep their relationship secret for a year. Sara Roosevelt's plans did not work, however, and, after a sixteen-month engagement, Anna Eleanor Roosevelt married Franklin Delano Roosevelt on March 17, 1905. President Theodore Roosevelt, who was in town for the St. Patrick's Day parade, gave the bride—his niece—away. The wedding made the front page of the *New York Times*.

Although Eleanor clearly loved her husband, married life was difficult from the start. Sara Roosevelt chose their first home—a small brick dwelling three blocks from her own residence—hired the staff, chose all the interior decorations, and became Eleanor Roosevelt's most constant companion. Within a year, a daughter (Anna) was born, followed in rapid succession by James (b. 1906), Franklin (b. 1909), who died soon after birth, Elliott (b. 1910), Franklin (b. 1914), and John (b. 1916). She later described this period in *This Is My Story*: "For ten years I was always just getting over having a baby or about to have one, and so my occupations were considerably restricted." Moreover, as the Roosevelt family grew, in 1908 Sara Roosevelt gave the couple a town house in New York City that was not only adjacent to her own home but also had connecting doors on every floor. Eleanor Roosevelt was miserable, recalling that she was "simply absorbing the personalities of those about me and letting their tastes and interests dominate me." All that started to change in 1911, when Dutchess County elected Roosevelt to the New York State Senate. He asked his wife to leave Hyde Park and to set up a home for the family in Albany. Eager to leave the ever-vigilant criticism of her mother-in-law, Eleanor Roosevelt tackled the move with enthusiasm and discipline. "For the first time I was going to live on my own," she recalled twenty years later. "I wanted to be independent. I was beginning to realize that something within me craved to be an individual."

By the time Roosevelt left Albany to join the Wilson administration two years later, Eleanor Roosevelt had begun to view independence in personal and political terms. Franklin had led the campaign against the Tammany Hall bloc in the senate as his indignant wife watched in fascination as the machine attacked its critics. Outraged that a political machine could vindictively deprive its critics of the means of supporting themselves, Eleanor Roosevelt lost a great deal of the naivete that had characterized her earlier attitude toward government. "That year taught me many things about politics and started me thinking along lines that were completely new." Roosevelt agreed, later telling Ruby Black, his wife's

friend and early biographer, that Albany "was the beginning of my wife's political sagacity and co-operation."

Consequently, when Roosevelt was appointed assistant secretary of the navy in autumn 1913, Mrs. Roosevelt knew most of the rules under which a political couple operated. "I was really well schooled now. . . . I simply knew that what we had to do we did, and that my job was to make it easy." "It" was whatever needed to be done to complete a specific familial or political task. As Eleanor Roosevelt oversaw the Roosevelt transitions from Albany to Hyde Park to Washington, coordinated the family's entrance into the proper social circles for a junior cabinet member, and evaluated her husband's administrative and political experiences, her independence increased as her managerial expertise grew. When the threat of world war freed cabinet wives from the obligatory social rounds, Eleanor Roosevelt, with her commitment to settlement work, administrative skills, disdain for social small talk, and aversion to corrupt political machines, entered the war eager for new responsibilities.

World War I gave Mrs. Roosevelt an acceptable arena in which to challenge existing social restrictions and the connections necessary to expedite reform. Eager to escape the confines of Washington high society, she threw herself into wartime relief with a zeal that amazed her family and her colleagues. Her fierce dedication to Navy Relief and the Red Cross canteen not only stunned soldiers and Washington officials but shocked herself as well. She began to realize that she could contribute valuable service to projects that she was interested in and that her energies did not necessarily have to focus on her husband's political career. "The war," observed Ruby Black, "pushed Eleanor Roosevelt into the first real work *outside her family* since she was married twelve years before."

Emboldened by these experiences, Mrs. Roosevelt began to respond to requests that she play a more public political role. When a navy chaplain, whom she had met through her Red Cross efforts, asked her to visit shell-shocked sailors confined in St. Elizabeth's Hospital, the federal government's facility for the insane, she immediately accepted his invitation. Appalled by the quality of treatment the sailors received, as well as by the shortage of aides, supplies, and equipment, Eleanor Roosevelt urged her friend Secretary of the Interior Franklin Lane to visit the facility. When Lane declined to intervene, Mrs. Roosevelt pressured him until he appointed a commission to investigate the institution. "I became," she wrote, "more determined to try for certain ultimate objectives. I had gained a certain assurance as to my ability to run things, and the knowledge that there is joy in accomplishing good."

The end of the war did not slow Mrs. Roosevelt's pace nor revise her new perspective on duty and independence. In June 1920, while she was vacationing with the children at Campobello Island in Canada, Roosevelt received the Democratic nomination for vice president. Although both her grandmother and mother-in-law strongly believed that "a woman's place is not in the public eye" and pressured Eleanor Roosevelt to respond to press inquiries through her social secretary, she developed a close working relationship with her husband's intimate adviser and press liaison, Louis Howe. Invigorated by Howe's support, she threw herself into the election and reveled in the routine political decisions that daily confronted the ticket. By the end of the campaign, while other journalists aboard the Roosevelt campaign train played cards, Louis Howe and Eleanor Roosevelt could frequently be found huddled over paperwork, reviewing Roosevelt's speeches and discussing campaign protocol.

When Republican Warren G. Harding won the 1920 election, the Roosevelts returned to New York. Franklin practiced law and planned his next political move as his wife considered her options. Dreading "a winter of four months in New York with nothing but teas and luncheons and dinners to take up [her] time," Eleanor Roosevelt "mapped out a schedule" in which she spent Monday through Thursday in New York

City and the weekend in Hyde Park. She declined invitations to sit on the boards of organizations that wanted to exploit her name rather than use her energy, opting instead to join the Women's City Club, the National Consumers League, the Women's Division of the Democratic State Committee, and the New York chapters of the League of Women Voters and the Women's Trade Union League.

Despite her labeling the 1920s as a time of "private interlude" in *This I Remember*, in the seven-year span between the onset of her husband's paralysis and his campaign for the New York governorship, Eleanor Roosevelt's political contributions and organizational sagacity made her one of New York's leading politicians. While still fervently committed to democratic ideals, she recognized that ideology alone does not provide the votes and skills necessary to win elections. Repeatedly she goaded women's and other reform groups to set realistic goals, prioritize their tasks, and delegate assignments. Her pragmatism attracted attention within the party and women's political organizations. Soon the *New York Times* publicized her clout, referring to her on April 8, 1928, as the "woman [of influence] who speaks her political mind."

After working with attorney Elizabeth Read and her partner, the educator and consumer activist Esther Lape, Eleanor Roosevelt agreed to chair the Legislative Affairs Committee of the League of Women Voters and to represent the league on the Women's Joint Legislative Committee. Each week she studied the *Congressional Record*, examined legislation and committee reports, interviewed members of Congress and the state assembly, and met with league officers to discuss the information she had gathered. Each month she assembled her analyses and presented a report for league members, outlining the status of bills in which the organization was interested and suggesting strategies by which it could achieve its legislative goals. Moreover, she also frequently spoke out at these monthly assemblies on pressing nonlegislative issues such as primary reform, voter registration, and party identification. Recognizing the extensive contributions she had made, the league elected her its vice chairman eighteen months later, after Eleanor Roosevelt skillfully arbitrated a hostile internal dispute.

Ruby Black saw this time as the period when "Eleanor Roosevelt was traveling, not drifting, away from the conventional life expected of women in her social class." Mrs. Roosevelt agreed, later labeling the last part of 1920 as the beginning of "the intensive education of Eleanor Roosevelt." Polio did not strike her husband until the following summer; consequently, she was already in a position to keep the Roosevelt name active in Democratic circles before illness sidelined her husband.

Throughout September 1922, Eleanor Roosevelt, Nancy Cook, Marion Dickerman, and future New York Congresswoman Caroline O'Day traveled throughout the state to encourage the formation of Democratic women's clubs. Their organizational efforts created such strong support among the Democratic rank and file that at the state convention in Syracuse the women present demanded that Mrs. Roosevelt, Marion Dickerman, and Caroline O'Day each be considered as the party's nominee for secretary of state. The following month, as Democratic Women's Committee vice president and finance chairman, Eleanor Roosevelt edited and wrote articles for the *Women's Democratic News*, discussing campaign strategies and the fall election.

By 1924, Eleanor Roosevelt had joined the board of the bipartisan Women's City Club, whose major objectives were to inform women about pressing political and social issues, introduce them in a pragmatic way to governmental operations, and organize lobbying and publicity campaigns for club-sponsored issues. During her four-year tenure as a board member of the club, Mrs. Roosevelt chaired its City Planning Department, coordinated its responses on housing and transportation issues, chaired its Legislation Committee, pushed through a reorganization plan, arbitrated disputes over child labor laws, promoted workmen's compensation, and, in a move that made

banner headlines across New York State, strongly urged the adoption of an amendment to the penal law legalizing the distribution of birth control information among married couples.

Not all of the Roosevelts' friends supported her activism. Indeed, Eleanor Roosevelt's political prominence created some in-house sarcasm among the governor's advisers. That May, Josephus Daniels taunted his former assistant secretary in a letter dated May 8, 1924, that he was glad not to be "the only 'squaw' man in the country."

Such inside joking did not curtail Eleanor Roosevelt's political exposure. She attended the 1924 Democratic National Convention as chair of the women's delegation to the platform committee and as New York governor Al Smith's liaison to women voters. When the committee rejected her requests, and the convention refused to choose Smith as its standard-bearer, she returned to New York undaunted. "I took my politics so seriously," she uncharacteristically recalled in *This Is My Story*, "that in the early autumn I came down to the state headquarters and went seriously to work in the state campaign."

Assiduously, Eleanor Roosevelt courted voters throughout the state. New Yorkers living in the rural areas often neglected by the party heard her personalized appeals for support. She pledged to keep their interests in front of the party leadership if the farmers would continue to make their demands known and to vote Democratic. But she also appealed to voters' more basic instincts. Despite her aversion to Tammanyesque practices, Eleanor Roosevelt occasionally participated in her own version of negative campaigning, even if the candidate was a member of her own family. The Republicans had nominated her cousin, Ted Roosevelt, for governor. Without a second thought, Eleanor Roosevelt tailed her cousin around the state in a roadster topped with a giant steaming teapot, in a flagrant attempt to associate him with Teapot Dome corruption.

Eleanor Roosevelt then took to print to promote her candidates with the same level of energy she had displayed in her speeches. She expanded her audience, broadened her themes, and carefully tailored her remarks. Within the next twelve months, she continued her regular articles for the League's *Weekly News* and *Women's Democratic News*, and she published four substantive political articles in publications ranging from the popular women's magazine *Redbook* to the more scholarly journals *Current History* and *North American Review*.

So strong an impression did her organizational and administrative campaign skills make on the state's professional politicians that Belle Moskowitz and Al Smith both recruited her energies for Smith's 1928 presidential campaign. A longtime supporter of Smith, Eleanor Roosevelt agreed to coordinate preconvention activities for the Democratic Women's Committee. The *New York Times Magazine* recognized her increasing political clout and featured a lead article on her influence in its April 8, 1928, issue. Ironically, as a result of this continuous activity, by the time her husband received the Democratic Party's nomination for governor, Eleanor Roosevelt was better known among the faithful party activists than was Franklin Roosevelt.

The 1928 election presented a new challenge to both Roosevelts. New York state law prevented Al Smith, the Democratic presidential nominee, from seeking reelection as governor, and Smith wanted Roosevelt to succeed him. This decision placed Eleanor Roosevelt squarely in opposition to her husband's most trusted aide, Louis Howe. Howe vigorously opposed Roosevelt's candidacy and Roosevelt, following Howe's advice, refused to take Smith's phone calls. Smith, whose chief political adviser was a woman, appreciated the scope of Eleanor Roosevelt's expertise and the influence she held in her husband's innermost political circle. Consequently, Smith turned to Eleanor Roosevelt, who had enthusiastically endorsed his candidacy and who was the only individual who might counteract Howe's opposition, to intercede with Franklin. Eleanor Roosevelt agreed, phoned her husband, told him that "she

knew he had to do what he felt was expected of him," handed the phone to Smith, and left to address a Smith campaign rally.

However, this does not mean that Eleanor Roosevelt unequivocally endorsed her husband's electoral aspirations. She feared that his victory would undermine all her autonomy. "It became clear," James Roosevelt wrote in 1976, "that she felt if father won, she would lose" the autonomy she had worked so painstakingly to develop.

By the early 1920s, the Franklin Roosevelt–Eleanor Roosevelt relationship had begun to move away from an alliance defined by marital responsibilities and more toward a professional collaboration between peers. Mrs. Roosevelt's discovery in 1918 of her husband's affair with Lucy Mercer, her social secretary, destroyed marital intimacy and encouraged her to look elsewhere for closeness. While both treasured their friendship with Louis Howe and Roosevelt enjoyed most of his wife's associates, the separate strong attachments the Roosevelts formed with different coworkers and companions were the rule rather than the exception in the Roosevelt household.

Indeed, the few old friends and Democratic Party commitments the Roosevelts shared were enough to sustain a friendship, but not an intimate one. Competing pursuits and divergent communities encouraged the Roosevelts to follow different paths and to develop separate lifestyles. "It is essential," Eleanor Roosevelt responded in August 1930, when *Good Housekeeping* asked her to define "What Is a Wife's Job Today," for the woman "to develop her own interests, to carry on a stimulating life of her own." As a result, by the time Roosevelt was elected governor, each had developed independent personal and political support systems.

With her ties to reform movements and women's political associations expanding, Eleanor Roosevelt carefully and deliberately developed her own network. Caroline O'Day and Elinor Morgenthau became her lifelong intimate friends. With Democratic Women's Committee colleague Nancy Cook and her partner Marion Dickerman, with whom Eleanor Roosevelt taught and who would later administer the Todhunter School for Girls in New York City, Eleanor Roosevelt built Val-Kill, her home away from the Roosevelt house.

While the Roosevelts both expanded their levels of commitment to the state Democratic Party and promoted the same candidates, they began to form different views of the political process. Although both Roosevelts realized that politics was part ego, part drive, and part conviction, they differed as to which component they valued the most. If politics were part game and part crusade, Eleanor Roosevelt tolerated the game for the sake of the crusade. To her dismay, her husband enjoyed all its aspects. To the extent that Roosevelt failed to reverse this trend, he could no longer depend upon his wife's unqualified support. Consequently, in 1932, Eleanor Roosevelt responded to a friend who confessed to voting for Norman Thomas by saying that "if [she] had not been married to Franklin," she, too, would have voted for the Socialist candidate.

This does not mean, however, that once Franklin Roosevelt assumed the governorship, Eleanor Roosevelt played the game more than she struggled for reform. The dilemma that the return to Albany presented Eleanor Roosevelt was one of continuing independence: one of time management rather than political fidelity. Her bid for personal freedom was a more strenuous and long-lasting campaign than her husband's 1928 run for office had been.

Thus, Eleanor Roosevelt was not thrilled with the prospect of returning to Albany—a goldfish bowl in which all her movements would be both confined by and interpreted through her husband's political prestige. She told son James, who recalled this conversation in *My Parents*, that "she knew that [FDR] had wanted her to become active in politics primarily to keep his case in the public eye," and that he "would expect her to move into the shadows if he moved into the limelight." This depressed her immensely. As Marion Dickerman later told Roosevelt biographer Kenneth S. Davis, Eleanor Roosevelt's "dread" was so strong that it fostered

a rebellion that "strained at the leash of her self-control."

Yet Mrs. Roosevelt also realized that her political expertise and her new support system were an outgrowth of, and therefore a by-product of, her relationship with her husband. Never did she fully expect him to withdraw from public life or expect that she would be immune from its scrutiny. Instead, Eleanor Roosevelt concentrated on how to find the most appropriate manner in which to promote two careers at once—how best to pursue her separate interests and not undermine her husband's public standing.

The three keys to her freedom—the Democratic Women's Committee (DWC), the Todhunter School for Girls, and Val-Kill—lay outside Albany. Therefore, the extent to which Mrs. Roosevelt could maximize her independence was directly parallel to the extent to which she could efficiently divide her life between the governor's mansion and the family's East 65th Street residence in New York City. She knew how threatening this would be to some pundits. So, immediately after the election, Eleanor Roosevelt launched her own media campaign to make the press treat her various activities in the most positive light possible. On the day of Franklin's inauguration as governor, November 11, 1928, when a *New York Times* reporter asked her what her new schedule would be, Eleanor Roosevelt responded that although she would resign her DWC positions, she would still support the furniture factory at Val-Kill and commute to New York City three days a week to continue her government and English literature classes and to fulfill her administrative responsibilities at Todhunter.

Eleanor Roosevelt's duties in New York City did not preclude political contributions to Franklin Roosevelt's administration. She successfully lobbied Democratic National Chairman John Raskob for increased allocations to the Democratic State Committee and raised seed money for the Women's Activities Committee. Furthermore, in Albany and in other locales throughout the state that she visited,

Eleanor Roosevelt began to apply the political finesse she had demonstrated earlier in arbitrating League of Women Voters disputes to resolve disagreements within Franklin's inner circle. With her friend Henry Morgenthau, Mrs. Roosevelt pressured her husband to invite both Republican and Democratic mayors, rather than just the officials who supported Roosevelt's goals, to the State Mayors' Conference. She regularly arbitrated conflicts between Roosevelt intimates Louis Howe and Jim Farley, and acted as a political stand-in when her husband would not or could not participate in the discussion.

Eleanor Roosevelt's contributions were not limited to crisis management. Aware of how difficult it was for a politician and his staff to face unpopular decisions, Mrs. Roosevelt championed the appointment of individuals who had the nerve to disagree with Roosevelt. She lobbied successfully for Frances Perkins's appointment as state secretary of labor and for Nell Schwartz to fill the vacancy Perkins's appointment had left on the State Industrial Commission. Believing that she knew former governor Smith better than her husband did, Mrs. Roosevelt strongly objected to his retaining any of Smith's cabinet. In particular, she opposed Belle Moskowitz's appointment as the governor's personal secretary and Robert Moses's reappointment as secretary of state, writing to her husband in Warm Springs, Georgia, on November 13, 1928, that "by all signs Belle and Bob Moses mean to cling to you. If you are not careful," she continued, "you will wake up to find R.M. Secretary of State and B.M. running Democratic publicity at the old stand unless you take a firm stand." Furthermore, she testified before various Senate committees in behalf of protective labor legislation and was not afraid to criticize her husband's plan for unemployment insurance.

The 1932 presidential campaign assaulted Eleanor Roosevelt's adaptability with increasing frequency. Although she supported her husband's political ambitions out of loyalty to both him and the Democratic Party, she astutely recognized that she would encounter attacks if she continued to pursue her individual projects with the same vigor that she had applied in the past. For his part, Franklin Roosevelt continued to promote the image of "his Missus" as part of the Roosevelt team. Nevertheless, Eleanor Roosevelt knew that this was a political screen designed to enhance her symbolic value to the campaign. What her future role would be was uncertain.

Therefore, once the election was decided in her husband's favor, Eleanor Roosevelt turned to the press to test her public standing. Whereas during the race she continued to declare to interviewers that she "would be very much at home in Washington" if her husband were elected, she confided her dread to reporters she trusted. Riding in a day coach to Albany with Lorena Hickok, who covered Mrs. Roosevelt's activities for the Associated Press wire service, on November 9, 1932, Eleanor Roosevelt unburdened her thoughts for the record: "I never wanted it even though some people have said that my ambition for myself drove him on. . . . I never wanted to be a President's wife." Fearful that her seeming lack of support for her husband would be misunderstood, she clarified her stance:

> For him, of course, I'm glad—sincerely. I could not have wanted it any other way. After all I'm a Democrat, too. Now I shall have to work out my own salvation. I'm afraid it may be a little difficult. I know what Washington is like. I've lived there.

The American press, like the American public, was divided over how professionally active a First Lady should be. Although Eleanor Roosevelt's preinaugural activities were in the same fields as the positions she had held while she was the governor's wife, criticism of her commercial radio and journalism contracts increased. Suddenly, Eleanor Roosevelt found herself ridiculed in such diverse publications as the *Harvard Lampoon*, the *Hartford Courant*, and the *Baltimore Sun*. By February 1933, the press was increasingly interpreting her professionalism as commercialism. As Lorena Hickok recalled in *Eleanor Roosevelt: Reluctant First Lady*:

> [A]ll through January and February and right up until March 2, the day they left for Washington, Eleanor Roosevelt continued to do the things she had always done. The papers continued to carry stories about her. And some people continued to criticize her. They just could not get used to the idea of her being "plain, ordinary Eleanor Roosevelt."

Although Eleanor Roosevelt admitted to her friend that she would "curtail somewhat her activities" because she "suppose[d] [she] had made some mistakes," Mrs. Roosevelt adamantly refused to abandon the expertise she had worked so diligently to achieve. Aware of the criticism her position would provoke, she argued that she had no choice but to continue. "I'll just have to go on being myself, as much as I can. I'm just not the sort of person who would be any good at [any] job. I dare say I shall be criticized, whatever I do."

Eleanor Roosevelt's aversion to any other role was so strong that in the week before Roosevelt's presidential inauguration, she impetuously wrote to Dickerman and Cook that she was contemplating divorce. She told Hickok, in a quotation for the record, that she "hated" having to resign her teaching position at Todhunter, saying "I wonder if you have any idea how I hate to do it." Increasingly sympathetic to her dilemma and aware of the potential repercussions of such statements, Hickok, in her November 11, 1932, Associated Press piece, portrayed Mrs. Roosevelt as upbeat and confident: "The prospective mistress of the White House thinks people are going to get used to her ways, even though she does edit *Babies—Just Babies*, wears $10 dresses, and drives her own car."

Clearly, when Eleanor Roosevelt entered the White House in March 1933, she did so reluctantly. Although she supported her husband's aims and believed in his leadership ability, she feared that his

political agenda—in addition to restricting her movements and curtailing her independence—would force her to minimize the political issues she held nearest and dearest to her heart. As soon as Franklin Roosevelt won the election, he asked his wife to resign her positions with the Democratic National Committee, the Todhunter School, the League of Women Voters, the Non-Partisan Legislative Committee, and the Women's Trade Union League. She then announced that she would no longer take part in commercial radio events and that she would refrain from discussing politics in her magazine articles. Though she tried to avoid it, public expectation was redefining her career, and it hurt. "If I wanted to be selfish," she had confessed earlier to Hickok, "I could wish that he had not been elected."

Questions "seethed" in Eleanor Roosevelt's mind about what she should do after March 4, 1933. Afraid of being confined to a schedule of teas and receptions, she volunteered to do a "real job" for the president. She knew that Ettie Rheiner (Mrs. John Nance) Garner served as an administrative assistant to her husband the vice president, so the First Lady tried to convince the president to let her provide the same service. When the president rebuffed her offer, trapped by convention, she begrudgingly recognized that "the work [was FDR's] work and the pattern his pattern." Bitterly disappointed, she acknowledged that she "was one of those who served his purposes."

Nevertheless, Mrs. Roosevelt refused to accept a superficial and sedentary role. She wanted "to do things on [her] own, to use [her] own mind and abilities for [her] own aims." She struggled to carve out an active contributory place for herself in the New Deal. That was not to be a challenge easily met. Dejected, she found it "hard to remember that [she] was not just 'Eleanor Roosevelt,' but the 'wife of the President.'"

Eleanor Roosevelt entered the first hundred days of her husband's administration with no clearly defined role. Her offers to sort the president's mail and to act as his "listening post" had been rejected summarily. Moreover, the press continued to pounce on each display of the First Lady's individualism. When she announced in an Inauguration Day interview with the *New York Times* that she planned to cut White House expenses by 25 percent, "simplify" the White House social calendar, and serve as Franklin's "eyes and ears," reporters discovered that she was just as much news after the inaugural as she had been before.

Mrs. Roosevelt's relations with the press during the spring and summer of 1933 did nothing to curtail their interest. On March 6, two days after her husband became president, she held her own press conference, at which she announced that she would "get together" with women reporters once a week. She asked for their cooperation. She wanted to make the general public more aware of White House activities and to encourage their understanding of the political process. She hoped that the women reporters who covered her would interpret—especially to American women—the basic mechanics of national politics.

Despite Mrs. Roosevelt's initial intention to focus on her social activities as First Lady, political issues soon became a central part of the weekly briefings. When some members of her press corps tried to caution her against speaking off the record, she responded that she knew some of her statements would "cause unfavorable comment in some quarters . . . [but she was] making these statements on purpose to arouse controversy and thereby get the topics talked about."

Eleanor Roosevelt then made the same argument to the public when she accepted an offer for a monthly column from *Woman's Home Companion*. Announcing, in August 1933, that she would donate her monthly $1,000 fee to charity, the First Lady then proceeded to ask her readers to help her establish "a clearinghouse, a discussion room" for "the particular problems which puzzle you or sadden you," and to share "how you are adjusting yourself to new conditions in this amazing changing world." Titling the article "I Want You to Write to Me," Eleanor Roosevelt rein-

forced the request throughout the piece. "Do not hesitate," she wrote, "to write to me even if your views clash with what you believe to be my views." Only a free exchange of ideas and discussion of problems would help her "learn of experiences which may be helpful to others." By January 1934, 300,000 Americans had responded to her request.

From her first days in the White House, her desire to remain part of the public propelled Eleanor Roosevelt's New Deal agenda. She greeted guests at the door of the White House herself, learned to operate the White House elevator, and adamantly refused Secret Service protection. Yet there also were signs that she intended to be a serious contributor to the Roosevelt administration. She converted the Lincoln bedroom into a study and had a telephone installed. She urged her husband to send Hickok on a national fact-finding tour for the Federal Emergency Relief Association in the summer of 1933. She prodded the administration to appoint women to positions of influence throughout the New Deal programs. And, when the Washington press corps refused to admit its women members to its annual Gridiron dinner, Eleanor Roosevelt gleefully threw herself into planning a "Gridiron Widows" banquet and skit for women officials and reporters.

When Eleanor Roosevelt read Hickok's accounts of the squalid conditions in the West Virginia coal town of Scott's Run, she was appalled and moved immediately to address the problem. She met with Louis Howe and Secretary of the Interior Harold Ickes to argue that the Subsistence Homestead provision of the National Industrial Recovery Act would help address the community's problems. She succeeded, and became a frequent visitor to the new community—Arthurdale. There she was photographed square dancing with miners in worn clothes and holding sick children in her lap. That image—when linked with her strong commitment to building the best living quarters the funds could provide—served as a lighting rod for critics of the

New Deal, and they delighted in exposing each cost overrun and each program defect.

While most historians view Eleanor Roosevelt's commitment to Arthurdale as the best example of her influence within the New Deal, that assessment is too one-dimensional to reflect the breadth of her commitment to democratic reform. The First Lady did more than champion a single antipoverty program. Continuously she urged that relief be as diverse as the constituency that needed it. "The unemployed are not a strange race. They are like we would be if we had not had a fortunate chance at life," she wrote in 1933. The distress they encountered, not their socioeconomic status, should be the focus of relief. Consequently, she introduced programs for groups not originally included in New Deal plans; supported other programs that were in danger of elimination or having their funds cut; pushed the hiring of women, blacks, and liberals within federal agencies; and acted as the administration's most outspoken champion of liberal reform.

Eleanor Roosevelt did not immediately begin to push programs. Rather, as her actions to modify the Federal Emergency Relief Administration (FERA) and the Civil Works Administration (CWA) show, she waited to see how the programs that Roosevelt's aides designed were put into operation, and then lobbied for improvements or suggested alternatives. When the needs of unemployed women were overlooked by FERA and CWA planners, Mrs. Roosevelt lobbied first to have women's divisions established within both agencies and then to have specific women appointed as program directors. She then planned and chaired the White House Conference on the Emergency Needs of Women and monitored the Household Workers' Training Program, which was born during the conference.

Mrs. Roosevelt addressed the problems of unemployed youth with the same fervor that she applied to women's economic hardships. That, too, was not a politically popular position for her to take. The unemployed youth of the 1930s underscored sev-

eral fears that adults had for society. Conservatives saw disgruntled young people as a fertile ground for revolutionary politics, while progressives mourned the disillusionment and apathy spreading among American youth.

The First Lady thought that camps of the Civilian Conservation Corps (CCC), while providing temporary relief for some youth, did not meet the need. Furthermore, because the camps were supervised by military personnel and provided instruction only in forestry, she believed that an additional program tailored to the special needs of young people was urgently required. In mid-1933, she pressured Harry Hopkins, head of the Federal Emergency Relief Administration, to develop a youth program that would provide a social rather than a militaristic focus. Eleanor Roosevelt argued that the specific problems facing youths needed to be recognized, but only in a way that fostered a sense of self-worth. By providing job skills and education, she hoped that the program would foster a sense of civic awareness, which, in turn, would promote a commitment to social justice. Then young people would be empowered to articulate their own needs and aspirations and to express those insights clearly.

Although historians disagree over how major a role Eleanor Roosevelt played in establishing the National Youth Administration (NYA), her imprint upon the agency's development is indelible. Established by an executive order signed by Roosevelt on June 26, 1935, the NYA was authorized to administer programs in five areas: work projects, vocational guidance, apprenticeship training, educational and nutritional guidance camps for unemployed women, and student aid. Clearly, her preference for vocational guidance and education triumphed over the CCC relief model.

Moreover, the First Lady was both the agency's and the young people's natural choice for confessor, planner, lobbyist, and promoter. She reviewed NYA policy with agency directors, arranged for NYA officials and youth leaders to meet with Roosevelt in and out of the White House, served as the NYA's intermediary with the president, critiqued and suggested projects, and attended as many NYA state administrators' conferences as her schedule allowed. Last but not least, she visited at least 112 NYA sites and reported her observations in her speeches, articles, and "My Day," the daily column she began in 1936. Mrs. Roosevelt took such satisfaction in the administration that when she briefly acknowledged her role in forming the agency, she did so with an uncharacteristic candor: "One of the ideas I agreed to present to Franklin," she wrote in *This I Remember*, "was that of setting up a national youth administration. . . . It was one of the occasions on which I was very proud that the right thing was done regardless of political consequences."

While she listened to the concerns of youth, Eleanor Roosevelt also met with unemployed artists and writers to discuss their concerns. They asked for her support for a Public Works Arts Project (PWAP). She agreed immediately and attended the preliminary planning meeting. Sitting at the head table next to Edward Bruce, the meeting's organizer, Eleanor Roosevelt knitted while she listened to Bruce propose a program to pay artists for creating public art. Advocating a program in which artists could control both form and content, Bruce recruited supporters for a federally financed work appropriate for public buildings. Sitting quietly through most of the discussion, the First Lady interrupted only to question procedure and to emphasize her support of the project.

Mrs. Roosevelt became PWAP's ardent public and private champion. When PWAP artists were sent to CCC camps in mid-1934 and produced over 200 watercolors, oil paintings, and chalk drawings portraying camp life, Eleanor Roosevelt enthusiastically opened their "Life in the CCC" exhibit at the National Museum. When 500 PWAP artworks were displayed at Washington's Corcoran Gallery, she dedicated the exhibit and declared that, in addition to their artistic merit, the works liberated society greatly by expressing what many people could find no words to describe.

After Bruce was appointed PWAP director, he proposed that artists be eligible for Works Progress Administration (WPA) programs. Immediately Bruce solicited Mrs. Roosevelt's support. She agreed that artists were in need of government aid and supported the WPA venture, in the process entering the internal dispute over whether FERA should fund white-collar programs. With the support of FERA administrator Harry Hopkins, Eleanor Roosevelt lobbied her husband to endorse Bruce's concept. The president agreed, issuing an executive order on June 25, 1935, that created the Federal One Programs of the Works Progress Administration: the Federal Writers Project, the Federal Theater Project, and the Federal Art Project (formerly PWAP).

Eleanor Roosevelt continued to run administrative interference after the programs were in operation. When Jean Baker, director of the WPA Professional and Service Products Division, gave in to pressure from conservatives who wanted to place the program under local control, Mrs. Roosevelt convinced Hopkins that Baker should be replaced. Hopkins agreed, and filled Baker's post with Eleanor Roosevelt's close friend Ellen Woodward.

Mrs. Roosevelt also continued to promote the project despite its increasingly controversial image. When Hallie Flanagan, director of Federal Theater Project, asked for assistance in convincing Congress that the Federal Theater Project was not a heretical attack on American culture, Eleanor Roosevelt agreed on the spot. The First Lady told Flanagan that she would gladly go to Congress because the time had come when America must recognize that art is controversial and that controversy is an important part of education.

Despite the fervor with which Eleanor Roosevelt campaigned for a more democratic administration of relief through the establishment of women's divisions, NYA, and the three Federal One programs, these efforts paled in comparison to the unceasing pressure she placed upon the president and the nation to confront the economic and political discrimination facing African

Americans. Although the First Lady did not become an ardent proponent of integration until the 1950s, throughout the 1930s and 1940s she nevertheless persistently labeled racial prejudice as undemocratic and immoral. African Americans recognized the depth of her commitment and consequently kept faith with Roosevelt because his wife kept faith with them.

Mrs. Roosevelt's racial policies attracted notice almost immediately. Less than a week after becoming First Lady, she shocked conservative Washington society by announcing she would have an entirely black White House domestic staff. By late summer 1933, photographs appeared showing her discussing living conditions with black miners in West Virginia, and the press treated her involvement in the anti-lynching campaign as front-page news. Rumors of the First Lady's "race-baiting" actions sped across the South with hurricane force.

Eleanor Roosevelt refused to be intimidated by rumor. She mobilized cabinet and congressional wives for a walking tour of Washington's slum alleys to increase support for housing legislation then before Congress. After being intensively briefed by civil rights leader Walter White, the First Lady toured the Virgin Islands with Lorena Hickok in 1934, investigating conditions for herself, only to return agreeing with White's initial assessments. In 1935, she visited Howard University's Freedman Hospital, lobbied Congress for increased appropriations, and praised the institution in her press conferences. The president's disapproval kept her from attending the 1934 and 1935 National Association for the Advancement of Colored People (NAACP) conventions; however, his cautiousness did not affect her support of the organization. Indeed, she telegraphed her deep disappointment to the delegates. She then joined the local chapters of the NAACP and National Urban League, becoming the first white Washington resident to respond to the membership drives. And, in contrast to her husband, who refrained from actively supporting anti-lynching legislation, a very public Eleanor Roosevelt refused to leave the Senate gallery during the filibuster over the bill.

As the 1936 election approached, Eleanor Roosevelt continued her inspections and finally convinced her husband to let her address the NAACP's and National Urban League's annual conventions. When the *New Yorker* magazine published the famous cartoon of miners awaiting her visit, the First Lady aggressively defended her outreach to minorities and the poor in a lengthy article for the August 24, 1935, issue of the *Saturday Evening Post*. She directly attacked those who mocked her interest. "In strange and subtle ways," she began, "it was indicated to me that I should feel ashamed of that cartoon and that there was certainly something the matter with a woman who wanted to see so much and know so much." She refused to be so limited, she responded to those "blind" critics who refused to be interested in anything outside their own four walls.

The liberal and conservative press gave such actions prominent coverage. When Eleanor Roosevelt addressed the National Urban League's annual convention, NBC Radio broadcast the address nationally. When she visited Howard University and was escorted around campus by its Honor Guard, the *Georgia Woman's World* printed a picture of her surrounded by the students on its front page, while it castigated the First Lady for conduct unbecoming to a president's wife. Mainstream press such as the *New York Times* and *Christian Science Monitor* questioned the extent to which Mrs. Roosevelt would be "a campaign issue."

Eleanor Roosevelt increased her civil rights activism in her second term as First Lady. She continued her outspoken advocacy of anti-lynching legislation, served as an active cochair of the National Committee to Abolish the Poll Tax, spoke out in favor of National Sharecropper's Week, urged Agricultural Adjustment Act administrators to recognize the discriminatory practices of white landowners, pressured FERA administrators to pay black and white workers equal salaries, and invited African-American guests and entertainers to the White House. With NYA administrator Mary McLeod Bethune, she convened the National Conference of Negro Women at the White House and publicized the agenda that the conference promoted. She also pressured the Resettlement Administration to recognize that black sharecroppers' problems deserved attention and lent her active endorsement to the Southern Conference on Human Welfare (SCHW).

Often the public stances Mrs. Roosevelt took were more effective than the lobbying she did behind the scenes. When the First Lady entered the SCHW's 1938 convention in Birmingham, Alabama, police officers told her that she would not be allowed to sit with Bethune, because a city ordinance outlawed integrated seating. Mrs. Roosevelt then requested a chair and placed it squarely in the aisle between the groups, highlighting her displeasure with Jim Crow policies. In February 1939, the First Lady resigned from the Daughters of the American Revolution (DAR) when the organization refused to rent its auditorium to the internationally known black contralto Marian Anderson. She then announced her decision in her newspaper column, thereby transforming a local act into a national disgrace. When Howard University students picketed lunch stands near the university that denied them service, Mrs. Roosevelt praised their courage and sent them money with which to continue their public education programs. And when A. Philip Randolph and other civil rights leaders threatened to march on Washington unless the president acted to outlaw discrimination in defense industries, Mrs. Roosevelt took their demands to the White House.

By the early 1940s, Eleanor Roosevelt firmly believed the civil rights issue to be the real litmus test for American democracy. Thus she declared over and over again throughout the war that there could be no democracy in the United States that did not include democracy for African Americans. In *The Moral Basis of Democracy* she asserted that people of all races have inviolate rights to property: "We have never been willing to face this problem, to line it up with the

basic, underlying beliefs in Democracy." Racial prejudice enslaved blacks; consequently, "no one can claim that . . . the Negroes of this country are free." She continued this theme in a 1942 article in the *New Republic*, declaring that both the private and the public sector must acknowledge that "one of the main destroyers of freedom is our attitude toward the colored race." The First Lady went on: "What Kipling called 'The White Man's Burden,'" she proclaimed in a July 1942 issue of *American Magazine*, is "one of the things we can not have any longer." Furthermore, she told those listening to the radio broadcast of the 1945 National Democratic Forum, "democracy may grow or fade as we face [this] problem."

When, during World War II, Eleanor Roosevelt dared to equate American racism with fascism and argued that to ignore the evils of segregation would be capitulating to Aryanism, hostility toward her reached an all-time high. Newspapers from Chicago to Louisiana covered the dispute and numerous citizens pleaded with J. Edgar Hoover, director of the Federal Bureau of Investigation (FBI), to silence her. Refusing to concede to her opponents, she continuously asserted that if the nation continued to honor Jim Crow, America would have defeated fascism abroad only to defend racism at home.

Eleanor Roosevelt said the same things in private that she did in public. Whether interceding with the president for Walter White, Mary McLeod Bethune, A. Philip Randolph, or W.E.B. DuBois; raising money for Howard University or Bethune-Cookman College; investigating discrimination black women encountered while stationed at the Women's Auxiliary Army Corps base in Des Moines, Iowa; pressing the Fair Employment Practices Commission to investigate complaints; or supporting antisegregation campaigns and antilynching legislation, the First Lady pressed to keep civil rights issues at the top of the domestic political agenda. Consequently, throughout the war years, her standing with civil rights leaders increased while her standing with some key White House aides decreased.

Eleanor Roosevelt also angered some White House aides by her insistent demand that New Deal reforms continue during wartime. Vowing that she would not put the New Deal away in storage, the First Lady pressured Roosevelt's aides, liberal leaders, and concerned Americans to remember that there was an economic emergency in addition to a military one. Thus, by the 1944 presidential election, the two camps within the Roosevelt administration had become even more clearly defined.

When Franklin Delano Roosevelt died on April 12, 1945, Eleanor Roosevelt was well prepared personally and politically for the challenges facing her. She had close confidants, colleagues, and friends to turn to for support. And, although she was hurt to discover that Lucy Mercer had been with her husband when he suffered his fatal stroke, she quickly recovered and resumed her commitments.

The question Mrs. Roosevelt faced in 1945 was what her public role would be. Invitations poured into the White House, her apartment in New York City, and her home at Val-Kill. Now that she was no longer First Lady, Eleanor Roosevelt was anxious to leave the White House. Within a week of the president's death, she coordinated his funeral, responded to friends' condolences, oversaw the boxing of possessions acquired and documents generated during her twelve years in Washington, said good-bye to colleagues and staff, and pondered her future. Despite the intensity of this schedule, Mrs. Roosevelt made time on April 19 to host a farewell White House tea for the women's press corps. Although the reception was a private affair, Eleanor Roosevelt did answer some questions for the record. After scoffing at various rumors of her own political ambitions, she declared that her only aspirations were journalistic ones. Yet, the next evening, after arriving in Manhattan, she faced those questions for a second time. Confronted by a small group of photographers and reporters outside her Washington Square apartment, she refused to comment on their speculations. "The story," she said, "is over."

Despite these denials, politicians, pundits, and the public openly speculated on what actions Eleanor Roosevelt should take next. Speaker of the House Sam Rayburn and New Jersey Congresswoman Mary Norton urged Mrs. Roosevelt to join the American delegation to the conference charged with planning the United Nations. Secretary of the Interior Harold Ickes pleaded with her to run for the U.S. Senate, while New York Democratic Party leader Ed Flynn argued that she should be the Empire State's next governor. Others proposed that she be the new secretary of labor. Even the syndicated columnists Joseph and Stewart Alsop belatedly joined the conjecture, satirically suggesting that their cousin become President Truman's new political "medium."

Close friends and the press reinforced this expectation. As they rode the train from Roosevelt's Hyde Park funeral back to Washington, Henry Morgenthau, Jr., recommended that Roosevelt's estate be settled as soon as possible so that Eleanor Roosevelt could speak out to the world, arguing that it was most important that her voice be heard. After encouraging her friend to take a brief rest, Lorena Hickok reminded Mrs. Roosevelt that she was independent now, freer than she had ever been before, and that a very important place awaited her. The Associated Press agreed, succinctly summarizing the pressures confronting Eleanor Roosevelt on April 14, 1945, with this front-page headline: "Mrs. Roosevelt Will Continue Column; Seeks No Office *Now*."

Eleanor Roosevelt had her own expectations about the future; however, unlike her friends and the press, she was undecided about what actions she should take to achieve them. Fearing that her public life had died along with her husband, Eleanor Roosevelt struggled to set her own course. Although she declared her determination not to be seen solely as a former First Lady, she feared that, without the ear of the president, she would lose the influence she had struggled so diligently to attain. At times she succumbed to these anxieties only to encounter jocular criticism from those closest to her. When a self-pitying Eleanor Roosevelt informed young friends that she merely wanted to write, visit her family, and live a peaceful life, Trude Lash teasingly suggested that they all go buy Mrs. Roosevelt a lace cap as a retirement gift.

As Eleanor Roosevelt reflected on her life, she drew confidence from the way she had handled previous political expectations. During her years in New York, she had managed her career as teacher, journalist, and political organizer without discounting her responsibilities as the Empire State's First Lady. In the White House, she had revolutionized the role of First Lady by constantly acting in ways that were new to the position. She was the first (and only) First Lady to hold regular press conferences, write a daily newspaper column, publish books and articles, travel the nation on speaking tours, chair national conferences in the White House, address national conventions of social reform organizations, give a keynote address at her party's presidential convention, represent her nation abroad, travel across battlefields, and direct a governmental agency. Clearly, she had numerous skills that could be applied to politics outside the White House.

Yet these new boundaries did not mean that new politics would follow. Eleanor Roosevelt had no plans to forsake the goals and ideals of the New Deal. In fact, she planned to do the exact opposite. If Franklin Roosevelt had abandoned his New Deal objectives to win the war and had resented her insistent wartime references to domestic problems, she anticipated that his successor would be even less likely to pursue the controversial reforms that the president had postponed. She recognized that if the New Deal were to reenter the political arena, she would have to assist in orchestrating its return. Whether she did this by promoting candidates or policy was up to her. The path she selected was not the pivotal point in her strategy. What was important was that she selected a mode of operation that allowed her the greatest leeway in pursuing her own goals while she protected her husband's legacy.

For the next seventeen years of her life, until her death on November 7, 1962, Eleanor Roosevelt carefully walked this line. She published *This I Remember*, the memoirs of her years in the White House. She gladly lent her name to Democratic Party fund-raisers, campaigned for local, state, and national candidates, and hosted events commemorating her husband's major accomplishments.

But it was Mrs. Roosevelt's efforts as a politician in her own right that made her post–White House years unique. President Truman appointed her to the U.S. delegation to the United Nations, where she stunned delegates with her political finesse by overseeing the drafting and unanimous passage of the Universal Declaration of Human Rights. Although her seven-year service to the United Nations was one of the most fulfilling assignments of her life, Eleanor Roosevelt did not confine herself to one organization or one cause.

Worried that Roosevelt's death had deprived liberals of the leadership they needed to make America a more just democracy, Mrs. Roosevelt pressured Democratic officials and liberal leaders to practice what they preached. Comfortable with her own power, she remained uncomfortable with both consensus liberals and Communist-front sympathizers. She remained dissatisfied with President Truman, and he entered the election of 1948 without her endorsement. Yet as disappointed as she was with the Democratic Party in 1948, she refused to abandon the Democrats to promote a third party that was not sure of its membership or its principles.

Eleanor Roosevelt entered the Eisenhower presidency committed to making the Democratic Party less glued to the consensus agenda of price controls and fair deals, and more supportive of racial justice and tolerant of political dissent. Indeed, her perception of racial justice grew as she aged. She was not a complacent supporter of civil rights. She served on the national board of directors for the NAACP, CORE, and other major civil rights organizations. Her friendships with civil rights leaders and her experience chairing investigations of race riots, visiting internment facilities, and combating violent segregationist backlashes continually exposed her to the brutal nature of American racism. Soon the Ku Klux Klan had placed a bounty on her head. The number of death threats she received for her civil rights stance increased.

The First Lady's involvement with Democratic Party leaders and liberal interest groups also showed her on a daily basis the superficial nature of liberal commitment to racial justice. Gradually she moved away from counseling patience and working within the system, to supporting those activists who staged grand public events designed to force the political system to recognize the shallowness of its promises.

Eleanor Roosevelt simultaneously struggled to support civil liberties while criticizing American Communist activism. Once again uncomfortable with the stringent dictates of vital center liberalism, she frequently opposed Cold War liberals who argued that communism had no place in American politics. Not only was she the first nationally prominent liberal to oppose Joseph McCarthy, but she was also the only liberal to oppose the House Un-American Activities Committee and the Smith Act from its inception. Despite the rapidity with which Adlai Stevenson, Arthur Schlesinger, and other liberals deserted Alger Hiss after his conviction, Eleanor Roosevelt refused to let her disappointment in Hiss's judgment dictate her reaction to his conviction. That placed her in heated conflict with Richard Nixon, whom she viewed as one of the most dangerous men in America.

Discouraged by Stevenson's defeats in the 1952 and 1956 elections, Eleanor Roosevelt approached the campaign of 1960 with mixed emotions. Convinced that the party needed a new, vigorous vision to win the election and implement reform, she nevertheless could not convince herself that John F. Kennedy was the answer to the liberals' dilemma. His moderation on civil rights, his evasion on McCarthy, his reliance on machine politics, and his father's conduct during World War II only reinforced Mrs. Roosevelt's opposition to his election. Yet Kennedy realized that he needed her support and traveled to Hyde Park to meet with her. She was still not convinced that he was a true liberal, but she was willing to give him a chance. By October, when Kennedy made concessions to civil rights, Eleanor Roosevelt actively campaigned for him. After Kennedy was sworn in, he appointed her as chair of the President's Commission on the Status of Women.

Eleanor Roosevelt spent the last two years of her life tired and in pain, but she rarely curtailed her schedule. Battling aplastic anemia and tuberculosis, she nevertheless continued to speak out on issues relating to racial justice, world peace, and women's rights. Outraged by the violence the Freedom Riders encountered in Mississippi and Alabama, and discouraged by the tepid response of the Kennedy administration, Eleanor Roosevelt eagerly agreed to a request from CORE in May 1962 to chair a public hearing charged with investigating law enforcement officials' acts against the protesters. She returned home to Hyde Park, where she struggled to complete her last book, *Tomorrow Is Now*, in which she stressed the need for racial, political, and social justice. She died on November 7, 1962, in a New York City hospital at the age of seventy-eight.

BIBLIOGRAPHICAL ESSAY

The papers of Anna Eleanor Roosevelt are housed in the Franklin D. Roosevelt Library in Hyde Park, New York. The papers are voluminous and are divided into two sections: 1884–1945 and 1945–1962. Those interested in investigating Mrs. Roosevelt's life should also consult the following collections, which are also housed at the Roosevelt Library: Franklin D. Roosevelt papers, Lorena Hickok papers, Molly Dewson papers, Henry Morgenthau papers, the Eleanor Roosevelt Oral History Project, Anna Roosevelt Halstead papers, the Franklin D. Roosevelt, Jr., papers,

Joseph P. Lash papers, and the Democratic Women's Committee papers.

Material relating to Eleanor Roosevelt that is not included in the Roosevelt Library can be found in the following collections in the Library of Congress: NAACP papers, CORE papers, Edith Helm papers, Agnes E. Meyer papers, and the Democratic Study Group papers. There is also a substantial collection of information related to her in the Adlai E. Stevenson papers, housed in the Princeton University Library. Joseph Lash has published two collections of Eleanor Roosevelt's correspondence— *Love, Eleanor* (New York, 1982) and *World of Love, Eleanor* (New York, 1984)—which reflect her political and personal opinions.

Eleanor Roosevelt was a prolific writer. She wrote four autobiographies—*This Is My Story, This I Remember, On My Own*, and *The Autobiography of Eleanor Roosevelt*—as well as several monographs, the most important of which are *It's Up to the Women, This Troubled World, The Moral Basis of Democracy*, and *Tomorrow Is Now*. Her column "My Day" was published six times a week from 1936 until 1962 and is a wonderful source for her daily activities and political position. She also wrote over 200 articles, the most important of which can be found in Allida M. Black, *What I Want to Leave Behind: The Essential Essays of Eleanor Roosevelt* (Brooklyn, N.Y., 1995). Allida M. Black, ed., *Courage in a Dangerous World: The Political Writings of Eleanor Roosevelt* (New York, 1998), is an additional important collection of her writings.

Maurine Beasely has edited all the remaining transcripts from the First Lady's press conferences, *The White House Press Conferences of Eleanor Roosevelt* (New York, 1983), and assesses Mrs. Roosevelt's career as a journalist in *Eleanor Roosevelt and the Media* (Urbana, Ill., 1987). Susan Ware's study *Beyond Suffrage: Women in the New Deal* (Cambridge, Mass., 1981), clearly illustrates Eleanor Roosevelt's influence within the administration and reform circles.

There have been dozens of works published about Eleanor Roosevelt. Of biographies by contemporaries close to her, the best are Lorena Hickok, *Eleanor Roosevelt: Reluctant First Lady* (New York, 1962), and Ruby Black, *Eleanor Roosevelt* (New York, 1940).

Although many have tried to portray her life, most biographers create a superficial, one-dimensional portrait of Eleanor Roosevelt. Blanche Wiesen Cook's *Eleanor Roosevelt: Volume One* (New York, 1992) is a thorough and thoughtful reconstruction of her life before the White House. Because this essay focuses on Eleanor Roosevelt's political career, readers seeking information on the First Lady's emotional and romantic commitments before 1932 should consult Cook's excellent discussion. Cook continues the story of Eleanor Roosevelt's life in *Eleanor Roosevelt: Volume 2, 1933–1938* (New York, 1999). Joseph P. Lash's *Eleanor and Franklin* (New York, 1970) is the most comprehensive study of Mrs. Roosevelt's White House years published to date, despite its protective slant. Joan Hoff Wilson and Marjorie Lightman's anthology *Without Precedent: The Life and Career of Eleanor Roosevelt* (Indianapolis, 1984) supplies a scholastic assessment of Eleanor Roosevelt's political education and political performance before and during her tenure as First Lady. Doris Kearns Goodwin, *No Ordinary Times: Franklin and Eleanor Roosevelt, the Home Front in World War II* (New York, 1994), offers a differing perspective on Mrs. Roosevelt's emotional and political relationships.

Unfortunately, Eleanor Roosevelt's post–White House career has not yet received full treatment. Lash's *Eleanor: The Years Alone* (New York, 1972) presents only a cursory depiction of her activities after her husband's death. The only serious study of her contribution to diplomacy is Jason Berger's *A New Deal for the World* (New York, 1981). Allida M. Black's *Casting Her Own Shadow: Eleanor Roosevelt and the Shaping of Postwar Liberalism* (New York, 1997) discusses Eleanor Roosevelt's evolving commitment to civil rights, civil liberties, and Democratic Party reform.

★★★   ★★★

Elizabeth Virginia (Bess) Wallace Truman

(1885–1982)

First Lady: 1945–1953

Debbie Mauldin Cottrell

Elizabeth Virginia (Bess) Wallace was born in Independence, Missouri, on February 13, 1885, the oldest child of David Willock Wallace and Margaret "Madge" Gates Wallace. Her siblings were Frank Gates Wallace, George Porterfield Wallace, David Frederick Wallace, and a sister, Madeline, who died in infancy. The Wallaces were part of the upper social echelon in the small, rural town of Independence, located about twelve miles east of Kansas City.

Bess's mother's family, the well-established and wealthy Gateses, never fully accepted her handsome but unstable father. He was elected Jackson County treasurer in 1888 and 1890, and was appointed a customs surveyor in Kansas City, but these positions were interspersed with unemployment. They also failed to produce a salary sufficient to meet the expectations of his privileged wife. As a young girl, Bess became aware of the financial strain within her family and also felt much responsibility shift to her when her mother's emotional and physical health failed.

Bess exuded a strength that her mother lacked. Confident and athletic, she excelled at tennis and ice-skating, and was known for her remarkable whistle that could bring her younger brothers quickly home. At the same time, her mother ensured that Bess acquired the social skills appropriate to her status, such as ballroom dancing. Bess developed many friendships, one of the closest being with her next-door neighbor and lifelong friend Mary Paxton, who later became the first female graduate of the journalism school at the University of Missouri.

Bess stayed close to her father into her high school years, and she became more deeply aware of the depths of his unhappiness. Increased debt and pressure to take care of his family led David Wallace to seek release in alcohol. As her father's drinking problem became more and more public, Bess's mother refused to recognize and deal with the issue. Despite this unsettled state of affairs at home, Bess thrived in high school and was an excellent student. Though academically capable of joining her friends who planed to enroll at prestigious colleges and universities, Bess knew that her family could not afford such a future for her.

Bess's life was irrevocably affected by her father's suicide in June 1903. In addition to her own loss, she felt the impact her father's death had on her mother, who in many ways never recovered from the shame and grief her husband's death brought. It became clear in the aftermath of her father's death that Bess would have to become the leader of her family. She never blamed or criticized her mother for her father's death, and understood that this tragedy had forced a shift in their roles. In many ways, Bess would be more of a parent than a daughter to her shattered mother for the rest of their lives.

After her husband's death, Madge Wallace and her four children moved into the Gates family mansion on North Delaware Street in Independence. Following a year (1903–1904) in Colorado Springs, Colorado, Bess and her family returned to Independence. Bess's grandparents saw to it that she enrolled at the prestigious Barstow School in Kansas City in 1905. She was a strong and popular student and athlete, but did not follow the course of most Barstow students, who went on to elite eastern colleges. Instead, she returned home to Independence to care for her mother and help with her younger brothers.

At this time Bess became reacquainted with Harry Truman, whom she had known since they were children and his family moved to Independence from a farm in Grandview, Missouri, south of Kansas City. Bess had never paid much attention to the poor, bespectacled, piano-playing newcomer who clearly occupied a lower social status in the world of Independence than she did. He, however, was keenly aware of her from their first encounter at Sunday school at the First Presbyterian Church. He always said he fell in love with Bess there, when she was five years old.

By 1910, when Harry returned a cake plate to the Wallace-Gates home while visiting his cousins who lived nearby, the differences in their lives, still present, seemed less significant than during their school years. They began a cautious, deliberate, and careful friendship—aware of the challenges in building a relationship while he worked the family farm in Grandview and she cared for her mother in Independence. Harry left no doubt of his fondness for Bess and his desire to be a permanent part of her life. As the surviving letters he wrote to her at this time demonstrate, he persistently worked to gain her affection and was never deterred by setbacks or hesitations on her part. Three and a half years after becoming reacquainted, Harry and Bess became engaged. Several years later, after Harry returned from service in World War I, the couple was married on June 28, 1919, at Trinity Episcopal Church in Independence. She was thirty-four, and he was thirty-five.

Following a honeymoon in Chicago, Detroit, and Port Huron, Michigan, the Trumans returned to Independence and moved in with Mrs. Wallace in the Gates homestead, an action they both accepted as inevitable, given Madge's dependence on her daughter. As a newlywed Bess Truman helped her husband with his new haberdashery business, corresponded with friends, and pursued an active social life in Independence. Their early years of marriage were difficult however, for the haberdashery business failed, Mrs. Truman suffered two miscarriages, and she had to accept, unwillingly, that her husband was planning to shift his career to politics. Her lack of enthusiasm for this career choice had several sources: the unseemly aspects of politics did not fit her background, nor did this seem the best route to financial security—an issue of some concern, given her own family life. Nevertheless, Bess Truman supported her husband's decision and even met with his constituents in his absence after he was elected judge for the Eastern District of Jackson County in 1922. As his political career rose and fell, she devoted herself to maternal duties, following the birth of their only child, Mary Margaret, in 1924.

Bess Truman was a devoted mother, but also a strict one who believed in instilling discipline in her young daughter and who, at times, believed her husband was too lenient with Margaret. As her daughter later recalled in her biography of her mother, being called Marg, which only her mother called her, "still resounds in my ears with orders, impatience, and discipline." Long after her own athletic days had passed, Bess Truman frequently pushed her daughter to be more athletic than Margaret was inclined to be.

In 1934 Bess Truman was a reluctant, though loyal, supporter of her husband's successful bid for the U.S. Senate. She detested the ongoing attacks against him, especially those that emphasized his connection to the Pendergast machine in Kansas City. After his victory, she dreaded the move to Washington but found its small-town Southern atmosphere to be more welcoming than she had expected. Still, her emotional ties to her family, particularly her mother, in Independence remained strong, and she frequently returned to Missouri with her daughter, leaving her husband behind in Washington. Despite this distance, Bess Truman was actively involved in her husband's career—keeping up with staff members, offering advice on votes, and reminding him of the media's reaction to him. She spent enough time in Washington to have a growing number of friends and a sense of security as her husband's rank in the U.S. Senate increased in stature.

In July 1941, Bess Truman was officially put on the payroll in her husband's office. Though it was not unheard of for members of Congress to put their relatives on their payrolls at this time, some viewed it as a questionable practice. It is not clear exactly what Mrs. Truman did for her $2,400 annual salary, but Harry Truman did raise concern about negative publicity from this situation when his name was mentioned as a possible vice presidential candidate in 1944.

The possibility of his vice presidential candidacy created some anguish for both Harry and Bess Truman, not only because of her being on his payroll but also because of concerns that her father's suicide would be exposed if Senator Truman became part of the Democratic Party's presidential ticket. As her husband weighed his obligations to his party against his desire to stay in the Senate, Mrs. Truman did not demand that he refuse the nomination. Despite her own very strong reservations, particularly given the health of President Franklin Roosevelt, she let her husband make his own decision. In her biography of her mother, the Trumans' daughter later credited this approach on her mother's part to "an invisible line in their partnership that Bess never crossed—a line that divided a wife's power over her husband between influence and control."

Harry Truman's resistance to the nomination was worn down at the Democratic National Convention in Chicago in July 1944, and when the convention was over, he had been selected as the vice presidential nominee. In the days immediately after this event, Bess Truman found the inevitable spotlight most uncomfortable, and insisted that she would not comment on public issues with which her husband would be dealing. To her husband, she made it clear that she would join him in campaigning only in a very limited fashion and would not leave Independence for the rest of the summer. Though the campaign proved to be grueling and lonely for Harry Truman, both Trumans were relieved that it did not prove to be as dirty as expected and that the death of David Wallace did not become an issue. After the Democratic ticket victory in November, Bess Truman's major concern was the toll the campaign and his future work as vice president would take on her husband's health. Ironically, this was a greater worry for her than the rumors of the rapidly declining health of President Roosevelt.

Bess Truman had served as second lady for less than three months when Franklin Roosevelt died on April 12, 1945. For most of this time she harbored the hope that her husband's load would be lightened as World War II came to a close. Though not particularly enamored of her new role, she resumed her part in the social life of Washington that she had come to know as a senator's wife. She also participated in the war effort as a volunteer with the Washington United Service Organization (USO). The transition that came after April 12 was probably the most difficult of her life, as she mourned the death of President Roosevelt, worried about what would face her husband in the days ahead, and tried to adjust to her new, and most public, role as First Lady. Her old friend from Independence, Mary Paxton Keeley, wrote to her in May 1945 that "yours is the hardest job I have ever known any woman to undertake but I have never known you to do anything that you did not do well." Bess Truman's response indicated her own emotional distress, as well as her determination, at this time: "I think you have sized up the situation pretty well. We are not any of us happy to be where we are but there's nothing to be done about it except to do our best—and forget about the sacrifices and many unpleasant things that bob up."

Almost immediately, Bess Truman found herself confronting issues related to how much she would continue in the style of Eleanor Roosevelt as First Lady, a distinctive style the country had experienced for more than twelve years. Some assumed that Bess Truman, a Midwestern housewife who had centered her life on her family, felt inadequate when compared to Eleanor Roosevelt. A close look at Mrs. Truman's approach to serving as First Lady, however, reveals that it was not inadequacy that concerned her as much as maintaining her sense of self. Though she appreciated and respected Mrs. Roosevelt's style, she wanted no part of imitating it or trying to be something she was not. Reflecting on how she felt on the first night of being First Lady, Mrs. Truman later said that it concerned her that the country would have to get used to a new and different First Lady after so many years. According to biographer Jhan Robbins, she knew that "I couldn't possibly be anything like her. I wasn't going down in any coal mines."

One of the first areas where Mrs. Truman had to exert her own style was in her relations with the media. Eleanor Roosevelt offered to hold a press conference at which she would introduce Bess Truman to the female White House press corps, and thus set the stage for continuing Mrs. Roosevelt's weekly press conferences. At first, Mrs. Truman assumed this was a standard requirement for First Ladies, and she agreed, from a sense of duty, to participate. But when a discussion with Frances Perkins, Franklin Roosevelt's secretary of labor, revealed that the press conferences were unique to Mrs. Roosevelt, Bess Truman quickly determined that she would not perpetuate this tradition. Subsequently, her contacts with the press were handled through Reathel Odum, Mrs. Truman's personal secretary, or Edith B. Helm, the social secretary. They held regular press briefings and provided Mrs. Truman's written responses to questions submitted to her via these two assistants. In this way, Mrs. Truman quickly established her own approach to dealing with the media without cutting off all access to the First Lady.

Because of her determination to preserve her identity, and because her predecessor had been so different from her, Bess Truman recognized that she would have to establish her own rules and policies for operating as First Lady, and would have to adhere to them firmly and consistently. When the American Cancer Society sought her assistance in March 1949, Mrs. Truman responded:

Though I am deeply interested in the work of the American Cancer Society and am glad to do what I can to promote the program which the Society has outlined, I feel that I should explain to you that I have never made any addresses over the radio or done any public speaking. This is a rule which I have followed steadfastly ever since I have been in the White House and as I have declined other requests to speak in behalf of many worthwhile projects, I feel that it would be most unfair to depart from this rule now.

What might be viewed as reluctance, rigidity, or a lack of desire to use her position aggressively must also be seen as a strong internal belief that her own approach was adequate to the task, regardless of how unlike Eleanor Roosevelt's it was.

As First Lady, Bess Truman separated her position into two distinct roles—a public role that she filled with a firm commitment both to keeping her identity intact and to showing a sense of responsibility about the position, and a private role that allowed her to continue to share fully in the life of her husband and to be his adviser and confidante. Although the second of these roles was probably the more significant, and certainly was the one she most cherished and enjoyed, it was the first one that usually got more attention and that has continued to be used as the basis for observations about her.

Soon after determining that her relationship with the press would be different from Mrs. Roosevelt's, Bess Truman exhibited another sign of independence from her predecessor. Invited to attend a tea given in her honor by the Daughters of the American Revolution (DAR) at Constitution Hall in October 1945, Mrs. Truman readily accepted. Her participation was roundly criticized by Congressman Adam Clayton Powell, Jr., who noted that his wife, the pianist Hazel Scott, had been denied the opportunity to perform in Constitution Hall because she was black. The First Lady, whom Powell referred to as the "Last Lady" (which earned him permanent banishment from the White House by President Truman), was horrified at the controversy generated by this incident, but she was determined not to be intimidated or to allow politics to dictate her social life.

She spoke out against racism but did not change her plans. In a letter to Powell, which appeared in the *New York Times* on October 13, 1945, she noted:

> Personally, I regret that a conflict has arisen for which I am in no way responsible. In my opinion my acceptance of the hospitality is not related to the merits of the issue which has since arisen. I deplore any action which denies artistic talent an opportunity to express itself because of prejudice against race or origin.

Powell and others drew a contrast between Mrs. Truman and Eleanor Roosevelt, who had resigned from the DAR when black singer Marian Anderson had not been allowed to perform at Constitution Hall because of her race. In the aftermath of the DAR tea controversy, Americans sent Bess Truman their reactions, which were mixed. Letters in the White House Social Office Files in the Truman Library from October 1945 provide a sample of the range of responses. "Please accept my thanks for your courageous refusal to yield to intimidation and especially for repudiating the example of your calculating predecessor," wrote one man. Another letter writer noted "shock" at Mrs. Truman's decision and asked, "Why give lip service against race prejudice if you give body present to its practice?" This episode reinforces the sense that Bess Truman was determined to remain herself and to carry out her public role as she saw fit. To her, the public part of her job was necessarily difficult and brought few rewards.

Her reaction to public prying into her daughter's life was even more negative. When Reathel Odum told her that a society reporter for the *Washington Star* was asking why Margaret Truman had remained in Independence at one particular time instead of returning to Washington, Bess Truman sent a message to her secretary that Margaret was finishing some voice lessons back in Missouri. Then, she added with some resignation that Odum should provide this detail to the reporter so that false rumors would not circulate or untrue stories be printed. The First Lady indicated that she would rather tell the reporters it was none of their business, but knew she could not do that. On another occasion, when a reporter called Odum to inquire what the First Lady would wear to an upcoming tea, Mrs. Truman was less charitable, telling her secretary to indicate that it was none of the reporter's damn business. The secretary edited Mrs. Truman's response, saying that the First Lady had not yet made up her mind. When a reporter interviewed Bess Truman in 1947, the First Lady gave brief but clear answers to indicate that being in the White House was not her preference, nor would she wish the role of First Lady on her daughter, nor would she ever want to be president herself or expect any woman to fill that role.

Bess Truman put considerable energy into her public role as official hostess. She reinstituted a formal White House social season, hosting afternoon teas, state receptions, and other events. She also maintained her ties to a variety of women's clubs, including her Independence bridge club, the P.E.O. Sisterhood, the Daughters of Colonial Wars, and the Red Cross Motor Club.

As committed as the First Lady was to preserving herself in the public eye, she was equally determined to maintain the open, accessible, and equal relationship she had enjoyed with her husband throughout their married life. It was this role as his close adviser that she cherished and enjoyed most, and looked forward to most as First Lady. Bess Truman was accustomed to being very involved in the daily decisions, challenges, and activities of her husband. She was used to critiquing him, to encouraging him, to pointing out ways he could be better. She was used to daily talks or letters. The relationship she knew and understood as his wife was one marked by mutual dependence and respect. Those who knew the Trumans well noted that Bess Truman was the pillar of strength in her husband's life. This went far beyond the notion of making his life more comfortable, and spoke to her ability to support her husband

from a position of honesty, strength, and love. Though Mrs. Truman may have talked about having no desire to be anything more than a wife and mother, her family and close friends recognized that in her family, that was in no way a limited role. Her daughter said she was the spark plug of the family; the family joke was that if the three Trumans became a vaudeville act, with the president playing the piano and daughter Margaret singing, Bess Truman would surely be the manager.

Early in her husband's presidency, Bess Truman felt that this role was being diminished. She was particularly concerned, even angry, in the summer of 1945 when she realized that her husband had determined to drop the atomic bomb on Japan without talking to her about it. (She was in Independence at the time.) The Truman's daughter, Margaret, wrote in her biography of her mother that she reluctantly faced the fact that at this time "she had become a spectator rather than a partner in Harry Truman's presidency." To realize that this role of partner might not exist, or at best might be marginalized, was a major setback. It led to tension between the president and First Lady that lasted for several months, and caused Mrs. Truman to appear rather detached at the beginning of her public role as First Lady. Gradually, after spending some time away from the White House as well as having her beloved Independence bridge club visit her in Washington, she got past her anger and realized she could reestablish her role as the president's closest adviser. By the summer of 1946, she and her husband had resumed their nightly discussion of issues and personalities, and continued it for their remaining years in Washington.

Though it is difficult to know how much impact her adviser role had on the presidency, it is not difficult to see that it was a significant part of the life of Bess Truman. Her legacy as First Lady lies in her sense of self, her independence, and her ability to serve effectively in this role without rearranging any of the other roles that she cherished. It has been noted that, apart from the DAR tea incident, Mrs. Truman was rarely criticized as First Lady. Many Americans sensed in her an appealing level of integrity and security. She has been credited with being an early advocate of women's rights because of her inherent belief that women were as good as men, which led her to encourage her husband to appoint more women to high-level government positions. The phrase "full partner" has been applied frequently to her relationship with her husband. After the Trumans left Washington and returned to Missouri, the *Los Angeles Times* had this to say about Bess Truman on January 18, 1953:

> She has been a model First Lady. . . . This is not to say that every First Lady must elect the retiring role that Mrs. Truman chose, but to express the feeling most Americans share that she always has been simply herself, a genuine and gracious lady, without any desire to capitalize on her husband's office or to mirror its importance.

Throughout their years in the White House, Mrs. Wallace lived with the Trumans, although she never developed much respect or fondness for her son-in-law. Bess Truman managed to remain committed to both her husband and her mother, although maintaining a sense of family balance was not always easy. Ninety-year-old Madge Wallace died in the White House on December 5, 1952, shortly before the Trumans returned to Independence for good.

By the time the Trumans left the White House in 1953, after President Truman determined not to seek reelection, the Washington female press corps had come to see Bess Truman as a friend, and held a luncheon in her honor. By 1982, Mrs. Truman was ranked fifteenth in an overall survey of First Ladies, a rating which rose to eleventh by 1993. Her ratings for integrity were in the top five in both surveys.

After their White House years, the Trumans returned to Independence, where they were active in civic life. They also traveled to Hawaii and Europe, and remained close to their daughter, Margaret, who married Clifton Daniel in 1956 and subse-

quently provided the Trumans with four grandsons. After Harry Truman's death in 1972, Mrs. Truman lived alone. She had a mastectomy in 1959, and she later suffered from arthritis and other ailments. She died at her home in Independence on October 18, 1982, at the age of ninety-seven.

In assessing Bess Truman's time in the White House, it is instructive not to confuse private with noninfluential. It is also important not to assume that her traditional manner confined her to a limited role. Evidence suggests that she separated out the roles required of the First Lady, using some parts to sustain her and help her endure the other parts that were less pleasant. She had the self-confidence to establish her own traditions as First Lady, even as successor to someone who had held the post for twelve years and who had approached the job very differently than she did. Bess Truman once noted that in terms of her predecessors, she found Elizabeth Monroe particularly interesting. This First Lady, with whom she shared a first name, followed the outgoing and very public Dolley Madison. Monroe, too, was more quiet and retiring, but was unquestionably devoted to her hard-drinking politician husband. This observation speaks to the self-awareness and independence of the woman from Independence who approached her job as First Lady on her own terms, and used her position quite effectively to achieve the goals she thought were appropriate for Harry Truman's wife.

BIBLIOGRAPHICAL ESSAY

No official collection of Bess Truman papers exists, and very little of the body of her correspondence remains. The Harry S. Truman Library in Independence, Missouri, does have other helpful materials, however. Particularly noteworthy are the Mary Paxton Keeley Papers, the Office of Social Correspondence files, the records of the White Social Office, the White House Central Files in the President's Personal File category, and the papers of Reathel Odum (Bess Truman's personal secretary) and Alonzo Fields (chief butler at the White House). The letters Harry Truman wrote to

Bess are preserved in the library, and many of them were published in Robert H. Ferrell, ed., *Dear Bess: The Letters from Harry to Bess Truman, 1910–1959* (New York, 1983).

Researchers seeking information beyond the Truman Library should consult the Edith B. Helm, Bess Furman, and Katie Louchheim Papers in the Manuscripts Division of the Library of Congress, as well as the Frances Perkins Oral History Project at Columbia University. Other helpful sources on Bess Truman include Margaret Truman, *Bess W. Truman* (New York, 1986) and *Souvenir* (New York, 1956); and Jhan Robbins, *Bess & Harry: An American Love Story* (New York, 1980). More recent studies on Harry Truman include some treatment of Bess, such as David McCullough's *Truman* (New York, 1992) and Alonzo Hamby's *Man of the People: A Life of Harry S. Truman* (New York, 1995). Bess Truman's obituary appeared in the *New York Times* on October 19, 1982.

★★★ ★★★

Mamie Geneva Doud Eisenhower

(1896–1979)

First Lady: 1953–1961

Mark Young

Mamie Geneva Doud was born on November 14, 1896, in Boone, Iowa, the second child of John Sheldon Doud and Elvira Mathilde Carlson Doud. She had an older sister, Eleanor, and two younger sisters, Ida Mae and Mabel Frances. The Douds were a prosperous family, and they provided Mamie and her sisters with a privileged upbringing.

Mamie's father, John Doud, was born in Rome, New York, in 1870. He was the son of a wealthy wholesale grocer. The Doud family moved west to take advantage of the better business opportunities afforded in the growing city of Chicago. When the city developed into a railroad hub, the elder Doud recognized the lucrative potential of establishing a meatpacking company in Chicago. Later he opened another meatpacking house in Boone, Iowa, a smaller boom town farther west. In 1893, John Doud moved to Boone to manage his father's meatpacking operation, and he eventually acquired control of the business.

As the head of one of the larger concerns in Boone, Doud soon came to the attention of another well-to-do businessman, Carl Carlson. Doud eventually married one of Carlson's daughters, Elvira Mathilde, in 1894. Elvira was sixteen and John was twenty-three. Two years later, Mamie was born. Nine months after Mamie's birth, Doud sold his successful meatpacking business and moved the growing family to Cedar Rapids, Iowa, in search of better financial opportunities. In Cedar Rapids,

Mamie's earliest memories were of the winter sleigh rides and the train trips on weekends to visit her Carlson grandparents in Boone.

While John Doud prospered in Cedar Rapids, the first of many ailments shook his family. By the age of twenty-four, Elvira had given birth to four children and had gone into a "decline." Her husband hired domestic help for his wife, but marital difficulties may have contributed to the deterioration in her health. Doctors informed Doud that the labors of raising four children, combined with the harsh Iowa winters, were a strain for Elvira. By 1903 not only was his wife's health in jeopardy, but one of his daughters faced a serious illness. When she was seven, Mamie suffered a bout of rheumatic fever that damaged the valves on the left side of her heart, leaving her with a chronic problem that would limit her activities later in life.

John Doud was now a wealthy man, and at the age of thirty-six he moved his family to Colorado, where the climate would be better for Elvira. The Douds settled in a fashionable part of Denver and participated in many of the city's cultural offerings. Because of the delicate health of her older sister, Eleanor, who died at seventeen, Mamie became her father's favorite daughter. Nicknamed "Puddy" by her father, she was strong-willed and showed signs of independence. However, her father, typical of early twentieth-century heads of households, made it clear that he was the unqualified boss and she must remain obedient.

As was the case with many women of her generation, Mamie's formal education after the eighth grade was sporadic. She attended East Denver High School and the Mulholland School in San Antonio intermittently. During the school term of 1914–1915, she matriculated at Miss Wolcott's School, a finishing school for the daughters of prominent Denver families. Though Mamie was a dependable and good student, her father believed higher education was superfluous for society girls, who would learn more at home by observation or with tutors. Furthermore, numerous family trips inter-

rupted her education. Mamie never experienced the rigors and challenges of advanced studies, but she possessed common sense and self-confidence.

Beginning in 1910, the Doud family spent the winters in the milder climate of San Antonio, Texas, out of consideration for the family's health. Every winter they rented a large house in the fashionable part of San Antonio. Mamie made her society debut in San Antonio in 1915. A pretty, vivacious woman, she attracted suitors, many from the local military bases. One day in October 1915, two army acquaintances introduced her to another officer, Dwight David "Ike" Eisenhower. Despite warnings that Ike had a reputation as a woman hater, Mamie pursued and captivated him. He was different, she later recalled, not like "those lounge lizards with patent leather hair" she was used to in Denver.

Their courtship was not smooth. Though friendship blossomed quickly, the romance evolved at a slower pace. Initially, Mamie continued to see other men. After one evening out, Mamie returned to find her father and Eisenhower waiting on the front porch. Eisenhower found in Mamie a "charmingly saucy" woman. He proposed on Valentine's Day 1916, though it was a month before he could formally ask Mamie's father for permission to marry her. Doud initially worried how Mamie would reconcile herself to living on the income of an army officer with a paycheck of only $141.67 a month. He overcame his reservations after Mamie convinced him she could adjust to a more stringent lifestyle as an army wife. The wedding date, originally set for November, was moved up to July 1, because of the chance that Ike might be sent to Mexico, where General John J. Pershing was pursuing Pancho Villa.

In many respects the Eisenhowers complemented one another quite well: both had independent streaks, but they did not clash. She was more refined in social graces, he was more rough-hewn. He was from an emotionally distant family, whereas she was from a family that was demonstrative. He was from a poor family, brought up valuing the worth of a dollar. Her privileged up-bringing had insulated her from the lessons he had learned. Yet by the White House years, Mamie Eisenhower was a confirmed coupon clipper. During her husband's time in the army, wherever they were posted, their quarters became "Club Eisenhower," reflecting her ability to create an atmosphere free of tension.

The wedding took place at the Doud home in Denver. Mamie Doud's marriage to an unknown from outside the Denver community shocked many of her family's friends and acquaintances. Arriving at the Doud home early on the wedding day, Eisenhower won over the skeptics with his friendly manner and his handsome appearance. After a brief honeymoon at El Dorado Springs, outside of Denver, the Eisenhowers were off to Abilene, Kansas, so Mamie could meet her in-laws. This short stopover revealed much of her character, as well as what she would face in the future. She won over her in-laws by declaring that she now had brothers. But she also learned a lesson in coping with the desires of her husband. He went off to play poker with some old friends until 2 A.M., ignoring her urgent pleas to return earlier. He preferred to determine his schedule according to his own priorities.

Mamie Eisenhower gradually reconciled herself to the lot of an army wife: her husband absent for days or weeks at a time, low pay, and inadequate housing. Her first home at Fort Sam Houston, formerly her husband's two-room bachelor quarters, did not even have a kitchen. Soon after their return to San Antonio, Mamie Eisenhower was shocked to find her husband preparaing to leave for maneuvers. In words she would always remember, he said: "Mamie, there's one thing you must understand. My country comes first and always will. You come second." She also adjusted to her husband's independence that sometimes bordered on neglect. When conditions seemed unbearable, she sought refuge by staying with her parents for a few weeks or more.

These adjustments seemed negligible when Mamie Eisenhower learned in early 1917 that she was pregnant. On September 24, 1917, Mamie gave birth to Doud Dwight Eisenhower, nicknamed "Icky." In 1919, the Eisenhowers moved to Laurel, Maryland, because they had been transferred to Camp Meade. Their room in a boarding-house had electricity only from nightfall to eight in the morning, and the bathroom was down the hall. Meals were supplied at another boardinghouse. After ten days, Mamie Eisenhower packed up Icky and herself, and went to stay with her parents.

Mamie Eisenhower's recurrent stays at her parents' home because of poor housing or his military duties revealed a deep emotional attachment to her parents and the life she knew before marriage. With her parents, she was waited on by servants, had a nurse to look after the baby, and lived in a very protective and comforting home. Ironically her trips home reflected independence, not dependence. She was running away from conditions which seemed incapable of providing her with the lifestyle she desired. Furthermore, Eisenhower's parents, who were aging, came to rely on her for emotional support whenever she returned to their home. When she eventually returned to her husband's side, she had to subsume her desires to his military career. Undoubtedly, this situation created unresolved tension for her.

In 1921 the Eisenhowers experienced the greatest tragedy of their marriage: young Icky died of scarlet fever. Because of the severity of his condition and the lack of treatment for the highly contagious disease, Icky was quarantined and his parents could only wave to their dying son through a window. When Icky died, Mamie Eisenhower was alone in bed, sick with grief, and her husband was at the hospital. The guilt of being apart from her son in his last days stayed with her for years. Her husband rarely spoke about the loss of Icky, and Mrs. Eisenhower suffered because of his avoidance of the subject. This resulted in an estrangement between them.

In 1922 the Eisenhowers sailed for Panama, their next post. The conditions that confronted them upon arrival are best described as primitive. The legs of their bed stood in pans of kerosene to keep various bugs, including large cockroaches, from crawling into bed with them. When they went to sleep that first night, a bat descended upon them. Furthermore, they often dealt with an infestation of rats.

During her first months in Panama, Mamie Eisenhower stayed active in army wives' organizations. Most notable was her role in helping to build a maternity hospital for the Puerto Rican soldiers' wives, who were not able to receive treatment at the regular U.S. Army hospital. The Jim Crow army of the 1920s maintained segregated facilities on its military bases. These policies extended to Puerto Rican citizens, but Mamie Eisenhower recognized that decent health care for babies was an issue regardless of race.

In Panama the Eisenhowers came under the tutelage of General Fox Conner and his wife, Virginia. General Conner was responsible for developing his young protégé, so the two officers often discussed military campaigns and tactics. Mrs. Conner provided a similar function for Mrs. Eisenhower, who felt both physically and emotionally neglected by her husband. Pictures of her at the time depict a gaunt woman living in a jungle environment with wild animals, exotic diseases, and many uncertainties. Virginia Conner, who recognized the signs of a disintegrating marriage, took Mamie Eisenhower under her care. She encouraged her to work at saving the marriage, telling her to "vamp" her husband. Mrs. Eisenhower created a new hairstyle for herself, which included the bangs that she would be famous for thirty years later.

The marriage stabilized when Mamie Eisenhower became pregnant for a second time. Impending childbirth also provided a reason for her to return home, and she left Panama for Denver, where the couple's second son, John Sheldon Doud, was born in August 1923. Dwight Eisenhower was able to obtain a leave to be present for the birth. The familiar and comfortable surroundings of her parents' home, the presence of her husband, and the birth of a healthy baby boy all created a happy and serene atmosphere for Mrs. Eisenhower.

On her return to Panama, she recommitted herself to making the marriage work. However, Mamie Eisenhower suffered what would now be termed a postpartum depression. The raw and wild conditions in Panama had not improved during her absence. Though the Douds provided a nurse for their daughter and new grandson, Mamie Eisenhower still found Panama inhospitable. The most worrisome aspect was the possible health problems for her newborn son—a real concern to a mother who had lost one child to disease. After a few months in Panama, Mrs. Eisenhower returned to Denver. Her husband, hardly the doting father and husband, was frequently absent for days, if not weeks, at a time.

During the remainder of the 1920s and 1930s, the Eisenhowers were assigned to Fort Leavenworth, Kansas; San Antonio, Texas; Paris, France; the Philippines; and Washington, D.C. Some of the assignments proved interesting, especially Paris, where "Club Eisenhower" opened up again with frequent parties for American civilians and military personnel based in the French capital. In 1935, Dwight Eisenhower went to the Philippines as General Douglas MacArthur's assistant, to help develop a Philippine army. To Mamie Eisenhower the pending tour of duty in the Philippines conjured up unpleasant memories of Panama. With her hsuband already in the Philippines, she delayed her departure for a full year to avoid interrupting their son's schooling. However, once she joined her husband in Manila, she quickly learned to appreciate the life of a high-ranking colonial official's wife. She enjoyed the social life in which American officials participated, and she developed a close-knit group of friends who were always up for a game of bridge or mah-jongg. Included in this circle was Jean MacArthur, the general's wife. In 1939, when the Eisenhowers returned to the United States, Mamie Eisenhower saw her stay in the Philippines as enjoyable but was also glad to be leaving the islands.

The start of World War II in Europe caused the usually lethargic army to move a little faster. Dwight Eisenhower began a series of assignments that in 1943 resulted in his appointment as Supreme Commander Allied Expeditionary Force. Though Mamie Eisenhower was justly proud of her husband, she began a period of stress, loneliness, and media scrutiny. The army did not provide the necessary support system for her new role. She had no secretarial support for the avalanche of letters she received and no media advisers like those provided for the generals. She had never experienced such public intrusions into her life, but the war years provided good training for realities that would remain with her for the rest of her life. When her husband went to Britain in 1942, Mamie Eisenhower was left behind. Her only contact with him, except for a brief visit in 1944, was through a voluminous exchange of letters. Not until 1945 were they reunited.

The Wardman Park Hotel in Washington, D.C., became home for Mamie Eisenhower and the other generals' wives during the war years. In many respects these women helped to cushion her from the demands of the news-starved press and to make the duration of her husband's absence bearable. Nevertheless, this new scrutiny of and intrusion into her life caused problems. Mrs. Eisenhower was very careful of what she said and how she behaved in public. She recognized that anything she did that was the least bit questionable could reflect badly on her husband and also, in the war effort, would not set a good example. She worked at the military canteen in Washington and refused public appearances that could be construed as frivolous.

During the war years, gossip about her possible alcoholism first surfaced. Mamie Eisenhower's circle of friends protected her, but items still appeared in the press. Her brother-in-law, Milton Eisenhower, wrote to her husband that her drinking did not appear to be out of the ordinary. Mrs. Eisenhower was probably suffering from Ménière's disease, a problem of the inner ear that affected her balance. The resulting falls and bruises generated speculation about what caused her to stumble into furniture. When the disease flared up, she needed a steady hand to support her as she entered a taxi. Such incidents spurred gossip about a supposed drinking problem.

The wartime separation sparked rumors that Dwight Eisenhower was having an affair with his British driver, Kay Summersby. The pictures of him and his military family often included the young and pretty Summersby. Mamie Eisenhower knew that some members of her husband's military entourage had wartime romances. Ruth Butcher, a friend whose husband, Harry Butcher, served on Dwight Eisenhower's staff, endured the same rumors. In letters to his wife, Dwight Eisenhower constantly affirmed his love and devotion. In a letter dated Valentine's Day 1944, he reminded his wife that it was "28 years ago I brought over the West Point class ring" as an engagement ring. He told her, "I'm lucky to have had you to see or send a message to every Valentine Day for 28 times," and he closed his letter to her with "I love you—always." But this was small comfort to a woman under constant press scrutiny and separated from her husband by the Atlantic Ocean.

After the war, the Eisenhowers reunited and the gossip about wartime romances abated. Their life changed both economically and personally with his new appointments. His memoirs of the war, *Crusade in Europe*, guaranteed sufficient income for a comfortable retirement. Mamie Eisenhower received her first mink coat as they began to enjoy some previously unobtainable creature comforts. The Eisenhowers bought a farm near Gettysburg, Pennsylvania, the first home they had ever owned, as their eventual retirement home. After a stint as president of Columbia University (1948–1951), Dwight Eisenhower accepted the position of Supreme Allied Commander of NATO. When he returned to Europe for his new duties, he brought his wife with him. In 1952, the Eisenhowers prepared for their first political campaign in response to public outpourings of support.

Mamie Eisenhower proved to be good at politics. In her husband's presidential campaigns in 1952 and 1956 she built enthusiasm with Republican women. Since World War II she and her family had appeared in news accounts as the all-American family. Such stories surely garnered support among family-minded voters. Dwight Eisenhower agreed with the assessment of a family friend that the only person working harder than himself in the 1952 campaign was his wife. She was not hesitant to let her husband know whom she liked in regard to politics. Richard Nixon was one of her favorites during the 1950s.

When Mamie Eisenhower began her duties in January 1953, she was the first First Lady to wholeheartedly welcome the traditional aspects of the role in over a generation. The preceding First Ladies found the job an imposition on their lifestyle, although for very different reasons. Eleanor Roosevelt completed the process begun by Lou Henry Hoover of remodeling the First Lady's duties away from those of a ceremonial figurehead and into those of a social justice and policy advocate. Bess Truman had no desire for the position, whatever its focus. She preferred Independence, Missouri, to Washington, D.C., and thus left the White House empty of the First Lady for extended periods of time. Mamie Eisenhower, accustomed to military postings, saw the White House as just another temporary home, and quickly acclimated herself to the new surroundings. Whereas Eleanor Roosevelt politicized the position of First Lady and Bess Truman found it an inconvenience, Mrs. Eisenhower reveled in her new role. Mrs. Roosevelt and Mrs. Truman both disliked the social role of the First Lady, but she saw it as a perk. However, to her the position of First Lady was more than parties; it entailed being a gracious, pleasant hostess and representative of the American people.

Mamie Eisenhower never considered her role as First Lady as anything more than hostess and wife to the president. When her husband finished work in the Oval Office, she required the family quarters to be free of work-related stress. Likewise, she rarely intruded into her husband's work area. She visited the Oval Office only four times while First Lady. This absence from her husband's work is reflected in the fact that she is mentioned only fifty-one times in her husband's two-volume presidential memoirs. Rarely and only in subtle ways did Mamie Eisenhower advise her husband. For example, suggesting the inclusion of a prayer at his first inaugural was the limit of her activity. Her policy of not intruding into her husband's domain was an arrangement they had worked out for over forty years.

Mamie Eisenhower was the last First Lady to uphold the tradition of a silent and publicly demure persona for presidential spouses. She rejected the model of activism undertaken by the last Republican woman to be first lady, Lou Henry Hoover, just as much as she avoided the style of Eleanor Roosevelt. Instead, she preferred to take the noncontroversial, behind-the-scenes supporting role that she had played throughout her husband's military career. Mamie Eisenhower learned that the newspapers and magazines were preoccupied with questions about whether she should shake hands with her gloves on or off and the minutiae of how many hands she shook in a week. After every social occasion at the White House, the newspapers scrutinized table decorations, her jewelry, her dress, and any gossip that may have arisen at the reception. To later generations this reporting on the First Lady might look frivolous. However, it reflected what the American public expected of their First Lady.

One subject the press was fascinated with was Mamie Eisenhower's hairstyle, the famous "Mamie bangs." She had adopted her hairstyle in Panama, and continued with it for the rest of her life. Critics viewed it as unbecoming for a First Lady. Some saw it as frivolous, while others thought the style was more appropriate for a teenager or young woman than for a woman in her fifties. Mrs. Eisenhower received letters imploring her to change her hairstyle, but she steadfastly refused to alter her appearance. As long as her husband liked her hair, that was all that mattered.

Another area of attention was the numerous articles devoted to Mamie Eisenhower's wardrobe. She caught flak for her taste in dresses. She preferred off-the-rack American dresses rather than expensive French designer ones. At formal receptions she often wore strapless gowns that critics claimed were more appropriate for a younger woman. Mrs. Eisenhower ignored her detractors, stating that she might be a grandmother, but that did not mean she always has to dress like one. Furthermore, her appearance on the New York Dress Institute's list of the twelve best-dressed women every year she was in the White House was its own reply to her critics.

After nearly two decades of deprivation because of the Great Depression and the Second World War, the American people relished the postwar economic boom of the 1950s. In many ways Mamie Eisenhower mirrored this new postwar consumer culture, with her many dresses, her jewelry, and her role in the renovation of the Gettysburg farm. Even the postwar baby boom was reflected in part by the Eisenhowers' relationship with their own grandchildren. The American public saw many picture stories of White House functions featuring the doting grandparents.

Health concerns for herself and her husband consumed a large part of Mamie Eisenhower's time as First Lady. She conducted her morning business from bed, whether it was phone calls, correspondence, or reading the newspaper. Mrs. Eisenhower felt that staying in bed to conduct business would conserve her energy, and was important to good health for women over the age of fifty. This practice, she thought, gave her more vitality and freshness in her public appearances.

Starting in 1955, Mrs. Eisenhower's health concerns shifted from herself to her husband. His heart attack that year led her to urge his retirement after one term in office. However, after conferring with Dr. Howard Snyder, the presidential physician, she came away with the belief that retirement might put more stress on her husband. However, by the end of his second

term his health was still declining. During the 1960 presidential race she asked Republican nominee Richard Nixon to reject any campaign help from Dwight Eisenhower, to prevent a possible heart attack.

Mamie Eisenhower treated the White House as an eight-year post. She redecorated the rooms that the family occupied and created a familiar home environment. As in all their previous twenty-eight homes, she hung a small picture near the elevator that declared "Bless this House." Her attitude toward the staff was friendly and courteous, yet at all times strict protocol was followed. Though she was known as a stickler for a clean White House, especially with regard to footprints on the carpet, she also was informal with staff, keeping them posted on the president's health through each medical emergency.

Mrs. Eisenhower took an interest in the White House staff, always giving personal Christmas and birthday gifts. She was concerned with the families of personnel—once she invited Chief Usher, J. B. West, and his wife aboard a campaign plane going to Iowa so West could visit his father in Des Moines. West described her as "gay, breezy, open—we all got to know her better than we did any other First Lady because she let us in on almost everything that went on in her life, and she took an interest in everything in ours." As a former army wife, Mamie Eisenhower was familiar with hierarchical management. These skills extended to her White House years, when she employed the model of a military base commander's wife who must maintain a functioning base. However, her concern for a functioning White House ended at the Oval Office. Her generosity did not include the presidential secretarial pool or her husband's personal secretary, Ann Whitman. They were in his domain, and because of their close work with him, she was uneasy toward them, her feelings sometimes bordering on jealousy.

Mamie Eisenhower considered the White House living quarters her domain. A frugal administrator of the Executive Mansion budget, she often perused the Washington newspapers for the best deals on food items. She held firm against wasteful spending at the taxpayers' expense, often telling staff and friends "don't run it on the Eagle." Officially, she had only one secretary, Mary Jane McCaffree, who in 1953 was the first person to be listed in the *Congressional Directory* as an employee of the First Lady. However, there was also a staff of stenographers to help with the correspondence. Mrs. Eisenhower replied to most of the letters sent to her, believing that those who took the trouble to write deserved a personal answer. Her diligence in this matter showed at the end of the administration, when it was revealed that over half a million letters were in the White House Social Office records. These letters depict a First Lady who was popular with the American public. Concerned citizens both sought her advice and offered advice to her.

The final years in the White House brought some unexpected embarrassment to Mrs. Eisenhower. In 1958, the *Chicago Tribune* published the itinerary of one of her husband's weekend golf trips to Augusta, Georgia. That incident proved controversial because it included a 3,000-mile detour to Phoenix, Arizona, which allowed Mamie Eisenhower and two friends to visit the Elizabeth Arden Maine Chance health spa. The publicity about the trip, its extravagant appearance, and its travel cost to taxpayers created a media flap. Furthermore, the president's trips to the Augusta National Golf Course, whose wealthy members had built a private bungalow and dubbed it "Mamie's Cabin," gave the appearance that the Eisenhowers where losing their common touch.

After leaving the White House in 1961, the Eisenhowers retired to their farm in Gettysburg, Pennsylvania. During these years, Mamie Eisenhower enjoyed the company of her husband on a scale she had never had in the past. With Jacqueline Kennedy she cochaired the fund-raising for the National Cultural Center (renamed the Kennedy Center for the Performing Arts). She continued to appear on lists of the ten most admired women in her retirement years. She comforted her husband as his health declined in his final years. He died in 1969, and she lived for another ten years. In her final years she devoted her time to her grandchildren and correspondence with friends, and successfully weathered a renewal of interest in the Summersby rumors. Mamie Eisenhower died on November 1, 1979, and was buried in Abilene, Kansas, next to her husband and their young son, Icky. She can best be described as his adjunct; she was also his loyal supporting partner who strove to be uncomplicated. Indeed, she remained simple to her husband and to the people she represented.

BIBLIOGRAPHICAL ESSAY

The Mamie Doud Eisenhower Papers are located at the Eisenhower Presidential Library in Abilene, Kansas. The collection is large, containing more than 500 boxes of letters, clippings, and ephemera. The bulk of the material dates from 1948 until her death. There is also an extensive oral history of Mamie Eisenhower. The library contains other collections and oral histories of people close to the Eisenhowers.

There is no scholarly monograph on Mamie Eisenhower to date. Her granddaughter Susan Eisenhower provides the best work available covering the entire life of Mrs. Eisenhower in *Mrs. Ike* (New York, 1996). Dwight Eisenhower's *At Ease: Stories I Tell to Friends* (New York, 1967) is an open memoir of his life with anecdotes of his wife and other highlights of their life together. Other useful works include Lester David and Irene David, *Ike and Mamie: The Story of the General and His Lady* (New York, 1981); and D. L. Kimball, *I Remember Mamie* (Fayette, Iowa, 1981). Two early books are Dorothy Brandon, *Mamie Doud Eisenhower: A Portrait of a First Lady* (New York, 1954); and Alden Hatch, *Red Carpet for Mamie* (New York, 1954). Both of these works cover Mrs. Eisenhower from birth to the White House years.

Gil Troy's *Affairs of State: The Rise and Rejection of the Presidential Couple Since World War II* (New York, 1997) devotes thirty-six pages to the Eisenhowers' relationship and is the best scholarly treatment available. Betty Boyd Caroli, *First Ladies* (New York, 1995), is also useful. J. B. West, *Upstairs at the White House: My Life with the First Ladies* (New York, 1973), describes his work with Mrs. Eisenhower in the White House. Julie Nixon Eisenhower devotes a chapter to Mamie Eisenhower in her book *Special People* (New York, 1977).

On the topic of Dwight Eisenhower's possible wartime infidelity, see Kay Summersby, *Eisenhower Was My Boss* (New York, 1948), and the updated version that came after Merle Miller, *Past Forgetting: My Love Affair with Dwight D. Eisenhower* (New York, 1976). For a response to the Summersby book, see John S. D. Eisenhower, ed., *Letters to Mamie* (Garden City, N.Y., 1978). Stephen Ambrose's two volumes on Eisenhower provide a detailed look at Dwight Eisenhower and the role his wife played in his life: *Eisenhower: Soldier, General of the Army, President-Elect, 1890–1952* (New York, 1983) and *Eisenhower: The President* (New York, 1984). Mamie Eisenhower's obituary appeared in the *New York Times* (November 2, 1979).

★★★ ★★★

Jacqueline Lee Bouvier Kennedy Onassis

(1929–1994)

First Lady: 1961–1963

Betty Boyd Caroli

Jacqueline Lee Bouvier was born on July 28, 1929, in Southhampton, Long Island, New York. She was the elder of two daughters of Janet Lee Bouvier and John ("Jack") V. Bouvier III. Although much about Jacqueline's early years suggests luxury and privilege, her father's heavy drinking and the stormy relationship between her parents encouraged her to distance herself from much that went on around her, and she developed an inordinate insistence on guarding her privacy. She found pleasure in horseback riding, at which she excelled, and in drawing and poetry. She thus developed, as a youngster, the interests that would sustain her throughout her adult years. Her genuine respect for artists and their work helped shape not only her White House years but also those that followed.

In July 1940, Jacqueline's parents divorced. Two years later her mother married the twice-divorced Hugh D. Auchincloss. His former marriages (to Maria Chrapovitsky and Nina Gore Vidal) had produced two sons and one daughter; with Janet Lee, he would have another son and daughter. Stepfather Hugh Auchincloss offered little of the excitement Jack Bouvier had, but his wealth and continued success as a stockbroker provided a comfortable life for his expanding family. They divided their time between two estates—Merrywood in Virginia and Hammersmith Farm in Newport, Rhode Island.

Although Jacqueline and her younger sister, Lee, resided with their mother, they went away to school at a young age. At the age of fifteen, Jacqueline enrolled at Miss Porter's in Farmington, Connecticut. In 1947, she entered Vassar (then a woman's college) in Poughkeepsie, New York, and after completing two years, she opted for the then-popular junior year abroad and chose Paris. Completing a final year of study at George Washington University in the nation's capital, she graduated in 1951.

Before his death in 1957, Jack Bouvier exerted a strong influence on his daughter. Remarkably handsome, he enjoyed a wide reputation as a womanizer and liked to surround himself with beautiful, elegant women who maintained the allure of mystery and distance from those around them. John Davis, a Bouvier cousin, credits Jacqueline's father with helping her develop her own elegant style and the reserve that increased her attractiveness to many people and became her hallmark.

In August 1951, Jacqueline won first place in Vogue magazine's Prix de Paris contest, which involved several parts: quizzes on advertising, a composition, and an interview with Vogue editors. Rather than accepting the prize, consisting of a year's work on the magazine divided equally between Paris and New York, she opted for a full-time job at the Washington Times Herald, a job secured with her stepfather's help and the assistance of his friend Arthur Krock. Beginning there in late 1951, at $42.50 a week, she soon had her own byline—"Inquiring Photographer."

Little about Jacqueline's daily columns between 1951 and 1953 reveal her thinking on serious topics. In fact, the format of the short pieces offered little opportunity for depth or insight. The "Inquiring Photographer" posed a question and then reported the answer alongside the respondent's photograph. Questions tended toward the innocuous, such as "Have you done your Christmas shopping?" (November 21, 1952), rather than the more substantive "Should Eisenhower confer with General MacArthur before going to Korea?" (November 25, 1952). Some queries hinted at misogyny: "How could women be trained to be punc-

tual?" (July 8, 1952) or "Do women marry because they are too lazy to go to work?" (September 9, 1952). Jacqueline Bouvier apparently saw no reason to put the families of government leaders off-limits, and, when Richard Nixon was elected vice president in 1952, she sought out his six-year-old daughter to ask her thoughts on his fitness for the job. Tricia Nixon apparently saw high office as more trouble than pleasure, as she replied: "He's always away. If he's famous, why can't he stay home?" (November 7, 1952).

According to several accounts, including that of her cousin John H. Davis, who later wrote The Bouviers, Jacqueline was briefly engaged to John G. W. Husted, Jr., a "prominent New York banker's son," in 1951. She met John Fitzgerald Kennedy in May 1952, as he was completing a third term in the U.S. House of Representatives and preparing to run for the U.S. Senate. Even then, she understood he had higher political ambitions. Davis recalled that she had spoken to him at that time of John Kennedy but had dismissed him as "quixotic" because of his intention to become president. By the spring of 1953, Jacqueline and John Kennedy had evidently decided to marry, although the announcement was delayed in order to accommodate an article about him titled "The Senate's Gay Young Bachelor" that the Saturday Evening Post had scheduled to run on June 13.

The wedding took place on September 12, 1953, in St. Mary's Roman Catholic Church in Newport, Rhode Island. The ceremony was followed by a reception at Hammersmith Farm. Jack Bouvier, who was scheduled to escort the bride to the altar, became indisposed at the last minute, reportedly because of excessive drinking, so Hugh Auchincloss walked his stepdaughter down the aisle.

Jacqueline Bouvier's marriage into the Kennedy family—a family that was so different from her own—furnished fodder for generations of writers. Many of them, including John Davis, speculated that she found the escape from her own troubled kin a blessing but, at the same time, never became fully involved in the rambunctious shenanigans of the Kennedy clan. She found much of their fun boisterous and their sport overly strenuous. Family matriarch Rose Kennedy attempted to tutor her in domestic arrangements, as she did all her daughters-in-law, and the patriarch Joseph Kennedy evidently liked her style, but Jacqueline Kennedy remained something of an enigma to her husband's family—a confident person who knew her own mind and preferred to keep some distance from them.

The first few years of Jacqueline Kennedy's marriage included serious disappointments. Her husband underwent spinal surgery in 1954 and again in early 1955, the same year in which she suffered a miscarriage. The daughter she delivered in 1956 was stillborn, and her husband failed in his attempt to win the Democratic Party's nomination for vice president.

By 1957, the Kennedys' luck appeared to shift. Daughter Caroline Bouvier Kennedy was born on November 27, 1957, and John Kennedy's book *Profiles in Courage* (1956) won the Pulitzer Prize for biography that same year. The following year he was reelected to the U.S. Senate, and, by the time of the 1960 primaries, he stood ready to make a strong run for his party's nomination for the presidency.

Jacqueline Kennedy had never shown much interest in politics generally or in the campaign process that led to success. She had joined her husband's sisters and mother in the tea-party and coffee-klatsch routine when he ran in Massachusetts in 1958, because that was the expected routine of the female components of candidates' families at the time. But any speeches on her own, beyond the innocuous "glad to be here" comments, would have been unusual for a candidate's spouse. Wives of aspiring politicians had not yet learned the value of or developed a taste for campaigning on their own for their husbands. Early 1960 primaries in Wisconsin and West Virginia included the appearance of Jacqueline Kennedy, but only as part of a larger group effort involving her husband, other family members, and staff.

Even that limited and not entirely successful participation diminished after July 1960, when the Kennedys announced her pregnancy—another child was due late that year. The candidate's wife had not really warmed to the crowds, and some Kennedy staffers implied that the campaign would gain from her absence. Although her youth and vibrancy appealed to some voters, her reserve and upper-class Eastern reticence did not endear her to all audiences. According to one campaign worker, she showed little understanding of what most of her contemporaries in the Midwest thought or did. In one remarkable miscalculation, she suggested that a Wisconsin crowd join in singing "Southie is My Hometown," a song virtually unknown outside Boston.

Although her pregnancy caused her to withdraw from most public appearances, Jacqueline Kennedy continued to work for her husband's election. In a column entitled "Campaign Wife" that she wrote for the Democratic National Committee (which made it available to newspapers), she chatted amiably about being sidelined while her husband campaigned. She hosted a "television listening party" and helped launch a "Calling for Kennedy" campaign. Photographs appearing late in the campaign gave the impression that she continued to campaign actively. For example, the *New York Times* on October 30 carried a photo of her standing beside her husband and greeting a Manhattan crowd in Italian and Spanish—languages that she spoke less easily than French.

In a lighter vein—one that would prove dominant in the coverage of her activities—Jacqueline Kennedy showed a strong sense of fashion that reporters found immensely appealing. Maternity clothes, previously treated as unworthy of fashion writers' consideration, became the subject of much discussion as many photographs appeared, showing a visibly pregnant Mrs. Kennedy meandering along a Cape Cod coastline or sparring verbally with reporters. Rather than self-consciously concealing her expanding form, she appeared to flaunt it, choosing bright pink (then called "shocking" pink) slacks and oversized T-shirts. By the time of her husband's victory in November, she was more than eight months pregnant but posed beside him in an elegant sleeveless dress for a family portrait.

Early media attention to Jacqueline Kennedy, although enormous, involved several contradictions. Much of the writing treated her as a pampered princess who spent excessively on clothing. When one intrepid journalist tried to pin her down on the exact total of her annual clothing bill, and suggested a specific figure, she replied that she could not spend as much as that unless she wore sable underclothing. The more common journalistic treatment included raves about whatever she chose to don—and accolades appeared even from the anthropologist Margaret Mead, who wrote in the February 1962 issue of *Redbook* that Jacqueline Kennedy had "gladdened the eye" of the entire nation and awakened it to its cultural heritage. Millions of American women copied her fashion lead, making the bouffant hair style, low-heeled pumps, and sleeveless sheath dresses enormously popular.

In August 1960, well before the results of the election came in, the Kennedy camp prepared to make Jacqueline Kennedy a successful First Lady by hiring Letitia Baldrige to assist her. Slightly older than the prospective First Lady, Baldrige shared two schools with her—Miss Porter's and Vassar—and considerable interest in Europe. Baldrige had worked in both Paris and Rome as social secretary to the American ambassadors, and she had a strong sense of the socially correct. As a child she had lived in Washington, D.C., where her father served as congressman, so she understood the need to assess the political consequences of any action.

In the last months of the 1960 campaign, Jacqueline Kennedy evidently worked out with Baldrige the details of what she meant to accomplish as First Lady. Her ideas on the subject were not sharply formed. She made vague promises about working for some cause or project, as many of her predecessors had done, and she suggested that her attention would go to international education or exchange programs for youth. By the time of the election, however, her ideas had shifted, and, within a week of victory, she announced that she intended to concentrate on restoring the White House to its original splendor. Although she did not confine her activities to one project (she also served in a sponsoring or leadership capacity to the American Association of Maternal and Infant Health, the American Cancer Society, and the Girl Scouts, and shared with Mamie Eisenhower honorary chairmanship of the National Cultural Center—later renamed the Kennedy Center), her main concern was with White House restoration.

The presidential household was traditionally the province of the First Lady—at least since the days of Dolley Madison—and its furnishings and social events were evaluated as an indication of her tastes and interests. The hours of its accessibility to tourists, the number of guests and seating arrangements at formal dinners, the refurbishing of carpets and draperies had all been her domain, and it was the rare president, notably James Monroe and Chester Arthur, who had intervened.

Jacqueline Kennedy moved quickly to stake out her claim to a decisive role as First Lady. Within weeks of the election, and days of giving birth to a son, John, Jr., she announced through her social secretary that she meant to make the president's home a "showcase" for American artists and talent. Not everyone approved, partly because of ungrounded fears that emphasis would be on modern or abstract art, thus altering the mansion's appearance. The First Lady's staff quelled much of this criticism by announcing that contemporary culture would be represented by performing artists, while "Early American" would continue to characterize the public rooms.

Although oversight of this sizable mansion might have seemed a manageable task, it was rendered more difficult by the need to walk a narrow line, erring neither on the side of excess nor of inattention. Americans have held differing opinions, over the years, on whether their president's house should epitomize the very best that the nation has to offer or whether it should serve as a democratic reminder that leaders should live simply, much as their countrymen do. Jacqueline Kennedy's announcement that she intended to put the "best" inside the White House placed her in the elitist camp with all the political detriments that entailed. History-minded advisers noted that Grace Goodhue Coolidge had not done her husband any good in the 1920s by heading a campaign to encourage donations of valuable antiques to the White House. The Kennedys had already taken some flak because of their enormous family wealth (which permitted, according to many accounts, Joseph Kennedy to bequeath $1 million to each of his nine children), and the president did not relish the prospect that his wife's restoration project would draw attention to his own privileged background.

Jacqueline Kennedy persisted in her plan to restore (she disliked the word "redecorate") the presidential home in spite of the fact that she was, she admitted, "warned, begged, and practically threatened" to leave it alone. She persevered, she explained, because she recalled her excitement at visiting the mansion when she was a youngster of twelve, and she did not think the rather shabby interior that she saw on her tour with Mamie Eisenhower would produce the same effect on young tourists in 1961.

Jacqueline Kennedy may well have been encouraged by others. The National Society of Interior Designers had already shown interest in improving the White House interior by working for two years to raise $100,000 to purchase early American antiques. In June 1960, the society made its presentation to President and Mrs. Eisenhower, who announced that the furniture would be used in the oval Diplomatic Reception Room on the ground floor, the first room in the mansion to be furnished entirely with authentic antiques.

To assist her in making decisions about selecting artwork and exhibiting it, Jacqueline Kennedy enlisted several experts whose names were announced in late January 1961: William Walton, artist and Kennedy friend; David E. Finley, chairman of the Commission of Fine Arts; and John Walker, director of the National Gallery. With their help she arranged to borrow paintings from the Boston Museum of Fine Arts, the Metropolitan Museum of Art, and the National Gallery of Art for display in the public and private quarters.

In an effort to raise money for other acquisitions, the First Lady helped establish the White House Historical Association, founded on November 3, 1961. It sought to "enhance understanding, appreciation and enjoyment of the White House." Officially organized as a "not-for-profit historical and educational organization" composed of persons appointed by the president, the association oversaw the publication of guidebooks and other educational materials about the presidential home and the families who have lived there. In the first three decades of its existence, the association raised more than $8 million for additional acquisitions to the White House collection and for the cleaning and refurbishing of the interior.

The idea for raising funds through the sale of guidebooks evidently had the support of the First Lady from the beginning. At $1 per copy (the initial price) *The White House: An Historic Guide* was an immediate success, first going on sale on July 4, 1962, in the east wing. The initial printing of 250,000 copies sold out in a few months, and another 3 million would sell over the next two decades. Besides bringing in several million dollars (the price quickly rose), the book appealed to visitors who wished to carry home a souvenir of their tour of the White House. Some critics objected to the president's home being commercialized in this way, but the success of the sales silenced much of the opposition.

The association's work was facilitated by legislation that the First Lady endorsed. Passed by the 87th Congress in September 1961, the law made all the mansion's furnishings of "artistic or historic importance" the "inalienable property" of the White House. Presidents and their families could no longer give away or otherwise dispose of pieces that they did not care for or wish to use. President Chester Arthur had reportedly authorized the carting off of several wagonloads of furnishings not to his liking when he refurbished the Executive Mansion in the 1880s, and Theodore Roosevelt was generous in passing out small mementos. On one occasion a visiting friend remarked that his wife would relish having one of the Monroe plates, and Roosevelt obligingly opened the cabinet and took one out.

Jacqueline Kennedy's move to stop such largesse, a move backed by the force of law, encouraged Americans to donate valued items to the White House. Assured that the furniture and art would remain at 1600 Pennsylvania Avenue, donors offered treasured chairs and desks that earlier presidents and their families had used. Some of these items, such as the typewriter once used by President Wilson, had primarily historical significance, but others, such as the 1767 portrait of Benjamin Franklin that was donated by Walter Annenberg, were of enormous value.

New staff members were required to list the holdings of the Executive Mansion and its recent acquisitions, and Jacqueline Kennedy devised a strategy that would permit an expert to supervise the task. In March 1961, she arranged for a part-time curator, Lorraine Pearce, to come on loan from the Smithsonian, and Pearce began the enormous inventory task. She listed new donations in a special catalog, much like that put out by a museum. After Jacqueline Kennedy left the White House, President Johnson issued an executive order that made a full-time curator a permanent part of the White House staff, and the curator continued to operate out of a small office on the ground floor of the White House.

With new attention focused on the White House and the assurance that its contents were protected by law, its collection of furnishings and artwork grew. A complete list of the items acquired between 1961 and 1964 was published in the first issue of *The White House Collection*. Each item was categorized as Furniture, Furnishings (such as glassware, textiles, and ceramics), Fine Arts (paintings, prints, and sculpture), or Documents, and its description and provenance recorded. Among the most prized donations was one of the Empire armchairs that President Monroe had ordered from France in 1817; other important pieces were purchased with "general funds."

In deciding about decorating matters, Mrs. Kennedy engaged the help of a Frenchman, Stephane Boudin, who previously had supervised the Malmaison restoration outside Paris. Boudin's choices did not find universal approval, and some observers charged that the result was a White House "too Frenchified" to be either appropriate for an American chief executive or an accurate representation of the building's history. Some of his choices had been expensive, and critics were particularly angered to hear that he had encouraged the acquisition of old French wallpaper when new paper of comparable quality could have been purchased more cheaply.

These arguments about cost and taste overshadowed coverage of the efforts that Jacqueline Kennedy personally put into the restoration project. She went in "working clothes" to sift through the storerooms and find suitable pieces for exhibition. Some items, once seen only on special occasions by important visitors, were put on permanent display. The gilt plateau centerpiece, a delight to dinner guests since 1817 and described as the "chief historic treasure of the White House," was placed in the State Dining Room so that every tourist could enjoy it. The collection of vermeil pieces, given to the White House in the 1950s by American heiress Margaret Thompson Biddle, became the focus of one entire room on the ground floor.

For most of the twentieth century, the ground and first floors of the White House were considered public, while the second and third were reserved for the private use of the president's family. Presidential families could make changes to accommodate specific needs or interests, and Jacqueline Kennedy introduced several. She installed a kitchen and dining room on the second floor, so that her family would not have to trek downstairs to eat or have trays delivered upstairs.

Although the private areas were off-limits to most visitors, crowds flocked to see the restored public rooms. To accommodate those who could not make the trip to Washington, the First Lady agreed to accompany television crews through the White House for a special program that was taped and then broadcast on February 14, 1962. More than 46 million Americans watched as the First Lady drew attention to the president's house as a national monument and to the fact that the president's wife had come to have special responsibility for overseeing it. After the previous restoration of the building was completed in 1952, President Truman had led television cameras on an abbreviated tour. Jacqueline Kennedy's tour, however, lasted a full hour, and provided a more extensive view for the public. Although she dodged some of the interviewer's more controversial queries, such as what responsibility the federal government should take for promoting the arts, she lent her own considerable glamour to a topic formerly deemed stodgy and uninteresting.

Although Jacqueline Kennedy was the first presidential spouse born in the twentieth century, she approached the job of First Lady much as earlier women had. When asked about her agenda, she repeatedly focused on what her predecessors had been doing since the founding of the republic—making their husbands comfortable and their children happy. In her case, the children were both young—less than five years of age when their father took the oath of office—thus necessitating arrangements unusual for the family of a chief executive. No president since Theodore Roosevelt had brought such a young family into the White House (although several recent presidents, including Herbert Hoover, Franklin Roosevelt, and Dwight Eisenhower had welcomed young grandchildren to stay for extended periods). Arrangements for the schooling of daughter Caroline and for her security and privacy, as well as that of John, Jr., preoccupied their mother.

Although the Kennedys used a country estate, Glen Ora, which they leased near Middleburg, Virginia, and summered at the Kennedy compound in Hyannisport on Cape Cod, they resided principally in the White House. The First Lady organized a school for daughter Caroline on the top floor and invited a few children her age to join her there, thus eliminating the need for tight security had she attended classes elsewhere. A new playground on the south lawn was shielded from easy public view.

Relations with the press were complicated during the Kennedy administration because of the First Lady's ambivalence toward it. Her desire for personal privacy pushed her to keep reporters at a distance, and more than one of them complained of her insensitivity to their need to report what the public wanted to know about the president's family. She would look right through them, one reporter recalled, and act as though she wished they would all disappear. She saw the job of her husband's press secretary, Pierre Salinger, as keeping crowds away and preserving her privacy and that of her children.

On the other hand, the First Lady had worked as a journalist and recognized the value of a positive column or a flattering photo. She cooperated in making pictures of herself with her children available so that they could be released at a propitious time. Salinger recalled that during the First Lady's visit to India, the president suggested that Salinger distribute some of the pictures she had made before going, so that the nation could be exposed to the image of a healthy, happy family in the White House.

Jacqueline Kennedy planned several social events at the White House as overtures to the press. One of her first parties, given in April 1961, honored newswomen. The Kennedys initiated the custom of inviting a few representatives from the press to join their predinner cocktail hour with honored guests upstairs before joining the larger list of invitees downstairs.

Much of the reporting on the First Lady was extremely flattering, and her popularity quickly spread to other nations. Polish magazines debated the "Jackie look," and an Argentine poll named her "Woman of the Year." In part, her popularity resulted from her international appeal. She was not the first president's wife to have been educated abroad, but her youth and beauty, combined with her fashion flair and ability in languages, multiplied her admirers abroad.

In accompanying the president on several highly publicized trips, Jacqueline Kennedy enhanced her appeal. In May 1961, after a short journey to Ottawa, Canada, she accompanied the president to Europe, where she reportedly impressed Prime Minister De Gaulle with her knowledge of French history and helped ease contacts between the prime minister and her husband. In Vienna, a few days later, she charmed Premier Khrushchev, who reportedly asked to shake her hand before the president's. Residents of both cities greeted her enthusiastically, and it was on this trip that President Kennedy made his much-quoted introduction of himself (reported in the *New York Times* on June 3, 1961) as "the man who accompanied Jacqueline Kennedy to Paris." A trip in December of that year offered her the chance to speak in Spanish to crowds in Venezuela and Colombia. In June 1962, she accompanied her husband to Mexico.

Much of Jacqueline Kennedy's travel during her years as First Lady was for pleasure rather than business. On these trips she was accompanied by her sister, Lee Radziwill, rather than the president. In 1961, the former Bouvier sisters visited Greece and the Greek islands; in March 1962, their destinations were India and Pakistan after a stop in Rome. Later that summer they returned to Italy, accompanied this time by four-year-old Caroline Kennedy. Lee Radziwill and her husband also accompanied Jacqueline Kennedy to Greece in October 1963, when she sailed on Aristotle Onassis's yacht in the Aegean.

Jacqueline Kennedy's personal travel was an innovation. Previous First Ladies had limited themselves to domestic trips—such as Mamie Eisenhower's spa stays or Bess Truman's visits to Missouri—or to short journeys abroad in the interests of the nation—such as Eleanor Roosevelt's trips to England and to the Pacific during World War II to inspect the troops. Whether she intended it or not, Jacqueline Kennedy thus opened the possibility that her successors would be able to follow more of their own interests, even while exposed to the scrutiny that a First Lady had come to expect.

Jacqueline Kennedy reshaped the expectations of what a presidential spouse could do in other ways as well. She frequently begged off public appearances, even those she had agreed to attend. Sometimes she sent a substitute in the form of the vice president's wife, her mother-in-law, her secretary, or even the president, and she did not shrink from excusing herself from public duties that she did not wish to perform. Frequently she cited her health, until reporters noted that just a mention of her sinuses could bring a laugh from their colleagues. Sometimes she insisted that her children required her presence.

The First Lady's staff began to expand in the early 1960s. Pamela Turnure, a twenty-three-year-old former staff member from John Kennedy's Senate days, took the position of press secretary to the First Lady. A graduate of Colby Junior College and Mt. Vernon Junior College, Turnure had little experience dealing with the press. Pierre Salinger, the president's press secretary, handled all but the most routine announcements. Nevertheless, a press aide became an accepted part of the First Lady's staff, and each of Jacqueline Kennedy's successors made an appointment to that job.

Since much of Jacqueline Kennedy's work as First Lady involved White House restoration, she relied on experts and advisers outside the normal boundaries of staff. Many worked only briefly or were simply "on loan" so that their tenures cannot be easily verified or evaluated. Letitia Baldrige, who acted as social secretary until June 1963, when she left to work at the Merchandise Mart in Chicago, was succeeded by Nancy Tuckerman, an old friend and former roommate of the First Lady's.

The social secretary's task expanded as Mrs. Kennedy sought to use White House events to emphasize the glamour and taste that she hoped would be associated with her husband's administration. The president's official entertaining had historically aroused controversy among his countrymen, as some championed an elitist leader who put forth the nation's best foot while others wanted their chief executive to entertain on the level that most Americans did. The nation has never reached consensus on which model it prefers, and First Ladies of both camps have become enormously popular. Following Mamie Eisenhower's emphasis on popular favorites such as Lawrence Welk, Jacqueline Kennedy took a place in the "elitist" camp.

Her innovations in entertaining included several highlights. A state dinner for the president of Sudan in October 1961 featured professional actors in scenes from the plays of William Shakespeare. The platform on which they performed in the East Room was billed as the first permanent stage ever constructed for the White House. Many internationally famous musicians, including Alexander Schneider and Pablo Casals, entertained White House guests. To underscore her desire to honor great Americans, she scheduled a dinner for forty-nine Nobel Prize winners living in the Western Hemisphere at the time. She thus provided President Kennedy with the opportunity to offer his much-quoted observation that this was arguably the most august assemblage ever to eat at the White House "except perhaps when Thomas Jefferson dined alone."

Capital watchers remarked on a change in White House food. After a long string of rather undistinguished chefs, French-born René Verdon was hired to serve up fare with names that few Americans felt comfortable pronouncing. A "typical menu," served to intimate friends and family, included courses of "consommé julienne" and "crème brûlée." Rather than using the large banquet "E" or "U" table formations that previous administrations had adopted, Jacqueline Kennedy preferred smaller, round tables—each seating ten—to facilitate conversation. The reception line was abolished in favor of a more casual approach

in which the president and honored guests could mingle. She experimented with innovations at state dinners and arranged for one to take place at Mt. Vernon, President Washington's home on the Potomac, even though guests had to be transported by boat from the capital.

For all her reputation as a big spender, the First Lady did not order new White House china. She managed with the remnants of other sets left by her predecessors. In purchasing new glassware, she departed from standard practice and selected a simple, unmarked glass rather than the ornate, costly, cut patterns that had always graced the president's table. The plain glasses from a West Virginia factory sold for less than $10 a dozen at the time, and resembled those used in thousands of American homes. Since the glass was unmarked, it held little value for White House guests who might be tempted to carry off a souvenir. Fewer replacements were needed. But that was not the explanation given by the First Lady, who said she made her choice in the hope of assisting an economically depressed part of the nation.

Her lack of interest in politics kept Jacqueline Kennedy from accompanying her husband on many trips, but in November 1963, following a vacation of her own in the Greek islands, she agreed to go to Texas. Her depression following the death of her newborn son, Patrick Bouvier, in August 1963, had apparently diminished, and she consented to add her own popular image to her husband's attempt to mend a rift that had developed among Texas Democrats. Vice President Lyndon B. Johnson and his wife were also in Dallas. Thus it happened that for the first time in American history, a vice president was on hand at the time of the chief executive's assassination and could be sworn in within minutes of his death.

The oath-taking of Lyndon Johnson aboard *Air Force One*, although delayed to await the arrival of Jacqueline Kennedy, occurred ninety-nine minutes after John Kennedy's death. In her pink, bloodspattered suit, she stood to the new president's left as he pledged to lead the nation.

Jacqueline Kennedy's presence was unprecedented. No woman widowed as First Lady had attended the inauguration of her husband's successor—even Eleanor Roosevelt had not gone to the west wing when Harry Truman took the oath of office in April 1945, although she was only a few hundred feet away in the residence at the time. Mrs. Kennedy's presence, recorded in a much-reproduced photo, helped assure Americans, at a very troubled time, when no one seemed to know what had happened in Dallas or who was responsible, that leadership had passed in a legitimate way to the next in command.

In arranging the details of John Kennedy's funeral, his thirty-four-year-old widow took charge in a way that no one could recall having seen equaled. Not since 1901 had a president been assassinated, and William McKinley's widow, suffering from a series of misfortunes and health problems, had been unable to handle many details on her own. Several of her nineteenth-century predecessors had not even had the fortitude to attend their husbands' funeral services. Widowed First Ladies of the twentieth century (Harding and Roosevelt) had attended the funerals and helped with arrangements but had had neither the heart nor the flair for directing the drama that marked John Kennedy's funeral.

Staffers recalled that Jacqueline Kennedy asked them to begin preparations even before the plane carrying her and her husband's body from Texas landed in Washington. She took as her example the services of Abraham Lincoln, assassinated nearly a century earlier, and specified that the catafalque upon which the coffin lay in the East Room duplicate that in the Lincoln funeral. Whether at services in the rotunda of the Capitol with a child on each side or walking between her brothers-in-law following the coffin from the White House to St. Matthew's Cathedral, she made a strikingly poignant picture. Then the young widow met privately with world leaders who came to show their respect. Millions of people who watched her on television understood that they would never forget the image.

As Jacqueline Kennedy prepared to vacate the White House, she faced several problems, including that of finding a place for herself and her children to live. President Johnson agreed to let Caroline's school class continue until the end of the semester, and diplomat Averell Harriman offered the Kennedys his Georgetown house after they moved out of the White House in early December 1963.

Amid her other planning, Jacqueline Kennedy sought to ensure that her husband's abbreviated presidency would not be forgotten. She arranged for a plaque, noting the number of days that "John Kennedy and his wife Jacqueline" had lived there, to be placed over the mantel in their second-floor bedroom. She also made a request—which President Johnson honored but which she later admitted she regretted—to change the name of the Florida space center. According to her oral history, deposited in the Lyndon Baines Johnson Library, she would not have requested the name change if she had known that the name Cape Canaveral went back to the time of Columbus. Although President Johnson renamed both the place and the space center for John Kennedy on November 29, 1963, the place resumed its historic name in 1973, while the facility remained the John F. Kennedy Space Center.

In other ways, Jacqueline Kennedy appeared preoccupied with preserving her husband's place in history. A week after the funeral, she summoned the writer Theodore White to Hyannis, where she encouraged him to write about the Kennedy administration as "Camelot." According to one of White's biographers, the widow spoke with him for several hours and then edited his article before he phoned it in to *Life*, where it appeared on December 6, 1963. The two-page article referred only briefly to the lines from "Camelot," but it apparently hit a popular chord and established a permanent association between the magical kingdom and the early 1960s. Many critics, including Kennedy staffers such as Arthur Schlesinger, Jr., insisted that the tag was inaccurate.

In 1964, Jacqueline Kennedy purchased an apartment at 1040 Fifth Avenue, New

York City, and she moved her family there in September. When Aaron Shikler was selected to paint her portrait for the White House, she chose that apartment as the setting. Wearing a long robe, without any particular style that would locate her in time, she stands near a table holding objects that have nothing at all to do with American history. Thus, the First Lady whose attachment to fashion is perhaps clearer than that of most is represented in the White House portrait gallery in a pose that defies association with any particular period or place.

Inasmuch as she left the White House when she was thirty-four, Jacqueline Kennedy faced the prospect of many more years on her own. Unlike most other presidential widows, she chose to remarry. In October 1968, within months of her brother-in-law Robert Kennedy's assassination in Los Angeles, Jacqueline Kennedy wed Greek tycoon Aristotle Onassis on his private island Skourpios. Only one previous presidential widow (Frances Cleveland) had remarried after her husband's death, and she had chosen a mate considerably more palatable to her admiring countrymen. Onassis's enormous wealth, Greek citizenship, age (he was twenty-three years older than Mrs. Kennedy), reputation for womanizing, and habitually aggressive business dealings made him an unworthy candidate—in the view of many people—for marriage to the woman who had become something of a national icon. Those who knew her suggested that she sought a protector from what she perceived as dangers for herself and her children, protection that the enormous wealth of Onassis could provide.

Whatever her reasons for the marriage, Jacqueline Kennedy Onassis spent considerable time separated from her husband. Her children remained in school in New York, and she was often with them. Aristotle Onassis appeared in the company of other women, including a prior romantic attachment, the opera singer Maria Callas. The death of Aristotle Onassis's only son in 1973 apparently strained relations even more between him and his wife. When he died in 1975, his widow was not with him,

but she attended his funeral and issued a statement that stopped short of announcing her love for him. According to her cousin John H. Davis, in his book *The Kennedys*, the statement accurately reflected her feelings about Onassis. He had "rescued" her at a time when her life "was engulfed with shadows," she said, and he had "meant a lot" to her. Estimates of her inheritance vary from about $20 to $26 million, the bulk of his estate going to his daughter.

The basis of Jacqueline Kennedy Onassis's appeal has never been fully explored. Her youth (she was only thirty-one when she became First Lady) endeared her to many, and her flair for style pleased others. Although demure and quiet in her presentation of herself, she nevertheless expressed strong opinions on a variety of subjects and refused to conceal her well-developed mind. At a time when the model of femininity was a kind of brainless beauty, she presented the possibility that one woman could combine intelligence and glamour. Yet her breathy, childlike voice suggested immaturity and powerlessness.

Much of her popularity resulted from the fact of television's taking her image into so many millions of homes. In many ways, she was the first White House chatelaine of the television age. Mamie Eisenhower had chatted amiably with Edward R. Murrow in a *Person to Person* interview in 1956, but for all her emphasis on youthfulness, she could not appeal to viewers in the same way as a successor who was young enough to be her daughter. Jacqueline Kennedy's use of television in the White House tour, and in other more abbreviated instances, helped acquaint a nation with her beauty, her poise, and her genuine interest in her photogenic children.

Although Americans occasionally commented privately that John and Jacqueline Kennedy did not appear to have a close marriage, journalists failed to report on what they observed as his meetings with other women. His birthday celebration on May 19, 1962, did raise some eyebrows because of the nature of the entertainment and the absence of his wife. Held as a Democratic

Party fund-raiser at Madison Square Garden in New York City, the festivities featured Marilyn Monroe singing in breathy, suggestive tones to "Mr. President" while the First Lady, reportedly riding in Virginia, was conspicuously absent. After John Kennedy's death, numerous stories appeared in print describing his relationships with other women: one of them was a first-person account. Judith Exner published *My Story* (New York, 1977), in which she described intimate visits with President Kennedy in the White House through 1961 and early 1962.

These rumors may have contributed to Jacqueline Kennedy Onassis's reluctance to write her own account of her White House years—a task that each woman who followed her as First Lady has taken for granted (except Patricia Nixon, whose daughter Julie performed the task for her). Jacqueline Kennedy apparently kept no diary, and for the three decades that followed her White House years, she refused to give interviews on that period in her life. The exception is a short oral history on the subject of the Kennedys' relationship with the Johnsons, now in the Lyndon B. Johnson Library. Her interview with *Publishers' Weekly* in April 1993 was limited to questions about her work as an editor.

Following her husband's death in 1975, Jacqueline Kennedy Onassis began working as an editor at Viking Press. She left after two years, following a disagreement over a book that Viking had contracted to publish. The move to Doubleday, where she began in 1978 as an associate editor, was facilitated partly by her friend and former White House social secretary, Nancy Tuckerman, who was then employed there. As senior editor, Mrs. Onassis worked three days a week, editing about a dozen books a year. Most were nonfiction—many in the arts and others by writers she found particularly interesting, such as Bill Moyers and the Egyptian Nobel Prize winner Naguib Mahfouz.

Although Jacqueline Kennedy Onassis occasionally made a public appearance to draw attention to one of the books she had edited, she did so rarely, and she shunned

political activities in favor of those involving art and architecture. As a member of the board of the American Ballet Theatre, she frequently attended rehearsals, including one in which her ailing friend Rudolf Nureyev conducted for the first time the American Ballet Theatre orchestra in *Romeo and Juliet*. Her efforts to preserve Grand Central Station are credited with the success of that project. Even before leaving Washington she had spoken of the need to build the John F. Kennedy Library, and she devoted considerable time to that effort, helping to choose architect I. M. Pei and then to draw attention to the library by attending its dedication and other events held there. During the last twelve years of her life, although she did not marry again, she appeared often in public with Maurice Tempelsman, a Belgian-born diamond dealer who remained married to his first wife.

In early 1994, Mrs. Onassis was diagnosed as having non-Hodgkins lymphoma, the treatment for which (including chemotherapy) resulted in medical complications. Surgery for bleeding ulcers followed. After numerous short hospitalizations, she returned to her Fifth Avenue home on May 18, 1994, and the next evening she died. As reported in the *New York Times* on May 21, her son, John, Jr., noted that she had died "in her own way and on her own terms," surrounded by family, friends, and the things she had loved. Enormous attention from the entire nation and abroad focused on her death, partly because it had been so unexpected.

Although she had been a parishioner at St. Thomas More Church on 89th Street, a few blocks from her apartment, her funeral took place at St. Ignatius Roman Catholic Church on Park Avenue, where she had been baptized and confirmed. The larger church was selected partly because of the need to accommodate several hundred persons, although the funeral services were billed as private.

Along with her two children, Caroline and John, Jr., and her brother-in-law, Edward Kennedy, Maurice Tempelsman played a prominent part in her funeral service on May 23, riding with her children to the church and reading a poem, "Ithaka." John Kennedy, Jr., prefaced his own remarks at his mother's funeral by noting that he and his sister had searched for the themes that had shaped her life, and in the end they had selected three: love of words, emphasis on family, and desire for adventure.

Burial took place at Arlington National Cemetery near the graves of her first husband and the two children who had predeceased them: the unnamed, stillborn daughter and son Patrick Bouvier Kennedy, who had died in infancy in August 1963.

Although First Lady for less than one full term (from January 20, 1961, until November 22, 1963), Jacqueline Bouvier Kennedy captured enormous public attention within the United States and abroad, and that attention continued for the three decades that followed her residence in the White House. One of the most written-about of all presidential spouses, she became the subject of numerous books, countless articles, and several dramatic treatments. But, because she refused to cooperate with most of these efforts, they tended to concentrate on the glamorous and more superficial aspects of her White House tenure rather than explore the thinking that led her to compile the record that she did.

Following the death of John F. Kennedy, Jr., in an airplane accident on July 16, 1999, numerous books and articles appeared, reassessing the recurring role of tragedy in the Kennedy story.

BIBLIOGRAPHICAL ESSAY
The John Fitzgerald Kennedy Library in Boston has compiled a research guide on its holdings particularly relevant to Jacqueline Bouvier Kennedy Onassis. More than 200 of the oral history transcripts refer to her, and some make multiple references. Not all are open to the public, although the status of many changes each year. A transcript of the interview she gave to Joe B. Frantz on January 11, 1974, in New York City is deposited at the Lyndon Baines Johnson Presidential Library in Austin, Texas, and is open for research.

The Kennedy Library has opened the first 100 boxes of the White House Social Files, and other boxes may be seen with the permission of the chief archivist. There is no finding aid. The library has no list of Jacqueline Kennedy Onassis's speeches, appearances, or staff, but it does have copies of several of her "Campaign Wife" articles. All quotations, except those for which a source is cited in the text of this essay, come from Betty Boyd Caroli, *Inside the White House* (New York, 1992).

Although no doctoral dissertation focuses entirely on Jacqueline Kennedy Onassis, two devoted to First Ladies include consideration of her role: Barbara Oney Garvey, "A Rhetorical-Humanistic Analysis of the Relationship Between First Ladies and the Way Women Find a Place in Society" (Ph.D. diss., Ohio State University, 1978), and Myra G. Gutin, "The President's Partner: The First Lady as Public Communicator, 1920–1976" (Ph.D. diss., University of Michigan, 1983). The Gutin dissertation was published as *The President's Partner* (Westport, Conn., 1989).

Jacqueline Kennedy Onassis's cousin, John H. Davis, in *The Bouviers* (New York, 1969), offers an account of her early life and relationships with her family. His later book, *The Kennedys: Dynasty and Disaster* (New York, 1984), explores her relationship with her husband's family after his death.

Although her household staff reportedly signed pledges not to discuss or write about their work for the Kennedys, even after retirement, several employees published books: Letitia Baldrige, *Of Diamonds and Diplomats* (Boston, 1968), provides the perspective of the First Lady's social secretary; Maud Shaw, *White House Nanny* (New York, 1965); and Mary Barelli Gallagher, *My Life with Jacqueline Kennedy* (New York, 1969), a memoir by her personal secretary. After her death, many of her friends and employees talked more willingly about her and their relationship with her. Among the many books that appeared, two relied heavily on new interviews: Edward Klein, *All Too Human: The Love Story of Jack and Jackie Kennedy* (New York, 1996); and Christopher

P. Anderson, *Jack and Jackie: Portrait of an American Marriage* (New York, 1996).

Books that document the White House years include Carl Sferrazza Anthony, *First Ladies*, vol. 2 (New York, 1991); and Mary Van Renssalaer Thayer, *Jacqueline Kennedy: The White House Years* (Boston, 1967). Thayer's account lacks footnotes but is based on the First Lady's White House Social Office files. Anthony's treatment of Mrs.

Kennedy cites specific interviews that he conducted as well as files at the Kennedy Library.

Considerable audiovisual material on Jacqueline Kennedy is available, including *A Tour of the White House with Mrs. John F. Kennedy*, produced by CBS News, and available at the Kennedy Library. Her obituary appeared in the *New York Times* on May 21, 1994.

★★★ ★★★

Claudia Alta Taylor (Lady Bird) Johnson

(1912–)

First Lady: 1963–1969

Lewis L. Gould

Claudia Alta Taylor was born in Karnack, Texas, on December 22, 1912, to Thomas Jefferson "T. J." Taylor and Minnie Patillo Taylor. Her parents were married in 1900 and already had had two sons: Thomas, Jr,. and Antonio. When Claudia was a child, she acquired the nickname "Lady Bird," which stayed with her for the rest of her life. Comparing her to the ladybird beetles of East Texas, an African-American cook in the family said that the child was as pretty as a lady bird. Her efforts to shake loose from the nickname during her youth proved futile.

Claudia's mother was a cultured, intelligent woman who found life in East Texas somewhat confining and dull. Her marriage to "T. J." Taylor experienced much strain

before their daughter was born. Minnie Taylor read the classics to her daughter and visited the opera in Chicago. Claudia remembered little about her mother, except that she had fostered in her a lifelong love of reading. Their time together was brief. Pregnant at the age of forty-four, Mrs. Taylor fell down the stairs in September 1918. A miscarriage and blood poisoning ensued, and she died. Her father tried to bring up his daughter by himself, but he soon realized that he needed help.

A maiden aunt, Effie Patillo, came from Alabama to rear the youngest Taylor. T. J. Taylor was making a success of his store and extensive landholdings near Marshall, Texas. It was a lonely life for the little girl, and Claudia often escaped into the nearby woods around Caddo Lake. She recalled how she grew up hearing "the wind in the pine trees of the East Texas woods." She learned the names of the flowers and nurtured a love for the landscape and the natural world. She dreamed of travel and the great world beyond her home.

Claudia attended schools in Karnack and nearby Jefferson. She graduated from Marshall High School at the age of fifteen. Her classmates predicted that she would travel extensively. Too young for college, she attended St. Mary's School for Girls in Dallas for two years. In the fall of 1930 she entered the University of Texas in Austin. Her love affair with the city and its surroundings was immediate. At the university she majored in history, wrote articles for the *Daily Texan*, and was publicity manager for the University of Texas Sports Association, a group of female athletes.

Claudia Taylor's social life was varied. Friends recalled that she dated a number of men and made it clear to each of them that she hoped to marry a man who would make a mark in the world. She had her own car and a charge account at Neiman-Marcus in Dallas. Her father refused, however, to let her join a sorority. She earned a B.A. degree in the spring of 1933. She then stayed on for another year to obtain a journalism degree as well. Her plans for life after graduation were vague during the summer of 1934. She expected to spend some time in Karnack redecorating her father's house, and then she wanted to find work on a newspaper as a drama critic. The options for a talented woman in Texas in 1934, in the depths of the Great Depression, were limited.

In the late summer, a friend introduced her to Lyndon B. Johnson, who was then an aide to a member of Congress from Texas. The twenty-six-year-old Johnson impressed her as a tall, good-looking man. She said later that she had met something remarkable, but she was not sure just what that was. To her surprise, Johnson proposed to her during their first day together. Although she declined, they had established an emotional bond. He gave her a book about the effects of Nazism on Germany—an indication of the immediate seriousness of their relationship. He also took her to meet his parents. On his way back to Washington, he stopped in Karnack to meet her father. T. J. Taylor's verdict was that his daughter, after dating boyish youngsters, had finally brought home a suitor who looked like a man.

The couple conducted a long-distance romance by mail and telephone for several months. Johnson wrote about their shared interests and talked of the cultural events they would see together in Washington. The impetuous Johnson did not stop there. He drove to East Texas in early November to propose to Claudia once again. After some hesitation and consultation with Aunt Effie, she decided to drive with him to Austin to visit one of her friends. On the way, Johnson persuaded her to go ahead with marriage. He called some friends in San Antonio, who worked out the problem of obtaining a license on short notice. They were married there on November 17, 1934, and honeymooned in Mexico.

The Johnsons had some adjustments to make to one another. Lyndon Johnson had a fiery temper and he expected his wife to cater to his whims—large and small. He had little real interest in cultural matters, especially the theater, which she loved. She was bookish; he rarely read anything but political letters and memoranda. He criticized her clothes and embarrassed her in front of their friends. She learned to endure his cutting words once she accepted that he was trying to encourage her to make the most of her talents. Later, she would urge those around Lyndon Johnson to bear his tirades and sudden mood swings, and to consider working with him a great adventure.

Lyndon Johnson came to depend on his wife's judgments and patience as elements of stability in his active and hectic life. He knew that she was an excellent judge of people and their motives. She became adept at soothing the injured feelings that he caused. Among the many people who served him, she was the only one in whom he could have absolute trust and confidence that she placed his interests first.

Despite his respect and affection for his wife, Lyndon Johnson was on occasion unfaithful to her with other women. She gave no visible sign that she was aware of his infidelities. She knew, however, that such episodes were transitory and that her best strategy was to wait for them to stop. A divorce would have ended Johnson's political career. In the process, she developed unusual self-control and patience.

After their wedding, the Johnsons lived briefly in Washington. Then, in August 1935, Johnson was named director of the National Youth Administration (NYA) for Texas. They moved back to Austin for two years. Both Johnsons were proud of the system of roadside parks that the NYA created in Texas to put young people to work.

In February 1937, the incumbent congressman in the Tenth District in Central Texas died, and Lyndon ran for the vacant seat. Mrs. Johnson contributed $10,000 from her mother's estate to aid the campaign. Her father quietly donated another $25,000. Her role in the ensuing race was to be the supportive wife. Johnson won a hard-fought campaign as a supporter of Franklin D. Roosevelt and the New Deal.

Once Johnson returned to Washington, Mrs. Johnson found herself quite busy. Her husband's Texas constituents made frequent visits to the nation's capital. She escorted them to the tourist sites in Washington, learning about the open spaces and the attractions of the city. The Johnsons' attempts to have children during the period before World War II resulted in several miscarriages.

In 1941, a U.S. Senate seat became available in Texas when the incumbent died suddenly. Johnson tried to move up politically in the special election that followed in July. Despite exhausting campaigning, he suffered a narrow defeat at the hands of the popular Texas governor W. Lee "Pappy" O'Daniel.

Within months, the United States was at war. Johnson had earlier joined the navy, and he went on active duty after the Japanese attack on Pearl Harbor in December 1941. He left in April 1942 for an inspection trip to the South Pacific. During his stint of military service, Johnson did not resign his congressional seat. Instead, Lady Bird Johnson was given the assignment of running his congressional office while he was away in uniform.

Mrs. Johnson found herself very much at home in the job. She had innumerable local problems to address. Rationing and housing policies affected the district, and there were letters to write to angry constituents, grieving relatives of the war dead, and local officials. It was a good political education for Mrs. Johnson. The experience gave her a renewed self-confidence in her own abilities. Johnson received word from his political associates that his wife was managing the office as well as he had.

Johnson returned home in July 1942 in response to President Franklin D. Roosevelt's order that members of Congress should stay with their legislative duties. After spending years in apartments, the Johnsons bought a home in Washington where Mrs. Johnson cultivated her own garden. On their frequent trips to and from Austin, she noted the changing landscape, the billboards that advertised products, the developments that altered nature, and the roadside flowers. Her interest in the environment was dormant at this time, but she was storing up impressions that would shape her decisions during the 1960s.

In 1943, the Johnsons embarked on a new venture that would affect their personal lives for two decades. Worried about their economic situation if an election defeat should force Lyndon to leave politics, they decided to invest in a radio station in Austin to build up their economic resources. The couple purchased Station KTBC with $17,000 that Mrs. Johnson received from the settlement of her mother's estate. The formal application to the Federal Communications Commission was in her name, and she was the owner of the station for legal purposes.

The station that the Johnsons acquired was small and not well run. It could reach only a limited, local audience. Taking over the actual operations, Mrs. Johnson cleaned up the decrepit facilities, hired new on-air talent, and sought sponsors for her programs. While her management role of the day-to-day business of the station was significant, Lyndon Johnson's influence with the Federal Communications Commission proved decisive in the early success of KTBC. Thanks to his lobbying, the station was allowed to broadcast twenty-four hours a day and to increase its transmitting power. His friendships with radio executives in New York brought KTBC lucrative advertising and national programming, especially from the CBS network.

It took time for the station to get out of debt, but by the mid-1950s, it had become the cornerstone of a multimillion-dollar media empire that the Johnsons built before their move to the White House in 1963. Her colleagues noted that Mrs. Johnson was an adept businesswoman. She learned how to read a balance sheet, and she expected those who worked with her to be as well prepared as she was. The station also served the Johnsons' political interests in Central Texas and gave them a powerful access to their constituents.

The couple's efforts to have children were also successful at this time. Their first daughter, Lynda Bird, was born in March 1944, and a second daughter, Lucy Baines Johnson, arrived in July 1947. As the family expanded, Mrs. Johnson became more involved with her husband's political career. She supported his decision to run for the U.S. Senate in 1948 when O'Daniel retired from politics and the seat again became open.

The campaign, against the popular former governor Coke Stevenson, was an exhausting one. Mrs. Johnson helped to organize the Women's Division and she toured the state with other campaign workers speaking to groups of women. Newspapers described her as a proven vote-getter even though her shyness about public appearances was evident. Throughout the summer of 1948, she wrote to friends across the state urging them to turn out to vote for Lyndon Johnson in the August runoff election. On the night before the balloting, she traveled to San Antonio to join her hus-

band. The car that took her there had two accidents on the way. She shrugged off the resulting bruises and worked through the end of the campaign. The Democratic voters gave Johnson a controversial eighty-seven vote margin, but he was the Senate nominee. He won the Senate seat outright in the November election.

After assuming his new post, Johnson acquired a ranch that belonged to members of his family on the Pedernales River between Fredericksburg and Johnson City. At first skeptical of the move, Mrs. Johnson became a convert to the beauties of the Texas Hill Country and its environment. She spent a large amount of time planting and cultivating what evolved into the LBJ Ranch. The experience strengthened her love of the Texas landscape and her concern for its preservation.

A medical crisis overtook the Johnsons in July 1955, when Johnson suffered a serious heart attack. Overweight and a heavy smoker, he needed to change his habits to avoid a recurrence of the heart problem that had nearly killed him. Mrs. Johnson supervised the low-fat diet he adopted and helped him break his lifelong smoking habit. From the heart attack onward, she monitored his health closely. Her efforts to change his intense and hard-driving habits in politics were less successful.

By the mid-1950s, Lyndon Johnson was being mentioned as a possible candidate for the presidency. Although he did not win the Democratic nomination in 1956, it was evident that his wife faced future national campaigns. She took a public speaking course through the Capital Speakers Club in 1959 to lessen her fears about appearing before audiences. Though she never lost her apprehensions about speeches, she improved her speaking style by the early 1960s. In time she developed an engaging and effective public presence.

The presidential campaign of 1960 thrust Mrs. Johnson into national politics in a decisive way. She had only a modest part in her husband's effort to defeat John F. Kennedy for the nomination, but she was a key adviser at the national convention when Kennedy asked Johnson to be his running mate. She did not want her husband to accept the vice presidency, but recognized that taking second place on the national ticket made sense for his long-range ambitions.

During the campaign for the Kennedy-Johnson ticket, Mrs. Johnson proved an important asset as the Democrats sought to hold the South against Republican inroads. She made several whistle-stop tours of Dixie that impressed the Kennedy people at national headquarters. Then came an incident that turned the tide toward the Democratic ticket in Texas. Four days before the voting, the Johnsons were in Dallas for a campaign appearance at the Adolphus Hotel. As they arrived for their scheduled event, they encountered several thousand ardent Republican partisans who had just seen their candidate, Richard M. Nixon, off to the airport. The crowd waved signs at the Johnsons, who had to cross the street into the throng to reach their destination. An ugly scene ensued as political passions flared. Mrs. Johnson was hit with a sign and other Republicans, particularly some Dallas women, spat at her. The unseemly episode produced a public backlash that contributed to the Democratic victory in Texas. That state in turn proved pivotal to Kennedy's victory. Robert Kennedy later said that Mrs. Johnson had carried Texas for his brother.

During the next three years, Mrs. Johnson received an invaluable preparation for the role of First Lady. Jacqueline Kennedy did not much like the ceremonial duties of a president's wife, and she was grateful for Mrs. Johnson's willingness to act as her surrogate. Mrs. Johnson got the title of Washington's best "pinch hitter." To help her with official responsibilities, Mrs. Johnson acquired a personal staff, including Bess Abell as her social secretary and Elizabeth ("Liz") Carpenter as her press secretary. The two women were capable and efficient, and they served Mrs. Johnson well.

Throughout the vice presidency, Mrs. Johnson accompanied her husband on the many foreign tours that he made for President Kennedy. She noted the trees and flowers in the African and Asian landscapes that she encountered. At home she was gaining a reputation for her charm and grace under pressure. She had not yet found a personal cause with which she was identified. Her interest in natural beauty was latent in all that she had done since her childhood; it awaited only the right circumstances to assert itself in her public life.

The Johnsons were on a speaking tour with the Kennedys in Dallas on November 22, 1963, when John F. Kennedy was killed. Mrs. Johnson felt, she said later, as though she were part of a Greek tragedy that played itself out before her eyes. Amid the grief and shock, she had to adjust to a new role in which the eyes of the people of the United States were focused on everything that she did.

She made some enduring contributions to the institutional role of the First Lady. She named the ebullient and lively Liz Carpenter as staff director and press secretary, two titles that had not been officially designated for any aide of the First Ladies before 1963. Bess Abell continued as social secretary. As her beautification programs developed, Mrs. Johnson's staff expanded. To oversee the operation out of the White House, Mrs. Johnson brought in Sharon Francis, a dedicated conservationist from the Interior Department. From within the White House itself, the First Lady drew on the talents of Cynthia Wilson in dealing with beautification work behind the scenes.

While Mrs. Johnson did not hold formal news conferences with the White House press corps, as Eleanor Roosevelt had done, she established a good rapport with the women journalists who covered her. Her press relations were notably warm with very few episodes of strain. She had little of the suspicion of journalists that marked the relations of Lyndon Johnson with the press corps.

Another important step was her decision to maintain a formal record of what she did in the White House. She started a diary in November 1963 that eventually grew to 1,750,000 words. She made time in her schedule to sit down with the files and clippings of what she had done each day or for several days. She then dictated her recollections into a tape recorder. Her staff knew that she should be left alone during these sessions. After she left Washington, she published about one-seventh of her diary as *A White House Diary* (1970). It provided a valuable account of her accomplishments, and shed much light on her relationship with her husband and his presidency.

Mrs. Johnson balanced family responsibilities with the duties of the First Lady. Both of her daughters were married during the Johnson presidency. As for her husband, she monitored his health closely and tried to ease the burdens of his work. She was well briefed on the issues he confronted. He gave her important speeches to read in advance and consulted her on many issues. Her exact role in Lyndon Johnson's decision-making is still cloudy, but all the available evidence indicates that she was a significant element in the key moments of his presidency.

The first priority for the Johnsons in 1964 was winning election to a full term. Mrs. Johnson encouraged her husband to remain a presidential candidate in August when he talked of perhaps withdrawing from the race. During the fall campaign she made a very visible whistle-stop tour of the South in the "Lady Bird Special." She withstood hecklers from the supporters of Barry Goldwater in the region and helped to woo Democratic officials back to the national ticket. The train was a rollicking experience for those who took it, especially the reporters who covered the First Lady. Her political skill was instrumental in limiting Republican gains in Dixie in 1964.

Following her husband's landslide election victory, Mrs. Johnson had to make decisions about the causes she wished to pursue during the four years ahead. Because of her long-standing interest in children, she became a high-profile supporter of the Head Start program to assist preschool children in obtaining the skills they needed for success in education. Working with Sargent Shriver, who headed the Office of Economic Opportunity, she visited Head Start classrooms and made speeches in behalf of the program. When funding for Head Start was in trouble in Congress, she threw her influence behind continuation of the program.

The cause with which she became most identified, however, was the beautification of the natural environment. During 1964 she thought about such an initiative during trips in the West with Secretary of the Interior Stewart Udall. Their rapport about conservation issues emerged as they conversed about resource problems and possible solutions. Mrs. Johnson was also aware that her husband saw natural beauty and its preservation as a key element in the Great Society goals he announced in 1964.

In November 1964, Mrs. Johnson concluded that natural beauty was the area in which she should channel most of her energies as First Lady. Friends urged her to focus first on Washington, D.C., as a city where conservation ideas could be tried out on a workable scale. Advisers such as her old friend Elizabeth Rowe, Democratic Party activist Katherine S. ("Katie") Louchheim, and Udall told her that Washington needed refurbishing to make it a model for the nation. She decided that an initial concentration on Washington would be the best way to proceed. At the same time, she was aware of initiatives within the Johnson administration to preserve the beauty of the nation's roadsides through control of outdoor advertising and billboards on the highways. She prepared to move ahead with both aspects of the campaign for natural beauty during the winter of 1965.

The first step occurred in January when President Johnson included references to natural beauty in his State of the Union address—the first president to do so. A month later the president sent Congress a message devoted solely to beautification. Shortly thereafter Mrs. Johnson held the initial meeting of her First Lady's Committee for a More Beautiful Capital. It included Udall, Laurance Rockefeller, and Mary Lasker, a supporter of medical research and urban beauty. The initial phase of her work culminated with the White House Conference on Natural Beauty, held on May 24–25, 1965. The First Lady spoke to the gathering and attended many of the sessions, taking copious notes as she watched. The conference provided the beautification campaign with a high degree of favorable publicity.

Mrs. Johnson's work in Washington, D.C., operated on two tracks for the rest of her time in the White House. In dealing with the needs of the city that the tourists saw—the Washington of monuments and vistas—she collaborated with Lasker, Nash Castro of the National Parks Service, and her committee to publicize the needs of Washington for flowers, parks, and open spaces. The First Lady hosted a national television program about her campaign in 1965. She also used the publicity that the White House commanded to raise private donations for the city.

The key figure in the effort was Mary Lasker. Her own gifts helped to expand the number of flowers in Washington's parks, to plant cherry trees, and to landscape scenic areas. Beyond Mary Lasker's contributions, the First Lady involved herself with the improvement of Pennsylvania Avenue, encouraged Joseph Hirshhorn to make the gifts that became the Hirshhorn Museum, and worked with Nathaniel Owings to make the mall in front of the Capitol a more attractive setting.

To manage the flow of donations and to encourage popular support for the upgrading of Washington, Mrs. Johnson supervised the creation of the Society for a More Beautiful National Capital. Through this private group, the First Lady raised money for further enhancement of the city's appearance. Lasker, Rockefeller, and Carolyn Fortas— the wife of Supreme Court Justice Abe Fortas—were significant participants in the work of the society. By 1968, the society had collected more than $2.5 million for its activities. It had seen to the installation of hundreds of thousands of trees, plants, and flowers. The looks of major landmarks such as Pennsylvania Avenue, the Mall, and the Potomac shore were dramatically upgraded.

Although the society did not long survive after Mrs. Johnson left Washington, the legacy of her campaign for Washington's beauty endured. The flowers and trees that she and her associates planted in the 1960s were still blooming a quarter of a century later. Every spring in Washington, the residents said to each other when the flowers appeared: "Thank God for Lady Bird Johnson."

The First Lady knew that her campaign for Washington would not be fully successful if it ignored the condition of the African-American majority population of the nation's capital. Washington was a city that faced the difficult urban problems of poverty and despair that confronted the United States during the 1960s. Mrs. Johnson wanted her natural beauty endeavors to speak to the needs of Washington's inner city as much as to the places that the tourists visited.

Washington's city government was under the supervision of Congress during the 1960s. The First Lady reached into the local bureaucracy to find her link with the African-American community. She enlisted Walter Washington of the National Capital Housing Agency as her adviser on neighborhoods and their programs. She visited the places where people lived, and listened when Walter Washington told her of the needs of the local areas. Washington and the First Lady started with a cleanup campaign in the Second Precinct, where schools and parks would be spruced up and trash removed. Residents cooperated during the summer of 1965 to make the campaign a reality. The efforts that Walter Washington and Mrs. Johnson had begun continued into the next year for other parts of the city.

As the difficulties of working with the city government on her programs became clearer, Mrs. Johnson also enrolled the New York philanthropist Brooke Astor as a sponsor of her Washington efforts. The First Lady collaborated with another advocate of improving the inner city, Polly Shackleton. A longtime Democratic activist, Shackleton wanted to see expanded jobs programs for the black population at Washington's core. She joined her enthusiasm to that of Walter Washington to produce Project Pride during the summer of 1966. The 250 African-American youths who took part in the campaign beautified playgrounds and parking lots, hauled off trash and abandoned cars, and trapped rats.

To continue the program during 1967, Shackleton and Mrs. Johnson sought financial support from Laurance Rockefeller for Project Trail Blazers. Federal funds were being cut back in reaction against the president's Great Society initiatives in Congress. Rockefeller supplied enough money to put 110 children to work transforming a closed movie theater into a neighborhood museum for the Anacostia community in Washington and to set up play spaces near the former home of the nineteenth-century black leader Frederick Douglass. The program continued into 1968 before cutbacks in government funds and the urban riots of that year lessened support for what the First Lady had tried to do.

His work with the First Lady helped to propel Walter Washington into the post of mayor of the city of Washington—the first African American to occupy that position. When President Johnson reorganized the city's government in the spring and summer of 1967, he named Washington as the mayor as soon as Congress approved the new arrangement. The beautification work of Lady Bird Johnson had a significant effect on the future of one of the African-American leaders of the city.

These efforts were not all that Mrs. Johnson tried to do for the city of Washington. In late 1966 and early 1967, she also sponsored an ambitious campaign to revitalize the area around Capitol Hill, as a pilot program for what the Washington metropolitan area might accomplish. This idea began with another wealthy benefactor, Stephen Currier, who was married to a member of the wealthy Mellon family. Long interested in civil rights and social causes, Currier proposed to use some of his resources for improving the urban environment. He proposed that Mrs. Johnson find an innovative architect to design new landscapes for Capitol Hill and other parts of Washington. By the late summer of 1966,

Currier had identified the architect he wanted for the project: Lawrence Halprin of San Francisco.

On a trip to the West Coast during September 1966, Mrs. Johnson met Halprin and invited him to come east and consult with her staff about ideas for Washington. Plans went forward in the months that followed, underwritten with money from Currier, for Halprin to develop new projects such as small, vest-pocket parks, play spaces, and community recreation areas within the existing structures of the neighborhoods. Halprin laid his plans before Mrs. Johnson's committee in January 1967 and talked about how Washington could be transformed with some imaginative concepts that paralleled what he had done in San Francisco. Before the ideas could bear fruit, however, Stephen Currier and his wife died in a plane crash. The immediate enthusiasm for the Halprin program vanished.

The First Lady and her staff tried energetically to realize the vision that Currier and Halprin had presented during the remainder of 1967 and into 1968. They encountered obstacles from opposition within the district, the unwillingness of donors to complete a project that another rich person had started, and a general reduction in federal funds as the end of the Johnson presidency neared. Most of what Halprin had proposed was still on the drawing boards when Mrs. Johnson returned to Texas in 1969.

The overall legacy of Mrs. Johnson in Washington, D.C., is most clearly seen in the monumental areas of the city. What she tried to do in the inner neighborhoods could not make a dent in the poverty and racial tension that confronted the African-American residents. Nonetheless, within the very limited resources at her disposal, she tried hard to provide an example of what a partnership between the private and public sectors could do to meet the urban issues of the 1960s. She was an important figure in the history of the nation's capital, with an effect that transcended her time as First Lady.

The natural beauty campaign also involved Mrs. Johnson in one of the most arduous and bitter legislative battles of her husband's presidency—the struggle to secure the passage and enforcement of the Highway Beautification Act of 1965. The drive to control billboards along the nation's highways was gathering momentum during the 1950s. The opposing sides were not evenly matched. Advocating billboard regulation were the garden clubs and their female members, urban planners, and the growing but still small cadre of what would become environmentalists by the next decade. Arrayed against them were the owners of billboards, including the Outdoor Advertising Association of America (OAAA), the operators of the tourist attractions that billboards publicized, and the labor unions whose members worked at hotels, restaurants, and roadside establishments. Congress responded readily to the pressures from the industry that decided which candidate obtained advertising space at election time.

There had been tentative legislative efforts to set up billboard rules during the Eisenhower and Kennedy years. Those laws were flawed and ineffective. Critics of outdoor advertising denounced billboards vigorously during these years in magazine articles and books. Because of the power of the billboard lobby, however, it did not seem likely that much constructive action would be taken as 1964 ended.

Mrs. Johnson became a new element in the political equation. Late in 1964 the president called the secretary of commerce to convey the First Lady's interest in seeing junkyards cleaned up. The department responded that the junkyard problem could be addressed with existing laws. For billboard regulation, it proposed that the administration push for more advanced laws. President Johnson knew that any campaign to control the use of outdoor advertising would produce strong opposition from the industry. To achieve the goals that his wife had identified, he embarked on a strategy to split the billboard forces. He designated a close aide, Bill Moyers, to negotiate with the OAAA to see if a measure acceptable to the advertisers could be produced. Moyers talked with Phillip Tocker, a lawyer and lobbyist for the OAAA.

These discussions resulted in draft legislation that the president announced at the Natural Beauty Conference in May 1965. When it became known, however, that the administration had written the proposed law with the section of the industry that operated billboards in urban areas, there was a storm of opposition from the roadside councils that disliked outdoor advertising. The OAAA had difficulty in delivering the support of its own membership as well. A nasty and prolonged fight loomed on Capitol Hill.

The battle over what became the Highway Beautification Act of 1965 drew the First Lady deeply into the contest. She talked with Walter Reuther of the United Auto Workers to enlist his backing. The word was soon all over Washington that Lyndon Johnson was insisting on passage of the bill that his wife wanted so badly. He promised to get it enacted for her if he possibly could.

By mid-September 1965, the bill was being considered by a subcommittee of the Committee on Roads, chaired by John Kluczynski, a Democrat from Illinois. The White House believed that the bill had to come out of the panel no weaker than when the lawmakers began considering it. At meetings to plot legislative strategy, Mrs. Johnson was in attendance as lists of wavering representatives were prepared. She was assigned a group of people to call, including Kluczynski. Her telephone conversation with him helped to bring a satisfactory bill closer to House passage.

This episode represented a significant expansion of the role of the First Lady. It was unprecedented for the president's wife to be part of the legislative planning of the administration and to exercise her influence directly with lawmakers in behalf of specific bills. In the fight over highway beautification, Lady Bird Johnson pushed out the boundaries of what First Ladies could do in Washington in behalf of their favorite causes.

When the legislation reached the House floor, it was evident that victory would not be easy. Opponents of the law made much of Mrs. Johnson's interest. The *Congressional Record* for October 7 contained some of their denunciations of her alleged influence. One congressman styled the law "the President's wife's bill." Representative Robert Dole, a Kansas Republican, proposed to strike the title "Department of Commerce" wherever it appeared in the law and substitute instead the words "Lady Bird." The House defeated that proposal on a voice vote. When Democrats criticized Dole for his actions the next day, he responded, according to the *Congressional Record* for October 8, "that when one chooses to step down from the pedestal of the dutiful preoccupied wife of the President, or other public official, and to wade into the turbulent stream of public controversy, one must expect to, at least, get her feet wet."

In the end, the bill cleared both the House and Senate, and Lyndon Johnson signed it into law on October 22, 1965. Passage of the Highway Beautification Act was a clear victory for Mrs. Johnson and her campaign for natural beauty. She had exercised the implicit power of the First Lady to push serious legislation through Congress. At no other time would enactment of billboard regulation even have been possible. In that sense, Mrs. Johnson's success represented a unique achievement in the historical evolution of the institution of the First Lady.

Victory came at a high price. To appease the billboard forces, the law had been seriously weakened as it moved through Congress. The most important change was the requirement that the government pay billboard owners monetary compensation before a billboard could be taken down. That clause would complicate efforts to make the law meaningful in the years after it was passed. Many environmentally minded opponents of billboards thought that the White House had given up too much to the industry. Neither its friends nor its enemies were very pleased with the Highway Beautification Act when it was first passed.

The battle that raged in Congress over the adoption of the billboard law did not end the controversy. Despite their earlier endorsement of the administration's law, the OAAA moved to a position of outright opposition once the measure was on the statute books. The First Lady and her allies waged an incessant campaign between 1965 and 1969 to keep the Highway Beautification Law alive and reasonably effective. In the process, her involvement with Congress and its deliberations became even greater and more extensive than it had been in 1965.

During the two years after enactment of the Highway Beautification Law, the billboard industry endeavored to water down the new measure. Mrs. Johnson and her staff monitored the process by which the Commerce Department implemented regulations to enforce the statute. Throughout 1966 the First Lady found that congressional support was eroding for a vigorous regulatory policy toward outdoor advertising. Money for billboard control was deleted from the 1966 federal highway act.

Mrs. Johnson remained committed to the anti-billboard campaign in 1967. She sought stronger enforcement through the appointment of a coordinator of highway beautification in the Bureau of Public Roads who agreed with her goals. The First Lady had to fend off attacks on the law from members of Congress and persistent criticism from the roadside control groups who wanted an even tougher law on the books. It became clear that the White House would be hard pressed to save the Highway Beautification Act at all; a stronger version was politically impossible. Even within the federal government, other agencies used billboards for advertising in ways that undercut what Mrs. Johnson was trying to do.

The goal of the Johnson administration in 1967 was to remove funding for billboard regulation from close congressional scrutiny through the establishment of a trust fund for paying billboard operators to take down their signs. Congress rejected the idea but did provide some appropriations for the law. The tide was running against this natural beauty reform on Capitol Hill. The

First Lady decided, after consulting with the president's legislative aides, to make another effort to secure funding in 1968.

It did not happen. The trust fund idea was stalled in a House committee and the legislative leadership sliced the appropriation for billboard regulation down to $8.5 million. Nonetheless, Mrs. Johnson lobbied as hard in 1968 as she had in 1965 for positive congressional action to keep billboard control alive as a policy. The Federal-Aid Highway Act of 1968 delivered a serious blow to the anti-billboard forces but there was virtually nothing that the White House could do but to accept the meager results of what had once been such an ambitious program.

With the passage of the 1968 law, Mrs. Johnson's involvement with highway beautification as First Lady came to an end. In the years after 1969, the Highway Beautification Act of 1965 was often criticized as an ineffective piece of legislation that had actually promoted the interests of the billboard owners. If that was, in fact, the case, it was not Mrs. Johnson's fault. The law that was enacted in 1965 was as strong a measure as the political forces in Congress that year would have allowed. Without the support of the First Lady and the president, no billboard regulation law of any kind could have been passed. The choice that Mrs. Johnson faced was doing something to advance the cause of natural beauty on the highways or making no progress at all. She was the political catalyst that gave billboard regulation a chance to survive throughout the 1960s.

Mrs. Johnson's beautification work as First Lady went beyond her efforts in behalf of Washington, D.C., and her campaign to control the spread of billboards. She was a visible public advocate for the principle of natural beauty throughout the years after 1965. She traveled to endangered areas and alerted her fellow citizens to the state of the nation's natural heritage. The speeches that she made further stimulated public interest in matters relating to the environment and its protection. She asked Americans to consider whether a democratic society had to settle for the lowest common denominator or whether beautiful and important projects to safeguard the environment could be supported and sustained.

The trips she made to wilderness refuges and scenic places were frequent during her years as First Lady. In 1966, she toured the Big Bend region of Texas with Udall. About 100 people, including seventy reporters, accompanied her as she rafted down the Rio Grande. She made similar visits to the California redwoods and the Pacific Coast in 1966, two trips through New England in 1967, and another swing through Texas with a group of foreign editors in April 1968. The publicity she garnered and the interest that her campaign evoked across the country increased the demands on her time as a speaker beyond what she could fulfill. Her staff devised a speakers bureau of cabinet wives and other volunteers that worked effectively through 1966 until the requests for surrogates for Mrs. Johnson diminished.

Mrs. Johnson also reached out to the business community in her conservation campaign. She approached oil companies about upgrading the appearance of their service stations. She also collaborated with insurance companies and grocery store chains to help in beautifying urban neighborhoods. Similar attempts to enlist bottling companies and highway contractors proved less rewarding. On the whole, the First Lady was disappointed that she did not get more support from business at all levels.

Despite the strong endorsement that President Johnson provided for her environmental goals, the First Lady had to push the agencies of the federal government to achieve positive results. There was no outright opposition. Instead, she faced the reluctance of male bureaucrats to supply enthusiastic approval of what many of them saw as a feminine crusade. Within those limits, however, Mrs. Johnson gave her backing to a youth conference on natural beauty in 1966, which in turn led to various volunteer efforts in behalf of local beautification projects. She also supported the National Historic Preservation Act, passed by Congress in 1966.

The First Lady and her staff also monitored closely the work of the Citizen's Advisory Committee on Recreation and Natural Beauty after President Johnson created it by executive order in May 1966. Mrs. Johnson made sure that she had staff members such as Liz Carpenter and Sharon Francis at the meetings of the panel. She also took an active role in the appointments of the committee's members, including some discreet lobbying to see that more women were named. She was given an informal but important advisory role in the selection process that suggested how she had expanded the role of the First Lady during her husband's presidency.

As environmental problems spread during the mid-1960s, interested groups implored the First Lady to give her public backing to their causes. When the prospect of dams on the Colorado River threatened the continued existence of the Grand Canyon in 1966, she received a flood of mail asking her to speak out against the proposal. She had to tread gingerly, as the administration was supporting the dams for Arizona, and her role was not crucial in defeating the project. The mail that came in attested to the degree that the public regarded her as a voice for conservation within the administration.

The attempt to create a national park for the California redwoods aroused fears among environmental groups that the park would not be large enough to protect many of the old trees from lumber companies and developers. Mrs. Johnson's trip to California in 1966, her dispatching of Sharon Francis to investigate the controversy in 1967, and her quiet lobbying role with her husband contributed to the climate that enabled the Johnson administration to secure compromise legislation in 1968 that preserved some of the redwood growth.

As she carried on her beautification endeavors, Mrs. Johnson could not escape the political pressures that were gathering around her husband's administration in the wake of the Vietnam War. When she spoke at Williams College in Massachusetts and at Yale University in Connecticut during

the autumn of 1967, 1,200 silent protesters outside the hall at Yale made the situation a difficult one for the First Lady. She wanted to know what people were thinking, but she wondered if she should speak again on college campuses.

Lyndon Johnson's support for his wife's work was unstinting throughout their time together in the White House. He made it clear on numerous occasions that she moved him with gentle firmness to push ahead with conservation policies. The president noted that they had been a partnership for thirty years; he would come to meetings that she had with officials and private citizens about her natural beauty goals and give his support to what she was doing.

By 1967, however, they faced personal decisions about the president's political future. Worried about her husband's health and his ability to survive another term in the White House, Mrs. Johnson did not want him to suffer a crippling illness, like the one that enfeebled Woodrow Wilson in 1919. She saw what the agony about the Vietnam War and the social turmoil domestically was doing to her husband as the months passed. In their private conversations, the Johnsons decided as early as 1967 that he would not be a candidate for president again in 1968. The question then became when to make the announcement. She began to give quiet hints to her staff that they should not expect to serve another four years. In discussions with friends, such as Texas governor John Connally and Supreme Court Justice Abe Fortas, they concluded that sometime in early 1968 would be the most suitable time to make a formal withdrawal statement.

The right moment did not come during the early weeks of 1968, and the issue was still in doubt when Mrs. Johnson spoke with her husband on January 17. He decided not to make an announcement during his State of the Union Address that evening. The following day, the First Lady held one of her events devoted to the activities of women. She called them "Women Doer Luncheons," and they brought together at the White House women who had achieved distinction in their fields or who were interested in a current social issue. They had become one of the features of her regular schedule. The topic for the luncheon on January 18 was crime in the streets, a controversial subject at a time when urban rioting had become a fact of American life.

One of the guests that day was the African-American singer and actress Eartha Kitt. During a question period, the entertainer made a lengthy statement about the impact of the Vietnam War on the nation's young people. Kitt charged that the administration was taking children and sending them off to war in Vietnam. Mrs. Johnson put down Kitt's words in her own *White House Diary*: "We send the best of this country off to be shot and maimed. They rebel in the streets. They take pot and they will get high."

It was an emotional moment for the First Lady. She told herself to remain calm and dignified. She told Kitt that the existence of the war in Southeast Asia should not mean that everyone should abandon efforts for the improvement of society. The room broke into applause when Mrs. Johnson had finished. The episode soon became a national controversy. Kitt charged that her career suffered because of her Vietnam War statement. The First Lady received public approval for her comments, but the incident revealed the extent to which the war in Vietnam had polarized opinion in 1968.

The next two months were crowded with events. In the wake of the Tet Offensive in Vietnam, which shook public confidence in the war, the challenges to the president's reelection from Eugene McCarthy and Robert Kennedy, and the erosion of Lyndon Johnson's political base, the thoughts of the Johnsons returned to their projected statement of withdrawal from politics. Throughout those troubled weeks, the First Lady fretted continually about the worrisome state of the president's health. By March 31, 1968, Lyndon Johnson had decided to make his surprise departure from political life.

The First Lady approached the occasion with mixed feelings, but she was convinced that her husband had done the right thing.

She instructed her staff that they should make the most of the time that remained in the White House. In a busy round of activities, she escorted foreign editors on a tour of Texas, spoke out for conservation causes, and tried to get more legislation through to safeguard natural beauty. She took special pride in the changes that Congress made to amend the Land and Water Conservation Act of 1964. Mrs. Johnson believed that the use of revenues from mineral leases to increase the fund was an innovation that foreshadowed what other administrations did for the environment during the 1970s.

As the end of the administration approached, the White House staff looked for ways to continue Mrs. Johnson's work into the next presidential term. The idea was explored of making the First Lady's Committee for a More Beautiful National Capital permanent by executive order. In a memorandum from White House aide Matthew Nimetz to presidential assistant Joseph Califano, dated July 31, it was stated that "the First Lady has never been given official duties by law or executive order, and this would be a break with tradition." Califano advised Mrs. Johnson that any formal action to extend the life of her committee would not be appropriate. Mrs. Johnson was careful during those last months not to take any actions that would be seen as obligating her successor as First Lady.

During her last weeks in the White House, Mrs. Johnson received praise from across the nation for the work she had accomplished for natural beauty. An island in the Potomac River was named Lady Bird Johnson Park. Commentators concluded that she had expanded the role of the First Lady in significant ways and had raised the national awareness of conservation permanently. The members of her committee honored her with gifts to Washington, D.C., of more flowers and trees. Her aide, Sharon Francis, was quoted as saying to her: "You made us all better people, Mrs. Johnson."

Mrs. Johnson had a significant impact on the institution of the First Lady. Her appointment of Liz Carpenter as chief of staff laid the foundation for the subsequent expansion of the bureaucratic apparatus that served the wife of the president. Mrs. Johnson was the first president's wife since Eleanor Roosevelt to identify herself with a substantive cause. She revived a program of innovation for the First Lady that had been dormant for two decades. Her direct involvement with congressional legislation went well beyond what Mrs. Roosevelt had done. She took the ill-defined institution of the First Lady and revitalized it in ways that foreshadowed the activism of Betty Ford, Rosalynn Carter, and Hillary Rodham Clinton.

Her return to Texas did not mark the end of her work for the environment. She created a program to reward employees of the Texas Highway Department for their efforts in behalf of highway beautification. The occasion became an annual event that often featured celebrities such as Laurance Rockefeller and Mary Lasker. The experience laid the groundwork for what would become the National Wildflower Research Center.

In the city of Austin, which she valued so much, she gave her time and energy to the improvement of the river that runs through the center of the community. The Town Lake Beautification Project on the Colorado River led to a hike and bike trail—surrounded by trees—that hikers, bicyclists, and joggers used in the years that followed.

Lyndon Johnson lived on in slowly declining health until 1973. Following his death, his widow pursued business and personal interests for the ten years that followed. In January 1977, President Gerald Ford awarded Mrs. Johnson the Presidential Medal of Freedom. She was a member of the Board of Regents of the University of Texas at Austin, a skillful manager of the extensive radio and television interests that her family retained, and a quiet supporter of Democratic candidates in state and national races. A growing number of grandchildren claimed much of her attention. She told her daughters that her own sense of feminism also expanded at this time.

As she neared her seventieth birthday in 1982, Mrs. Johnson decided to embark on another beautification-related endeavor.

She announced on December 22, 1982, that she was donating sixty acres east of Austin and $125,000 toward the creation of the National Wildflower Research Center. It would be, she said in newspaper accounts at the time, "her last hurrah." In her own words to journalists, Mrs. Johnson said that the donation would serve as payment for the space she had occupied in the world. The friends who helped her in Washington—Laurance Rockefeller and Mary Lasker—came to her assistance with generous gifts once again. Helen Hayes added her support to the campaign to raise money for the center.

During the 1980s, the Wildflower Center expanded to a national membership that exceeded 7,500 people. Symposia on wildflower research topics were frequent events, and the center sponsored projects to develop uses of wildflowers across the country. The results were encouraging. Using wildflowers reduced mowing and maintenance costs for highway departments in many states, sometimes up to millions of dollars annually. In the early 1990s, the center moved from its original site east of Austin to a development in the southwestern part of the metropolitan area.

Throughout her eighth decade, Mrs. Johnson planned to reduce her busy schedule of events and commitments. She even made occasional announcements to that effect; however, there is little evidence that she fulfilled her plan. She wrote a best-selling book, *Wildflowers Across America*, with Carlton Lees in 1988, made speeches and appearances, and remained a loyal supporter of Democratic and feminist causes. In April 1988, she received a Congressional Gold Medal and President Ronald Reagan welcomed her back to the White House.

Mrs. Johnson's eightieth birthday was a time of gala celebrations at the Lyndon Baines Johnson Presidential Library, as her friends gathered to honor her and her accomplishments. For the occasion, the director of the LBJ Library wrote a volume, *Lady Bird Johnson: A Life Well Lived* (1992), that brought together her words and the memories of her friends to evoke the many events and causes in which she had participated. At the conclusion of the book, Mrs. Johnson is quoted as saying: "There's been so much in my life, and I almost feel like pinching myself and saying, 'Did all of this happen to me? Is this really me, living this?'"

Even Mrs. Johnson's energy and efficiency could not stave off the effects of advancing age. During the summer of 1993, she suffered a slight stroke and recurring episodes of dizziness. Macular degeneration impaired her vision and left her unable to read. The honors for her kept pouring in. In 1997 the Wildflower Center was renamed the Lady Bird Johnson Wildflower Center. A year later the LBJ Library opened a permanent exhibit on her life, and in 1999, Secretary of the Interior Bruce Babbitt gave her a lifetime achievement award from the National Conservation Initiative.

Mrs. Johnson figured significantly in the development of the First Lady's role during the second half of the twentieth century. Because of the circumstances by which her husband became president in 1963, and the memories of the glamour that Jacqueline Kennedy brought to the White House, Mrs. Johnson was somewhat overshadowed by her predecessor during the 1960s. With the passage of time, however, the importance of Mrs. Johnson to the history of First Ladies has become clearer. She was the first activist wife of a president since Eleanor Roosevelt a generation earlier. In her lobbying for the Head Start program and the environment, Mrs. Johnson went beyond what Mrs. Roosevelt had done and became a direct participant in the environmental policy-making of her husband's administration. Her support for the beautification of Washington, D.C., represented a major contribution to the improvement of the nation's capital. Around the nation, she stimulated an awareness of the problems of natural beauty that moved thousands of citizens to take similar actions in their own local communities. She was a crucial catalyst in the attempt to limit blight on the nation's roadsides and to curb the spread of billboards. Whatever its later failures, the Highway Beautification Act of 1965 could not have been enacted without her influence and the impetus she gave to the anti-billboard drive.

The work that Mrs. Johnson began as First Lady became the theme of her years after the White House. She extended and developed her beautification campaign in Texas and across the nation through the National Wildflower Research Center. The wives of state governors and other women in politics came to see her for ideas about how they could influence public policy. Mrs. Johnson did not simply pursue beautification as a campaign in Washington, then cast it aside once she was out of politics. Instead, it became the defining principle of her career for a quarter of a century.

Mrs. Johnson's importance as First Lady can be identified with her well-focused interest in environmental questions between 1965 and 1969. Her initiatives helped impart a concern for these issues into the public mind with a skill and political adroitness that placed her in the front rank among women in American history and First Ladies in the twentieth century.

BIBLIOGRAPHICAL ESSAY

The personal papers of Claudia Alta Taylor Johnson at the Lyndon B. Johnson Presidential Library are not yet open for research. The library does have, however, seventeen boxes of records relating to her beautification work in the White House Social Files. This group of records also contains the more than 1,000 boxes of the alphabetical files of her correspondence as First Lady. The library will review for research purposes and open materials from this collection. The Liz Carpenter subject and alphabetical files in the White House Social Files are also useful. The library contains the originals of Mrs. Johnson's White House Diary. The diary is still closed to researchers in its manuscript form, but may be opened during the next several years. There are relevant files relating to Mrs. Johnson in the papers of Lyndon Baines Johnson.

Manuscript collections outside Austin that contain information about Mrs. Johnson include the records about her family in the Harrison County Courthouse, Marshall, Texas; the Katie Louchheim and Nathaniel Owings Papers, Manuscripts Division, Library of Congress; and the Maurine Neuberger Papers, University of Oregon, Eugene.

Mrs. Johnson has written two important works. *A White House Diary* (New York, 1970) represents one-seventh of the original. It is an excellent source for her own attitudes toward her years in the White House and is valuable for her insights into what her husband was doing as president. *Wildflowers Across America* (New York, 1988), written with Carlton Lees, is a good statement of her views toward the natural world during the period after she left the White House.

There is no biography of Mrs. Johnson based on all of her personal papers. Ruth Montgomery, *Mrs LBJ* (New York, 1964); and Marie Smith, *The President's Lady: An Intimate Biography of Mrs. Lyndon B. Johnson* (New York, 1964), were written while she was First Lady. Liz Carpenter, *Ruffles and Flourishes* (College Station, Tex., 1992), was originally published just after the Johnson presidency, and is an engaging memoir by the First Lady's staff director. A modern examination of the First Lady's role in the 1960s is Lewis L. Gould, *Lady Bird Johnson and the Environment* (Lawrence, Kans., 1988). The quotation from residents of Washington appears in this book. Robert Dallek, *Lone Star Rising: Lyndon Johnson and His Times, 1908–1960* (New York, 1991), is the most balanced and insightful treatment of the Johnsons and their marriage. Harry Middleton, *Lady Bird Johnson: A Life Well Lived* (Austin, Tex., 1992), published on the occasion of her eightieth birthday, is a volume of pictures and memories. Mrs. Johnson's quoted memory of her girlhood appears in the Middleton volume.

Jan Jarboe Russell, *Lady Bird: A Biography of Mrs. Johnson* (New York, 1999), is based on interviews by a journalist and emphasizes the trials of the Johnson marriage and the impact of Lyndon Johnson's infidelity. Lewis L. Gould, *Lady Bird Johnson: Our Environmental First Lady* (Lawrence, Kans., 1999), appraises her role in the White House.

★★★　　★★★

Thelma Catherine (Patricia) Ryan Nixon

(1912–1993)

First Lady: 1969–1974

Carl Sferrazza Anthony

Although christened Thelma Catherine, the wife of the thirty-seventh president of the United States would always be known as "Patricia," or just "Pat," Nixon. Born late in the night on March 16, 1912, in a mining tent in Ely, Nevada, Thelma Catherine Ryan was nicknamed "Pat" by her father, William Ryan, when he returned home from his work as a silver miner. His calling her his "St. Patrick's Babe in the Morn" was a tribute to his heritage as the son of Irish immigrant parents. Her mother, Kate Halberstadt Bender Ryan, a native of southern Germany who was widowed with two children, married Ryan after she immigrated to the United States. Patricia was thus the only twentieth-century president's wife to be a first-generation American.

The Ryan family, including two sons, Tom and Bill, moved to a ten-acre truck farm in the small southern-California town of Artesia, outside of Los Angeles, later renamed Cerritos. "It was very primitive," Patricia later said:

> It was a hard life. . . . I didn't know what it was like not to work hard. I worked right along with my brothers in the fields, really, which was lots of fun. We picked potatoes; we picked tomatoes, we picked peppers and cauliflowers. . . . When I got older I drove the team of horses. . . .

Kate Ryan died of cancer when Patricia was fourteen, and the teenager assumed the traditional role of housewife for her family while continuing to work on the farm. When her father died of lung silicosis three years later, Patricia supported her two brothers as housekeeper. She worked to bring in money to keep her family together during the devastating Depression. "I don't like to think back to that time," she later said.

An excellent student, Patricia saw education as her opportunity to see the world outside of the small town and to improve her lot. While nursing her father during his final illness, for example, she had not only taken a shorthand class between working on the farm and attending high school, but also had begun saving for higher education. Graduating from high school with honors, she enrolled at Fullerton Junior College. To pay for school, she worked after early household chores at six in the morning. She scrubbed down the marble steps of the local bank, cleaned the bank as janitor, and then worked in the bank as a teller. Only after a day's work could she take a trolley car and attend college classes. "In any type of occupation requiring the meeting of the public, Pat will be a great success," wrote one of her professors.

In 1931, Patricia seized a chance to see the world by offering to drive an elderly couple across the country to New York. She settled there for two years and worked first as secretary. After taking a radiology course at Columbia University, she was employed as a radiology technician at a Catholic hospital in the Bronx. Courted by doctors and enjoying her independence, she found her most rewarding and moving moments in the wards of terminally ill children. On winter nights, she often helped them out for sleigh rides on a nearby hillside, recalling those dark evenings as "among the most haunting of my life." She wrote to her brothers in California that "the world is what we make of it, so let's make ours a grand one."

In the summer of 1933, Patricia made her first trip to Washington, D.C., and visited the White House. Several months later she attended a dinner at which President and Mrs. Franklin D. Roosevelt were also present. As a youth, Patricia campaigned for and would have voted for fellow Irish

Catholic Al Smith in 1928. She was registered as an independent but focused on completing her education, not politics.

Returning to California, Patricia Ryan enrolled in the University of Southern California. Again she put herself through school—working as an extra in Hollywood films, a clothing model at a department store, a dental technician, a science professor's assistant, and a telephone operator. Her Shakespeare teacher, Frank Baxter, recalled that one would see her working in the cafeteria at lunch, in the library afterward, and as a research assistant at night. "She stood out from the empty-headed overdressed little sorority girls of that era like a good piece of literature on a shelf of cheap paperbacks," said Baxter.

In 1937 Patricia earned her degree in merchandising, along with a teacher's certificate. She graduated cum laude with enough credits to gain the equivalent of a master's degree—the first president's wife to reach such a level of higher education. Although she had hoped to develop a career in marketing, she accepted an offer to teach typing and shorthand at Whittier High School in southern California. She also assumed a multitude of responsibilities, including faculty adviser to the student Pep Committee, cheerleader coach for sporting events, and director of student theatrical productions. Sensitive to students who had to work as she had, particularly Mexican Americans, she was still a strict teacher. One former student recalled that she expected

> clockwork punctuality from us and we absorbed the gentle hint that questions to her should be prefaced by her name. . . . Miss Ryan followed the book. She allowed no compromises, no errors, no second-rate job. Perfection and high standards were the only things she accepted.

While auditioning for the Whittier Community Players production of the Alexander Wollcott-George S. Kaufman play *The Dark Tower* in the autumn of 1938, she met fellow actor and Whittier lawyer Richard M. Nixon. Nixon was immediately struck by the sight of the "beautiful and vivacious young woman with titian hair," and said he instantly fell in love. He quickly pursued her and announced that "someday I am going to marry you."

For nearly three years Nixon wooed Pat Ryan, even driving her to dates with other beaus and waiting for her to finish, then taking her home. Ambitious for a political career, he envisioned her as part of his future life. He wrote to her that she was "destined to be a great lady," and that they must marry because "it is our job to go forth together and accomplish great ends and we shall do it too." He found her unwilling to open up her early traumas to him, and he thought she had a "strangely sad but lovely" smile.

Pat developed a deeper respect and love for Richard as time went on. "I admired Dick Nixon from the very beginning," she later recalled, "but I was having a very good time and wasn't anxious to settle down." However, she took seriously his revealed hope. As she told a friend, "He's going to be president someday." After one of their frequent evening drives out to the beach at San Clemente, Patricia accepted his marriage proposal. They were wed on June 21, 1940, at the famous Old Mission Inn, in Riverside, California.

After a short honeymoon in Mexico, Pat Nixon continued to work full-time as a teacher, contributing to their savings. The couple set up housekeeping in a small apartment above a car garage in Whittier, California. With the outbreak of World War II, Nixon took a post in Washington, D.C., as an attorney for the Office of Price Administration. There, Pat Nixon worked as a secretary for the Red Cross but later qualified as a price analyst for the Office of Price Administration (OPA), the only woman in an otherwise all-male division.

When Nixon joined the U.S. Navy and held a variety of positions around the country, his wife went with him. While he was in the Pacific, she settled in San Francisco and worked again as an OPA economic analyst. Living there alone, she enjoyed her independence but wrote daily to her husband, who did likewise. She sent him books by

authors ranging from Karl Marx to Guy de Maupassant.

After Nixon returned to California, he was courted by the Whittier Republican Party, in which he had been active as an attorney, to run in the Twelfth Congressional District as a candidate for the House of Representatives in 1946. Nixon first consulted his wife about entering politics. Her primary concern was having sufficient funds to campaign. She offered to donate their savings—several thousand dollars that they had planned to put toward a home—to his campaign. Just six hours after giving birth to their first daughter, Patricia, called Tricia, on February 21, 1946, Mrs. Nixon was researching stacks of congressional records. She wanted to familiarize herself and her husband with the views and voting record of the incumbent, Jerry Voorhis, Nixon's Democratic opponent. She wrote and edited campaign literature, typed and printed it, and hand-distributed it. Nixon won the election, and the family moved to Washington, D.C. A year later, Pat Nixon gave birth to her second child, Julie, on July 5, 1948.

Throughout Nixon's subsequent campaigns—for Congress again in 1948, the Senate in 1950, the vice presidency in 1952 and 1956, and the presidency in 1960—Pat Nixon played a substantive role behind the scenes. She attended the speeches of many of his opponents and took shorthand transcriptions of their exact words. She also critiqued her husband's speeches. Publicly, she appeared tireless, attending constant rounds of teas, coffees, luncheons, and other fundraisers for Republican women. People spoke of her down-to-earth nature, even in the most perfunctory of social situations, which went a long way toward humanizing the candidate. Although she proved to be an excellent campaigner, spending long hours each day focusing on individual voters, Mrs. Nixon later revealed that she disliked campaigning more than any other aspect of politics because it so often involved being attacked and having to attack one's opponent. She never made major policy speeches, but what began as welcoming remarks would evolve into more formal statements that would reflect her husband's agenda.

As a House—and later Senate—wife, Pat Nixon tried to keep her two daughters and the family's home life her priority. Although she attended the requisite political and social events, with and without Nixon, she never did so eagerly. As chair of a subcommittee on the House Un-American Activities Committee, her husband was developing a national reputation as an anticommunist, winning him a loyal core of supporters but vicious enemies as well. Politics, she said, produces "the most vicious people in the world." It made Mrs. Nixon all the more guarded. Meticulous in her personal grooming and clothing, she strove to be perfect at all of her public appearances, which led later to the derisive label "Plastic Pat." If some thought her robotic, however, those who knew her best understood that she was struggling to protect her private life and family.

Her task was challenged in 1952 when Nixon was nominated as the Republican vice presidential candidate. Press reports claimed that he kept a "secret" fund to provide for political expenses. In the face of advice that her husband step down from the ticket, Pat Nixon told him, "We both know what you have to do, Dick. You have to fight it all the way to the end, no matter what happens." He followed her counsel and arranged to explain the fund to the American public on television, in the process revealing the family's finances. Mrs. Nixon balked at that, saying: "Why do we have to tell people how little we have and how much we owe? Aren't we entitled to at least some privacy?" Nixon replied that divulging all details was necessary, and his wife appeared with him on television, a strong but silent figure. Three times the candidate referred to her, stating that Mrs. Nixon was Irish and someone who didn't quit easily; that she was not on the Senate payroll, as many other Senate wives were; and that she had a cloth coat, not a mink coat. The "Checkers Speech," named after Nixon's reference to his daughters' little dog, not only turned the tide in Richard Nixon's favor, but made Pat Nixon a national figure.

As a vice presidential wife during the Dwight D. Eisenhower administration (1953–1961), Mrs. Nixon frequently appeared at daytime functions in First Lady Mamie Eisenhower's stead, and the latter called her "my Rock of Gibraltar." As part of what became known as the "Dick and Pat team," Mrs. Nixon joined her husband on his many international junkets and developed her own public schedule, visiting orphanages, hospitals, and even a leper colony. By doing so in many underdeveloped nations, Mrs. Nixon raised a previously unacknowledged consciousness of women as active public figures. "Everywhere I went," she said proudly, "it helped women." Privately, however, she wrote to a friend, "I would like to do part-time work rather than all the useless gadding I am expected to do."

Politically, Mrs. Nixon was both astute and active, working for her husband on correspondence and scheduling and editing his speeches. While she did not publicly express her opinions during the 1950s, Patricia Nixon did have strong views. She personally distrusted Senator Joseph R. McCarthy, although she believed that the Wisconsin Republican's investigation into State Department employees who might be Communist sympathizers was warranted. She saw the vice presidency as a "dead end." However, when there was a "dump Nixon" movement by Eisenhower loyalists during the 1956 presidential campaign, Pat Nixon told her husband, "No one is going to push you off the ticket." She was not enamored of President Eisenhower, who was folksy in public, viewing him as seeing her husband only from a politically expedient perspective.

By her international travel and frequent appearances at political functions, and her photogenic nature at such events, Pat Nixon developed the role of "Second Lady" into a far more public one than had previously been the case. *Time* magazine in 1960 pronounced her "one of the U.S.'s most remarkable women—not just a showpiece Second Lady, not merely part of the best-known team in contemporary politics, but a public figure in her own right."

Such recognition proved useful in Nixon's 1960 race for the presidency against Democratic Senator, John F. Kennedy. The Republican National Committee held a "Pat Week" of national rallies and women's events. One of their press releases stated that "When you elect a President you are also electing a First Lady. . . . The First Lady has a working assignment. She represents America to all the world. Pat Nixon is . . . uniquely . . . qualified." There were "Pat for First Lady" buttons, posters, and bumper stickers created, all to appeal to large numbers of traditional housewives—like Pat Nixon—who were heavily courted by the Republican Party during the 1950s. Pat Nixon even defended herself against charges that, as a woman, she was too political. She said that her work was

reflective of women all over America taking an active part, not only in political life but all activities. There was a day when they stayed at home . . . but they have emerged as volunteers for the cause they believe in.

The press briefly attempted to draw a race between the candidates' wives, Jacqueline Kennedy and Patricia Nixon, by comparing their clothing styles and expenditures, but both women resisted being drawn into it.

When Nixon lost the presidency by the closest popular vote margin in history and conceded his defeat on live television, Patricia Nixon was seen publicly crying for the first time. She declared herself happy to be "out of the rat race" of politics, and settled into the life of a lawyer's wife in Beverly Hills, California. She strongly advised her husband not to run for governor in 1962, although he did, and lost. In early 1963 the Nixons moved to New York City, where Mrs. Nixon went to work part-time as a receptionist and stenographer in Nixon's office, going by the name "Miss Ryan."

In 1968, amid the rancor of bitter debate about the nation's continued presence in Vietnam, calls for radical changes of women's roles, urban riots, and campus unrest, Nixon was again nominated for the presidency. It was a move Pat Nixon did not favor. Upon her husband's election, Mrs. Nixon put aside her own misgivings, and publicly expressed her belief that "he alone was capable of solving some of the problems" of the torn nation.

Through the programs, projects, and causes that she assumed as First Lady, Pat Nixon made a conscious attempt to emphasize the individual American, the "common man." It was, at times, an effort that the media overlooked because of larger national priorities, or derided as hokum in an era when previously accepted values were being questioned. Still, Mrs. Nixon persisted quietly, and those anonymous individuals who somehow directly benefited from her effort appreciated her concern and greatly praised her for it. She reveled in the symbolic aspect of being First Lady when it put her in touch with average citizens.

As one of her staff members explained, Pat Nixon was "aware of what contact with the 'First Lady' meant to the average American who might have the chance to be around her." United Press International reporter Helen Thomas, who later became dean of the White House press corps, said that Pat Nixon was "the warmest First Lady I covered and the one who loved people the most. . . . Sharp, responsive, sensitive . . . concerned about people's feelings."

Mrs. Nixon's most immediate response to the individual was through management of her personal correspondence. Although thousands of letters were written to her each week, Mrs. Nixon instructed her director of correspondence, Gwen King, to direct several hundred letters to her. In the private quarters, Mrs. Nixon spent upwards of five hours a day personally answering those citizens who had written to her. If someone asked for federal assistance, Mrs. Nixon not only directed the letter to the proper agency, but also responded through the East Wing, much as a congressional office operates. As the First Lady explained, "When a letter arrives from the White House in a small town, it's shown to all the neighbors, and often published in the local paper. It's very important to the people who receive it."

In the Washington community, Pat Nixon began "Evenings in the Park," a series of local summer concerts for inner-city youth. She held one program on the White House lawn, and attended another on the Washington Monument grounds, despite the large number of antiwar and "Black Power" protesters who shouted down the national anthem. She took groups of other underprivileged children on trips on the presidential yacht, and visited several day camps that the private sector supported.

When Mrs. Nixon refurbished several state rooms of the White House in 1970 and 1971, she greatly expanded the fine arts and furniture collection. The First Lady focused specifically on trying to complete the collection of life portraits of presidents and their wives, and managed to obtain portraits of James Madison and Louisa Adams. The Philadelphia Academy of Fine Arts agreed to make a permanent loan of their Gilbert Stuart life portrait of Dolley Madison only after Pat Nixon personally intervened with the institution. Making the refurbished mansion as accessible as possible to the public was among her most important but least acknowledged legacies.

With a constant emphasis to her staff that the mansion was "the people's house," Pat Nixon opened the grounds to the public for the first time since the mid-twentieth century by initiating autumn and spring tours. She arranged for special tours to be conducted for groups of the blind and deaf, and made the complex handicapped-accessible. For those visitors who did not speak or read English, the First Lady offered guide pamphlets printed in several languages. To ease the burden of those waiting in long lines around the outside gate of the White House, she had a recorded history of the mansion placed at intervals along the fence in boxes. She provided display cases containing historic treasures for those who were waiting inside. She ordered lights around the mansion lit at night so that it was visible from the air or street. During the winter, she had the fountains turned on. At Christmas, being sensitive to working parents, she initiated "Candlelight Tours" of the yuletide-decorated mansion in the evening hours.

On February 18, 1969, Pat Nixon announced that as First Lady she would encourage a "national recruitment program," enlisting thousands of American volunteers. Although no formal network of volunteers was developed by the White House, her staff named "volunteerism" as her "project." Genuinely believing in the power of mass voluntary effort to change aspects of small communities, Mrs. Nixon explained, "Our success as a Nation depends upon our willingness to give generously of ourself for the welfare and enrichment of the life of others."

The First Lady's initial domestic solo mission was inspecting ten "Vest Pockets of Volunteerism" community programs. Matching volunteers with pressing social problems, she said, "can often accomplish things that legislation alone cannot. This is where I think I can help, encouraging . . . those 'small, splendid efforts.'"

Besides the tours, which brought public attention through local news stories, Mrs. Nixon and her staff also scanned newspapers and correspondence for volunteer projects and sent unsolicited commendation letters, which were usually printed locally. She also used the White House to honor local groups that had formed in response to a community problem or an outstanding individual volunteer.

Pat Nixon became formally associated with the quasi-government-funded National Center for Voluntary Action. She attended its annual awards ceremonies, conferred with leaders at the Washington headquarters, and participated in a briefing on the center's objectives held at the State Department. She became an advocate of the Domestic Services Volunteer Act of 1970, an official declaration of Congress formulated with the help of the center, although she did not testify before Congress nor associate politically with the act.

The First Lady paralleled the administration's domestic agenda by "going into the field" and inspecting public works projects related directly to Nixon's programs, illustrating for the press the issues that the president was simultaneously raising. For example, when Richard Nixon attended a Chicago environmental meeting, his wife spent the day inspecting a land reclamation center, an example of thermal pollution, and several conservation projects, as well as dedicating a strip of undeveloped park. When he met with law enforcement officials in Denver, she toured a rehabilitation home for juvenile delinquents.

After Nixon first spoke of the "energy crisis," the First Lady led a press tour of a model home that conserved energy. She also highlighted a program known as "Legacy of the Parks," which turned federally developed, protected, and maintained lands over for community recreation. In a series of colorful ceremonies, Pat Nixon transferred nearly 50,000 such federal acres to state and local control. She was a member of the President's Committee on Employment of the Handicapped, and honorary chair of the Department of Health, Education, and Welfare's "Right to Read" program.

Pat Nixon was most noted overseas for her "personal diplomacy," particularly during the trips she made with her husband in 1972 to the Soviet Union and the People's Republic of China. In China, dressed in her bright red coat, Mrs. Nixon became a living symbol of America for the entire world, via the live broadcast and press coverage of her every move around Peking, from farm communes to classrooms.

When Mrs. Nixon made several goodwill trips without the president, she did so with the official, but temporary, rank of "the president's ambassador." In January 1972, she made a solo visit to three African nations—Ghana, the Ivory Coast, and Liberia. In all three nations, she addressed congresses and met with leaders, discussing American state policy on Rhodesia and South Africa.

In June 1970, following a devastating earthquake in remote areas of Peru (80,000 were killed; 80,000 left homeless), the First Lady personally arranged with national volunteer organizations to gather food, clothing, and medical supplies, and launched a

"volunteer American relief drive." She then led the outreach herself, traveling into the treacherous Andes mountain range in a small helicopter with ten tons of supplies. Upon her return, she maintained a network of fund-raising and volunteer efforts in continuing relief work. Peru awarded her the Grand Cross of the Sun, the oldest decoration in the Western Hemisphere, and she was universally praised in North and South America for her accomplishment. The "profound significance" of her campaign, said Lima's *La Prensa*, improved United States–Peru relations.

Mrs. Nixon was the most traveled First Lady up to her time. One of her first foreign trips with the president, for example, included Guam, India, the Philippines, Indonesia, Pakistan, Romania, England, and South Vietnam. In South Vietnam, the First Lady entered the combat zone. In an open-air helicopter just eighteen miles from Saigon, on her way to a military hospital, she caught sight of American troops scattered in the jungle below. At her side throughout were military guards with machine guns and bandoliers.

The First Lady publicly supported the U.S. presence in Southeast Asia, in agreement with her husband's policy. After speaking with servicemen on active duty, she said, "I feel that they know a great deal more about the conflict there than many of us do at home. . . . Our servicemen [are] proud to be helping to defend freedom there." Yet, when she learned that four rock-throwing antiwar protesters had been killed at Kent State University in 1970 after being fired upon by Ohio National Guardsmen, she was in "disbelief" and "appalled by the tragic deaths."

Like those of her husband, Mrs. Nixon's appearances were often met by antiwar protesters. On one occasion, colored confetti was thrown at her as protesters chanted, "If this was napalm, you would now be dead"—a reference to the deadly jellied gasoline used in Vietnam. During one campus appearance, however, she warmly embraced protesters in beards and beads, one wearing a peace button.

The president was sensitive to the respect awarded to the symbol of the First Lady. He wrote memoranda about entertaining or household details that he believed brought greater dignity to his wife's position. He was also sensitive to his wife as a human being, and how much she should be asked to do for the administration. "She's very good *onstage*, so to speak," he said in an interview, "even though she prefers not to be onstage."

A formality in the marriage was illustrated by his sending memos to her about small matters, yet part of that was his nature of meticulous chronicling. Nixon speechwriter William Safire believed that, as the president's partner, Mrs. Nixon shared his "prejudices and scar tissue." Her press secretary, Connie Stuart, thought that Nixon "never wanted her hurt . . . because of . . . his work. He wanted her protected and insulated." This resulted in a different dynamic to their marriage. As daughter Julie wrote, her mother had once "been intimately involved in negotiations and decisions," but as of 1969, when they entered the White House, she "would never play that kind of role. . . . My father tried increasingly to separate his political and personal life."

Mrs. Nixon regularly read and marked the daily "Presidential News Summary," administration studies, and issue papers. She attended the first Nixon administration cabinet meeting and a "domestic briefing." Her advice, delivered strictly in private, could often be pointed and critical, according to accounts left by her husband and his advisers. While she did not unravel the details of specific problems, she offered a "strategic, stylistic approach" to issues facing his presidency, according to Connie Stuart. When Vice President Spiro Agnew attacked the press for its "distorted picture" of the nation, the First lady "privately questioned" the administration's "wisdom of speaking out so bluntly through Agnew."

On several women's issues, however, Pat Nixon did speak out. On the issue of abortion, for example, she stated that she felt it was a "private decision." When there was a vacant seat in the Supreme Court, she went first to the press, telling them that she believed a woman should be appointed to fill the vacancy, then persistently lobbied the president, unsuccessfully. Her strong and vocal support of the Equal Rights Amendment (to the point that she included an open pro-ERA letter in the official program of the 1972 Republican National Convention) derived not only from her personal experience as a woman working with male colleagues in her many jobs earlier in life, but also from her own political perspective. During a trip to Yugoslavia, she had remarked that both its parliament and the U.S. Congress should have more women representatives. She encouraged women to run for office, and stated that she would vote for a qualified woman candidate, even if she were not a Republican. Mrs. Nixon even posed publicly in pants.

Press coverage of Patricia Nixon did not capture her personality. A primary reason for this was that Mrs. Nixon did not want a high press profile for herself, and she responded with the same general answers to press questions. In terms of television interviews, she was extremely uncomfortable being recorded, and she also prevented her print interviews from being taped. With Vietnam, the women's rights movement, and later Watergate, among many other social issues dominating the coverage of the Nixon era, Mrs. Nixon's activities and statements were not perceived as being substantive copy.

Mrs. Nixon kept her office in the family quarters, while her staff occupied the East Wing. Her first press secretary, Gerry van der Huevel, lasted only nine months. H. R. Haldeman, the president's chief of staff, replaced her with Connie Stuart, who also served as de facto chief of staff to the First Lady. Haldeman later removed Stuart. The First Lady's third press secretary, Helen Smith, kept a low profile, but was popular with the press, particularly during Watergate, for her blunt honesty. Mrs. Nixon's social secretary for the full term was Lucy Winchester. Press aide Patti Matson doubled in the role of advance woman, who prepared for personal appearances and trips for the First Lady.

For the first two years of Nixon's term, daughter Tricia lived in the mansion with her parents. She married Edward Finch Cox on June 12, 1971, in the first White House garden wedding. After Nixon's 1968 election, but before his 1969 inauguration, their younger daughter, Julie, married David Eisenhower, the grandson of President Eisenhower. The Eisenhowers and Nixons had remained close following Nixon's term as vice president during the Eisenhower administration. The bond grew even stronger because of the sense of being under siege that gripped the White House, first because of Vietnam and then because of the Watergate scandal.

Richard Nixon's renomination in 1972 saw the popular Pat Nixon addressing the Republican National Convention. She made several lengthy campaign trips, criss-crossing the length of the nation on her own. She wanted the president to have a second term, not for any personal reasons but because she wanted, as she told her daughter, "to see congressional action on the crucially important welfare reform, health care, and environmental proposals." As President Nixon recorded, "The road had been hardest of all for Pat. . . . My deepest hope was that she felt that it had all been worth it."

Although Nixon won the election, the growing Watergate scandal overshadowed his second administration. Pat Nixon maintained that she "only [knew] what [she] read in the newspapers" about the break-in at Democratic Party headquarters, the secret taping system of her husband in his office, or the concerted effort by the president's staff—many claim at his explicit direction—of a "cover-up" of the Watergate investigation. When she learned the details of Watergate, Mrs. Nixon strongly defended her husband to the press, maintaining that he was innocent of the many charges made against him, but offered that the tapes should have been destroyed when they were still personal property.

Publicly, she assumed an upbeat attitude about her reaction to Watergate. "By block-ing out the negatives, the positives focus more prominently in my mind. A long time ago, I learned that if I worry about what might happen, my energies are sapped." Privately, however, she grew deeply disturbed about the president's becoming "closed off" into "his own world" and relying too heavily on the advice of a small circle of advisers. Pat Nixon had never had a good working relationship with the president's chief of staff, Haldeman, and his aide, John Ehrlichman. On many occasions, both men attempted to overrule decisions that Mrs. Nixon and her staff had made. As House and Senate committees probed Watergate, Mrs. Nixon was relieved to see Haldeman and Ehrlichman resign during the spring of 1973.

When the threat of impeachment of President Nixon became real in late July 1974, Pat Nixon advised her husband not to resign because of the blanket criminal indictment that might ensue. Instead, she suggested that he fight the articles of impeachment one by one. Once he had decided to resign, however, and announced it to the nation, she immediately began packing their personal items for transportation the next day to their home, La Casa Pacifica, in San Clemente, California, on the Pacific Ocean.

Pat Nixon appeared with her husband in the East Room on August 9, 1974, when he delivered his televised farewell to his staff. She walked with him down the red carpet on the south lawn, to a waiting helicopter, with Vice President and Mrs. Gerald Ford, who were now to replace President and Mrs. Nixon. At noon, as the Nixons were flying back to California, Richard Nixon ceased being president.

Despite exaggerated media reports, Mrs. Nixon did not become a complete recluse at San Clemente. Rather, she lived quietly amid old friends, as well as her two daughters and their husbands, outside of public life. She attended the 1975 dedication of a local high school named in her honor, and donated a wishing well to it. In 1976, however, Mrs. Nixon suffered a debilitating stroke. Through a rigorous occupational therapy program, she recovered use of the stricken limbs on her left side. When she suffered another minor stroke in 1982, she again fully recovered. Other health problems plagued the First Lady, however. She suffered from emphysema, a degenerative spinal illness, and cancer of the mouth.

Although her energy was limited, Pat Nixon lived a full life, particularly after she and her husband moved to be near their daughters—first to a New York City town house, then a large Saddle River, New Jersey, home in a wooded area, and finally a Park Ridge, New Jersey, town house. Often in the company of her four grandchildren, Mrs. Nixon went on local outings and frequently to favorite old haunts in New York. She also accompanied former president Nixon back to China on his first return trip there after his presidency. These retirement years, Richard Nixon wrote, gave the couple "a chance to spend a lot of time together. We've discovered, in this time . . . that we need each other. We've grown closer than ever before."

Patricia Nixon emerged most publicly in July 1990 at the two-day dedication celebration at the Richard Nixon Birthplace and Library in Yorba Linda, California. At a private reception, she delivered a short welcome address to the crowd and participated in all of the public ceremonies. In September 1991, she again appeared publicly with her husband, along with Lady Bird Johnson, Gerald and Betty Ford, Jimmy and Rosalynn Carter, George and Barbara Bush, and Ronald and Nancy Reagan, at the dedication of the Reagan Library.

Stricken with lung cancer during the winter of 1992–1993, Patricia Nixon died just one day after her fifty-third wedding anniversary, surrounded by her husband and daughters, on June 22, 1993. Her husband died ten months later, and was buried beside his wife at the Nixon Birthplace and Library.

Patricia Nixon was a transitional First Lady at a time in American history when so much that had been traditionally accepted as part of the culture was in flux or being questioned. She provided an image of sta-

bility to her husband's administration. Although she did not participate in policy, she served as a strong symbol for the United States overseas and for the administration at home. In step with her times, she was a progressive woman in terms of her views on equality for her sex. From her own difficult early years to the White House, her life illustrated the mythical "American Dream." Her interest in the individual and making the White House accessible at a time when her husband was often under attack stood in sharp contrast to the image that his "palace guard" crafted of an "imperial presidency."

BIBLIOGRAPHICAL ESSAY

The best primary source on Patricia Nixon is her daughter Julie Nixon Eisenhower's biography, *Pat Nixon: The Untold Story* (New York, 1986). It reproduces, often in full, her private and public correspondence with her husband, daughters, friends, and staff members, as well as contemporary newspaper and magazine articles about and interviews with Pat Nixon, and many other useful documents unobtainable to the researcher.

The second best source is *RN: The Memoirs of Richard Nixon* (New York, 1978), which contains many of President Nixon's diary and calendar notes and reflections on Mrs. Nixon, her public role and private life, how she reacted to Vietnam and Watergate, and her foreign trips.

The other biography of Mrs. Nixon is Lester David, *The Lonely Lady of San Clemente: The Story of Pat Nixon* (New York, 1978). It does not present an in-depth analysis of her, nor provide much substance about her work as First Lady beyond the superficial facts. It does contain some contemporary newspaper accounts of her activities as "Second" and First Lady, as well as portions of print interviews. An example of her daily schedule as First Lady is reprinted in the appendix. There is interesting information on Pat Nixon in Irwin F. Gellman, *The Contender: Richard Nixon, The Congress Years, 1946–1952* (New York, 1999).

President Nixon's official memos to his wife are reprinted in Bruce Oudes, ed.,

From the President: Richard Nixon's Secret Files (New York, 1989). There is information about her relations with the White House staff in H. R. Haldeman, ed., *The Haldeman Diaries: Inside the Nixon White House* (New York, 1994). Helen Thomas left a detailed account of Pat Nixon's activities in China in her book *The President's Trip to China* (New York, 1972). Books that provide useful information about Mrs. Nixon include Allen Drury, *Courage and Hesitation: Notes and Photographs of the Nixon Administration* (Garden City, N.Y., 1971); William Safire, *Before the Fall: An Inside View of the Pre-Watergate White House* (Garden City, N.Y., 1975); John D. Ehrlichman, *Witness to Power* (New York, 1982); J. B. West, *Upstairs at the White House* (New York, 1973); and Henry Kissinger, *Years of Upheaval* (Boston, 1980). Unless otherwise noted, all quotations are from Carl Sfer-razza Anthony, *First Ladies: The Saga of the Presidents' Wives and Their Power*, vol. 2, *1961–1990* (New York, 1991).

Ladies' Home Journal (February 1972) carried a cover story interview of Patricia Nixon by Lenore Hershey, which presented Mrs. Nixon's feminist views. *People* magazine (May 27, 1974) ran a cover story that provided previously unpublished information on her reaction to Watergate and the Nixon marriage.

Mrs. Nixon's pre–White House papers were donated to the Richard Nixon Library in 1993 and will soon be available for limited research. Her post–White House papers will also be housed there. The White House Papers, at the Nixon Research Project in the Washington, D.C., area, are under the supervision of the National Archives. The best obituary of Mrs. Nixon appeared in the *New York Times* on June 24, 1993.

★★★ ★★★

Elizabeth Ann (Betty) Bloomer Ford

(1918–)

First Lady: 1974–1977

John Pope

Elizabeth Ann Bloomer was born April 8, 1918, in Chicago. She was the daughter of William Stephenson Bloomer, a conveyor-belt salesman, and Hortense Neahr Bloomer. She longed to be called Elizabeth but was always called Betty. She had two older brothers, Bob and Bill, Jr. After living in Chicago and Denver, the family moved to Grand Rapids, Michigan, when Betty was two. They settled at 717 Fountain Street.

Because her father's job kept him on the road, Betty's mother ran the household; she was a strong, loving influence on her only daughter. In *The Times of My Life*, Mrs. Ford's first memoir, she described an episode at the family's summer cottage when her mother had tried to imbue her with courage as they watched a thunderstorm roll across Whitefish Lake:

I can still feel my mother's arms around me, holding me, as she stood out on the porch and we watched a storm come rolling in across the lake, waves swelling, thunder crashing, lightning slicing the sky, and my mother telling me how beautiful it was. I found out later she was scared to death, but she taught me not to be afraid; I was safe in those arms.

Betty had a happy childhood, playing the tomboy with her long-suffering siblings. When she was eight, she started dance lessons, embarking on a course that would eventually lead her to Carnegie Hall. Besides taking lessons, she taught dance in a hall she rented from a family friend, entertained hospitalized children, and read voraciously about all sorts of dance. She especially liked modern dance for the way its practitioners could express themselves, and she dreamed of a career in this liberating art. Dance, she said in her first memoir, "was my happiness."

When Betty was eleven, the stock market crashed. To make extra money, she worked Saturdays modeling dresses for tearoom customers in Herpolsheimer's Department Store. She earned $3 each lunch before rushing off to teach the fox trot, waltz, and Big Apple to youngsters who paid fifty cents apiece.

As a teenager during the Depression, Betty came under the influence of another strong woman, Eleanor Roosevelt. In her role as Franklin D. Roosevelt's social conscience, the First Lady barnstormed the country to see how people lived. She danced the Virginia reel, descended into coal mines, commiserated with families in their shacks, and reported on what she saw and learned to the president and to millions of newspaper readers in her column, "My Day." In an interview with Carl Sferrazza Anthony, Mrs. Ford later said: "[Mrs. Roosevelt] eventually became a role model for me because I liked her independence. . . . I really liked the idea that a woman was finally speaking out and expressing herself rather than just expressing the views of her husband. That seemed healthy."

But Betty's life wasn't all dance and idealism. When she was sixteen, her father died of carbon-monoxide poisoning while working on the family car. It was an accident; the car was in a garage and the day was hot and humid.

After she finished Central High School in 1936, Betty longed to go to New York and study dance. Her mother said no—not until she turned twenty. Betty persisted. They compromised: she was allowed to spend the next two summers studying at the Bennington School of Dance at Bennington College in Vermont, where she worked not only with legendary dancer-choreographer Martha Graham, but also with such dancers

as Louis Horst, Doris Humphrey, Jose Limon, Charles Weidman, and Hanya Holm.

Graham was the dominant influence for the girl from Grand Rapids. This small, striking woman, a pioneer in modern dance, was tough and demanding— the kind of woman who would poke a pupil's back with a knee to straighten it—and her exercise regimen made Betty's muscles knot. Nevertheless, her pupil said years later, "I worshiped her as a goddess. . . . More than anyone else, she shaped my life."

Between summers, Betty felt she was marking time in Grand Rapids, where she modeled, joined the Junior League, and taught dance. After the second summer, she knew she wanted to work with Graham, but she didn't ask Graham's permission until after her troupe performed at Ann Arbor. To Betty's great delight, Graham said yes.

Betty and Natalie Harris, her Bennington roommate, took an apartment in Manhattan's Chelsea section, within walking distance of Graham's studio near Washington Square. Since Graham could pay only $10 a performance, her dancers had to find other work. Betty registered as a Powers model; she spent days modeling hats, dresses, and furs, and took dance classes at night.

Harris was tapped for Graham's main group; Betty was picked for the auxiliary troupe. Though that kept her from traveling with Graham because Graham couldn't afford the expense, being an auxiliary dancer was good enough to get Betty onstage with the other Graham dancers before an audience that filled Carnegie Hall. But Betty Bloomer had another force to reckon with: her mother. After a two-week visit to New York, Hortense Bloomer could see that her daughter was serious about a career as a dancer and, therefore, impervious to her pleas to come home. Mother and daughter struck another compromise: Betty agreed to go back to Grand Rapids for six months, with permission to return to New York if nothing worked out.

Back home, Betty became known as the Martha Graham of Grand Rapids. She started a troupe that introduced religious dance to the city, and taught dance in school and at night, including—to her family's dismay—one night a week in a school in an all-black district. She was even briefly engaged. She returned to Herpolsheimer's as assistant to the fashion coordinator. The six-month test period came and went; Betty, a woman with her own apartment and her own circle of friends, was having a good time. Among the men she dated was Bill Warren, who had taken her to her first dance when she was twelve. She liked him, she said in her first memoir, because he was a good dancer, a good athlete, and not at all stuffy. Although the United States had by then entered World War II, Warren's diabetes kept him out of the service.

Betty gave up her apartment to move in with her mother and her mother's new husband, Arthur Meigs Godwin. Neither approved of Warren, so she sneaked out to see him. But the Godwins' mood seemed to change when Betty and Bill announced their engagement. In fact, the wedding was performed in the Godwins' living room, and the reception was in the garden. It was the spring of 1942; Betty Bloomer Warren was twenty-four.

The marriage didn't last. In *The Times of My Life*, Betty referred to that phase of her life as "the five-year misunderstanding." The Warrens moved from one city to another in the Midwest and East as Bill Warren tried one job and then another, moving himself and his wife in with his parents in Grand Rapids between jobs until he decided what to try next. He sold insurance in Maumee, Ohio; worked for the Continental Can Company in Syracuse, New York; and sold furniture up and down the East Coast for the Widdicomb Furniture Company of Grand Rapids. Along the way, Betty worked in a Toledo, Ohio, department store and taught dance at a university there. While the Warrens lived outside Syracuse, she worked on the production line in a frozen-food factory, sorting and boxing produce. When the Warrens returned to Grand Rapids, Betty Warren went back to Herpolsheimer's, this time as its fashion coordinator, a job in which she trained models, staged fashion shows, and

traveled to New York City to check out new clothing lines.

Her life in those years was hardly dull. One evening in Maumee, around dinner time, she pulled out a 20-gauge shotgun and bagged one of the dozens of rabbits that hopped around their home. But she wasn't happy. When he wasn't off selling furniture, Bill was hanging out in bars with his fellow salesmen. She sometimes went along on these drinking excursions. "The things that had made our dating so amusing made the marriage difficult," she wrote in her first autobiography. "No matter how many somersaults I turned, it wasn't enough to keep him home."

Just as Betty became angry enough to write him telling him not to bother coming home from his latest selling trip, Warren's boss called to say that Bill was sick in Boston in a diabetic coma and wasn't expected to live. Betty Warren flew to Boston and learned how to give him insulin injections. "All of the time the question kept snaking through my mind, What am I doing here when I no longer love this man?" she wrote. "But I told myself I had no choice."

After six weeks, Warren was allowed to go home. He and his father went by train; Betty drove her father-in-law's car back to Grand Rapids. Bill Warren slept on a hospital bed in his parents' house. His wife slept upstairs and vowed to plunge so deeply into her job at Herpolsheimer's that she wouldn't have time to think about her miserable life. She was twenty-seven. Then, Warren had to move into a hospital. Betty went to see him every night after work before heading home to their apartment; it was, she recalled "a terrible experience." After two years, Warren recovered, and Betty began divorce proceedings.

"Bill didn't put up much of a struggle," she later wrote:

I took a dollar in settlement (you had to have some sort of settlement to make it legal) and it was finished. I was twenty-nine years old, and I didn't want to hear from anybody about my marriage having been a failure. I didn't fail, but it's a long time ago and nothing's gained by going into the details. Lots of Bill's friends resented the fact that I'd divorced him. That was only natural, but frankly, by then I didn't give a hoot.

Betty's marriage ended in 1947. Although she professed to have no interest in getting married again, friends persuaded her to meet Gerald R. Ford, a World War II veteran, fledgling lawyer, and handsome bachelor. When he called for a date, Betty tried to put him off, saying that her divorce wasn't final and that she had to work late on the next day's fashion show. But she relented and agreed to meet him for a few minutes at a bar. "The next time I looked at my watch, an hour had passed," she later wrote. "That's how it began."

Once Betty's divorce became final, she and Ford dated regularly, and he taught her how to ski. They were falling in love. When he left for his annual Christmas ski holiday at Sun Valley, Idaho, she gave him a stocking full of gifts, including a pair of argyle socks she had knitted herself—albeit several sizes too large—and a pipe lighter with this inscription: "To the light of my life."

Ford proposed in February 1948. Actually, Betty wrote, "He just told me he'd like to marry me. I took him up on it instantly, before he could change his mind."

But, Ford said, the wedding would have to wait until fall because he was going to run for Michigan's Fifth District seat in the U.S. House of Representatives. The Republican primary, in which he defeated U.S. Representative Bartel "Barney" Jonkman, was in September, and the general election would be held November 2. The marriage was scheduled for October, in the home stretch of his campaign, in Grand Rapids. She was thirty; he was thirty-five.

It was a frantic time. Betty worked while Ford campaigned. At night they tried to attend parties given for them. When there were no parties, Betty spent nights licking envelopes at his headquarters while he made speeches.

The tempo didn't let up even for their wedding. Shortly after they arrived at the Peninsula Club for their rehearsal dinner,

Ford had to dash off to make a speech, returning in time for dessert. The next day—October 15, 1948—Ford campaigned until early afternoon, arriving barely in time for the 4 p.m. ceremony at Grace Episcopal Church. Although he had changed into his gray pinstripe suit, the groom was still wearing his brown shoes—dusty from a farm appearance—instead of his shiny black pair. The bride wore a sapphire blue satin dress and, she said, "her heart in her eyes."

The Fords' wedding kicked off a frenetic weekend. The ceremony was held on a Friday so the newlyweds could get to Ann Arbor to see the University of Michigan, Ford's alma mater, play Northwestern the next day. They dined at the Town Club and stayed up late, even though they had to get up early the next day for a pregame brunch in their honor. Michigan won the game. Then they drove eighty-eight miles to Owosso, Michigan, because candidate Ford had been invited to sit on the platform at a rally held in a freezing football stadium with Thomas Dewey, the Republican presidential candidate. Dewey, who had been born in Owosso, was governor of New York.

They had planned to spend the night in Detroit, but didn't arrive until 3 A.M. On Sunday, they toured the city and returned to Ann Arbor the next day for lunch with faculty friends before heading home to Grand Rapids. But, when they reached home, Ford had to dash to a political meeting. Betty Ford opened a can of tomato soup and made two cheese sandwiches.

The nonstop campaigning paid off. Ford won—one of the few Republicans to prevail that November—and the couple moved to a Washington apartment at 2500 Q Street Northwest. After his 1954 reelection convinced Ford that the district was his for as long as he chose to run, the family built a house at 514 Crown Drive in Alexandria, Virginia, where they stayed until they moved into the White House nearly two decades later. The couple had four children: Michael (b. 1950); John, better known as Jack (b. 1952); Steven (b. 1956); and Susan (b. 1957).

With a growing family, a husband constantly at work on Capitol Hill or on the campaign trail, and the mountain of charitable and social duties expected of a congressional spouse, Mrs. Ford had to assume a variety of roles. She was a Cub Scout den mother, a rooter at Little League games, program director of the Congressional Wives Prayer Group, a Sunday school teacher, and a volunteer worker for crippled children.

Like other Washington wives, Betty Ford became "a virtual political widow," biographers Edward and Frederick Schapsmeier wrote, because Congressman Ford was away so much—280 days one year. "Although initially resenting it, Mrs. Ford never complained. Soon she accepted such a way of life as the norm." The loneliness—and demands on her time—increased after Ford unseated Charles Halleck in January 1965 to become House minority leader. At one point, the Schapsmeiers wrote, Ford awoke early one morning—after coming in late the night before—to find this note on his pillow: "Glad to see you home again. Hello, from Susan."

In the summer of 1964, two days before leaving on a family vacation, Mrs. Ford awoke with a pain in her neck. It turned out to be a pinched nerve—the result, perhaps, of straining across a four-foot-wide counter to open a kitchen window. The pain was intense, forcing her to spend weeks in bed. Since surgery was not feasible for that condition, or for the spinal arthritis she developed, painkillers were prescribed to provide her with some relief. She eventually developed a dependence on them, a condition that continued through her time in the White House.

These were tough years. Besides physical pain, Mrs. Ford had to endure her husband's long absences, which made her virtually a single parent. She watched other congressional marriages crumble, and she succumbed to a drinking problem that she did not acknowledge for more than a decade. Finally, in 1965, after years of keeping her misery inside, she snapped and started crying uncontrollably. "I felt as though I were doing everything for everyone else, and I was not getting any attention at all," she wrote. "I was so hurt that I'd think, I'm going to get in the car, and I'm going to drive to the beach, and nobody's going to know where I am. I wanted them to worry about me. I wanted them to recognize me."

Betty Ford started seeing a psychiatrist twice a week. The doctor acted as a sounding board—someone to whom she could tell things that she could tell to no one else. "I've often said I'd lost my feeling of self-worth," she wrote, "and that's what sent me for help. I think a lot of women go through this. Their husbands have fascinating jobs, their children start to turn into independent people, and the women begin to feel useless, empty. . . . Jerry and I talked it over, and we came to the conclusion that my mental state had a lot to do with my physical illness. . . . I don't believe in spilling your guts all over the place, but I no longer believe in suffering in silence over something that's really bothering you. I think you have to get it out and on the table and discuss it, no matter what it is."

Mrs. Ford's sessions did not address her underlying addiction problems, mainly because she did not discuss them; at that time, she was in deep denial about them. Mrs. Ford later wrote that she had refused to admit her alcoholism for years because she feared it might embarrass her husband. Nevertheless, the help she received was important, and she said so, as First Lady, before a psychiatrists' convention. She earned a standing ovation because her candor helped eliminate some of the stigma surrounding psychiatric care. In her typically offhand style, she refused to see what the big deal was: "There was nothing terribly wrong with me. I just wasn't the Bionic Woman, and the minute I stopped thinking I had to be, a weight fell from my shoulders."

In 1968, Richard M. Nixon was elected president, and Gerald Ford, still House minority leader, thought he might become speaker of the House. But the Democrats kept control of Congress. In 1972, after Nixon started to restore ties with China, the

Fords went to China with House Majority Leader Hale Boggs and his wife, Lindy. They had an extraordinary trip. She was impressed by sea-slug dinners and an operation for an ovarian tumor performed with acupuncture anesthesia. They returned in time to jump into the campaign for Nixon's re-election.

There had been a break-in at the Democratic headquarters in the Watergate complex in June 1972, but that seemed to have no impact on the electorate: Nixon carried forty-nine states. However, the Democrats held on to their majorities in both houses of Congress, and Ford, acknowledging that he probably never would become speaker, promised his wife he would retire when Nixon left the White House in January 1977.

But destiny intervened. On October 10, 1973, less than a year after Nixon was sworn in for a second term, Vice President Spiro T. Agnew resigned after pleading no contest to charges of accepting kickbacks from contractors while he was governor of Maryland. Two nights later, in an incongruously upbeat White House ceremony complete with mariachi music, Nixon announced that he had picked Ford to be his new vice president—the first vice president selected under the terms of the Twenty-fifth Amendment. As the Nixons and Fords stood together in the East Room, acknowledging applause and posing for pictures, Nixon leaned over to offer congratulations to Mrs. Ford. "Congratulations or condolences?" she said in a stage whisper.

Ford, a genuinely popular man on Capitol Hill, won Senate confirmation easily. With Mrs. Ford standing by his side, he was sworn in by Chief Justice Warren E. Burger on December 6, 1973, before a joint session of Congress. "I wore a bright orange wool crepe dress and a broad smile," Mrs. Ford wrote. "If I had known what was coming, I think I probably would have sat right down and cried."

Suddenly, reporters wanted to interview the new vice president and his family. Mrs. Ford established her reputation for candor when Barbara Walters asked for her opinion on the 1973 U.S. Supreme Court decision legalizing abortion. "I said I agreed with the Supreme Court's ruling," Mrs. Ford wrote, "that it was time to bring abortion out of the backwoods and put it in the hospitals where it belonged."

Meanwhile, investigations into the deepening Watergate scandal continued. As calls for Nixon's impeachment grew louder, Ford started to look more and more like the next president. But Nixon seemed determined to stay on, even after the House Judiciary Committee voted in the summer of 1974 to impeach him on three counts. Then, on August 5, 1974, Nixon released the tape containing what came to be known as the "smoking gun": a June 23, 1972, conversation in which Nixon told H. R. Haldeman, his chief of staff, to get the CIA to halt an FBI investigation of the Watergate break-in, claiming the inquiry would jeopardize national security. That was the last straw. Nixon steadily lost even his staunchest defenders in both houses of Congress. His allies told him that if he did not quit, he probably would become the first president to be impeached by the House and convicted by the Senate.

On August 8, 1974, Nixon announced his resignation in a nationally televised speech. He left the White House the next day, after an emotional East Room farewell, and Gerald R. Ford was sworn in moments later as president—the first person to hold the two highest offices in the land without winning either in a national election. After taking the oath of office as the thirty-eighth president of the United States, he declared that he was indebted "to no man and to only one woman—my dear wife, Betty." With that statement, the new president let the nation know how vital a partner Betty Ford had become in their marriage, in his quarter-century in the House of Representatives, and, most recently, in the vice presidency.

As Mrs. Ford stood next to him, the new president proclaimed to anxious Americans, "Our long national nightmare is over." But the nightmare wasn't over. On September 8, 1974, Ford pardoned his predecessor, and the nation was furious. Almost overnight, Ford's Gallup approval rating plummeted from 71 percent to 49 percent, and he was booed while making a speech because spectators suspected he had cut a deal with Nixon. Jerald terHorst, his press secretary, quit in protest. Ford acted alone in making this decision, his wife wrote, but she supported him, saying the country had to move beyond Watergate—and the possibility of a months-long trial that could paralyze the nation. Though both Fords have consistently said they felt the pardon was the right thing to do, they also have agreed that it probably cost Ford the 1976 election.

Later that month, the Fords had a crisis much closer to home. Acting on a friend's suggestion, Mrs. Ford went for a routine annual checkup on September 26. The doctor found a suspicious lump in her right breast. A specialist recommended a biopsy—a surgical procedure—as quickly as possible; if the tumor proved malignant, the breast would have to be removed immediately, while Mrs. Ford remained under anesthesia.

The Fords agreed but told no one. In fact, Mrs. Ford went through her full schedule on September 27, including a Salvation Army luncheon, the dedication of the LBJ Memorial Grove of 500 white pines along the Potomac, and a tour of the White House's private rooms for Lady Bird Johnson and her daughters. Those duties done, Mrs. Ford headed for Bethesda Naval Hospital for surgery the next day.

The lump turned out to be cancerous, and surgeons performed a radical mastectomy, removing her right breast and some of the supporting muscle, as well as lymph nodes in her armpit. Since doctors found cancer in three nodes, she would have to undergo chemotherapy—via pills—to keep the disease from spreading. Her husband said receiving that news was "the lowest and loneliest moment" of his presidency; he sat at his desk and cried.

But Mrs. Ford insisted on seeing the positive side of her ordeal because, she said, it gave her an idea of the influence she could have. "Lying in the hospital, thinking of all those women going for cancer checkups

because of me, I'd come to realize more clearly the power of the woman in the White House," she wrote in her first memoir. "Not my power, but the power of the position, a power which could be used to help." After all, she said in a 1994 interview, "if a First Lady was afflicted with breast cancer and had to have a mastectomy, it made it possible that others could be, too." That awareness that her plight brought—and the attention it drew to a subject that had been only whispered about—"saved a lot of lives," she said.

One life was that of Happy Rockefeller, the wife of Nelson Rockefeller, whom Ford would pick to be his vice president. Because of the attention given Mrs. Ford's condition, Rockefeller said, Happy went in for a checkup—just in time. She wound up losing both breasts to cancer.

With the White House's cooperation, Mrs. Ford's mastectomy received wide, candid coverage. In the 1994 interview, she said this probably had more impact than anything else she did as First Lady. "No one had talked about mastectomy publicly before," she wrote in her autobiography. "Since then, it's never gone underground again, which is great. I've never regretted it." By the time Mrs. Ford returned to the White House two weeks after checking into the hospital, her office had received more than 50,000 cards, letters, and telegrams—10 percent from women who had had mastectomies—and thousands of dollars, which Mrs. Ford gave to the American Cancer Society.

By emphasizing her importance on his inauguration day, Ford had provided a preview of the important role Betty Ford would assume in so many aspects of American life. For although the Fords occupied the White House for less than two and a half years, Mrs. Ford became the most outspoken First Lady since Eleanor Roosevelt—a staunch advocate of abortion rights, the Equal Rights Amendment, and the appointment and election of more women to important governmental offices. By candidly discussing her own psychotherapy, she helped remove some of the stigma associated with mental illness. And by going public with details of her breast cancer and mastectomy, she focused national attention on what had been a seldom-discussed disease, making millions of people aware of its destructive potential and probably saving thousands of lives.

In recognition of her work, *Time* magazine named Mrs. Ford one of its Women of the Year for 1975—an accolade no other First Lady had received. The honor was especially significant because her husband was the only president since Herbert Hoover not to be named Man of the Year. Moreover, her approval ratings often were higher than her husband's.

Mrs. Ford's role as an activist, she said in a 1994 interview, was a natural outgrowth of the widespread influence of Eleanor Roosevelt and her own relationships with such strong women as her mother and the legendary dancer-choreographer Martha Graham. From their example, and from experience as a politician's wife, she said, "I got the confidence to be a spokesperson."

It seemed absolutely natural to her to apply this self-assurance to issues as personal as her battles with breast cancer and substance abuse or as public as the campaigns for abortion rights and the Equal Rights Amendment: "I've always felt that if I've got a problem, the best way to handle it is to address it and do what I need to do about it and be honest and get on with my life."

As soon as she could, Mrs. Ford resumed her activities, which included preparing for state dinners, decking out the White House for Christmas, and getting Ford to sign an executive order establishing a National Commission on the Observance of International Women's Year. While that had no legal force, Mrs. Ford said, it was important because it put the administration on record in support of women and their struggle for equality. When the president asked his wife if she wanted to make a statement before he put pen to paper, Mrs. Ford replied, "I just want to congratulate you, Mr. President. I am glad to see you have come a long, long way. She lobbied for the Equal Rights Amendment in speeches and by telephon-

ing legislators in Illinois and other states in behalf of ratification. She occasionally wore an outsize, pro-ERA button lest anyone miss the point, and, she said, she was proud to be picketed for her own political views.

In June 1975, Betty Ford went to New York to honor her mentor, Martha Graham, at a benefit gala for Graham's troupe. Her escort was Woody Allen, who wore black sneakers with his tuxedo. Rudolf Nureyev, wearing a gold jockstrap designed by Halston, and Dame Margot Fonteyn danced Graham's "Lucifer," and Mrs. Ford gave her former teacher a bouquet. She later successfully lobbied for Graham to receive the Presidential Medal of Freedom, the nation's highest civilian honor.

While her evening in New York attracted attention, nothing else Mrs. Ford did that summer was so newsworthy as her appearance on *60 Minutes* in August. In an interview with Morley Safer, Mrs. Ford reiterated her support of the Equal Rights Amendment and legalized abortion, said that marijuana smoking had become as routine as beer drinking, suggested that premarital sex might lower the divorce rate, and said that she wouldn't be surprised if her daughter, then eighteen, were to announce that she was having an affair. "I think she's a perfectly normal human being, like all young girls," she said. "If she wanted to continue it, I would certainly counsel and advise her on the subject. And I'd want to know pretty much about the young man."

The reaction, which is on file at the Gerald Ford Library, was astonishing. By October, the mail totaled more than 33,000 pieces, with letters opposing her opinion outnumbering those supporting it by two to one. The Woman's Christian Temperance Union censured her, the reactionary *Manchester* (New Hampshire) *Union-Leader* called her "A Disgrace to the White House" in a front-page editorial, and a Texas minister excoriated her "gutter-type mentality." One letter writer, saying Mrs. Ford was no lady, suggested she resign.

Once the tone of these comments became public, Mrs. Ford's supporters rallied, praising her candor. One letter writer called her "a crusader in the finest tradition of Eleanor Roosevelt," and an eighty-three-year-old woman who dubbed herself "The Last of the Puritans" wrote: "I am deeply grateful that we have someone in the White House who thinks integrity is more important than political advantage. Many thanks for your refreshing example." Mrs. Ford's approval rating in a survey conducted by pollster Louis Harris soared from 50 percent to 75 percent. She provided the perfect capper for the episode. She sent Safer a photograph of herself with this inscription: "Dear Morley, If there are any questions you forgot to ask—I'm grateful. Betty Ford."

By this time, "The role of women in American society was shifting, and she perfectly mirrored it," Carl Sferrazza Anthony wrote. "Mrs. Ford believed that she had to become visible and active. 'I suppose a First Lady could possibly be like Bess Truman, but it's unlikely.'" John Robert Greene, a student of the Ford presidency, offered another explanation: "It is quite possible that the nation, in a transition period in its thinking regarding women's rights, accepted Mrs. Ford's candor because it had already been so impressed with her courage."

But Betty Ford's service in the White House was not all political, however. She realized the symbolic importance of her role, and she became philosophical about it. She told Anthony that the First Lady is "the heart of the nation," while the president is "the mind," and she suggested that presidents' wives receive a salary as official hostesses—and a better staff than the vice president's. She was a busy hostess, presiding over 34 state dinners and 600 other events in slightly less than two and a half years.

She also was aware of her ability to turn the White House into a showcase for all things American. She used Steuben glass and Native American reed baskets as centerpieces. Old wooden spools from a New England textile mill became candle holders. At state dinners, where she mixed china patterns from previous administrations, she banished E-shaped arrangements in favor of circular dining tables, following a style Jacqueline Kennedy had initiated. Although

it adhered to what she called the less formal style of Michigan, there was a political purpose to this, too, she said in a 1994 interview: this format let her get more women—especially those deserving high office—at the president's table.

Mrs. Ford lobbied tirelessly to get more women appointed to high office, frequently using a strategy she called "pillow talk": taking advantage of the time at the end of the day when no one else was around. Among Ford's female appointees were Anne Armstrong, the first woman ambassador to Great Britain, and Carla Hills, secretary of housing and urban development. Mrs. Ford tried to get her husband to appoint a woman to succeed William O. Douglas on the Supreme Court, but he chose John Paul Stevens.

In October 1975, the First Lady addressed the International Women's Year Congress in Cleveland. In the speech, which is part of the collection at the Gerald Ford Library, she had to walk a fine line, according to Sheila Rabb Weidenfeld, her press secretary. While pressing for the Equal Rights Amendment, Mrs. Ford had to stress that ERA's passage would have no effect on the family. And, while urging women to excel in business, she had to be careful also to extol women who chose to be homemakers. Betty Ford succeeded. "Being ladylike does not require silence," she said. "I spoke out on this issue because of my deep personal conviction. Why should my husband's job or yours prevent us from being ourselves?" Speaking to homemakers, Mrs. Ford said, "We just take the 'just' out of 'just a housewife' and show our pride in having made the home and family our life's work. Downgrading this work has been part of the pattern in our society that downgrades individual women's talents in all areas."

This tension between old and new expectations for women was something the First Lady encountered every day, and, she wrote in her memoir, it was rough:

One day, I'd be greeting women stockbrokers in the Map Room, congratulating them for having got out of their kitchens and into the stock market. The next day, in the same room, I'd be greeting a Home-makers' Seminar, and congratulating house-wives for having stayed in their kitchens.

Although she had held many paying jobs, Mrs. Ford had followed a more or less tra-ditional path for women since her marriage, devoting her energies to her husband and children, and she refused to apologize. In one speech, she said, "Anyone who feels good about what she's doing in the home should have the same sense of liberation."

Trying to reach out to traditionalists and progressives was no small challenge, but people apparently felt the First Lady did a good job. Just a few months after her *60 Minutes* appearance, the Harris survey quoted in the November 11 issue of the *Detroit Free Press* showed that Mrs. Ford was "one of the most popular wives of a president to occupy the White House. . . . Betty Ford has a wide and deep following in the mainstream of American life, and surely must be judged a solid asset to her husband in the White House."

In December 1975, the Fords returned to China, taking their daughter with them. Although serious talks were conducted, and although all three Fords had an audience with Mao Zedong, the memorable pictures from that trip were of Mrs. Ford in a ballet school, dancing with the students and hav-ing a wonderful time. She seemed happiest when she was dancing—whether she was cutting up with members of the Alvin Ailey troupe, doing the bump with Tony Orlando at the 1976 Republican National Conven-tion, or, at the 1976 Gridiron Dinner, per-forming a soft-shoe to the tune of "Once in Love with Amy" and earning a standing ovation from the Washington political and media establishment.

Those last two performances came in a hectic year, when she was making the rounds of primary states as her husband was seek-ing a four-year presidential term in his own right. Sporting a "Vote for Betty's Husband" button, she rode in parades, visited festivals, spoke at luncheons and dinners, and even adopted a "handle"—"First Mama"—as

part of the CB radio craze. In a burst of good humor, she took to the airwaves her-self, telling truckers: "Please keep on talkin' for President Ford. We appreciate your help in keeping the Fords 10-20 at 1600 Pennsylvania Ave. Happy trip."

On September 25, 1976, President and Mrs. Ford boarded the steamboat *Natchez* for a ride along the Mississippi River from Lutcher, Louisiana, to New Orleans, accom-panied by local and national politicians, squadrons of reporters, and a bevy of women in hoop skirts. At stops along the way, they worked the crowds on the riverbank, and President Ford stood on flimsy deck chairs to wave. Mrs. Ford grabbed him from behind to keep him from falling, muttering in mock earnestness, "I'll never leave you. Never." It was a day for puckish fun, reported in several stories in the September 27 issue of the (New Orleans) *States-Item*. Besides making a CB broadcast over the ship-to-shore radio, the First Lady also discussed her pendant, which resembled a set of ice tongs. "It's a nutcracker," she said, smiling naughtily at an interviewer. "I'm saving it in case I find some nuts that I think need cracking."

It was hardly all fun. Campaigning was hard work, and the stress aggravated her pinched nerve and arthritis. Consequently, she increased her intake of painkillers. When she combined the medication with alcohol, she slurred her words. In such sit-uations, observant reporters were curious, but even Sheila Weidenfeld said she wasn't sure what was going on. In such situations, the press secretary formed a one-person fence to shield her boss from reporters. Once, Weidenfeld said, when she con-fronted Mrs. Ford about her pain, the First Lady replied: "I've lived with it for twelve years. I've learned to hide it. I can't let it show." In public, she projected her usual upbeat nature, telling Frances Spatz Leighton in an interview: "Either way the election turns out, I win. If my husband loses, I win more of his time. If he wins . . . then I have the chances to continue own work." "She was a public person with her own agenda," Myra G. Gutin and Leese E.

Tobin wrote. "The country perceived her this way as well."

The election was a close one. Jimmy Carter beat Ford by fifty-seven electoral votes, 297 to 240. His victory margin was nearly 1.7 million votes—about 2 percent of the total number of ballots cast. The morning after his defeat, Ford's voice had given out, so Mrs. Ford read his concession speech for him in the White House press room. Although she had long urged her husband to leave public office, she told *U.S. News & World Report* that the method of leaving—being voted out—came as a shock: "The trauma—the manner in which we had to leave Washington—intensified my internal stress, which in turn, caused an increase in my medication."

Betty Ford's condition did not improve in retirement, because Ford was still busy traveling on the political, lecture, and golf tournament circuits. Once again his wife was alone, this time in their new home in Rancho Mirage, California, where the Fords had moved because the hot, dry, desert climate would be best for her arthritis. Her dependence on alcohol and painkillers continued. Finally, in April 1978, her family confronted her and told her she had to get help. Two days after her sixtieth birthday, Betty Ford checked into Long Beach Naval Hospital for treatment. The program was tough, but she later acknowledged that it probably saved her life. "I don't think everybody has to stop drinking," wrote Mrs. Ford, who was the daughter and sister of alcoholics. "I just think *I* had to stop drinking. When I add up the amount of pills I was taking, and put a drink or two on top, I can see how I got to the breaking point."

When word got out that she had been admitted for treatment, encouraging mail started pouring in. So did newspaper stories and editorials that cheered her—once again—for her candor in confronting a difficult problem that most people ignored. "Whatever combination of emotional and psychological stress and physical pain . . . brought her to this pass, she is, characteristically, determined to overcome it," the *Washington Post* said in an April 25 editorial. "And she is unafraid and unembarrassed to say so."

Betty Ford emerged from treatment free from her dependence on alcohol and painkillers. However, her arthritis and pinched nerve have remained chronic, sometimes keeping her awake at night, so she has resorted to moist heat, exercise, traction, special pillows, and prayer. "I've always been a religious person," she said in her second autobiography, "so I find a lot of strength in that." Her stay at the hospital made her aware of the widespread problem of alcohol and drug abuse, and she started thinking about doing something about it. She and a group of her friends, including Bob Hope and the tire magnate Leonard Firestone, a recovering alcoholic, started raising money for the center that would bear her name—and become world-famous as a haven for people with alcohol and drug abuse problems.

The Betty Ford Center in Rancho Mirage was dedicated October 3, 1982. There was music and there were speeches, most notably Gerald Ford's. Saying he was speaking for their children and grandchildren, he told his wife, "We're proud of you, Mom. . . . We want you to know that we love you." Then, as he discussed his wife's recovery, his voice broke—the first time that had happened in public since he had told reporters she would be all right after her mastectomy.

Patients at the center have included such celebrities as Elizabeth Taylor, Liza Minnelli, Mickey Mantle, and Johnny Cash, as well as hundreds of ordinary people with substance abuse problems. There is no special treatment for anyone; everyone goes through the same rigid regimen, which starts with physical and psychological evaluations and continues with lectures and individual and group sessions. Though the Betty Ford Center has become known for the celebrities who have been treated there, the famous people have to wait their turn on its list with the Medicaid recipients.

Because the center bears her name and because she heads the board that runs it,

Mrs. Ford said in her second book that she feels she has been given a great honor and a great burden:

> Even if nobody else holds me responsible, I hold myself responsible.... It's hard to make anyone understand what it's like to have your name on something, to be given credit for things you haven't done. I've been at meetings where someone turned and thanked me, and I hugged the person and said, "Don't thank me, thank yourself, you're the one who did it. With God's help."

Since 1979, when she started talking about building it, the Betty Ford Center has become the focus of her life outside her home. "I'm able almost on a daily basis to see the positive results," she said in a 1994 interview. "I see patients arriving. A week, two weeks later, they're so improved and feel so positive about themselves. It's so rewarding. It's probably the most positive thing I could do."

Betty Ford's work at the center—helping people who had no voice, supporting a cause that few championed—is a logical continuation of what she did in the White House. In only two and a half years, Mrs. Ford became the most important feminist First Lady in the six decades between Eleanor Roosevelt and Hillary Rodham Clinton because she dared to speak her mind about such causes as abortion rights, the Equal Rights Amendment, and matters of health—specifically, psychiatric treatment and breast cancer.

Mrs. Ford delivered strong messages on tough topics, but that wasn't the only reason she seemed so outspoken. She followed Patricia Nixon, a quiet, shy woman who hated politics and seemed to spend her public time gazing adoringly at her husband. The country was in turmoil during the Nixon years, alive with calls for change of every kind, but Mrs. Nixon decided her principal chore as First Lady would be traditional and "safe": the encouragement of volunteer work.

After five years of a silent First Lady, many people had become conditioned not

to expect too much from that side of the White House. Then came Betty Ford. Unlike some political couples who spend their lives preparing for the presidency, the Fords never intended to occupy the White House. Consequently, Mrs. Ford managed to avoid the image makeovers that some politicians' wives undergo. She was never pressured to forsake her independence, integrity, and great good humor. In her first memoir, she wrote, "I figured, okay, I'll move to the White House, do the best I can, and if they don't like it, they can kick me out, but they can't make me be somebody I'm not."

Nobody ever tried to muzzle the outspoken—but never strident—Betty Ford as she spoke out on such issues as women's rights, abortion rights, and increased attention to women's health issues. Her staunchly conservative husband consistently supported her, even though he occasionally quipped that her candor might cost him votes. Betty Ford was determined to be an activist from the beginning—she made ratification of the Equal Rights Amendment one of her goals when she became First Lady—and the White House gave her a fine platform for speaking out and enlisting allies.

But some of her activity—perhaps her most significant achievement—was the result of a cruel turn of fate. After her mastectomy, Mrs. Ford's natural openness led her to encourage more frank talk about breast cancer. She became a heroine—and, indeed, a lifesaver—to millions of women, including many who probably could not abide some of her feminist politics.

The combination of personality and circumstance made Betty Ford a valuable First Lady who could not have been more in touch with her times. While this loyal wife and devoted mother of four never posed a threat to women who chose to stay home, she was smart enough to encourage the changes feminism was beginning to make. Mrs. Ford also was canny enough to exhort women to take advantage of these changes and make conditions even better.

By the mid-1970s, what had been known as women's liberation reached the grassroots level. More and more women were working outside the home, and more and more of them were demanding better jobs, better pay, a role in determining their health care, and bigger roles in politics. As women across the country were finding their own voices, they could look to the White House for a sterling example of a woman whose brave, outspoken voice had made a difference.

BIBLIOGRAPHICAL ESSAY

The two best sources about Betty Ford are her two books of memoirs, *The Times of My Life* (New York, 1978) and *Betty: A Glad Awakening* (Garden City, N.Y., 1987). In the books, written with Chris Chase, Mrs. Ford serves up not only the details of her life but also a great deal of insight and wit. Since she has continued to be publicly active after leaving the White House, both books are necessary to understand and appreciate her work.

Besides these books, I drew on my access to Mrs. Ford as a reporter on the 1976 campaign. See John Pope, "Bean Bandwagon Boosts Ford's Bid," "Betty's Model Campaigner," and "Ford Sails, Crowd Hails," all from the (New Orleans) *States-Item* (September 27, 1976). In 1994, working through her assistant, Ann Cullen, I set up a telephone interview in which Mrs. Ford discussed such topics as her mastectomy, her work with the Betty Ford Center, and the influences that helped make her an activist in the White House. I am grateful for Mrs. Ford's willingness to help me, and for being such a delightful interview subject.

The papers of Betty Ford are in the Gerald R. Ford Presidential Library in Ann Arbor, Michigan. In addition, material pertaining to her and her activities is in many other collections there. The holdings are exhaustive; the staff is overwhelmingly helpful. For more information, write to the Gerald R. Ford Library at 1000 Beal Avenue, Ann Arbor, MI 48109-2114.

Leesa E. Tobin, an archivist at the library, has been not only a wellspring of information about the library's holdings but also a source of insight in her article "Betty Ford as First Lady: A Woman for Women,"

Presidential Studies Quarterly 20 (Fall 1990): 761–767. Tobin Gutin and Myra G. Gutin discussed Mrs. Ford's impact on the Ford presidency during Hofstra University's April 1989 colloquium. Their essay " 'You've Come a Long Way, Mr. President': Betty Ford as First Lady," is in Bernard J. Firestone and Alexej Ugrinsky, eds., *Gerald R. Ford and the Politics of Post-Watergate America* (Westport, Conn., 1993), vol. 2, 623–632.

Helpful books about Betty Ford are Carl Sferrazza Anthony's *First Ladies: The Saga of the Presidents' Wives and Their Power*, vol. 2, *1961–1990* (New York, 1991), and Edward I. Schapsmeier and Frederick H. Schapsmeier's *Gerald R. Ford's Date with Destiny: A Political Biography* (New York, 1989).

Although White House staff members can be counted on to write books about their experiences, the output from the Ford team isn't very insightful about Mrs. Ford. Probably the best of the lot is *First Lady's Lady: With the Fords at the White House* (New York, 1979) by Sheila Rabb Weidenfeld, Mrs. Ford's press secretary. Other books from Ford administration staff members include *Palace Politics: An Inside Account of the Ford Years* (New York, 1980) by Robert T. Hartmann, chief of staff to Vice President Ford and counselor to President Ford; and John J. Casserly, *The Ford White House: The Diary of a Speechwriter* (Boulder, Colo., 1977). James Cannon, *Time and Change: Gerald Ford's Appointment with History* (New York, 1994), by President Ford's assistant for domestic affairs, is instructive because it shows how both Fords have consistently worked as a team. John Robert Greene's *The Presidency of Gerald R. Ford* (Lawrence, Kans., 1995) offers a good summary of Mrs. Ford's personality and her appeal, suggesting that people tolerated her outspokenness because they had been impressed by her courage in facing cancer.

Among magazine articles published while the Fords were in the White House that might help researchers are "A Fighting First Lady," *Time* (March 3, 1975); the January 5, 1976, issue of *Time*, in which Mrs. Ford was named one of the magazine's Women of the Year for 1975; and a *Newsweek* cover story on Mrs. Ford in the December 29, 1975, issue. John Pope, "Ford Blew Cover off Breast Cancer," [New Orleans] *Times-Picayune* (September 27, 1999), is a retrospective look at Mrs. Ford's revelation about her breast cancer in 1974.

★★★   ★★★

Eleanor Rosalynn Smith Carter

(1927–)

First Lady: 1977–1981

Kathy B. Smith

Eleanor Rosalynn Smith was born in Botsford, Georgia, on August 18, 1927, to Wilburn Edgar Smith and Francis Althea (Allie) Murray. She was named Rosalynn after her maternal grandmother, who was called Rosa. Rosalynn had two younger brothers, Jerry and Murray, and a younger sister, Lillian Althea.

Rosalynn's mother was the only child of a very religious family. She had a strict Baptist father and a devout Lutheran mother, Rosa Wise, and Sundays were observed with verse learning and Bible reading. Allie's father, a farmer and Botsford's postmaster, was known to all as "The Captain." As a high school student, Allie met her future husband, Edgar Smith, who drove her school bus. She studied home econom-

ics at Georgia State College for Women in Milledgeville and graduated with a teaching certificate.

Edgar Smith, nine years older than Allie, was described by Rosalynn in her memoirs as tall and handsome. He was a strict father who, in addition to driving the school bus, operated an auto repair shop, worked in a store on weekends, and cultivated his farm outside of Plains, Georgia. A respected member of the community, Smith was elected town councilman. The family experienced financial hardships after his death from leukemia in 1940, at the age of forty-four. Allie was left with four children, aged four to thirteen, to support.

Prior to her father's death, Rosalynn had a happy, small-town childhood in Plains. She enjoyed reading, playing with her dolls, basketball, studying, and playing with friends. Her best friend was Ruth Carter, the younger sister of Jimmy Carter. The churches of Plains were the center of social life, and with a Lutheran grandmother, a Baptist grandfather, and Methodist parents, Rosalynn went to functions at all three churches. The school she attended had fewer than 150 students in eleven grades, and was the other center of Rosalynn's childhood. She studied hard and graduated from Plains High School in 1944 as class valedictorian.

Both her parents were strong positive influences on Rosalynn. She took to heart her father's admonition to better herself and take care of her family. Her mother helped Rosalynn develop a strong internal moral code by not establishing strict rules of conduct. She expected her children to do the right thing. These high expectations and the altered family circumstances after her father's death placed a heavy burden on Rosalynn. Reflecting on this time, she wrote, "I had to be very strong—or appear to be strong. But I wasn't." She cared for her three younger siblings and helped her grieving mother.

Rosalynn's grandmother Rosa Murray died a year after her father. Her grandfather sold his farm and came to live with her family. "That's when I saw my mother develop into a strong, independent person, assuming full responsibility for the family, and asking no help or charity from anyone," Rosalynn recalled. "This made a deep impression on me." Rosalynn's mother supported her family by sewing, selling the milk and butter from their one cow, working in the school cafeteria and in a grocery store, and finally, by working a full-time in the Plains post office until she was forced to retire at age seventy. Rosalynn did not have to contribute to the family's income because the house on South Bond Street was mortgage-free when her father died, there was rental income from their farm, and Allie had inherited some money from her mother. When, as a teenager, Rosalynn worked as a shampooer in a beauty parlor, it was to earn her own spending money.

Rosalynn's social life took a decisive turn in the summer of 1945 when twenty-year-old James Earl "Jimmy" Carter, a midshipman at the U.S. Naval Academy and older brother of her best friend, Ruth, came home on leave. Three years older than Rosalynn, he had seen her only as a friend of his sister's until that summer. Ruth conspired to have Rosalynn come to clean up the Pond House, built by Carter's father, which was a setting for community parties. Jimmy Carter and Rosalynn cleaned the house and talked that day, and the next day they went to a movie. After the movie, Carter's mother asked him if he liked Rosalynn. He responded, "She's the girl I want to marry."

While Jimmy Carter was at Annapolis from July until December, they wrote frequently. He proposed to Rosalynn in December, but she turned him down because she felt it was too soon. Moreover, she planned to finish her education at Georgia Southwestern, a junior college in Americus. Her ultimate plan was to graduate from her mother's alma mater, Georgia State College for Women.

By the time Rosalynn visited Annapolis for the first time—on the weekend of George Washington's birthday—they were carrying on an almost daily correspondence; and when he again proposed marriage, she accepted. Her mother was pleased, but Carter's family had some reservations. Earl Carter had great ambitions for his son into which a seventeen-year-old friend of his daughter did not fit. Even Ruth was a little protective of her special relationship with her brother. Jimmy's mother, Lillian, in Rosalynn's words, "was my only champion. Miss Lillian was always for the underdog."

On July 7, 1946, Rosalynn married Jimmy Carter in the Plains Methodist church. Although they had not sent out invitations, the church was packed with family and friends. After a honeymoon in the mountains at Chimney Rock, North Carolina, they moved to Carter's first naval post at Norfolk, Virginia, in August 1946.

Rosalynn Carter was forced to become very self-sufficient and independent as a navy wife. Her husband was assigned to the

USS *Wyoming*, which was at sea Monday through Thursday of every week. He had additional duty on ship one night of the two in port, and every third weekend he was at sea. With her husband home only one or two days a week, Mrs. Carter coped by herself until she gave birth to their first son, John William "Jack" Carter, on July 3, 1947.

Jimmy Carter was chosen for the prestigious submarine school at New London, Connecticut, in 1948, and the family moved there. For the first time in two years of marriage, he had regular hours and was home at night. These were years when the Carters' lifelong interest in self-improvement led them, according to Mrs. Carter, to study music, poetry, art, and dancing. The family next moved to Hawaii. Their second son, James Earl "Chip" Carter III, was born there on April 12, 1950. Jimmy Carter then qualified for submarines and earned his dolphin insignia.

The Carters next spent five months in San Diego, California. There, Rosalynn Carter ran the household and cared for the couple's two small children. Her husband joined the family on weekends.

Jimmy Carter was again assigned to New London, Connecticut, to duty on the USS *K-1*, a small submarine that was the first new ship built by the U.S. Navy after World War II. On August 18, 1952, Rosalynn Carter's birthday, Donnel Jeffrey "Jeff" Carter was born. Jimmy Carter subsequently qualified to command submarines, and was chosen by Admiral Hyman Rickover to join the nuclear submarine program.

The family's last move while Jimmy Carter was in the navy was to Schenectady, New York. There they awaited the completion of the reactor for the USS *Seawolf*, the second nuclear submarine, to be built. Then, fate changed the Carters' path. Earl Carter died of cancer, leaving the family business adrift. Jimmy Carter learned on his return to Plains that his father had been quietly helping many families for years. Looking at his life from a new perspective, he decided to leave the navy and return home to take over the business. According to Rosalynn Carter, the most serious argument of

their marriage ensued. She loved their life in the navy and the independence she had achieved. She returned unhappily to Plains in 1953. Initially they lived with Lillian Carter, but soon moved to new public housing a block away. After a few months they rented a house, and later moved to a house close to Lillian Carter's home. Because of a severe drought the peanut crop failed in 1954, and their income that year was less than $200.

Times improved for the Carters, and the peanut warehouse and associated business expanded. Rosalynn Carter soon began taking care of the accounts and weighing in the farmers' trucks during the harvest. She was a full partner in the business. The independence that she had feared leaving behind in the navy emerged in her business dealings. Her self-confidence is revealed in her recollection that her husband expected those who helped him to figure out how to do things on their own: "I knew more about the books and more about the business on paper than Jimmy did." Just as she had managed the family's personal finances through the navy years, she now wrote the checks and balanced the books for the rapidly growing family business.

Their increasing affluence enabled the Carters to travel to Florida, New Orleans, and Mexico, and to attend stock car races and Atlanta Braves baseball games. There was also time for golf and for classes on great issues, great books, and speed-reading, as well as dance lessons. Though they were socially active, they were relatively unknown in the larger social circles of the state. They considered themselves best friends and reserved much of their time for work. As Rosalynn Carter observed, "I've never had time for friends . . . I've always worked too hard."

Jimmy Carter's first brush with politics came in 1962, when, on his thirty-eighth birthday, he committed to run for the state senate. Rosalynn Carter made phone calls and campaigned door-to-door. She referred to herself more as "a political partner than as a political wife, and never felt put upon." The election was marred by significant voting irregularities. The Quitman County ballot box was found under the bed of the county boss's daughter, unsealed and empty. Jimmy Carter won the write-in election (his first political office), leaving his wife to run the business for two and a half months during each of the next four years. (He was reelected in 1964.) She proudly reported that Carter was called home only once, when the brick warehouse collapsed and spilled tons of peanuts in the street. She handled her husband's state senate correspondence along with running the business and raising three sons.

After twenty-one years of marriage and with sons aged twenty, seventeen, and fifteen, Rosalynn Carter, in her words, became "happily pregnant." She worked every day at the warehouse until Amy Lynn was born on October 19, 1967. For the next six months she cared for Amy at home and kept the business accounts.

When Amy was two years old, Jimmy Carter again ran for governor. (He had failed to win the Democratic primary in 1966.) In a well-orchestrated campaign in which the whole family was active, Rosalynn Carter left Amy with her mother while she traveled. This experience led her to sympathize with working mothers who have to leave their young children.

In the 1970 gubernatorial campaign, Mrs. Carter traveled widely in Georgia without her husband. From morning to night she handed out brochures and asked people to vote for her husband. Personal contacts and interviews were easier for her than speeches. For times when she was pushed into "saying a few words," she had memorized prepared remarks. Her discussions with citizens during this campaign revealed to Rosalynn Carter how often mental illness in a home meant severe financial hardship. She would later return to this theme many times. All her efforts came to fruition when Jimmy Carter became the seventy-sixth governor of Georgia and she became the governor's wife.

The move from Plains to Atlanta ushered in a significant growing period for Rosalynn Carter. She emerged as a public figure in her own right, and for the first time encountered what she termed "fishbowl living." Her first year as the governor's wife was an unhappy one in which she felt "trapped by my schedule and by the security." Still striving for perfection, she always tried to have herself and active, three-year-old Amy meticulously groomed. These unrealistic goals were shed as the governor's mansion became more her home.

Rosalynn Carter's predecessor, Mrs. Lester Maddox, had had a very different style. There was no staff trained to Mrs. Carter's preferences, and she had no personal background to draw upon for the extensive and formal social activities that she was expected to oversee. The initial mistakes were learning experiences, and enabled the Carters to put their own stamp on the governor's home. The number of visible, uniformed security guards in the mansion was decreased. Rosalynn Carter arranged fresh flowers from the grounds and hung artwork by Georgians on the ballroom walls. The populist theme of living in the "People's House" was implemented with Sunday afternoon open houses for everyone living in selected congressional districts. The invitations to visit with the state's first family were placed in local newspapers and announced on local radio stations.

The many formal functions required a sizable wardrobe of long dresses. Since five women in the family wore size 6 or 8, they pooled their long dresses and kept them in a large, second-floor closet; Rosalynn Carter always had first choice from the collection. Only a blue gown she had worn at her husband's inauguration was excluded. It was no wonder, then, that she raised eyebrows by wearing the same gown she had worn at her husband's gubernatorial inauguration, at his presidential inauguration.

During the early years in Atlanta, Rosalynn Carter renewed her religious faith, gaining a deeper sense of her own spiritual identity. In her words, "I am constantly aware that God is with me to help me through the difficult times."

Jimmy Carter encouraged his wife to take a public role. After she had turned down all requests for speaking appearances for six months, he asked her to present an outline of his mental health program before the Georgia Association for Retarded Children. Rosalynn Carter took the assignment reluctantly, gave her speech nervously, and was predictably unhappy with the results. She felt bad because even though her husband sympathized with her, his expectations for her had not been met. She wrote that "he had always thought I could do anything and he never accepted 'no' or 'I can't' as an answer or excuse from anyone." A few months later, she overcame most of her fear of public speaking when she gave an address about the governor's mansion to the Atlanta Women's Chamber of Commerce.

Shortly after his inauguration, Jimmy Carter established the Governor's Commission to Improve Services to the Mentally and Emotionally Handicapped. As a member of the commission, Rosalynn Carter toured state hospitals and reported back to the commission. Ultimately, the state mental health system was overhauled, with the number of community mental health centers increasing from 23 to 134 during the Carter years. Mrs. Carter also volunteered one day a week at Georgia Regional Hospital. She described her work with the mentally ill as the most rewarding thing she did as the governor's wife.

A visit to Lady Bird Johnson's ranch with members of the Atlanta Garden Club helped Rosalynn Carter start the Georgia Highway Wildflower Program. She also worked with another First Lady, Betty Ford, as chairperson of the southeastern tour of Artrain, a six-railcar moving museum of art.

In 1973 the Carters covered 1,550 miles on the backroads of Georgia, renewing personal contacts and building support for Governor Carter's state reorganization plans. They moved down opposite sides of the street, shaking hands, before climbing in their car to travel to the next town, factory, or gathering place.

Rosalynn Carter's work with the Women's Prison Committee of the Commission on the Status of Women improved the prison housing conditions and established a work-release center in a home that had once served as a Carter campaign headquarters.

By the end of his term as governor, Jimmy Carter was prepared to run for president, and his wife encouraged him to do so. So on April 14, 1975, eighteen months before the election, Rosalynn Carter drove off with Edna Langford, Jack Carter's mother-in-law and the wife of a Georgia state senator, to visit Democratic activists and to campaign in Florida. The two women shook hands, distributed brochures, and went to all the radio and television stations they could find, offering to give interviews. Many times the stations wanted the unexpected interview but did not know what to ask, so Rosalynn Carter had five or six questions ready to hand out. Careful lists were kept of all contacts made during the trip. Mrs. Carter returned home from her trip with four hints: stop at the courthouse, look for large radio antennas, stay in people's homes, and muster the courage to intrude.

The Carters were partners in the campaign as they were in most of their endeavors. During the nomination campaign, Mrs. Carter set her own itinerary, wrote her own speeches, and returned home to be with her family on weekends. The strategy of campaigning apart from her husband allowed the campaign to increase its coverage. Campaigning without her husband also forced Rosalynn Carter to educate herself on the issues that were important to the constituencies she addressed. Although she did not view campaigning as her vocation, she realized that it was crucial if her husband was to beat all the other Democratic candidates. She was a good campaigner and enjoyed meeting the people much more than soliciting funds, which she did in the summer of 1975 to meet the federal requirement for matching campaign funds.

At the 1976 Democratic National Convention in New York City, Rosalynn Carter saw Ohio give its votes to her husband, ensuring his nomination. She said, "It was one of the most thrilling moments of my life. We had worked for it, planned for it, and knew it would come." The Carter team, in her opinion, had won the nomination.

During the 1976 general election campaign, Rosalynn Carter flew in a private chartered plane. She visited forty-two states, accompanied by her press secretary, Mary Finch Hoyt, and her secretary, Madeline MacBean. Once again, the Carters campaigned separately but were together to watch the returns on Election Night. The former Georgia peanut farmer won the election, becoming the thirty-ninth president of the United States. Rosalynn Carter, tempered by years of public exposure, was ready for the White House.

Historians have routinely given Rosalynn Carter high marks for her role as First Lady. In fact, her rating is much higher than her husband's position in the ranking of presidents. Elements that influenced her success included her relations with the president, her organization of her staff, her communication and political skills, her personality, and her focus on her goals.

The mutual respect and love between the Carters enhanced Rosalynn Carter's influence and effectiveness. In his memoirs, *Keeping Faith*, Jimmy Carter describes how they "were full partners in every sense of the word." There had been no other sweethearts for either of them, and they had shared the experience of raising a family, running a business, and campaigning successfully for the offices of state senator, governor, and president. Emphasizing the strength of their relationship, he continued:

> We communicate easily, and often we have the same thoughts without speaking. We had been ridiculed at times for allowing our love to be apparent to others. It was not an affectation but as natural as breathing.

Jimmy Carter admired his wife's appearance, but significantly, he also described her as having superb political judgment. Biographer Howard Norton, in *Rosalynn*, relates that in a rare comment on her daughter-in-law, Miss Lillian said "She can do anything in the world with Jimmy. He listens to her. He thinks she has a great mind." Ultimately, Norton writes, these views led to what the president described as "an absolutely unconstrained relationship. There is very seldom a decision that I make that I don't first discuss with her."

The office of the First Lady was reorganized into the following divisions: projects and community liaison, press and research, schedule and advance, and social and personal. The initial full-time staff of eighteen was increased during the term to twenty-one plus volunteers. Mary Finch Hoyt, who had been press secretary to Eleanor McGovern and Jane Muskie in their husbands' national campaigns, was appointed press secretary. A more controversial appointment, however, was made in August 1979 when Edith J. Dobelle, the former chief of protocol at the State Department, was hired for the newly created position of chief of staff for the First Lady. This new senior staff position placed her at the same rank and salary as Hamilton Jordan and as the president's national security adviser, Zbigniew Brzezinski.

The First Lady went to her office almost every day when she was not traveling. A perfectionist, Mrs. Carter was a tough but informal manager. Striving for efficiency in using her valuable time, she had a picture of the White House printed that she signed with an Autopen instead of signing by hand. And to answer schoolchildren's questions, the First Lady's office produced a booklet titled *The White House . . . It's Your House, Too*, written as if the White House was seen through Amy Carter's eyes.

Rosalynn Carter's attention to communication and political considerations further enhanced her success. On April 26, 1979, in a speech before New York Women in Communications, she said, "I think we are fortunate to be in the communications business—and I would like to include myself in your field today. We can choose our message. We can affect attitudes. We have influence." While in the White House she gave over 500 speeches and delivered remarks before many groups visiting the White House. Her speeches were delivered clearly, in a softly modulated Southern accent. While campaigning, her ability to give the same speech repeatedly and have it come across as fresh and sincere was a major asset.

The First Lady did not hold press conferences, but she was accessible to the press for comments. Mrs. Carter bridled at the press's attempt to focus more on her appearance and social activities than on her substantive work. For instance, on the day the mental health commission findings were announced, more press coverage was given to the Carters' decision not to serve hard liquor on the state floor of the White House than to the commission's report. The press focused, not always positively, on Rosalynn Carter's unusually high level of access and influence in the Carter administration. Her controlled manner made for a far less open relationship with the press than her predecessor, Betty Ford, had achieved.

President Carter and his wife agreed that she was the more political of the pair. According to Rosalynn Carter, she had greater concern about popularity and winning reelection. This led to disagreements over the timing of public announcements, with the First Lady often losing her arguments for political awareness. For example, she suggested that the divisive Panama Canal treaties wait until the second term, and that the federal budget cuts in social programs dear to the hearts of New York City Democrats not be announced just days before the New York presidential primary.

While in the White House, Rosalynn Carter took Spanish lessons three days a week, violin lessons (with Amy), and a speed-writing course with the president. She studied foreign policy and domestic issue briefings on a regular basis. After reviewing the information, she had strong opinions, which she frequently presented to her husband.

Though friendly and gracious, Rosalynn Carter did not develop a large network of friends. The president and the First Lady described themselves as best friends and did not feel the need to reach out for other intense social contacts. Rosalynn Carter had a firm sense of responsibility for others that had been honed in her childhood and

nurtured by her strong religious beliefs. Impatient with inaction, she strove to achieve her goals.

Rosalynn Carter's main roles as First Lady were as social leader, adviser, representative, campaigner, and policy or project advocate. Although social responsibilities were not as central for her as they have been for some First Ladies, she carried out her social duties conscientiously. She left the White House before choosing a Carter china pattern (which she regrets), and she did not use all the money set aside for refurbishing the personal quarters. She did, however, work on setting up trust funds to provide a permanent source of money to maintain the White House furnishings. The First Lady's natural frugality expressed itself in White House entertaining. She often chose the least expensive menu offered to her by the chef, and she invited only half the total number of guests to dinner; the rest, to the following entertainment.

Rosalynn Carter's social secretary, Gretchen Poston, helped arrange a White House welcome for nearly 100 heads of state during Jimmy Carter's first twenty months as president. Although protocol abounds with rules, Mrs. Carter contended that "real protocol is warmth and putting your guests at ease, an important part of Southern hospitality, not just rules."

The Carters discontinued the printing of White House menus with French terms. They instituted more events to which families were invited, such as picnics on the lawn, and they generally had an informal social style that some Washingtonians criticized. White House social events included the first reception in the White House for American poets, the first reception for Armenian Americans, and the first musical festival featuring African Americans. Consistent with the Carters' populist theme, through 1979 a series of Sunday afternoon performances by American artists was taped by the Public Broadcasting Service (PBS) for national transmission. In a November 19, 1980, *Washington Post* article, Donnie Radcliffe reported that Rosalynn Carter said the White House "was an open, friendly, warm place where there were more 'ordinary people' invited than ever before."

Rosalynn Carter's role as the president's closest adviser added to the evolutionary history of First Ladies. Other First Ladies had been active advisers to their husbands, but no previous president was as open in acknowledging his use of his wife's advice. In *Keeping Faith*, Jimmy Carter openly discussed how he turned to his wife for "sound advice on issues and political strategy." She was kept fully informed of everything going on in the administration except for some top-secret security matters. President Carter confided that "it was most helpful for me to be able to discuss questions of importance with her as I formed my opinions."

The president invited his wife to attend cabinet meetings so that she would know more about what was going in the administration. She accepted this unprecedented invitation when her schedule permitted. The First Lady sat on the side of the room with other staff members during cabinet meetings and quietly took notes. Her silent presence enhanced her reputation as the president's adviser and gave detractors evidence of her exaggerated "copresidency." The First Lady was also included in national security briefings.

Examples of advice from Rosalynn Carter to the president abound. During the 1978 congressional campaign she supported the theme of morality, and in the second presidential debate in 1980, she approved the president's reduction of the recitation of facts and figures. Some memos and correspondence from the president's staff were directed to the First Lady for her comments. She suggested the termination of U.S. oil purchases from Iran after the hostage crisis, and after cabinet members agreed, the sales stopped. Regarding the Camp David Accords, President Carter wrote in his memoirs, "Rosalynn was a partner in my thinking throughout the Camp David negotiations."

Mrs. Carter was also consulted on major appointments, including the vice president. Her office maintained a list of qualified women used by President Carter to appoint an unprecedented number of women to high-ranking positions.

Presidential speeches, from the 1976 Inaugural Address through the energy speeches, received the First Lady's constructive comments. She argued that the July 1979 energy speech, popularly known as the malaise speech, should emphasize the positive features of America and the improvements being made. Obviously, her advice was not always taken: "Though I could seldom sway him when his mind was made up, he always listened." Although her privileged position in policy discussions was new for the institution of the First Lady, it was merely a continuance of the lifelong habits of the Carters.

Rosalynn Carter was sent to Boston to greet Pope John Paul II, the first pope to visit the United States. Like First Ladies before her, she also stood in for the president at numerous foreign ceremonial occasions.

In November 1979, days after the Iranian hostage crisis began, the First Lady visited the Sakeo refugee camp on the Cambodia–Thailand border. She walked among the tents, touching, talking to, and holding the inhabitants. The film crew covering her visit brought pictures of the misery home to America. The refugee camp workers had told Mrs. Carter of the desperate need for a single coordinator for all relief efforts. She relayed this information to Kurt Waldheim, the U.N. secretary-general, and asked that other nations not be told it was a U.S. initiative. Sir Robert Jackson, who had directed the U.N. Bangladesh relief efforts, was quickly named relief coordinator.

The First Lady used her media access to promote American relief efforts. Public service spots showing the film shot at the camp were used. She discussed the issue on the *Today* show; gave speeches, including one at the Council of Foreign Relations; held fund-raisers at the White House; and helped spur the formation of the National Cambodian Crisis Committee and the Cambodian Crisis Center. President Carter directed that the U.S. quotas for refugees from that area be increased and that the level of support be raised.

Rosalynn Carter's 1977 trip to Latin America was an example of a First Lady representing the president in a policy-making setting. Her grueling schedule covered seven Latin American countries—Jamaica, Costa Rica, Ecuador, Peru, Brazil, Colombia, and Venezuela—and over 12,000 miles in thirteen days. This unprecedented foreign policy trip by a First Lady began on May 30, 1977. Eleanor Roosevelt had traveled abroad as a representative of the president during World War II, but her mission had not been to explain American foreign policy to heads of state.

Rosalynn Carter was asked by the president to make the trip because his own schedule allowed him to make only one trip, to the Economic Summit in London. Vice President Walter Mondale was traveling to the NATO allies, Secretary of State Cyrus Vance was scheduled for a tour of Africa, and the president was left with the high-priority area of Latin America uncovered.

Earlier that month, in a May 3 address, President Carter had described the First Lady as his political partner, whom he would send for substantive talks with Latin American leaders. She was asked to bring home reports on ways to improve relations with Latin America. She explained her charge as emphasizing the foreign policy themes of the Carter administration. These themes included an emphasis on human rights policy and nuclear arsenals while stressing the unique nature of each country. According to her account she was instructed not to (1) defend any policy errors of the past, (2) promise anything or tell countries what to do, or (3) discuss specific aid packages.

The goodwill surrounding her trip declined when President Carter signed the treaty establishing Latin America as the world's first nuclear weapons–free zone four days before her departure. Then, while she was en route, he signed the American Convention on Human Rights on June 1. Both of these measures were resented by some Latin American countries (especially Brazil, which signed neither) as interferences in their domestic affairs.

The First Lady was accompanied by Bob Pastor, the national security adviser for Latin American affairs, and Terry Todman, assistant secretary of state for Latin America. The American ambassador to each nation joined her when she met the head of state.

Rosalynn Carter's official meetings began with a very brief summary of the new administration's foreign policy as it pertained to Latin America and the Caribbean. The First Lady made this statement to "let the leaders know I was informed and could enter into a productive conversation." She took notes throughout every meeting, and subsequently wrote talking points on a card she kept in her purse and reviewed during rides to receptions and other meetings with the heads of state. Following an official meeting, Mrs. Carter sent a comprehensive memorandum to the president and the State Department, "leaving it to the experts in Washington to interpret." With the daily phone calls to the president and the usual embassy correspondence, her trip was well documented.

Rosalynn Carter spoke to the question of credentials when she wrote "and who is closer to the president, who better has his ear than his wife . . . I was *determined* to be taken seriously." To this end she continued her Spanish classes from 9:00 A.M. to noon on Tuesdays, Wednesdays, and Fridays. She also received twenty-six hours of briefings from scholars, officials from the State and Treasury departments, the National Security Council, the Organization of American States (OAS), and special assistant to the president for national security, Zbigniew Brzezinski. Her background reading included historical studies of U.S.–Latin American relations, her husband's speeches, and Latin American literature.

At official meetings Mrs. Carter occasionally received notes from the U.S. officials suggesting questions or follow-up responses. She asked the Latin American diplomats to be blunt with her so that she could accomplish her mission. In a speech given soon after her return, she explained her mission: (1) Latin American nations needed to know the new president, and he needed to know them; (2) there was a need to explain firsthand three major foreign policy speeches by President Carter at the United Nations, the OAS, and the University of Notre Dame; and (3) "I felt I could establish a personal relationship between these leaders and my family, which is very important."

In her role as representative of the Carter administration and the U.S. government, Rosalynn Carter was met by heads of state in every nation that she visited. Her first stop, in Jamaica, included a seven-hour private talk with Prime Minister Norman Manley. He expressed concerns about Western intentions to overthrow his government because of his ties to Fidel Castro, the trade deficit, and Jamaica's need for aid. Rosalynn Carter remarked that "as it turned out, my duties throughout the trip were heavier than the president's in his own official visits. I assumed the official responsibilities *plus* the chores of a First Lady."

Discussions in Costa Rica centered on the request that the United States raise the quota on Costa Rican beef and that Costa Rica increase its investigations into human rights violations in OAS nations. Initially, President Daniel Oduber included his wife at the meeting, signaling his impression that it was a social visit, and pointedly directed his answers to the First Lady's questions to male U.S. officials. As the talks progressed, however, his wife left, and President Oduber addressed the First Lady directly.

In Ecuador, Rosalynn Carter was the first high-ranking U.S. representative to visit that country in almost twenty years. Vice President Nixon was the last such visitor in 1959, and he had been pelted with eggs. There was an anti-U.S. demonstration by approximately 150 students and some Molotov cocktails were thrown, but the First Lady was never directly confronted. The scheduled ninety-minute meeting with government leaders stretched to three hours and covered the controversy over the U.S. ban on Israel's sale of its Kafi jets with American-made engines, and the U.S. trade restrictions placed on Ecuador subsequent to its raising of oil prices.

In Peru, President Morales Bermudez began discussions on a cautious note but warmed to the substantive discussion of arms buildup, and extended their meeting to three hours. Rosalynn Carter dominated all Lima newspapers on June 5, and her activities were reported on radio and television. Her press conference received full coverage, and an editorial in *La Crónica* on file at the Carter Library said:

> The visit of Mrs. Carter is an opportunity to broaden and strengthen the understanding and collaboration between both nations. . . . Mrs. Rosalynn Carter's visit will leave a permanent remembrance and sincere bond of friendship between Peru and the U.S.A.

U.S.–Brazilian relations were in a strained state when Rosalynn Carter met with President Ernesto Geisel. She later wrote, "My mission was to try to ease the tension between our countries by explaining the Carter policies on human rights, nuclear nonproliferation, and the arms race." The White House Press Office summary of June 8, 1979, reported that a close aide to President Geisel said that the leader "attaches enormous significance to his talks with the First Lady."

After checking with her husband, the First Lady visited two American missionaries who had been detained without contact with diplomatic officials and treated inhumanely. Although she told reporters that she sympathized with the missionaries and would take their personal messages back to President Carter, she did not openly criticize Brazil's actions. An editorial by Carlos Conde in *O Estado de São Paulo* included the following appraisal: "Clearly the intention is that her trip is not just protocol as was Pat Nixon's. . . . As a good politician, Carter knows that his wife will be less constrained than a diplomat in saying and hearing things in Latin America."

In Colombia, a country friendly to the United States, Rosalynn Carter's discussion centered on drug trafficking and the detention of over sixty Americans on drug charges.

A change in the tone of the visit was evident when the farewell champagne reception for wives became a gathering of American and Colombian officials.

Official meetings in Venezuela focused on the U.S. denial of preferential trade status to that nation following its increase in the price of oil. Although Rosalynn Carter was ill at the end of her trip, she had missed only one event in Venezuela.

The Latin American trip, clearly substantive in nature, was perceived by the participants as successful. The largest circulation newspaper in Rio de Janeiro, *O Globo*, on June 5 described her trip in these positive terms: "In her capacity of almost a member of the Carter Cabinet, Rosalynn comes to express . . . her husband's concern with institutional, economic and arms issues and respect for human rights."

There were many positive reactions to the use of the First Lady in this political manner. For example, on June 4, 1977, the *Chicago Sun-Times* wrote: "First Lady Rosalynn Carter is making America proud. The close friendships she has evoked . . . in her Latin America visit are valuable . . . in a process of upgrading U.S.–Latin American relationships." *CBS Evening News* said on June 4: "Rosalynn Carter continues her South American tour, acting as a two-way conduit of views, not a negotiator."

NBC Nightly News on June 6 concluded, "After one week of her trip, Mrs. Carter has played the role of the wife of a head of state while discussing the fine points of foreign policy with foreign leaders. One Ecuadoran official said she was well prepared and surprised them with her intelligence." The *Richmond Times-Dispatch* wrote on June 10 that Rosalynn Carter's preparations "do not qualify her as a Latin American expert, but . . . this may not be a bad thing."

Upon her return on June 12, a correspondent for *CBS Evening News* said, "What started as a rather doubtful mission has apparently ended successfully." On June 13 the same program showed President Carter telling reporters that "she has succeeded almost to perfection, and has affirmed Latin American relations with the United States as ones of close cooperation and equality of approach to common problems."

This unusual role for a First Lady did not pass without criticism. Rosalynn Carter recalled that a U.S. diplomat, back from a long tour in Brazil, said, "Latin women still are in the state that women were in back in the nineteenth century in Europe and the United States. They are decorative, useful at home and that's all." She responded that the same cultural factor led some congressmen to oppose her trip "because I was a woman going into very male territory."

The First Lady's legitimacy as a representative was also questioned when reporters in Jamaica asked if she had the right to speak for the president. In *Newsweek*, on June 20, Meg Greenfield continued this discussion by stating that if Mrs. Carter acted as a diplomat, she should be accountable to the American people. Bob Wiedrich, writing for the *Chicago Tribune*, hoped that "President Carter would stop using members of his family as ex-officio representatives of the American people who voted him into office."

An editorial in the Brazilian paper *O Estado* stated, "No matter how well informed she may be, Mrs. Carter will lack the indispensable experience to negotiate with GOB [Government of Brazil] authorities who have a tradition of negotiators [*sic*] which dates back to imperial times."

In an example of less overt criticism, Betty Boyd Caroli argued in her book *First Ladies* that since all Mrs. Carter's subsequent trips were more traditional, her husband may not have viewed the experiment as fully successful. There is, however, no direct evidence that the president was anything but pleased.

Rosalynn Carter believed that a First Lady was in the position to accomplish many things. Her list of projects was organized by state and subject, but mental health was given the highest priority. She worked to change the nature of government assistance to the mentally ill. "I wanted to take mental illness and emotional disorders out of the closet, to let people know it is all right to admit having a problem without their fear of being called crazy."

In the first month after his inauguration, President Carter signed an executive order establishing the President's Commission on Mental Health. Unexpectedly, he was informed by the Justice Department's Office of Legal Counsel that his wife could not chair that commission. The president was prohibited from appointing a close relative, such as a wife, to a civilian position. Carter could not find a way around this restriction, so the First Lady was designated honorary chair. Dr. Tom Bryant was named chairman and executive director, and the president's special assistant for health issues, Peter Bourne, acted as coordinator for the First Lady and the twenty commissioners. The commission covered specialized subjects through the use of thirty task forces and over 450 volunteers.

The need for such a commission was clear. There had been no national assessment of how the nation was meeting the mental health needs of the citizens since a 1961 report given to President Kennedy. A 1965 commission had investigated the health needs of children, but the recommendations were never implemented. The president's commission was scheduled to give an interim report, followed by a final report to the president in April 1978. President Carter also made it clear that there would not be much new money to implement the recommendations. With this timetable and such cautious expectations, the commission launched a series of public hearings across the country.

Rosalynn Carter took a very active role in the commission. She attended many public meetings and toured mental health facilities nationwide. On April 22, 1977, Marjorie Hunter, writing for the *New York Times* about the commission's first official meeting in Chicago, said, "Mrs. Carter was soft-spoken, but displayed a steely determination as she almost imperceptibly took over the direction of the meeting from the official chairperson, Dr. Thomas E. Bryant, an old family friend." At the first public hearing of the commission in Philadelphia on May 27, the First Lady assured reporters that the commission was not merely a public relations operation. It would produce "something to give to Jimmy. This is not just for show."

This promise was fulfilled when the commission issued its report containing 117 recommendations, including eight major ones. Rosalynn Carter used the media to highlight the report by appearing on *Good Morning America* and the *MacNeil-Lehrer Report* on April 27, 1978, the day the president received the findings. The recommendations included an emphasis on community health care centers, inclusion of treatment of mental illness in health insurance programs, aid to personnel working in rural areas and the inner cities, and an increased commitment to research and programs for the prevention of mental illness.

The president quickly ordered that the recommendations, which did not require congressional action, be assigned timetables for implementation. Unfortunately, Secretary of Health and Human Services Joseph Califano did not implement the recommendations as quickly as the First Lady had hoped. Finally, she found it necessary to go directly to the president and to James McIntyre at the Office of Management and Budget to get things moving.

The commission's recommendations were part of the Mental Health Systems Act which was submitted to Congress by President Carter in 1979. Rosalynn Carter actively lobbied for passage of the bill by giving speeches on mental health and inviting numerous involved groups to the White House for briefings. The preceding February she had testified before the Subcommittee on Health and Scientific Research of the Senate Human Resources Committee in support of the commission's recommendations. This was the first time since 1945, when Eleanor Roosevelt had testified before a congressional committee, that a First Lady testified.

The Mental Health Systems Act was passed and funded by Congress in September, and was signed by the president in October 1980. Unfortunately, the significantly different agenda of the incoming Reagan administration halted much of the funding needed to implement the act. Some results lasted beyond the initial Reagan cutbacks, however. The Office of Prevention was created in the National Institute of Mental Health (NIMH), and the changes in the training program of the NIMH that addressed the goal of altering the government's approach to mental health continued to go forward.

Consistent with her beliefs in community-based services for the mentally ill, Mrs. Carter supported the Green Door project in Washington, D.C. It served the chronically mentally ill by establishing a house (with a green door) where patients could go, and cook and perform other household chores.

Another chronic need Rosalynn Carter had identified during her campaign travels was services for the elderly. Following her campaign years she continued to visit senior centers and homes, and supported a task force which took stock of all the federal programs for the elderly. Her interest in senior citizens grew naturally from her teenage years, when her grandfather had lived with her family, as well as from more recent events—her mother's forced retirement when she turned seventy and her mother-in-law's joining the Peace Corps at age sixty-eight. Rosalynn Carter presided at the White House Conference on Aging held in May 1977 and at the National Council on Aging meeting. She lobbied Congress in support of the Age Discrimination Act, the Rural Clinics Act, Social Security reform, and bills to contain escalating hospital costs.

Mrs. Carter's work with Betty Bumpers, the wife of Dale Bumpers, U.S. senator from Arkansas, culminated in a national childhood immunization program, Every Child by Two. The program's goal was to promote the immunization of all American children on schedule from birth to the age of two years. Implementation of the program helped to make measles rare in the United States.

Rosalynn Carter wrote in her memoirs that her greatest disappointment in all her White House projects was the failure of the Equal Rights Amendment (ERA) to be ratified. Both Carters lobbied for its passage

with personal phone calls to state legislators. Mrs. Carter wrote letters, gave speech-es, and attended fund-raisers. One of the more unusual events was the February 18, 1978, fund-raising dance in Tampa, Florida, where the First Lady was raffled off as a dance partner. She responded to critics of her actions by informing the press that the political activities were paid for by the Democratic National Committee. Much news media attention was gained when Rosalynn Carter joined Betty Ford and Lady Bird Johnson to support the ERA at the Houston conference celebrating the International Women's Year in 1977. Although the Equal Rights Amendment was not ratified, she worked to promote appointments of women to federal positions. The Carter administration excelled, for the standards of that time, in appointing women to high-level positions.

The First Lady was raised in a small, Southern town where a sense of community pride and involvement ran strong. She carried this faith in community activism into her White House projects. She traveled across the country promoting volunteerism as a way to tackle social problems such as unemployment. For example, on July 27, 1978, she hosted a daylong "First Lady's Employment Seminar" in Washington, D.C. Paying their own expenses, 200–300 delegates from a wide range of groups and regions came to share information and learn how other communities had responded to their unemployment situations.

Washington, D.C., was Rosalynn Carter's community during her White House years, and she quickly became involved in local concerns. The commission of Washington General Hospital asked for her help in increasing the number of volunteers. The First Lady's support helped encourage the involvement of a radio announcer and a number of other private individuals and groups. She even painted a wall in the hospital reception room. A nursing education program for geriatric patients was filmed at D.C. General, and Mrs. Carter introduced each segment of the series, titled *The Rosalynn Carter Nurses Training Program*. The success of the volunteer involvement was apparent when the hospital regained its accreditation.

The Community Foundation of Greater Washington got a boost from the First Lady's support and became a thriving organization that provided grants for neighborhood programs for the young, the old and the mentally ill. She left the Camp David peace summit to attend a White House luncheon to build business support for the foundation.

A White House breakfast for 230 businessmen in May 1977 was the setting for the First Lady to promote William Milliken's Project Propinquity. This program focused on retraining ghetto youth, and through the First Lady's promotion, Milliken received $2.7 million of federal funds and an office. In *Rosalynn*, Howard Norton relates that a reporter said Milliken's project was supported because it had the "Three F's—Faith, Fundraising and First Lady."

On June 10, 1980, the National Mental Health Association and the D.C. Mental Health Association combined to name Rosalynn Carter "the volunteer of the decade." Acknowledging her contributions to the Washington community, the D.C. City Council gave her a special commendation in December 1980. She also received two honorary degrees: a Doctor of Humane Letters from Morehouse College and a Doctor of Humanities from Tift College.

International matters also received the First Lady's attention. She actively lobbied congressional wives to influence their husbands in support of the Panama Canal treaties. She helped to found, and served as honorary chair of, the Friendship Force, a professional adult exchange program. Rosalynn Carter traveled widely both with the president and alone on official missions, and she openly shared her advice on the two major events during the Carter administration—the Camp David peace summit and the Iranian hostage crisis. Her diary of 200 typed pages covering the thirteen-day Camp David meeting provided a fascinating human account of the summit for her autobiography.

Rosalynn Carter participated in midterm campaigning for Democratic congressional candidates in 1978 and undertook major campaign duties in the presidential race of 1980. Two major foreign policy events—the taking of American hostages in Iran on November 4, 1979, and the Russian invasion of Afghanistan on December 27, 1979—affected the president's campaigning. Carter wrote in his autobiography: "I did not ignore the Democratic primary contests, but depended on Fritz, Rosalynn and others to do the campaigning while I concentrated on the Iran crisis and my other duties." If he ran, Senator Edward Kennedy of Massachusetts was expected to capitalize on the president's low public opinion rating and capture the Democratic nomination. Kennedy did run, but intensive campaigning helped Jimmy Carter win his renomination for president at a divided convention.

Rosalynn Carter played an important role in securing the nomination and launching the uphill general election battle against a Republican Party united behind Ronald Reagan. She campaigned throughout the country, and until two days before the election, she believed victory could be theirs. The poor economic conditions, the American hostages in Iran, a divided Democratic Party, and a united Republican campaign led to an overwhelming Reagan victory. Reagan took all but six states, and the Republicans won a majority in the Senate. There were bitter moments after the election, but on Inauguration Day Mrs. Carter's spirits were high. She knew as she rode beside her successor, Nancy Reagan, that the American hostages were finally coming home.

Rosalynn Carter was an effective First Lady and strengthened the position of First Lady by her activities. She set a precedent by hiring a chief of staff, with a high senior staff rank, to serve her office. Her advice was both sought and listened to by the president. The office of First Lady became a base for strong lobbying efforts on issues ranging from the Panama Canal treaties to the ERA to mental health. Rosalynn Carter became the second First Lady—Eleanor Roosevelt was the first—to testify before Congress. She took an unprecedented role in representing the United States at substantive policy discussions with foreign leaders, and she raised mental health and concerns for the elderly to new levels of public awareness. Even her role as an independent, full-time campaigner set Rosalynn Carter apart from most other First Ladies. As First Lady, she consistently received higher rankings than her husband received in rankings of presidents.

The Carters returned to Plains, Georgia, in 1980, and picked up the strands of their private life. Mrs. Carter's autobiography, *First Lady from Plains*, was published three years later. It was number 1 on the *New York Times* best-seller list and stayed there for eighteen weeks in 1984. Together the Carters wrote a book highlighting volunteerism and healthy living, *Everything to Gain* (1987). In 1994 Rosalynn Carter's book for caregivers, written with Susan Golant and reflecting her own personal experience of caring for a terminally ill grandfather and dying father in her youth, *Helping Yourself Help Others*, was published. Her most recent book, *Helping Someone with Mental Illness: A Compassionate Guide for Family, Friends and Caregivers*, also written with Susan Golant, earned the Outstanding Book Award in the service category from the American Society of Journalists and Authors in 1999.

Rosalynn Carter continues to be active in projects of the Carter Presidential Center, where she serves as vice chair of the board of trustees. Some of these projects have involved extensive foreign travel with her husband. For example, in February 1999 she accompanied President Carter and other delegates to observe Nigeria's presidential election.

The Carters also work together on building sites in America and abroad under the auspices of Habitat for Humanity. Mrs. Carter became a member of its board of advisers in 1984. This nonprofit organization accepts no state or federal funds to support the building of homes for the poor. The prospective homeowners must work on their houses and their neighbors' houses, and pay the low actual cost over twenty years.

Rosalynn Carter continues to pursue her interest in mental health in many ways. She hosts the annual Rosalynn Carter Sympo-

sium on Mental Health Policy and is chair of the Carter Center Mental Health Task Force, an advisory group advocating positive changes in mental health policy that was founded in 1991. The Rosalynn Carter Georgia Mental Health Forum, held regularly at the Carter Center, provides an opportunity for state mental health caregivers to discuss their common concerns. The Rosalynn Carter fellowships for mental health journalism were established by the Carter Center to promote a more positive portrayal of individuals with mental illness.

Rosalynn Carter is honorary chair of the board of directors of the Rosalynn Carter Institute (RCI). The institute was founded in 1987 at Georgia Southwestern State University, her alma mater, and focuses on caregiving by both families and professionals. RCI provides educational programs for caregivers, supports research on caregiving, and offers a policy forum for discussing the caregiving process.

Speaking out on the topic of mental health is a regular activity for Mrs. Carter. She founded the International Committee of Women Leaders for World Mental Health in 1991 and spoke at their meeting in Helsinki, Finland, in 1996. In March 1994, Mrs. Carter and Betty Ford testified before the U.S. Senate Labor and Human Resources Committee, urging the inclusion of mental health and substance abuse benefits in the national health care plan. Similarly, Mrs. Carter and Nancy Domenici, wife of Republican Senator Pete Domenici of New Mexico, visited Capitol Hill in May 1995 to support protection of mental health benefits in the face of federal Medicaid and Medicare restructuring.

Rosalynn Carter has received many honors since leaving the White House, including the Presidential Citation from the American Psychological Association, honorary fellow of the American Psychiatric Association, board member emeritus of the National Mental Health Association, and, in 1990, distinguished fellow of the Emory University Institute for Women's Studies.

The Carter's received the Presidential Medal of Freedom, the highest civilian honor, on August 9, 1999. In his remarks at the award presentation, President Clinton said, "Rosalynn Carter will always be remembered as a pioneer on mental health and a champion of our children."

With her husband, Rosalynn Carter continues to work on projects which, in their words, involve "promoting good for others."

BIBLIOGRAPHICAL ESSAY

Rosalynn Carter's personal papers are not available for research at the Jimmy Carter Library in Atlanta, Georgia. The Carter Library does contain source material on her in the White House Central File, the Speechwriter's Office File, the Press Office files of Jody Powell, and the Administration Office files of Hugh Carter. The records of the President's Commission on Mental Health are open, and are contained in twenty-six boxes. There are also interviews with Rosalynn Carter and a number of her staff in the library's oral history collection.

Rosalynn Carter's autobiography, *First Lady from Plains* (Boston, 1984), was used in this essay to express her feelings and viewpoints; most quotations, unless otherwise indicated, come from that source. No biography of Rosalynn Carter has yet been written using all her personal files. *Everything to Gain*, written with Jimmy Carter (New York, 1987), provides an interesting view of their post–White House years. Discussion of Mrs. Carter's role as First Lady is found throughout Jimmy Carter's memoirs, *Keeping Faith* (New York, 1982).

With Susan Galont, Rosalynn Carter has written two books dealing with caregivers: *Helping Yourself Help Others: A Book for Caregivers* (New York, 1994) and *Helping Someone with Mental Illness: A Compassionate Guide for Family, Friends and Caregivers* (New York, 1998).

Biographies that provide good background material include Howard Norton's *Rosalynn* (Plainfield, N.J., 1977) and Richard Hyatt's *The Carters of Plains* (Huntsville, Ala., 1977) Edna Langford and Linda Maddox, *Rosalynn: Friend and First Lady* (Old Tappan, N.J., 1980), is written from friends' viewpoints.

Books on First Ladies which include useful chapters on Mrs. Carter are Diana Dixon Healy's *America's First Ladies* (New York, 1988); Paul F. Boller, Jr.'s *Presidential Wives* (New York, 1988); Alice E. Anderson and Hadley V. Baxenbale's *Behind Every Successful President* (New York, 1992); Margaret Truman's *First Ladies* (New York, 1995); Carl Sferrazza Anthony's *The First Ladies*, vol. 2 (New York, 1991); Betty Boyd Caroli's *First Ladies* (New York, 1987); and Myra Gutin's *The President's Partner* (New York, 1989).

Articles providing interesting insights into the life of Rosalynn Carter include Drummond Ayres, Jr. "The Importance of Being Rosalynn," *New York Times Magazine* (June 3, 1979); Linda Charlton, "Rosalynn Carter: Balancing Roles," *New York Times* (November 6, 1977); Faye Lind Jensen, "An Awesome Responsibility: Rosalynn Carter as First Lady," *Presidential Studies Quarterly* 20 (Fall 1990): 769–775; "Mrs. Carter Speaks Out," *New York Times* (July 14, 1983); "The President's Partner," *Newsweek* (November 5, 1979); Donnie Radcliffe, "Tears and Praise of the Steel Magnolia," *Washington Post* (November 19, 1985); Hugh Sidey, "Second Most Powerful Person," *Time* (May 7, 1979); James T. Wooten, "Mrs. Carter Sees Role Widening," *New York Times* (March 15, 1977).

Useful Web sites covering the activities of Rosalynn Carter include the home pages of the Carter Center (http://www.cartercenter.org/) and of the Rosalynn Carter Institute (http://rci.gsw.edu/). Both the *Carter Center News* and news releases from the Carter Center are sources for current information on a very active former First Lady.

★★★   ★★★

Nancy (Anne Frances Robbins Davis) Reagan

(1921–)

First Lady: 1981–1989

James G. Benze, Jr.

Anne Frances "Nancy" Robbins was born in New York City, the only child of Kenneth Robbins and Edith Luckett Robbins. Her date of birth is often officially given as July 6, 1923, but her birth certificate and high school and college records indicate the actual year of birth to be 1921. Although her given name is Anne (for her paternal great-great-great-grandmother), her mother called her Nancy.

When Nancy was born, her parents had been married for four years. Her father, originally from Pittsfield, Massachusetts, worked as a used car salesman in New Jersey. Her mother, who often claimed a Southern heritage and entertained guests with stories of life on her family's Virginia plantation, was actually born in Washing-

ton, D.C. Prior to her marriage, Edith Robbins was a moderately successful actress who had appeared in New York stage productions with such well-known actors as George M. Cohan and Spencer Tracy. She temporarily retired from the theater when Nancy was born.

By 1923, differences between Kenneth and Edith Robbins over where they would live and Edith's desire to return to the stage grew so great that they separated; they were divorced in 1928. Edith, who had custody of Nancy, had not given up her aspirations for a stage career, and needed money to support her daughter and herself. Because of the demands of touring, she placed Nancy in the care of her older sister, Virginia, and her husband, C. Audley Galbraith, who lived in Bethesda, Maryland, and were better able to provide the child with a stable, if modest, home life.

Over the next five years Nancy saw her mother only sporadically, usually when Edith was in New York for a stage production. On such occasions, she usually traveled to New York to be with her mother—trips that she remembered fondly. The separation from her mother was painful to Nancy. Most of Nancy Reagan's biographers point to the lack of consistent contact with her parents, and the resulting perceived lack of security in her childhood, as in part explaining the tremendous emotional importance she would place on her own marriage.

In late 1928, Nancy was introduced to her mother's new beau, the prominent Chicago neurosurgeon Loyal Davis. On May 21, 1929, Edith and Dr. Davis were married. Edith's remarriage was fortunate, for the Galbraiths were soon transferred to Atlanta and could no longer care for Nancy.

The Davises' marriage was in many ways an attraction of opposites. Edith, a Democrat, was by all accounts a gregarious, fun-loving, and outspoken woman who liked a good story—and liked it even better if it was at least slightly off-color. Dr. Davis, a conservative Republican, was much less outspoken, very strict, and extremely punctual. He did, however, love the theater, and at one time harbored acting aspirations of his own.

Her mother's remarriage changed young Nancy's life. She went from a lower-middle-class family in Bethesda, Maryland, to an affluent Presbyterian family living on Lake Shore Drive in Chicago. Moreover, for the first time in five years, Nancy was living with her mother.

Although she admitted to being initially a bit jealous of the attention her mother showed her stepfather, Nancy came to love and respect Dr. Davis. She was extremely happy when he finally adopted her; he had been reluctant to do so because her natural father was still alive. Nancy so respected Dr. Davis that his conservative political views influenced not only her political beliefs but also those of her future husband, Ronald Wilson Reagan.

Although Edith Davis's stage career ended with her remarriage, she remained friends with many actors and stage personalities. Thus, the Davis home often had visitors such as Spencer Tracy, Katharine Hepburn, and Walter Huston, all of whom helped fuel young Nancy's interest in the theater. While attending Girls' Latin School in Chicago, Nancy Davis not only played field hockey and was active in student government, but also got her first real taste of acting with the lead in her 1939 senior class production of (ironically) *First Lady*.

After graduation, Nancy entered Smith College. By her own admission, her weakness in math and science ruled out many traditional majors. Therefore, she was one of the few students to major in drama. While at Smith, Nancy appeared in some student productions, but most of her acting experience was in summer stock theater. Her most notable theater instructor at college was Hallie Flanagan of the Federal Theater project. At Smith, Nancy had her first serious romance; it ended with the young man's death in a railroad accident.

In 1943, Nancy Davis graduated from Smith with a Bachelor of Arts degree, then returned to Chicago to stay with her mother while her stepfather served in the U.S. Army in Europe. To keep busy and help support the family, she worked at Marshall Fields (a major department store) and as a nurse's aide.

However, Nancy Davis had not given up on her acting aspirations. She performed in summer stock theater whenever possible, and landed her first professional role (with the help of one of her mother's old friends, ZaSu Pitts) in a touring company performing *Ramshackle Inn*. The company eventually ended up in New York, where she landed a small role in a Broadway production of *Lute Song*, starring Yul Brynner and Mary Martin. In 1949, again with the help of her family's theater connections, she got her biggest break when Spencer Tracy helped arrange a screen test that resulted in her signing a beginner's contract with Metro Goldwyn Mayer.

Though Nancy Davis was never a major Hollywood star, her film career had its high points. In 1949, she appeared with Glenn Ford and Janet Leigh in *The Doctor and the Girl* and in a very lavish production of *East Side, West Side*. In total, Nancy appeared in eleven movies, including *Night into Morning* (1951), *It's a Big Country* (1951), and *Donovan's Brain* (1953)—almost always in supporting roles. However, she did garner some good reviews for her performances; A. H. Weiler of the *New York Times* described her as "beautiful and convincing" (May 19, 1950), and Lloyd Shearer of the *New York Herald Tribune* commended her for "good solid acting" (June 25, 1950).

Through her Hollywood career and an unusual set of circumstances, Nancy Davis met her future husband. In her memoirs, Mrs. Reagan remembers that in late 1949, while reading a Hollywood newspaper, she noticed her name on a list of Communist sympathizers. Given the "Red Scare" of the time (particularly strong in Hollywood), she was quite concerned. Not sure how to deal with the problem, she contacted Mervyn LeRoy, her director in *East Side, West Side*. In turn, LeRoy contacted the president of the Screen Actors Guild, Ronald Reagan. Reagan discovered that there was another actress by the same name, and at a dinner meeting with Nancy Davis, he explained the mix-up. (He later convinced the other Nancy Davis to change her professional name.) Some biographers of both Nancy and Ronald Reagan have suggested that Nancy had influential Hollywood friends who could make sure she wasn't confused with the other Nancy Davis. They suggest that her real goal was to meet the eligible Ronald Reagan, not to "clear" her name.

Although Nancy Reagan often said that her life began when she met Ronald Reagan, her future husband initially was not ready for marriage. Having just ended his marriage to Jane Wyman, and the father of a daughter, Maureen, and adopted son, Michael, he was not prepared for a new serious relationship. Over the next several years, though he and Nancy Davis dated often, they also dated others. After a few years of playing the field, Ronald Reagan was ready to settle down, and on March 4,

1952, Nancy Davis became Mrs. Ronald Reagan. On October 22, 1952, the Reagans' first child, Patricia Anne, was born, and in May 1958 their son Ronald, Jr., was born.

Nancy and Ronald Reagan were as much opposites as Edith and Loyal Davis had been. Ronald Reagan was amazed by his wife's familiarity with the Hollywood elite—that since childhood she had known Walter Huston and Spencer Tracy, and that she had actually dated Clark Gable. Moreover, he got along famously with her mother. They both loved to tell bawdy stories, and he would sometimes call Edith Davis on the phone to tell her his latest story. Ronald Reagan also admired Dr. Loyal Davis, whose strong conservative political opinions were partially responsible for his evolution from a liberal Democrat to a conservative Republican.

Nancy Reagan admired her husband's rise from humble circumstances, his having worked his way through Eureka College by washing dishes, and his refusal to feel sorry for himself. Naturally shy, she was attracted to his outgoing, gregarious personality. Ronald Reagan loved to talk and tell stories, and she loved to listen. Whereas she was something of a worrier, he was an eternal optimist. In fact, Nancy Reagan often described her husband as the most optimistic person she had ever met.

More important, the Reagans were deeply committed to one another and to their marriage, and became very protective of one another. Undoubtedly the depth of their commitment was at least partially the result of their past experiences: his unpleasant divorce from Jane Wyman and her difficulty with her mother's divorce and her happy remarriage.

Though Ronald and Nancy Reagan had very different backgrounds, in one important way their Hollywood experiences were very similar. They never became major stars, and insiders considered them as second-tier Hollywood actors. For Nancy Reagan, who like her mother gave up her career when she married, the lack of stardom was not a major concern. However, for Ronald Reagan, who had a family to support, his limited success was a significant problem. Although he had made some successful movies, including *Knute Rockne, All American* (1940) and *King's Row* (1942), by 1952 his Hollywood career was on the decline and he had difficulty getting what he considered acceptable parts. Fortunately, after a brief stint as a Las Vegas emcee, he was offered the job of official spokesman for General Electric. The position involved hosting a weekly television dramatic series, *General Electric Theater*, and traveling around the country giving speeches for the company at its factories and conventions.

For Ronald Reagan, this was an almost ideal job. He appeared in some *General Electric Theater* dramas, and he had a steady income and a number of perks associated with the job including a new all-electric home. As General Electric spokesman he perfected his public speaking abilities and made contacts that would be important for his future political career. During this period, Reagan's political conservatism—born out of his experiences as president of the Screen Actors Guild and furthered by his association with Dr. Loyal Davis—matured. In fact, as his speeches for General Electric became more conservative, he began to realize that his own politics had more in common with the Republican Party than with the Democrats. He soon decided to change his party affiliation.

This period was not nearly as easy for Mrs. Reagan. She was extremely supportive of her husband in his job as spokesman for General Electric. She traveled with him when she could, and also appeared in some of the *General Electric Theater* dramas. However, she was often left at home to raise their two young children by herself. Mrs. Reagan has frequently stated that this time, when she was a young, inexperienced, and overprotective mother, was one of the most difficult (if rewarding) periods of her life.

In 1962, Ronald Reagan lost his position with General Electric, at least partly because of the increasing political conservatism of his speeches. For the next several years he had to rely primarily on speechmaking for income. In 1964, with the help of his brother Neil, he was hired to host the television program *Death Valley Days*. Over the years, however, it was politics, not acting, that became Ronald Reagan's real interest. In 1960 he gave speeches as a Democrat for Richard M. Nixon, and in 1962 he officially changed his party registration to Republican. In 1964 he was cochairman of California Republicans for Barry Goldwater and stumped the state, giving speeches and raising money for the Goldwater presidential campaign. On October 27, 1964, Ronald Reagan made his national political debut with a passionate televised speech for Goldwater. It was well received, and drew contributions that added significantly to the coffers of the Goldwater campaign.

Barry Goldwater's crushing defeat by President Lyndon Johnson convinced Ronald Reagan that it was time for him to get off the sidelines and into the political game. Moreover, former actor George Murphy's defeat over Pierre Salinger in the race for a U.S. Senate seat from California proved that being a former actor was not necessarily an impediment to political success in California. While Ronald Reagan was considering his entrance into politics, he was approached by Henry Salvatori, finance chairman of the Goldwater presidential campaign, and Holmes Tuttle, a multimillionaire Republican fund-raiser, about entering the race for the governorship of California. With their backing, he quickly agreed to become a candidate.

Fortunately for candidate Reagan, Pat Brown, the two-term governor of California, did not consider him a serious threat. Unopposed in his own primary in 1966, Brown focused most of his attention on Reagan's Republican primary opponent, thus giving Reagan a free ride until the general election. Reagan, on the other hand, focused all of his attention and considerable rhetorical skills on Governor Brown. As the general election drew closer and a Reagan victory became more possible, the tone of the campaign became more bitter. When the votes were finally counted, Ronald Reagan had scored a major political upset, winning the election by almost 1 million votes.

For Nancy Reagan, this first experience of politics was something of a shock. She of course supported her husband's efforts, but she did not play much of a role in the campaign. She especially disliked giving campaign speeches. However, it was impossible to avoid making some appearances during the campaign. Therefore, Mrs. Reagan adopted a question-and-answer format for her appearances as an alternative to prepared speeches. Over time she became fairly comfortable with this format, and used it regularly in future campaigns. Even with her improving campaign skills, however, her clear preference was still to accompany her husband, sit in the audience, and listen attentively to his speeches.

The next eight years foreshadowed Mrs. Reagan's tenure as First Lady of the United States. She faced many of the same problems as the governor's wife that she later faced in the White House. In California, Mrs. Reagan was protective of her husband, sometimes to the point of being criticized for becoming too involved in his affairs. She also had a tendency to stir up controversy (even when that was not her intent), and often had a fairly stormy relationship with the press.

As the governor's wife, Mrs. Reagan often seemed to the public to be uninterested and uninvolved in many of her husband's policies as governor. However, she soon gained a reputation among the Reagan staff as being excessively committed to her husband's well-being—so much so that staff members sometimes described Mrs. Reagan as a lioness protecting her cub. For example, she would call the governor's staff to suggest that an item or two be dropped from her husband's schedule if she felt that he was being overworked. She also would let her husband know when she felt that a staff member did not have his best interests at heart.

Though some of his staff believed that Governor Reagan was henpecked, he always understood that his wife was concerned with his well-being, and rarely resisted her involvement. In fact, both Reagans realized the needs they filled in one another.

Mrs. Reagan needed to feel needed, and her husband required her constant attention. Far from resenting her involvement, he came to recognize and value her ability as a shrewd judge of character.

Probably Mrs. Reagan's biggest controversy involved the official governor's residence in Sacramento, a Victorian mansion built in 1877 that was quite run-down. Its downtown location—next to an American Legion hall, two gas stations, and a motel—was less than ideal. Mrs. Reagan made public her opinion that the mansion was an inappropriate residence for the governor of an important state such as California, and that, as a fire hazard, was a poor place to raise their son. After only four months, the Reagans moved out of the governor's mansion and into a twelve-room Tudor-style house in a quiet suburb of Sacramento, which they rented for $1,250 per month. There was quite a bit of public and press criticism about the Reagans putting on airs—being too good for the mansion that had served other governors and their families.

For the remainder of her husband's term, Mrs. Reagan's relationship with the press became increasingly strained. Some political reporters commented on what came to be called the "gaze": a glassy-eyed stare of rapt attention with head slightly tilted (suggesting that she did not have a thought in her head) that the governor's wife fixed upon her husband whenever he was speaking.

Ironically, some of the most severe criticism of Mrs. Reagan resulted from her effort to cultivate the press by agreeing to an in-depth interview conducted by novelist and essayist Joan Didion for *Saturday Evening Post*. The interview resulted in a scathing profile of Mrs. Reagan, titled "Pretty Nancy," published in the June 6, 1968, issue. In the profile, Ms. Didion described Mrs. Reagan as seeming to live in a perfect daydream world, full of phoniness and playacting, and characterized her as insincere and overly dramatic. Mrs. Reagan was very unhappy with the profile, and grew increasingly wary of the press.

However, not all of Mrs. Reagan's press coverage was negative. Though she was generally panned on the editorial pages, she often received accolades on the society pages. As the governor's wife she spent much of her time shopping in the most prestigious Beverly Hills stores, lunching with millionaire friends such as Betsy Bloomingdale, and attending society and cultural events around the state. Before long, Mrs. Reagan had cultivated an image of style and elegance. In 1968, she was named to the list of best-dressed women in the United States and was also the focus of an hourlong documentary for national television.

Mrs. Reagan became involved in a number of important causes. Both she and her husband were extremely interested in the plight of returning Vietnam veterans and of servicemen listed as missing in action. She was also a strong advocate of the Foster Grandparents program, which puts children with special needs in close contact with older adults.

The idea of a run for the White House occurred to Ronald Reagan well before he entered the 1976 presidential primaries. For example, in 1968 he had gone to the Republican National Convention as the favorite son candidate of California. The Nixon campaign undercut his chances by shrewdly wooing Barry Goldwater and Southern conservatives such as Strom Thurmond and John Tower, thereby isolating Reagan from his political base. After Richard Nixon's victory in the general election, Ronald Reagan and his advisers thought that perhaps he should have pursued the nomination more vigorously.

By 1976, Ronald Reagan was positioned to make a run for the Republican nomination. He had finished his second term as governor in 1974, and spent the intervening two years traveling the country as the most prominent spokesman for the conservative wing of the Republican Party, winning converts and picking up political IOUs in the process. In early 1974, Governor Reagan had met with a group of close advisers to discuss his presidential prospects. The biggest impediment to his candidacy was the incumbent Republican president, Gerald R. Ford. When President Ford chose Nelson Rock-

efeller as his vice president, Ronald Reagan concluded that the conservative wing was losing control of the Republican Party. Thus, he began to think seriously about running against President Ford.

Before Governor Reagan launched his campaign, one important adviser remained to be convinced—his wife. Mrs. Reagan (as protective of her husband as ever) did not want him to make the attempt if it would harm his health or damage his future chances. However, she finally gave her approval, and the campaign began.

Publicly, Nancy Reagan again played a very quiet role in the campaign. She made her usual question-and-answer campaign appearances, traveled with her husband, and attended his speeches. She subtly tried to draw a distinction between herself and First Lady Betty Ford, whom she thought was too outspoken and too interested in pushing her own agenda (support for the Equal Rights Amendment being the most obvious example).

Behind the scenes, however, Nancy Reagan was becoming a more important campaign adviser. Not only did she know her husband better than anyone else—how much rest he needed, that he was better early in the day than later in the day, and so on—but she also was assuming a more active role with campaign personnel. For example, she was a strong supporter of John Sears (who had taken the time to cultivate her) for campaign director. She did not support Lynn Nofziger, a longtime Reagan supporter, who as head of Citizens for Reagan had raised millions of dollars for the campaign but, she felt, had not served her husband very well in California. As a result, Sears gained control of the campaign, and Nofziger was limited to coordinating the campaign effort in California.

Although the 1976 campaign was not successful, it resulted in the Reagan team's being better prepared for the 1980 campaign. During the 1980 campaign Mrs. Reagan's involvement in selection of campaign personnel became even more apparent. In the campaign's early days, she intervened to settle an ongoing battle for control of the campaign between Lynn Nofziger and John Sears, the official campaign director. With her support, Sears remained head of the campaign.

When John Sears found himself at loggerheads with longtime Reagan aide Michael Deaver, Mrs. Reagan arranged a meeting of Sears, Deaver, and her husband at the Reagans' home to try and reconcile their differences. When the differences could not be resolved, Michael Deaver left the campaign. Ironically, however, John Sears's position in the campaign became less secure. In challenging Deaver, he took on one of the few people in the campaign who, Mrs. Reagan felt, understood her husband almost as well as she did. Thus, when Ronald Reagan lost the Iowa caucuses to George Bush and fell behind Bush in the New Hampshire polls, both Reagans felt that Sears had to be removed. Soon John Sears was gone from the campaign and Michael Deaver and Lynn Nofziger were back.

After Ronald Reagan won the Republican nomination but made some opening blunders in the general election campaign, Mrs. Reagan insisted that a more centralized campaign command structure was needed. As a result, Stuart Spencer, who had guided the Reagan gubernatorial campaigns, was approached about directing the Reagan presidential campaign. Knowing Nancy Reagan's important role in the campaign, the first thing he wanted to know was whether she wanted him. Assured that she did, he signed on and helped lead the campaign to a successful conclusion. Mrs. Reagan played such a prominent role in the campaign that some political insiders wondered about her impact as First Lady, not only on personnel but also on policy.

To those outside the 1980 campaign, however, Mrs. Reagan's role seemed much the same as ever. She gave the same question-and-answer sessions she had always given. Occasionally, when the need was especially great, she would make a speech, but she was clearly most content to be by her husband's side at rallies, dinners, and receptions—always well groomed and usually smiling graciously.

As in 1976, when her "opponent" had been Betty Ford, Nancy Reagan sought to underline the differences between herself and First Lady Rosalynn Carter. When asked by the press whether she intended to have as substantive a role in policy decisions as Mrs. Carter, Mrs. Reagan replied that she did not think it was proper for First Ladies to sit in on cabinet meetings, and that though her husband sometimes discussed issues with her, she served merely as a sounding board and rarely made any suggestions. In fact, however, her role in the presidential campaign indicated more involvement in the president-elect's affairs than she was willing to admit.

During the campaign, some of the younger (most often female) members of the press corps were often critical of Mrs. Reagan. Some of the criticism had more to do with style than with substance, focusing on the "gaze," the way she sat, the way she presented herself (which some saw as artificial and pretentious), and the deference she paid to her husband. She was also criticized for her unwillingness to address issues of substance—particularly women's issues.

Fortunately for the Reagan campaign, such criticism did not affect the outcome of the election, and in November 1980, Ronald Reagan won a decisive victory over President Jimmy Carter.

Although Mrs. Reagan was First Lady for two presidential terms (the first women since Mamie Eisenhower to be First Lady for that long), her impact on the position will probably not be judged as being of major historical significance. For example, her only "first" as First Lady was the minor claim to being the first First Lady to cohost a morning television talk show. What was most interesting and important about Mrs. Reagan's years as First Lady was the prolonged national debate that took place over the proper role of a First Lady, with her performance being either praised or condemned, depending on how the position of First Lady was defined.

During the 1980s, it seemed as if the nation could not make up its mind about what kind of First Lady it desired. Some Americans clearly desired an activist First Lady, and early in President Reagan's first term, his wife made these people long for Eleanor Roosevelt or Rosalynn Carter. Other Americans desired a First Lady who supported her husband but stayed out of politics, limiting herself to "safe" causes and hosting White House affairs. Ironically, by the end of President Reagan's second term, Mrs. Reagan would make these people yearn for Mamie Eisenhower or Jacqueline Kennedy.

As a result, Nancy Reagan spent much of her time embroiled in controversy over her actions as First Lady. Her problems began with the inauguration. The Reagans planned a very different inauguration from that of the Carters, which had a "common man's," folksy, down-home air. Instead, they organized an inauguration of elegance and style. The Reagans, who had staged the most expensive inauguration in Sacramento's history, attempted to do the same for Washington, D.C. The Republican National Committee pumped more than $5 million into the Reagan inauguration. Free events (more than twenty at the Carter inauguration) disappeared, nor were there any $20 tickets for the Inaugural Ball, as there had been four years earlier. Tickets for the Reagan Inaugural Ball ranged from $100 for standing room to $2,000–$3,000 for a seat. The total cost of the inauguration exceeded $16 million.

Washington society's initial reaction to the Reagans was very favorable. In many ways, the Carters had never conformed to official Washington's image of a president and a First Lady. Suddenly high fashion, opulent dinners, limousines, and the flaunting of wealth were in style. Letitia Baldrige, chief of staff and social secretary for Jackie Kennedy and longtime Washington insider, helped the transition by introducing the Reagans to the Washington social scene and overseeing the selection of Mrs. Reagan's staff.

The press also got caught up in the excitement of the inauguration and the arrival of Mrs. Reagan at the White House. Prior to the inauguration, leading news

magazines such as *Time*, *Newsweek*, and *US News & World Report*, as well as personality magazines such as *People*, reported Mrs. Reagan's plans to bring style back to the White House. No detail was too small to be ignored. Stories were written on the types of gowns the First Lady preferred (by designers James Galanos and Bill Blass), the style of her hair (lightly frosted by Monsieur Mark), her decorator (Los Angeles interior decorator Ted Graber), and her closest friends (best represented by Betsy Bloomingdale)—all described as world-class partygoers and -givers, and as movers and shakers in California society.

For Mrs. Reagan, whose stated preference in First Ladies leaned toward Jacqueline Kennedy, style and elegance were an essential part of fulfilling the role. When she received her tour of the White House from Rosalynn Carter, she felt that the official presidential residence was drab, dreary, and uninviting—not at all a place fit for entertaining the heads of other countries. Therefore, Mrs. Reagan set out to refurbish the White House raising funds through private donations. The First Lady also decided that the White House china, which was cracked and missing many pieces, needed to be replaced. This was paid for primarily through private donations.

However, elegance can easily cross over into elitism, and the First Lady was soon subjected to a barrage of criticism for being ostentatious. The press that had been so enthusiastic about the Reagan style ran stories criticizing Mrs. Reagan. For example, the cost of the redecorating of the White House, being paid for by private donations, quickly exceeded $800,000. With much of the donated money being tax deductible (in the 50 percent tax bracket), money was indirectly being spent from the public treasury. The same could be said for the $200,000 spent on new china.

The heaviest criticism was directed at Mrs. Reagan's expensive taste in clothing (such as the $5,000 gown worn for the Inaugural Ball). It was widely reported that she had accepted an unspecified number of gowns on loan from her favorite designers and that she had not returned them. This was a departure from the practice of previous First Ladies, and the Internal Revenue Service investigated whether the practice violated the Ethics in Government Act.

In response, Mrs. Reagan noted that wearing gowns donated by prominent fashion designers was a common European practice, and would be good advertising for the American fashion industry. To stop the criticism, she said that she would donate the gowns to notable American fashion museums. In reality, though, after very publicly donating a couple of gowns, Nancy Reagan returned to her previous habits.

A *Newsweek* poll published on December 21, 1981, provides evidence that the general public was equally unhappy with the First Lady. It showed that she had about the same public approval rating as Mrs. Carter at the low point of the Carter presidency (26 percent for Mrs. Reagan versus Mrs. Carter's 19 percent), and that 62 percent of those polled thought that Mrs. Reagan put too much emphasis on style and elegance, given the country being in a recession at the time. In addition, 61 percent felt that she was less sympathetic to the problems of the poor and disadvantaged than other First Ladies had been. However, the White House claimed that the public was not nearly as concerned about these issues as the press, and indeed, there was some support for their position in the same poll. For example, 57 percent of the respondents generally approved (versus 26 percent disapproving) of the way Mrs. Reagan was handling the job of First Lady.

The White House staff became concerned about the "Nancy problem" and the possible negative effect she might have on the president's reelection chances in 1984. Soon the president's closest advisers met to discuss methods of rehabilitating Mrs. Reagan's negative image. Their first conclusion was that she would have to keep contact with her fun-loving California crowd to a minimum and tone down the parties, designer dresses, and traveling hairdressers.

Second, she would have to make an effort to cultivate the press. The first step

in this effort occurred on March 29, 1982, when the First Lady appeared on stage at the annual Gridiron Dinner dressed in old, ill-fitting, ragged clothes and sang a self-deprecating song (set to the tune of "Secondhand Rose") about wearing secondhand clothes. The press reviews of her performance, focusing on her ability to poke fun at herself, were extremely favorable.

Third, Mrs. Reagan had to find a cause—something that would show her serious and caring side. In fairness to the First Lady, she had been involved in the antidrug cause, the servicemen missing in action, and the Foster Grandparent program before reaching the White House. The White House seized upon her antidrug efforts as a way to help improve her image. By the autumn of 1985, Mrs. Reagan had appeared on twenty-three talk shows to discuss drugs and her "Just Say No" program, cohosted an episode of the television show *Good Morning America* focusing on the drug problem (the first First Lady to cohost such a show), and hosted a two-hour documentary on drug abuse for PBS. Also in 1985 she invited seventeen First Ladies from other countries to a drug summit in Washington and Atlanta. That same year, the Nancy Reagan Drug Abuse Fund was established through the tax-exempt Community Foundation of Greater Washington as a vehicle for raising funds to fight drug abuse. Among the programs supported by the fund was Phoenix House, a residential drug treatment center for teenagers.

The campaign to improve her image worked remarkably well. Mrs. Reagan's press coverage become much more positive—including a cover story in *Time* and an hour-long special on NBC, both very favorable. However, an even more significant change took place in public opinion. A *New York Times*/CBS News poll in January 1985 found that the First Lady's popularity was even greater than the president's (72 percent favorability for Mrs. Reagan versus 62 percent favorability for President Reagan). An NBC News poll found her approval/disapproval ratio at nearly 69 percent to 9 percent. When respondents were asked what they most admired about her, the most frequent response was "she supports the President, and *acts like a First Lady should*" (emphasis added).

In three years, a very well organized public relations campaign emphasizing Mrs. Reagan's more compassionate and caring qualities had erased her earlier elitist image and made her seem much more in touch with the concerns of average Americans. Her involvement in the antidrug cause also provided the First Lady with some seriousness, and helped overcome the still common criticism of her as a political and intellectual lightweight. By 1985, Mrs. Reagan had successfully remade her image to fit the public's perception of a First Lady more closely.

Her staff ably aided Mrs. Reagan in transforming her image. Her press secretary and public relations adviser, Shelia Tate, helped Mrs. Reagan devise a strategy to win over the Washington press. Other members of Mrs. Reagan's staff included the social secretaries Muffie Brandon, Gail Hodges, and Linda Faulkner; chief of protocol Lee Annenberg; and personal assistant Jane Erkenbeck. One position that was difficult to keep filled was Mrs. Reagan's chief of staff. Peter McCoy held the position for several years, but he was blamed for her early negative public image and was dismissed. Another chief of staff, Lee Verstandig (handpicked by Michael Deaver), lasted only four weeks. In truth, Mrs. Reagan preferred to act as her own chief of staff, which greatly diminished the influence of the position.

By the end of President Reagan's second term in office, his wife was accused by many of having too much influence, dominating her husband, and being a "dragon lady." The event that precipitated the controversy occurred in 1987, when President Reagan's chief of staff, Donald T. Regan, was fired (seemingly at the urging of Mrs. Reagan, because she believed that he was not acting in the president's best interest).

Mrs. Reagan has never denied that she thought Donald Regan was not serving the president well, and she did recommend to the president that he be replaced. She also has stated, however, that she did not have the kind of power within the White House

to have Regan removed all by herself. She argued that firing Donald Regan was the president's decision to make; that if it had been up to her, Regan would have been gone much sooner; and that she only gave the president the kind of supportive advice a husband should expect from his wife.

Donald Regan had a different interpretation of the situation. He felt that the First Lady pressured the president to order him to resign, and that she even went so far as to request the help of Michael Deaver and Stuart Spencer in planting negative stories in California papers that the president was sure to read. According to Regan, they also enlisted the aid of William Rogers, former secretary of state, and Robert Strauss, chairman of the Democratic National Committee, to help convince the president that Donald Regan should be dismissed.

The affair touched off a mini firestorm of controversy, with Mrs. Reagan being compared with Edith Wilson, who was accused of running President Woodrow Wilson's affairs during his serious illness. Some members of Congress pointed out that the Regan affair, coming on the heels of the Iran-Contra scandal, only served to confirm that the president was disengaged not only from policy-making but also from the personnel process of his own administration.

Although the timing of the situation worked against Mrs. Reagan, it was precisely Donald Regan's mishandling of the Iran-Contra scandal that was one of the major criticisms the First Lady had of the president's chief of staff. She concluded that he was not giving the president good advice, and that he was more interested in protecting his own image than that of Ronald Reagan.

Although Mrs. Reagan argued in her memoirs that her involvement in the Donald Regan affair was unique, the First Lady had a long history of helping to choose the men and women who would serve her husband. There was the example of her participation in the hiring and firing of key staff during the 1980 presidential campaign. In addition, many important staff members from the Reagan administration have described specific instances of Nancy Reagan's influence in key personnel decisions. For example, she is reported to have vetoed the appointment of Lynn Nofziger as the president's press secretary, and to have played a pivotal role in the switch of William Clark from national security adviser to secretary of the interior, and in the ousting of Raymond Donovan as secretary of labor and of Margaret Heckler as secretary of health and human services.

By this time it was also generally well recognized that Mrs. Reagan exerted a great deal of control over the president's schedule (and in fact had done so since he was governor of California)—not just when the president was recovering from his several surgeries, but also in the scheduling of the Bitburg trip (1985) and the Geneva (1986) and Reykjavik (1986) summits. She has always believed that she knows the personal needs of her husband better than anyone else. One of the best ways she could help him was to ensure that he was not overworked.

In addition to being involved in personnel decisions and scheduling, the First Lady was sometimes accused of managing the president; for example, she surreptitiously supplied him with key phrases when he seemed at a loss for words. The best-known example was the president's "doing everything we can" response (1984) when questioned by the press about what America could do to bring the Soviet Union to the negotiating table on arms control.

An area of Mrs. Reagan's influence that was less well substantiated was the degree to which she became involved in policy issues. Although the Reagans share a core philosophy of conservatism, the First Lady is generally considered to be the more pragmatic. Some biographers suggest that she was responsible for getting the president to soften some of his more conservative ideological positions. She supposedly convinced him to tone down his "evil empire" rhetoric toward the Soviet Union and to aggressively pursue arms control with the Soviets. The First Lady is also thought by many to have urged the president to "back burner" many social issues (such as abortion) that she considered divisive.

What makes it so difficult to judge the exact degree of Mrs. Reagan's influence in her husband's administration is that she tended to exert her influence in the traditional ways of First Ladies—out of the public eye, when she was alone with the president or with his closest and most trusted staff. The Donald Regan case generated so much additional controversy because Mrs. Reagan's influence became much more public and thus nontraditional; it not only made the First Lady seem overinvolved in the administration's affairs, but also made her husband look correspondingly weak at a time when he could least afford it. Thus, to some, Mrs. Reagan had gone well beyond the conventional role of First Ladies—hosting dinners, supporting their husbands, and involving themselves in the appropriate good causes.

While First Lady, Nancy Reagan also had to deal with a number of personal problems that were made much more difficult by her position in the public eye. The most obvious example was John Hinckley's 1981 assassination attempt on her husband. For all the jokes made by President Reagan after he was shot (I'd rather be in Philadelphia, etc.), his situation was much more critical, and his recovery more difficult than the public was led to believe. At the time of the assassination attempt the president, although in very good physical shape, was hardly a young man. He had been shot in the chest with a .22 caliber handgun and had lost a great deal of blood; doctors estimated that if he had arrived at the hospital five minutes later, he might have died. The president had to undergo major surgery to remove the bullet and subsequently developed an infection and fever.

For Mrs. Reagan, who has always been deeply concerned about her husband's health, the situation was a nightmare made worse by the fact that there was so little she could do. She had to face the possibility that the president might not recover—a vividly real scenario for her in the immediate aftermath of the shooting, when she had difficulty getting to see the president or receiving accurate information. Once the president started to recover, Mrs. Reagan took responsibility for his convalescence. She carefully coordinated his image to the press and public, all the while continuing to meet the many demands of her own busy schedule.

Nancy Reagan had to go through much the same trauma again in 1985, when her husband underwent major cancer surgery. Once more the First Lady had to deal with her own fears, manage the president's recovery, coordinate his schedule, stage-manage his image, and keep her own commitments. At the same time, she often saw the details of the president's operation and prognosis for recovery spread across the front pages of newspapers and as lead stories on the nightly television news.

In October 1987, Mrs. Reagan had to face her own medical crisis when doctors found a malignant tumor in her left breast. After being apprised of her options, she decided to undergo a mastectomy. This decision was soon subject to public debate. Critics of her decision argued that a lumpectomy combined with radiation treatments would have been a better choice, and that by choosing a mastectomy, she might have deterred other women from seeking treatment, even though they might be candidates for less traumatic procedures. One doctor even remarked that the First Lady had set the treatment of breast cancer back ten years. Mrs. Reagan deeply resented this criticism, and argued that the choice of treatment for breast cancer is a decision each woman must make for herself. Because she is a compulsive worrier, the First Lady made the choice that gave her the most peace of mind. She was not recommending that every woman make the same decision.

While Mrs. Reagan was First Lady, her parents died—Loyal Davis in 1982 and Edith Davis in 1987, shortly after the First Lady's surgery for breast cancer. Although they had been ill for some time, their deaths (particularly that of her mother) were very difficult for the First Lady.

Creating even more controversy for Mrs. Reagan was her relationship with her children. Even before President Reagan's election in 1980, there had been considerable strain between the Reagans and their children. Nancy Reagan never developed a close relationship with her two stepchildren, Maureen and Michael. As First Lady, her relationship with them was often the subject of media stories. Both President and Mrs. Reagan were criticized in the national press for not making more of an effort to see Michael Reagan's children. Throughout the Reagans' years in the White House, there were indeed extended periods of estrangement between Michael and his parents that kept the latter apart from their grandchildren.

Aside from some of the usual tensions between parents and sons, the Reagans' relationship with Ron, Jr., remained fairly close. A much more difficult and more widely reported relationship was between the Reagans and their daughter Patti Davis, who changed her name from Reagan to distance herself from her father's political views and career. Nancy Reagan notes in her memoirs that the relationship between Patti and herself was strained almost from the beginning. Patti was a headstrong child, and Mrs. Reagan, by her own admission, was an inexperienced mother who often wanted to control her children's lives.

The most difficult point in the family relationship came when Patti published a thinly veiled autobiographical novel titled *Homefront* (1986), whose main characters were a politically ambitious television star and his superficial wife who sacrificed their family for political success. The novel became an immediate topic of numerous press accounts, and the president and First Lady were asked many questions about the book. At the time they claimed not to be bothered by the novel, noting that it was a piece of fiction. However, Mrs. Reagan was deeply wounded by her daughter's portrayal of her family, and it was hard to attempt to reconcile their differences while she was in the White House.

Given the extraordinary press scrutiny of First Ladies in general and of Mrs. Reagan in particular, it is remarkable that the First Lady's interest in astrology remained secret for as long as it did. The general press and public were first made aware of her interest with the 1988 publication of *For the Record: From Wall Street to Washington*, Donald Regan's memoirs of his two years as President Reagan's chief of staff.

Regan describes Mrs. Reagan as relying on a West Coast astrologer named Joan Quigley to provide detailed advice about planning President Reagan's schedule—so much so that nearly every move and decision made by the Reagans during this period was cleared with her. For instance, according to Regan, the First Lady's astrologer influenced the scheduling of the Reagan–Gorbechev Washington summit. After preparing the astrological charts for both men, she determined that 2 P.M. on December 8, 1987, was the most advantageous time for them to sign the intermediate-range nuclear force treaty. Regan asserts that other major events scheduled on the basis of Joan Quigley's advice included the Reykjavik summit, the Bitburg trip, and even the president's surgery in 1985.

In her memoirs, Mrs. Reagan attempted to clarify the situation. She noted that although she had met Joan Quigley as far back as the 1980 presidential campaign, it was not until after President Reagan was shot in 1981 that the First Lady began to rely on her advice. At that point, Joan Quigley demonstrated to Mrs. Reagan that the astrological charts she had prepared foretold that the period around March 30, 1981, would be an extremely dangerous period for the president. Emotionally shaken by the attempt on the president's life, Nancy Reagan began to rely on Quigley's advice, figuring that it was an extra way of ensuring that no harm would come to her husband. She has adamantly argued that at no point during the Reagan administration were political or policy decisions influenced by astrology, that only the president's schedule—which days were good or bad for him and particularly which days were safe for him to travel out of town—was affected.

In hindsight, Mrs. Reagan may be correct in feeling that the story was overplayed. However, the First Lady also has not been completely forthcoming about her interest in astrology. Though she may have relied on Mrs. Quigley's advice only since 1981, both Reagans have always been superstitious, observing such harmless rituals as knocking on wood and never walking under ladders. More to the point, numerous confidants of Mrs. Reagan have noted that she has relied on the advice of astrologers at least since 1967, when her husband was governor of California. In fact, she is reported to have relied heavily on the advice of Jean Dixon, another noted astrologer, until she fell out of favor with Mrs. Reagan and was replaced by Joan Quigley. Ronald Reagan was known to have had his astrological charts regularly done in his acting days, although there is no evidence to suggest that he took them as seriously as his wife did while she was First Lady.

Having survived the great astrology scandal, President and Mrs. Reagan left the White House in January 1989, after George Bush was elected president. They returned to California to live on a Bel Air estate. Mrs. Reagan has kept busy writing her memoirs, serving on the board of directors of Revlon, and pursuing her interest in the antidrug campaign.

Although no longer First Lady, Nancy Reagan has not been able to leave all the controversy behind her. Once the Reagans had left the White House, the Internal Revenue Service began to take a second hard look at the First Lady's practice of accepting dresses, jewelry, and furs from some of the nation's top designers, and keeping many instead of turning them over to fashion museums. The IRS contended that the apparel constituted taxable income, and is reported to have imposed upon President and Mrs. Reagan an estimated $1 million bill for back taxes, interest, and penalties. The matter was settled by the Reagans. The case reportedly was referred to the criminal division of the IRS, which declined to take action.

The specifics of Nancy Reagan's continuing efforts in the antidrug area have generated some controversy, particularly over funding. The core of her antidrug efforts while First Lady, the Nancy Reagan Drug

Abuse Fund, was originally established under the auspices of the Community Foundation of Greater Washington. When the fund was created, the foundation board stipulated that any money raised was the sole property of the foundation. In the autumn of 1988, Community Foundation officials were surprised to find out that Mrs. Reagan no longer wanted them to administer "her" fund. She intended to take all the fund's assets back to California to establish her own charitable foundation, the Nancy Reagan Foundation, which would support grants for community-based programs such as Phoenix House and the "Just Say No" program.

The directors of the Community Foundation felt that, given the stipulations under which the Nancy Reagan Fund was created, any revenues from the fund were technically the property of the Community Foundation. However, they also realized that it was the appeal of the former First Lady's name that raised most of the revenue, and were reluctant to publicly argue the point with her. Therefore, on July 6, 1989, the foundation presented Mrs. Reagan's new foundation with a check for $3,625,674.76. Today, the Nancy Reagan Foundation, with Mrs. Reagan as its executive director, has assets exceeding $4 million.

Within the limits of her new life, Nancy Reagan remains active in the antidrug campaign. In 1995, she and former drug czar William Bennett testified before the House Subcommittee on Government Reform and Oversight. They stated that in their opinion, the gains made by antidrug forces during the late 1980s and early 1990s were being eroded by the lack of a strong antidrug message from the Clinton administration. In 1997, Nancy Reagan was awarded the International Child Care Award for her efforts in the "Just Say No" program.

The most significant problem Mrs. Reagan has faced since leaving Washington has been her husband's diagnosis with Alzheimer's disease. In 1995, she and her husband announced that they had joined with the national Alzheimer's Association to establish the Ronald and Nancy Reagan Research Institute. It is designed to expand on the Alzheimer's Association's existing programs to bring together leading scientific minds from around the world and drug and biotechnology companies to speed information exchange and find treatments, preventions, and cures.

President Reagan's condition has continued to decline, and the former First Lady has taken on the exhausting role of full-time caregiver. She watches over her husband with the same protective eye as when he was president. Friends describe her as often mentally exhausted, under a great deal of strain, and frequently lonely.

Nancy Reagan has even become a surrogate speaker for her husband, appearing on his behalf at important functions. In 1996 she addressed the Republican National Convention and received a very warm reception from the delegates. In 1997 she spoke for him at the dedication of the George Bush Presidential Library.

The period in which Nancy Reagan was First Lady was historically important in helping define that institution. A fascinating debate was played out in the press and in the minds of the public as to exactly what role a First Lady should play. Nancy Reagan herself will probably not be considered among the most important First Ladies. She did not seek to expand the duties of the position by taking on new responsibilities, like the legislative efforts of Lady Bird Johnson, nor did she attempt to use the position as a "bully pulpit" to address political issues that she thought were crucial, as Betty Ford had done. Nancy Reagan's most visible effort to become involved—her "Just Say No" program—seemed as much designed to improve her own image as to reduce drug abuse.

Only lately had it become clear how politically important Mrs. Reagan was in the affairs of her husband's administration. The most recent histories of the Reagan presidency are unanimous in noting her influence on at least some of the key personnel decisions in the Reagan White House and her impact on the president's schedule. In addition, there is a growing consensus that Mrs. Reagan informally exerted substantial influence regarding some policy decisions. For example, she felt that social issues such as abortion and school prayer were politically unpopular, and that the president should emphasize economic issues instead. Nancy Reagan also wanted her husband's legacy to include peace with the Soviet Union, and with Michael Deaver and George Schultz, she argued strongly for new arms control negotiations.

In a 1988 poll of historians about First Ladies, Nancy Reagan ranked ahead only of Mary Lincoln. But as the histories of the Reagan administration are written and read, her standing will undoubtedly improve, and she will be seen as one of the more interesting and controversial presidential wives of the twentieth century.

BIBLIOGRAPHICAL ESSAY

Nancy Reagan's papers are currently stored at the Reagan Library, 40 Presidential Drive, Simi Valley, California. Though her personal papers are not available, the library does make available many official records pertaining to the Office of the First Lady, including the records of many staff members and materials related to her antidrug campaign. All Reagan Library materials related to Nancy Reagan are available under the Freedom of Information Act (in accordance with the 1978 Presidential Records Act). Carl Anthony, "She Saves Everything: The Papers of Nancy Reagan," in *Modern First Ladies*, ed. Nancy Kegan Smith and Mary C. Ryan (Washington, D.C., 1989), discusses the voluminous nature and possible contents of Mrs. Reagan's personal papers.

Mrs. Reagan's first autobiography, *Nancy* (New York, 1980), deals primarily with her life before Ronald Reagan ran for governor. Her second autobiography, *My Turn: The Memoirs of Nancy Reagan* (New York, 1989), though not completely accurate historically, provides the First Lady's perspective on such areas of controversy as her image and relationship with the press, her relations with her children, her interest in astrology, and her overall role in the Reagan presidency.

Though there are no biographies of Mrs. Reagan based on her personal papers, those which do exist include Chris Wallace's *First Lady: A Portrait of Nancy Reagan* (New York, 1986); Frances Spatz Leighton's *The Search for the Real Nancy Reagan* (New York, 1987); and, by far the most controversial, Kitty Kelley's *Nancy Reagan: The Unauthorized Biography* (New York, 1991). Kelley's book is exhaustively researched, but clearly slanted against Mrs. Reagan and loosely sourced. Mrs. Reagan has published, *I Love You, Ronnie: The Letters of Ronald Reagan to Nancy Reagan* (New York, 2000).

Biographies of both Ronald and Nancy Reagan include Laurence Leamer's *Make Believe: The Story of Ronald and Nancy Reagan* (New York, 1983) and Bill Adler's *Ronald and Nancy: A Very Special Love Story* (New York, 1985). President Reagan's memoirs, *Ronald Reagan: An American Life* (New York, 1990), describe the extraordinarily close relationship of the president and First Lady, but provide few details on her influence.

Many of the memoirs of members of the Reagan administration—including Michael Deaver's *Behind the Scenes* (New York, 1987); Donald T. Regan's *For the Record: From Wall Street to Washington* (New York, 1988); and Larry Speakes's *Speaking Out* (New York, 1988)—provide much insight into Nancy Reagan's role in the Reagan White House.

Three of the Reagan children—Patti Davis in *Homefront* (New York, 1986), Michael Reagan in *Outside Looking In* (New York, 1988), and Maureen Reagan in *First Father, First Daughter* (Boston, 1989)—provide limited insights into their complex relationships with their mother/stepmother.

Works that attempt to place the former First Lady in a larger cultural context include Garry Wills, *Reagan's America: Innocents at Home* (New York, 1985); and James G. Benze, Jr., "Nancy Reagan: China Doll or Dragon Lady," *Presidential Studies Quarterly* vol. 20, no. 4 (Fall 1990): 777–790.

Recent histories of the Reagan presidency—such as William Pemberton, *Exit with Honor* (Armonk, N.Y., 1997); Deborah Hart Strober and Gerald S. Strober, *Reagan: The Man and His Presidency* (Boston, 1998); Dinesh D'Souza, *Ronald Reagan: How an Ordinary Man Became an Extraordinary Leader* (New York, 1997); and James M. Strock, *Reagan on Leadership* (Roseville, Calif., 1998)—devote considerable effort to assessing Nancy Reagan's impact on her husband's presidency. Their overall conclusion is that she had more influence than is generally acknowledged, particularly in convincing President Reagan to begin a dialogue on arms reduction with the Soviet Union.

★★★　　★★★

Barbara Pierce Bush

(1925–)

First Lady: 1989–1993

Myra Gutin

Barbara Pierce was born in New York City on June 8, 1925, the third of four children born to Marvin Pierce and Pauline Robinson Pierce. The Pierces were socially prominent in affluent Rye, New York. Barbara's great-great-great-uncle was President Franklin Pierce (1853–1857); her mother was the daughter of an Ohio Supreme Court justice. At the time of Barbara's birth, Marvin Pierce was the assistant to the publisher of the McCalls publishing company; by 1946 he had risen to president of the company.

The four Pierce children were strongly influenced by their mother. They developed a love of reading and learned to care about the feelings of other people. Pauline Pierce, a cultured woman with many interests, was

an avid gardener, and a collector of china, antiques, and furniture. Barbara thought that Pauline was a very good mother; unfortunately, the two did not enjoy a positive relationship. However, Barbara's relationship with her father was affectionate and warm.

Barbara attended public school through sixth grade, the private Rye Country Day School for the next four years, and was then sent to Ashley Hall, an exclusive boarding school in Charleston, South Carolina, for her final two years of high school. She was popular and happy at Ashley Hall, and participated in the student council and drama club.

During Christmas break in 1941, her junior year at Ashley Hall, Barbara attended a dance at the Round Hill Country Club in

Greenwich, Connecticut. George Herbert Walker Bush, also called "Poppy" (a family nickname; George was named in honor of his maternal grandfather), a senior at Phillips Academy, spotted Barbara across the room and asked a friend for an introduction to the slender young woman with reddish-brown hair. Barbara was immediately attracted to George and later recalled that her future husband was so attractive and charismatic that when he was in the room, she had difficulty breathing. Bush was equally enamored of Barbara, and the couple spent much of the evening becoming acquainted.

Barbara and George saw each other the next evening at another dance, and George asked Barbara for a date. After Christmas vacation, Barbara returned to Ashley Hall with stories about Poppy Bush. The couple began an ardent and voluminous correspondence. Her Ashley Hall friends observed that Barbara was in love with her new beau.

The relationship was overshadowed by World War II. George was accepted at Yale, but decided to defer his admission and enlist in the U.S. Navy. Shortly after graduation from Phillips Academy he left for preflight training at Chapel Hill, North Carolina. Barbara and George saw little of each other for the next ten months as Barbara was completing her senior year in high school and George was sent to Minnesota and Texas for further flight training. Their correspondence continued unabated. In June 1943, Barbara graduated from Ashley Hall and George was commissioned an ensign after completing his training as a navy pilot.

Home on leave, George invited "Bar" to spend time with him at his family's summer home at Kennebunkport, Maine. At the conclusion of seventeen days together they told their families that they intended to be married. In spite of their youth (Barbara was eighteen, George nineteen), neither family opposed the marriage, since George was scheduled to be shipped overseas and Barbara was about to embark upon her freshman year at Smith College.

Reflecting on her first year at Smith, Barbara later told reporters that she wouldn't want to have anyone look at her grades; she was much more involved in playing sports—she was captain of the freshman soccer team—and having fun than in academic pursuits. Later she admitted that at that time, she wasn't very interested in education, she was just interested in George Bush.

Barbara and George became formally engaged in December 1943. They set a wedding date for December 19, 1944. A few months later, George shipped out to join a fighter squadron in the South Pacific.

Barbara returned to Smith for her sophomore year, but dropped out shortly after the start of the semester. She was preoccupied with her upcoming wedding. Years later she would come to regret her decision to leave college, but at the moment, it seemed the right thing to do.

George Bush began flying missions against the Japanese in March 1944. On September 2 of that year his plane was shot down over Chichi Jima, one of the Bonin Islands. He was rescued by a U.S. submarine and was out of touch with his family and Barbara for a month. Bush's parents were told that their son was missing in action; they sought to keep the news from Barbara. Barbara was already worried because she hadn't received a letter from George in a long time. She was vastly relieved when Dorothy Bush called to inform her that George was alive and well after his ordeal.

Bush's squadron was rotated home for holiday leave, and he arrived in Greenwich on Christmas Eve. The young navy pilot had missed his wedding day but the nuptials were rescheduled, and George Bush and Barbara Pierce were married on January 6, 1945. Mrs. Bush has since stated that her marriage was the turning point in her life.

After a honeymoon in Sea Island, Georgia, Bush rejoined his squadron to receive further training for the final assault on Japan. He moved from Florida to Michigan to Maine to Virginia. Barbara Bush joined him wherever she could, and lived in constant dread that his squadron would be called up to take part in the Japanese action. Both Bushes were grateful when President

Truman announced Japan's surrender and the end of World War II on August 14, 1945. Because of his distinguished combat record (fifty-eight sorties), Bush was in one of the first groups to be released from active duty in September 1945.

A few weeks later, the Bushes set up housekeeping in New Haven, Connecticut, so that George Bush could begin his long-delayed college education at Yale University. With thousands of returning servicemen, he was able to enroll in a special program that would allow him to graduate in less than three years. The respite at Yale was a happy time for the young couple. Money was tight, for they were living on funds that George Bush had saved from his military paychecks. To bolster their finances, Mrs. Bush worked at the Yale Coop—the campus store—until the birth of their first child, George Walker Bush, Jr., in July 1946. The elder Bush did well academically and socially at Yale, graduating Phi Beta Kappa, serving as captain of the varsity baseball team (Barbara Bush was the official team scorekeeper) and as president of Delta Kappa Epsilon fraternity, and being inducted into the secretive and exclusive Skull and Bones Senior Society. Both Bushes became active in the United Negro College Fund, which George Bush headed on the Yale campus.

Barbara Bush had always assumed that she and her husband would settle down in New England, not far from the Bush and Pierce families, and raise their own children. However, her husband became excited by tales of fortunes to be made in the oil and gas business in Texas. In the fall of 1948, therefore, he headed south to Odessa, Texas, and his first job as an equipment clerk with the International Derrick and Equipment Company (Ideco). His wife and young son soon followed. Barbara Bush, at first reluctant to leave the East, later reflected that the move was probably good for her marriage and that she and her husband were forced to grow up quickly.

After a year in Odessa, Bush was promoted to a drilling-bit salesman and the family moved to California. The nomadic life continued as they lived in Huntington Park, Bakersfield, Whittier, Ventura, and Compton. It was also during this time that the Bushes experienced a tragic loss. In October 1949, Pauline Pierce was killed in a freak accident when her husband swerved his car to avoid spilling a cup of hot coffee that his wife had placed on the front seat. Marvin Pierce lost control of the car and slammed into a stone wall. He sustained broken ribs and facial contusions; Pauline died instantly. Concern for his daughter's health prompted Pierce to persuade Barbara Bush, seven months pregnant with her second child, not to fly east for her mother's funeral. Many years later, Mrs. Bush told an interviewer that she regretted not attending her mother's funeral or spending time with her father during his convalescence. In December 1949, Pauline Robinson ("Robin") Bush, named in memory of her maternal grandmother, was born.

Dresser Industries, the parent company of Ideco, moved the Bushes back to Midland, Texas. A few months after his return, Bush and a friend set up their own oil firm, the Bush-Overbey Oil Development Company, with financial help from Bush's uncle. By 1953, the company had merged with another independent oil firm to become Zapata Petroleum.

Both George and Barbara Bush understood that they came from privileged backgrounds and had been taught that from whom much is given, much is expected. Perhaps for that reason, they became active in the Midland community, starting the YMCA, establishing three banks, and raising funds for the United Way and Cancer Crusade. Both taught Sunday school at the local Presbyterian church. The Bush family welcomed a third child, John Ellis ("Jeb") Bush, born in 1953.

When Jeb was a few months old, Mrs. Bush noticed that three-year old Robin was tired and listless. A checkup by the pediatrician revealed that the child had an acute case of leukemia. The doctor told the Bushes that Robin had only a few weeks to live; they were advised not to treat the disease and to let the child die peacefully. Her parents instead chose an aggressive course of action. Robin was admitted to Memorial Sloan-Kettering Cancer Institute in New York and, although she received the most up-to-date drug therapies, she died in October 1953 after lingering for seven months.

The Bushes were devastated. Three decades later Mrs. Bush recalled that she nearly fell apart, so intense was her grief. She remembered that she had been the strong one during Robin's illness, but after their daughter's death, it was George Bush who gave his wife strength, refusing to let her withdraw, and helping her to grieve and share their loss. They received strong support from friends, neighbors, family, and their two young sons. There would always be reminders of Robin; in particular, Mrs. Bush's reddish-brown hair turned white as a result of the ordeal. Over time their depression lifted. The change was aided in large measure by their rapidly expanding family: Neil Mallon was born in 1955, Marvin Pierce was born in 1956, and Dorothy ("Doro") Walker was born in 1959.

The child-rearing years of the 1950s and 1960s were arduous for Barbara Bush. Her husband was away much of the time building his business, and she was charged with the myriad tasks involved with running a home and rearing children. While generally content with the children, Barbara Bush acknowledged that she was "dormant" during this era of diapers, constant trips to the pediatrician, and countless Little League games.

Neighbors and old friends were of the opinion that Barbara Bush was supermom. Hers was the house where the neighborhood kids congregated. She was also the family disciplinarian, screaming at and occasionally spanking one of the children if she felt the situation warranted such action. Firm yet loving, Barbara Bush created a home filled with caring and warmth. There was a price to be paid, of course; there were times when Barbara was lonely and thought that she would scream if the children didn't say something intelligent. Occasionally she felt resentful and jealous of her husband, rarely home, who seemed to be having a wonderful time traveling around the world,

developing opportunities. An astute businessman, Bush enjoyed the success he had hoped to achieve in Texas. By his late thirties, George Bush was a millionaire.

A special challenge confronted Mrs. Bush when her son Neil was diagnosed with dyslexia. For years she worked tirelessly to help him overcome his reading problems. Many observers have suggested that it was this experience that sparked Mrs. Bush's interest in literacy, although she claims that this was not the case. It simply seemed to her that things would be better if people could read, write, and comprehend.

The year 1959 saw the Bushes leave Midland for Houston. In 1962, local Texas Republicans asked Bush to run for chairman of the Harris County Republican Party. The Bush family had a tradition of public service (George's father, Prescott Bush, Sr., was a U.S. senator from Connecticut) and George Bush was eager to continue that tradition. The campaign for chairman was rough and dirty as the Bushes barnstormed through all of Harris County's 189 precincts. During this time, Bush discovered a previously hidden asset—his wife. Barbara Bush enjoyed politics. Her warmth and extroverted personality played well on the campaign trail; she was adept at small talk and rarely forgot a name. However, untrue or unfair statements provoked immediate and sometimes caustic responses from Mrs. Bush. She had to learn to control herself, to hold back. Years later she would comment that not only was she outspoken, but she was also honest—not the optimum mix for an aspiring politician's wife. Nevertheless, Bush was elected chairman of the Harris County Republican Party.

Bush lost his bid for the U.S. Senate in 1964, the year of Lyndon Johnson's presidential landslide. The defeat did nothing to dampen his enthusiasm for politics. In 1966, he was elected to the U.S. House of Representatives; he was reelected in 1968. In 1970, Bush made another attempt at winning a Senate seat. Despite enthusiastic support from President Richard Nixon, Bush was defeated again. Over the next decade, however, he was appointed to a variety of posts in the Nixon and Ford administrations, including ambassador to the United Nations (1971–1973), chairman of the Republican National Committee (1973–1974), U.S. envoy to China (1974–1975), and director of the Central Intelligence Agency (1976–1977).

Mrs. Bush was an enthusiastic political wife and perfect helpmate. While a congressional wife she had begun to hone her skills in public speaking by assembling a slide show on the gardens of Washington, D.C.; the presentation was given to Texas constituents and other groups. Public speaking did not come easily, however; a former staff member recalled that Mrs. Bush's knees would knock, but she persisted, working hard on the substance and delivery of remarks. She also wrote a monthly newspaper column discussing current issues for her husband's Seventh Congressional District constituents.

As the U.S. ambassador to the United Nations, Bush lived in the ambassador's official residence in the Waldorf Towers at the Waldorf-Astoria Hotel in New York City. There, Mrs. Bush entertained, attended sessions of the General Assembly, and did volunteer work at the Memorial Sloan-Kettering Cancer Institute.

Mrs. Bush reportedly opposed her husband's decision to accept the chairmanship of the Republican National Committee in 1973. Watergate had plunged the party and the country into near social and political upheaval, and Mrs. Bush felt that her husband should avoid the quagmire and maintain the country's perception that he was a statesman. Bush, ever the party loyalist, believed that Republicans needed him to coordinate efforts at damage control. He accepted the assignment.

In 1974, as a reward for his efforts in behalf of his party, President Ford selected Bush to head the U.S. Liaison Office in Beijing. Barbara Bush adored China; it was her favorite of all her husband's posts. Much like Lou Henry Hoover, a former First Lady who had lived in China at the beginning of the century, the Bushes traveled as much as they could—usually by bicycle—studied Chinese, and immersed themselves in the

country's art, history, and culture. This time together was so special that the Bushes were reluctant to return to Washington when President Ford summoned Bush to head the Central Intelligence Agency (CIA).

The CIA assignment was especially difficult for Mrs. Bush. She had loved China and had hoped to have more time there. In addition, the Bush "nest" was empty—all the children were out of the house and involved in their own endeavors. Security restrictions at the new job made it impossible for the couple to discuss many of George Bush's activities. Moreover, the women's movement was in high gear, stressing professional achievement, and Mrs. Bush felt like a failure. She felt that her work was devalued—even denigrated—in the prevailing social climate; all she had done since her marriage to George Bush thirty years before—raising five children and providing emotional support for her husband—was thought to be of dubious value. She was depressed for months but never consulted a physician, resolving to tackle the problems on her own. She threw herself into volunteer work, devoting hundreds of hours to the Washington Home—a hospice where she did all types of jobs, from washing patients' hair to changing bedclothes. Capitalizing on her China experiences, Barbara Bush assembled a slide show on the country that she presented to various audiences; her speaker's fees were donated to charity. Eventually, with her husband's help and understanding, she came to believe that she had made the right decision in deciding to be a homemaker and helpmate.

In 1979, George Bush declared his intention to run for the Republican nomination for president. For much of 1979 and until her husband withdrew from the presidential race in May 1980, Mrs. Bush and the rest of the Bush family were on the road trying to help him achieve his dream.

Mrs. Bush, usually accompanied by a single aide, flew on commercial airliners and barnstormed through every state but Alaska. As the wife of an almost unknown politician (despite Bush's many Washington posts), she worked continuously to increase name recognition among the nation's Republicans. Sometimes she attended five or six events a day; she was away from home for weeks at a time. Initially she presented her China slide show to audiences as a way to introduce them to George Bush. Later, she went on to give more formal campaign discourses. As a result of the campaign, Mrs. Bush became an engaging, polished public speaker.

During this time, Barbara Bush learned to deal with unending, sometimes hurtful criticism. People frequently ridiculed her size and her white hair. On one occasion, according to biographer Pamela Kilian, at a fund-raiser where Bush's mother Dorothy was present, someone came up to Barbara and introduced her to another guest as George Bush's mother. During the 1988 presidential campaign, *Saturday Night Live* presented a skit that dramatized this supposedly funny incident for a national audience. Reportedly, Barbara Bush failed to appreciate the humor.

George Bush emerged the victor in the 1980 Iowa caucuses and his campaign seemed to pick up momentum, but he ran a distant second to former California governor Ronald Reagan in the New Hampshire primary and many other state contests. In late May, Bush announced that Reagan had sewn up the nomination and that he was dropping out of the race.

Both George and Barbara Bush professed surprise when Reagan offered Bush the number two spot on the national ticket. Mrs. Bush, who was delighted for her husband, learned almost immediately that she would have to submerge her own opinions (pro–Equal Rights Amendment, and purportedly pro-choice) and ideas, and support the Republican platform and Ronald Reagan. She did this willingly and, once again, took to the hustings as she had done during the primaries. In November, the Reagan–Bush ticket overwhelmed President Jimmy Carter and Vice President Walter Mondale.

In January 1981, when Bush assumed the vice presidency, Barbara Bush was a seasoned political veteran with almost twenty years of experience. She announced that her national project would be a cause dear to her heart—literacy. She had worked to increase national literacy for many years, and she believed that the root of many of America's problems was the inability to read.

During Bush's eight years as vice president, Barbara Bush participated in over 500 literacy events all over the United States. In addition, she performed requisite political duties: appearances before visiting groups, meetings with Republicans, official entertaining, and travel. She also continued her charity work.

During the 1984 Reagan–Bush reelection effort, Barbara Bush functioned in much the same manner as she had in 1980. This time, however, she campaigned as the wife of the vice president. There were no more commercial flights and carrying her own bags through airports. Her cause and her hair had become well known to the public. She was universally well liked, and her speeches generated larger, more enthusiastic audiences.

One incident that occurred during the campaign demonstrated that Mrs. Bush could become testy when she felt that her husband was the target of unfair criticism. Barbara Bush became annoyed with Democratic vice presidential nominee Geraldine Ferraro, who had told reporters that the Bush family wealth insulated them from the problems of most Americans. Barbara Bush told reporters that Ferraro's family was probably more affluent than the Bushes and she couldn't say the word that best described Ferraro, but it rhymed with rich. The story received national coverage. Mrs. Bush later telephoned Mrs. Ferraro to apologize for the crack. In November, the Reagan–Bush ticket was reelected by a wide margin.

George Bush took center stage in 1988 as he emerged from Ronald Reagan's shadow to make his own run for the presidency. With Indiana senator Dan Quayle as his vice presidential running mate, Bush led the national electoral effort against Massachusetts governor Michael Dukakis and Texas senator Lloyd Bentsen (who had defeated Bush for the Texas Senate seat in 1970).

The 1988 presidential campaign saw Barbara Bush again turn to the slide show to introduce her family to the voters. She toured the country with a collection of pictures showing the Bush family in Maine, enjoying the grandchildren; George Bush standing at the Great Wall of China, and meeting with world leaders. She told reporters that she wouldn't be involved in policy-making like Rosalynn Carter, nor would she seek to influence presidential decision-making. She would tell her husband what was on her mind—she always had—but she did not feel it was incumbent upon her to tell the press when they disagreed. She was reticent about addressing policy questions on the campaign trail and demurred, saying that she didn't mind discussing the issues but didn't feel particularly well informed about them.

Barbara Bush campaigned throughout the primaries both with and without her husband. At the 1988 Republican National Convention she was introduced to the delegates through a video presentation, then gave a speech to educate them about the human side of George Bush, his family, and his values. Reporters had written that the Bushes weren't physically demonstrative in public and that the Dukakises were perceived as being much warmer. The Bushes countered by holding hands, smiling at one another, and touching more frequently. The strategy seemed to pay dividends, and the "affection gap" narrowed.

In October, less than three weeks prior to the election, a rumor circulated through both campaigns that the *Washington Post* was about to publish a story about George Bush's alleged extramarital affair with a former staff member. When Barbara Bush heard the story, she told campaign staffers that it was ridiculous and to disregard it. She expressed surprise that campaign strategists were even disturbed by the rumor. To reporters she quipped that Mr. Bush couldn't stay up past ten o'clock. When the story persisted, Mrs. Bush abandoned humor and labeled the charges malicious and vicious. The Bush campaign dealt with the question by pointing to George Bush, Jr., who told

Newsweek that he had asked his father directly if he had ever been involved in a relationship with another woman. The answer was an emphatic no. The rumor would follow Bush into office and would surface again during the 1992 presidential campaign. However, the charges apparently had little effect on the public; George Bush decisively defeated Governor Dukakis on Election Day.

For eight years Barbara Bush had the opportunity to observe the activities of First Lady Nancy Reagan. The two women were not close; some observers suggested that Mrs. Reagan did not like the Bushes and never invited them to visit upstairs at the White House. Mrs. Bush was unfailingly cordial to the First Family, and did her best to stay in the background and let Mrs. Reagan enjoy the national spotlight. She probably received an education in the ways in which the White House podium might be most effectively utilized—for example, Mrs. Reagan's "Just Say No" project—and what to avoid—china, designer dresses, and astrologers.

If Americans were put off by the Hollywood glamour of Nancy Reagan, they embraced the down-to-earth, size fourteen, faux-pearl-wearing Barbara Bush. By the time she became mistress of 1600 Pennsylvania Avenue, the "Silver Fox" (as she was nicknamed by her children) had already made twenty-nine different homes for her family in seventeen cities. Another departure from the Reagan era became readily apparent when the Bushes announced that their five children and twelve grandchildren would be frequent visitors to the White House. In January 1989, Barbara Bush was well prepared to undertake the duties of First Lady, having served a long internship as the wife of a businessman, congressman, ambassador, head of the CIA, and vice president. She was already associated with a national project. Disciplined and organized, she was equal to the rigors of the office of First Lady.

There was never any question that Barbara Bush's White House project would be literacy. Having worked in the area for years, she was both knowledgeable and committed. In 1988, Mrs. Bush was quoted in the *Chicago Tribune*'s August 14 issue: "Literacy fits in with so many other things. If more people could read, fewer people would have AIDS. There would be less homelessness. I'm absolutely convinced of that." She felt that most of society's ills—crime, violence, drug abuse, teenage pregnancy, and a host of others—flowed from the inability to read.

Barbara Bush told her staff that literacy was her major and volunteerism was her minor. She cared deeply about the volunteerism aspect of the program and believed that it was in keeping with "the thousand points of light" her husband described in his speech accepting the Republican nomination for president. She, too, wanted to work for a kinder, gentler America. Her concern extended to AIDS sufferers, day-care centers, and the homeless. Thousands of people wrote to the First Lady asking what they could do to be part of her literacy program. She wrote back, "Go out and help a neighbor who needs help, then you'll be part of my program."

Shortly after becoming First Lady, Barbara Bush established the Barbara Bush Foundation for Family Literacy—a private, Washington-based concern that solicited grants from public and private organizations to support literacy programs. As honorary chair of the foundation, Mrs. Bush kept track of the literacy programs that applied for and were awarded grants. The First Lady was also a sponsor of Laubach Literacy International and the Business Council for Effective Literacy. Profits from Mrs. Bush's 1984 book *C. Fred's Story* (anecdotes about the Bush family's cocker spaniel) were earmarked for major literacy organizations. A later book written by Mrs. Bush, *Millie's Book* (1990), examined life in the White House from the perspective of Millie, a springer spaniel who was C. Fred's successor. All royalties from the volume (approximately $1 million) were directed to Mrs. Bush's foundation.

Barbara Bush used the national news media to carry her message about literacy.

In September 1990 she began hosting a ten-part Sunday evening radio show titled *Mrs. Bush's Story Hour*, during which she read books to children. The programs, which aired on ABC radio and were carried by many ABC affiliates, were scheduled for a time when children would be most likely to hear the stories. Later, the books that Mrs. Bush had read were sold on audio tape cassettes as part of the "Read Me a Story" collection. In the cassette box, buyers found a reprint of the Barbara Bush Family Foundation tips for reading. The cassettes were sold at department stores and bookstores. The entire program enjoyed great success.

Barbara Bush also appeared on the Oprah Winfrey show to discuss literacy and education with the popular afternoon talk-show host. The First Lady was a great admirer of Winfrey, who was a mentor to young girls; she was giving back to the community, and Mrs. Bush commended her for that. The discussion between the two women kept literacy before the American public. In addition, Barbara Bush wrote an article titled "Parenting's Best-Kept Secret: Reading to Your Children" that appeared in the October 1990 issue of *Reader's Digest*. The piece reached millions of readers.

As First Lady, Mrs. Bush took part in hundreds of literacy events. She traveled to schools, Project Head Start centers, day-care facilities, and General Educational Development (GED) graduations across the nation. When the First Lady visited a location, she told her hosts and hostesses that she wanted to highlight literacy or education, not Barbara Bush. She said, "We're here so that people will know what's going on in their community." Then she would ask her sponsors what they wanted her to tell the press who would write stories about the event, and whether they needed contributions or volunteers. She offered to help them in any way possible.

In the early months of her White House tenure, Mrs. Bush was diagnosed with Graves disease—a thyroid condition that causes double vision and swollen eyes. Treatment consisted of radiation therapy and medication. The problem did little to slow the First Lady's pace. In fact, members of her staff commented on Barbara Bush's great energy and said that she was probably one of the busiest First Ladies ever, delivering several hundred informal and formal speeches. A majority of her discourse was devoted to literacy; even when she wasn't discussing literacy directly, she made reference to her project because she felt that every mention of literacy, every discussion of the issue, heightened people's awareness of the problem.

Barbara Bush told her speechwriters that she wanted her talks to be short and funny, and to leave her listeners with something to remember. Her speeches were a collaborative effort among her chief of staff, press secretary, deputy press secretary, staff members (sometimes the president's speechwriters), and herself. She would make decisions about adding to texts or deleting material. The First Lady practiced her speeches but felt free to ad-lib when she spoke to audiences, frequently including a topical reference. Occasionally she would survey an audience's mood, put aside her prepared text, and speak extemporaneously. Anna Perez, Barbara Bush's former press secretary, commented that Mrs. Bush had perfect comedic timing, and that she could use a pause or silence to build dramatic tension or set off a punch line.

Two speeches during her White House tenure were instrumental in developing and sustaining a national perception of Barbara Bush as a deeply caring individual and the quintessential good sport. Though separated by two years and given for different purposes, the speeches combined the literacy message with Barbara Bush's philosophy of life and, to a lesser extent, administration policy and concerns. The first speech, the commencement address to the Wellesley College class of 1990, took place on June 1, 1990.

The speech had been preceded by controversy. Two months prior to the commencement, 150 students presented Wellesley president Dr. Nanerl Keohane with a petition protesting the selection of Mrs. Bush as commencement speaker. The petition charged that the First Lady had been recognized because of her husband; she did not represent the type of professional woman that the college sought to educate; her designation as graduation speaker, they argued, contradicted the Wellesley experience.

Barbara Bush reacted with calm and graciousness, as she observed in the *New York Times*, on May 4, 1990, that the protesters were twenty-one years old and were "looking at life from that perspective. . . . I don't disagree with what they're looking at." She went on to suggest, however, that she might have some worthwhile ideas to share with the members of the class of 1990. Demonstrating the wry sense of humor and understanding that made her one of the most popular First Ladies of the twentieth century, Mrs. Bush commented, according to author Carl Sferrazza Anthony, "Much ado about nothing. I understand it. Even I was twenty once."

President Bush, questioned about his response to the controversy, underscored his wife's comments by telling reporters that the young women of Wellesley could learn much from his wife's model of unselfishness, her exemplary conduct as a mother, and her advocacy of literacy. Perhaps most important, according to the president, Barbara Bush was "not trying to be something she's not."

Mrs. Bush's appearance went forward as planned. She was accompanied to Massachusetts by Raisa Gorbachev, Russia's First Lady, who was visiting the United States with her husband. Mrs. Bush announced that Mrs. Gorbachev would also have some comments to make to the graduates.

The First Lady used self-deprecating humor and an earnest tone to lecture her listeners. She opened her presentation by noting wryly that she was well aware that she had not been the class of 1990's first choice as commencement speaker: "I know that you wanted [author] Alice Walker, known for *The Color Purple* [she added puckishly, 'Guess how I know?']; instead you got me, known for the color of my hair." Mrs. Bush acknowledged the relatively recent movement toward cultural diversity when she continued her speech: "Diversity like anything else worth having requires effort. Effort to learn about and respect differences, to be compassionate with one another, to cherish our identity and to accept unconditionally the same in others."

Mrs. Bush told the graduates that they should make three important choices: Believe in something larger than yourself; find the joy in life; and cherish human connections with family and friends: "At the end of your life, you will never regret not having passed one more test, not winning one more verdict or not closing one more deal. You will regret time not spent with a husband, a child, a friend or a parent." She concluded her remarks by saying, "Who knows? Somewhere out in this audience may even be someone who will one day follow in my footsteps and preside over the White House as the president's spouse. And I wish him well."

The speech, reported in the *New York Times* on June 2, 1990, was interrupted numerous times by laughter and enthusiastic applause, and drew uniformly favorable responses. Mrs. Bush had risen to the challenge and won over much of her audience. While some remained steadfast in their opposition to the First Lady, a new petition circulated by a group of students and released just prior to the speech commended the selection of Barbara Bush and celebrated "all the unknown women who have dedicated their lives to the service of others." The petition urged Mrs. Bush to take a strong stand on day care, cuts in welfare, and gaps in wages between men and women. Mrs. Bush's speech left no doubt as to the Bush administration position on family values, which would become a major issue in the 1992 presidential campaign.

A second speech, Mrs. Bush's speech to the Republican National Convention in August 1992, developed two major themes: George Bush's worthiness and capability to continue as the nation's chief executive, and family values.

The First Lady's speech was preceded by comments delivered by AIDS activist Mary Fisher and "second lady" Marilyn Quayle.

The atmosphere among the more than 2,000 delegates was unsettled as Mrs. Bush strode to the podium. Fisher had exhorted the convention and the administration to place AIDS at the top of its agenda with a presentation that left listeners teary-eyed.

Mrs. Quayle was the "heavy" of the evening, almost defiantly proclaiming that she had made a decision to leave the practice of law, work in her husband's political campaigns, and raise their children. She told the delegates that most women love being mothers or wives, and that these roles gave life a richness not available through professional accomplishments. Though not mentioned by name, she implied that Hillary Rodham Clinton—an attorney, working mother, and the wife of Democratic presidential nominee Bill Clinton—was a less-than-fit mother and the symbol of antifamily values. Quayle's speech, delivered in a combative tone, energized some but also appalled many of her listeners.

By contrast, Barbara Bush's speech was both conciliatory and calming. She told the convention that their warm welcome made her feel wonderful, "but then I always feel wonderful when I get to talk about the strongest, the most decent, the most caring, the wisest, yes, and the healthiest man I know . . . [George Bush]." Utilizing humor and a touch of sarcasm, she told delegates that something wasn't quite right. After all, they had heard from President Ronald Reagan, President Gerald Ford, Secretary Jack Kemp, Senator Phil Gramm—and Barbara Bush?

Barbara Bush told her listeners that she didn't want to give a speech; instead she wanted to have a conversation about family values. She said, "When we speak of families, we include extended families, the neighbors, even the community itself." Families in the 1990s faced difficult challenges; there was more violence, more crime, and more promiscuity. Still, Mrs. Bush was heartened by many of the families she'd spoken with around the country: "The parents we've met are determined to teach their children integrity, strength, responsibility, sharing, love of God, and pride in being an American. However you define family, that's what we mean by family values." Mrs. Bush's remarks suggested that the Republican Party could accommodate any configuration of family and that the party was the guardian of families.

According to the First Lady, family was the primary concern of Barbara and George Bush. Her five children had been far from perfect, but they still came home. Families were the strength of the country and, she added, "While the White House is important, the country's future is in your house, every house, all over America." Then Mrs. Bush introduced her five children and twelve grandchildren. George P. Bush, the oldest grandchild, added a personal testament about his grandfather as he briefly addressed the convention.

The speech was another triumph for Barbara Bush. It received an enthusiastic reception from convention delegates and garnered positive press reviews. Mrs. Bush's comments didn't have the searing immediacy of Mary Fisher's, nor was she perceived to be abrasive like Marilyn Quayle. She was Barbara Bush, the nation's first grandmother, and defender and protector of family. Of particular interest were the things she chose not to say. There were no veiled references to Hillary Rodham Clinton or to abortion, two topics other convention speakers had found impossible to resist. Mrs. Bush's speech also provided a perfect segue into Labor Secretary Lynn Martin's speech nominating George Bush for a second term in office.

Her immense popularity and her national discussion of family values seemed to justify the First Lady's selection as a speaker at the Republican National Convention. Just prior to the convention, the First Lady had created controversy when she told reporters that abortion did not belong in the party platform. Barbara Bush had long been suspected of harboring pro-abortion sympathies, but she stated that she wasn't either pro or con on the abortion issue. Instead, she said that abortion was a private matter, and should be left out of platforms and conventions.

Barbara Bush had also been critical of Republican national chairman Rich Bond, who had excoriated Hillary Clinton for views on family she had expressed in a journal article. Mrs. Bush told reporters that Bill Clinton, not Hillary, was running for the job of chief executive. A former staff member said that Mrs. Bush thought that criticism of Mrs. Clinton was both wrong and stupid.

Her former chief of staff, Susan Porter Rose, said that Mrs. Bush enjoyed campaigning if it was for George Bush, but that the First Lady was also effective in supporting the candidacies of others. Another staff member asserted that Mrs. Bush understood her responsibilities and discharged them fully. She knew that she was helping George Bush by trying to elect Republican members of Congress. A much sought-after speaker, Barbara Bush campaigned for various Republican candidates during midterm elections. These actions established a precedent; while previous presidential wives had campaigned for their husbands, no other First Lady had campaigned by herself during the off-year elections for members of her husband's party. Her selection as campaigner for members of Congress and other Republicans attested to Mrs. Bush's popularity and political value.

Approximately 30 to 40 percent of Barbara Bush's White House tenure was devoted to ceremonial activities. Her day began at dawn with exercise, reading six newspapers, watching the morning news programs, breakfast, and conversation with her husband. This was followed by planning sessions, speech sessions, and various events including luncheons, teas, and receptions, preferably for non-profit groups. The First Lady believed that a White House tea or reception was an excellent way to raise the visibility of a group. During an average week, Mrs. Bush traveled two or three times to advance literacy and education.

Mrs. Bush bristled at criticism of her family, especially her husband. Arriving at the 1992 Republican National Convention, Mrs. Bush forcefully told reporters to give her son Neil an opportunity to clear his name in the Silverado Savings and Loan scandal. She was furious with Ann Richards (who later became the governor of Texas), who had heaped sarcasm on George Bush in her keynote address to the 1988 Democratic National Convention. She was equally incensed at those who implied that George Bush was a wimp. In spite of her anger and frustration, Barbara Bush was sensitive to the fact than anything she said might reflect on her husband, and she didn't want him to have to expend any of his political capital to clean up after her. Most of the time she deflected comments or refrained from commenting at all. The latter was a reaction to the 1984 Ferraro debacle; she told the press that "the poet laureate has retired."

There is some evidence that the Bushes disagreed, at times, on public policy issues. For example, when a sniper used an assault weapon to shoot and kill five children in a Stockton, California, school yard, Mrs. Bush told the press that she strongly opposed assault weapons. Her statement ran counter to Bush administration policy (Mr. Bush supported assault weapons at that time; later, he would alter his stance). In another instance, Barbara Bush supported the idea of women serving in combat situations if they were qualified to fight (women were prohibited from combat at that time).

Mrs. Bush probably influenced presidential decision-making on a number of issues. Like many of her predecessors, she sent mixed signals, saying that she would not be influential but promising to provide impartial opinions about a range of topics. There are some indications (Mrs. Bush's papers are not yet available for scholarly use; to obtain information about her from the Bush Library, one must file a Freedom of Information Act request) that Barbara Bush was influential in private while maintaining public silence. The Bushes habitually discussed issues, and there is no reason to believe that this arrangement ceased when they moved to the White House. The president solicited the First Lady's opinions, and she served as a sounding board for some of her husband's initiatives. She had good judgment and common sense, and

rendered evaluations of some Bush administration personnel.

Barbara Bush was the president's conscience on social issues; one reporter recalled the First Lady's saying that she had lobbied the president to increase AIDS funding. Mrs. Bush's influence may well have been the decisive factor in the president's decision to sign the National Literacy Act of 1991 and increase funding for Head Start in 1990. She may also have been an advocate for the Hate Crimes Statistics Act signed into law in 1990. Mrs. Bush openly invited gay men and lesbians—those frequently affected by hate crimes—to attend the ceremony.

A former staff member characterized Barbara Bush's press relations as both good and productive. Anna Perez, who had worked previously on Capitol Hill, directed the press office. Mrs. Bush had one rule for dealing with the press: Everything was on the record ("If I said it, I said it," she told her press secretary). She also insisted on accuracy. If she requested certain information, she expected accurate, up-to-date data. Press aides couldn't respond to the First Lady by saying "I think" or "I believe." The First Lady told her staff that if they didn't know the answer to a question, they had to go out and supply her with the correct response; she didn't want to have to face two dozen reporters, provide them with information, and learn later that she had been wrong.

Barbara Bush did not hold formal press conferences, but she saw reporters with some frequency. Occasionally she would have lunch with approximately six to eight reporters and would then invite a few upstairs to the family residence to join her for informal conversation. These press roundtables were all on the record and reporters were sent transcripts of the discussions.

The press was always invited to travel with the First Lady. Her office scheduled pretrip briefings, and Mrs. Bush was accessible for "press availabilities." She would take questions about any topic, but retained the right to refuse to answer any question that she deemed inappropriate. It was not always easy to have national coverage of the First Lady's literacy project, but when Mrs. Bush traveled, the coverage was plentiful and often excellent.

She was unafraid of the fourth estate—as the press is sometimes called. On one occasion she told reporters that she had been working out and that they shouldn't attempt to tangle with her or she would throw them over her shoulder. When Hillary Rodham Clinton made the traditional postelection victory visit to the White House, Mrs. Bush advised her (perhaps more than half seriously) to avoid reporters at all costs.

Mrs. Bush was a well-liked First Lady whose popularity ratings frequently exceeded those of the president. At the end of 1989, her first year in the White House, she was ranked number three in the Gallup Poll's annual Most Admired Woman poll. At the end of 1990, she was ranked number two; in 1991 and 1992, she was ranked number one.

The presidential campaign of 1992 tested Mrs. Bush's intestinal fortitude and storied good humor. A year before, at the height of his popularity following the Persian Gulf War, George Bush appeared to be unbeatable. Now he seemed all too vulnerable as he faced tough opposition from within his own party as well as from Democrats. A political cartoon from the campaign shows George Bush in boxing gloves sitting on the shoulders of an oversized Barbara (also in boxing gloves). The implication was that the First Lady, about three times as popular as the president, was being counted on to bring life to George Bush's reelection bid.

While she didn't plan strategy or tactics, Mrs. Bush attended many 1992 campaign meetings. When she took to the hustings, Mrs. Bush spoke to audiences about the differences between Bill Clinton's Arkansas and George Bush's America. She told listeners about George Bush the businessman, the war hero, the president, the father. She and the president maintained separate schedules but occasionally campaigned together. Mrs. Bush would not give her opinion on certain policy issues but would

respond by saying, "Let me tell you what George Bush thinks about that. . . ." Despite the Bush family's furious campaigning, voters seemed to prefer the change promised by Bill Clinton; the Democrat won a decisive victory in the presidential election.

Barbara Bush was very disappointed that her husband lost the 1992 presidential election. She felt that he was the best man for the job and that America had lost out on his experience and commitment. However, she had extraordinary perspective: she had seen wins and losses; she had been through a presidential resignation, four assassination attempts, four national campaigns, and two defeats. There is an ebb and flow to politics, and life would go on.

On January 20, 1993, George and Barbara Bush became private citizens for the first time in almost three decades. The former First Lady continues to lead an active life. She travels and speaks about literacy all over the United States (when she gives an address, she is frequently accompanied by a new reader), and she continues to be intimately involved in the work of the Barbara Bush Foundation for Family Literacy. She also serves on the board of the Mayo Clinic, entertains, and visits with her large family. She watched with pleasure when her son George W. Bush was elected governor of Texas in 1994 and reelected in 1998. She also applauded when son Jeb was elected governor of Florida in 1998. George W. Bush's candidacy for president in 2000 had her quiet support behind the scenes and she stood with pride on the west front of the Capitol when he was sworn in as the forty-third president on January 20, 2001. Mrs. Bush has also encouraged former aides of her husband to assist in rehabilitating the historical image of her husband's presidency.

Barbara Bush made no enduring changes in the institution of First Lady. She broke no new ground, fostered no innovations. She combined some of the best characteristics of her predecessors: the caring of Eleanor Roosevelt, the quiet but steady influence of Bess Truman, the honesty and candor of Betty Ford. Perhaps Barbara

Bush demonstrated to the nation that the office of First Lady can be flexible, that it can accommodate all types of personalities and concerns. She gave the office a blend of formality and informality. Former press secretary Anna Perez commented, "She made it look easy—and it wasn't. She led with grace, humor, wit and her willingness to be herself."

It is important to note that Barbara Bush never responded to situations as a politician. Although she was politically savvy, she always perceived situations from the perspective of a mother. While this might have seemed unsophisticated and simplistic to some, a majority of Americans were touched by the First Lady's no-nonsense yet nurturing responses to problems. She supported Project Head Start because she wanted young, disadvantaged children to have an equal chance in life. She fought for literacy because the myriad problems that might affect children and adults could be traced to the inability to read. She was a strong proponent of family because, in her opinion, it is the strength of the country. Some observers said that Mrs. Bush was a voice for compassion in the administration; others heard her voice and concern in some of the president's speeches.

At the beginning of the Bush administration, Mrs. Bush was asked by Charlotte Saikowski of the *Christian Science Monitor* what she would like to be remembered for, four or eight years hence. She replied in the Monitor's issue of February 16, 1989, "I hope people will say, 'She cared; she worked hard for lots of causes.'" Barbara Bush worked tirelessly to promote literacy and education, family values, and concern for others. We associate Lady Bird Johnson with the environment, Rosalynn Carter with mental health, and Barbara Bush with the ability to read and to care.

BIBLIOGRAPHICAL ESSAY

The author wishes to thank Susan Porter Rose, former chief of staff for Barbara Bush, and Anna Perez, former press secretary to Barbara Bush, for their time and comments.

The personal papers of Barbara Bush will not be available for research until January 20, 1998. They will be housed at the George Bush Presidential Library, Texas A&M University, College Station, Texas.

Mrs. Bush's autobiography, *Barbara Bush: A Memoir* (New York, 1994), records her views on her years as First Lady. It is based on her extensive diaries. Mrs. Bush has written two other books: *C. Fred's Story* (Garden City, N.Y., 1984) and *Millie's Book* (New York, 1990). In both books, Barbara Bush writes from the perspective of her dogs.

The best biographies of Barbara Bush are Pamela Kilian, *Barbara Bush: A Biography* (New York, 1992); and Donnie Radcliffe, *Simply Barbara Bush: A Portrait of America's Candid First Lady* (New York, 1989). Kilian's work is well-researched, but she had no access to Mrs. Bush, whereas Radcliffe had covered the First Lady for the *Washington Post*. Her observations are helpful in understanding the pressures of being First Lady and the way in which Barbara Bush responded to them. Another source worth consulting is Ann Grimes, *Running Mates* (New York, 1990). Grimes traveled with both the Bush and the Dukakis presidential campaigns, and provides revealing insights into the 1988 presidential race from the perspective of Mrs. Bush and Kitty Dukakis. Carl Sferrazza Anthony offers some interesting insights about Barbara Bush, based on her first year as First Lady, in *First Ladies: The Saga of the Presidents' Wives and Their Power*, vol. 2 (New York, 1991).

Mrs. Bush's commencement address to the Wellesley College Class of 1990 may be found as "Choices and Change; Your Success as a Family," *Vital Speeches of the Day* (July 1, 1990): 549. Her remarks to the Republican National Convention in 1992 were printed as "Family Values: The Country's Future Is in Your Hands," *Vital Speeches of the Day* (September 15, 1992): 718.

Two books about George Bush that contain information about his wife are Fitzhugh Green, *George Bush: An Intimate Portrait* (New York, 1989); and Webster Griffin Tarpley and Anton Chaitkin, *George Bush: The Unauthorized Biography* (Washington, D.C., 1992). George Bush's autobiography is not yet published. Herbert S. Parmet, *George Bush: The Life of a Lone Star Yankee* (New York, 1997), sheds a good deal of light on Mrs. Bush's role in her husband's life. George Bush, *All the Best, George Bush: My Life in Letters and Other Writings* (New York, 1999), has much information on Mrs. Bush.

For articles about Mrs. Bush, see Jean Libman Block, "The Best Time of Life Is Now," *Good Housekeeping* (November 1989):155; Bernard Weinraub, "A Down-to-Earth Tenant for an Exclusive Address," *New York Times* (January 15, 1989); Margaret Carlson, "The Silver Fox," *Time* (January 23, 1989); Christine Saikowski, "At Home in the White House," *Christian Science Monitor* (February 16, 1989); and Paula Chin and Maria Wilhelm, "In the Eye of the Storm," *People* (October 1990): 82. Mrs. Bush talks about her post–White House activities in James Brady, "In Step with Barbara Bush," *Parade* (September 25, 1994):18.

★★★ ★★★

Hillary Rodham Clinton

(1947–)

First Lady: 1993–2001

Lewis L. Gould

Hillary Rodham was born in Chicago, Illinois, on October 26, 1947, the oldest child and only daughter of Hugh Rodham and Dorothy Howell Rodham. The Rodhams later had two sons. Hillary's father ran a small textile business in Chicago. In 1950 the family moved to Park Ridge, Illinois, where Hillary grew up. It was a Chicago suburb, conservative, Republican, and very much a white bastion. The Rodhams emphasized education for their children, and Hillary soon demonstrated that she was a gifted student. Her mother encouraged her to choose any career that she wanted to pursue; her father stressed the need for high academic achievement.

Hillary attended Maine East High in Park Ridge for three years, then completed high school at Maine South. She was involved with her class newspaper, the student council, and the cultural values committee. As a junior, Hillary was elected vice president of her class but lost the race to be president the following year. Her academic record was distinguished, and she was named to the National Honor Society. She requested that the National Aeronautics and Space Administration (NASA) send her information about becoming an astronaut. NASA told her that women were not accepted for astronaut training, a response that astonished her.

Hillary Rodham played an active role in the youth programs of the First United Methodist Church in Park Ridge. In 1961 Donald G. Jones joined the church staff as chancellor of the young people's group. Interested in theology as it applied to the problems of society, Jones took members of the group to the inner city of Chicago to see the living conditions of the African-American and Hispanic residents. In April 1962 Hillary and her fellow youth group members heard a speech by the Reverend Martin Luther King, Jr., that urged an end to racial injustice. After the speech she met Dr. King—a significant moment in her life. Before Jones left Park Ridge in 1963, he had introduced the youth group to such religious writers as Paul Tillich and Reinhold Niebuhr, men who would shape Hillary's outlook on the world and politics.

In high school, Hillary adhered to the Republican views of her family and community. In 1964 she campaigned for the Republican presidential candidate, Senator Barry M. Goldwater of Arizona, as a "Goldwater Girl." When she graduated, Hillary was in the top five percent of her class. Her classmates voted her most likely to succeed.

Hillary applied to Smith College and Wellesley College, both in Massachusetts. She was accepted by the latter, and in September 1965 enrolled as a member of the class of 1969.

At Wellesley, Hillary's opinions began to track the moderate ideas of John Lindsay and Nelson Rockefeller of New York. In the winter of 1968 she farther departed from her roots when she worked for the presidential candidacy of Senator Eugene McCarthy of Minnesota during the New Hampshire primary. By then Hillary regarded the Vietnam War as a major mistake. After Dr. Martin Luther King, Jr., was assassinated on April 4, 1968, she took part in protests on the Wellesley campus. Not yet twenty-one when voter registration in Illinois concluded, she could not vote in the election of 1968, but she later said that she would have cast a ballot for Senator Hubert H. Humphrey, the Democratic nominee.

As a college student, Hillary Rodham displayed the same leadership ability that she had shown in high school. She moved up through the ranks of Wellesley's student government and was elected president at the end of her junior year. During her senior year, she wrote a thesis about the community-action programs of Lyndon Johnson's Great Society. She concluded that the War on Poverty did not do enough to address the problems that poor Americans confronted. Although Hillary drew on the ideas of the radical community organizer Saul Alinsky about the poor, she was never the socialist that later critics claimed.

The climax of Hillary Rodham's career at Wellesley, and her first taste of the national spotlight, came at her commencement in 1969. The college administration had asked Senator Edward Brooke, a Massachusetts Republican, to deliver the graduation speech. Students asked Wellesley's president to name a student speaker who would express their feelings about the turbulence that American society was undergoing. Hillary Rodham was named to give the speech on behalf of her class. Fellow students besieged her with ideas in the days before the commencement ceremonies. By graduation day, she had a prepared text ready for delivery. Her father was in the audience as the proceedings began.

As she listened to Brooke's speech, she became convinced that his remarks were inadequate to the challenges that she and her fellow graduates were facing. Improvising her comments to respond to him, she replied to his statements and offered her own vision of what the times demanded. "The challenge now," she said, "is to practice politics as the art of making what appears to be impossible, possible." *Life* magazine carried passages from her speech and ran her picture. It was an auspicious end to her rewarding undergraduate experience at Wellesley.

Hillary Rodham had decided that law school offered her the best preparation for the career in public service that she planned to pursue. Choosing between Harvard and Yale, she found the activism of Yale more suited to her future involvement in government and politics. So, in September 1969, Hillary Rodham was one of the thirty women in the entering class of 160 students at Yale Law School.

Rodham's years at Yale continued the combination of involvement and achievement that marked her education at Wellesley. She developed an interest in law as it applied to poor children and served as an intern with Marian Wright Edelman, an advocate for disadvantaged youngsters. For one summer with Edelman's Washington research project, Rodham dealt with such issues as migrant workers and their children. She resolved to delve more deeply into the legal aspects of how children were treated in American society.

Until 1971, Hillary Rodham's romantic involvements, though sometimes passionate, had not reached the stage of engagement or marriage. In September 1970, however, William Jefferson "Bill" Clinton had entered Yale Law School. Clinton had completed his undergraduate education at Georgetown University and had held a Rhodes Scholarship at Oxford University. A native of Arkansas who talked nonstop about his home state, he was a year older than Hillary Rodham when their paths crossed. They had noticed one another on earlier occasions, but their first meetings took place in the Yale Law School library. Hillary Rodham noticed Bill Clinton staring at her across the library. She walked over to him and said, according to several biographers, "Look, if you're going to keep staring at me, and I'm going to keep staring back, I think we should at least know each other. I'm Hillary Rodham. What's your name?"

They soon paired off professionally in the law school and in their private lives. The two were a team in the Barristers' Union competition at Yale that featured mock trials. A friend watching them together in action told Clinton's biographer, David Marannis: "Hillary was very sharp and Chicago, and Bill was very *To Kill a Mockingbird*."

Though they did not win their case, their commitment to one another deepened. During the fall of 1971, her third year in law school, they shared a house in New Haven. At Christmas, Clinton visited her parents and won over her skeptical mother. The Rodhams still worried about Clinton's evi-

dent intention to pursue a political career in Arkansas, however.

In 1972, although she could have graduated, Hillary Rodham decided to remain in New Haven for an additional year. She applied for admission to a program at the law school that was devoted to children's rights. Out of this experience she refined the research she had done with Marian Edelman and prepared an article for the *Harvard Educational Review*, titled "Children and the Law." In it she argued that "the phrase 'children's rights' is a slogan in search of definition," a process that her essay sought to advance. In one celebrated passage, she discussed how society dealt with individual rights in "a dependency relationship" such as the one between children and parents. "Along with the family," she wrote, "past and present examples of such arrangements include marriage, slavery, and the Indian reservation system." Nineteen years later, her Republican opponents would allege that she had equated marriage with slavery. Later during the 1970s she published other articles and a book chapter about children's rights.

During the summer of 1972, Hillary Rodham joined Bill Clinton in Texas, working as an organizer for the presidential campaign of Democratic candidate Senator George McGovern of South Dakota. Though the campaign effort failed and Richard Nixon carried Texas in the fall, Bill Clinton and Hillary Rodham were making the friends who in time would give them a network of supporters throughout the national Democratic Party.

Hillary Rodham and Bill Clinton graduated from Yale Law School in the spring of 1973. He returned to Arkansas to teach at the University of Arkansas Law School and to prepare to run for Congress. She went to Cambridge, Massachusetts, to work for Marian Edelman at the Children's Defense Fund. For the moment, at least, she had not committed herself either to Clinton or to Arkansas. Early in 1974 she was hired as a staff attorney for the House Judiciary Committee that began to consider impeachment proceedings against President Richard

Nixon as a result of the burgeoning Watergate scandal. Although Hillary Rodham worked largely out of the public eye, Republican partisans marked her as one of the young agents of Nixon's political downfall.

Following the abrupt end of the Judiciary Committee assignment, Hillary Rodham decided to move to Arkansas and take a teaching position at the University of Arkansas Law School in Fayetteville. Bill Clinton was in the middle of his congressional race, and she emerged as his campaign manager. On the night Clinton lost, Hillary Rodham argued with another campaign aide about strategy, and heated words were exchanged. Twenty-six years later, during the 2000 Senate campaign, the aide told an unfriendly biographer of the Clinton marriage that Rodham had uttered an anti-Semitic slur during the episode. Few objective analysts credited the story because the person who made the allegation had serious memory problems and emotional difficulties in his past.

Hillary Rodham decided to remain in Arkansas. She liked the atmosphere there, she liked her work, and, of course, she liked Clinton, who was pressing her to get married during the first half of 1975. While considering his proposal and looking for possible alternatives, Rodham approached a Marine Corps recruiter about obtaining a commission as an attorney in that branch of the armed services. She did not reveal this initiative until 1994, when she reported that the recruiter had discouraged her in sexist terms and urged her to try the army.

Hillary Rodham and Bill Clinton were married on October 11, 1975, in a small ceremony that included family and close friends. They honeymooned in Acapulco, Mexico, along with most of the Rodham family. Returning to Fayetteville, Hillary Rodham (she retained her maiden name) resumed her legal work and teaching. The following year Bill Clinton was elected attorney general of Arkansas, and the couple relocated to the state capital of Little Rock. Hillary Rodham moved onto the larger and more complex stage of Arkansas state politics, with its interlocking networks of friends, political allies, and potential hazards for the unwary.

Shortly after her arrival in Little Rock, Hillary Rodham received a job offer from the Rose Law Firm, the most powerful private legal institution in the state. The Carter administration appointed her to the board of the Legal Services Corporation. She became a founder of Arkansas Advocates for Children and Families, a nonprofit organization that called for greater rights for children in the state. Both Bill Clinton and Hillary Rodham found their lives to be promising and rewarding in a public sense. Behind the scenes, however, there may have been strains. Years later, an Arkansas woman named Juanita Broaddrick would claim that Bill Clinton had raped her in 1978, and in 1998 Clinton would concede to a grand jury that he had had a sexual encounter with Gennifer Flowers in 1977.

In 1978 Bill Clinton announced his candidacy for governor of Arkansas. He won the Democratic nomination easily and trounced his Republican opponent in the fall election.

The couple thought about starting a family at this time, and they looked to their financial future. Hillary Rodham managed their finances. In 1978 she began trading in commodities futures—a venture that continued until the summer of 1979. On her initial investment of $1,000 she made an ultimate profit of $100,000. Fifteen years later, when the episode came out in the press, critics alleged that she must have received special treatment to have gained such large returns on her small investment. Advice on managing her portfolio had come from her friend James Blair, a lawyer who later was associated with Tyson Foods, a major Arkansas employer. The person who handled her trading account, Robert L. "Red" Bone, had a checkered career as a commodities speculator. In the 1990s some Republicans suggested that she had been allocated these returns as a kind of legal bribery to pay for influence with her husband.

Another investment that the Clintons made in 1978 proved to have more far-reaching consequences. They joined their friends James and Susan McDougal in forming the Whitewater Development Company. The Clintons used borrowed money to make a $200,000 investment in property in northwestern Arkansas. Neither Bill Clinton nor Hillary Rodham was involved in James McDougal's savings and loan enterprise, Madison Guaranty Savings and Loan. The Whitewater Company was not a success in the early 1980s, and the Clintons made continuing interest payments on their bank loan. The records of the transactions indicate that the Clintons were the victims of Jim McDougal's dishonesty and that they lost money on their investment in the Whitewater venture.

Meanwhile, during her husband's first term as governor, Hillary Rodham pursued her busy round of causes and commitments, including service on a task force on rural health care in Arkansas. In 1979 she became a partner in the Rose Law Firm. That same year she announced that she was pregnant, and she gave birth to a daughter, Chelsea, on February 27, 1980.

By the time Bill Clinton began to campaign for reelection, political observers in Arkansas saw problems for his candidacy. One source of voter resentment was Hillary Clinton, and reports circulated about unhappiness with her decision not to take her husband's name. After a difficult primary battle, Governor Clinton was a narrowly defeated by Republican Frank White in the 1980 general election. The Clintons were devastated by the loss.

Reports of problems in the Clinton marriage arising from Bill Clinton's extramarital affairs dogged the couple during this period. Hillary Rodham's family remained her top priority, and she became an important element in the political comeback that Bill Clinton mounted in 1981 and 1982. Most important, she decided that she should be known as Hillary Clinton, so that anger over her name would not cost her husband an election victory. She also paid attention to her appearance with the help of a fashion consultant who advised her about cosmetics and dress. She learned how to practice the politics of friendship and per-

sonality that was so much a part of the Arkansas environment. Bill Clinton won the 1982 election, and the Clintons had another opportunity to serve the people of Arkansas.

The major initiative that the reinstated governor pursued was reform of the state's antiquated system of public education. He named his wife to chair the Education Standards Committee that would overhaul the schools. During the two years that followed, she toured the state to gather information about the educational needs of Arkansas. The specific proposals that came out of the work of Mrs. Clinton's committee tracked what had been done in other states. The panel advocated smaller classes and tests of the performance of students throughout their careers. To move the necessary tax increase that would fund the reforms through the Arkansas legislature, it was coupled with a test of the basic skills of the state's teachers. The requirement angered educators, who deemed the examination an affront to their profession. African Americans called the test a concession to racist elements in the state, but it proved to be the key to enactment of the educational program.

For her achievements in education reform, Hillary Clinton garnered national honors. An Arkansas newspaper dubbed her Woman of the Year, and *Esquire* magazine placed the Clintons among the 272 members of the baby-boom generation who were leaving their mark on the United States. She continued her many activities in behalf of children. Her law career prospered as she joined the boards of such corporations as Wal-Mart and TCBY, a yogurt shop franchiser. She handled the family's increasingly complex personal finances as well.

The Whitewater Development Company participated in the financial excesses of the 1980s. James McDougal had headed Madison Guaranty Savings and Loan, an institution that went bankrupt and was placed in receivership by the federal government. In the 1990s, critics raised questions about the links between the Clintons and Madison Guaranty Savings and Loan.

They focused on the following issues: Had Mrs. Clinton acted ethically when the Rose Law Firm engaged in negotiations over the future of Madison? The evidence indicates that her name was once mentioned in a letter from Rose Law Firm to an Arkansas state regulator, but her role and eventual profit as a member of the firm were both small. Had she pressured state regulators for special treatment? The evidence indicates that she did not. Did she and her husband earn personal profits from these transactions? If anything, they suffered losses. As an independent counsel concluded in 2000, there was no basis for criminal indictments against Mrs. Clinton for her role in Madison.

The political success that Bill and Hillary Clinton achieved in Arkansas led many in the Democratic Party to speculate about the presidential chances of the youthful governor and his brilliant wife in 1988. In July 1987, Bill Clinton announced that he would not be a candidate for the Democratic nomination the following year. He noted that Chelsea Clinton was only seven years old, and stressed his commitment to his family's well-being. Other observers noted that since marital infidelity had destroyed the candidacy of Senator Gary Hart of Colorado, Bill Clinton might have held back for similar reasons. Hillary Clinton remained a highly successful professional, and in 1988 she was named by the *National Law Journal* as one of the hundred most influential attorneys in the United States.

Bill Clinton won a fifth term as governor in 1990. His opponent in the Democratic primary, Tom McRae, denounced his record. When the challenger held a news conference in Little Rock on May 16, 1990, Hillary Clinton appeared and attacked McRae's statements about her husband. The episode helped the governor win the primary and defeat his Republican opponent in the fall.

As 1992 approached, the Clintons once again considered whether he should make a race for the White House. President George Bush seemed unbeatable to many Democrats, and few high-profile candidates from

the Democratic Party had entered the race by mid-1991. During the summer Governor Clinton decided to become a candidate; he announced his entry into the presidential contest on October 3, 1991. He and his wife met with Washington reporters in mid-September. They said that their marriage had experienced its share of problems, but stressed their commitment to one another and the strength of their relationship. For the moment the issue of their marriage and its problems seemed to be behind them.

By early January 1992, however, the question surfaced once again as tabloid newspapers and television reporters repeatedly asked Hillary Clinton about stories in Arkansas that her husband had been unfaithful. The campaign bombshell came on January 23, 1992, when the supermarket tabloid the *Star* broke a story about an alleged affair that Bill Clinton had had with a woman in Arkansas named Gennifer Flowers. Though many parts of her recollections proved to be false or erroneous, Flowers reiterated her charge that she and the Arkansas governor had had a twelve-year sexual relationship. In 1998 Bill Clinton admitted to one sexual encounter with her. In 1992 the revelation threatened to torpedo his candidacy just as he was emerging as the front-runner for the Democratic presidential nomination.

To counter Flowers's charges, the Clintons appeared on *60 Minutes*, the CBS television news magazine, in an interview that aired on January 26. The program ran just after the Super Bowl, to the largest possible nationwide audience. The couple acknowledged problems in the past but deflected the allegations of infidelity without directly contradicting them. At a key moment during the interview, Hillary Clinton said: "I'm not sitting here because I'm some little woman standing by my man like [country singer] Tammy Wynette. I'm sitting here because I love and respect him, and I honor what he's been through and what we've been through together. And you know, if that's not enough for people, then heck, don't vote for him."

Her reference to Wynette caused a flap among country music fans, but for the most part Hillary Clinton's declaration helped reduce the damage that the Flowers episode had done to her husband's presidential hopes. She affirmed that their marriage was strong, and since she had forgiven Bill Clinton for any transgressions, the rest of the country should do the same.

Bill Clinton came in second in the New Hampshire primary, an impressive comeback after his candidacy had seemed to be on the ropes. During the month that followed, he emerged as the leader for the Democratic presidential nomination. More and more press attention focused on Hillary Clinton: her appearance, her statements, and her personal business affairs. More than any potential First Lady of her era, she aroused intense passions in the electorate. The press discussed her headbands at length until she finally stopped wearing them. Reporters also looked into the Whitewater Development Company and its ties to the Clintons, but a report from the campaign on their financial activities and the continuing success of Bill Clinton's candidacy put the issue to rest for the time being.

One incident in March underlined the sensitivity of Hillary Clinton's visible role in her husband's presidential campaign. Speaking in Chicago on March 16, 1992, she told a reporter, "I've done the best I can to lead my life. I suppose I could have stayed home and baked cookies and had teas." The press pounced on the statement, and radio talk shows reverberated with angry denunciations of Hillary Clinton as having demeaned traditional women and their homemaking priorities. Republican strategists began to think that she might be a weak spot for her husband, and they focused closely on her writings and her public life.

In an interview published in *Vanity Fair*, Hillary Clinton mentioned a rumor that President George Bush had had a mistress, a story that the press seemed reluctant to probe. When the magazine came out, a flap ensued, and Mrs. Clinton apologized. Meanwhile, Republicans focused more attention on her legal writings during the early 1970s. Roger Stone, a Republican operative, wrote in the *New York Times* on May 18, 1992, that "Hillary Clinton is exceedingly polarizing." On the eve of the Republican National Convention, party chairman Rich Bond, in a speech reported in the August 13, 1992, issue of the *News & Observer* of Raleigh, North Carolina, charged that Mrs. Clinton had "likened marriage and the family to slavery. She has referred to the family as a dependency relation that deprives people of their rights."

At the Republican National Convention in Houston in late August, the most fiery speech against Mrs. Clinton came from sometime presidential candidate and television personality Pat Buchanan. He told the delegates that she believed "that twelve-year-olds should have the right to sue their parents, and Hillary has compared marriage and the family as institutions to slavery—and life on an Indian reservation."

The strategy of attacking Hillary Clinton backfired. Voters who disliked Mrs. Clinton were inclined to vote for George Bush anyway. Undecideds in the electorate, particularly women, reacted negatively to her vilification. Criticisms of her writings often ripped her words out of context or distorted them to prove a political point. As those facts became more clear, the attacks on Mrs. Clinton worked against those who made them. By the fall of 1992 Hillary Clinton had become an asset as her husband's campaign for the White House approached victory.

Hillary Clinton's experience in 1992 was uncommon among prospective First Ladies. Usually, questions about the views and role of the wife of a potential president come up after the election or during the early months of the new administration. For Hillary Clinton, however, the scrutiny had begun in New Hampshire and continued unabated until November 1992 and beyond. Her professional career, her clear policy-making role close to her husband, and her espousal of many of the feminist ideas of the 1970s and 1980s made her seem a harbinger of the new American woman who was emerging as a force on the national scene.

Once Bill Clinton had been elected president, the question arose about the role that his wife would play in the administration. In keeping with their promise that the American people would get two presidents for the price of one, Mrs. Clinton made it clear that she intended to have a policy role in the White House. Along with the traditional offices in the east wing of the mansion, she also received an office in the west wing, the exclusively male area of the White House in earlier administrations. Her office informed the press that she would be known officially as Hillary Rodham Clinton.

Mrs. Clinton assembled a thirteen-person staff of her own to help carry out her priorities as First Lady, a somewhat smaller number than her immediate predecessors had had. She selected Margaret Ann "Maggie" Williams as her chief of staff, the first African American to hold the post. For the position of press secretary, Mrs. Clinton selected Lisa Caputo; Neel Lattimore and Karen Finney became deputy press secretaries. For scheduling director, the First Lady appointed Patti Solis, a Hispanic woman.

Her staff had much to do. Because of Mrs. Clinton's place in the public spotlight, she received a large amount of mail— approximately 500,000 letters by mid-1995. Her active schedule and involvement in the workings of the administration meant that she operated at a hectic and exacting pace. After the euphoria of the inauguration, the Clintons experienced a rocky first month in the White House. As problems arose about the selection of a female attorney general, for example, questions surfaced about Mrs. Clinton's political instincts as they related to her role in appointments to major posts.

Her important position in the administration became apparent one week after the inauguration. On January 25, 1993, the president named her to head the panel that would prepare a new health care plan for submission to Congress. She thus became the leading figure on the president's team to sell his major policy goal to the nation. Soon she began to appear at events around the country, making the argument for changes in health care. Early in February the First

Lady went to Capitol Hill to meet with lawmakers about the issue. Her visit was a success; representatives and senators responded positively to her lobbying appearance. She outlined the nature of the problem that Congress confronted in dealing with health issues, and she promised to consult closely with them in shaping legislation.

By this time, an undercurrent of opposition to Mrs. Clinton had emerged. The election of Bill Clinton had energized the right wing of American politics. The venom with which they attacked the president extended to the First Lady. In a fund-raising "Hillary Alert," the American Conservative Union said that Mrs. Clinton's "radical agenda includes special privileges for homosexuals, feminists, abortionists, and other left-wing kooks." Not since Eleanor Roosevelt during the 1940s had a First Lady aroused such intense animosity from her political enemies.

Opponents of heath care reform filed suit during the winter of 1993, charging that the President's Task Force on National Health Care Reform, the panel that Hillary Rodham Clinton headed, could not hold its deliberations in secret because that violated the Federal Advisory Committee Act (1972). The Justice Department argued in response that the First Lady was a de facto government employee, and thus not covered by the provisions of the law. The case went to the Federal Court of Appeals, and the judges decided in June 1993 that Mrs. Clinton was in effect a government official, as the Justice Department had maintained. The impact of the ruling was important in the institutional history of the office of the First Lady because it set out for the first time the basis for the position of the president's wife in American government.

Personal difficulties interrupted the early months of Hillary Rodham Clinton's tenure as First Lady. Her father, Hugh Rodham, became seriously ill in March 1993, and the First Lady rushed to his bedside in Little Rock. He died on April 7, 1993. A day earlier, Mrs. Clinton made one of the significant speeches of her career at the University of Texas at Austin. She told the audience of 14,000 people: "We need a new politics of meaning. We need a new ethos of individual responsibility and caring." The speech attracted great attention and debate about what the First Lady meant. A month after that speech, however, the firing of employees in the White House travel office produced another controversy over whether the First Lady was responsible for their ouster.

Then tragedy set the stage for future problems for the president and First Lady. On July 20, 1993, deputy White House counsel Vincent Foster committed suicide. Within days of his death, news reports linked White House aides to the removal of records and files regarding the Clintons and their Arkansas real estate investments from Foster's office. That these records belonged to the Clintons and were not subject to inquiries when no crime was alleged, received little notice. Behind the scenes, momentum began to build for further investigations of the Clintons before they came to Washington. There were even whispers that Mrs. Clinton and Foster had been romantically involved, charges for which no evidence existed.

One of the high points of Hillary Clinton's role as First Lady came in September 1993, when she testified before a House committee on the administration's health care plan. She was the third First Lady to appear before Congress; Eleanor Roosevelt and Rosalynn Carter had preceded her. Mrs. Clinton demonstrated impressive skill in handling the lawmakers. The health care campaign had gotten off to a sparkling start, thanks to her political talents. At the same time the administration and the president were getting themselves established with the approval of the North American Free Trade Agreement (NAFTA) and the improving economy.

In October and November 1993, however, the good news began to wane as political and news media questions about the Clintons and their Arkansas business reappeared. Press reports revealed that the Resolution Trust Corporation, which handled bankrupt savings and loan firms, had sent the Department of Justice a criminal referral about Madison Guaranty Trust and the Whitewater real estate venture in which the Clintons had been involved. The referral, which was immediately leaked to the press, mentioned the Clintons as possible witnesses in the inquiry. No criminal wrongdoing on their part was alleged.

Political opponents clamored for the appointment of an independent counsel or special prosecutor to examine the entire matter. The First Lady opposed the selection of a counsel for some time. She believed that the Clintons should not agree to a partisan fishing expedition into their record in Arkansas. It was unprecedented for the president and his wife to be investigated for actions that had occurred before they came to the White House. The political pressure during the winter of 1994 proved to be too strong to withstand. In the end, President and Mrs. Clinton accepted the appointment of Robert Fiske to look into the Whitewater affair.

During the same period, reporters broke stories about Hillary Rodham Clinton's commodity trading ventures and the profits she had realized. Many critics contended that her profit-making success cast doubt upon her earlier denunciations of the alleged greed and excesses of the 1980s, during the Reagan and Bush administrations. Some on the Right alleged that the episode reflected apparent illegal behavior on her part.

The First Lady answered the charges relating to Whitewater and commodity trading in a press conference on April 22, 1994. Addressing the reporters by herself at the White House for over an hour, she responded to all the queries that were put to her. Her impressive display of emotional reserve under fire quieted some of the attacks upon her. During the summer of 1994, however, her troubles continued. A woman in Arkansas, Paula Jones, accused the president of making sexual advances to her in 1991. Congressional hearings in July investigated controversial contacts between the White House and the Treasury Department. The dismissal of moderate Republican Robert Fiske as the Whitewater counsel and his replacement by a conservative Republican, Kenneth Starr, added to the difficulties that the Clintons confronted.

Meanwhile, the health care initiative encountered political trouble. By August 1994 the complex "Clinton Plan" was a continuing liability for the White House. Some of its problems arose from mistakes early in the administration, such as the clumsy handling of the press. The budget battle of 1993 and the Whitewater controversy further eroded the political capital of the White House.

In retrospect, however, many of the basic criticisms leveled against the First Lady and the administration's health care proposals were greatly exaggerated. The Clinton plan would have been mandatory for all Americans because serious health care reform would have been impossible if large numbers of the population were left out. The health alliances that the administration proposed would have provided more choices than many Americans received from private insurance. Other aspects of the plan tracked existing health care practices. As to the ostensible complexity of the Clinton plan, any proposal to deal with the intricacies of the nation's medical system would have been complicated, whether it came from the Left or the Right.

As the 1994 congressional elections approached, reports circulated that Hillary Rodham Clinton was planning to adopt a lower public profile in the months ahead. The Republican victories of 1994 underlined the wisdom of that course. Having gained control of Congress, Republican critics of the Clintons talked of intensive hearings about the Whitewater issue during 1995. Hillary Clinton reassessed her own role within the White House during November and December 1994, and she began the new year with a less visible public presence. Her focus was now on the older model of an activist First Lady. As Lady Bird Johnson and Rosalynn Carter had done, she intended to be an advocate for specific causes rather than a legislative manager, as she had been in the health care debate. Her staff declared that expanding

opportunities for women and children would claim more of her time.

Throughout 1995 Mrs. Clinton traveled widely and found ways to get her personal message across to the American people. In March 1995 she embarked on a twelve-day trip to Asia that included stops in Pakistan, Indian, Nepal, Sri Lanka, and Bangladesh. One of the highlights of the trip was the emergence of Chelsea Clinton as a figure in her own right. The Clintons had been successful in shielding their daughter from the scrutiny of the Washington press corps during the first term. On the tour Mrs. Clinton emphasized the crucial role of education as a force for improving the lives of women in Asia. The coverage of the tour was very favorable, a change from the difficulties of 1994.

Throughout the spring and summer of 1995, the First Lady remained very much in the political arena. She launched a syndicated weekly newspaper column to bring her views directly to the public, the first wife of a president to do so since Eleanor Roosevelt and her "My Day" column. In September 1995 Mrs. Clinton attended the United Nations Fourth World Conference on Women in Beijing, China, where she gave a hard-hitting speech attacking the policies of the host government that damaged the lives of women and children. A month later she traveled to South America for more meetings and speeches on the role of women in developing nations. Unknown to her, her husband had begun a sexual affair in the White House with a young intern named Monica Lewinsky.

Hillary Clinton's political fortunes reached another low point in early 1996 when her Rose Law Firm billing records subpoenaed by both independent counsel Kenneth Starr and Congress for several years turned up in the White House among memorabilia. Though the records supported her version of events in the 1980s, the discovery suggested a possible coverup. When the news broke, the *New York Times* conservative columnist William Safire called the First Lady "a congenital liar." The White House press secretary declared that had Bill Clinton not been president, "he would have delivered a more forceful response" by punching Safire in the nose. Starr subpoenaed the First Lady to testify before his grand jury, and Hillary Clinton became the first wife of a president to appear in such circumstances. She testified for four hours. Despite newspaper predictions that she would soon be indicted for perjury, there was no further legal action against her.

During the rest of 1996, Mrs. Clinton campaigned for her husband, saw Chelsea enter Stanford University, and prepared for a second term. In the year that followed Bill Clinton's reelection, the First Lady made visits to Argentina in October 1997 and to Russia and Central Asia the following month. Though legal difficulties persisted for her husband in the Paula Jones case in the federal courts, Hillary Clinton anticipated a productive second term as 1997 ended.

Then the Monica Lewinsky scandal broke in January 1998. Unaware of the extent of her husband's infidelity, the First Lady went on the *Today* show on January 27, 1998, and defended him. Many of his troubles, she said, arose from "this vast right-wing conspiracy against my husband since the day he announced for president." The charge of a concerted conservative effort to bring down Bill Clinton was true, but so was his sexual philandering that produced the Lewinsky crisis. Mrs. Clinton's comments were widely ridiculed, especially by her conservative enemies.

When President Clinton testified before the Starr grand jury in August 1998, his wife learned from one of his attorneys that her husband was going to acknowledge a sexual affair of some sort with Lewinsky. That meant the president had lied to his wife and daughter for months, even years. Other disturbing revelations marked this period. Juanita Broaddrick's charge that Bill Clinton had raped her in 1978 came out in February 1999. The strains that emerged within the Clinton family were evident to outside observers, but the couple went on through the rigors of the impeachment crisis and the 1998 elections toward the ulti-

mate crisis of the presidency. In the end, Bill Clinton survived impeachment in February 1999. For Hillary Clinton, it was time to look to her own political future.

Since 1997 Democrats in New York State had been talking up the possibility that she might run for the Senate seat that Daniel Patrick Moynihan would be vacating in 2000. The Democratic Party wanted to find a high-profile candidate to hold the seat against the expected campaign of Mayor Rudolph Giuliani of New York City. By October 1998 what seemed a long-shot endeavor became a more real possibility after the First Lady spent time campaigning for Democratic candidates in that year's congressional elections. In the winter of 1999, Mrs. Clinton said in a brief statement that she was giving "careful thought" to a Senate campaign.

During the summer the First Lady went to Senator Moynihan's farm, and then began a "listening tour" of upstate New York, where Democrats rarely did well. Republicans claimed that she was a "carpetbagger" who had no roots in New York, a theme that would intensify in the months to come. The Clintons purchased a house in Westchester County, and Mrs. Clinton was on the campaign trail. Some early problems with New York politics led to talk that she might not run, but she said in November 1999 that she would announce her candidacy.

The formal declaration came on February 6, 2000, and the First Lady began what would be a virtual nonstop campaign across the state. Meanwhile, Mayor Giuliani encountered marital and personal problems of his own. He announced that he had prostate cancer, was seeing "a very good friend" socially, and was separating from his wife. On May 19, 2000, the mayor withdrew from the race.

Congressman Rick A. Lazio immediately announced for the Republican nomination. He used the same carpetbagger theme that Giuliani had employed but never gained much traction in his campaign. A defining moment in the contest came during the first televised debate between Mrs. Clinton and her rival. In a discussion of campaign finance reform, Lazio left his podium and strode over to Mrs. Clinton, brandishing a pledge against campaign excesses that he urged her to sign. This invasion of the First Lady's personal space alienated women voters, and the Lazio campaign never recovered.

On election night, November 7, 2000, the First Lady, aided by the strong showing of Vice President Al Gore as the presidential candidate, trounced Lazio with 54 percent of the vote.

During the Senate campaign, Independent Counsel Robert Ray, who had replaced Kenneth Starr, announced that Mrs. Clinton would not face indictment over the White House travel office matter or the Whitewater issue. Hillary Clinton could begin her Senate career without any legal clouds over her future.

In the history of the institution of the First Lady, Hillary Rodham Clinton will occupy a unique place. By any standard, she was the most controversial presidential wife of the twentieth century, far eclipsing the turmoil that swirled around Eleanor Roosevelt in the 1930s and 1940s. She has a number of "firsts," some of them of dubious value, that grew out of her White House years. Mrs. Clinton was the first First Lady to manage a major policy initiative, in the health care plan of 1993–1994. Her appearance before the grand jury in 1996 was another, less welcome, breakthrough. Finally, in running for the Senate and winning while First Lady, she capitalized on the celebrity aspects of her position to her own political advantage.

In terms of her actual achievements as First Lady, however, the record is more mixed. Because of the glare of publicity and alleged scandal that surrounded her, Mrs. Clinton was not able to sustain an involvement with a cause or campaign with which her name can be associated. Children's rights, women's rights, health care, and world peace came and went at various times, but none emerged as the signature cause of her White House tenure.

More than any other presidential couple, the Clintons lived out the strains and strengths of their marriage in public. Hillary Clinton had to face the problems of a woman who had married a man with great political assets and corresponding personal and emotional weaknesses. Whether President Clinton was a "sex addict," as some critics charged, or a middle-aged man who never grew up, his behavior placed his wife in predicaments. One achievement of Hillary Rodham Clinton as First Lady may well be that she survived a series of emotional traumas that would have broken a less resilient person.

One intriguing issue for her biographers will be her capacity to polarize opinion about her across the country. To her admirers she was the embodiment of the modern woman who juggled career and family under the most difficult circumstances. As her success in the New York Senate race demonstrated, her life and personality struck a responsive chord with many Americans. For others on the Right, she was a more sinister figure who represented the evils that Bill Clinton brought to politics. They accused her of unlimited ambition and unbridled ruthlessness in her pursuit of power. At the same time, they depicted her as an impotent tool of her unscrupulous husband. As 2000 ended, conservatives freely predicted that a race for the White House lay in her future.

A final verdict on Hillary Clinton as First Lady is premature. How history will see her hinges on the record of the woman who follows her into the position, Laura Bush, and on Mrs. Clinton's own performance in the Senate. What seems appropriate to conclude is that the institution of the First Lady had never experienced anything like the eight years of Hillary Clinton, and will probably go through a quieter and less clamorous period after her departure from the White House in January 2001.

BIBLIOGRAPHICAL ESSAY

Because she will probably be a U.S. Senator until at least 2006, it is unlikely that any of Hillary Clinton's personal papers will be available in the near future. When her husband's presidential library opens in Arkansas, it will contain her White House Social Files and other records, but availability of those documents is also problematic for some years. Important information about her professional career in Arkansas can be found in U.S. Congress, Senate, *Investigation of Whitewater Development Corporation and Related Matters*, Senate Hearing 104–869, 20 vols. (Washington, D.C., 1997); U.S., Congress, House, *Investigation of the White House Travel Office Firings and Related Matters*, House Report 104–849 (Washington, D.C., 1996); and *The Starr Report* (Washington, D.C., 1998), about the impeachment of the president. Much information about her, most of it negative, can be found on the Internet.

Among the published writings of Hillary Clinton are *It Takes a Village and Other Lessons Children Teach Us* (New York, 1996); *Dear Socks, Dear Buddy: Kids' Letters to the First Pets* (New York, 1998); and *An Invitation to the White House* (New York, 2000). Claire G. Osborne, ed., *The Unique Voice of Hillary Rodham Clinton: A Portrait in Her Own Words* (New York, 1997), is a collection of excerpts from her public statements. Her legal articles on children are "Children Under the Law," *Harvard Educational Review* 43 (November 1973): 487–514; "Children's Policies: Abandonment and Neglect," *Yale Law Journal* 86 (June 1977): 1522–1531; and "Children's Rights: A Legal Perspective," in Patricia A. Vardin and Ilene N. Brody, eds., *Children's Rights: Contemporary Perspectives* (New York, 1979), 21–36.

Mrs. Clinton has been the subject of a large number of biographies during her years in the White House. In the second term, many of these books were strident partisan attacks on her character and record. Those that appeared at the outset of the Clinton administration include Rex Nelson with Philip Martin, *The Hillary Factor* (New York, 1993), emphasizing her Arkansas roots; Judith Warner, *Hillary Clinton: The Inside Story* (New York, 1993); Norman King, *Hillary: Her True Story* (New York, 1993); and Donnie Radcliffe, *Hillary Rodham Clinton: A First Lady for Our Time* (New York, 1993). The Warner and Radcliffe books have been updated since they first appeared.

The biographies that have criticized Hillary Clinton began with David Brock, *The Seduction of Hillary Rodham* (New York, 1996), which approached her from a conservative point of view—with perhaps more sympathy than the author intended. Joyce Milton, *The First Partner: Hillary Rodham Clinton* (New York, 1999), is a mixture of solid evidence and conjecture that reaches negative conclusions. Gaily Sheehy, *Hillary's Choice* (New York, 1999), advances a psychological explanation for Mrs. Clinton's commitment to her marriage that is often marked by factual errors. By 1999 book-length attacks on Mrs. Clinton had become a cottage industry among conservative authors. Examples of this genre are Barbara Olson, *Hell to Pay: The Unfolding Story of Hillary Rodham Clinton* (Washington, D.C., 1999), based largely on published sources; and Peggy Noonan, *The Case Against Hillary Clinton* (New York, 2000), which reveals as much about the author as it does about her subject.

Popularized studies of the Clinton marriage include Christopher Andersen, *Bill and Hillary: The Marriage* (New York, 1999); and Jerry Oppenheimer, *State of a Union: Inside the Complex Marriage of Bill and Hillary* Clinton (New York, 2000), which broke the report about Mrs. Clinton's alleged anti-Semitic remark in 1974. Roger Morris, *Partners in Power: The Clintons and Their America* (New York, 1996), is an analysis of their political career through 1992.

On the Whitewater controversy, a thorough guide is Joe Conason and Gene Lyons, *The Hunting of the President: The Ten-Year Campaign to Destroy Bill and Hillary Clinton* (New York, 2000). For the impeachment and Mrs. Clinton's response to it, two useful studies are Peter Baker, *The Breach: Inside the Impeachment and Trial of William Jefferson Clinton* (New York, 2000); and Jeffrey Toobin, *A Vast Conspiracy: The Real Story of the Sex Scandal That Nearly Brought Down a President* (New York, 1999). The best book on Bill Clinton's early life and his relationship with his wife is David Maraniss, *First in His Class: A Biography of Bill Clinton* (New York, 1995).

Press coverage of Mrs. Clinton has been extensive and all the relevant stories cannot be cited here. A good compilation of diverse views about Hillary Clinton is Susan K. Flinn, ed., *Speaking of Hillary: A Readers' Guide to the Most Controversial Woman in America* (Ashland, Ore., 2000).

★★★ ★★★

Laura Welch Bush

(1946–)

First Lady: 2001–

Lewis L. Gould

Laura Lane Welch was born in Midland, Texas, on November 4, 1946, the only child of Jenna Hawkins Welch and Harold Bruce Welch. Her father, a native Texan and son of a home builder in Lubbock, was a credit officer with a loan company where he rose to be branch manager in the 1950s. Later he operated a home building company out of his residence. Laura's mother was originally from Taylor and then El Paso, where her father was a postal worker and home builder. She kept the books for her husband's building enterprise. Neither of Laura's parents had graduated from college, and they wanted their daughter to achieve more in education than they had accomplished.

Jenna Welch raised her daughter with a love of reading. "She didn't go to bed unless you read to her," she recalled in July 2000. In elementary school Laura was a member of the Brownies and Girl Scouts, and studied ballet. During these years, Laura Welch took up smoking, a practice that continued until she was in her late forties. By the second grade she had also decided that she wanted to be a teacher. Addressing the Republican National Convention in July 2000, she recalled that "growing up, I practiced teaching on my dolls. I would line them up in rows for the day's lessons." In junior high school, one of her fellow students for a year was George Walker Bush, but the two did not know one another.

In 1961, Laura entered Robert E. Lee High School in Midland, and plunged into extracurricular activities such as the Junior Council and the *Rebelee*, the yearbook. Popular and attractive, she "dated a lot of guys but she was never seriously involved with anyone," according to a friend. In 1963 she participated in the "powder puff" football game in which the girls played and the boys provided the cheers. At the game, Laura met Michael Douglas, a star athlete and one of the most popular students at Lee. The couple dated several times, then apparently drifted apart.

On November 6, 1963, two days after her seventeenth birthday, Laura and a close friend, Judy Dykes, were driving to a party in Midland. It was shortly before eight o'clock on a clear night. At a highway intersection Laura was apparently distracted as they talked about clothes, and she ran the stop sign. Her car hit a Chevrolet Corvair driven by Michael Douglas. "She didn't see him, he didn't see her" was how a classmate remembered the event. Douglas suffered a broken neck and was dead on arrival at Midland Memorial Hospital. Laura and Judy Dykes suffered minor injuries, and were released from the hospital.

The funeral for Michael Douglas was held in Midland three days later. Laura and her family sent flowers but did not attend. Douglas was buried in Austin Memorial Park where his headstone reads "So Dearly Loved, Life Eternal." The 1964 *Rebelee* carried a poem about him to which Laura contributed. "His imprint lingers in the halls, / Where he walked only a while ago," read one verse.

Her classmates recall that the incident deeply affected Laura Welch. "It took the heart and life out of her. She kind of disappeared for a few weeks," said one friend. Another friend said, "It made Laura realize every act has consequences that cannot be escaped." The legal consequences for Laura Welch were slight. No charges were filed in the case, and she received no traffic ticket or suspension of her driving privileges.

When the press revealed what had happened in the spring of 2000, Laura Bush said that "it was crushing . . . for the family involved and for me as well." A spokesman for her said, "To this day, Mrs. Bush remains unable to talk about it." After a brief flurry of press interest, the episode was little discussed in the 2000 campaign and coverage of Laura Bush as a potential First Lady. Journalists who had examined the life of Hillary Clinton in the most minute detail displayed no interest in discussing any unanswered questions about the disposition of Michael Douglas's death as a legal matter or the long-term effect on Laura Bush.

After graduation from Lee High School, Laura Welch entered Southern Methodist University in Dallas in the fall of 1964. She majored in elementary education, and took courses in Shakespeare and children's literature. She joined Kappa Alpha Theta, one of the most prominent and socially prestigious sororities on a campus where money, football, and parties had a higher priority than academics in the 1960s. Laura's room in the sorority house was, according to a friend, "central headquarters for discussions." The political upheavals of the decade touched Laura lightly, if at all. Martin Luther King, Jr., visited the campus in 1966, but she did not recall the occasion when asked about it years later. There are few reports of her social life because her friends say little about any romantic involvements before her marriage. She graduated with a bachelor's degree in elementary education in 1968.

Following college, Laura began teaching second grade at Kennedy Elementary School in Houston. Many of her young students were African Americans, and the experience "opened my eyes" and made her "realize how unfair in a lot of ways life is." Though she was not political at this stage of her life, she considered herself a Democrat at a time when the Republicans were struggling to establish themselves in Texas. Laura lived in the Chateau Dijon apartment complex at the same time as George W. Bush. She resided on what she called the "sedate" side of the facility, whereas he hung out with the wilder crowd of young adults on the other side.

After several years in Houston, Laura enrolled in the Graduate School of Library Science at the University of Texas at Austin in 1970. She earned a master's degree in library science in 1972, then returned to Houston as a school librarian. Two years later she moved back to Austin, where she held a similar post at Dawson Elementary School. As she neared her thirtieth birthday, she had had a number of male friends but was not disappointed that marriage had not yet occurred.

Her friends in Midland were eager to introduce Laura to George Walker Bush, four months her senior, who had moved back to the city in 1975 to enter the oil business. After a brief time in the industry, Bush was thinking about a run for Congress in 1978. In late July 1977, during a visit to her parents, Laura agreed to meet George Bush at a barbecue given by their mutual friends Joe and Jan O'Neill. The couple clicked at once. "I think it was a whirlwind romance because we were both in our early thirties," she later said. Though mutual attraction was at the heart of their relationship, marriage also served other interests. A married congressional candidate in West Texas would have an advantage over a bachelor, and for Laura Welch her future husband promised more excitement than a school librarian's career would provide. Within three months, they had decided to get married, to the surprise of some of their friends. The small family wedding took place in Midland on November 5, 1977. Laura had just celebrated her thirty-first birthday.

The newlyweds were a blend of opposites. Until his marriage, George W. Bush had relied on the wives of his friends to do his laundry and was renowned for his general untidiness. His bride was neat and organized. Active, gregarious, and sometimes overbearing, George Bush was all energy and drive. He often drank too much, but few in his crowd regarded that behavior as a serious weakness. Laura Bush, on the other hand, was neat, quiet, and observant. She emerged as a steadying influence on her volatile husband. Yet Laura Bush also liked the excitement and sense of drama that surrounded her husband and his family.

Her independent streak became evident during one of her initial visits to the Bush summer home at Kennebunkport, Maine. One of the older women in the Bush clan noted that the family was about to begin one of its noisy and frenetic games, and asked Laura Bush, "And what do you do?" She shot back, "I read, I smoke, and I admire." Her relationship with her mother-in-law, Barbara Bush, was friendly but somewhat guarded.

Laura Bush's first challenge was her husband's campaign for Congress in 1978. During their courtship, she had made him promise that she would not have to give a speech for him. That pledge soon fell by the wayside. "We campaigned the whole first year of our marriage," she recalled in 1999. George W. Bush lost to his Democratic opponent and returned to the oil business. Within two years his father was elected as Ronald Reagan's vice president, and the younger Bush put his own political ambitions on hold.

On the surface, their marriage was not a political partnership. Laura Bush ended her career as a school librarian, campaigned with her husband in 1978, and then turned to volunteer causes and eventually motherhood. She has always emphasized that she rarely gives her husband advice, and she has also said that she does not seek his. "George is my husband and not my best friend, necessarily," she said to a Texas newspaper in February 1999, and she emphasized that "we don't have a lot of policy discussions where we philosophize." Whether this denial covers the whole of their personal and political interaction will not be clear for some time. Mrs. Bush has retained a circle of women friends with whom she takes trips and vacations. She remains far more bookish than her husband.

George and Laura Bush wanted to have a large family, but the first three years of their marriage were childless. As they began to think about adoption, Laura Bush learned that she was pregnant with twins. As their birth approached, doctors told Laura Bush that she had toxemia. She was hospitalized in Dallas, and the doctors warned George W. Bush: "Your children will be born tomorrow; either that or your wife's kidneys will fail." Their daughters, Barbara and Jenna, were born in November 1981. They were named for their grandmothers.

The Bush daughters grew up out of the spotlight during their father's years as governor and presidential candidate. They attended schools in Midland and Austin, and both graduated from Stephen F. Austin High School in Austin. Barbara Bush entered Yale University in 2000 and was regarded as the more studious of the two girls. Jenna studied at the University of Texas at Austin, where the press depicted her as fun-loving and high-spirited.

During the first half of the 1980s, the Bushes raised their daughters in Midland while George W. Bush tried to prosper during the hard times for the oil business. In the gloomy economic atmosphere, he partied hard and often drank too much. When he woke up in the mornings with a hangover, Laura would tell him that he should quit drinking. Her husband knew he had a problem with alcohol. In 1976 he was arrested for driving drunk during a Maine vacation. Nonetheless, his habits did not change. "George was very disciplined in a lot of ways—except for drinking," Laura said years later. In July 1986, after a drunken weekend in Colorado, George W. Bush concluded that he must stop drinking altogether. He later told his wife of his decision, and her pleasure was obvious. The lifestyle change proved to be permanent.

Within a few months of the sobriety pledge, George Bush sold out his oil interests, and in the summer of 1987 he moved his family to Washington to help his father's campaign for the presidency in 1988. After George Bush was elected president, his son and daughter-in-law moved back to Texas to reestablish a political base in his home state. A year later George W. Bush was among a group of investors who acquired the Texas Rangers baseball team. He managed the franchise.

Despite the family's growing wealth, their lifestyle in Dallas was modest. The Bush daughters attended private school, but otherwise the couple lived simply. Laura

Bush volunteered at a local hospital, taking care of babies with AIDS. She and her husband went to baseball games together. Laura Bush enjoyed the period out of the public spotlight and was not eager to see her husband reenter politics in the early 1990s.

After President George Bush lost his reelection bid in 1992, his oldest son felt free to run for governor of Texas. Laura Bush was one of the last members of his inner circle to agree to the campaign against the incumbent governor, Ann Richards. Laura asked her husband, "Are you sure you're going to ask our family to make a life change? Are you sure that this is something you really want to do?" Her doubts were overcome, and her husband announced his candidacy. Once the campaign began, she proved to be a strong and effective advocate for her husband's candidacy. He defeated Richards in 1994.

In Austin, Laura Bush quickly emerged as a proponent for reading, literacy, and children. Few wifes of Texas governors had been identified with political or social causes, but Mrs. Bush moved forward in a number of areas. Her high-profile endeavor was the Texas Book Festival, held at the state capitol each November from 1996 on. The goal of the festival was to raise money for book collections in the state's public libraries, and in its first three years the event brought in $600,000 for such purchases. By 2000 the festival had become an annual event for the state's literary community. Televised on C-Span, it publicized Texas writing and the diversity of the state's intellectual life.

The other major area of Laura Bush's concern in Texas was literacy as it related to early childhood development. Four initiatives became key elements of her approach. She advocated a "Ready to Read" project that involved prekindergarten Head Start programs. In addition, she sponsored a *Take Time for Kids* magazine about child-care issues, to be distributed to parents. Mrs. Bush also set up the First Lady's Family Literacy Project for Texas and endorsed family literacy programs administered through the University of Texas at Austin. Finally, she encouraged the "Reach Out and Read" program, in which medical personnel read to children as part of their regular checkups. These initiatives were carried out in collaboration with the Barbara Bush Foundation for Literacy.

These projects involved only modest sums of money from the Texas state budget during Governor Bush's tenure, and they did not envision an extensive governmental structure to sustain them. Laura Bush accomplished these goals despite a staff of one. She proved very effective as an advocate with the legislature even though she disclaimed any interest in lobbying lawmakers. During the 1999 legislative session, she worked in the background with Democrats to keep funding for her literacy efforts in the budget.

Howard Welch died in April 1995 of the effects of Alzheimer's disease, and his daughter added a commitment to fighting that malady to her personal agenda. She also served as honorary chair of the "First Ladies Build" of Austin's Habitat for Humanity. In April 1999, Laura Bush said to a reporter, "I've had the opportunity to champion causes that I'm interested in. I've had an opportunity to make a difference in our state."

By every measure, Laura Bush was a very popular and well-regarded governor's wife. Her warmth and friendliness struck a chord with the people she met. A horse breeder in El Paso named one of his fillies Sweet Laura Bush. Her appeal stretched across party lines, and examples of direct criticisms of her record were virtually nonexistent after six years in the governor's mansion.

In April 1999, Southern Methodist University named a garden area and walkway outside its new library in honor of Laura Bush. A $250,000 donation to the university from Governor Bush made the promenade possible. "I had a wonderful experience at SMU," Mrs. Bush remarked. "I had some great teachers, especially in children's literature, who inspired me to become a teacher and librarian."

Following George W. Bush's sweeping reelection victory in 1998, speculations arose about his presidential ambitions for 2000. Once again his wife was not an enthusiastic early proponent of a run for the presidency. She reminded him again of the demands that such an endeavor would place on their daughters and their private lives. Nonetheless, when the decision to seek the presidency was made, she became a dedicated participant in her husband's bid for the White House.

At a time when the scandal involving President Bill Clinton and White House aide Monica Lewinsky was still fresh in the popular mind, Laura Bush emphasized in her campaign speeches that her husband would be a force for morality and dignity if he became president. "Americans want somebody . . . they do trust, someone . . . they feel like won't embarrass them but instead will make them proud," she told voters in Ames, Iowa, in July 1999.

During the fall of 1999, George W. Bush took time out from the campaign trail to honor his wife. Skipping a debate with five competitors for the Republican nomination in New Hampshire, he opted to attend ceremonies at Southern Methodist University, where his wife accepted a Distinguished Alumni Award. "New Hampshire is important," said Governor Bush, "but it's not nearly as important as being here with Laura tonight. There's going to be ample time to debate."

Laura Bush distinguished herself from First Lady Hillary Clinton more by her attitude toward the duties of that position than by direct criticism of Mrs. Clinton. Mrs. Bush made it clear that she would not push legislative programs herself or endeavor to lead on an issue such as health care, as Hillary Clinton had done in 1993–1994. She was, she said, "a traditional woman" who "would never run for office—that's just not my temperament." On the other hand, she did assure the Republican National Convention that she would "make early childhood development one of my priorities." How these competing commitments would be reconciled remained for the future to decide.

As her husband's hold on the Republican presidential nomination strengthened in the winter of 2000, Laura Bush became one of his primary assets in the race for the White House. George W. Bush's speeches reiterated that the best decision he ever made was to ask her to marry him in 1977. Sometimes the couple campaigned together. On other occasions Laura Bush canvassed with prominent Republican women and female members of the Bush family.

Election Day brought one of the closest presidential contests in American history, and the outcome was not settled for more than a month. Amid the uncertainty about her husband's prospects for the White House as the electoral votes of Florida hung in the balance, Laura Bush stayed out of the public eye. Few indications of what she planned to do as First Lady were disclosed during the awkward transition period. Friends in Washington asserted that she would look to predecessors in the position such as Rosalynn Carter for inspiration about pursuing programs.

Laura Bush also confronted a problem that no other incoming First Lady had faced. Her predecessor, Hillary Rodham Clinton, is a new U.S. Senator from New York, and the media attention on the former First Lady will be intense. Sharing the spotlight with Hillary Clinton and being asked to comment on her public statements as a senator will, at least in the first year, require a deft touch from the new First Lady.

The challenges of the role of First Lady would be formidable for Laura Bush. By the end of the twentieth century, the institution had acquired a bureaucratic character that required First Ladies to manage a small staff, deal with an importunate press corps, and identify with specific programs, such as literacy or mental health. Once she was in Washington, Laura Bush would have to move beyond the individualized role that she had played as the governor's wife in Texas. In a bitterly divided and partisan city, she would also confront pressures and strains that had not previously characterized her political life. More traditional than Hillary Clinton yet more activist than her mother-in-law, Barbara Bush, Laura Bush

took her place in the continuum of presidential wives in January 2001.

The early stages of her time in Washington were eventful. Her fashion choices received some press criticism which she and her new staff disregarded. At her husband's inauguration, she participated in "Laura Bush Celebrates American Authors" and she also visited public schools in the Washington area to promote literacy. She and the new president made it clear that they hoped the press would allow their daughters a zone of privacy. The new First Lady's most notable policy statement came the day before the inauguration. A television interviewer asked her whether the Supreme Court decision on *Roe v. Wade*, allowing legal abortions, should be overturned. "No, I don't think it should be overturned," Mrs. Bush replied. Her comment caused a negative response among those who opposed abortion, and the Bush White House brushed it off as her personal view and not that of the new president. How Laura Bush positions herself as First Lady on this and other matters remains unclear.

BIBLIOGRAPHICAL ESSAY

There are no biographies of Laura Bush as yet. Her personal papers will not be available until well after the end of her husband's presidency. Some information may exist at the George Herbert Walker Bush Presidential Library at Texas A&M University, but it will be difficult to obtain as long as Mrs. Bush is First Lady. The records of George W. Bush's governorship in Texas may shed some light on his wife's role in Texas when those materials become public. Searching for Laura Bush on the Web will produce links to many of the published sources cited below.

For now, the researcher must rely on newspaper sources and published biographies of George W. Bush and his family. There is a small file of clippings about Laura Bush at the Center for American History, the University of Texas at Austin, and Southern Methodist University in Dallas collects similar materials.

Laura Bush's writings and speeches include "Remarks of Laura Bush, Republican National Convention, July 31, 2000," from NPR Online; and, from her tenure as governor's wife in Texas, "Pleasures to Celebrate, Treasures to Preserve," *Texas Parks and Wildlife* (December 1998): 14; "First Lady's Challenge: A Call to Action, Early Childhood Development and Brain Research Conference" (December 10, 1998); Texas Commission on the Arts, "1st Lady of Texas Laura Bush Del Rio Speech," *Arts Texas* (February 1997), at www.arts.state.tx.us. For her comments on abortion, see "Laura Bush: Don't Nix Roe v. Wade," *Washington Post*, January 19, 2001.

Barbara Bush, *Barbara Bush: A Memoir* (New York, 1994), has some interesting comments from Laura Bush's mother-in-law. Elizabeth Mitchell, *W: Revenge of the Bush Dynasty* (New York, 2000); and Bill Minutaglio, *First Son: George W. Bush and the Bush Family Dynasty* (New York, 1999), are journalistic biographies of George W. Bush that provide insights into his marriage to Laura Bush.

The basic outline of Laura Bush's life can be found in Skip Hollandsworth, "Reading Laura Bush," *Texas Monthly* (November 1996): 120, 151–154; Julie Bonnin, "What Laura Wants," *Austin American-Statesman* (April 18, 1999); Richard L. Berke, "First Lady of Texas Plays a Firm Second Fiddle," *New York Times* (August 3, 1999); Patricia Ann La Salle, "Laura Bush: Leading for Literacy," *SMU Magazine* (Fall 1999): 20–22; Lois Romano, "Laura Bush Redefines Her Role," *Washington Post National Weekly Edition* (June 12, 2000): 9–10; Georgia Temple, "Jenna Welch 'Extremely Proud' of Potential First Lady," *Midland Reporter-Telegram* (July 30, 2000).

On the 1963 automobile accident, see "Lee High School Senior Dies in Traffic Mishap," *Midland Reporter-Telegram* (November 7, 1963); Daniel Jeffreys, "Texas Tragedy," *NYPost.com* (March 22, 2000); Jim Vertuno, "Report: Laura Bush in 1963 Car Wreck," *Salon.com* (May 4, 2000); George Kuempel, "Report Finds Crash Attributable to Mrs. Bush," *DallasNews.com* (May 4, 2000).

Other articles on Laura Bush that provide relevant information are Carolyn Barta, "Laura Bush Accepts SMU Award," *Dallas Morning News* (October 29, 1999); Lynn Shank, "Getting Personal with Laura," *Senior Lifestyles* (October 1999): 2–3 (about her father's Alzheimer's disease); and Georgia Temple, "Journalist Recalls Childhood Memories of Laura Bush," *Midland Reporter-Telegram* (July 27, 2000).

APPENDIX A

★ ★ ★ ★ ★

The Siena College First Lady Polls, 1982, 1993

The results in these polls derive from the Siena Research Institute survey of historians at 102 four-year colleges and universities in 1982 and 1993. Respondents rated the First Ladies on a scale of 1–5 in ten categories: background, value to country, integrity, leadership, intelligence, own person, accomplishments, courage, public image, and value to president. Results were converted to a scale of 100, with 60 representing an average score. This table compiles their ratings in the ten categories into an overall score.

The 1982 survey lists forty-two First Ladies, while the 1993 survey lists only thirty-seven. In the first survey, there are six cases in which the First Lady is not a wife (examples include nieces, sisters, and daughters), and a seventh case, Anna Harrison whose husband died a month after becoming president. Using feedback from the first survey, the SRI decided this information made the survey confusing and so decided to include only established First Ladies in the current survey.

These polls, conducted in 1982 and 1993 by the Siena Research Institute, are reproduced courtesy of the institute for the purposes of this volume only. The Siena Research Institute retains all rights to the results and tabulations of the poll and their permission must be secured before these poll results are reproduced in this or any other form.

Siena Research Institute First Lady Survey
First Ladies Ranked by Total Score

1993 Survey		1982 Survey	
1. Eleanor Roosevelt	93.65	1. Eleanor Roosevelt	93.29
2. Hillary Rodham Clinton	86.35	2. Abigail Adams	84.64
3. Abigail Adams	83.63	3. Lady Bird Johnson	77.45
4. Dolley Madison	77.42	4. Dolley Madison	75.39
5. Rosalynn Carter	77.38	5. Rosalynn Carter	73.84
6. Lady Bird Johnson	77.28	6. Betty Ford	73.43
7. Jacqueline Kennedy	74.67	7. Edith Bolling Wilson	71.76
8. Barbara Bush	74.03	8. Jacqueline Kennedy	69.51

Siena Research Institute First Lady Survey
First Ladies Ranked by Total Score (*continued*)

1993 Survey		1982 Survey	
9. Betty Ford	72.16	9. Martha Washington	67.45
10. Edith Bolling Wilson	70.72	10. Edith Kermit Roosevelt	65.35
11. Bess Truman	68.19	11. Lou Henry Hoover	63.51
12. Martha Washington	67.39	12. Lucy Webb Hayes	63.09
13. Lou Henry Hoover	63.90	13. Frances Folsom Cleveland	62.33
14. Edith Kermit Roosevelt	63.87	14. Louisa Adams	62.03
15. Lucy Webb Hayes	62.82	15. Bess Truman	61.70
16. Louisa Adams	62.26	16. Ellen Axson Wilson	61.52
17. Mamie Eisenhower	62.10	17. Grace Goodhue Coolidge	61.25
18. Patricia Nixon	61.78	18. M. Jefferson Randolph	61.02
19. Grace Goodhue Coolidge	61.71	18. Helen Herron Taft	61.02
20. Sarah Polk	61.30	20. Julia Dent Grant	60.74
21. Ellen Axson Wilson	60.82	21. Eliza Johnson	60.70
22. Frances Folsom Cleveland	60.35	22. Sarah Polk	60.52
23. Elizabeth Monroe	60.13	23. Anna Harrison	60.11
24. Eliza Johnson	59.98	24. Elizabeth Monroe	60.09
25. Helen Herron Taft	59.94	25. Mary Arthur McElroy	60.07
26. Julia Dent Grant	59.81	26. Emily Donelson	59.98
27. Julia Tyler	59.36	27. Julia Tyler	59.94
28. Lucretia Garfield	59.25	28. Abigail Fillmore	59.80
29. Caroline Scott Harrison	59.12	28. Harriet Lane	59.80
30. Letitia Tyler	58.62	30. Lucretia Garfield	59.76
30. Abigail Fillmore	58.62	31. Mamie Eisenhower	59.72
32. Ida Saxton McKinley	58.53	32. Martha Patterson	59.58
33. Margaret Taylor	58.32	33. Margaret Taylor	59.35
34. Jane Pierce	58.22	33. Caroline Harrison Scott	59.35
35. Florence Kling Harding	55.15	35. Letitia Tyler	59.33
36. Nancy Reagan	53.07	36. Angelica Van Buren	59.27
37. Mary Todd Lincoln	52.62	37. Patricia Nixon	58.45
		38. Jane Pierce	57.58
		39. Nancy Reagan	57.35
		40. Ida Saxton McKinley	57.03
		41. Florence Kling Harding	55.06
		42. Mary Todd Lincoln	52.86

APPENDIX B

★ ★ ★ ★ ★

Presidents and First Ladies, 1789–2001

President	Term	First Lady or Equivalent
George Washington	1789–1797	Martha Washington
John Adams	1797–1801	Abigail Adams
Thomas Jefferson	1801–1809	Martha Jefferson Randolph (daughter)
James Madison	1809–1817	Dolley Madison
James Monroe	1817–1825	Elizabeth Monroe
John Quincy Adams	1825–1829	Louisa Adams
Andrew Jackson	1829–1837	Emily Donelson Sarah Yorke Jackson (nieces)
Martin Van Buren	1837–1841	Angelica Van Buren (daughter-in-law)
William Henry Harrison	1841	Anna Harrison
John Tyler	1841–1845	Letitia Tyler (1841–1842) Julia Tyler (1844–1845)
James K. Polk	1845–1849	Sarah Polk
Zachary Taylor	1849–1850	Margaret Taylor
Millard Fillmore	1850–1853	Abigail Fillmore
Franklin Pierce	1853–1857	Jane Pierce
James Buchanan	1857–1861	Harriet Lane (niece)
Abraham Lincoln	1861–1865	Mary Todd Lincoln
Andrew Johnson	1865–1869	Eliza Johnson Martha Patterson (daughter)
Ulysses S. Grant	1869–1877	Julia Dent Grant
Rutherford B. Hayes	1877–1881	Lucy Webb Hayes
James R. Garfield	1881	Lucretia Garfield

Presents and First Ladies, 1789–2001 (*continued*)

President	Term	First Lady or Equivalent
Chester Alan Arthur	1881–1885	Mary Arthur McElroy (sister)
Grover Cleveland	1885–1889	Frances Folsom Cleveland (1886–1889)
Benjamin Harrison	1889–1893	Caroline Scott Harrison (d. 1892)
Grover Cleveland	1893–1897	Frances Folsom Cleveland
William McKinley	1897–1901	Ida Saxton McKinley
Theodore Roosevelt	1901–1909	Edith Kermit Roosevelt
William Howard Taft	1909–1913	Helen Herron Taft
Woodrow Wilson	1913–1921	Ellen Axson Wilson (1913–1914) Edith Bolling Wilson (1915–1921)
Warren G. Harding	1921–1923	Florence Kling Harding
Calvin Coolidge	1923–1929	Grace Goodhue Coolidge
Herbert Hoover	1929–1933	Lou Henry Hoover
Franklin D. Roosevelt	1933–1945	Eleanor Roosevelt
Harry S. Truman	1945–1953	Bess Truman
Dwight D. Eisenhower	1953–1961	Mamie Eisenhower
John F. Kennedy	1961–1963	Jacqueline Kennedy
Lyndon B. Johnson	1963–1969	Lady Bird Johnson
Richard M. Nixon	1969–1974	Patricia Nixon
Gerald R. Ford	1974–1977	Betty Ford
Jimmy Carter	1977–1981	Rosalynn Carter
Ronald Reagan	1981–1989	Nancy Reagan
George Bush	1989–1993	Barbara Bush
Bill Clinton	1993–2001	Hillary Rodham Clinton
George W. Bush	2001–	Laura Bush

Portrait Credits

★ ★ ★ ★ ★

Martha Washington	Library of Congress
Abigail Adams	Library of Congress
Dolley Madison	Library of Congress
Elizabeth Monroe	Library of Congress
Louisa Adams	Library of Congress
Anna Harrison	Library of Congress
Letitia Tyler	Library of Congress
Julia Tyler	Library of Congress
Sarah Polk	Ancestral Home of James K. Polk Columbia, Tennessee
Abigail Fillmore	Library of Congress
Jane Pierce	Library of Congress
Mary Todd Lincoln	Library of Congress
Eliza Johnson	Library of Congress
Julia Dent Grant	Library of Congress
Lucy Webb Hayes	Library of Congress
Lucretia Garfield	Library of Congress
Frances Folsom Cleveland	Library of Congress
Caroline Scott Harrison	Library of Congress
Ida Saxton McKinley	Library of Congress
Edith Kermit Roosevelt	Library of Congress
Helen Herron Taft	Library of Congress
Ellen Axson Wilson	Library of Congress
Edith Bolling Wilson	Library of Congress
Florence Kling Harding	Library of Congress
Grace Goodhue Coolidge	Library of Congress
Lou Henry Hoover	Herbert Hoover Library
Eleanor Roosevelt	Franklin D. Roosevelt Library
Bess Truman	Harry S. Truman Library
Mamie Eisenhower	Dwight D. Eisenhower Library
Jacqueline Kennedy	Library of Congress

Lady Bird Johnson	Center for American History, the University of Texas at Austin
Patricia Nixon	Nixon Presidential Papers Project, National Archives
Betty Ford	Gerald R. Ford Library
Rosalynn Carter	Jimmy Carter Library
Nancy Reagan	Library of Congress
Barbara Bush	Library of Congress
Hillary Rodham Clinton	The White House
Laura Bush	Corbis

INDEX

★ ★ ★ ★ ★

Murray, Rosa, 377, 378
Muskie, Jane, 382
My Memoir (Wilson), 244, 245
My Parents (Roosevelt), 291
My Story (Exner), 332

Nancy Reagan Drug Abuse Fund, 401, 405–406
Nancy Reagan Foundation, 406
National Amateur Athletic Federation, Women's Division of, 278, 279
National Association for the Advancement of Colored People (NAACP), 297, 301
National Center for Voluntary Action, 356
National Civic Association, 233, 235–236
National Cultural Center, 318, 324
National Gallery, 206, 325
National Institute of Mental Health (NIMH), 389
National Literacy Act of 1991, 420
National Trust for Historic Preservation, 244
National Urban League, 297
National Wildflower Research Center, 348, 349
National Women's Party, 253
National Youth Administration (NYA), 295–296, 298, 337
Neely, Esther Naomi, 249
Nevins, Allan, 166
New Deal programs, 294–299
New Jersey State Charities Aid Society, 232
Nichols, Roy Franklin, 110
Ninian, Edward, 121
Nixon, Julie, 332, 353, 358, 359, 360
Nixon, Patricia Ryan, 351–361, 374
    accomplishments and reputation of, 356–358
    activities and interests of, 352–353, 355–357
    childhood and youth of, 351–352
    courtship and marriage of, 352–354, 358
    death of, 360
    education of, 352
    as First Lady, 355–359
    health problems of, 359–360
    later years of, 359–360
    as mother, 353, 354
    personality and character of, 354, 358
    political activities of, 353–356
    public image and press coverage of, 354, 355, 358–359
    teaching career of, 352–353
    travels of, 352, 357, 360
    Watergate scandal and, 359
    women's issues and, 358
Nixon, Richard M., 301, 317, 322, 352–361, 367–368, 386, 396, 412, 413, 427, 428
Nixon, Tricia, 322, 332, 353, 358, 359, 360
Nofziger, Lynn, 398, 399, 403
Norton, Howard, 382, 390
Norton, Mary, 299
Nuryev, Rudolf, 370

Oak Hill, 43
O'Daniel, W. Lee (Pappy), 337, 338
O'Day, Caroline, 289, 290
Oduber, Daniel, 386
Odum, Reathel, 306, 307–308
Office of Price Administration, 353
Olcott, Charles, 187
Onassis, Aristotle, 328, 331
Onassis, Jacqueline Kennedy. *See* Kennedy, Jacqueline Bouvier

O'Neill, Jan, 441
O'Neill, Joe, 441
Ord, Edward O.C., 136
Outdoor Advertising Association of America (OAAA), 343, 345
Owen, Fred D., 178
Owings, Nathaniel, 341

Packard, Alpheus S., 107
Packard, Elizabeth Appleton, 107
Pastor, Bob, 385
Patterson, David T., 126, 128
Patterson, Eleanor, 267
Patterson, Martha Johnson, 126, 128, 129, 130
Payne, Anna (niece), 34
Payne, Anna (sister), 21, 22, 32, 34
Payne, Dolley. *See* Madison, Dolley Payne Todd
Payne, Isaac, 21, 23
Payne, John, 21, 22
Payne, John Coles, 21, 22, 24, 25, 32
Payne, Lucy, 21, 22, 24, 25, 28, 32
Payne, Mary, 21, 22, 23, 24–25
Payne, Walter, 21
Payne, William Temple, 21, 23
Peace Convention, 75
Pearce, Lorraine, 326
Peck, Mary Allen Hulbert, 231, 239, 241
Pendel, Thomas, 150
Perez, Anna, 417, 420
Perkins, Frances, 292, 306
Pershing, John, 269, 312
Philippines, Tafts' posting to, 216–218
Phillips, Carrie Fulton, 250
Phillips, James, 250
Pi Beta Phi, 261, 267
Pickens, Francis, 72
Pickering, Timothy, 16
Pickford, Mary, 265
Pierce, Barbara. *See* Bush, Barbara Pierce
Pierce, Benjamin, 108, 109
Pierce, Franklin, 105, 107–111, 409
Pierce, Franklin, Jr., 108
Pierce, Frank Robert, 108, 109
Pierce, Jane Appleton, 107–111
    childhood and youth of, 107
    courtship and marriage of, 107–108
    death of, 110
    as First Lady, 109–110
    health problems of, 108, 109, 110
    as mother, 108
    personality and character of, 108, 111
    reputation of, 111
Pierce, Marvin, 409, 411
Pierce, Pauline Robinson, 409, 411
Pitts, ZaSu, 394
Polk, James K., 63, 74, 82–89, 94–95
Polk, Jane Knox, 82, 83, 84
Polk, Ophelia, 84
Polk, Samuel, 82, 83
Polk, Sarah Childress, 35, 81–90, 151
    childhood and youth of, 81–82
    courtship and marriage of, 83–84
    death of, 89
    education of, 82
    as First Lady, 87–89
    health problems of, 88
    personality and character of, 83
    political life of, 85–87, 89–90

E 176.2 .A44 2001

AMERICAN FIRST LADIES

DATE DUE

Demco, Inc 38-293